6000 AWESOME FACTS

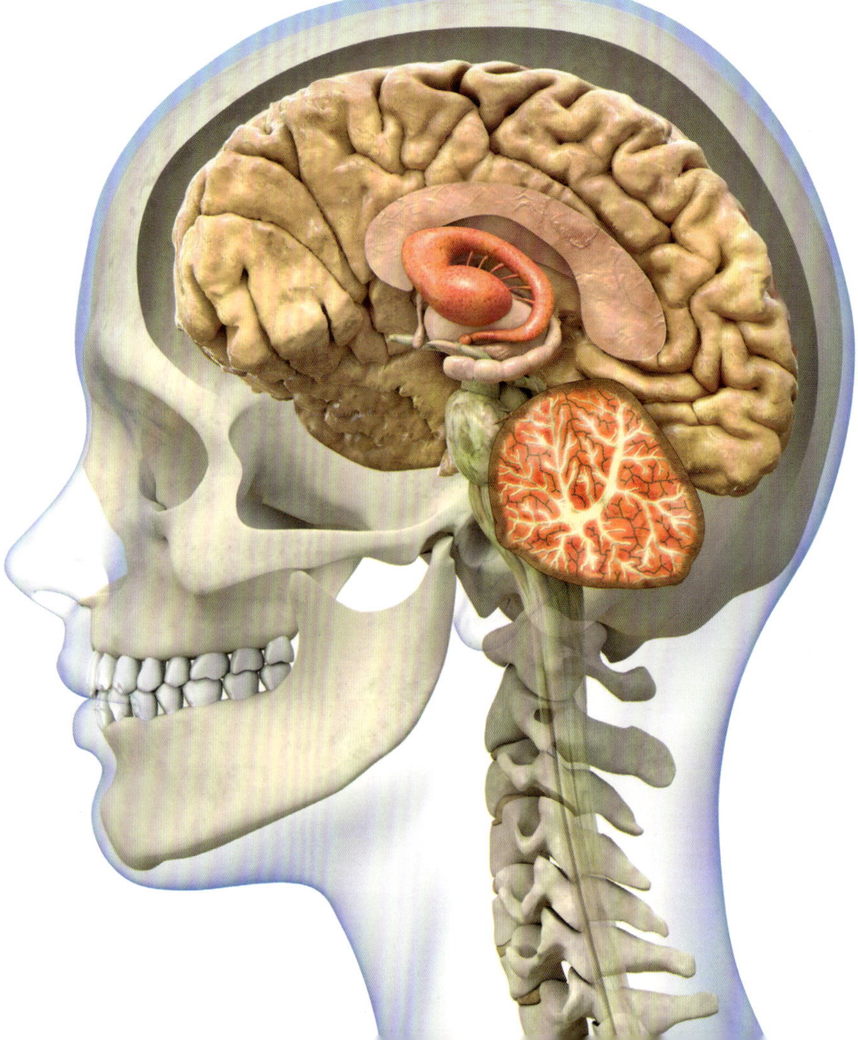

6000 AWESOME FACTS

Miles Kelly

First published in 2018 by Miles Kelly Publishing Ltd
Harding's Barn, Bardfield End Green, Thaxted, Essex, CM6 3PX, UK

2 4 6 8 10 9 7 5 3 1

Publishing Director Belinda Gallagher
Creative Director Jo Cowan
Editor Becky Miles
Design Manager Simon Lee
Image Manager Liberty Newton
Production Elizabeth Collins
Reprographics Stephan Davis, Darryl Du Plooy
Assets Venita Kidwai

ISBN: 978-1-78989-856-9

Printed in China

British Library Cataloguing-in-Publication Data
A catalogue record for this book is available from the British Library

Made with paper from a sustainable forest

www.mileskelly.net

CONTENTS

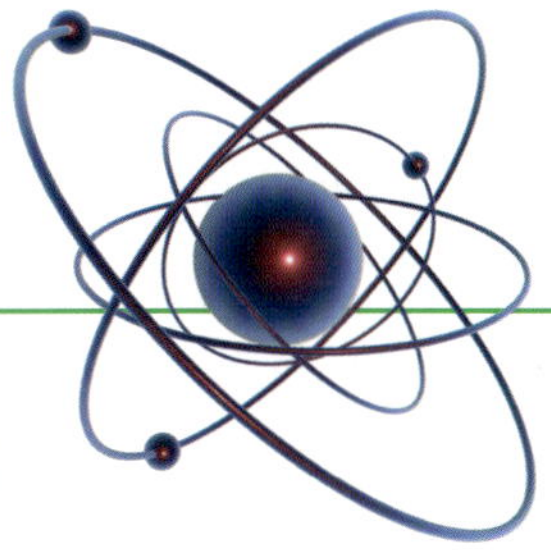

1000 SCIENCE FACTS 8

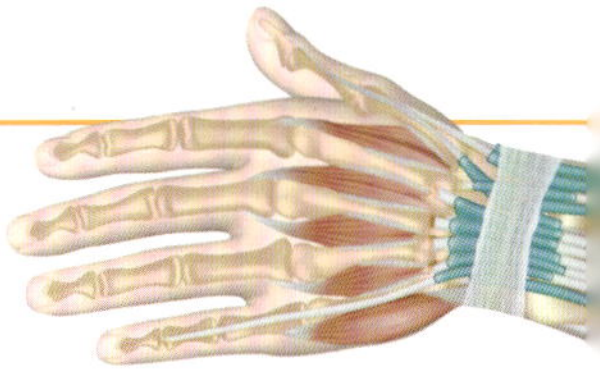

1000 HUMAN BODY FACTS 66

1000 PREHISTORIC LIFE FACTS 124

1000 MAMMAL FACTS 180

1000 BIRD FACTS 238

1000 SHARK FACTS 296

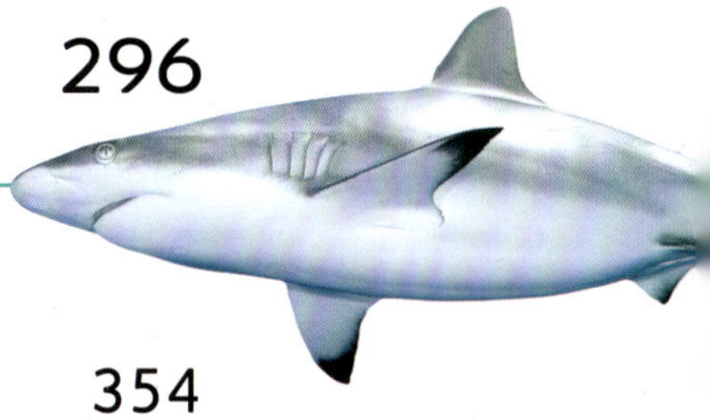

INDEX 354

ACKNOWLEDGEMENTS 382

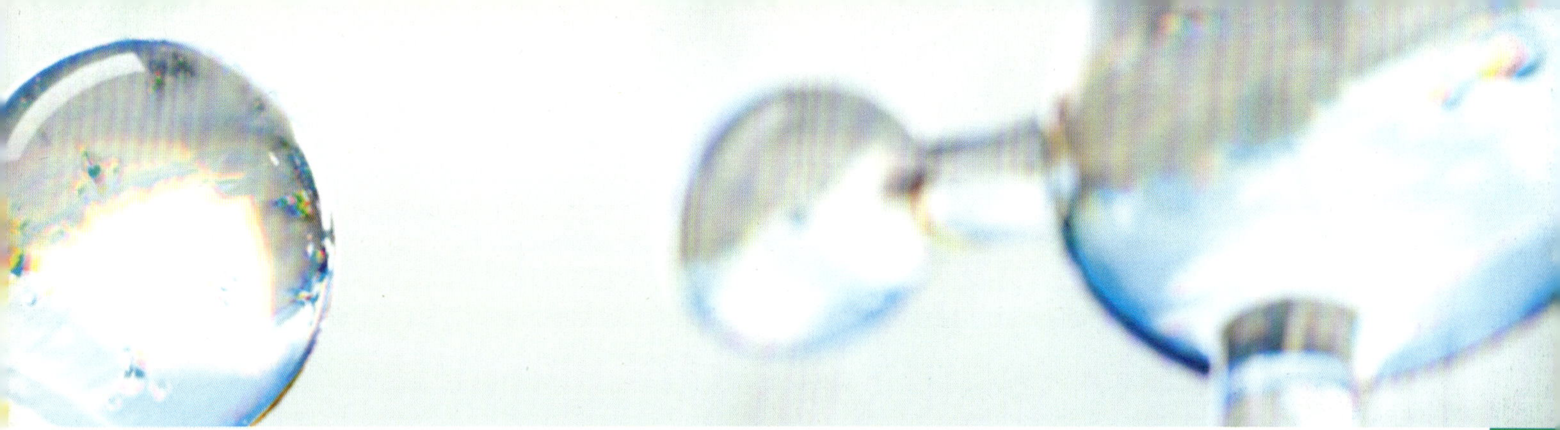

1000 SCIENCE FACTS

Chemicals of life

● **The study** of compounds that contain carbon atoms is called organic chemistry.

● **Organic chemistry** is so-called because originally scientists thought that carbon compounds were made by and occurred only in living things (the word 'organic' describes things that are related to living organisms). Organic chemicals are the basis of most life processes.

● **However, in 1828** German chemist Friedrich Wöhler made the carbon compound urea in his laboratory.

● **It is now known** that over 90 percent of all chemical compounds are organic.

● **Organic compounds** are used in a wide variety of products, including paints, plastics, food, drugs and oil.

● **Organic compounds** consist of carbon and hydrogen, often combined with other elements such as nitrogen, oxygen, phosphorus and silicon.

● **Compounds that consist** of hydrogen and carbon are called hydrocarbons. These are by far the largest groups of carbon compounds.

● **There are many** natural hydrocarbons in the human body including steroid hormones such as testosterone and cholesterol, which help build blood vessel walls.

● **Hydrocarbons and carbohydrates** are not the same. Hydrocarbons are made from carbon and hydrogen atoms, but carbohydrates contain oxygen atoms as well.

● **The oxygen** component of carbohydrates enables them to take a huge variety of forms essential for life.

● **Carbohydrates such as** starches and sugars are the basic energy foods of plants and animals.

● **Organic compounds** that are formed from rings of carbon atoms are called cyclic compounds.

◀ *Hummingbirds sip the nectar from flowers to get their essential energy source of carbohydrates.*

Forces

● **A force** is a push or a pull. It can make something start to move, slow down, speed up, change direction or change shape or size.

● **The greater a force**, the more effect it has.

● **Force is measured** in newtons (N). One newton is the force needed to speed up a mass of one kilogram by one metre per second every second.

● **When an object moves** there are usually several forces involved. When you throw a ball, the force of your throw hurls it forwards, the force of gravity pulls it down and the force of air resistance slows it down.

● **The direction and speed** of any movement depends on the combined effect of all the forces involved – this is known as the resultant.

DID YOU KNOW?

The thrust of Saturn V's rocket engines was 33 million newtons.

● **A force** has magnitude (size) and works in a particular direction.

● **A force can** be drawn on a diagram as an arrow, called a vector. The arrow's direction shows the force's direction and its length shows the force's strength.

● **Four fundamental forces** operate throughout the Universe. These are gravity, electric and magnetic forces (electromagnetic force) and nuclear forces.

● **A force field** is the area affected by a force. The field is strongest closest to the source.

◀ *When a boxer hits a punchball, the ball is moved by the force of their punch.*

Atoms

● **Atoms are the tiny particles** that make up every substance. An atom is the tiniest part of any basic substance. They are so small that you could fit two billion atoms on the full stop at the end of this sentence.

● **Atoms are mostly empty space**, dotted with a few even tinier particles, called subatomic particles.

● **Every atom** has a dense core (nucleus) made up of two kinds of particle: protons and neutrons. Protons have a positive electrical charge, and neutrons have none.

● **If an atom** were the size of a sports arena, its nucleus would be the size of a pea.

● **Smaller, negatively charged** particles called electrons whizz around the nucleus. Every type of atom has a different number of electrons.

● **Protons and neutrons** are made from different combinations of even smaller particles, called quarks.

▼ Inside every atom, electrons whizz around a dense nucleus built up from protons and neutrons.

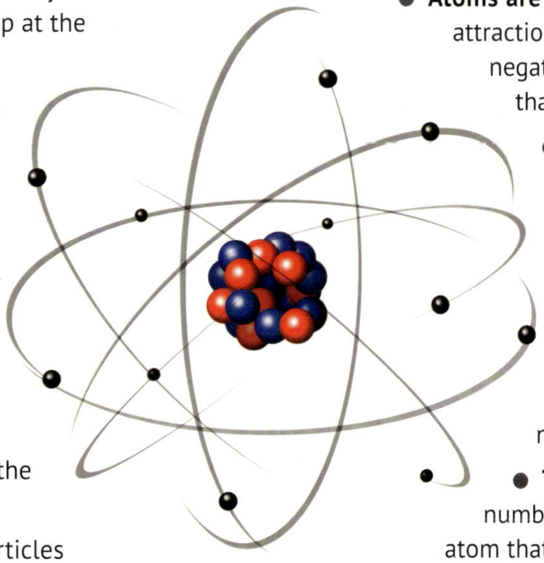

● **Atoms are held** together by the electrical attraction between positive protons and negative electrons, and the forces that hold the nucleus together.

● **All the atoms** that make up a chemical element are identical, so have the same number of protons. For example, an iron atom has 26 protons, while a gold atom has 79.

● **The number** of protons in an atom is known as its atomic number.

● **Typically**, an atom has an equal number of protons and neutrons. An atom that has an unequal number of protons and neutrons is called an isotope.

● **Atoms also** usually have an equal number of protons and electrons. An atom with an unequal number is an ion and has an electrical charge.

Energy

● **Energy is the capacity** of a system to do work. It has many forms, from chemical energy locked in sugar to mechanical energy in a speeding train.

● **Energy conversion** is when energy changes from one form to another.

● **When energy moves** from one place to another it is known as energy transfer.

● **Energy is never lost or gained**, it simply changes or moves. The total amount of energy in the Universe has always been the same.

● **Using energy** usually means converting it from one form to another. For example, when fuels are burned, chemical energy is changed into heat energy.

● **Potential energy** is energy that is stored up within a body or system ready for action.

● **The energy** in a coiled spring is an example of potential energy.

● **Kinetic energy** is energy that is possessed by an object because it is moving. A rolling ball has kinetic energy.

● **The greater an object's mass or velocity**, the greater its kinetic energy. A car has four times more kinetic energy at 40 km/h than at 20 km/h.

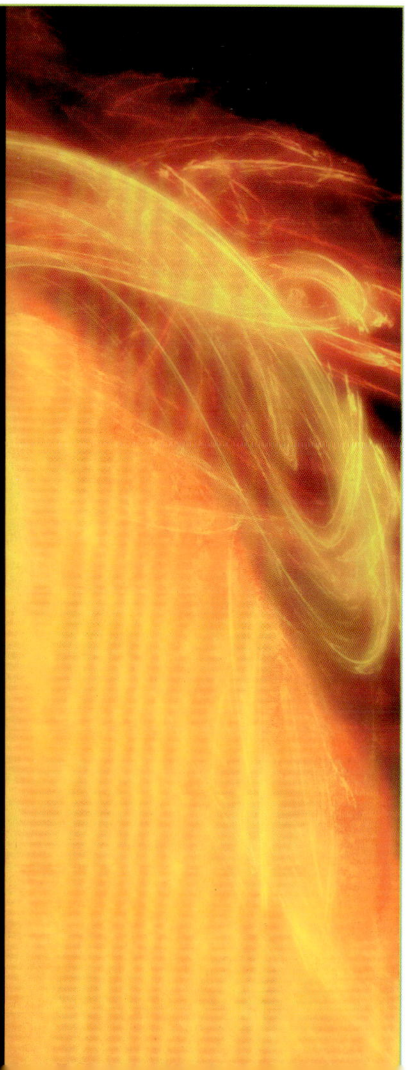

▶ Inside the Sun, nuclear energy in atoms is converted into heat energy, making the surface ferociously hot.

Space

- **A flat surface is two-dimensional.** The two dimensions – length and width – are at right angles to each other.
- **Any point** on a flat surface can be pinpointed exactly with two figures, one showing how far along the point is and the other how far across. These figures are called coordinates.
- **There are three dimensions** of space at right angles to each other: length, width and depth.
- **Any point** in space can be pinpointed with three figures, one showing how far along it is, one how high it is and a third how far across it is.
- **If an object is moving,** three dimensions are not enough to locate it. You need a fourth dimension – time – to pinpoint its location.
- **German mathematician** Hermann Minkowski laid the foundations for Albert Einstein's special theory of relativity in the early 1900s, when he realized that the three dimensions of physical space need to be combined with time.
- **Four-dimensional** space is called space-time.
- **After Minkowski's breakthroughs,** mathematicians began to develop special geometry to describe four dimensions.

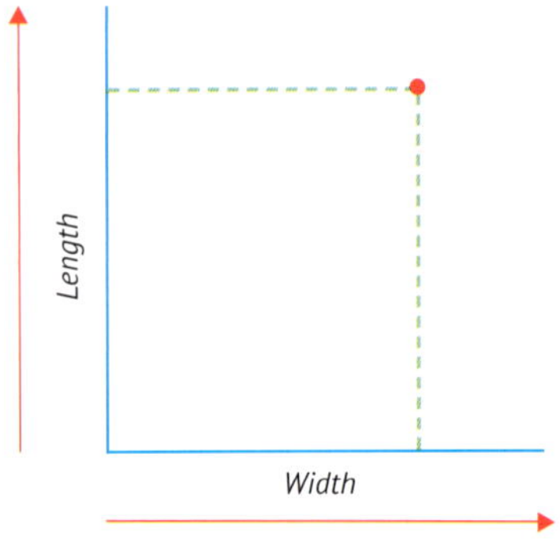

◀ *You can pinpoint a position on a surface with just two figures: length and width.*

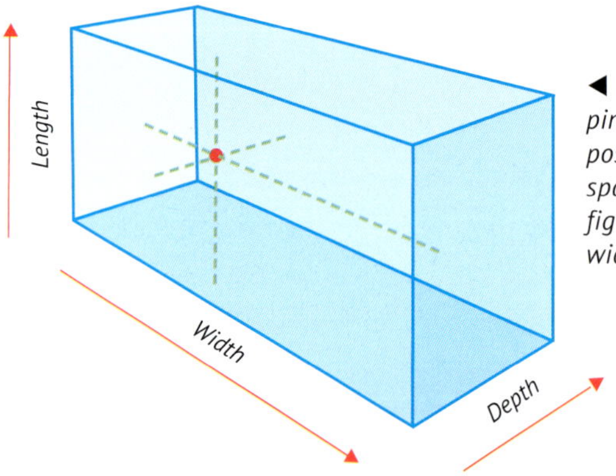

◀ *You can pinpoint a position in space with three figures: length, width and depth.*

Electricity

- **Electricity is energy,** and it is the major source of power for much of the industrialized world.
- **All the electrons** that make up every atom carry a tiny electrical charge. This is a force, which either pulls bits of atoms together (attracts them) or pushes them apart (repels them).
- **Some particles** (such as electrons) have a negative electrical charge. Others have a positive charge. Two particles with the same charge repel each other, while two particles with opposing charges attract each other.
- **Most atoms** have equal numbers of positive and negative particles, so they are usually balanced.
- **The movement of electrons** can produce an electric current – a flow of electricity.
- **A material** through which electrons (and electrical charges) flow, such as copper, is called a 'conductor'.
- **Materials that stop** electrons passing through, such as rubber, are called insulators.
- **Static electricity** is the accumulation of electric charge on an insulator. It is the result of electrons being shifted to the insulator by friction.
- **Electric charge** can be detected and measured with an instrument called an electroscope.

▼ *A lightning flash is a dramatic display of natural electricity.*

Time

▲ *The strontium atomic clock is thought to be more accurate than anything previously achieved.*

- **Time is measured** in seconds, minutes, hours, days, months and years.
- **A clock** is a device used to measure time.
- **Mechanical clocks are** controlled by mechanisms with repeating motions. Most clocks do not keep perfect time – they usually gain or lose at least a fraction of a second every day.
- **The standard worldwide time** has been set by atomic clocks since 1967. These are accurate to 0.001 sec in 1000 years.
- **Atomic clocks** are kept regular by the movement of certain atoms, such as caesium or strontium atoms.
- **Caesium atoms vibrate** at a rate of 9,192,631,770 times a second.
- **Strontium atoms are** even faster (and therefore even more accurate), at 429,228,004,229,952 times a second.
- **The strontium atomic** clock at JILA, a scientific institute in Colorado, USA, is the most accurate clock on Earth. It could run for 200 million years without gaining or losing a single second.
- **Time is** the fourth dimension (the other three being length, width and height). This suggests the theory that time could run forwards or backwards.
- **Distant stars** are so far away that their light can take many years to reach us. This means we see them as they were years ago, not as they are now.

DID YOU KNOW?

Einstein's theory of general relativity shows that time is affected by gravity, and runs slower nearer to strong gravitational fields such as stars.

Chemical reactions

- **A chemical reaction** is when two or more elements or compounds interact chemically, breaking old bonds between atoms and making new ones.
- **The chemicals** in a chemical reaction are called the reactants. The results are called the products.
- **The products** of a chemical reaction contain the same atoms as the reactants but in different combinations.
- **The products** of the reaction will have the same total mass as the reactants.
- **Reactions can be** reversible and irreversible. When irreversible, the products cannot be changed back into the reactants. For example, toasting bread causes an irreversible chemical reaction.
- **In a chemical reaction**, the elements that make up compounds can separate and recombine to form new compounds.
- **A catalyst** is a substance that speeds up or enables a chemical reaction to happen.
- **Nearly all reactions** involve energy. Some involve light or electricity, but most involve heat.
- **Reactions that give out** heat are called exothermic. Those that draw in heat are called endothermic.
- **Oxidation is a reaction** in which oxygen combines with a substance. Burning is oxidation – as the fuel burns it combines with oxygen in the air. Reduction is a reaction in which a substance loses oxygen.

▼ *Fire is the rapid oxidation of a substance, such as the chemicals in wood, in a process (combustion) that releases extreme heat and light. It also produces ash, gases and sometimes other particles. This mixture appears in the air as smoke.*

Computers

- **The information (data)** that a computer requires to work is stored in microchips – tiny structures of electronic components and their connections, which are produced in or on a small slice of silicon.
- **'Input' is** any form of getting data into a computer, such as typing, using a touchscreen, or taking from the internet or storage media. 'Output' is when the computer sends out results – by printing, showing on screen, playing sounds, sending over the internet or saving to storage media.
- **Microchips known as ROM** (read-only memory) carry a computer's basic working instructions.
- **These chips** contain data that a user can access but cannot alter.

DID YOU KNOW?

The IBM 'Roadrunner' computer at Los Alamos National Laboratory, USA, can make more than a quadrillion calculations in a second.

- **Microchips known as RAM** (random access memory) are the components that receive new data and user instructions and work in progress.
- **At the heart** of every computer is a powerful microchip called the CPU (central processing unit). This carries out the main processing – altering data (information) according to instructions from the application (program) and from the user.
- **Computers use a binary system**, storing and adding information as a series of on/off (one/zero) electronic pulses known as binary code.
- **A single digit** of binary code is known as a bit and eight bits make a byte. One million bytes is a megabyte (MB) and one billion bytes is a gigabyte (GB).

◀ *Improvements in the data capacity of chips and software programs have led to very sophisticated computer games, such as* Days Gone, *an action-adventure set in a post-apocalyptic world.*

Elements

- **Elements are** the Universe's basic chemicals. Each element is made from atoms with a particular number of protons (indicated by the element's atomic number).
- **Nearly 120 elements** have so far been recognized.
- **Chemists have organized** the elements into a table called the Periodic Table.
- **Of the most recently** identified elements, at least 20 were created by scientists and do not exist in nature.
- **The most** recently discovered elements all have large, heavy atoms.
- **Hydrogen** is the lightest element. It has an atomic number of 1.

DID YOU KNOW?

Scientists fired calcium atoms at californium atoms to create the element oganesson, which has an atomic number of 118 and the heaviest-ever atoms.

- **The heaviest** element that occurs naturally is osmium, with an atomic number of 76.
- **When elements combine** with other elements they form chemical compounds.

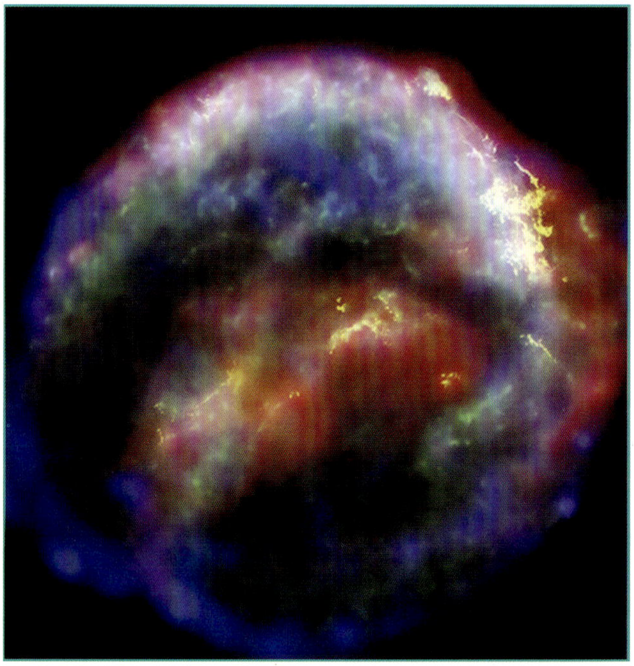

▲ *Iron and other heavy elements were created when smaller atoms were forced together in giant supernova explosions in space.*

- **New elements** are given temporary names based on their atomic number. For example, the new element with atomic number 116 was called ununhexium because un is Latin for 'one' and hex is Latin for 'six'. It is now called livermorium.

Electrons

- **Electrons are by far** the smallest of the three main, stable parts of every atom (the other two parts are protons and neutrons). In a normal atom there are the same number of electrons as protons.
- **Electrons are much smaller** than protons. They are more than 1800 times lighter. They have a mass of 0.000000000000000000000000000009109 kg. This can be written as 9.109×10^{-31} kg (10^{-31} is a short way of writing that the decimal point should be moved 31 places to the left).
- **Electrons were discovered** by English physicist J J Thomson in 1897 when he realized that the glowing rays made by electricity inside a glass tube (called a cathode ray tube) were actually streams of tiny particles. Until then, an atom was thought to be a solid ball.
- **Electrons are packets** of energy travelling around the nuclei of atoms.
- **Electrons have** a tiny negative electrical charge. This means they are attracted to positive electrical charges and pushed away by negative charges.
- **Electrons are attracted to the nucleus** because the protons in the nucleus have a positive charge that equals the negative charge of the electrons.
- **The distance between** the electron and nucleus depends on the energy level of the electrons. The greater an electron's energy, the farther it will be from the nucleus.
- **Although electrons** are usually shown circling a nucleus, as a planet circles the Sun, they do not quite do this. It is more accurate to think of an electron as a cloud around the nucleus.
- **Electrons are arranged** in shells, or 'energy levels', at different distances around the nucleus. Each shell can hold a particular number of electrons: the first shell can hold up to 2, the second up to 8, the third up to 18, the fourth up to 32, the fifth about 50, and the sixth about 72.

Carbon

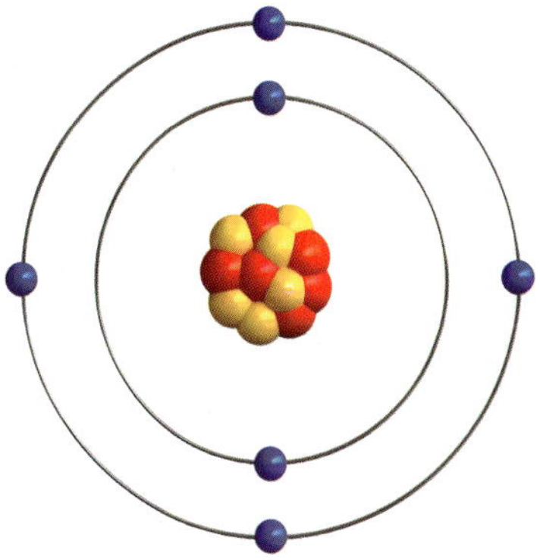

6 Protons 6 Neutrons 6 Electrons

Oxygen

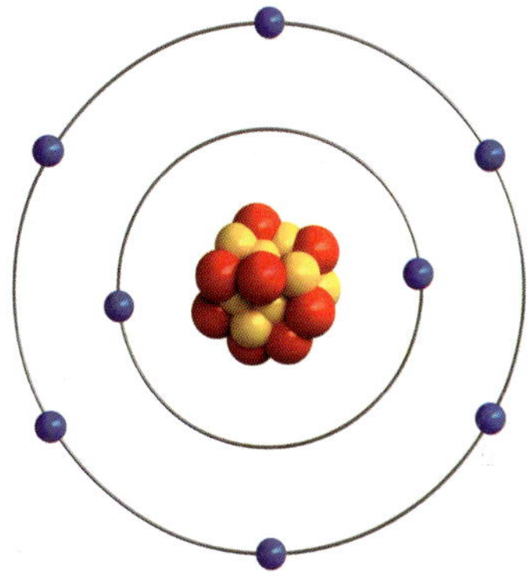

8 Protons 8 Neutrons 8 Electrons

Sodium

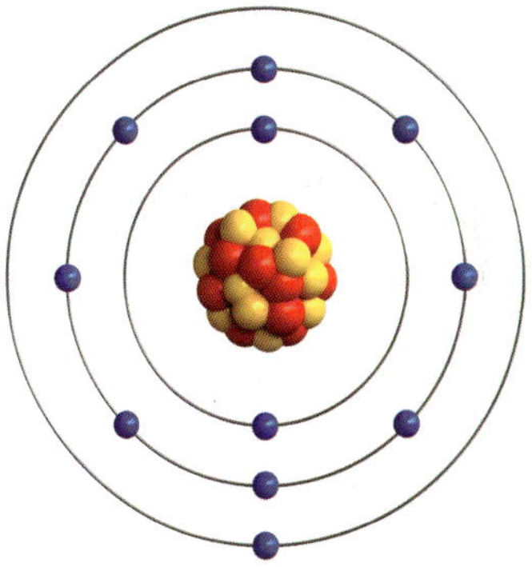

11 Protons 12 Neutrons 11 Electrons

Chlorine

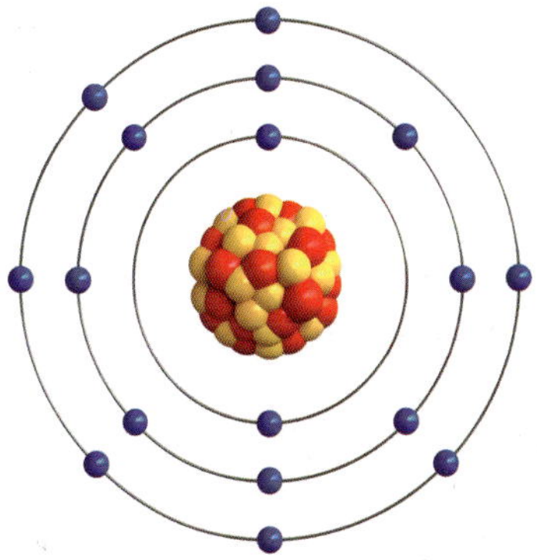

17 Protons 18 Neutrons 17 Electrons

▶ *Every type of atom has a different number of electrons. The electron shell structures for four common atoms are shown here.*

DID YOU KNOW?

In 2008, scientists filmed an electron moving using pulses of laser light. Each pulse lasted an attosecond (a billion billionths of a second).

Oxygen

DID YOU KNOW?

Most of the oxygen in the air is produced by marine organisms called algae.

● **Oxygen is the second** most plentiful element on Earth. It is a colourless, odourless, tasteless gas, and makes up 20.94 percent of the air.

● **Almost all living things** with more than one cell need oxygen to survive. Many bacteria (which have only one cell) can live without oxygen and some are even poisoned by it.

● **Oxygen becomes liquid** at −183.0°C. Liquid oxygen is pale blue in colour. It freezes at −218.4°C.

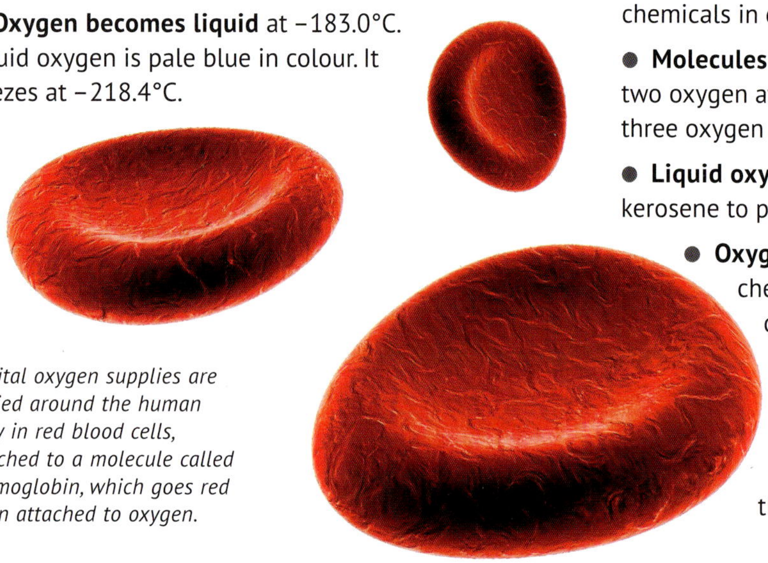

▶ *Vital oxygen supplies are carried around the human body in red blood cells, attached to a molecule called haemoglobin, which goes red when attached to oxygen.*

● **Living organisms** are dependent upon oxygen, because it joins with other chemicals in living cells, such as glucose, to release energy. This process is known as cellular respiration.

● **Oxygen is one of the most** reactive elements, so in the Earth's crust it is usually found joined with other chemicals in compounds.

● **Molecules of oxygen** in the air are made from two oxygen atoms. Molecules of the gas ozone have three oxygen atoms.

● **Liquid oxygen** (LOX) is combined with fuels such as kerosene to produce rocket fuel.

● **Oxygen was discovered** by both the Swedish chemist Carl Scheele and the English clergyman and scientist Joseph Priestley independently during the 1770s.

● **The word** 'oxygen' means acid-forming. Oxygen was named in 1779 by French scientist Antoine Lavoisier, who wrongly thought it to be a component of all acids.

Einstein

● **Albert Einstein** (1879–1955) was the most famous scientist of the 20th century.

● **Einstein was half German** and half Swiss, but when Hitler came to power in 1933, Einstein made his home in the USA.

● **Einstein's fame** rests on his two theories of Relativity.

● **His theory** of Special Relativity was published in 1905 while he worked in the Patent Office in Bern, Switzerland.

● **In 1905** Einstein also explained the photoelectric effect, showing that light can be used to produce electricity. From these ideas, photo cells were developed – these are used in solar panels and many other devices.

▶ *Einstein's equation $E=mc^2$ revealed the energy in atoms that is exploited to produce nuclear power.*

● **Einstein completed** his theory of General Relativity in 1915.

● **Einstein** was not satisfied with his theory of General Relativity as it didn't include electromagnetism. He spent the last 25 years of his life trying to develop a 'Unified Field Theory' to include it.

● **Einstein** was once reported to have said that only 12 people in the world could understand his theory. He denied saying it.

● **In 1939** Einstein urged US President Franklin Roosevelt to authorise work on nuclear bomb development because he knew the Nazis in Germany were close to developing their own nuclear weapons.

● **Einstein was married twice**. His first wife was Mileva Maric. His second wife Elsa was also his first cousin.

Solids, liquids and gases

● **Most substances** can exist in three states – solid, liquid and gas – known as the three states of matter.

● **Substances change** from one state to another as temperature and pressure change.

● **As temperatures rise** solids melt to become liquids. As they rise further, liquids evaporate to become vapours or gases.

● **The boiling point** is the maximum temperature a liquid can reach before it turns to gas, although liquids can partially evaporate at well below the boiling point.

● **The kinetic theory of matter** explains the changes from solid to liquid to gas in terms of the movement of the molecules.

● **The movement of molecules** depends on their energy. The more a substance is heated, the more energetic its molecules become.

● **Solids have** a definite shape because their molecules are bonded in a rigid structure, so they can only vibrate.

● **A liquid** flows and takes the shape of any container into which it is poured. This is because its molecules are bonded loosely enough to move over each other.

▶ In a plasma globe, electricity turns gases into a glowing, charged plasma filled with beams of light that move when a hand touches the globe's surface.

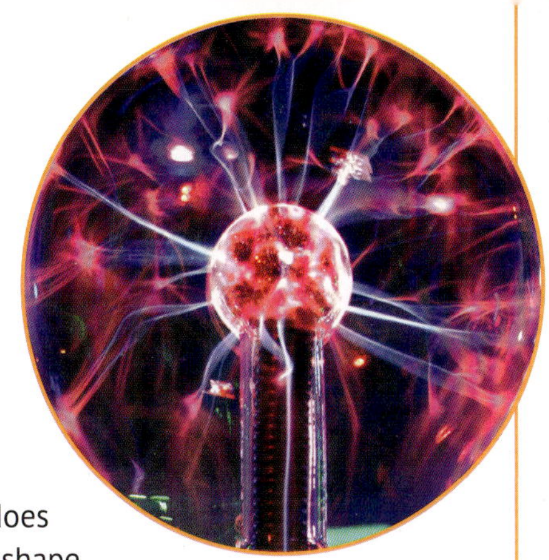

● **A gas**, such as air, does not have any definite shape or fixed volume. This is because its molecules are barely bound together at all, and are free to move around.

● **When a gas cools**, its molecules slow down until bonds form between them to create drops of liquid. This process is called condensation.

● **There are two other states of matter**. These are called plasmas and Bose-Einstein condensates.

● **Plasmas are** special gases in which all the particles are electrically charged. They are created by scientists for use in plasma TVs and neon lights, but occur naturally in space. Bose-Einstein condensates were created by scientists in 1995. They form when temperatures are so low that all the atoms almost stop moving.

Seeing the microworld

● **Microscopes are devices** used for looking at things that are normally too small for the human eye to see.

● **An optical microscope** uses a series of lenses to magnify an object. The latest optical microscopes can make a single molecule visible.

● **Electron microscopes** fire electrons at an object, which bounce off it onto a screen, making an image of them.

● **An electron microscope** can focus on an object that is one nanometre (one-billionth of a metre) across and magnify it five million times.

● **Scanning Electron Microscopes** (SEMs) work by scanning the surface of an object to magnify it by up to 100,000 times. They are so powerful that they can make individual atoms visible.

● **Transmission Electron Microscopes** shine electrons through thin slices of an object to magnify it millions of times.

● **The world's most powerful** transmission electron microscope is called the TEAM 0.5 microscope. It can show objects smaller than a hydrogen atom (the smallest of all atoms).

● **Scanning Acoustic Microscopes** use sound waves to see inside tiny opaque objects.

● **Scanning Tunnelling Microscopes** can make images of subatomic particles, which are the tiny particles that make up an atom.

◀ This image taken by a scanning tunnelling microscope reveals the exact shape of a fragment of DNA.

Electromagnetic spectrum

- **Electromagnetic radiation** is energy emitted by atoms. It travels in minute packets of energy called 'photons' that can behave either as particles or as waves.
- **Waves of electromagnetic radiation** can vary in length and frequency. The electromagnetic spectrum is the entire possible range.
- **The longest waves** are over 100 km in length, while the shortest are less than a billionth of a millimetre long.
- **The human eye** can see just a small range of wavelengths, known as visible light. Every colour we see has its own wavelength.
- **Infrared (IR)** is electromagnetic radiation given off by warm objects in waves just too long for the human eye to see. Ultraviolet (UV) is electromagnetic radiation given off by very hot objects in waves just too short for the eye to see.
- **Waves longer than light include**: terahertz (used for security body scans), microwaves (used in microwave ovens), and radio waves (used by radios, televisions, mobile phones and wireless networks). Longer waves are less energetic than short waves.

▼ *This satellite photo clearly shows all the 'near' IR (IR with waves shorter than heat) reflected by healthy vegetation, shown in red.*

▼ *X-rays are waves that can shine through many body tissues, just like light shines through paper. They are blocked by bone, so bones make shadows on medical photos taken with X-rays.*

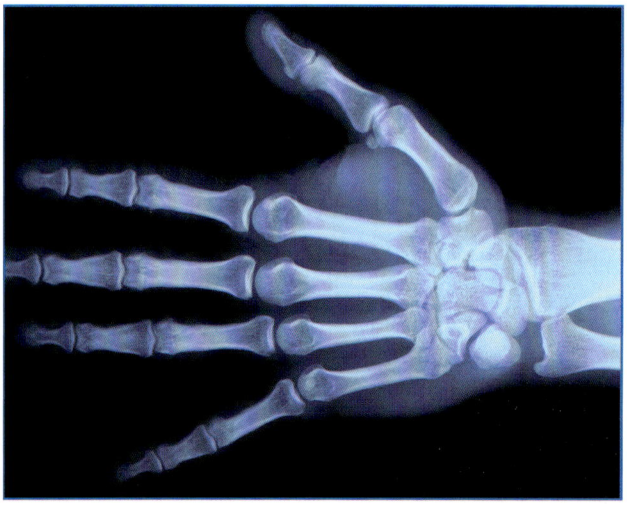

- **Waves shorter than light**, such as UV, X-rays and gamma rays, are very energetic, and can penetrate some solid materials that block light. That makes exposure to them dangerous.
- **UV in sunlight** in small doses tans the skin, but in large doses can cause skin cancer.
- **X-rays are harmless in brief doses** and are short enough to pass through most body tissues except bone. This is why they can be used to make medical X-ray photos.
- **Gamma rays** are dangerous even in small doses but they can be used in some body scans and to 'irradiate' seeds to stop them growing until needed.

DID YOU KNOW?

All electromagnetic waves travel at just under 300,000 km/sec – the speed of light.

▼ *The electromagnetic spectrum ranges from long wavelength, low energy radio waves to short wavelength, high-energy gamma rays.*

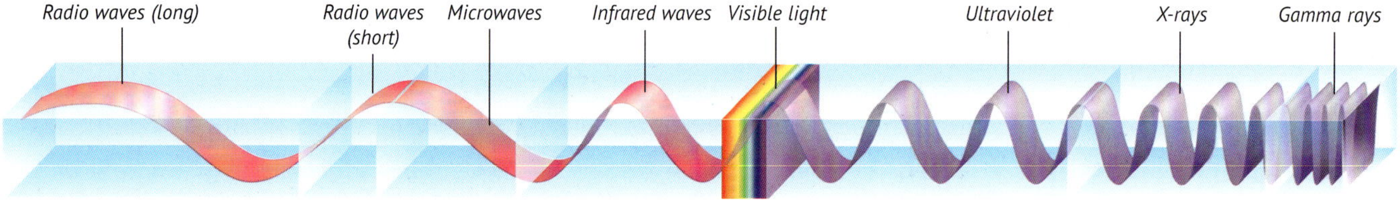

Magnets

- **A magnet is a material** in which the electrons are specially positioned so they all 'face' the same way, producing a magnetic field. This field can attract other materials that are magnetic (meaning they can have their electrons lined up in the same way). Iron is a strongly magnetic material.
- **A magnetic field** is the area around a magnet where its magnetic force can be detected.
- **A magnet** has north and south 'poles' near each end. The magnetic field is strongest at the poles.
- **'Like' poles** (the north poles of two magnets) repel each other, and 'unlike' poles (the north pole of one magnet and south pole of another) attract each other.
- **An electric current** creates a magnetic field. Earth has a magnetic field created by electric currents inside its iron core. The magnetic north pole is close to the geographic North Pole.

DID YOU KNOW?

If you cut a magnet in half you get two magnets, each with their own north and south poles.

- **If suspended freely**, a magnet will turn so that its north pole points to Earth's magnetic north pole.
- **The strength of a magnet** is measured in teslas. The Earth's magnetic field is 0.00005 teslas.
- **Magnetic materials** are made up of groups of atoms (domains). Each domain is a tiny molecular magnet with north and south poles.

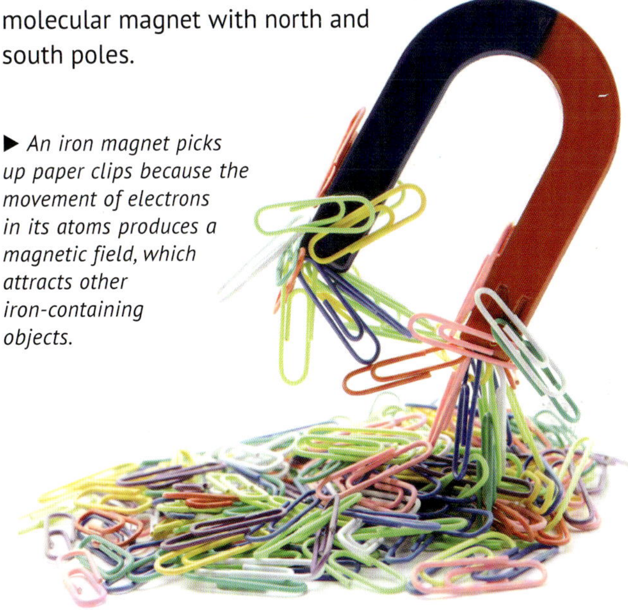

▶ *An iron magnet picks up paper clips because the movement of electrons in its atoms produces a magnetic field, which attracts other iron-containing objects.*

Pressure

- **Pressure is force** applied to a surface.
- **It is measured** as the force acting per unit area of surface. The standard unit of pressure is a pascal (Pa) or 1 newton per sq m (N/m^2).
- **The pressure at the centre of the Earth** may be 400 billion Pa. Steel can withstand 40 million Pa, while a shark bite can be 30 million Pa.
- **Pressure in a gas or liquid** is actually the assault of fast-moving molecules on surfaces around or within it.
- **An inflated bicycle tyre** feels firm because of the constant assault by air molecules on the inside of the tyre. Pumping pushes more air molecules into the available space and so increases pressure.
- **Pressures are greater** in liquids than in gas because liquids are denser. Pressure rises as you descend into the ocean because the density of water increases.
- **Air pressure** outside your body is balanced by the pressure of fluids inside your body. Without this internal pressure, air pressure would crush your body instantly.

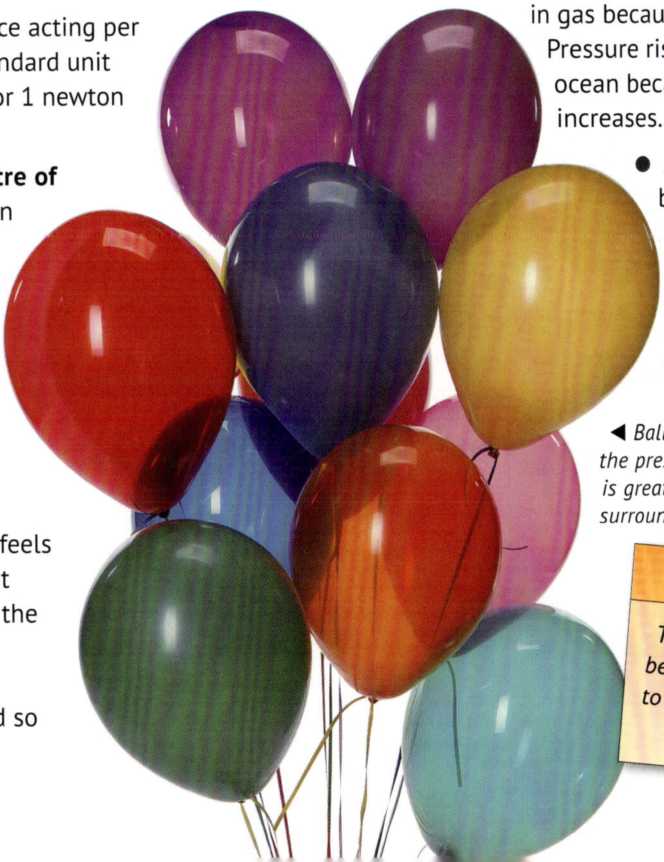

◀ *Balloons become inflated because the pressure of the air inside them is greater than the pressure of the surrounding air.*

DID YOU KNOW?

The water pressure 10,000 m below the surface is equivalent to seven elephants standing on a dinner plate.

Machines

DID YOU KNOW?

One of the world's biggest machines is the SMEC Earthmover, which is used in opencast mines in Australia. It weighs 180 tonnes and has wheels 3.5 m high.

- **In science**, a machine is a device that cuts down the effort needed to move a load. It works by modifying the force applied or changing its direction.
- **Simple machines** include levers, gears, pulleys, screws and wedges.
- **Complex machines**, such as cranes, are built up from combinations of simple machines.
- **Machines reduce the effort** by spreading the load over a greater distance or a longer time.
- **The mechanical advantage** (MA) is a measure of how effective a machine is. It is the ratio of the load to the effort needed to move it.
- **The velocity ratio** (VR) is the distance moved by the effort divided by the distance moved by the load.
- **In a perfect machine**, the VR would match the MA, but most machines are inefficient, with losses between the effort and the load due to forces such as friction (the resistance one surface encounters when moving over another).
- **Whenever a force moves an object**, scientists say work is done. Work is the force applied multiplied by the distance moved.

▶ *Enormous cranes are used to load containers onto large ships at ports around the world.*

- **The efficiency** of a machine is the ratio of the work done in moving the load to the work involved in applying the effort.
- **One of the world's biggest machines** is the SMEC Earthmover, which is used in opencast mines in Australia. It weighs 180 tonnes and has wheels 3.5 m high.

Faraday

- **Michael Faraday** (1791–1867) was one of the greatest experimental scientists of the 19th century.
- **Faraday was the son** of a poor blacksmith, born in the village of Newington in Surrey, England.
- **He started work** as an apprentice bookbinder but became assistant to the great scientist Humphry Davy after taking brilliant notes at one of Davy's lectures.
- **Faraday was said** to be Davy's greatest discovery.
- **In 1821** Faraday showed that the magnetism created by an electric current would make a magnet move and so made a very simple version of an electric motor.
- **In 1825** Faraday discovered the important chemical benzene.
- **In 1831** Faraday showed that when a magnet moves close to an electric wire, it creates, or induces, an electric current in the wire. This was discovered at the same time by Joseph Henry in the USA.

▲ *Faraday was a popular figure who gave a series of lectures to young people at the Royal Institution in London. These 'Christmas lectures' continue today.*

- **Using his discovery** of electric induction, Faraday made the first dynamo to generate electricity and so opened the way to the modern age of electricity.
- **In the 1840s** Faraday suggested the idea of lines of magnetic force and electromagnetic fields. These ideas, which were later developed by James Clerk Maxwell, underpin much of modern science.
- **Faraday was probably** the greatest scientific experimenter of all time.

Electric circuits

● **An electric circuit** is an unbroken loop of conducting material along which an electric charge may flow.

● **This flow of electricity** around a circuit is called an electrical current. It will only flow through a good conductor.

● **There are three basic components** in an electric circuit: a conductor, an energy source and an object for the circuit to power.

● **A conductor** is a substance that will permit electrical energy or heat to travel through it.

● **A current will only flow** if there is an energy force to push the electric charge. This force is called an electromotive force (emf).

● **An emf is created** by a battery or generator. Without an emf, charged electrons will just move randomly inside the conductor in different directions and not produce an electric current.

● **When a conductor** is connected to a battery, the negatively charged electrons are attracted to the battery's positive terminal, so they flow towards it, in one direction. The flow produces an electric current.

DID YOU KNOW?

The electrical resistance of dry skin is 500,000 ohms, whereas wet skin is just 1000 ohms.

● **Batteries give potential energy** to the electrons that come from it. The amount of electrical energy varies at different points in a circuit. This difference is measured in volts.

● **The rate** at which current flows is measured in amps. It depends on the voltage and the resistance (how much the circuit obstructs the flow of current). Resistance is measured in ohms.

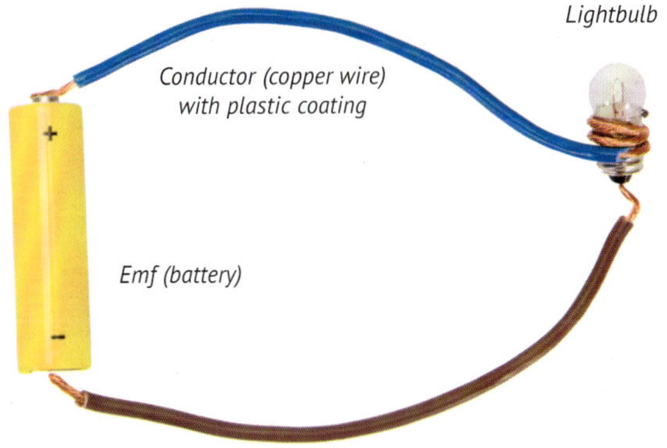

▲ *A battery provides the emf for an electric current to flow through the circuit and light the bulb.*

Chemical compounds

● **Compounds are substances** that are made when the atoms of two or more different elements join together.

● **The properties of a compound** are usually very different from the properties of the elements from which the compound is made.

● **Atoms in a compound** are joined chemically, and can only be separated by a chemical reaction.

● **All molecules** in a compound have identical combinations of atoms.

● **A chemical compound's scientific name** is usually a combination of the names of the elements that make it up, although it might have a different common name.

● **In the compound** sodium chloride (table salt), each molecule has one sodium and one chlorine atom.

● **The chemical formula** tells you which and how many atoms a molecule contains.

● **The chemical formula for water** is H_2O because every water molecule has two hydrogen (H) atoms and one oxygen (O) atom.

● **There are 118 elements** but they combine in different ways to form many millions of compounds.

● **Combinations of the same elements**, such as carbon and hydrogen, can form many different compounds. So, one carbon atom can combine with four hydrogen atoms to make methane (CH_4) or six carbon atoms can combine with six hydrogen atoms to make benzene (C_6H_6).

● **Compounds are either organic**, which means they contain carbon atoms, or inorganic.

▼ *Robot space probes landing on Mars have confirmed that it gets its red colour from rust – the chemical compound made when iron combines with the oxygen in water.*

Plastics

▲ *The spectacular, colour-changing exterior of the Allianz Arena, in Munich, Germany, is made from the fluorine-based plastic ETFE.*

● **Plastics are synthetic** (man-made) materials that can be easily shaped and moulded.

● **Plastics are polymers**, which are long chains of organic molecules.

● **Plastic gets its properties** from the way its polymer molecules are arranged.

● **Plastics are usually made** by joining carbon and hydrogen atoms to create ethene molecules, which are then strung together in long chains, sometimes with other molecules and atoms.

● **Long chains of molecules** that slide over each other easily make flexible plastics, whereas angled chains make rigid plastics.

● **Many plastics** are made from liquids and gases that are extracted from crude oil.

▶ *A pole vaulter's pole benefits from the lightness, strength and flexibility of fibreglass, made from plastic reinforced with tough fibres of glass.*

● **Thermoplastics** are soft and easily moulded when warm but set solid when cool. They are used to make products such as bottles and drainpipes.

● **Thermoset plastics**, which cannot be remelted once set, are used to make things like telephones and pan handles.

● **Plastic can be moulded**. Blow moulding uses compressed air to push plastic into a mould. Vacuum moulding uses a vacuum to suck plastic into a mould. In extrusion moulding plastic pellets are heated, then shaped by being forced through a nozzle.

● **Polycarbonate is easily moulded** but very durable (tough). It is used to make products such as smart phones.

● **Polystyrene is very light**. It is used to make products such as disposable coffee cups because it is a good insulator, meaning it does not get hot easily.

● **Polyvinyl chloride** (PVC) is a hard plastic, so it is used to make window frames. It can be softened with plasticizers to make anything from shoes to shampoo bottles.

● **Low-density polyethene** (LDPE) is a light, flexible plastic. It is used to wrap food.

● **High-density polyethene** (HDPE) is a tough but flexible plastic that is used for making products such as toys and rubbish bins.

● **Some plastics**, such as Teflon and tetrafluorethylene (ETFE), are made from carbon and fluorine rather than hydrocarbons (compounds of carbon and hydrogen).

DID YOU KNOW?

Polycarbonate is a plastic that is resistant to chemicals, so is used to make containers for medicine and industrial chemicals.

Halogens

- **Halogens are the non-metal** chemical elements fluorine, chlorine, bromine, iodine and astatine, which make salts when they form compounds with metals.
- **The word 'halogen'** means salt-forming.
- **Many salts in the sea** are compounds of a halogen and a metal, such as sodium chloride and magnesium chloride.
- **Together the halogens** form group 17 of the Periodic Table – elements that have seven electrons in their outer shells.
- **Fluorine and chlorine** are both gases. Fluorine is pale yellow, while chlorine is greenish in colour. Bromine is a red liquid, and iodine is a black solid.
- **Astatine** is an unstable element that only survives by itself briefly. It is usually made artificially.
- **Halogens are used** in lamps. As a halogen lamp heats, its tungsten filament starts to evaporate. Halogen gas combines with the atoms of tungsten redepositing them on the filament so the lamp burns for longer.

DID YOU KNOW?

Fluorides (fluorine compounds) are often added to drinking water to prevent tooth decay.

▼ Halogen lamps are very bright because the halogen gas means their tungsten filament can burn very hot.

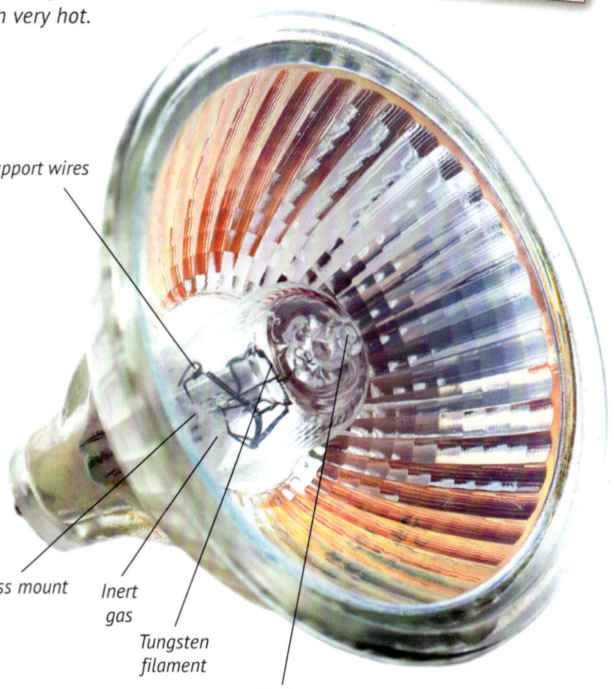

Turning forces

- **A force is** a push or pull – something that causes an object to move.
- **Forces always act in straight lines**, but when a force acts on an object that pivots or turns around a fixed point (a fulcrum), it creates a turning effect.
- **The size of the turning effect** is called the 'moment' by physicists and 'torque' by engineers. The further from the fulcrum the force is applied, the greater the moment.
- **A lever** is a simple machine consisting of a rigid bar that pivots about a fulcrum somewhere along its length.
- **In a Class 1 lever** the fulcrum is between the effort and the load. Pliers and scissors are Class 1 levers.
- **In a Class 2 lever**, the load is between the effort and the fulcrum. Screwdrivers and wheelbarrows are Class 2 levers.
- **In a Class 3 lever**, the effort is between the load and the fulcrum. Tweezers are a Class 3 lever.
- **A gear** is a toothed wheel that works with other toothed wheels to change the relation between the speed of a driving mechanism (such as a car engine) and the speed of the driven parts (the wheels).
- **The gear ratio** is the ratio of the number of teeth on two engaged gearwheels. A gear with 14 teeth needs to turn twice in order to turn a gear with 28 teeth once, giving a gear ratio of 2:1.
- **The larger the gear ratio**, the more the turning force is increased, but the slower the driven wheel turns.
- **Gears in a car** convert the rapid spinning of the engine's main shaft into the slower, more powerful turning of the driving wheels.

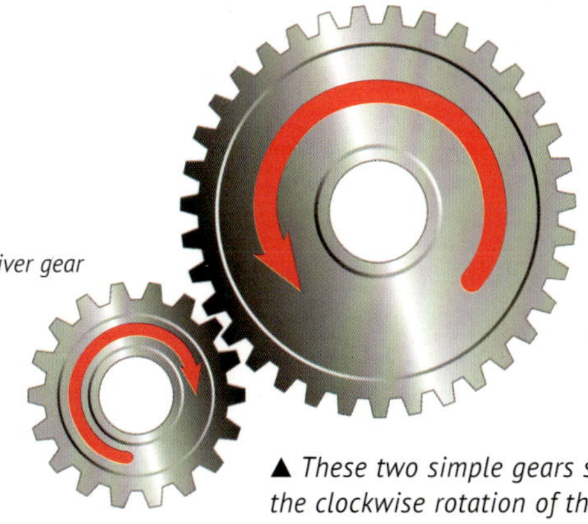

▲ These two simple gears show how the clockwise rotation of the smaller gear is converted to the anticlockwise rotation of the larger one.

New materials

- **Materials that are man-made** rather than occurring naturally are known as 'synthetic'.
- **Many synthetic materials**, such as plastics, are polymers – substances with long chains of organic molecules that are made up from lots of identical smaller molecules, called monomers.
- **Some polymers** are natural, such as the plant fibre cellulose.
- **The first synthetic polymer** was Parkesine. It was invented by Alexander Parkes in 1862.
- **The first successful** synthetic polymer was celluloid. It was invented by John Hyatt in 1869, and was soon used as photographic film.
- **Polymers can be** strung together to make light, strong fibres such as lycra.

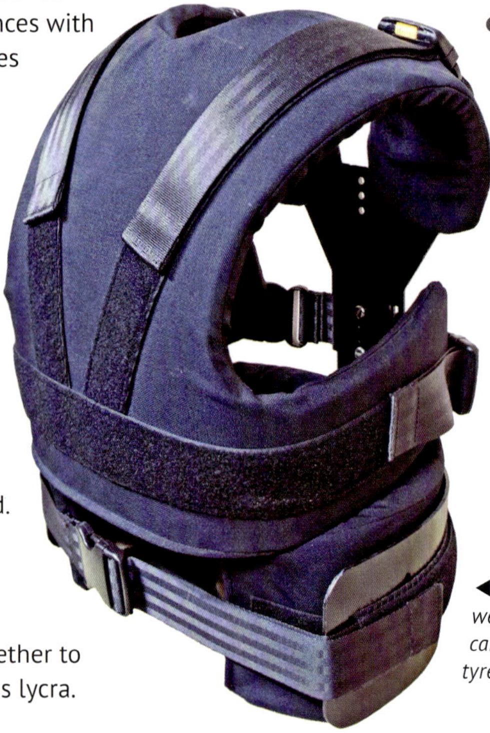

◀ *The material Kevlar has many applications. As well as being a component of bullet-proof vests, it can be used in the manufacture of things such as tyres, sails and musical instruments.*

- **The polymer nylon** was the first completely synthetic fibre. It was created by Wallace Carothers of the American company DuPont in the 1930s.
- **Kevlar is a fibre** developed by Stephanie Kwolek of DuPont in the 1960s. It is so light and tough it can be woven to make a bullet-proof vest.
- **Composites are new**, strong, light materials, made by combining a polymer with another material.
- **Carbon reinforced plastic** (CRP) is an incredibly strong, light material made by embedding tough fibres of carbon in a plastic.

Soaps and detergents

- **Soaps and detergents** are salts that can remove grease and dirt. They are known as surfactants.
- **Soaps are made** from natural compounds while detergents are made with synthetic chemicals.
- **Surfactants have special molecules**, which cling to dirt particles on surfaces and lift them away.
- **Surfactant molecules** are comprised of two parts. One part is hydrophilic (attracted to water), while the other is hydrophobic (repelled by water).
- **The hydrophobic tail** of a surfactant molecule digs its way into the dirt, while the hydrophilic head is drawn to the water.
- **Soap is made from** natural substances such as animal fats or vegetable oil combined with alkalis, such as sodium or potassium hydroxide. Most manufactured soaps also include perfumes, colours and germicides (germ-killers) as well as a surfactant.
- **Enzymes are molecules** that speed up chemical reactions. Certain enzymes can be added to detergents to help break down stains from natural substances such as blood, grease and starch.
- **Biosurfactants are natural** surfactants. Some bacteria and yeast produce biosurfactants that may be used to clean up oil spillages in the future.

▼ *Surfactant molecules on soap penetrate dirt with their water-hating tails, and so help lift the dirt off surfaces.*

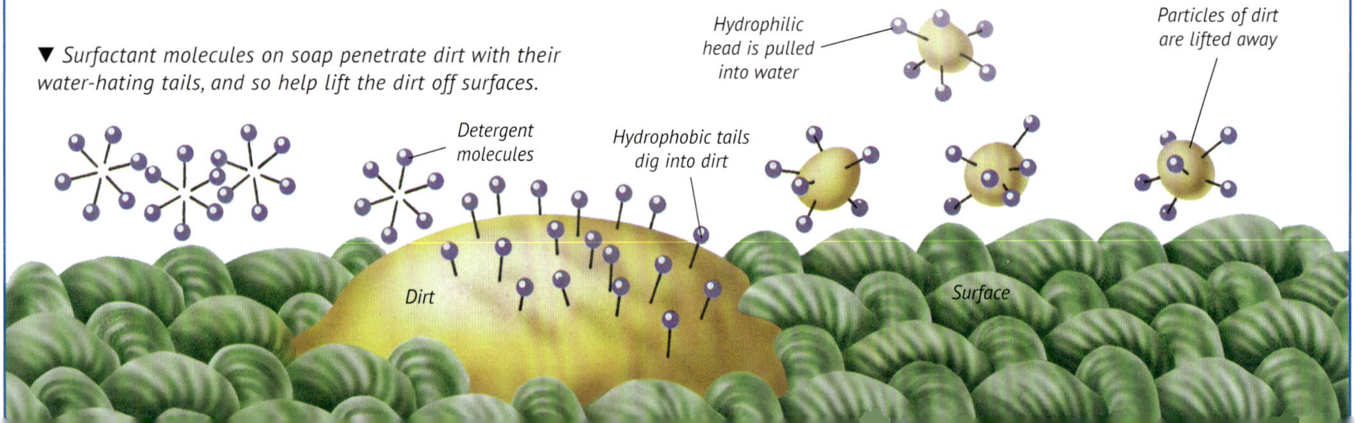

Sound

- **All of the sounds** you hear, from the whisper of the wind to the roar of a jet, are actually moving air.
- **Every sound** originates with something vibrating, like the strings of a guitar twanging to and fro. This makes the air vibrate too and the vibrations in the air carry the sound to your ears.
- **The vibrations** that carry sound through the air are called sound waves, which move by alternately squeezing air molecules together and then stretching them apart.
- **The parts of the air** that are squeezed are called condensations, and the parts of the air that are stretched are called rarefactions.
- **Sound waves** travel faster through liquids and solids than through air because molecules in liquids and solids are more closely packed together than air molecules.

DID YOU KNOW?

The speed of sound is around a million times slower than light. This is why you hear thunder after you see the flash of lightning that comes with it.

- **There is complete silence** in a vacuum (a space empty of all matter, even air) because there are no molecules to carry sound.
- **Sound travels** at 344 m/sec in air at 20°C, but 386 m/sec in air at 100°C. It travels at 1500 m/sec in water and about 6000 m/sec in steel.

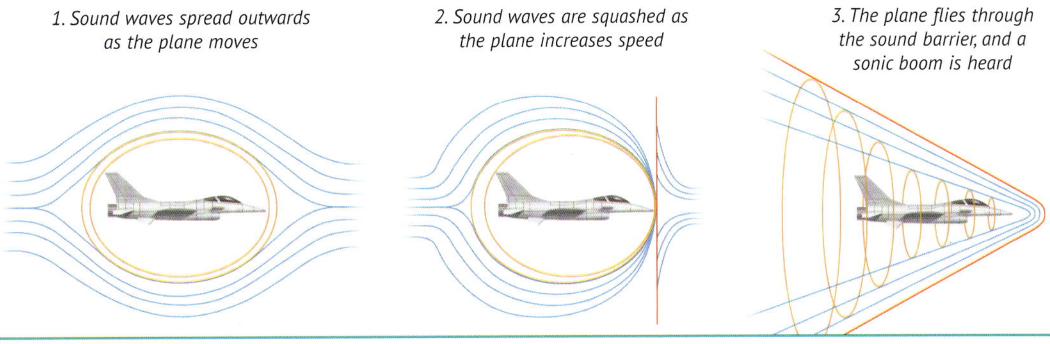

▶ *When an aircraft travels faster than sound, it squashes the air in front until it causes a 'sonic boom' as the air pops like a balloon.*

Lasers

- **A laser** is a device that creates an extremely focused beam of bright artificial light.
- **A beam of laser light** is so intense that it can punch a hole through steel, and is brighter than the Sun, in relation to its size.
- **Laser light** is the only known 'coherent' source of light. Coherent means that its light waves are all of the same frequency (wavelength) and all the same phase (the peaks and troughs of the waves all align).
- **Inside a laser** is a small space filled with either a gas, such as helium and neon, or a liquid or solid crystal, such as ruby. This is called the lasing material.
- **A burst of photons** (particles of electromagnetic radiation) excites atoms in the lasing material. The excited atoms emit photons. When the photons hit other atoms, they fire off photons too, which reflect up and down inside the space using mirrors.
- **The powerful laser beam** finally exits the space through a small hole in one of the mirrors.

DID YOU KNOW?

The word 'laser' is an abbreviation of Light Amplification by Stimulated Emission of Radiation.

- **Gas lasers** give a lower-powered beam suitable for delicate work such as eye surgery, while chemical lasers make intense beams for industrial uses.
- **Some lasers** send out a continuous beam, while pulsed lasers send out a high-powered beam at regular intervals.

▼ *Lasers provide a beam of energy so concentrated it can cut through steel.*

Crystals

▲ *Crystals often form from mineral-rich liquids on the lining of cavities in rocks called geodes.*

- **Crystals are particular kinds** of solids that are made from a regular arrangement, or lattice, of atoms or molecules. Most rocks and metals are crystals, as are snowflakes and salt.
- **Most crystals** have regular, geometrical shapes with smooth faces and sharp corners. They grow in dense masses, such as metals. Some crystals grow separately, such as grains of sugar.
- **Crystals were named** after chunks of quartz that the ancient Greeks called krystallos, which they believed were unmeltable ice.
- **Crystallization is the process** in which crystals form. It occurs when molten solids cool and solidify, or when liquids evaporate and the chemicals dissolved in them are deposited in a solid form.
- **A liquid crystal is a crystal** that can flow, like a liquid, but has a regular pattern of atoms or molecules, like a solid.
- **A liquid crystal** may change colour or go dark when the alignment of its atoms is disrupted by electricity or heat.

DID YOU KNOW?

The smallest crystals are microscopic, but occasionally crystals of a mineral such as beryl may grow to the size of telegraph poles.

- **Liquid crystal displays** (LCDs) use a tiny electric current to make the crystals twist light passing through them.
- **X-ray crystallography** uses X-rays to study the structure of atoms in crystals. It is widely used to study biological molecules, and is how we know the structure of many important life substances such as DNA.

Friction

- **Friction is a force** that acts to oppose the motion of two surfaces that are in contact with each other.
- **The type of friction** that prevents things sliding is known as static friction. The type of friction that slows sliding down is called dynamic friction.
- **The harder** two surfaces press together, the greater the force needed to overcome the friction.

◄ *Static friction keeps the tyres of a racing car firmly on the track. They only slide when the car skids as a result of stopping or turning too quickly.*

- **The coefficient of friction** (CF) is the ratio of the friction to the weight of the sliding object. Metal sliding on metal has a CF of 0.74, while ice on ice has a CF of 0.1.
- **This means** it is over seven times harder to make metal slide on metal than ice on ice.
- **Friction often** makes things hot. As the sliding surfaces are forced to slow down, some of the energy of momentum is turned into heat.
- **Fluid friction** occurs between two fluids, or between a fluid and a solid. Fluid friction makes thick fluids 'viscous' (flow less easily).
- **Oil reduces friction** by creating a film that keeps the solid surfaces apart.
- **Brakes use dynamic friction** to slow things down.
- **Drag is friction** between air and an object. It slows a fast car, or any aircraft moving through the air.

The Periodic Table

● **The Periodic Table** is a chart showing all of the known chemical elements. These are arranged in order of their atomic number, which is the number of protons the element has in the nucleus of each one of its atoms.

● **There are** 118 known elements. Of these, 98 are known to occur naturally on Earth, while the rest were created by scientists. Two of these, plutonium and neptunium, are now also known to occur naturally.

● **The table** was devised by Russian chemist Dmitry Mendeleyev in 1869. He realized that when elements were arranged by increasing atomic weight a pattern was displayed within groups of elements.

● **Mendeleyev left gaps** in places where he believed unknown elements would fall, predicting the existence of the elements gallium, scandium and germanium.

● **In the table**, the atomic number is shown in the top left corner of every element entry.

● **Atoms usually have** an equal number of electrons and protons, so as well as showing the number of protons an atom of the element has, atomic numbers also indicate the number of electrons it usually has.

● **The atomic mass** is shown in the bottom left of every entry. If you subtract an element's atomic number from its mass, the result (when rounded to the nearest whole number) is a guide to how many neutrons there are in that element's atoms. For example, calcium has an atomic mass of 40 and its atomic number is 20, so it has 20 neutrons in each of its atoms.

● **The vertical columns** in the table are called groups. The horizontal rows are called periods.

DID YOU KNOW?

The Periodic Table can be used to predict an element's qualities – such as its reactivity, conductivity and density – from its atomic mass alone.

● **As you move** across the table from left to right, the number of electrons in atoms increases.

● **Each group** is made up of elements with a certain number of electrons in their outer shell. This is what largely determines the element's character. All the elements in each group have similar properties.

● **Each period starts** on the left with a highly reactive alkali metal of group 1, such as sodium. Each atom of elements in group 1 has a single electron in its outer shell.

● **Every period ends** on the right with a stable 'noble' (colourless, odourless and tasteless) gas of group 18, such as argon. These elements have the full number of electrons in their outer shell and so they are unreactive.

● **By far the most common element** in the Universe is the simplest element, hydrogen. It was made in the first few minutes of the Big Bang and makes up about 74 percent of all known or visible matter.

▼ *In each row of the Periodic Table the atoms get heavier from left to right. Each column (up–down) contains elements with similar chemical features. Every element has a chemical symbol, name, atomic number and atomic mass. The table can be updated with new elements.*

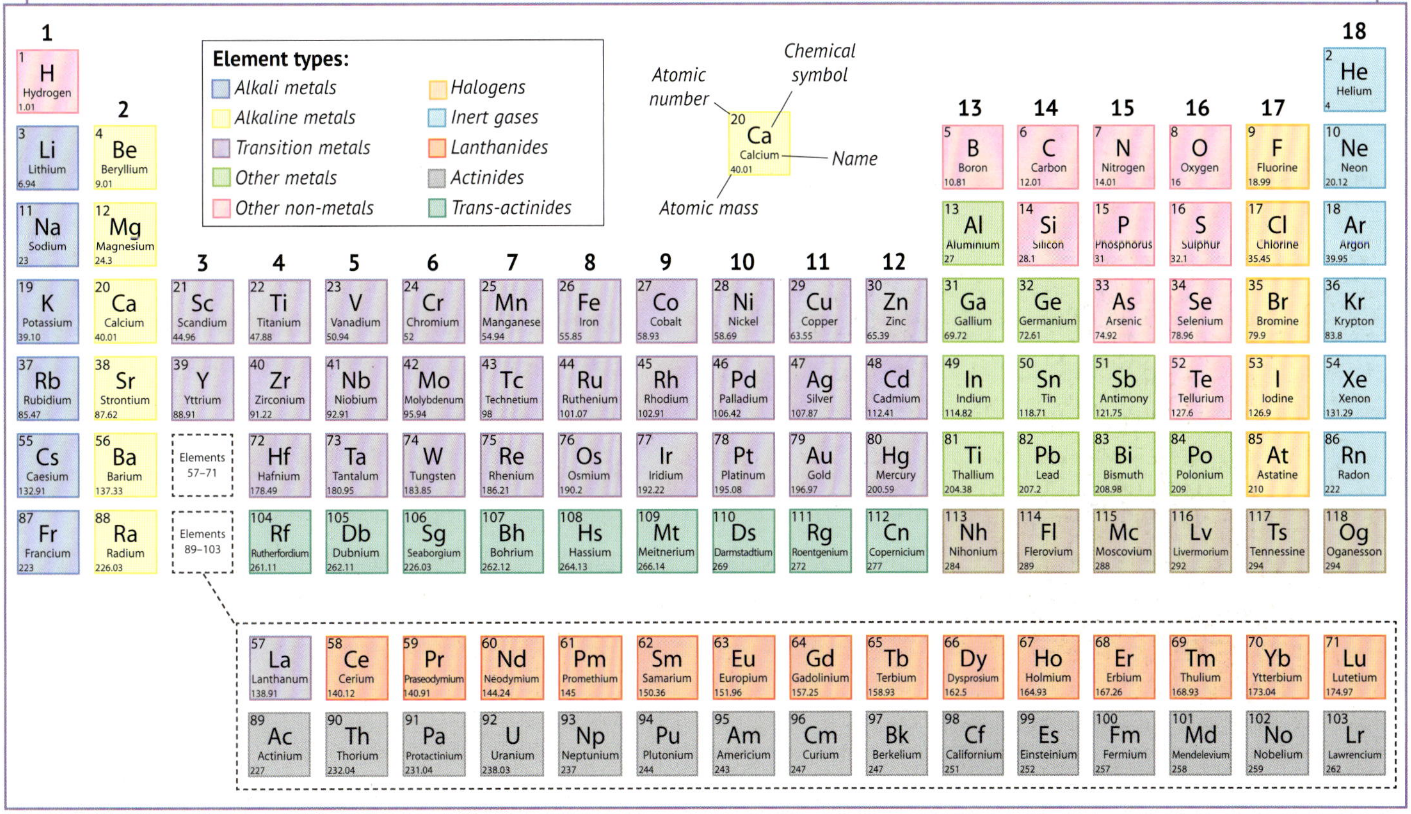

Lavoisier

● **Antoine Laurent Lavoisier** (1743–1794) was a brilliant French scientist who is regarded as the founder of modern chemistry.

● **He was elected** to the French Royal Academy of Sciences at the age of just 25 for an essay on street lighting. A year later, he worked on the first geological map of France.

● **Lavoisier earned his living** for a long while as a 'tax farmer', which meant he worked for a private company collecting taxes.

● **In 1771** he married 14-year-old Marie Paulze, who later became his illustrator and collaborator in the laboratory.

▶ *Hugely important in the history of chemistry, Lavoisier recognized and named the gases oxygen (in 1778) and hydrogen (in 1783).*

● **Lavoisier discovered** that water is a compound of hydrogen and oxygen.

● **He also** proved that burning involves oxygen.

● **Lavoisier** gave the first working list of chemical elements in his famous book *Elementary Treatise of Chemistry* (1789).

● **From 1776** Lavoisier headed research at the Royal Arsenal in Paris, developing gunpowder manufacture.

● **Lavoisier ran schemes** for public education, fair taxation, old-age insurance and other welfare projects.

● **However**, his good deeds did not save him. He was accused of fraud during the French Revolution and executed by guillotine in 1794.

Electromagnetism

● **Electromagnetism** is the combination of electricity and magnetism. Every electric current creates its own magnetic field.

● **Scottish physicist** James Maxwell (1831–1879) developed electromagnetic theory.

● **An electromagnet** is a strong magnet that is only magnetic when an electric current passes through it.

● **It is made** by wrapping a coil of wire (a solenoid) around a core of iron and passing an electric current through the wire.

● **Electromagnets are used** in most of the electric machines in use today, from ticket machines to telephones.

● **When an electric wire** is moved across a magnetic field, a current is created (induced) in the wire. This is the basis of every kind of electricity generation.

● **Electromagnets can be switched on and off**, unlike permanent magnets.

● **'Electromagnetic field'** describes the area around an electric or magnetic object in which the electromagnetic force is effective.

● **In a brain scan**, the patient's head goes inside a ring-shaped electromagnet and radio waves reveal slight changes in the field created by the brain.

▼ *Magnetic levitation (Maglev) trains use electromagnets to support the train above the rails by magnetic repulsion.*

Heat

- **Heat is a form of energy**. It is a result of the transfer of thermal energy.
- **Thermal energy** is the combined energy of moving molecules.
- **When you hold your hand** over a heater, the warmth you feel is actually the assault of billions of fast-moving molecules of air.
- **Heat is the combined energy** of all the moving molecules, whereas temperature is a measure of the average energy of the molecules.
- **The coldest temperature possible** is absolute zero, or –273.15°C. At this temperature molecules stop moving.
- **When you heat a substance**, its temperature rises because heat makes its molecules move faster.
- **The same amount** of heat will raise the temperatures of different substances by different amounts.

DID YOU KNOW?

Earth's interior produces 38 trillion watts of heat, which is 3600 times more than the entire daily energy consumption of the USA.

▲ *The heat of the Earth's interior can melt solid rock into fiery liquid lava.*

- **Specific heat** is the amount of energy required (measured in joules) to heat a substance by 1°C. This varies between different substances.
- **Latent heat** is the quantity of heat energy released or absorbed whenever a substance changes state without changing its temperature.
- **Sensible heat** is all the heat that is not converted to latent heat and so is free to move.
- **Heat spreads out** from its source. It heats up its surroundings while the source of the heat cools down.

Iron and steel

- **Iron is Earth's most** common element. It makes up 35 percent of the Earth, with most of it being in the core.
- **Iron is found** in iron ores (naturally occurring solid materials), rather than in its pure form. The ores are heated in blast furnaces to extract the iron.
- **Iron compounds** are described as ferrous or ferric.
- **Iron conducts heat** and electricity quite well and dissolves in water very slowly.
- **It is easily magnetized**, but also loses its magnetism easily.
- **Iron oxide** (rust) forms when iron combines with oxygen, especially in the presence of moisture.
- **Cast iron is iron** with 2–4 percent carbon and 1–3 percent silicon and is suitable for pouring into moulds.
- **Wrought iron** is almost pure. Carbon is removed to make it easy to bend and shape for railings and gates.

▶ *These cookers are made from steel made 'stainless' by adding chromium to keep it permanently shiny and smooth.*

DID YOU KNOW?

The chemical symbol for iron is Fe from the word ferrum, which is Latin for 'iron'.

- **Iron is made into steel** by adding traces of carbon. Steel is used in a variety of products including cars and railway lines.
- **Sixty percent** of all steel is made by the basic oxygen process where oxygen is blasted over molten iron to burn out impurities, leaving a small amount of carbon present.
- **Special alloy steels** such as chromium steels can be made from scrap iron (which is low in impurities) in an electric arc furnace.

Quantum physics

- **In the 1890s**, German physicist Max Planck showed that radiation from a hot object is not in the form of waves as everyone then thought.
- **Instead it is emitted** in tiny chunks of energy called quanta, which together behave like waves.
- **When light strikes certain atoms**, it creates electricity in what is called the photoelectric effect. Albert Einstein realized that this can be explained if light travels in quanta, not waves.
- **To Planck**, quanta were just a mathematical idea. Einstein showed they were real. Light quanta were later called photons.
- **In 1913**, Danish physicist Niels Bohr showed how the different energy levels for electrons in an atom can also be explained by quanta.
- **During the 1920s**, Erwin Schrödinger and Werner Heisenberg developed the idea of quantum energy levels in atoms to create a new branch of physics, called quantum physics.
- **Quantum physics** explains how electrons emit energy (radiation). It shows that an electron is both a particle and a wave, depending on how you look at it.
- **The development** of the technologies that gave us lasers and transistors came from quantum physics.

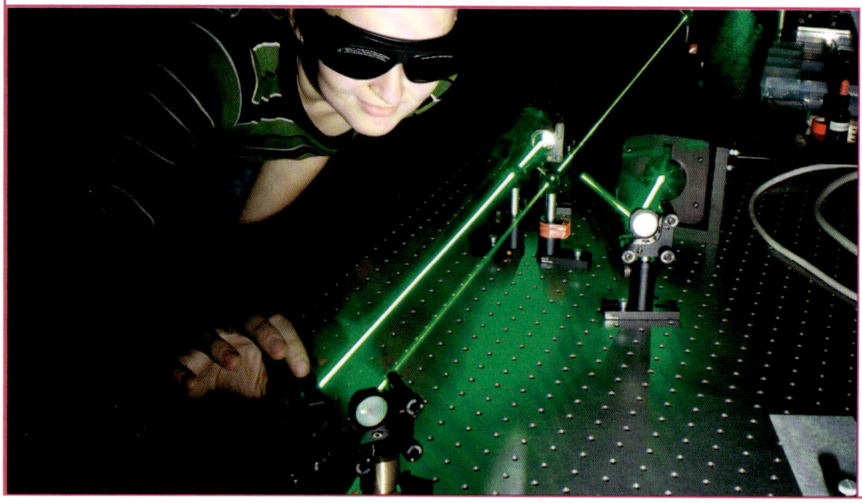

◀ *Experiments using laser beams are performed in a quantum optics lab.*

Metals

- **Most of all known elements** – in fact 75 percent of them – are metals.
- **Typical metals** are hard but also malleable, which means they can be hammered into thin sheets without breaking.
- **Metals are usually shiny**, strong, and conduct (transmit) heat and electricity well.
- **Instead of forming** separate molecules, metal atoms 'knit' together with metallic bonds to form lattice structures (regular three-dimensional arrangements).
- **All metals** have electron shells that are less than half-full. In chemical reactions metals give up their electrons to non-metals.
- **Most metals** occur naturally in the ground in rocks called ores. Gold, copper, mercury, platinum, silver and a few other rare metals occur naturally in their pure form.
- **Mercury** is the only metal that is liquid at normal temperatures. It melts at –38.83°C.
- **The element flerovium** (atomic number 114) was created in 1999. So few atoms of flerovium have ever been made that scientists can't tell what its properties are, but they think it might be a gas at room temperature, with properties of a heavy metal.

DID YOU KNOW?

Tungsten has the highest melting point of any metal – it melts at 3410°C.

▶ *The strength of steel is an essential component in skyscrapers such as the Petronas towers in Kuala Lumpur, Malaysia.*

Radioactivity

▶ *Some rocks naturally contain the isotope uranium-235. This decays radioactively over millions of years into lead-207. The decay happens at a constant rate, so scientists can tell the rock's exact age from the proportion of uranium-235 compared to lead-207. The higher the proportion of lead-207, the older the rock.*

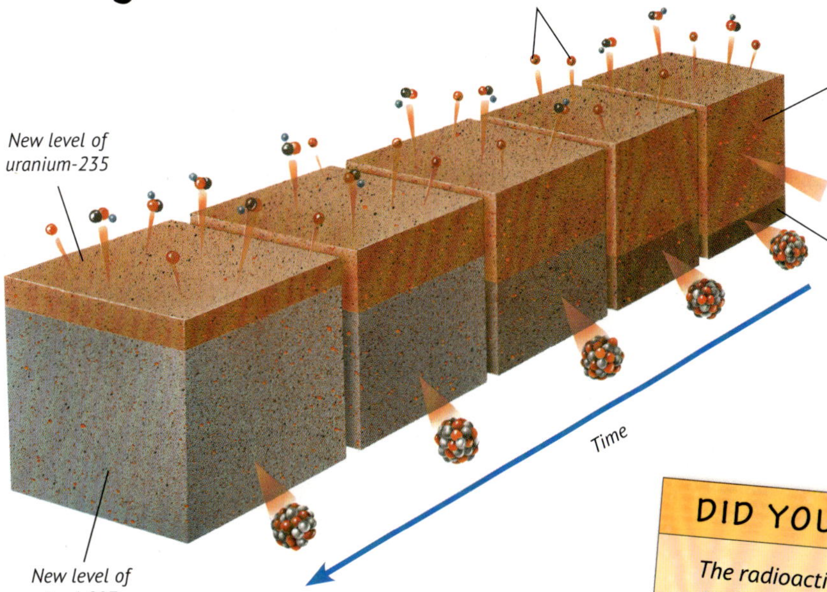

DID YOU KNOW?

The radioactive substance radium was once used to make glow-in-the-dark paints – until scientists realized how dangerous these substances can be.

- **Radioactivity** is the spontaneous disintegration of a certain kind of atom. As it breaks up, the atom emits little bursts of radiation.
- **These atoms** emit three kinds of radiation, called alpha, beta and gamma rays.
- **Alpha rays** are streams of alpha particles. These are made from two protons and two neutrons. Alpha rays can be stopped by a sheet of paper.
- **Beta rays** are streams of beta particles – these are electrons that are emitted as a neutron decays into a proton and an electron. Beta particles can penetrate aluminium foil.
- **Gamma rays** are electromagnetic waves of short wavelength and high energy. They can penetrate most materials and are the most dangerous form of radiation.
- **Radiation can be dangerous** because it can damage molecules in living cells when it collides with them. This can result in the cells becoming cancerous.
- **Isotopes** are atoms of the same element that contain the same number of protons and electrons as each other (as in normal atoms) but different numbers of neutrons.
- **A radioactive isotope** is called a radioisotope. Some atoms, such as uranium, are so unstable that all their isotopes are radioisotopes.
- **When a large**, unstable atomic nucleus disintegrates, it emits alpha and beta particles and becomes the atom of another element. This is called radioactive decay.
- **The half-life** of a radioactive substance is the time it takes for half of its radioactive atoms to decay. It is much easier to assess than the time it takes for all radioactivity to disappear.
- **All living things** contain carbon-14, a radioisotope of carbon. When an animal dies, carbon-14 leaks away at a steady rate, like a ticking clock. The amount of carbon-14 left in an animal's remains tells scientists how long ago it died. This is called carbon-dating.

Animals take in carbon-14 when they eat plant matter

After death, the carbon-14 begins to leak away

Carbon-14 in remains can be used to pinpoint date of death

◀ *Carbon-dating is one of a variety of ways radioactive decay is used to tell how long ago things happened, such as the death of a prehistoric mammoth.*

Light and atoms

- **Atoms give out light** when they gain energy by absorbing electromagnetic waves, or when hit by other particles.
- **Normally, atoms** are in a 'ground' state in which their electrons circle close to the nucleus, where their energy is at its lowest ebb.
- **An atom emits light** when it is excited (raised from the ground state) by taking in energy. When they gain energy, electrons move further away from the nucleus.
- **An atom** only stays excited for a fraction of a second before the electron drops back towards the nucleus.
- **When electrons** drop back, they release the energy they gained as a packet of electromagnetic radiation (a photon). Electrons drop towards the nucleus in steps.
- **Each 'step'** has its own energy level, so the energy of a photon depends precisely on how big the steps are.
- **Big steps** send out higher-energy short-wave photons such as X-rays.
- **The colour of the light** that an atom sends out depends on the size of the steps its electrons jump down.
- **Each kind of atom** has its own range of electron energy steps, so each sends out particular colours of light.
- **The range of colours** each kind of atom sends out is called its emission spectrum.
- **Atoms absorb light** as well as emitting it. A particular atom can only absorb particular wavelengths. This is known as an atom's absorption spectrum.

▼ *Astronomers can tell what distant stars are made of from the colour of light emitted by their atoms.*

Light fibres

DID YOU KNOW?

Fibre optic cables run along the seabed of the Atlantic and Pacific Oceans.

- **Optical fibres** are threads of transparent glass.
- **Fibre optic cables are** bundles of these threads that are used to transmit data.
- **For data to be transmitted** using fibre optics, it must be turned into a digital form (a series of on/off signals).
- **These signals** power a light source at the end of a fibre to pulse on and off. This coded light signal then travels along optical fibres until it reaches its destination, where circuits turn it back into an electrical signal.

- **A thin layer of wrapping** (cladding) surrounds each fibre to stop light spilling out. The cladding reflects all light back into the fibre, no matter how much the fibre twists and turns. This is called total internal reflection.
- **Single-mode fibres** are very narrow, so they require a laser light source, and are used for long-distance transmissions.
- **Multi-mode fibres** are wider than single-mode fibres, so they don't have to use lasers. They are less expensive, but unsuitable for long distances.
- **The largest cables** can carry hundreds of thousands of phone calls or hundreds of television channels.
- **Optical fibres** also have medical uses. An endoscope is a flexible tube containing bundles of optical fibres. Lenses at each end allow surgeons to view inside a patient's body.

◀ *Optical fibres allow huge amounts of information to be transmitted at the speed of light.*

Floating and sinking

- **When an object** is placed in liquid, its weight displaces (pushes away) a certain volume of the liquid.
- **A force called** 'upthrust' pushes upwards on the solid. This is equal in size to the weight of the displaced liquid.
- **If the upthrust** is equal to or greater than the object's weight it will float. This is called Archimedes' principle.
- **An object sinks** until its weight is equal to the upthrust of the water, at which point it floats. The ability of an object to float is called 'buoyancy'.
- **The density** of a substance is the ratio of its mass to its volume.
- **An object will only float** if it has the same density or is less dense than the liquid surrounding it.
- **A steel ship can float**, even though steel is denser than water, because its hull is full of air. The ship will sink to a point where enough water is displaced to match the combined weight of the steel and the air inside the hull, and then it will float.
- **Ships float** at different heights according to how heavily they are laden and how dense the water is.
- **Ships float higher** in sea water than in fresh water because salt makes sea water more dense.
- **Ships float higher** in dense cold seas than in warm tropical ones.

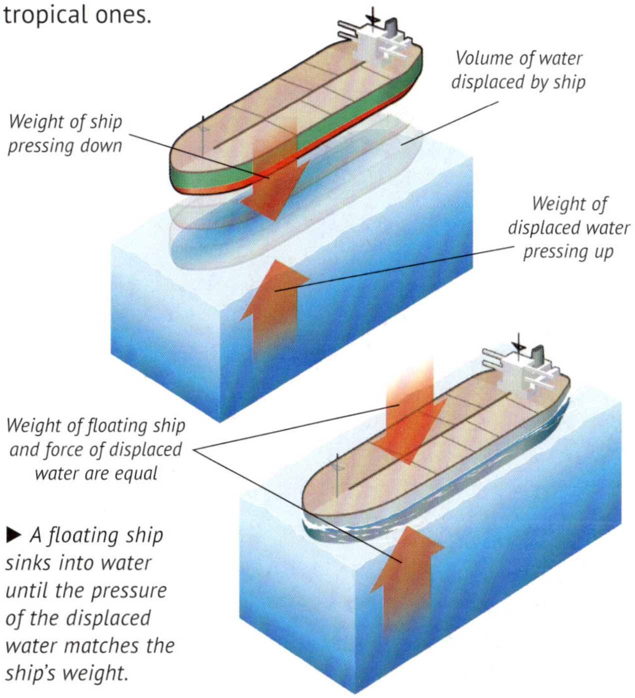

▶ *A floating ship sinks into water until the pressure of the displaced water matches the ship's weight.*

Electronics

- **Electronics is the technology** of electrical control systems, at the heart of everything from cars to mobile phones, hearing aids, activity trackers and computers.
- **Electronic components** control operations in these systems by switching tiny electrical circuits on and off.

▼ *Tiny electronic circuits are made by printing the circuit pattern on a copper-coated board, then dissolving away unwanted bits.*

- **Transistors are the key components** of every electronic system. They control the flow of electricity.

DID YOU KNOW?

A computer's Central Processing Unit (CPU) is made of a microprocessor – a chip containing all the circuits that carry out the computer's instructions.

- **A transistor** uses the properties of a semi-conductive material to control and amplify the flow of current through a circuit.
- **Diodes are transistors** with two connection points: an 'in' and an 'out'. They are simple switches, turning the current on or off.
- **Triodes are transistors** with three connection points: an 'in', an 'out' and a 'control'. They can amplify the current or reduce it.
- **A silicon chip** consists of thousands of transistors linked by thin metal strips, integrated (contained) within a single crystal (microchip) of the semiconductor silicon.
- **The electronic areas** of a chip are those treated with traces of chemicals, such as boron and phosphorus, which alter the conductivity of silicon.

Splitting the atom

- **Atoms were thought to be solid** and unbreakable until the 1890s. Then, in 1897, British physicist J J Thomson discovered that atoms contained even smaller particles, which he called electrons.
- **Scientists thought** electrons were embedded in the body of atoms. Then, in 1909, New Zealand physicist Ernest Rutherford fired alpha particles at gold foil. Most went straight through the foil, but a few bounced back.
- **Rutherford concluded** that atoms are empty space (which the alpha particles passed through) but that each has a tiny, dense nucleus at its centre.
- **In 1919**, Rutherford split the nucleus of a nitrogen atom with alpha particles and, in 1932, James Chadwick showed that the nucleus was made of two kinds of particle: neutrons and protons.
- **In 1933**, Enrico Fermi bombarded the nuclei of uranium atoms with neutrons, producing 'fission products' that were fragments of the original atoms.
- **German scientists** Otto Hahn and Fritz Strassman repeated Fermi's experiment in 1939 and found that the atoms created were a radioactive form of the much lighter element barium.
- **This indicated** that the uranium atom had split into two lighter atoms, a discovery that opened the way to releasing nuclear energy by fission.

▼ *You cannot actually see subatomic particles, but after they collide, they leave tracks behind them that can be recorded photographically.*

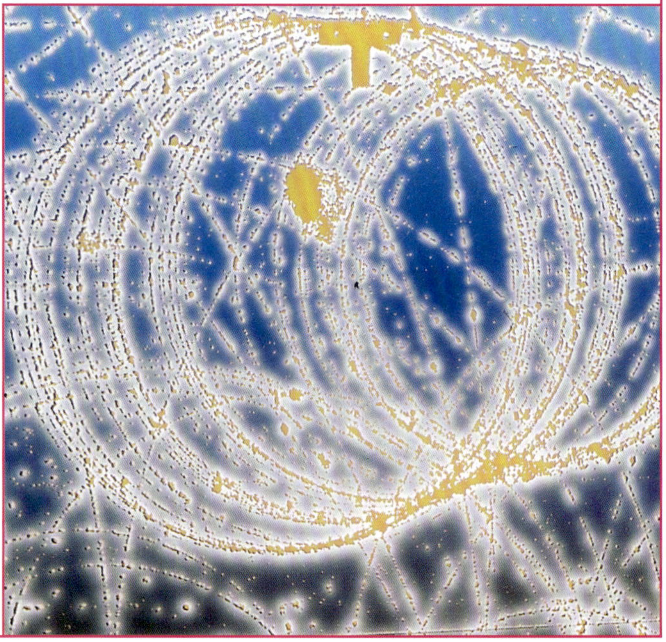

Heat movement

- **Heat moves** in three different ways: conduction, convection and radiation.
- **Conduction involves** heat spreading from hot areas to cold areas by direct contact. It works a bit like a relay race – energetic, rapidly moving or vibrating molecules bump into their neighbours, setting them moving.
- **Good conducting materials**, such as metals, feel cool to the touch because they carry heat away from your fingers quickly.

DID YOU KNOW?

Radiation transfers heat at the speed of light, so heat reaches us from the Sun in just eight-and-a-half minutes.

- **The best conductors of heat** are the metals silver, copper and gold, in that order.
- **Materials that conduct heat slowly** are called insulators. They help keep things warm by reducing heat loss. Wood is one of the best insulators. Water is also effective as an insulator.
- **Convection is the movement** of currents of hot and cold fluid (liquid or gas). An example of this is when warm air rises through cool air, as in a hot-air balloon.
- **Convection currents** are circulation patterns set up as warm air (or liquid) rises. Around the column of rising warmth, cool air (or liquid) continually sinks to replace it at the bottom.
- **Radiation is the spread of heat** as heat rays, that is, invisible waves of infrared radiation.
- **Radiation spreads heat** without direct contact.

◀ *A hot-air balloon contains air that is heated by a burner. The heat makes air molecules inside the balloon spread out, making the air inside the balloon lighter than the air around it, and the balloon rise.*

Telecommunications

● **Telecommunications** is the process in which data is transmitted almost instantaneously by electronic means.

● **Every communication system** requires three things to function – a transmitter, a communications link and a receiver.

● **Transmitters convert data** (text, images or sounds) into an electrical signal and send it. Telephones and computers are examples of transmitters.

● **Receivers pick up the electrical signal** and convert it back into its original form.

● **Communications links** carry the signal from the transmitter to the receiver.

● **They do this** in two main ways. Some give a direct link through telephone lines and other cables, while others are carried on radio waves through the air, via satellite or microwave links.

● **In the past**, telephone lines were mainly comprised of electric cables, which carried the signal as pulses of electricity. Today, telephone lines are mostly fibre optics, which carry the signals as coded pulses of light.

● **Communications satellites** are satellites orbiting the Earth in space. Telephone calls are beamed up on radio waves to the satellite, which then beams them back down to another part of the world.

▲ *Fibre-optic cables contain thin flexible fibres with a glass core. Usually laid underground, they transmit phone and TV signals.*

● **Microwave links** use very short radio waves to transmit telephone and other signals directly from one dish to another in a straight line across Earth's surface.

● **Mobile or cellular phones** transmit and receive phone calls directly via radio waves. Calls are picked up and sent on from a local aerial.

● **The information superhighway** is the network of high-speed links that is produced by combining telephone systems, cable TV and computer networks.

DID YOU KNOW?

Telephone calls crossing oceans are transmitted via satellite in one direction and via underwater cable in the other direction to avoid delays.

▼ *Using a GPS (Global Positioning System) receiver, anything on Earth can pinpoint its own location and navigate from place to place. The GPS is a network of about 30 satellites, plus the equipment to control and co-ordinate them.*

Light sources

● **The main source** of natural light on Earth is the Sun.

● **The brightness** (or 'luminous intensity') of a light source is measured in candelas (Cd), with 1 Cd having about the same luminous intensity as a small candle.

● **The Sun's surface** pumps out 23 billion Cd per square metre. Laser lights are even brighter, but very small.

● **The amount of light** falling on a surface is measured in lux, with 1 lux equalling the amount of light from a source of 1 Cd, from one metre away.

● **You need** around 500 lux to read by.

● **Some electric lightbulbs** are incandescent, which means that their light comes from a thin tungsten wire (filament) that glows when heated by an electric current.

● **Electric lights** were invented independently in 1878 by English physicist and chemist Joseph Swan and American inventors Thomas Edison and Hiram Maxim.

● **A fluorescent light** has a glass tube coated on the inside with powders called phosphors. Electricity causes the gases inside the tube to send out UV rays, which hit the phosphors, making them glow (fluoresce).

● **In a neon light**, a huge electric current makes the gas inside the tube electrically charged, causing it to glow.

◀ *At a concert, laser beams send out brilliant coloured shafts of light, each of a single wavelength.*

Weight and mass

DID YOU KNOW?

The largest stars in the galaxy have a mass 150 times bigger than the Sun – that's 3×10^{32} kg.

● **Mass is the amount of matter** in an object. Mass is not the same as weight. In physics, 'weight' refers to the force of gravity acting on an object. An object's weight varies according to its mass and the strength of gravity.

● **The weight of an object** can vary, but its mass is always the same, so scientists use units of mass to describe how heavy something is.

● **If you were standing on the Moon**, you would weigh only one sixth of your weight on Earth because the Moon's gravity is one sixth of the Earth's gravity, but your mass would be the same.

● **Objects weigh more** at sea level, which is nearer the centre of the Earth, than up a mountain.

● **The object** with the smallest known mass is a photon (a particle of energy), which has a mass of 5.3×10^{-63} kg.

● **The mass of the Earth** is 6×10^{24} (six trillion trillion) kg. The mass of the Universe is thought to be approximately 10^{51} (10 followed by 50 zeros) kg.

● **Density is the ratio** of the mass of a substance to its volume. It is measured in grams per cubic centimetre (g/cm^3).

● **The lightest solids** are silica aerogels made for space science, with a density of 0.005 g/cm^3.

● **The lightest gas** is hydrogen, at 0.00008989 g/cm^3. The density of air is 0.00128 g/cm^3.

● **The densest** solid is osmium, at 22.59 g/cm^3. Lead is 11.37 g/cm^3. A neutron star has a density of about one billion trillion g/cm^3.

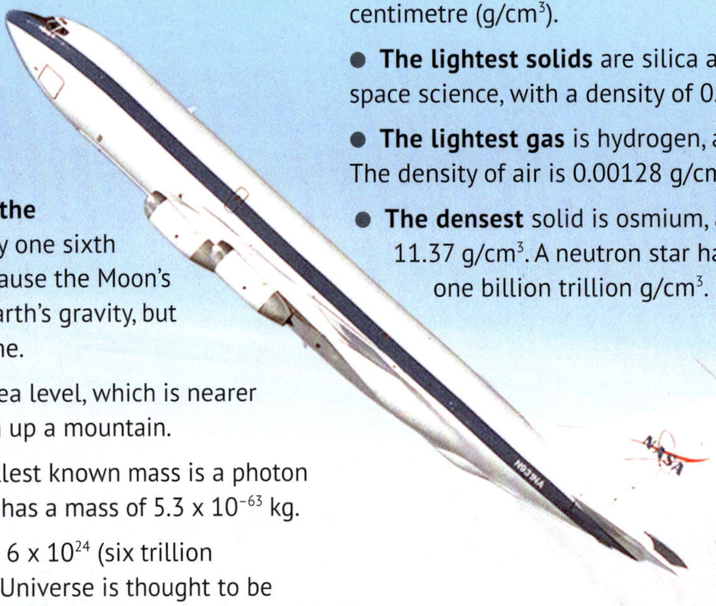

◀ *Experimental aircraft allow astronauts to feel the illusion of weightlessness for testing and training purposes.*

The Curies

- **Pierre and Marie Curie**, who were husband and wife, were the scientists who discovered the nature of radioactivity.
- **In 1903** they won a Nobel Prize for their work.
- **Marie Curie** (1867–1934) was born Marya Sklodowska in Poland. She went to Paris in 1891 to study physics.
- **Pierre Curie** (1859–1906) was a French lecturer in physics who discovered the piezoelectric effect in crystals. This discovery led to the development of devices from quartz watches to microphones.
- **The Curies** met in 1894 while Marie was a student at the Sorbonne. They married in 1895.
- **In 1896**, Antoine Becquerel found that uranium salts emitted a mysterious radiation that affected photographic paper in the same way as light.

◀ *The Curies' combination of brilliant insight with exact, patient work led to their historic breakthrough in discovering radioactivity.*

- **In 1898**, the Curies found the intensity of radiation was in exact proportion to the amount of uranium – so the radiation must be coming from the uranium atoms.
- **The Curies called** atomic radiation 'radioactivity'.
- **In July 1898**, the Curies discovered a new radioactive element. Marie called it polonium after her native Poland.
- **In December** the Curies found radium – an element even more radioactive than uranium.
- **In 1906** Pierre was killed by a tram. Marie continued to work, winning a second Nobel Prize in 1911.
- **Marie died** 28 years after Pierre from the effects of her exposure to radioactive materials, the dangers of which were unknown at that time.

Quarks

- **Quarks are the tiny elementary**, or fundamental, particles from which protons and neutrons are made up.
- **They are too small** for their size to be measured, but scientists have been able to measure their mass. The biggest quark is as heavy as an atom of gold. The smallest quark is 35,000 times lighter.
- **There are six types** of quark (known as flavours). They are up, down, bottom, top, strange and charm quarks.
- **Down, bottom and strange** quarks each carry one-third of the negative charge of electrons.
- **Up, top and charm** quarks each carry two-thirds of the positive charge of protons.
- **Quarks only exist** in combination with one or two other quarks. Groups of quarks are known as hadrons.
- **Three-quark hadrons** are called baryons and include protons and neutrons. Rare two-quark hadrons are called mesons.
- **A proton** consists of two up quarks (two parts positive two-thirds of a charge) and one down quark (one part negative one-third of a charge), so has a positive charge of 1.
- **A neutron** is made from two down quarks (two parts negative one-third of a charge) and one up quark (one part positive two-thirds of a charge). The charges cancel each other out, so a neutron has no charge.
- **The theory of quarks** was first proposed by American physicists Murray Gell-Mann and George Zweig in 1964.

▼ *This diagram illustrates the make-up of a drop of water, from molecule to quark. It shows how protons and neutrons are both made from different combinations of three quarks.*

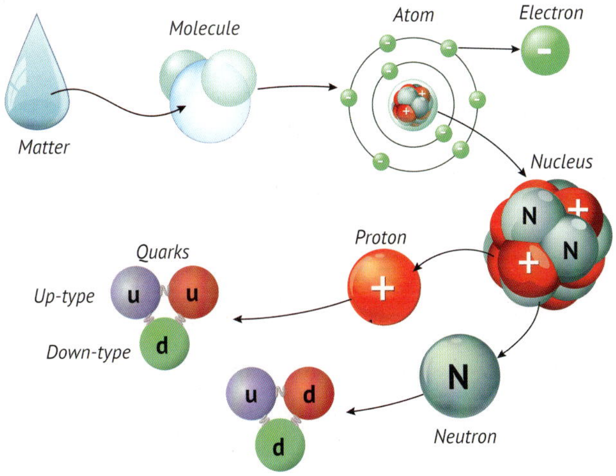

Hydrogen

▲ *Hydrogen bombs are among the most destructive of all nuclear bombs, a thousand times more powerful than basic atom bombs.*

- **Hydrogen is the lightest** of all gases and elements – a swimming pool full of it would weigh just one kilogram.
- **With just one proton** and one electron, hydrogen is the first element in the Periodic Table.
- **Of every 6000** hydrogen atoms, one has a neutron as well as a proton in its nucleus, making it twice as heavy. This atom is called 'deuterium'.
- **Some rare hydrogen atoms** have two neutrons as well as the proton, making them three times as heavy. These are called 'tritium'.
- **Hydrogen is the most common substance** in the Universe and makes up more than 90 percent of the Universe's weight.
- **Most hydrogen** on Earth occurs in combination with other elements, such as when it combines with oxygen to make water.
- **Pure hydrogen** occurs naturally in a few places, such as small underground pockets and as tiny traces in the air.
- **As one of the most** reactive gases, hydrogen is highly flammable, so it often bursts into flames.

▼ *The fuel cell in a hydrogen-powered car takes up a relatively high proportion of space in the vehicle.*

- **A hydrogen fuel cell** creates electrical power from a chemical reaction between hydrogen (the fuel) and oxygen (the oxidant).
- **In the future**, many cars could be powered by hydrogen fuel cells, which – unlike regular fuels – produce water, not polluting fumes.
- **Fuel for hydrogen-powered cars** could be made by using solar cells (electric cells that convert solar energy into electricity) to split water molecules into their component parts of hydrogen and oxygen.
- **Cars powered** by this method would essentially run on a clean mixture of water and sunlight!
- **A hydrogen bomb** is a thermonuclear weapon that uses a small nuclear explosion to fuse deuterium and tritium atoms together. It is called a thermonuclear weapon because of the high temperatures needed to fuse the deuterium and tritium atoms (100 million°C).

DID YOU KNOW?

Under extreme pressure hydrogen has the properties of a metal – the most electrically conductive metal of all.

▼ *The Mirai car by Japanese manufacturer Toyota was one of the first hydrogen fuel cell vehicles to be sold commercially.*

Scanning

- **A scanner** is an electronic device that traces out and builds up an image in lines.
- **Image scanners** convert pictures or text into a digital form that computers can read.
- **A photoelectric cell** inside the scanner measures the amount of light reflected from each part of the picture or document and converts this into a digital code.
- **Complex scanning devices** are used in medicine to produce pictures of internal organs or body parts. These include CT scanners, PET scanners and MRI scanners.
- **CT stands for** Computerized Tomography. In CT scanning, an X-ray beam rotates around the patient and is picked up by detectors on the far side to build up a 3-D image of the inside of the patient's body.
- **PET stands for** Positron Emission Tomography. In PET scanning, the scanner picks up positrons (positively charged electrons) sent out by substances injected into the blood. PET scans can show a living brain in action.
- **MRI stands for** Magnetic Resonance Imaging. MRI scans work in a similar way to CT scans, but use magnetism, not X-rays.
- **In an MRI**, the patient is surrounded by magnets, which cause all the protons of hydrogen atoms in the body to line up.
- **An MRI scan starts** as a radio pulse that changes the direction of spin of some protons. The scanner then detects radio signals sent out by these protons as they snap back into line.

▼ *MRI scanners are large machines that form a strong magnetic field around the part of the patient that is to be imaged.*

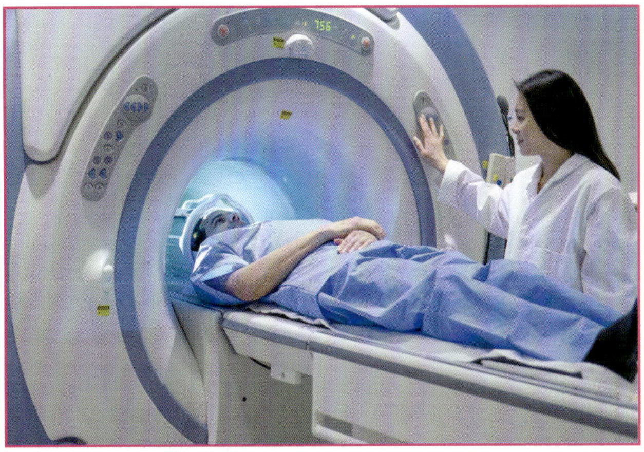

Velocity and acceleration

- **When an object** is moving in one direction at a constant speed, it is described as having uniform velocity.
- **The speed of the object** can be worked out using the following formula:

$$\frac{\textit{distance travelled (d)}}{\textit{time (t)}} = \textit{velocity (v)}$$

- **Acceleration is the rate** of change of velocity. When something speeds up (accelerates) it has positive acceleration. When something slows down (decelerates) it has negative acceleration.
- **Acceleration is typically measured** in metres per second per second (m/sec^2), meaning that in each second speed increases or decreases by so many metres per second. A rifle bullet accelerates down the barrel at 3000 m/sec^2. A fast car accelerates at 6 m/sec^2.
- **Earth's gravitational pull** causes freely falling objects to accelerate. The rate at which this happens is called g (acceleration of gravity). On Earth this rate is 9.8 m/sec^2.
- **In a rocket** travelling at 1 g the acceleration has little effect on passengers. At 3 g it becomes difficult to move, and if a force of 4.5 g keeps going for several seconds, passengers are likely to black out.
- **A plane takes off** at 0.5 g, while a car brakes at up to 0.7 g. A car crash can involve catastrophic forces of up to 100 g.

▼ *Sprinters develop their muscles to accelerate the body to the maximum velocity they can achieve in the shortest possible time.*

Air

- **Air is a mixture of gases**, dust and moisture.
- **The gas nitrogen** makes up 78.08 percent of the air. Nitrogen is usually unreactive, but sometimes reacts with oxygen to form oxides of nitrogen.
- **Oxygen makes up** 20.95 percent of the air. Animals breathe in oxygen, while plants give it out as they take their energy from sunlight in photosynthesis.
- **Earth's atmosphere** gained its oxygen from the billions of micro organisms that floated in the oceans of our world 2.4 billion years ago.
- **The air contains** very small quantities of the inert gases argon, neon, helium, krypton and xenon.
- **It also contains** a number of more reactive gases, including carbon dioxide, water vapour, ozone, sulphur dioxide and nitrogen dioxide.
- **In addition** to the atmospheric gases, there is water vapour in the air, which at any time and place can make up between 1 and 7 percent of the volume of air.
- **Carbon dioxide** is being continually recycled as it is breathed out by animals and taken in by plants in photosynthesis.
- **Ozone makes up** 0.00006 percent of the air. It is created by the action of ultraviolet radiation in sunlight on oxygen.
- **Hydrogen makes up** 0.00005 percent of the air, and is continually drifting off into space. It is gradually replenished from within the Earth.
- **Air is typically polluted** with gases, tiny solid particles (such as soot) and aerosols (tiny droplets).

▼ The Earth's atmosphere is just 100 km deep, proportionally less thick than the skin on an apple.

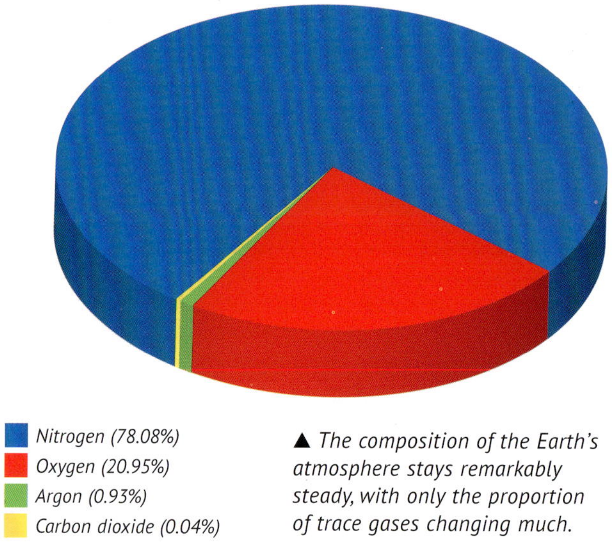

▲ The composition of the Earth's atmosphere stays remarkably steady, with only the proportion of trace gases changing much.

- **Some pollution is natural**, such as dust from storms, soot and smoke from forest fires, and ash from volcanic eruptions. However, a lot of pollution is now made by humans, including motor vehicle exhaust fumes and emissions from factories and power stations.
- **Man-made pollution** also adds gases such as carbon dioxide, methane, nitrous oxides and ozone to the air.
- **Particles from motor vehicle exhausts** can mix with fog to form smog, while soot particles can cause breathing problems such as asthma.
- **Carbon dioxide** created by burning oil and coal, and methane from cows and other animals are adding to the natural insulating effect of the atmosphere, so that the Earth is gradually getting warmer. This is called 'global warming'.
- **Rain is turned to acid** when sulphur and nitrogen compounds – emitted by coal and oil-burning power stations, factories and motor vehicles – dissolve in water vapour in the air.

DID YOU KNOW?

Air is a unique mixture that exists on Earth and nowhere else in the Solar System.

▼ Besides gases, air contains microscopic solid particles such as unburnt fuel and partially burnt soot, which are emitted by sources of pollutants such as car exhausts.

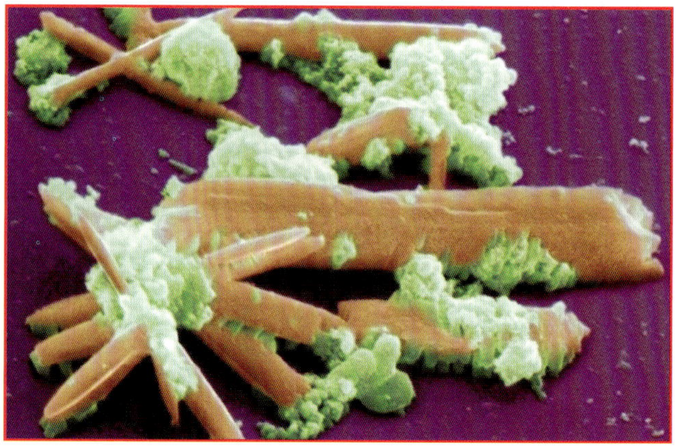

Relativity

● **Einstein was the creator of two theories** of relativity that have revolutionized scientists' way of thinking about the Universe. These are the 'special theory of relativity' (1905) and the 'general theory of relativity' (1915).

● **Time is relative**. It depends entirely on where you are and how you are moving when you measure it. Someone elsewhere will get a different measurement.

● **Distance and speed** are also relative. For example, if you are in a car and another car whizzes past you, the slower you are travelling, the faster the other car seems to be moving.

● **In his special theory of relativity**, Einstein showed that the speed of light is the fastest thing in the Universe.

DID YOU KNOW?

When astronauts went to the Moon, their clocks lost a few seconds. The clocks weren't faulty, but time actually ran slower in their speeding spacecraft.

● **He also showed** that the speed of light is constant (always stays the same) and realized that this would result in some strange effects on other objects moving at very high speeds.

▲ *Einstein's theory of general relativity showed that gravity warps space-time and so bends light rays around massive objects in space.*

● **For example**, if a rocket accelerated to near the speed of light, it would appear to shrink and its clocks would run more slowly as time stretched. If the rocket sped up and reached the speed of light, the clocks would stop altogether.

● **Einstein's general theory** of relativity showed that gravity bends space-time, leading scientists to predict the existence of black holes (points in space where gravity is so strong even light is pulled into them).

● **An eclipse of the Sun** in 1919 gave English scientist Arthur Eddington the opportunity to observe the Sun's gravity bending light, proving Einstein's general theory of relativity.

Hawking

● **Stephen Hawking** (1942–2018) was a British physicist famous for his ideas on space and time.

● **Hawking was born in** Oxford, England, and studied at Cambridge University, where he later worked as a professor.

● **Hawking's book** *A Brief History of Time* (1988) outlines his ideas on space, time and the history of the Universe since the Big Bang. It was one of the best-selling science books of the 20th century.

● **Hawking's contributions** to the study of gravity are considered to be the most important since Einstein's.

● **More than anyone else**, Hawking developed the idea of black holes – points in space where gravity becomes so extreme that it even sucks in light.

● **Hawking developed** the idea of a singularity, which is an incredibly small point in a black hole where all physical laws break down.

● **Hawking's work** provides a strong theoretical base for the idea that the Universe began with a Big Bang, starting with a singularity and exploding outwards.

● **Hawking suffered** from the paralysing nerve disease called amyotrophic lateral sclerosis (ALS). He could not move any more than a few hand and face muscles, but he got around in an electric wheelchair.

● **Hawking could not speak**, but he communicated effectively with a computer-simulated voice.

▼ *Stephen Hawking is one of the most famous modern scientists. He also made guest appearances in several popular TV series.*

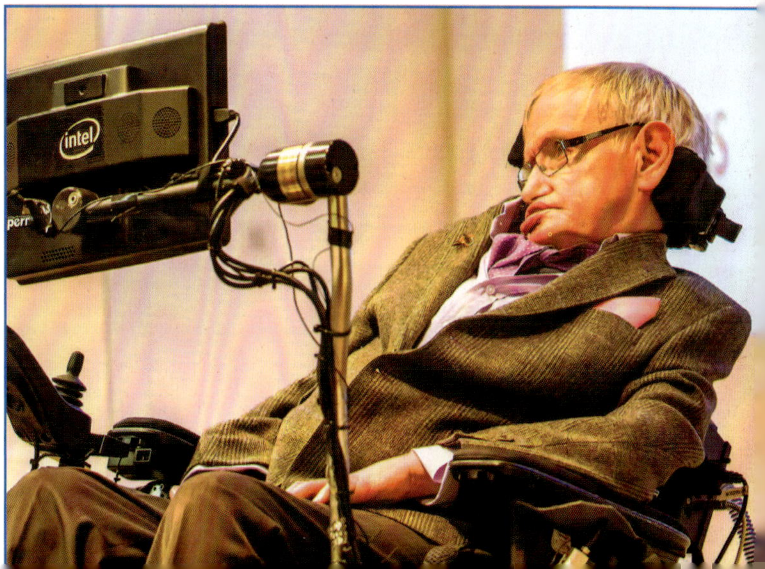

Temperature

- **Temperature is the measurement** of how hot or cold something is. The best known temperature scales are Celsius and Fahrenheit.
- **The Celsius (C) scale** is part of the metric system of measurements. It is named after Swedish astronomer Anders Celsius, who developed it in 1742.
- **Celsius is also known as centigrade** because water boils at 100°C, and cent is the Latin prefix for 100. Water freezes at 0°C.
- **In the Fahrenheit (F) scale** water boils at 212°F and freezes at 32°F.
- **To convert** Celsius to Fahrenheit, divide by 5, multiply by 9 and add 32.
- **To convert** Fahrenheit to Celsius, subtract 32, divide by 9 and multiply by 5.
- **The Kelvin (K) scale** is used by scientists. It is like the Celsius scale, but it begins at –273.15°C. This means that 0°C is equivalent to 273.15K.
- **Helium changes** from gas to liquid at –269°C. Petrol freezes at –150°C. The lowest air temperature ever recorded on Earth is –89.2°C.
- **A log fire burns** at a temperature of around 800°C. Molten magma is around 1200°C. The surface of the Sun is around 6000°C, while Earth's core is over 7000°C.
- **A lightning flash** reaches 30,000°C, while the centre of a hydrogen bomb reaches over 4,000,000°C.
- **The blood temperature** of the human body is normally around 37°C. Body temperature above 40°C is very hot, and below 31°C is very cold. Anything hotter than 45°C hurts if it touches your skin, although some specially trained people can walk barefoot on burning coals as hot as 800°C.

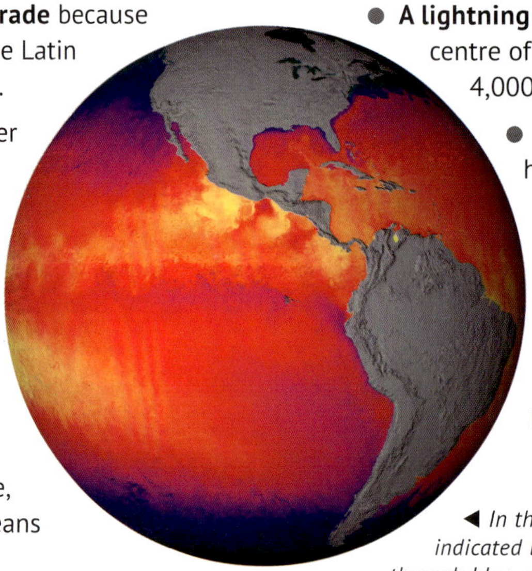

◀ *In this globe, sea surface temperature is indicated by colour, from the coldest waters (black) through blue, purple and red to the hottest, yellow.*

Colour

◀ *The shimmering blue of this butterfly is iridescence set up by tiny air pockets in the scales on its wings.*

- **Colour is** the way that our eyes see different wavelengths of light.
- **We see** the longest light waves as the colour red.
- **Waves that appear red** are about 700 nanometres (nm) in length (1 nm = 1 billionth of a metre).
- **The shortest light waves** – about 400 nm in length – are seen by human eyes as the colour violet.
- **Some light**, such as sunlight and the light from torches and ordinary lightbulbs, is actually a mixture of every colour, and is called white light.
- **The world around us** appears to us to be different colours because molecules in different surfaces reflect and absorb particular wavelengths of light.
- **The shimmering rainbow colours** that flash on surfaces such as peacock feathers, butterfly wings and soap bubbles are known as iridescence.
- **Iridescence can be caused** by the way a surface breaks the light, hitting it into colours.
- **It can also be caused by** interference, which occurs when an object has a thin, transparent surface layer. Light waves reflected from the top surface are slightly out of step with waves reflected from the inner surface, creating a pattern of light.

Oil and hydrocarbons

- **Oils are liquids** that do not dissolve in water but do burn easily. They are made from groups of carbon and hydrogen atoms.
- **There are three** main kinds of oil – essential oils, fixed oils and mineral oils.
- **Essential oils** are thin, perfumed oils from plants. They are used in flavouring and aromatherapy.
- **Fixed oils** are derived from plants and animals, such as fish oils and nut oils.
- **Mineral oils** come from petroleum, which is formed underground over millions of years from the remains of tiny marine organisms such as plankton.
- **Petroleum is a mixture** of organic compounds, most of which are hydrocarbons, combined with oxygen, sulphur, nitrogen and other elements.
- **Petroleum is separated** into different substances such as aviation fuel, petrol and paraffin by distillation.
- **In this process**, oil is heated in a distillation column, causing a mixture of gases to evaporate. Each gas cools and condenses at a different height, becoming a liquid or fraction (a mixture of liquids of similar boiling point), which is then drawn off separately.
- **There are different forms** of petroleum. These include crude oil and natural gas.
- **Crude oil** is usually thick and sticky, but it can vary in composition and colour, from jet-black Sudan oil to straw-coloured Texas oil.
- **The simplest hydrocarbon** is methane, the main gas in natural gas. Methane molecules are comprised of one carbon atom and four hydrogen atoms.
- **There are three** main kinds of hydrocarbon in oil – alkanes, aromatics and naphthenes. The proportion of each varies from oil to oil.
- **Alkanes have long**, chain-shaped molecules, aromatics have small, ring molecules and naphthenes have large ring molecules.

▲ *Crude oil from the ground must be separated at oil refineries to get useful materials such as petrol.*

- **Lighter alkanes** are gases such as methane, propane and butane (used in camping stoves). Candles contain a mixture of alkanes and they all make good fuels.
- **Alkenes are another type of hydrocarbon**. Ethene is the simplest alkene. It is also called ethylene (C_2H_4) and is used to make plastics.
- **Ethylene is also the basis** of many paint strippers and can be used to make ethanol – the alcohol in drinks such as wine.

DID YOU KNOW?

Petroleum is used to make a huge range of products from aspirins and toothpaste to candles and guitar strings.

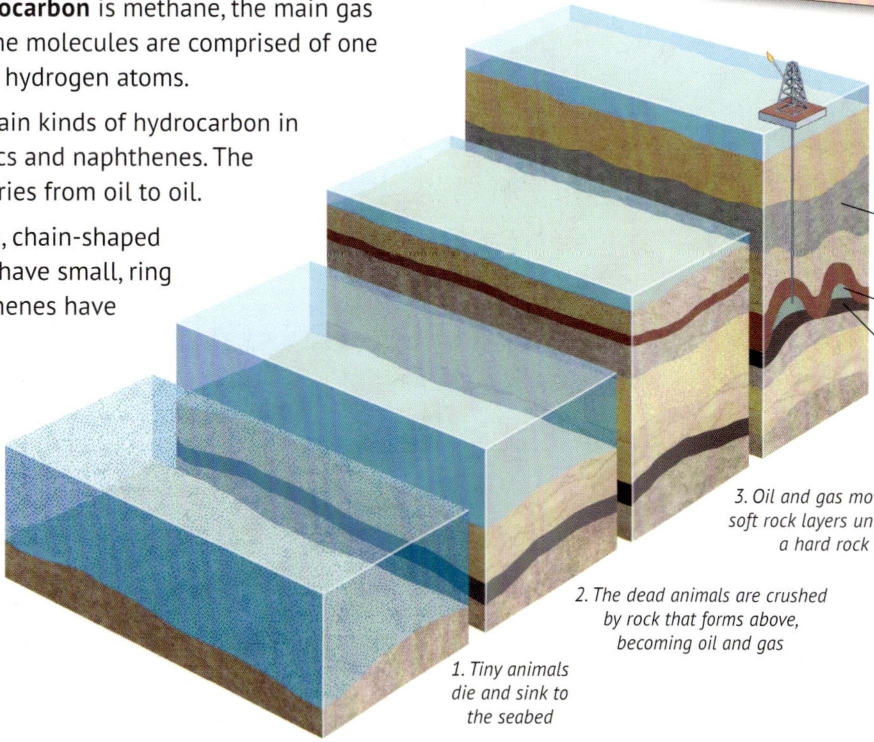

▶ *Oil forms in the ground over millions of years from the remains of microscopic sea creatures.*

Genetic engineering

▲ *Genetic engineers have created mice that glow green by giving them a gene from jellyfish called GFP (Green Fluorescent Protein).*

- **Genetics is the science of heredity**, which deals with how organisms pass on traits to their offspring.
- **A gene** tells an organism how to grow and live. It comes as a short section of chemical code on special molecules in every living cell called DNA.
- **Genetic engineering** involves deliberately changing the genes of organisms to give them different traits.
- **Scientists can alter genes** by snipping them from the DNA of one organism and inserting them into the DNA of another. This is called gene splicing.
- **Genes are cut** from DNA using biological 'scissors' called restriction enzymes. They are spliced into DNA using biological 'glue' called DNA ligase.
- **The CRISPR method** of gene editing uses specially manipulated DNA from bacteria to enter a cell and edit the cell's DNA to change a gene.
- **Once a cell** has altered DNA, every new cell it produces will also have the altered DNA.
- **By splicing new genes** into the DNA of bacteria, scientists can turn them into factories for making valuable natural chemicals.
- **In 2003**, scientists completed a map of the entire sequence of human genes, known as the human genome.
- **Genetically modified (GM) food** is produced from animals or plants that have had their genes altered. For example, a food crop can be genetically modified to make it resistant to pests.
- **Gene therapy** is an experimental science in which human genes are altered in order to cure diseases that are inherited from parents, or caused by faulty genes.
- **Cloning means** creating an organism with exactly the same genes as another. It takes DNA from a single donor and uses it to 'grow' a new life. The new organism has exactly the same genes as the donor of the DNA.

Motion

- **Every movement** in the Universe is governed by laws. Three of the most important of these laws were described by English scientist Isaac Newton (1643–1727).
- **Newton's first law of motion** states that an object accelerates, slows down or changes direction only when a force is applied to it.
- **Newton's second law of motion** states that the acceleration of an object depends on how heavy the object is, and on the size of the force that is acting on it.

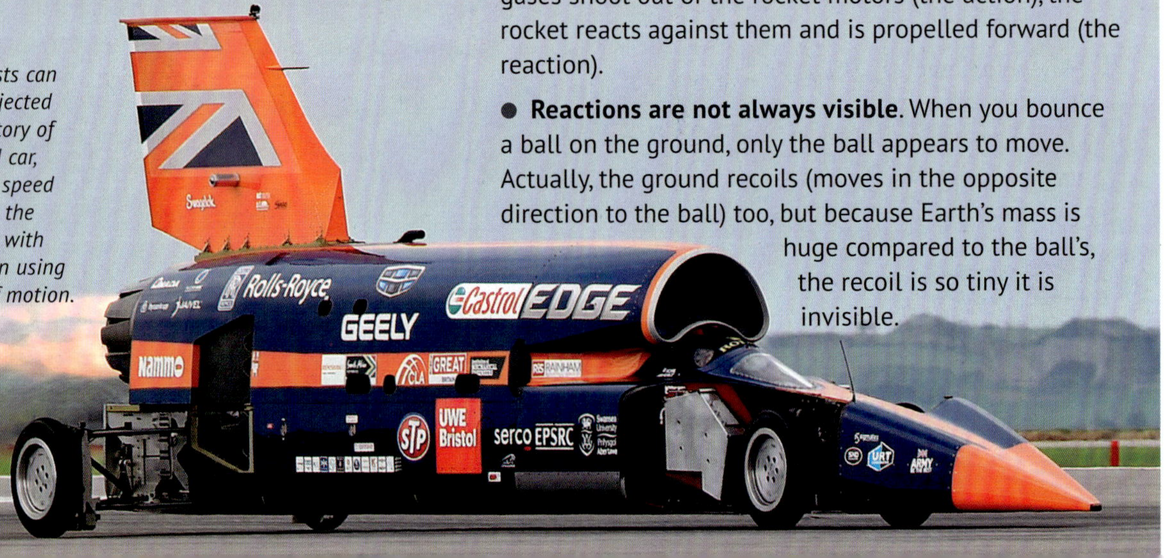

▶ *Rocket scientists can calculate the projected speed and trajectory of a rocket-powered car, such as the land speed record-contender the Bloodhound SSC, with pinpoint precision using Newton's laws of motion.*

- **The greater the force** acting on an object, the more it will accelerate.
- **The heavier** an object is (the greater its mass) the less it will be accelerated by a particular force.
- **Newton's third law of motion** states that when a force acts one way, an equal force acts the opposite way. 'To every action, there is an equal and opposite reaction'.
- **Rocket engines** depend on Newton's law. As the hot gases shoot out of the rocket motors (the action), the rocket reacts against them and is propelled forward (the reaction).
- **Reactions are not always visible.** When you bounce a ball on the ground, only the ball appears to move. Actually, the ground recoils (moves in the opposite direction to the ball) too, but because Earth's mass is huge compared to the ball's, the recoil is so tiny it is invisible.

Mixing colours

- **There are three** primary (basic) colours of light – red, green and blue.
- **These three colours** can be mixed to make any other colour by varying their proportions.
- **The primary colours** of light are called additive primaries, because they are added together to make other colours.
- **Each additive primary** is one third of the spectrum of white light, so combining all three makes white.
- **When two additive primaries** are added together they make a third colour, called a subtractive primary.
- **The three subtractive primaries** are magenta (red plus blue), cyan (blue plus green) and yellow (green plus red). They, too, can be mixed in various proportions to make other colours.
- **Surfaces appear as certain colours** to human eyes because they soak up some of colours that make up white light and reflect the others. The colour the eye perceives is a combination of the colours reflected.
- **Each subtractive primary** soaks up one-third of the spectrum of white light and reflects two-thirds of it.
- **Mixing two** subtractive primaries soaks up two-thirds of the spectrum. Mixing all three subtractive primaries soaks up all colours of the spectrum, making black.
- **Two subtractive primaries** mixed make an additive primary. Cyan and magenta make blue, yellow and cyan make green, yellow and magenta make red.

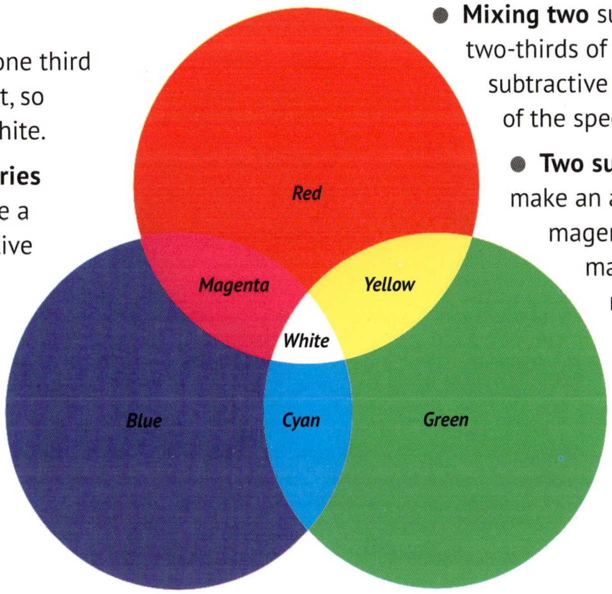

◀ *Each circle is a primary colour of light (red, green, blue). Where they overlap you see the subtractive primaries (magenta, cyan, yellow).*

Molecules

- **A molecule** is two or more atoms that are bonded (held) together.
- **The atoms** of the element hydrogen can exist only in pairs, or joined with atoms of other elements. A linked pair of hydrogen atoms is known as a hydrogen molecule.
- **The atoms in a molecule** are held together by chemical bonds (forces of attraction).
- **The structure** (shape) of a molecule depends on the arrangement of bonds that hold its atoms together.
- **Molecules made from atoms** of different elements are called compounds. Most molecules like this are made of just two or three kinds of atom.
- **The smallest part** of a compound that can exist independently is the molecule.

DID YOU KNOW?

Molecules can contain many thousands or millions of atoms.

- **If the atoms** in the molecule of a compound were separated, the compound would cease to exist.
- **Chemical formulas** show the make-up of a molecule or compound. For example, the formula for ammonia is NH_3. This tells you that an ammonia molecule consists of one nitrogen atom and three hydrogen atoms.
- **The molecular mass** is the sum of the atomic masses of all atoms making up a molecule.

▼ *Molecules of carbon dioxide gas (CO_2)are made from two atoms of oxygen and one of carbon.*

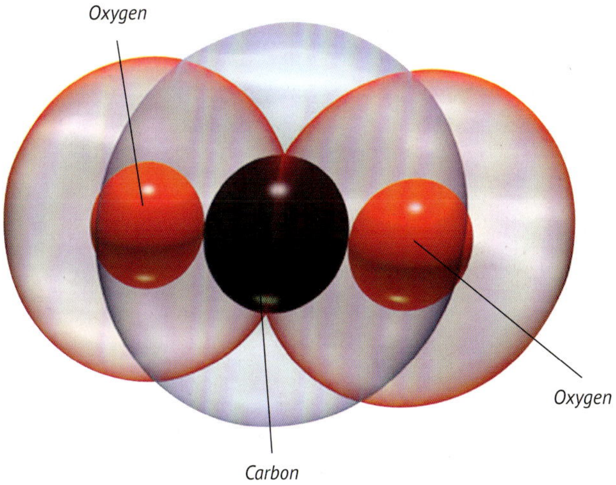

Aluminium

- **Aluminium is by far** the most common metal on Earth's surface, making up 8 percent of the Earth's crust.
- **Aluminium** never occurs naturally in its pure form – it is typically found combined with other chemicals in ore (rocks that contain minerals).
- **Pure aluminium** was first made in 1825 by Danish scientist Hans Ørsted.
- **The major source** of aluminium is layers of the soft ore rock bauxite, which is mostly aluminium hydroxide.

▶ *The aluminium ore bauxite forms deep, powdery layers where it is found in the tropics.*

- **Alum powders** made from aluminium compounds are used in the process of dyeing fabric.
- **Aluminium is silver** in colour when freshly made, but it quickly forms a layer of white oxide on its surface when exposed to air. This protects the pure aluminium underneath and means it is very slow to corrode.
- **Aluminium oxide** can crystallize into one of the hardest minerals, corundum, which is used to sharpen knives.
- **Aluminium melts** at 650°C and boils at 2450°C. It is also one of the lightest of all metals.
- **Each year 21 million tonnes** of aluminium are made, mostly from bauxite dug up in Brazil and New Guinea.

▼ *Duraluminium (aluminium with a little copper and manganese) is widely used for building aircraft because it is so light and tough.*

Particle physics

- **There are three** basic, stable subatomic particles (electrons, protons and neutrons), but scientists have also found more than 200 other particles. Most kinds of particles also have anti-particles, with the same mass but opposite electrical charge.
- **Cosmic rays** contain short-lived particles. These include muons, a type of particle that flashes into existence for a few microseconds just before the cosmic rays reach the ground.

DID YOU KNOW?

The world's largest and highest-energy particle accelerator, the Large Hadron Collider (LHC) at CERN, Switzerland, opened in September 2008.

- **Smashing atoms** inside particle accelerators creates short-lived, high-energy particles such as taus and pions and three kinds of quark – charm, bottom and top.
- **Particle accelerators** are huge machines set inside tunnels. They use powerful magnets to accelerate particles through a circular tube at high speeds, and then smash them together.
- **Scientists classify particles** using the Standard Model, in which they are divided into elementary particles and composite particles.
- **Elementary particles** are basic particles that cannot be broken down into anything smaller.
- **There are three groups** of elementary particles – quarks, leptons and bosons.

◀ *This is one of two huge particle physics detectors that form part of the LHC particle accelerator at CERN in Switzerland.*

Stretching and pulling

● **Elasticity is the degree** to which a solid can return to its original size and shape after being stretched, squeezed or deformed.

● **A force** that misshapes a material is called a stress.

● **All solids** have some elasticity but some, such as rubber, nylon and coiled springs, are very elastic.

● **A solid will return** to its original shape when stress stops, as long as the stress does not exceed its elastic limit (the point at which a material loses elasticity).

● **The amount** that a solid is stretched or squeezed when under stress is known as 'strain'.

● **Hooke's law**, named after English scientist Robert Hooke (1635–1703), states that the amount of strain is directly proportional to the amount of stress.

DID YOU KNOW?

Some types of rubber can be stretched 1000 times beyond their original length before reaching their elastic limit.

● **The amount** by which a solid stretches under a particular force – the ratio of stress to strain – is known as its elastic modulus.

● **Solids that have a low** elastic modulus, such as rubber, are more elastic than those with a high modulus, such as steel.

● **Steel can only be stretched** by one percent before it reaches its elastic limit. However, if steel is coiled into a spring shape, this can still allow for a huge amount of stretching and squeezing.

◀ *Bungee jumpers rely on precisely judging the elastic limits of the cord to bring them gently to a halt before they hit the ground.*

Television

● **Television (TV) relies** on a phenomenon called the photoelectric effect, in which electrons are emitted by a substance when it is struck by photons.

● **TV cameras** have three sets of tubes containing photocells. Each set reacts to a colour of light – red, green or blue – to convert the picture into electrical signals.

● **The sound signal** from microphones is then added.

● **Older TV broadcasting** (analogue) used the varying strength of radio signals to carry information for pictures and sound.

● **Digital broadcasting** carries information in the form of millions of on/off signals every second.

● **Modern TV sets** have flat screens, which took over from older, heavier, box-like glass-screen displays known as CRTs (cathode-ray tubes).

● **A plasma screen** has millions of tiny compartments (cells), and two sets of wire-like electrodes at right angles to each other.

● **Each cell** can be 'addressed' by sending electrical pulses along two electrodes that cross that cell.

● **These electrical pulses** heat the cell's gas into plasma, making a coloured substance (phosphor) glow. Millions of pulses every second at different 'addresses' all over the screen build up the overall picture.

▼ *Plasma screens provide a brilliant flat picture built up from millions of tiny cells filled with a plasma of gas.*

Visible light

- **When we refer to 'light'** we usually mean visible light, which is the only form of electromagnetic radiation that we can see.
- **During the day** light appears to be all around us, but only a few things are actually sources of light.
- **Light sources include** stars (such as our Sun), flames (such as with lit candles), and electric lights.
- **Most objects** are visible to us because they reflect the light that is produced by light sources. If something is not a light source and does not reflect light, we cannot see it, such as a black cat at night, for example.
- **Light travels** in straight lines, called rays. Light rays change direction if they are reflected off or pass through an object or substance, but still remain straight.
- **When light strikes a surface**, some or all of it is reflected. Most surfaces scatter light in all directions, which makes the surface visible to the human eye.
- **Mirrors and other shiny surfaces** reflect light in exactly the same pattern in which it arrived, producing a visible 'mirror image'.
- **When light passes** between different materials, such as the air, a glass and the water in the glass, it changes direction slightly. This is known as 'refraction'.
- **If the path of a light ray** is blocked, a shadow forms. Most shadows have two regions – the umbra and penumbra.

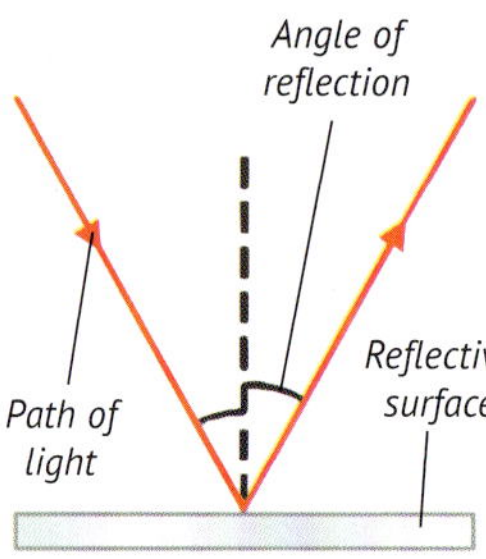

◀▲ *We see light rays reflected together from a mirror at the same angle that they arrived, so they show a clear image (left). A mirror that isn't flat reflects them at different angles, distorting the image (above).*

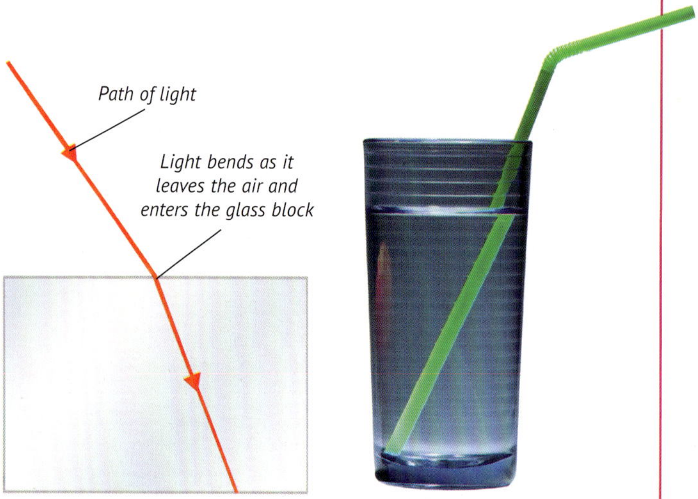

▲ *Light travels more slowly through glass than air, and if a ray enters glass at an angle it is bent or refracted, which is why the drinking straw shown here appears to be broken.*

- **The umbra** is the dark part where light rays are blocked altogether. The penumbra is the lighter rim where some rays reach.
- **If light rays** hit an object and are reflected off it, the object is described as being 'opaque'.
- **An object** that light rays can pass through but which mixes the light on its way through, such as frosted glass, is known as 'translucent'.
- **Anything that light** can pass through undistorted, such as glass, is described as being 'transparent'.

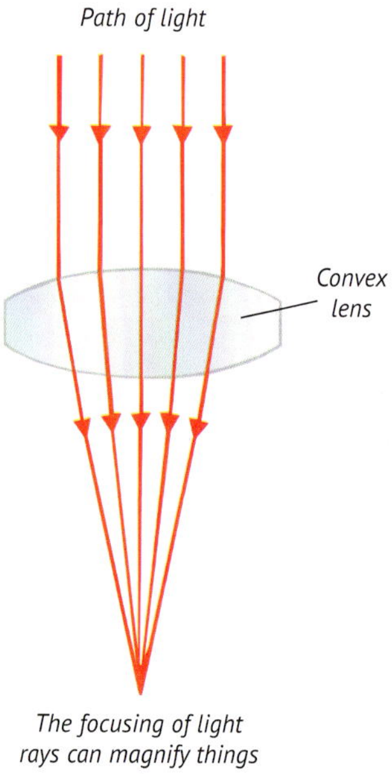

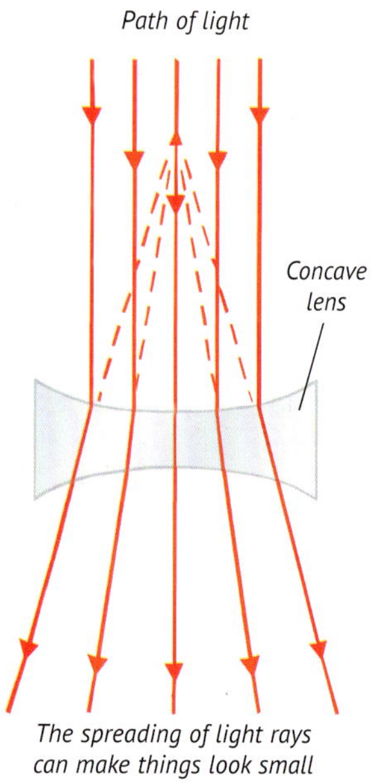

▲ *The curved surface of a glass lens refracts light. Bowed 'convex' lenses bend light rays in. Dished 'concave' lenses spread them apart.*

DID YOU KNOW?

Some scientists think the human eye is so sensitive that a single photon (particle) of light can be registered by its cells.

Huygens

- **Christiaan Huygens** (1629–1695) was one of the greatest scientists of the 1600s.
- **He was born** to a wealthy Dutch family in The Hague, in Holland.
- **Huygens studied law** at the University of Leiden and the College of Orange in Breda before turning to science.
- **He worked with his brother** Constanijn to grind lenses for very powerful telescopes.
- **With his powerful telescope**, in 1655 Huygens discovered that what astronomers had thought were Saturn's 'arms' were actually rings. He made his discovery known to people in code.
- **Huygens discovered** Titan, one of Saturn's moons.
- **He also built** the first accurate pendulum clock.
- **Responding to Newton's theory** that light was 'corpuscles' (tiny particles), Huygens developed the theory that light is waves in 1678.
- **Huygens described light** as vibrations spreading through a material called ether, which is literally everywhere and is made of tiny particles.

▲ *Christiaan Huygens was the leading figure of the Golden Age of Dutch science in the 17th century, making contributions in many fields.*

- **The idea of ether** fell out of favour in the late 19th century, but not the idea of light waves.
- **Huygens' wave idea** enabled him to explain refraction simply. It also enabled him to predict correctly that light would travel more slowly in glass than in air.

Engines

- **Engines are machines** that convert fuel into movement. Most work by burning fuel to make gases that expand rapidly as they get hot.
- **Engines that burn fuel** to generate power are called 'heat engines'. The burning process is called 'combustion'.
- **Internal combustion engines**, such as those in cars and jets, burn fuel on the inside.
- **In car and diesel train engines**, hot gases swell inside a 'combustion chamber' and push against a piston or turbine.

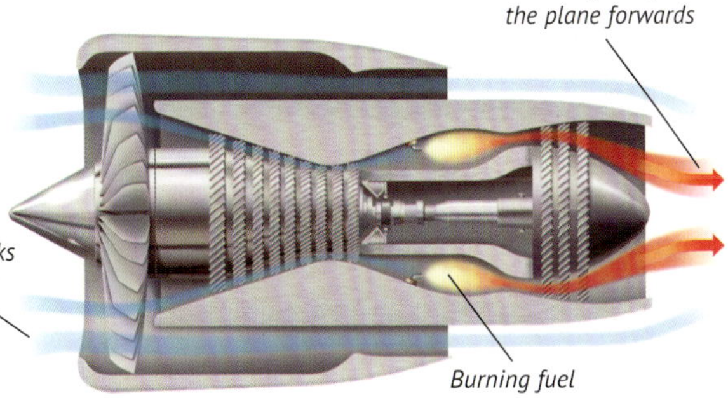

▲ *In a turbofan jet engine, cold air mixes with hot gases to produce thrust.*

- **External combustion engines**, such as those in steam engines, burn fuel on the outside in a separate boiler that makes hot steam to drive a piston or turbine.
- **The most common** fuels for motor vehicles are petrol and diesel, but reserves of these are limited.
- **Some engines** now burn biofuels, which are made from plants such as maize.
- **Petrol, diesel and biofuels** create gases that pollute the air, so some engines now use hydrogen.
- **Engines with pistons** that go back and forth inside cylinders are called reciprocating engines.
- **In four-stroke engines** (used in most cars) the pistons go up and down four times for each time they are thrust down by the hot gases.
- **In jets and rockets**, the hot gases swell, pushing against the engine as they shoot out of the back.
- **In a jet engine**, air is taken in at the front, compressed by fans, sprayed with fuel and ignited. The burning gases swell, blast past more fans (the turbine) and through the back of the engine to thrust the plane forwards.

Solutions

- **A solution** is a liquid that has a solid dissolved within it.
- **Tap water** is a solution because it contains a number of dissolved solids, such as minerals.
- **When a solid dissolves**, its molecules separate and mix completely with the molecules of the liquid it is in.
- **The liquid** in a solution is called the solvent.
- **The solid dissolved** in a solution is the solute.
- **As a solute dissolves**, the solution becomes more concentrated (stronger) until at last it is saturated.
- **This means that** no more solute will dissolve – there is literally no more room in the solvent.
- **If a saturated solution is heated** the solute will expand, making room for more solute to dissolve.
- **If a saturated solution cools** or is left to evaporate (the process in which a liquid turns into a vapour) there is less room for the solute. This will cause the solute to precipitate (come out of the solution).
- **Precipitated solute molecules** often link together to form solid crystals.

DID YOU KNOW?
Ancient alchemists searched for a universal solvent in which all substances would dissolve.

▲ *Stalagmites and stalactites form when water containing dissolved calcium carbonate evaporates, leaving solid calcium carbonate behind.*

Moving particles

- **Molecules are constantly moving**. The speed at which they move depends on temperature.
- **Heat gives molecules** extra energy, making them move faster.
- **In 1827**, Scottish botanist Robert Brown examined microscopic pollen grains in water and saw they were moving. They were being knocked by moving molecules too small to be seen. This is called Brownian motion.
- **In a solid**, molecules can't move around freely. This means that you can pick up solids, whereas liquids just slip through your hands.
- **Liquid molecules** can slide past each other, so they can flow to take the shape of whatever is holding them.
- **Without the movement** of liquid molecules materials would not move in and out of the cells in our bodies.
- **The atoms in a gas** are so far apart that they zoom about freely in all directions.
- **At absolute zero** (written as 0 K or –273.15°C), the movement of atoms and molecules slows down and comes to a complete standstill.

DID YOU KNOW?
The Sun's heat causes air molecules at the edge of the atmosphere to move so fast that many escape Earth's gravity and zoom off into space.

▶ *The movement of molecules increases dramatically as substances change from solid to liquid to gas.*

Inertia and momentum

- **Inertia is the property** that causes a body to resist any change in speed caused by a force. For example, a ball on a level surface doesn't move because inertia keeps it where it is. A kick provides the force to make it move.

▼ *The inertia of a ball on the ground will be overcome when the momentum of a moving foot kicks it, and the ball will move.*

- **Momentum is an object's mass** multiplied by its velocity (the rate at which it moves in a particular direction).
- **Inertia and momentum** depend on mass, so a large force is needed to slow down or speed up a heavy object.
- **When a moving object** strikes another object (when you kick a ball, for example), the momentum of the moving object (your foot) is transferred to the object it strikes (the ball), making it move.
- **This is known as** the law of conservation of momentum.
- **The momentum** of a spinning object is called angular momentum. When a spinning skater draws their arms close in to their body, their spin diameter (the circle they are making) is smaller than it would be if their arms were outstretched, and their body automatically spins faster.
- **For the same reason**, a satellite orbiting close to the Earth travels faster than one orbiting farther out.
- **A spinning top** remains upright while it is moving because its angular momentum is greater than the pull of gravity.

Internet

- **The internet** is a vast network (organized system) connecting millions of computers around the world.
- **Devised in the** 1960s when the US Army developed a network called ARPAnet to link computers, the internet is now used by people for everything from buying cinema tickets to keeping in touch with friends.
- **To link to the internet** via phone lines, a home computer's output must be translated into the right form with a modem or router.

- **Computers** connect to the internet through an Internet Service Provider (ISP).

DID YOU KNOW?

In 2015, there were more than 3 billion internet users around the world, over 40 percent of the global population.

- **Each ISP** is connected to a giant computer called a main hub. There are about 100 main hubs worldwide.
- **Some links between** hubs are made via phone lines while others are made via satellite. Links between hubs are called fast-track connections.
- **The World Wide Web** was invented in 1989 by English computer programmer Tim Berners-Lee of the CERN laboratories in Switzerland.
- **The Web makes special links** called hyperlinks between web pages.
- **Clicking on a link** automatically takes someone to data on another site or page.

◀ *Mobile phones can now access the internet by picking up radio signals sent out from service providers.*

Nuclear power

- **Nuclear power** harnesses the huge amount of energy that binds together the nucleus of every atom in the Universe. It is an incredibly concentrated form of energy.
- **Nuclear energy is** released through nuclear fission, in which the nuclei of atoms are split.
- **One day scientists** hope to release energy by nuclear fusion, in which nuclei are joined rather than split. This process occurs naturally in the Sun.
- **Nuclear reactors** do not burn fuel to produce their energy. Instead, they use pellets or rods of a fuel called uranium dioxide, an isotope of uranium.
- **Just 3 kg of uranium fuel** provides enough energy for a city of one million people for one day.
- **The earliest nuclear reactors** were designed to make plutonium for use in nuclear weapons. Magnox reactors make plutonium and electricity.
- **Pressurized water reactors** (PWRs) are now the most common kind of nuclear reactors. They were originally used in submarines.
- **Like coal- and oil-fired power stations**, nuclear power stations heat water to make steam to drive the turbines that generate electricity. But in nuclear power stations the heat comes from splitting uranium atoms in the fuel in a slow, controlled nuclear reaction.
- **Every stage of the nuclear process** creates dangerous radioactive waste that may take 10,000 years to become safe. Some mildly radioactive liquid waste is pumped out to sea. Gaseous waste is vented into the air. Solid waste is mostly stockpiled underground.

DID YOU KNOW?

One kilogram of deuterium (an isotope of hydrogen) provides the same amount of energy as 3 million kg of coal.

▼ *The exact layout of nuclear power plants varies, but they are all essentially giant boilers, designed to use nuclear reactions to heat water to create steam to drive the turbines that generate electricity.*

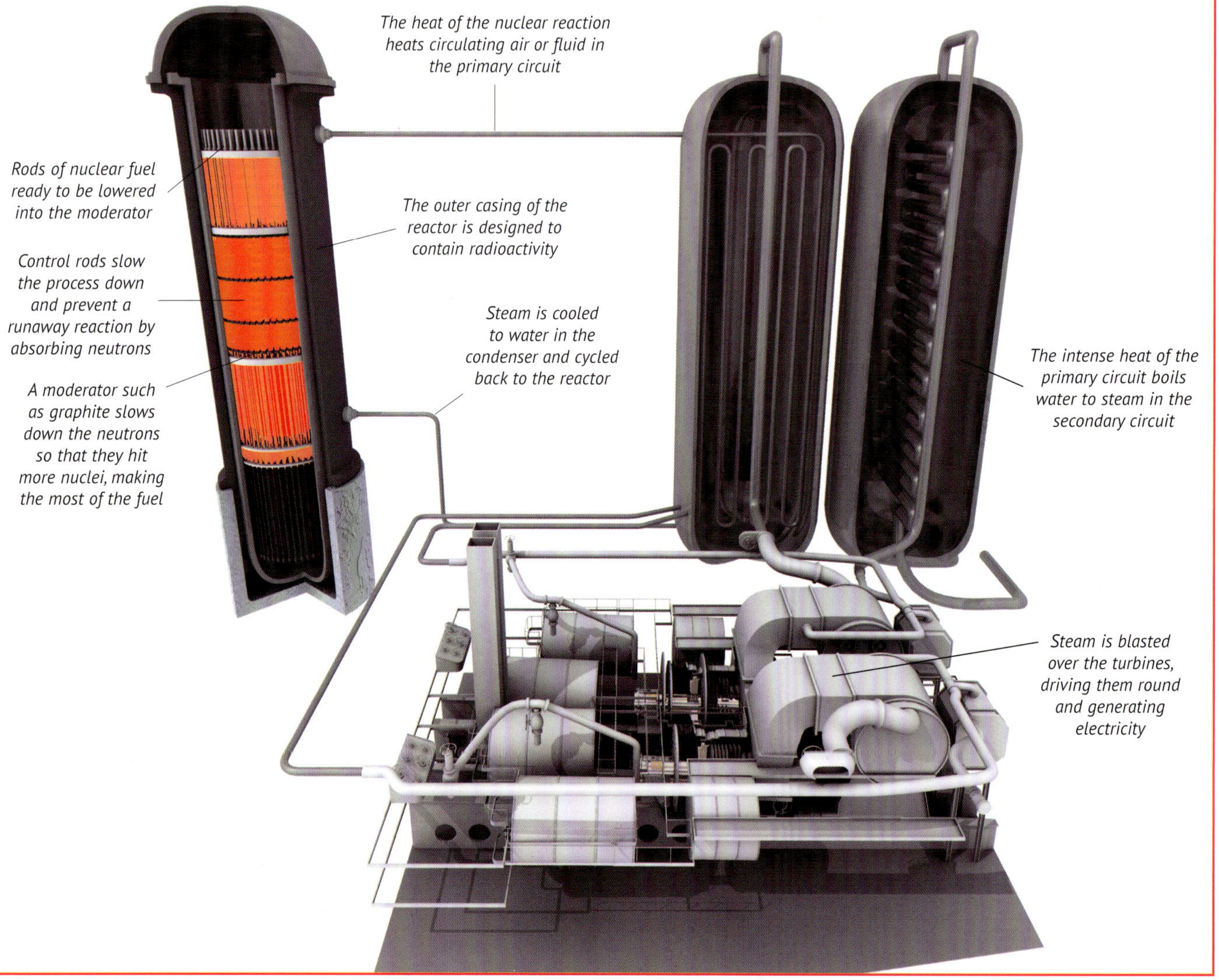

Vectors

▶ *Skiing downhill at 30 km/h is a vector quantity because it represents a magnitude (30 km/h) and a direction (downhill).*

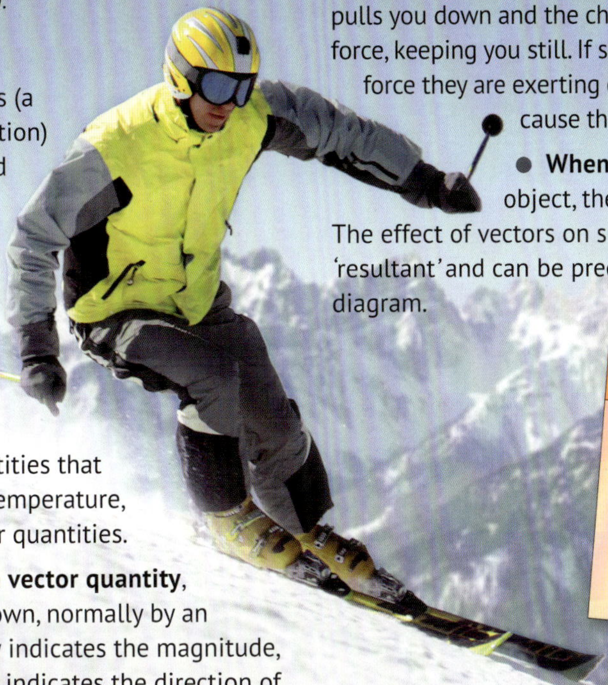

● **Vector quantities** are forces (a push or pull in a specific direction) that have magnitude (size) and direction.

● **Velocity, force and acceleration** are all vector quantities. Gravity, jet propulsion and the wind, for instance, can be seen as vectors.

● **Scalar quantities** are quantities that have a size but no direction. Temperature, density and mass are all scalar quantities.

● **When a value is given to a vector quantity,** the direction must also be shown, normally by an arrow. The length of the arrow indicates the magnitude, and the direction of the arrow indicates the direction of the force.

● **Objects can be affected** by a combination of vector quantities at the same time. If you sit on a chair, gravity pulls you down and the chair pushes you up with equal force, keeping you still. If someone pushes the chair, the force they are exerting combined with gravity may cause the chair to tip over.

● **When several vectors** affect an object, they may act at different angles. The effect of vectors on such an object is called the 'resultant' and can be predicted by drawing a geometric diagram.

DID YOU KNOW?

Vector charts are used to predict the weather because they describe both speed and direction – invaluable for showing the course of winds or storms.

Newton

● **Sir Isaac Newton** is one of the greatest scientists in history. His book *The Mathematical Principles of Natural Philosophy* (1687) is perhaps the most influential science book ever written.

● **Newton** was born in 1643 in Woolsthorpe in Lincoln, England, and died in 1727.

● **As a boy**, he often made mechanical devices such as model windmills and water clocks.

● **His theory of gravity** enabled scientists to explain how the Universe is held together.

● **Newton** said that his theory of gravity was inspired by seeing an apple fall from a tree.

● **He invented** an entirely new branch of mathematics called calculus. Independently, German mathematician and philosopher Gottfried von Leibniz (1646–1716) also invented it.

● **Newton** was a Member of Parliament, president of the Royal Society and master of the Royal Mint, where he found a way to make coins more accurately.

● **Newton** discovered that sunlight is a mixture of all colours.

● **He spent** much of his life studying astrology and alchemy.

● **The interference patterns** from reflected surfaces such as a soap bubble are called Newton's rings.

▼ *Newton discovered that when sunlight shines through a prism, its rays are bent, each colour to a different degree. When the light emerges from the far side of the prism, it splits into a spectrum – all the colours of the rainbow.*

Moving light

- **Light is the fastest thing** in the Universe, travelling at a speed of 299,792,458 m/sec.
- **One method** used to remember this figure is from the number of letters in each word of the following sentence: 'We guarantee certainty, clearly referring to this light mnemonic'.
- **For centuries** scientists debated whether light travels as waves or as particles (photons). It is now thought to do both.
- **Light waves** have peaks and troughs, like waves in the sea.

DID YOU KNOW?

An area the size of a pin head in direct sun receives one thousand billion photons in a single second.

- **If two beams** of light meet, they interfere with each other.
- **Constructive interference** occurs when the peaks of two light waves align, creating a single, brighter beam.
- **Destructive interference** occurs when the peaks of a light wave align with the troughs of another. This causes the beams to cancel each other out.

- **Light rays from the Sun** can be converted into other forms of energy. Solar photovoltaic (PV) converter panels (solar panels) are made of two or more layers of semi-conducting material, such as silicon.
- **When incoming** solar rays strike the silicon, it knocks out electrons that are conducted away by a metallic grid as an electric current.

◀ *In solar panels, the impact of photons of light on atoms generates electricity.*

Holograms

- **Holograms** are three-dimensional photographic images made with laser lights.
- **Holography was invented** by Hungarian-born British physicist Dennis Gabor in 1947, but its use was limited until laser light became available in 1960.
- **The first holograms** were made in 1963 by American scientist Emmett Leith and his University of Michigan research partner Juris Upatnieks, and Russian scientist Yuri Denisyuk.
- **Holograms are made** by splitting a beam of light from a laser in two. One part is reflected off the subject onto a photographic plate. The other (called the reference beam) is shone directly onto the plate.
- **The interference** between the light waves in the reflected beam and the light waves in the reference beam creates the hologram in microscopic stripes on the plate.
- **Some holograms** only show up when laser light is shone through them, while others, such as those used in credit cards and bank notes to stop counterfeiting, work in ordinary light.
- **Holograms can be used** to view objects that microscopes cannot reach. As long as an object can be reached by laser light, a hologram can be taken and its image reconstructed.
- **In 2008**, scientists developed a new method of making changing (dynamic) holograms, allowing these holograms to be made much larger and with better resolution than was previously possible.

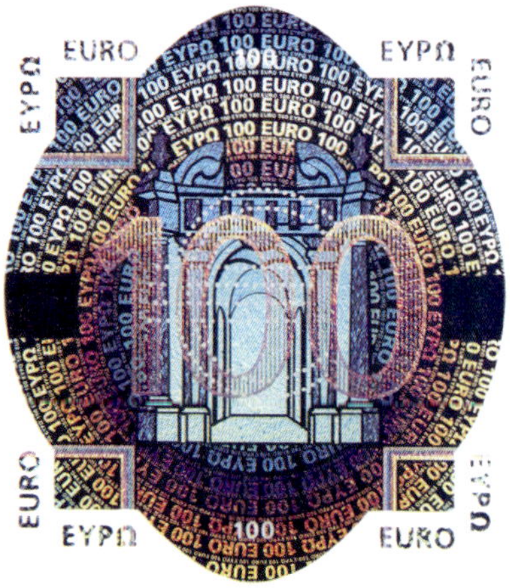

- **In the future**, this type of hologram may have applications in medicine, the emergency services and many other fields.

▲ *Holograms are very hard to forge, so are used on banknotes to prevent counterfeiting.*

Sound measurement

● **The loudness (volume) of a sound** is usually measured in decibels (dB). One decibel is one-tenth of a bel, the unit of sound named after Scottish-born American inventor Alexander Graham Bell.

● **Decibels** were originally only used to measure sound intensity, but are now used to compare electronic power output and voltages too.

● **An increase** of 10 points on the decibel scale means that a sound has increased by ten times, not just doubled.

● **The quietest sound** audible to human ears is 0 dB, and we can only hear a change in a sound's volume if it is of 1 dB or more.

● **A rustle of leaves** or a quiet whisper is 10 dB. Quiet talking is 30–40 dB, and loud talking is about 60 dB.

● **The noise level** on a city street is about 70 dB. Thunder is around 100 dB, while the loudest scream ever recorded was 128.4 dB. A jet taking off is 110–140 dB.

● **The loudest sound** ever made by human technology was an atom bomb, at 210 dB.

● **The amount of energy** in a sound is measured in watts per m^2 (W/m^2). A sound of 0 dB is one thousand billionths of 1 W/m^2.

DID YOU KNOW?

Listening to sound levels of over 100 dB for long periods of time causes deafness in humans.

▼ *A range of different sounds on the decibel scale.*

10 dB	40 dB	70 dB	100 dB	140 dB	210 dB
Rustling leaves	Talking	City street	Thunder	Jet take-off	Atom bomb

Copper

● **Copper has been in use** for over 10,000 years. It was one of the first metals used by humans.

● **It is one of the few metals** that occurs naturally in a pure form, but most of the copper we use today comes from ores that contain copper, such as cuprite and chalcopyrite.

● **The biggest deposits** of pure copper are found in volcanic lavas in the Andes Mountains in Chile.

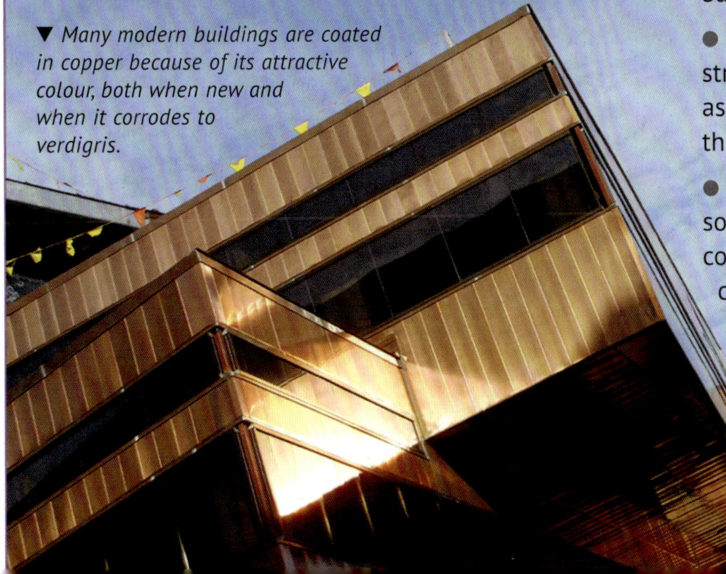

▼ *Many modern buildings are coated in copper because of its attractive colour, both when new and when it corrodes to verdigris.*

● **Chile accounts** for around a third of the world's copper production.

● **Copper is by far** the best low-cost conductor of electricity, so it is widely used for electrical cables.

● **It is also** a good conductor of heat, so it is used to make saucepan bases.

● **Copper is so ductile** (easily stretched) that a copper rod as thick as a finger can be stretched out thinner than a human hair.

● **After being exposed to the air** for some time, copper gets a thin green coating of copper carbonate. This is called verdigris, which means 'green' in Greek.

DID YOU KNOW?

Copper is essential to your health. Traces of it help to transport oxygen around your body, maintain hair colour and make hormones.

▶ *Probably the best known copper structure in the world is the Statue of Liberty in New York City. Erected in 1886, it had turned verdigris by the early 20th century.*

Electric power

● **In a power station**, electricity is created by a generator. In a generator, coils of wire are typically driven around between electromagnets to induce an electric current in the coils.

● **The magnets** in the generator in most large power stations are turned by turbines, which have blades like fans.

● **In some power stations**, the turbine blades are turned either by steam heated by burning fossil fuels such as coal or gas, or with nuclear fuel. In others, they are turned by moving water (hydro-electric power) or wind.

● **Simple dynamos** generate a direct current (DC) – an electric current that always flows in the same direction.

DID YOU KNOW?

The world's biggest hydro-electric power station is the Three Gorges Dam in China. It has a generating capacity of 22,500 megawatts.

● **Power station generators** are alternators. They give an alternating current (AC) – a current that continually swaps direction.

● **Electricity from power stations** is distributed around a country in a network of cables known as the grid.

● **Power station generators** generate upwards of 25,000 volts. This is too much to be used safely in homes, but too little to transmit over long distances.

● **To transmit** electricity over long distances, the voltage is boosted to 400,000 volts by transformers.

● **It can then be transmitted** through high-voltage cables. Near its destination, voltage is reduced to a level safe for use in homes.

◀ *Some power station transformers deal with half a million volts. Step-up transformers boost voltage, while step-down transformers reduce it for daily use.*

Archimedes

● **Archimedes** (*c.*287–212 BC) was one of the first great scientists. He created the sciences of mechanics and hydrostatics.

● **He was a Greek** who lived in the city of Syracuse, Sicily (when Syracuse was a Greek city state). Hieron II, king of Syracuse, was one of his relatives.

● **Archimedes' screw** is a pump supposedly invented by Archimedes. It scoops up water with a spiral device that turns inside a tube. It is still used in the Middle East.

● **To help defend** Syracuse against Roman attackers in 215 BC, Archimedes invented many war machines. They included a giant 'claw' – a grappling crane that could lift galleys from the water and sink them.

● **He analyzed** levers mathematically. He showed that the load you can move with a particular effort is in exact proportion to its distance from the fulcrum.

● **Archimedes discovered** that things float because they are thrust upwards by the water.

● **Archimedes' principle** shows that the upthrust on a floating object is equal to the weight of the water that the object pushes out of the way.

◀ *It is said that Archimedes came up with the idea of measuring specific gravity while getting in the bath, as this statue in Haifa, Israel demonstrates. He was so thrilled, he ran into the streets shouting 'Eureka!' (meaning 'I've got it').*

● **Archimedes** realized he could work out the density of an object by comparing its weight to the weight of water it pushes out of a jar when submerged.

● **Archimedes** used density to prove that a goldsmith had not made King Hieron's crown of pure gold.

● **Archimedes** was killed by Roman soldiers when collaborators let the Romans into Syracuse in 212 BC.

Thermodynamics

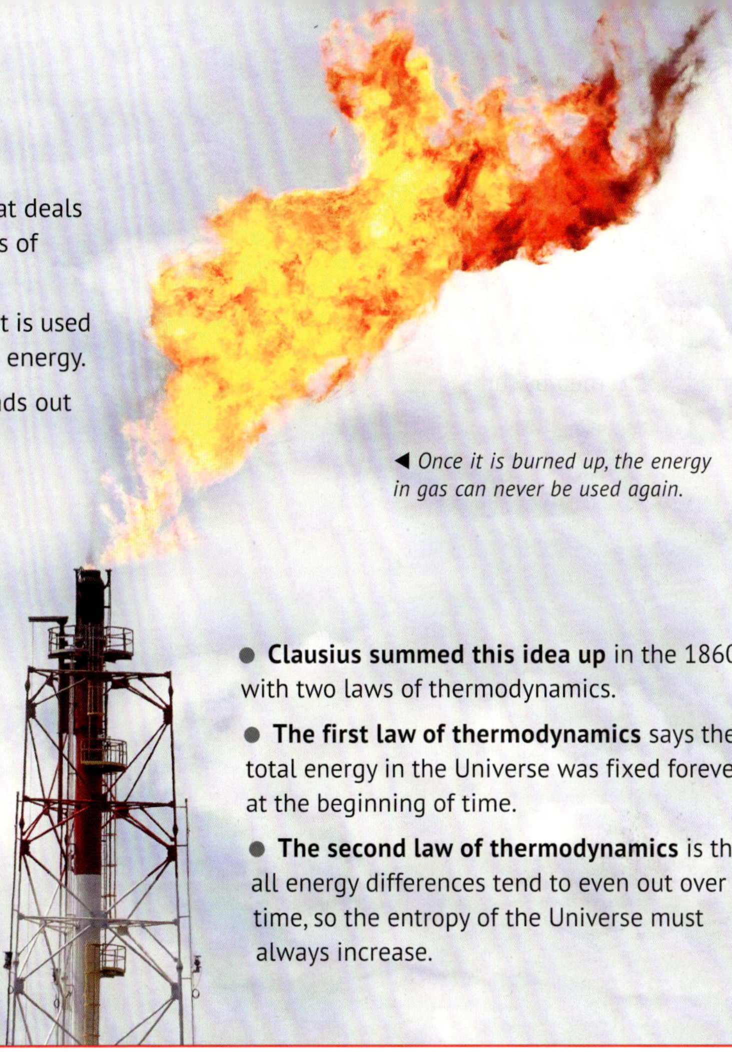

● **Thermodynamics** is the branch of science that deals with the relations between heat and other forms of energy.

● **Energy cannot be destroyed**, but every time it is used some of it is converted from other types to heat energy.

● **Energy that turns into heat** dissipates (spreads out thinly in all directions) and is hard to use again.

● **Scientists use the word** 'entropy' to describe how much energy has become unusable. The less energy available for doing work, the greater the entropy.

● **German physicist Rudolf Clausius** invented the word 'entropy' in 1868 to describe how everything happens because energy naturally moves from hot, high energy areas to cold, low energy areas.

● **Energy flows** from hot areas to cold until both are equal. Once this 'equilibrium' is reached, there is no longer any energy difference to make things happen. Entropy is said to be at a maximum.

◀ Once it is burned up, the energy in gas can never be used again.

● **Clausius summed this idea up** in the 1860s with two laws of thermodynamics.

● **The first law of thermodynamics** says the total energy in the Universe was fixed forever at the beginning of time.

● **The second law of thermodynamics** is that all energy differences tend to even out over time, so the entropy of the Universe must always increase.

Musical sounds

● **Like all sound**, a musical note is created by a vibration of air. Musicians control the frequency and volume of these vibrations to play tunes.

● **The pitch (level)** of a musical note depends upon the frequency of the vibrations.

● **Sound frequency** is measured in hertz (Hz), which refers to the number of waves per second.

● **Human ears** can hear sounds within a frequency range of 20–20,000 Hz.

▶ The shape of the saxophone controls the vibrations of air blown into it to create a musical sound.

● **Middle C** on a piano measures 262 Hz. A piano has a frequency range from 27.5–4186 Hz.

● **The highest singing voice** can reach the E above a piano top note (4350 Hz), while the lowest is 20.6 Hz.

● **Few sounds** have only one pitch. Most have a fundamental (low) pitch and higher overtones.

● **The frequency** at which an object naturally vibrates is called its resonant frequency.

● **A musical note** can shatter glass if its frequency coincides with the resonant frequency of the glass.

◀ The sound of a violin is created by the regular vibrations of the strings as the bow is drawn across them.

Glass

- **Glass is made** from heating together sand, soda ash (sodium carbonate) and limestone (calcium carbonate).
- **Silica is a hard**, glassy solid found in sand. Glass can be made from silica alone, but it has a very high melting point (1700°C), so soda ash is added to lower its melting point.
- **Adding a lot of** soda ash makes glass too soluble in water, so limestone is added to reduce its solubility.
- **To make sheets of glass**, 6 percent lime and 4 percent magnesia (magnesium oxide) are added to the mix.
- **To make glass for bottles**, 2 percent alumina (aluminium oxide) is added to the basic mix.
- **The cheapest glass** is green because it contains small impurities of iron.

DID YOU KNOW?

Glass is five times as strong as steel in tension (the force under which a material is stretched).

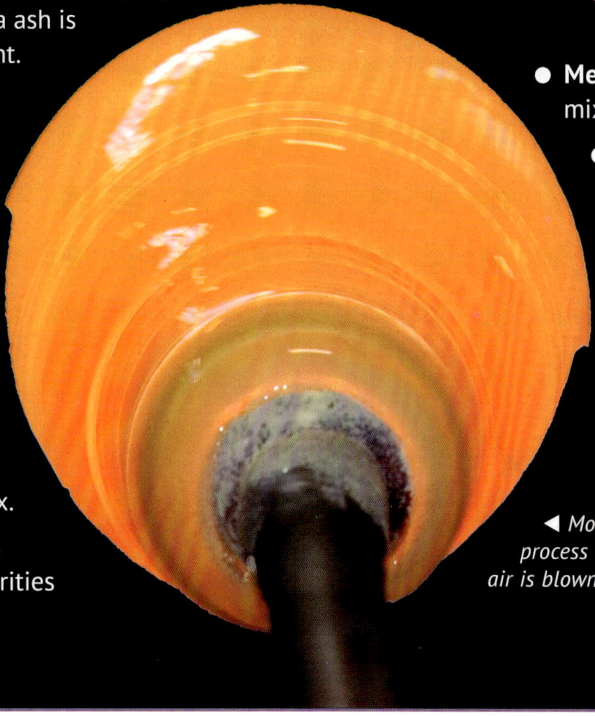

- **Metallic oxides** are added to the mix to make different colours.
- **Unlike most solids,** glass is amorphous (not made of crystals) so it does not have the same rigid structure as other solids.
- **When glass is extremely hot** it flows slowly like a thick liquid.

◀ *Molten glass is shaped by a process called 'glass-blowing' in which air is blown into it through a tube.*

Digital recording

- **Digital recording** is a process in which sounds or pictures are recorded as a series of digits.
- **The difference** between an analogue signal or recording and a digital one is that the analogue can have any value in a continuous range, whereas the digital can only have distinct 'steps' of a fixed size.
- **So, on an analogue clock** the second hand can be at any place between, say, 1 and 2, whereas a digital clock display jumps from one number to the next.
- **As a digital signal** is only sent in whole steps, there is no space for 'interference' – the noise sometimes heard on analogue recordings. So, with digital systems, there is no interference.
- **This is because** the recorder simply sends only the digital code of the recording to the player, which may be a TV, a computer or a music system. The player then simply recreates the original sound from the digital code.
- **Digital radio and TV broadcasts** can be very clear, because the digital code is always the same no matter how strong or faint the signal.
- **Digital reproduction** allows faint sounds and pictures to be amplified without any distortion.

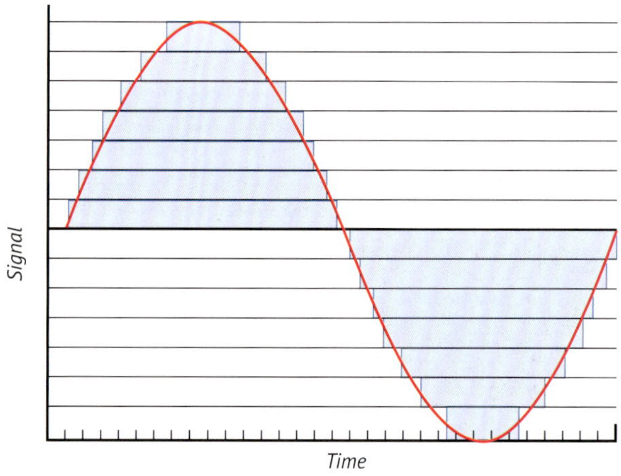

▲ *A digital signal is measured in steps as opposed to an analogue signal, which is continuous.*

- **It is possible** to process digital images by computer to accentuate some qualities and play down others.
- **Mathematically compressing** the data in a digital recording allows very detailed 'high resolution' recordings to be made and transmitted, including mp3 sound recordings and High Definition TV pictures.
- **Digital recording and compression** enables huge amounts of recorded music to be stored on mobile phones and tiny mp3 players.

Time travel

▲ *Gravity bends the fabric of space-time. Could it ever be bent so much that we could travel through time just as we travel through space?*

● **Einstein showed** that time runs at different speeds in different places, and that it is just another dimension like length, width and depth.

● **This has led** to the suggestion that at some point it may be possible for humans to travel through time to the past or future.

● **Einstein stated that** it is impossible for anyone to move through time, because it would involve moving faster than light. Even if they reached light speed, time would stop and they would not be alive.

● **The concept of time travel** causes theoretical problems for the relationship between cause and effect. A famous example is the idea of a man who travels back to a time before his parents were born and kills his grandfather. That would mean one of his parents could not have been born, and therefore he himself could not have been born. If so, then how could he have killed his grandfather? It's impossible to answer this paradox (contradictory statement).

● **During the 1930s**, American mathematician Kurt Gödel suggested that time travel might be possible by bending space-time. Scientists have since suggested all kinds of weird ideas for technology that could bend space-time, including gravity machines. The most powerful benders of space-time are black holes.

● **English physicist** Stephen Hawking believed that black holes cannot be used for time travel because everything that goes in to a black hole shrinks to a singularity (an unimaginably small point).

● **Hawking also argued** that if time travel were possible, we would meet visitors from the future.

● **Some scientists believe** black holes may be linked by wormholes (tunnels through space-time) to reverse black holes called white holes, where matter is ejected.

● **US astronomer Kip Thorne** argued that wormholes might be used for time travel. He also argues that there are infinite possible lines of cause and effect, so the grandfather paradox is irrelevant.

● **Wormholes may form links** between different areas of the Universe. However, Hawking's theories suggest that wormholes are so unstable that they would break up before they could be used for time travel.

▼ *Black holes in space suck in even light, but could artificially created black holes be the doors to wormholes – tunnels through space-time that could be used for time travel?*

Radiation

● **Radiation is energy** transmitted in the form of waves or particles. It can travel through empty space or through matter.

● **Electromagnetic radiation** is energy that travels as photons at the speed of light.

● **Particulate radiation** is bigger particles shot out by atoms at slower speeds.

● **Particulate radiation** includes cosmic rays (streams of particles from the stars) and 'radioactivity' that occurs when certain large atoms degrade (break down).

● **Radiation can be harmful**. It can damage and kill human, animal and plant cells.

● **Some bacteria can survive** a dose of radiation 10,000 times stronger than that which a person would survive.

● **Radioactivity** is commonly measured in becquerels. The radiation dose a victim receives is measured in roentgens. The dose they absorb is measured in grays.

● **An accident** at the Chernobyl nuclear power station in the Soviet Union in 1986, released large amounts of radiation into the atmosphere, killing 32 people outright and contaminating millions of acres of land.

● **The natural radioactivity** of a Brazil nut is about six becquerels. This means that six atoms in the nut break up every second.

● **There is always** a low level of radiation present in the environment – from the Universe, the gas radon that leaks from the ground, and from human activities, such as X-rays, that use radiation.

◀ *Some of the fuel burned in nuclear power stations becomes highly radioactive after being used and must be disposed of safely.*

Water

DID YOU KNOW?

The human brain is 85 percent water, and bones are about 33 percent water.

● **Water is the only substance** that exists as a solid, liquid and gas at normal temperatures. It melts at around 0°C and boils at around 100°C.

● **Water's boiling point** varies according to atmospheric pressure. It is 100°C at sea level, but just 68°C on the top of Mount Everest, where atmospheric pressure is low.

● **Ice is less dense** than water, which is why ice forms on the surface of ponds and why icebergs float.

● **Water is one of the few substances** that expands as it freezes, which is why pipes burst during cold weather.

● **Water is a compound** made of two hydrogen atoms and one oxygen atom. It has the chemical formula H_2O.

▼ *Icebergs float because ice is less dense than water.*

● **The way in which water molecules** are drawn together creates a lot of surface tension. This is what pulls water drops into globules.

● **Water covers 71 percent** of Earth's surface – in its oceans, seas, rivers and lakes. In addition, there is around 1.6 percent in the ground and 0.001 percent in the air as vapour, clouds and rain.

● **Some of the world's water** (2.4 percent) is frozen as glaciers and ice caps, but global warming reduces this.

● **Liquid water** may also occur elsewhere in space – frozen beneath the surface of the Moon; under the surface of Saturn's moon, Enceladus; and on Jupiter's moon Europa. Ice is present on Mars, and on Saturn's moon, Titan.

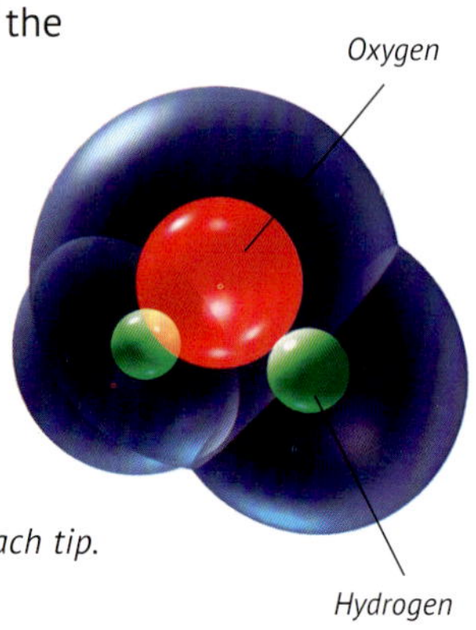

▶ *Water's V-shaped molecule has an oxygen atom (red) at the base and an hydrogen atom (green) at each tip.*

Echoes and acoustics

- **An echo** is a reflection of sound off an object or surface that is heard slightly after the direct sound.
- **Our ears** can only hear an echo if it comes back more than 0.1 second after the original sound. In 0.1 seconds, sound travels 34 m, so our ears can only hear echoes that are reflected back from surfaces at least 17 m away.

- **When standing in a valley** surrounded by mountains, you may hear a sound echoed many times over.
- **Smooth, hard surfaces** give the best echoes because they cause a minimum amount of disruption to the sound waves reflecting off them.
- **Acoustics** is the study of how sounds are created, transmitted and received. It also refers to the sound properties of a building.
- **Concert halls** are designed to use echoes effectively to project sound. If a hall has too much echo, echoing sounds will interfere with new sounds, but a complete absence of echoes results in a muffled, lifeless sound.
- **The sound of live music** can be heard fading after musicians have stopped playing. This delay is called the reverberation time. Concert halls typically have a reverberation time of 2 sec. A cathedral may reverberate for up to 8 sec, giving a less defined sound.

◀ *Acoustic engineers have installed sound cushions to reduce echoes from the vast dome of London's Royal Albert Hall, thereby improving sound quality.*

Acids and Alkalis

- **Acids are solutions** that are made when certain substances containing hydrogen dissolve in water.
- **Hydrogen atoms** have a single electron. When acid-making substances dissolve in water, the hydrogen atoms lose their electron, becoming positively charged ions (an ion is an atom that has gained or lost electrons).
- **The strength** of an acid depends on how many hydrogen ions (H^+) form.
- **Mild acids**, such as acetic acid (found in vinegar), have a sharp or sour taste.
- **Strong acids**, such as sulphuric acid, are highly corrosive (they dissolve metals).
- **A base** is the opposite of an acid. Weak bases such as baking powder taste bitter and feel soapy. Strong bases such as caustic soda are corrosive.
- **A base that dissolves** in water is called an alkali. Alkalis contain negatively charged ions – typically ions of hydrogen and oxygen, called hydroxide ions, OH^-.
- **When you add an acid** to an alkali, both substances are neutralized (they cancel each other out). The acid and alkali react together forming water and a salt.

DID YOU KNOW?

Hydrochloric acid is found in the human stomach and is essential for digestion. It has a pH of between 1 and 2.

- **The strength of an acid** can be measured on the pH scale. The strongest acid has a pH of 1. The strongest alkali has a pH of 14. Pure water has a pH of about 7. It is neutral – neither acid nor alkali.
- **Chemists use indicators** to test for acidity. An indicator is a substance such as litmus paper that changes colour depending on the pH of a solution.

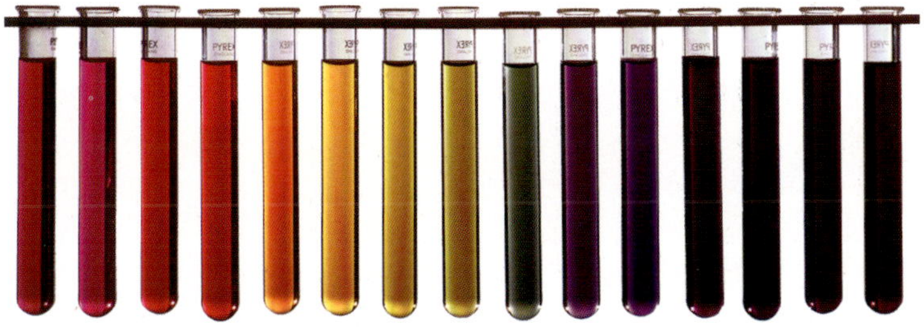

▲ *A universal indicator is a mix of dyes that changes colour over a pH range of 0–14 and is used to test a solution's acidity or alkalinity.*

Carbon

- **Carbon is the fourth** most abundant element in the Universe after hydrogen, helium and oxygen. Carbon was made inside stars.
- **The word** 'carbon' comes from the Latin word carbo, meaning 'charcoal'.
- **Carbon atoms have space** for four electrons in their outer shells, so carbon forms over ten million compounds.
- **Pure carbon** occurs in five major allotropes (forms). These are: diamond, graphite, amorphous carbon, fullerenes and carbon nanotubes.
- **Diamond, graphite and amorphous carbon** form naturally, while fullerenes and carbon nanotubes are mostly created artificially.
- **Diamond is the hardest natural substance** on Earth. Natural diamonds were made deep in the Earth billions of years ago. They were formed by huge pressures as the Earth's crust moved, and then brought nearer the surface by volcanic activity.
- **Diamonds are made** from incredibly strong networks of carbon atoms, each joined to four others in a tetrahedral (pyramidal) arrangement.

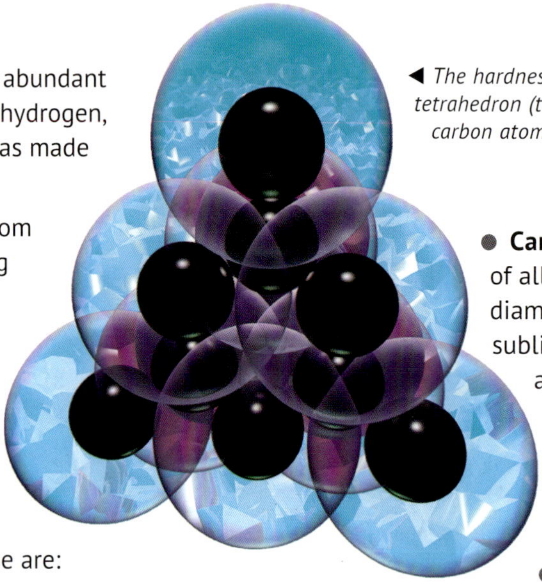

◀ *The hardness of diamonds comes from the very strong tetrahedron (three-sided pyramid) patterns that the carbon atoms are arranged in.*

- **Carbon has the highest melting** point of all elements. The melting point of diamond is about 3550°C, but it usually sublimes (goes straight from solid to gas), at around 3800°C.
- **Graphite is the black carbon** used in pencils. Its atoms are arranged in sheets that slide over each other, so it is quite soft.
- **Amorphous carbon** is the black soot residue that is left behind when candles and other objects burn.

▶ *Natural diamond is one of the world's hardest substances, forged by pressure deep down in the Earth billions of years ago.*

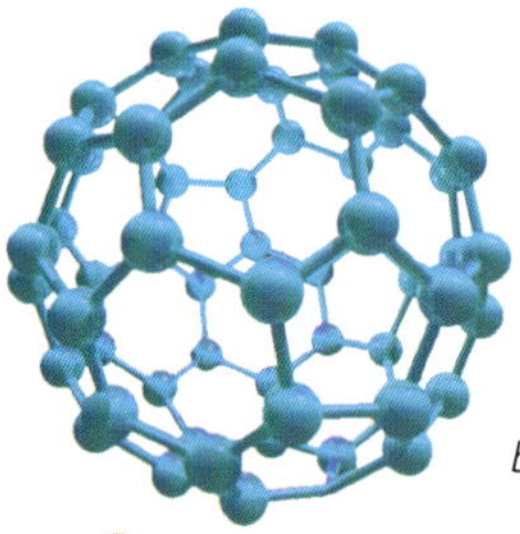

▼ *Scientists can make tough new forms of carbon called fullerenes by knitting together carbon atoms in balls and tubes.*

- **Fullerenes are big molecules** made of 60 or more carbon atoms linked together in a tight cylinder or ball. The first was made in 1985. They were named after the American architect R Buckminster Fuller, who designed a geodesic (Earth-shaped) dome that is constructed on the same structural principles.
- **Carbon nanotubes** are tubes of carbon atoms measuring a few nanometres across. (A nanometre is a billionth of a metre.)
- **They are** 20 times as strong as steel, and can bend and conduct electricity 1000 times better than copper.
- **In the future** carbon nanotubes may be used to make the ultimate small computers, or to make a lift to an orbiting space station.

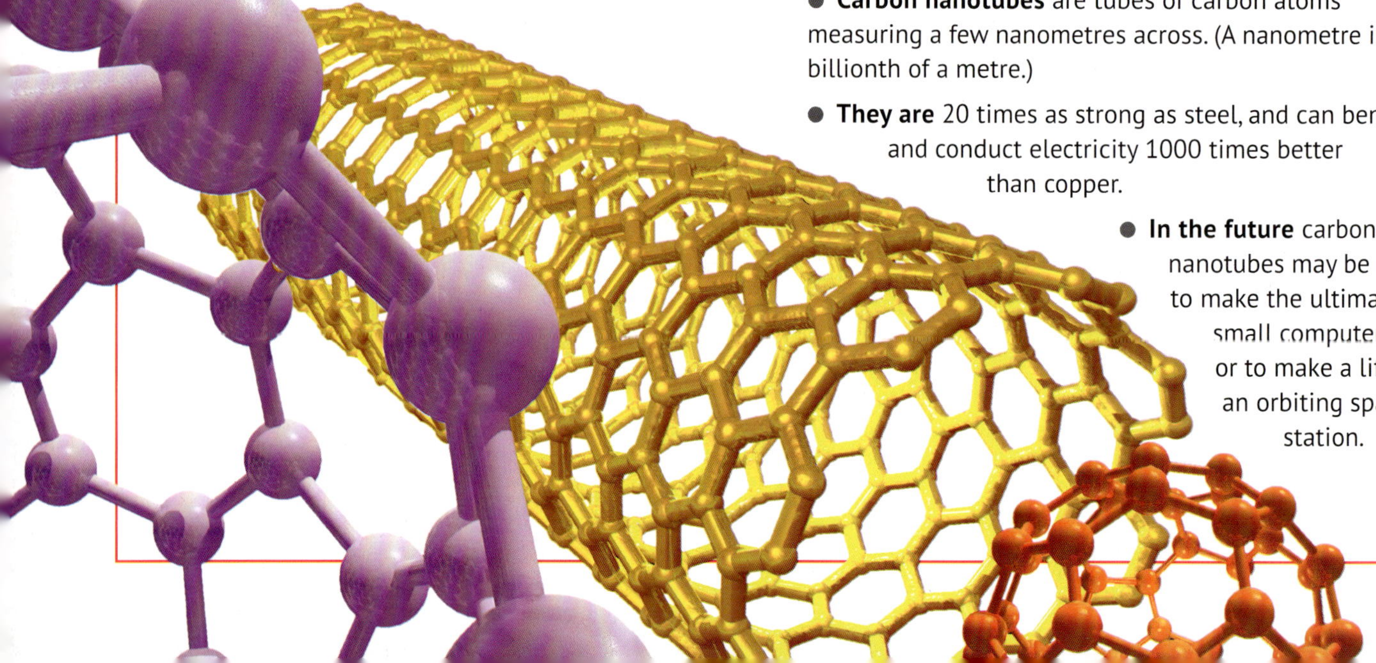

Chemical bonds

- **Chemical bonds** link atoms together to form molecules.
- **Atoms bond** in different ways by using the electrons in their outer shells.
- **Atoms are stable** when their outer electron shell has all the electrons it can hold. Atoms that don't have a full outer shell will form bonds with other atoms to gain, lose or share electrons to attain a full outer shell.
- **There are two ways** of doing this: forming ionic bonds and forming covalent bonds.
- **Covalent bonds form** when both atoms need more electrons to be stable; ionic bonds form when one atom needs more electrons and one needs fewer to be stable.
- **Ionic bonds occur** when atoms with just a few electrons in their outer shell 'donate' them to others with just a few missing from their outer shells.
- **The atom** that loses electrons becomes positively charged and the atom that gains electrons becomes negatively charged. The two atoms are then drawn together by the electrical attraction of opposites.
- **When sodium** forms an ionic bond with chlorine to create the sodium chloride (table salt) molecule, an electron is transferred from the sodium atom to the chlorine atom.
- **Covalent bonds** occur when atoms share electrons.
- **The shared electrons** are negatively charged, so they are all equally drawn to the positive nuclei of both atoms. The atoms are held together by the attraction between each nucleus and the shared electrons.

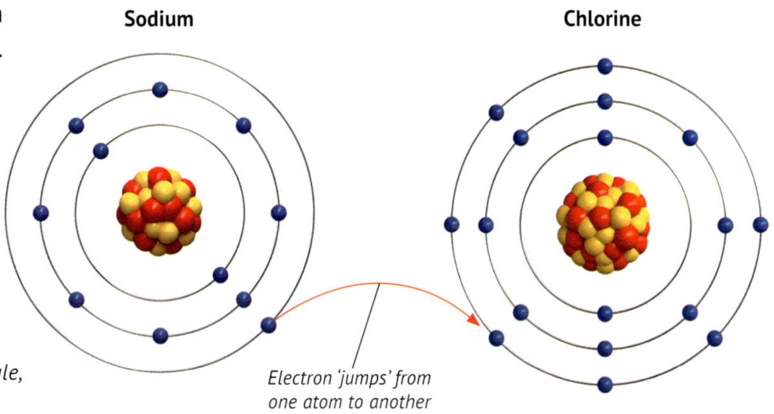

▶ *To make the ionic bond in a sodium chloride (table salt) molecule, a sodium atom donates an electron to a chlorine atom.*

Nitrogen

- **Nitrogen makes up** 78.08 percent of the air. Like oxygen, it is a colourless, tasteless, odourless gas.
- **Unlike oxygen**, nitrogen is inert (unreactive), but it is still vital to life.
- **Nitrogen becomes liquid** at −196°C and freezes at −210°C.
- **Liquid nitrogen can be used** to freeze substances so quickly that they are practically undamaged by the freezing process.
- **Foods such as fruit** can be preserved (made to stay fresh for longer) by being sprayed with liquid nitrogen.
- **Lightning supplies** the energy for reactions between nitrogen and oxygen. The result is nitrogen oxide, which combines with moisture to form around 250,000 tonnes of nitric acid per day, which is washed into soil by rain.

DID YOU KNOW?

When you 'crack' your knuckles, the noise you hear is actually popping bubbles of nitrogen gas, which is formed from the fluid in the joints.

- **Compounds of nitrogen** are called nitrates and nitrites. Both are important soil nutrients that help plants grow.
- **During a deep-sea dive**, water pressure can affect a diver's lungs, by causing extra nitrogen to dissolve in the blood. If the diver surfaces too quickly the nitrogen forms bubbles, causing a painful condition known as 'the bends', which can be fatal.

▶ *Liquid nitrogen is so cold, it can be used to make ice cream in less than ten minutes.*

Nuclear energy

- **The nucleus** at the centre of each atom is bound together with huge amounts of energy.
- **Releasing the energy** from the nuclei of millions of atoms can generate a huge amount of power, known as nuclear power.
- **Any reaction** that causes a change in the nucleus of an atom is known as a nuclear reaction.
- **Nuclear power** is used as an energy source for the creation of electricity and the explosion of atomic bombs.
- **Nuclear fusion** is the process in which small atoms such as deuterium, a form of hydrogen, are fused together to release nuclear energy. It is a natural form of this process that causes stars to glow.
- **Nuclear fission** is a process in which neutrons are fired at the large nuclei of atoms such as uranium and plutonium so that they split, releasing energy.

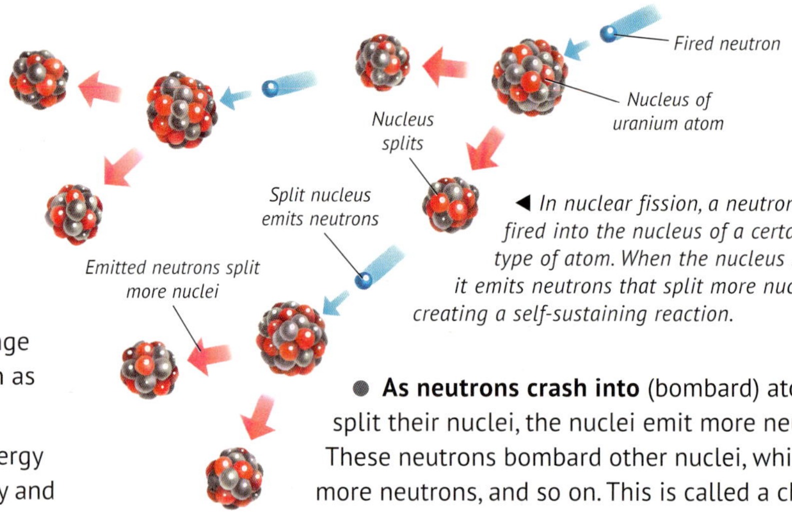

◀ *In nuclear fission, a neutron is fired into the nucleus of a certain type of atom. When the nucleus splits, it emits neutrons that split more nuclei, creating a self-sustaining reaction.*

- **As neutrons crash into** (bombard) atoms and split their nuclei, the nuclei emit more neutrons. These neutrons bombard other nuclei, which emit more neutrons, and so on. This is called a chain reaction.
- **An atom bomb** (A-bomb) is one of the two main kinds of nuclear weapon. It works by an explosive, unrestrained fission of uranium-235 or plutonium-239.
- **A hydrogen bomb** (H-bomb), or thermonuclear weapon, uses a conventional explosion to fuse the nuclei of deuterium atoms in a gigantic nuclear explosion.

Spectrum

- **A spectrum** (plural: spectra) is a range of different wavelengths of electromagnetic radiation.
- **The spectrum of visible light** can be seen as a band of colours if you shine a beam of white light through a prism.
- **The white light** is broken up into its spectrum of colours by the prism which refracts (changes the direction of) short wavelengths of the light more than longer ones.
- **This causes the light** to split into bands of colour ranging from violet (shortest wavelength) to red (longest).
- **The order of colours** in a spectrum is always red, orange, yellow, green, blue, indigo, violet.
- **You can remember** this from the first letter of each word in the phrase: 'Richard Of York Gave Battle In Vain'.

▶ *A narrow beam of white light is split into a spectrum by refraction as it passes through a prism.*

DID YOU KNOW?

Spectral analysis can reveal the elements that are contained in anything, from a distant galaxy to a drug.

- **Infrared** is light made of waves too long to be visible to the human eye.
- **Ultraviolet** is light made of waves too short to be visible to the human eye.
- **Spectral analysis** is the study of the spectrum created when a solid, liquid or gas glows.

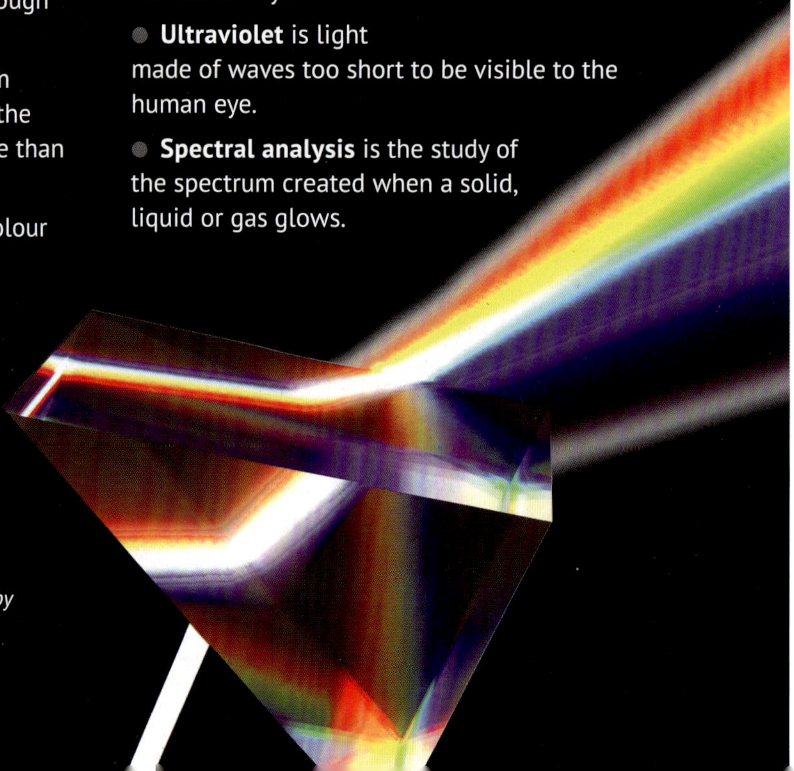

Energy conversion

● **Energy is measured** in joules (J). One J is equal to the amount of energy involved in moving a force of 1 newton (N) a distance of 1 m. A kilojoule (kJ) is 1000 J.

● **Energy used to be measured** in calories, but these are now only used when referring to the energy content of foodstuffs and related energy expenditure through exercise.

▼ *A wind turbine converts the kinetic (movement) energy of the wind into electric energy.*

● **One calorie** is 4.187 J. One kilocalorie (Cal) is 1000 calories.

● **While you are asleep** your body uses 60 Cals per hour. For an average-sized adult man, an hour of reading or watching television uses 80 Cals, while an hour of running uses 600 Cals and an hour of hard physical work uses around 350 Cals.

● **'Work' is the transfer of energy** that occurs when a force moves an object. The work done is the amount of energy (in J) gained by the object.

● **The work rate** (the rate at which energy is changed from one form to another) is known as the power.

● **The power of a machine** is the amount of work it does divided by the length of time it takes to do it:

$$\text{power} = \frac{\text{work done}}{\text{time taken}}$$

● **A transducer** is a device that converts electricity into different forms – such as sound, light or motion – or vice versa. A loudspeaker is an example of a transducer.

● **Earth's coal reserves** contain a total of 2×10^{23} J of energy. A thunderstorm has 10^{11} J.

Calcium

● **Calcium is a soft**, silvery white metal. It does not occur naturally in its pure form but is widely found as a compound (mixture of two elements).

● **It is the fifth** most abundant element on Earth.

● **Calcium is one of six** alkaline earth metals that make up group 2 of the Periodic Table.

● **Most calcium compounds** are white solids called limes. These include substances such as chalk, porcelain, enamel (found on teeth), cement, seashells and limescale.

● **The word** 'lime' comes from the Latin for 'slime'.

● **Quicklime is calcium oxide**, so-called because when water drips on it, it twists and swells as if it is alive ('quick' is the Old English word for 'living').

● **Slaked lime is calcium hydroxide**. It may be called 'slaked' because it slakes (quenches) a plant's thirst for lime in acid soils.

● **Limelight was the bright light** used by theatres to light performances in the days before electricity. It was made by placing a flame of burning hydrogen and oxygen over a cylinder of calcium oxide.

● **Limelight was replaced** by electric lighting, but its use is why famous people are sometimes referred to as being 'in the limelight'.

● **Calcium adds rigidity** to bones and teeth and helps to control muscles. Milk, cheese and green leafy vegetables are good sources.

◀ *Eggshell is made almost entirely from calcium carbonate.*

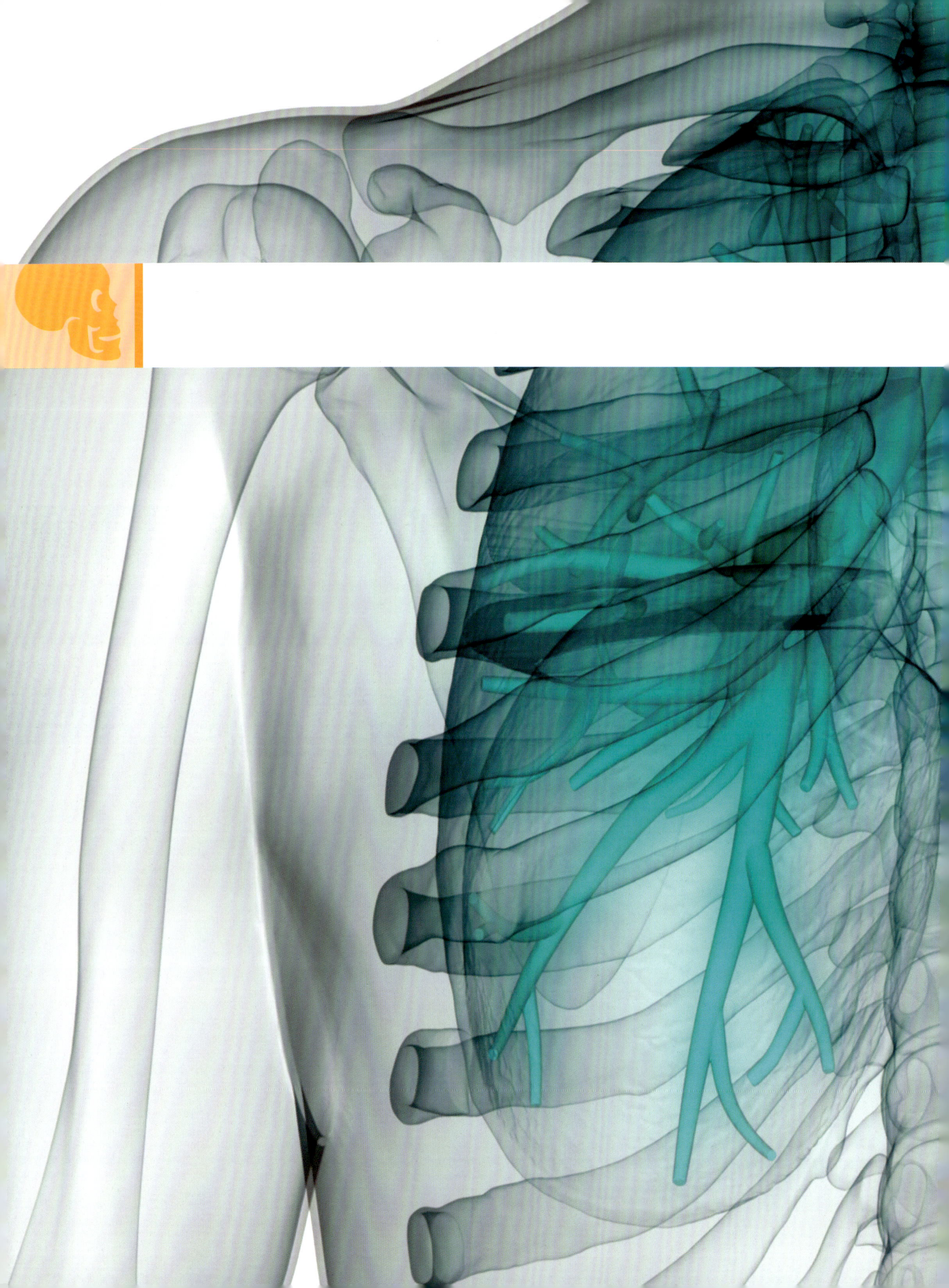

1000 HUMAN BODY FACTS

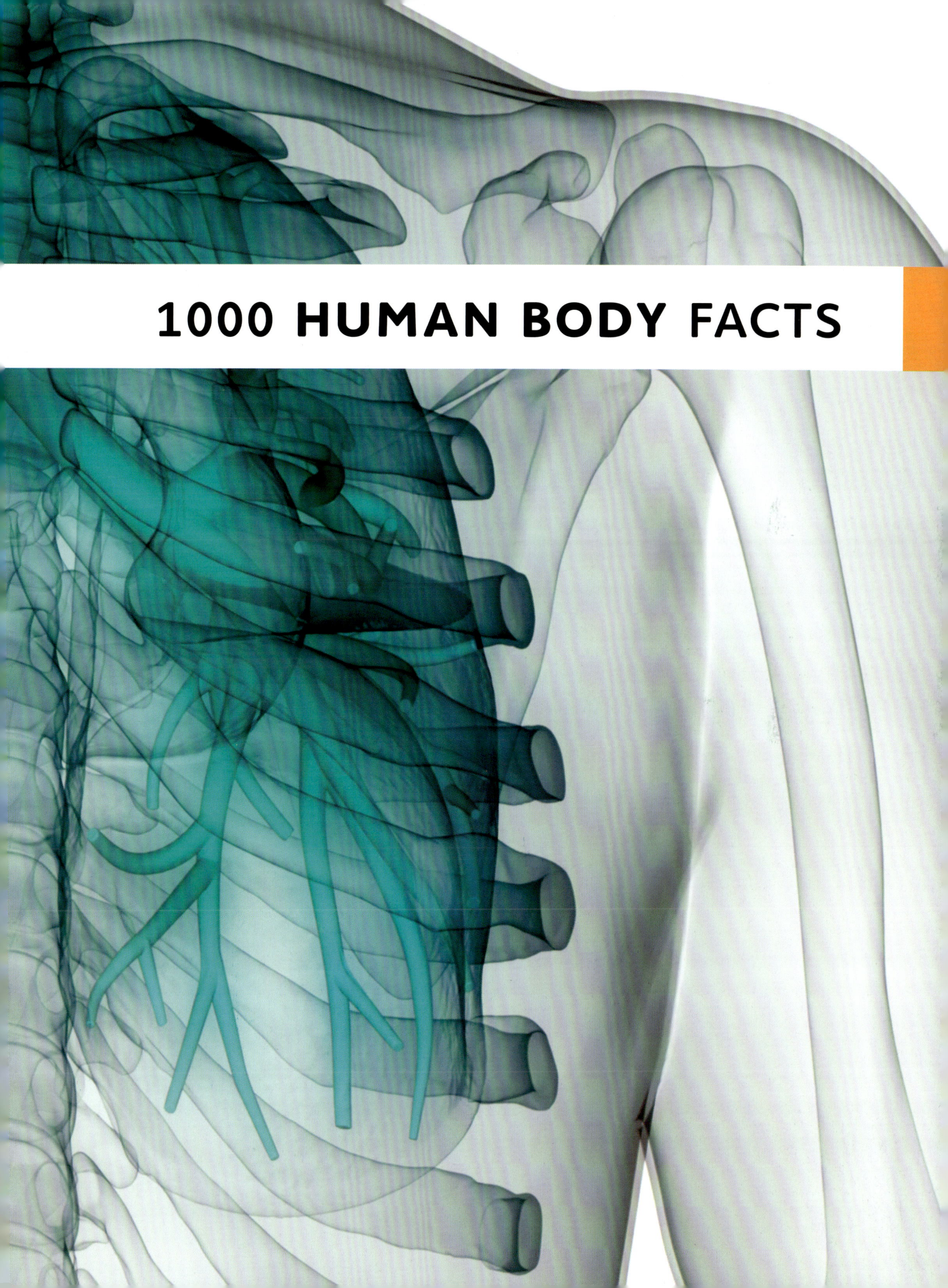

Body systems

● **Your body systems** are interlinked – each has its own task, but they are all dependent on one another.

● **The skeleton** supports the body, protects major organs, and provides an anchor for the muscles.

● **The nervous system** is the body's control and communications network.

● **The digestive system** breaks down food into chemicals that the body can use to its advantage.

● **The immune system** is the body's defence against germs. It includes white blood cells, antibodies and the lymphatic system.

● **Water balance** inside the body is controlled by the urinary system. This removes extra water as urine and gets rid of impurities in the blood.

● **The respiratory system** takes air into the lungs to supply oxygen, and lets out waste carbon dioxide.

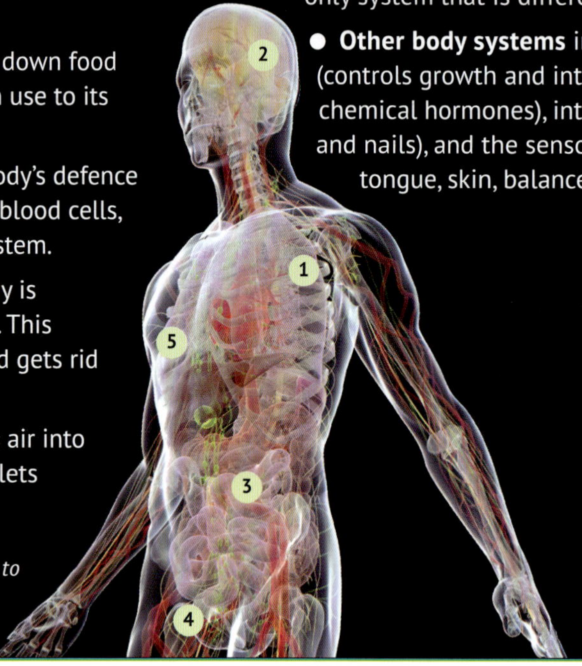

▶ *Our body systems all work together to keep us alive.*

● **The reproductive system** is the smallest of all the systems. It is basically the sexual organs that enable people to have children. It is the only system that is different in men and women.

● **Other body systems** include the hormonal system (controls growth and internal co-ordination by chemical hormones), integumentary system (skin, hair and nails), and the sensory system (eyes, ears, nose, tongue, skin, balance).

DID YOU KNOW?

The reproductive system is the only system that can be removed without threatening life.

KEY SYSTEMS
1 Skeleton Without the skeleton, the body would have no structure
2 Nervous system Nerves carry messages between the brain and the rest of the body
3 Digestive system Our digestive systems give us energy
4 Urinary system The urinary system helps to remove waste
5 Respiratory system This system allows the body to breathe

Anatomy

● **Anatomy is the study** of the structure of the human body.

● **Comparative anatomy** compares the structure of our bodies to those of animals' bodies.

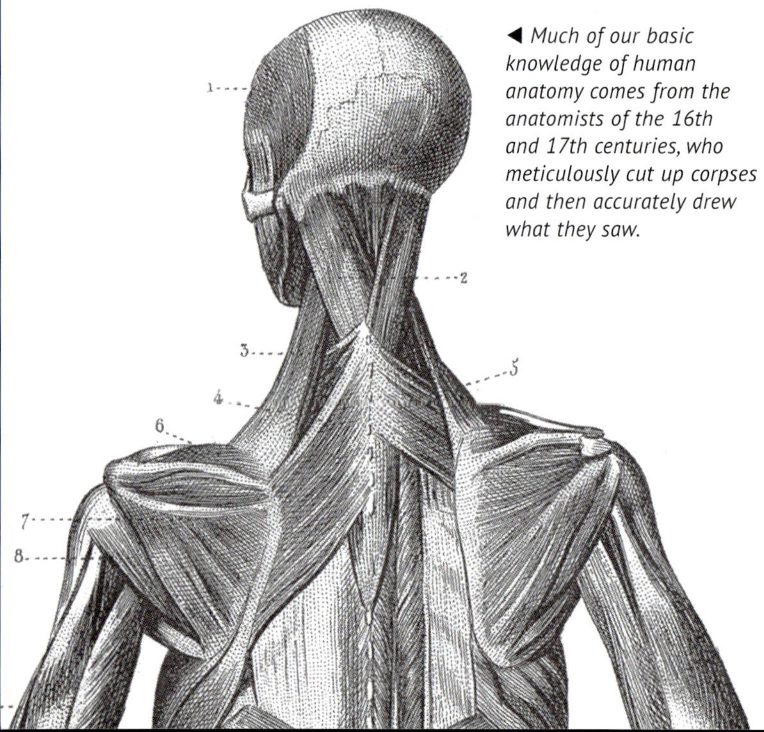

◀ *Much of our basic knowledge of human anatomy comes from the anatomists of the 16th and 17th centuries, who meticulously cut up corpses and then accurately drew what they saw.*

● **The first great anatomist** was the ancient Roman physician, Galen (AD 129–199).

● **The first great book** of anatomy was written in 1543 by the Flemish scientist Andreas Vesalius (1514–1564). It is called *De Humani Corporis Fabrica* ('On the Fabric of the Human Body.')

● **In order to describe** the location of body parts, anatomists divide the body into quarters.

● **The anatomical position** is the way the body is positioned to describe anatomical terms – upright, with the arms hanging down by the sides, and the eyes, palms and toes facing forwards.

● **The central coronal plane** divides the body into front and back halves. Coronal planes are any slice across the body from side to side, parallel to the central coronal plane.

● **The ventral** or anterior is the front half of the body.

● **The dorsal** or posterior is the back half of the body.

● **Every part** of the body has a Latin name, but anatomists use a simple English name if there is one.

The nervous system

● **The nervous system** is the body's control and communication system, made up of nerves, the spinal cord and the brain.

DID YOU KNOW?

The longest and largest nerve is the sciatic nerve, which is as wide as your thumb.

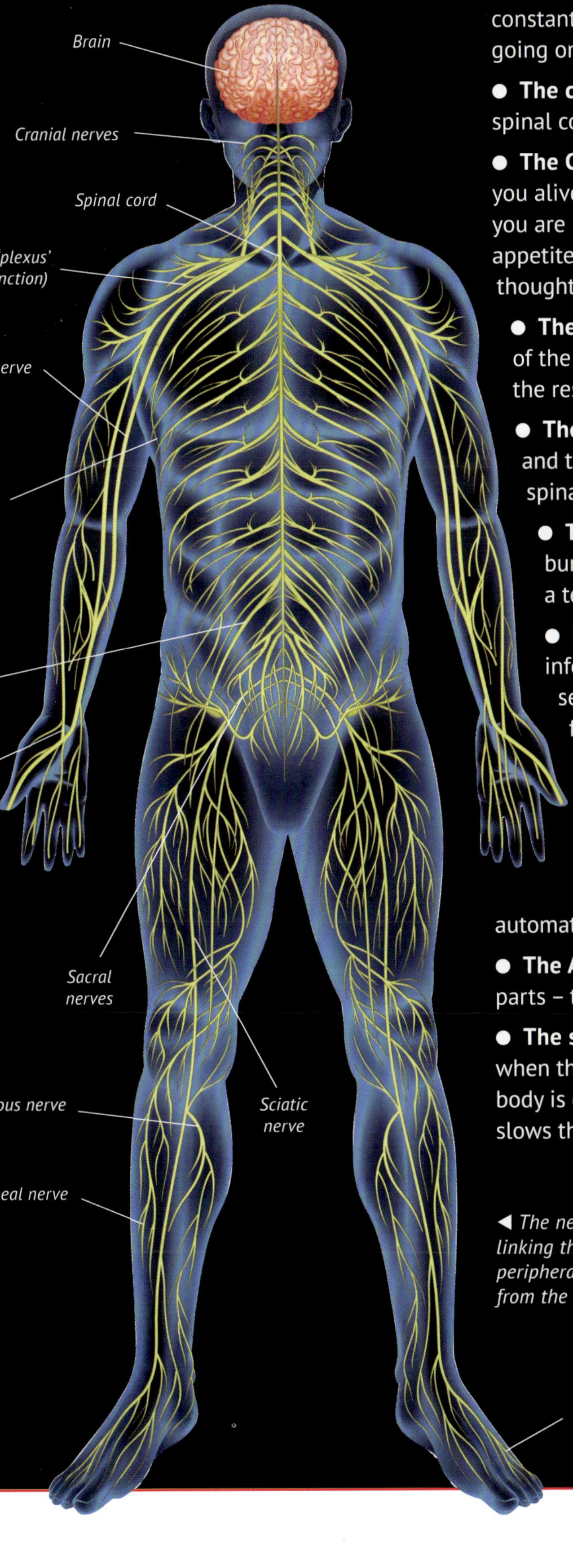

● **Nerves carry instant messages** from the brain to every organ and muscle – and send back a constant stream of data to the brain about what is going on both inside and outside the body.

● **The central nervous system (CNS)** is the brain and spinal cord.

● **The CNS** maintains all bodily functions that keep you alive, and can adjust according to the environment you are in. For example, it controls body temperature, appetite and breathing. The CNS is also the source of thoughts, emotions and memories.

● **The peripheral nervous system (PNS)** is made up of the nerves that branch out in pairs from the CNS to the rest of the body.

● **The PNS** are the 12 cranial nerves in the head, and the 31 pairs of spinal nerves that branch off the spinal cord.

● **The nerves of the PNS** are made up of long bundles of nerve fibres, arranged like the wires in a telephone cable.

● **Nerves that contain only fibres** that send information to the brain from the body are called sensory nerves. Nerves that only send signals from the brain to the body are called motor nerves. Mixed nerves contain both types of nerve fibre.

● **The autonomic nervous system (ANS)** is the body's third nervous system. It controls all internal body processes, such as breathing, automatically, without you even being aware of it.

● **The ANS** is split into two complementary (balancing) parts – the sympathetic and the parasympathetic.

● **The sympathetic system** speeds up body processes when they need to be more active, such as when the body is exercising or under stress. The parasympathetic slows them down.

◀ *The nervous system is an incredibly intricate network of nerves linking the brain to every part of the body. The nerves of the peripheral nervous system branch out to every limb and body part from the central nervous system (the brain and spinal cord).*

Central nervous system

DID YOU KNOW?

The CNS sends out messages to more than 640 muscles around the body.

- **The central nervous system** (CNS) is made up of the brain and the spinal cord (the nerves of the spine). It is responsible for collecting information from all the other nerves in the body, processing data and sending out appropriate responses.
- **The CNS** contains billions of densely packed interneurons – nerve cells with very short connecting axons (tails).
- **A surrounding bath of liquid** called cerebrospinal fluid cushions the CNS from damage.
- **There are 86 main nerves** branching off the CNS. These are 12 pairs of cranial nerves and 31 pairs of spinal nerves and are collectively called the Peripheral Nervous System (PNS).
- **Cranial nerves** are the 12 pairs of nerves that branch off the CNS out of the brain.
- **Spinal nerves** are the 31 pairs of nerves that branch off the spinal cord.

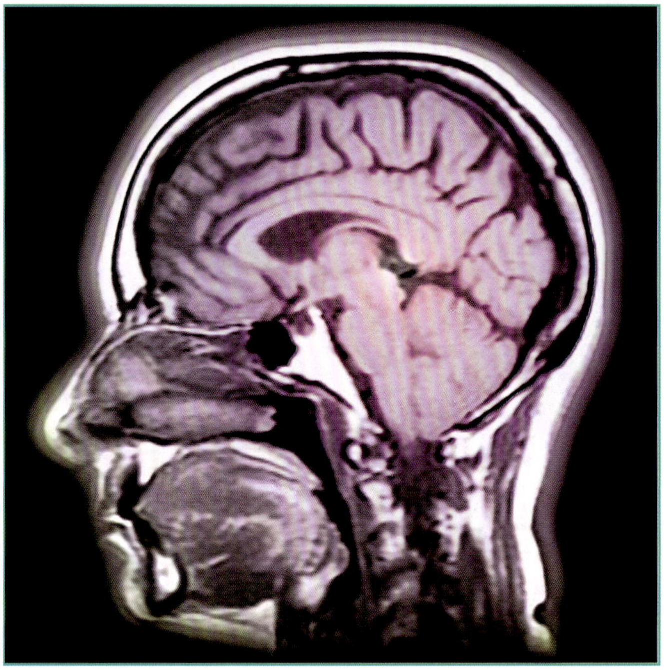

▶ *The brain's cortex (outer layer) is only 5 mm thick, but flattened out would cover an area almost as big as an office desk, and contains at least 50 billion nerve cells.*

Peripheral nervous system

- **The peripheral nervous system** (PNS) consists of the 12 pairs of cranial nerves in the head and the 31 pairs of spinal nerves that branch off the spinal cord.
- **Spinal nerves** can be divided into groups: there are eight pairs of cervical nerves in the neck, 12 pairs of thoracic nerves in the chest, five pairs of lumbar nerves in the abdomen, five pairs of sacral nerves in the lower back and one pair of coccygeal nerves at the base of the spine.
- **Several of the spinal nerves** combine to form collections of nerves called nerve plexuses.
- **Located in the head**, the cervical plexus provides the nerves that supply the neck and shoulders.
- **The plexus** in the neck and upper arm is called the brachial plexus and supplies the arm and the upper back.

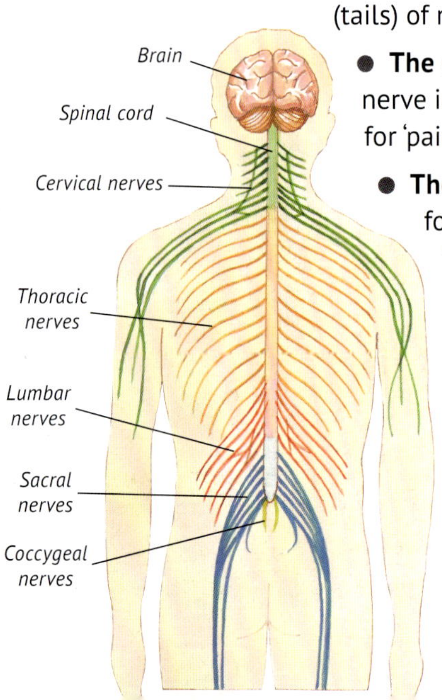

- **Nerves in the abdomen** are provided by the solar plexus.
- **The lumbar plexus** contains nerves that supply the abdomen and the leg muscles.
- **Long bundles** of nerve fibres make up the nerves of the PNS. These are in turn made from the long axons (tails) of nerve cells, bound together.
- **The sciatic nerve** to each leg is the longest nerve in the body. Its name comes from the Latin for 'pain in the thigh'.
- **The ulnar nerve** controls the muscles in the forearm, hand and fingers. When you hit your 'funny bone' you are actually bruising this nerve.
- **Pins and needles** occur when you pinch one of your peripheral nerves by sitting awkwardly or holding an arm or leg in a funny position for a long time.

◀ *Spinal nerves branch off the spinal cord in pairs, with one nerve on either side. They are arranged in four groups, and there is one pair between each of the 32 vertebrae.*

Nerve cells

● **Nerves are made of cells** called neurons that link up like beads on a string.

● **Neurons are spider-shaped cells**. They have a cell body, a number of slender projections (dendrites) from the cell body that receive signals, and a long tail-like projection called an axon, which can be up to one metre long.

● **The axon** ends in fan-shaped swellings called axon terminals that transmit the nerve impulse to other nerve cells by linking with the cell body or the dendrites.

● **Neurons cannot multiply** like other body cells, so they cannot be replaced if they are damaged. However, neurons have a long life and can live for over 100 years.

● **Neurons need** a plentiful supply of oxygen and glucose to keep working.

● **The outer skin** (membrane) of a neuron is electrically active. A nerve signal is a series of electrical pulses each lasting about 0.001 sec that passes along the axon to another nerve cell.

● **These electrical pulses** are created by the movement of electrically charged body salts (sodium and potassium) in and out of the nerve cell.

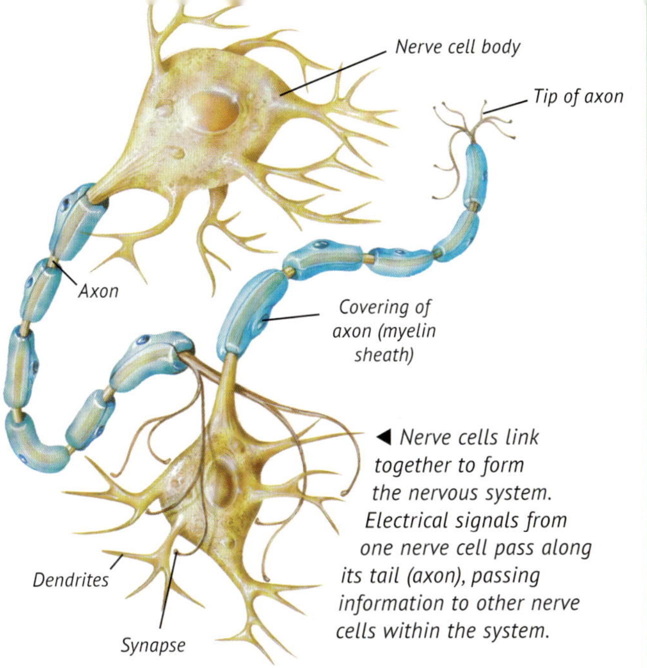

◀ Nerve cells link together to form the nervous system. Electrical signals from one nerve cell pass along its tail (axon), passing information to other nerve cells within the system.

● **The axons of long-distance nerves** are insulated by a sheath of a fatty substance called myelin. This stops the electrical signal from weakening as it travels.

● **With myelin**, nerve signals travel at 100 m/sec. Without myelin the signals travel at 1–2 m/sec.

● **When myelin is damaged**, such as with the disease multiple sclerosis, nerves don't communicate properly, causing a range of debilitating symptoms.

Synapses

● **Synapses are the gaps** between nerve cells.

● **When a nerve signal** goes from one nerve cell to another, it must be transmitted (sent) across the synapse by neurotransmitters.

● **Neurotransmitters are chemicals** used to relay, amplify (increase) and alter electrical signals between a neuron and another cell.

● **Droplets of neurotransmitter** are released into the synapse whenever a nerve signal arrives.

● **As the neurotransmitter droplets** lock onto the receiving nerve's receptors, they fire the signal onwards.

● **Each receptor site** on a nerve-ending only reacts to certain neurotransmitters.

● **Sometimes several signals** must arrive before enough neurotransmitter is released to fire the receiving nerve.

▶ Nerve signals are transmitted across a synapse as chemical messengers called neurotransmitters. These lock on to receptors on the receiving nerve.

● **Scientists have identified** more than 40 neurotransmitter chemicals.

● **Dopamine** is a neurotransmitter that works in the parts of the brain that control movement and learning.

● **Serotonin** is a neurotransmitter that is linked to sleeping and waking up, and also to your mood.

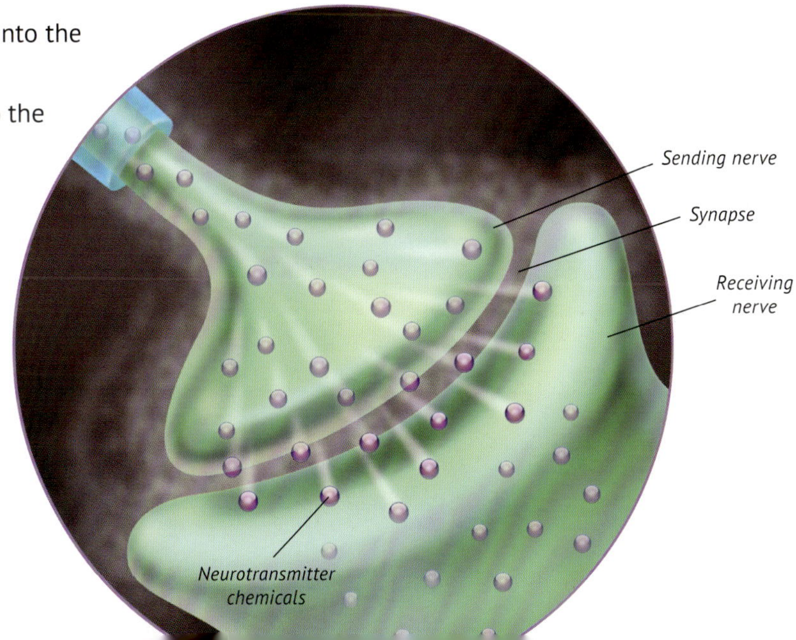

Inside the head

- **Your head contains** many delicate, soft structures that are necessary or important for a healthy life. These are surrounded by protective layers of tissue and bone to help prevent them from getting damaged.
- **The skin of the scalp** covers the bony skull, which forms a protective cage for the brain and supports the other soft structures inside the head.
- **Inside the skull** the brain is protected by three levels of membrane called the meninges.
- **The innermost membrane is the pia mater**, then comes the arachnoid and then the dura mater, which consists of two layers.
- **The illness meningitis** is an infection of these meninges.
- **The brain is bathed** by a clear, colourless liquid called cerebrospinal fluid (CSF).
- **This is produced within spaces** inside the brain called ventricles, and its main job is to act as a cushion, or shock absorber, for the brain and spinal cord.
- **CSF also carries nutrients** to the brain tissue and takes away wastes.
- **It circulates around the brain** between the arachnoid and the pia mater, following a particular route.
- **Sometimes a doctor** may need to take a sample of CSF to look for certain illnesses. They get it from the bottom of the spinal cord in a procedure called a lumbar puncture.

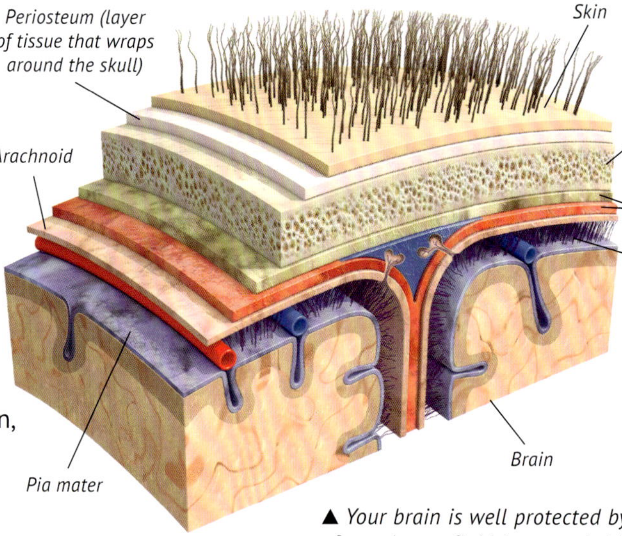

▲ *Your brain is well protected by layers of membrane, fluid, bone and skin.*

The skull

- **The skull** (cranium) is the hard bone case that protects your brain.
- **It looks like** it is a single bone. In fact, it is 22 bones, cemented together along rigid joints called sutures.
- **The dome** on top is called the cranial vault. It is made from eight curved pieces of bone fused (joined) together.
- **A newborn baby** has soft spots called fontanelles in its skull where the bones are not fully joined together. They join slowly over about 18 months.
- **As well as the sinuses** of the nose, the skull has four large cavities.
- **These are the cranial cavity** for the brain, the nasal cavity (the nose) and two orbits for the eyes.

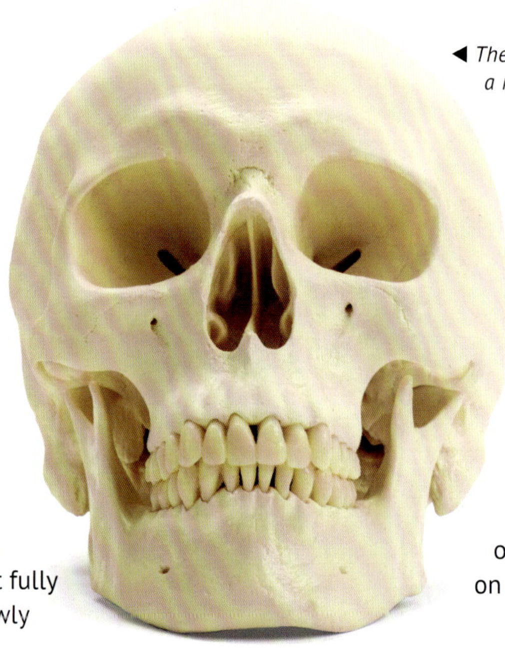

◀ *The skull holds and protects the brain. It is made of a number of bones that fuse together.*

- **There are holes in the skull** to allow blood vessels and nerves through, including the optic nerves to the eyes and the olfactory tracts to the nose.
- **The biggest hole** is in the base of the skull. It is called the foramen magnum, and the brain stem goes through it to meet the spinal cord.
- **In the 19th century**, people called phrenologists thought they could work out people's characters from little bumps on their skulls.

DID YOU KNOW?

Archaeologists can use computer analysis of ancient skulls to reconstruct the faces of people who died long ago.

The brain

- **The brain** is a delicate organ made up of more than 100 billion nerve cells (neurons). It is protected by the skull, three membrane (skin-like) layers (meninges) and a pool of clear fluid called cerebrospinal fluid (CSF).
- **Each neuron** is connected to as many as 25,000 other neurons – so the brain has many trillions of different pathways for nerve signals.
- **In an adult**, the brain makes up about 2 percent of the weight of the body.
- **The human brain** is far bigger in relation to the body than the brains of most other animals.
- **About 0.85 l of blood** shoots through your brain every minute. The brain may be as little as 2 percent of your body weight, but it demands 15 percent of your blood supply.
- **The cerebral cortex** is the outer layer of the cerebrum or upper part of the brain.
- **The brain** is divided into two halves (hemispheres). The right hemisphere controls the left side of the body and the left hemisphere controls the right side of the body.
- **Underneath the hemispheres** lie the parts of the brain that control automatic bodily functions, such as breathing, swallowing and sleep. The parts of the brain involved in these activities include the brainstem, midbrain (at the top of the brainstem), thalamus and hypothalamus.
- **The cerebellum** mainly controls body co-ordination and balance. It lies at the back of the skull under the cerebral hemispheres.
- **The corpus callosum** is the broad band of fibres joining the two hemispheres of the brain.
- **The basal ganglia** is group of structures linked to the thalamus at the base of the brain and is involved in coordination and movement.
- **The hippocampus** is the part of the brain that is linked to moods, willpower, learning and memory.

DID YOU KNOW?

It is now possible for scientists to grow human brain cells.

▼ *Protected by your skull, your brain is made up of many different but interconnected parts with different jobs to do.*

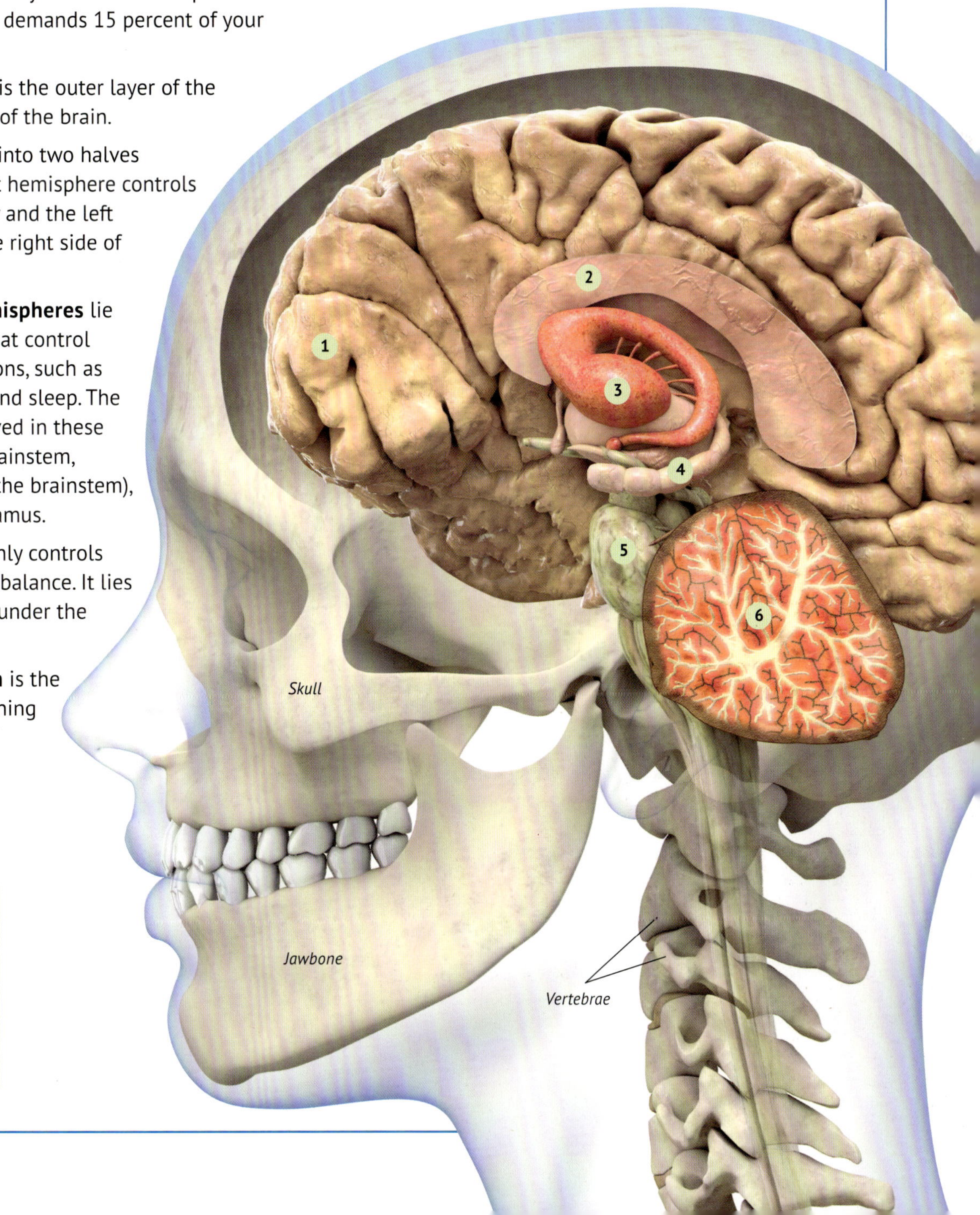

1	*Cerebrum*
2	*Corpus callosum*
3	*Basal ganglia*
4	*Hippocampus*
5	*Brainstem*
6	*Cerebellum*

The cerebral cortex

- **A cortex** is the outer layer of any organ.
- **The name of the brain's cortex** is the cerebral cortex. It is the outer layer of the cerebrum, which is the biggest part of the brain.
- **It consists of a layer** of nerve cells around the brain, which are also known as 'grey matter'.
- **The cerebral cortex** is where many signals from the senses are registered in the brain. It is also where conscious thoughts happen.
- **The visual cortex** is the part of the cerebral cortex where all of the things you see are registered in the brain.
- **The somatosensory cortex** is the place where a touch on any part of the body is registered, and each part of the body is represented in the somatosensory cortex.
- **The motor cortex** sends out signals telling body muscles to move.
- **The prefrontal cortex** is the most complicated area of the cerebral cortex because it is linked to your personality, reasoning ability, imagination, behaviour and your ability to learn complex things.
- **A human's cerebral cortex** is four times as big as that of a chimpanzee, about 20 times as big as a monkey's, and about 300 times as big as a rat's.

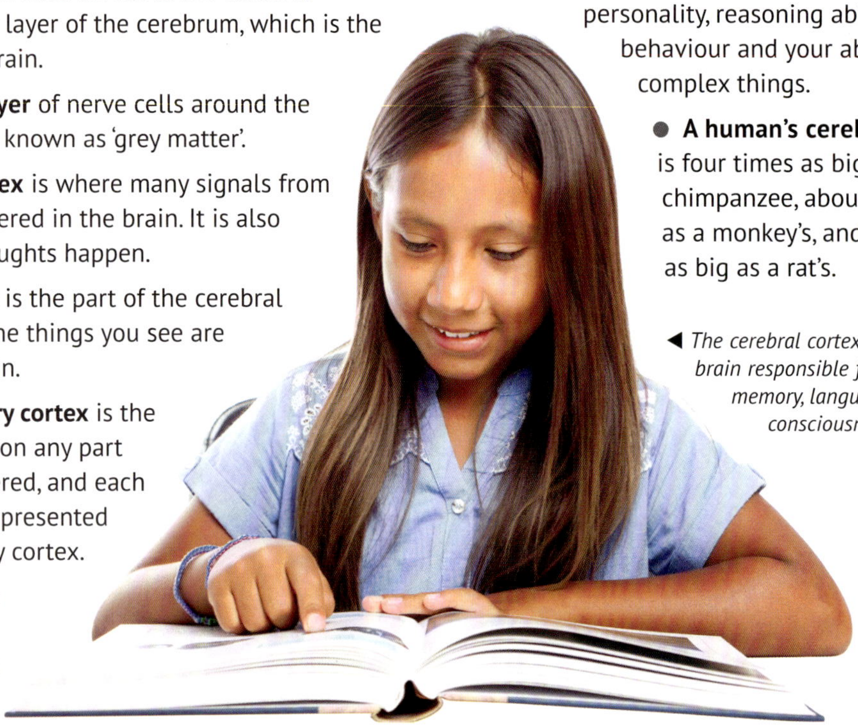

◀ *The cerebral cortex is the part of the brain responsible for intelligence, memory, language and consciousness.*

The spinal cord

- **The spinal cord** is the bundle of nerves that runs down a tunnel in the middle of the backbone.
- **It is the route** for all nerve signals travelling between the brain and the body.
- **The spinal cord** can work independently of the brain, sending out responses to the muscles directly. This is called a reflex response.
- **The outside** of the spinal cord is made up of the long tails (axons) of nerve cells and is called white matter.
- **The inside** is made up of the main nerve bodies and is called grey matter.
- **The spinal cord** is about 43 cm long and 1 cm thick. It stops growing when you are about five years old.

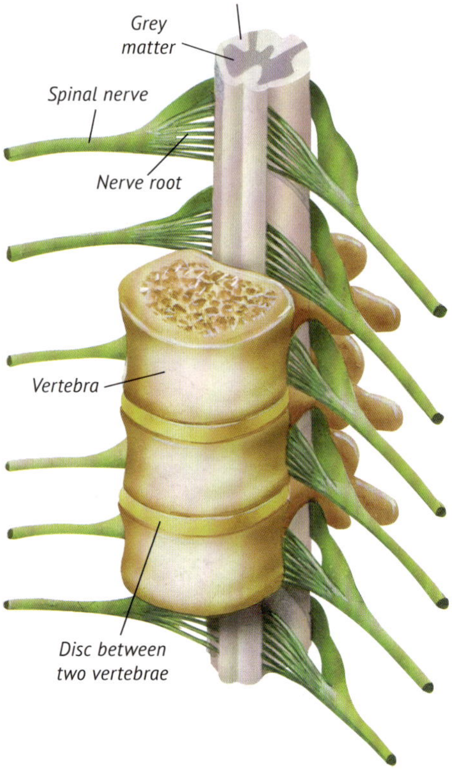

◀ *The spinal cord is encased in a tunnel in the backbone at the back of each vertebra. Nerves branch off to the body in pairs either side.*

- **Damage to the spinal cord** can cause paralysis.
- **Injuries below the neck** can cause paraplegia – paralysis below the waist.
- **Injuries to the neck** can cause quadraplegia – paralysis below the neck including both arms and legs.
- **Descending pathways** are groups of nerves that carry nerve signals down the spinal cord – typically signals from the brain for muscles to move.
- **Ascending pathways** are groups of nerves that carry nerve signals up the spinal cord – typically signals from the skin and internal body sensors going to the brain.

Reflexes

- **Reflexes are muscle movements** that are automatic. They happen without you thinking about them.
- **Inborn reflexes** are those you were born with, such as shivering when you are cold.
- **The knee-jerk** is an inborn reflex that makes your leg jerk upwards when the tendon below your knee is tapped.

DID YOU KNOW?

Athletes often have lightning reflexes – their bodies react faster than their brains can process.

- **Primitive reflexes** are reflexes that babies have for a few months after they are born.
- **The grasping reflex** is a primitive reflex. It causes a baby's hand to automatically grip anything it touches.
- **Conditioned reflexes** are learnt through habit, as certain nerve pathways are used again and again.
- **Conditioned reflexes** help you do anything, from holding a cup to playing football without thinking.
- **Reflex reactions** occur when your safety demands an automatic response, such as when you touch something hot or step on something sharp.
- **Reflex reactions** bypass the brain. The alarm signal from the body part that has detected the pain sets off motor signals in the spinal cord to make you move.
- **A reflex arc** is the nerve circuit from sense to muscle via the spinal cord.

◀ *Even babies have reflexes – automatically grasping anything put into the palms of their hands.*

Sensory nerves

- **Sensory nerves** are those that carry information to the brain from sense receptors all over the body.
- **Each sense receptor** in the body is linked to the brain by a sensory nerve.
- **Most sensory nerves** feed their signals to the somatosensory cortex at the top of the brain.
- **Massive bundles** of sensory nerve cells form the nerves that link major senses, such as vision, hearing, balance, taste and smell, to the brain.
- **Sensory information** from other regions of the body is carried by the paired spinal nerves that carry information to and from the brain. Each spinal nerve is associated with an area of the body.
- **In the skin**, many sense receptors are simply 'free', exposed sensory nerve-endings.

- **The brain interprets the signals** from sensory nerves in the skin so that you can tell the difference between touch, pain, hot and cold.
- **Different parts of the body** are more sensitive to these differences than others. This is because of the different amount of somatosensory cortex in the brain devoted to each region of the body.
- **Electrical signals** from the sensory receptors of the body travel to the brain along specific nerve pathways called ascending tracts.
- **Once the sensory signal** reaches the brain, processing of the information allows you to work out what the sensation (sensory signal) actually means. This is called sensory perception. For example, whether pressure on the skin is uncomfortable and where on the body it is felt.

◀ *Some of our most pleasant feelings, such as being hugged or stroking a pet, are sent to the brain by sensory nerves.*

Motor nerves

- **Motor nerves** tell your muscles to move.
- **Every major muscle** in the body has many motor nerve-endings that instruct it to contract (tighten).
- **Motor nerves cross over** from one side of the body to the other at the top of your spinal cord. This means that signals from the right side of the brain go to the left side of the body, and vice versa.
- **Each motor nerve** is paired to a receptor called a proprioceptor on the muscle and its tendons. This sends signals to the brain to say whether the muscle is tensed or relaxed.
- **If the strain** on a tendon increases, the proprioceptor sends a signal to the brain, which then adjusts the motor signals to that muscle to make it contract more or less.
- **Motor nerve signals** originate in a part of the brain called the motor cortex.
- **All the motor nerves** (apart from those in the head) branch out from the spinal cord.
- **The gut** has no motor nerve-endings but plenty of sense endings, so you can feel it but you cannot move it consciously.
- **Motor neuron disease** is a disease that attacks motor nerves within the central nervous system.

◀ *Motor nerves fire to make muscles move.*

Cranial nerves

- **The cranial nerves** – part of the peripheral nervous system – are found in the head. There are 12 numbered pairs.
- **Cranial Nerve I** is called the olfactory nerve. It is an entirely sensory nerve carrying signals to the brain about smell.
- **Cranial Nerve II**, the optic nerve, is a sensory nerve that carries information about vision to the brain.
- **Cranial Nerves III, IV and VI** are the oculomotor, trochlear and abducent nerves, which control eye movement.
- **Cranial Nerve V**, the trigeminal nerve, carries sensory information from the skin of the face and inside the nose to the brain, and controls the jaw muscles.
- **Cranial Nerve VII**, the facial nerve, controls the movement of the facial muscles to give expressions, and carries the sense of taste from the front of the tongue to the brain.
- **Cranial Nerve VIII** is called the vestibulocochlear nerve. It carries mostly sensory information about balance and hearing from the ear to the brain.
- **Cranial nerve IX, X and XI** are the vagus nerve, the glossopharyngeal nerve and the accessory nerve. Together, they control swallowing.
- **The glossopharyngeal nerve** also carries taste information from the back of the tongue.
- **The vagus nerve** also controls many other functions including heart rate.
- **Cranial Nerve XII**, the hypoglossal nerve, controls the muscles of the tongue used when speaking and swallowing.

▼ *The ability to smile is due to the action of the facial nerve, which sends signals from the brain to the muscles of the face.*

Thinking

- **Some scientists** claim that humans are the only living things that are capable of conscious thought.
- **Most thoughts** appear to take place in the cerebrum (situated at the top of the brain), and different kinds of thought are linked to different areas. These are called association areas.
- **Each half of the cerebrum** is divided into four rounded segments called lobes: two at the front (frontal and temporal lobes) and two at the back (occipital and parietal lobes).
- **The frontal lobe** is linked to your personality and is the area in which your ideas form.
- **The temporal lobe** is the area in which you hear and understand what people say to you.
- **The occipital lobe** is the area in which you work out what your eyes are seeing.
- **The parietal lobe** is where you register touch, heat and cold, and pain.
- **The left side of the brain** (left hemisphere) controls the right side of the body. The right side (right hemisphere) controls the left side.
- **One half of the brain** is always dominant (in charge). Usually, the left is dominant, which is why 90 percent of people are right-handed.

▶ *The brain thinks and plans all the time.*

Smell

- **Smells are scent molecules** that are carried in the air and breathed in through your nose.
- **The human nose** may be able to tell the difference between many millions of different chemicals.
- **Inside the nose**, scent molecules are picked up by a patch of olfactory cells called the olfactory epithelium.
- **Extensions of the cells** pass through a piece of bone in the base of the skull to the olfactory bulb.
- **The olfactory bulb** then sends the electrical signals to the part of the brain that recognizes smell.
- **The part of the brain** that deals with smell is closely linked to the parts that deal with memories and emotions. This may be why smells can evoke memories.
- **By the age of 20**, you will have lost 20 percent of your sense of smell. By 60, you will have lost 60 percent of it.

DID YOU KNOW?

The female hormone oestrogen increases the sense of smell, so women are more sensitive to smells than men.

▼ *Olfactory cells have micro-hairs facing into the nasal chamber to detect small particles.*

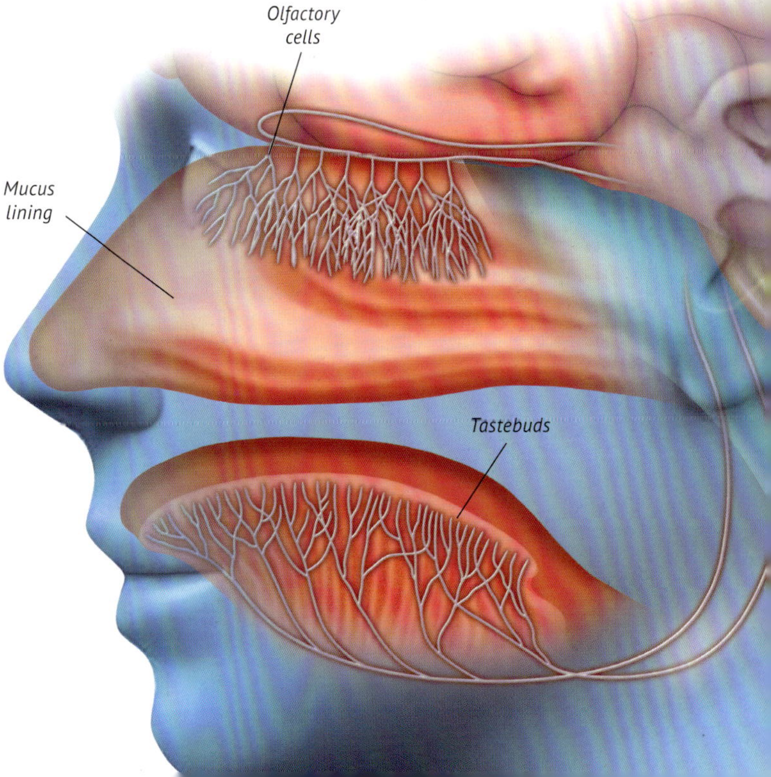

Hearing

- **The ear** is a complex organ containing the mechanisms for hearing and balance.
- **Pinnae** are the ear flaps on the sides of your head that collect and funnel sound.
- **When the eardrum vibrates** it shakes three bones called ossicles – the smallest bones in the body.
- **The three ossicle bones** are the malleus (hammer), the incus (anvil) and the stapes (stirrup). They sit in a small air-filled chamber called the middle ear.
- **When the ossicles vibrate**, they transmit the vibration to the fluid of the cochlea (the organ of hearing).
- **The cochlea** is a fluid-filled organ that contains thousands of hair cells. These cells detect frequencies of vibration and send this information to the brain.
- **The semicircular canals** are three fluid-filled canals containing nerve endings that detect head movement. Messages from these nerve endings help the brain to control balance.
- **The Eustachian tube** connects the middle ear chamber to the back of the nose and top of the throat. It keeps the air pressure inside the ear equal to the pressure outside your head.
- **Your ears can 'pop'** when pressure builds up inside the ear and then suddenly escapes down the Eustachian tube.

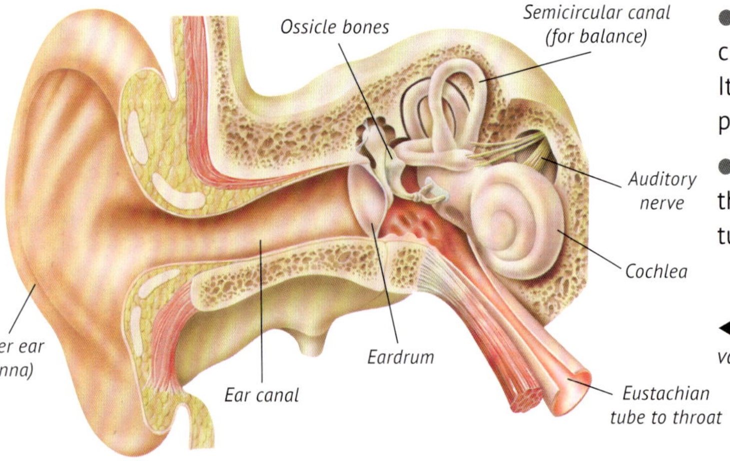

◀ *The ear is a delicate, complex structure that can pick up the tiny variations in air pressure created by a sound.*

Vision

- **Your eyes** enable you to see things because they focus the light rays reflected from objects to produce a sharp image on the lining at the back of the eye.
- **The back of the eye** is lined with millions of cells. This lining is called the retina, and it registers the picture and sends signals to the brain via the optic nerve.
- **The pupil** is the dark circular opening in the front of the eye which varies in size to regulate the amount of light entering the eye.
- **The cornea** is a glassy dish across the front of your eye. It allows light rays through the pupil into the lens.
- **The iris** is the coloured ring around the pupil. The iris narrows the size of the pupil in bright light and widens it when light is dim.
- **The lens** is just behind the pupil. It bends and focuses the image onto the back of the eye.
- **The image on the retina** is upside down because the light rays are bent. The brain turns the image the right way up when interpreting the information.
- **There are two kinds** of light-sensitive cell in the retina – rods and cones. Rods can work even in dim light, but cannot detect colours. Cones respond to colour.
- **Some kinds of cone** are sensitive to red light, some to green and some to blue.
- **Each of your eyes** gives you a slightly different view of the world. Your brain combines the two views to give an impression of depth.

DID YOU KNOW?

You have 200 eyelashes on each eye to protect them from dust.

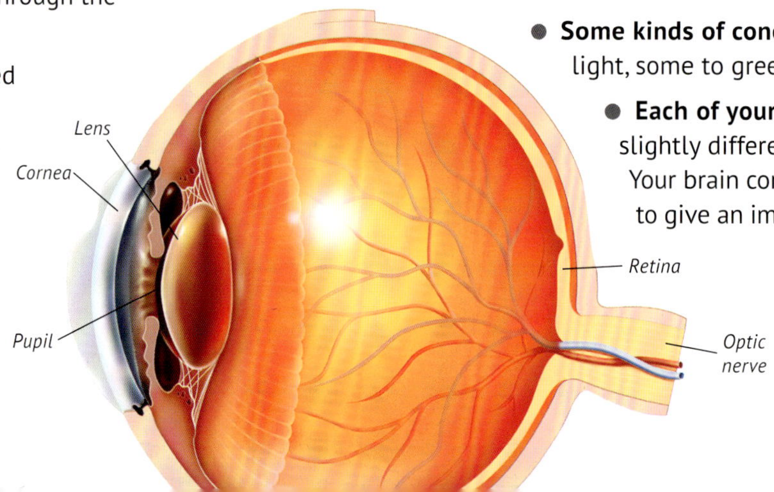

▶ *Jelly-like vitreous humour in the main body of the eye holds the eye's shape and keeps everything in place.*

Taste

- **Taste allows you to tell** whether food is safe to eat or should be avoided.
- **Taste receptors** detect food chemicals dissolved in saliva (spit) in the mouth. They are found mainly on the tongue's surface inside structures called taste buds.
- **Taste buds** are tiny cups that contain taste receptor cells. Long projections on these cells stick out of the taste bud so that they are always in saliva.
- **There are around 10,000 taste buds** on the tongue. There are also a few inside the cheeks and in the throat.
- **When a food chemical** is detected, the taste receptor sends a signal via the facial nerve to the brain.
- **Taste and flavour** are different – there are at least five basic tastes, and many flavours.
- **The detection of flavour** is an interaction between the senses of taste and smell. Food tastes bland when you have a cold because you lose this interaction when your nose is blocked.
- **The basic tastes** are umami (savoury), sweet, salty, sour and bitter.
- **Different parts of the tongue** are more sensitive to one of these five basic tastes than the others. The tip of the tongue is most sensitive to sweetness, for example.
- **As well as taste**, the tongue can also feel the texture and temperature of food.

▼ *This powerful microscope picture of the surface of the tongue shows in pink the papillae which contain the taste buds.*

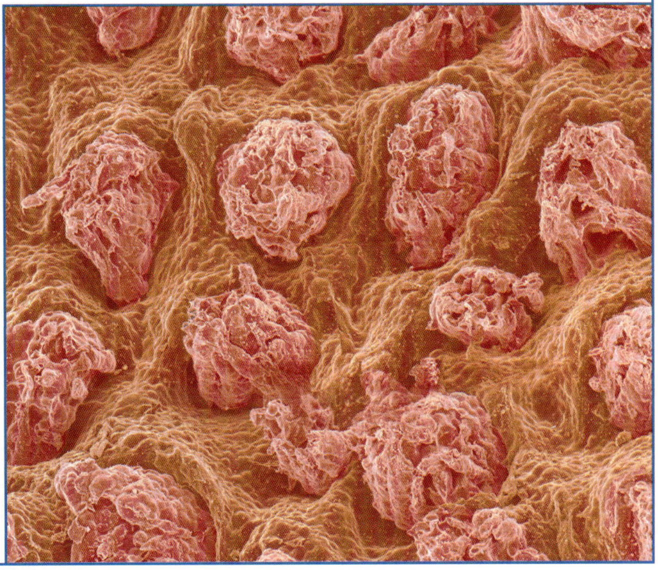

Touch

- **Nerve endings in the skin** can detect touch, pressure, pain, heat and cold.
- **There are sense receptors** everywhere in your skin, but places like your face have more than your back.

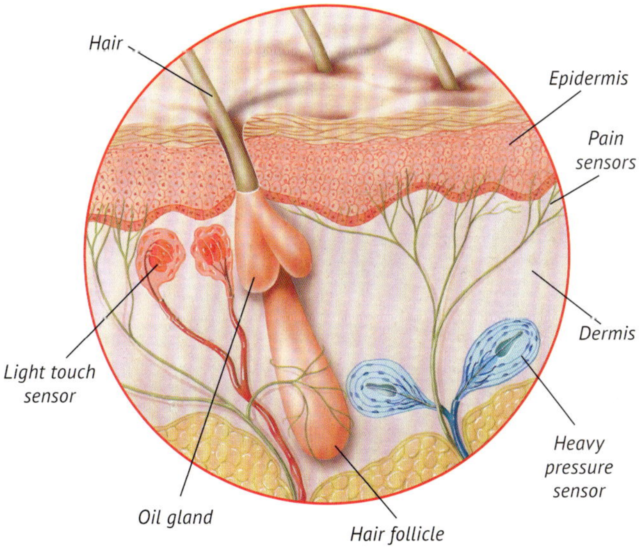

◀ *This magnified view shows touch sensors beneath the skin.*

- **There are 200,000** heat and cold receptors in your skin, as well as 500,000 touch and pressure receptors, and nearly 3 million pain receptors.
- **When we touch something**, pressure on the skin causes the receptors to move, sending signals to the brain for it to interpret.
- **Free nerve-endings** respond to all kinds of skin sensation and are almost everywhere in your skin.
- **There are specialized receptors** in certain places, each named after their discoverer.
- **Pacini's and Meissner's corpuscles** react instantly to sudden pressure.
- **Krause's end-bulbs**, Merkel's discs and Ruffini's corpuscles respond to steady pressure.
- **Krause's end-bulbs** are also sensitive to cold.

DID YOU KNOW?

The speed of nerve signals from the skin to the brain varies according to the amount of pressure the sensors in your skin feel.

Balance

- **To stay upright**, the body sends a continual stream of data about its position to the brain – and the brain tells the body how to move to keep its balance.
- **Balance** is controlled in many parts of the brain, including the cerebellum.
- **The brain** finds out about the position of the body from many sources, including the eyes, the semicircular canals in the ears and proprioceptors.
- **The semicircular canals** are three fluid-filled loops in the inner ear that detect head movement, including nodding, shaking and turning your head. They also detect how fast the head is moving.
- **Proprioceptors** are position and stretch sensors that are found in skin, muscles, tendons and in every joint.
- **Your inner ear** contains a maze of bony chambers called the bony labyrinth, which contains your organs of balance.
- **Your first organ of balance** detects the position of your head. Your second organ of balance detects rotational movements of your head.
- **The nerve interactions** between the sensory organs of balance and the brain are complex. They are designed to keep the eyes focused and to allow quick adjustments of position to stop you falling.
- **When conflicting information** is received by the brain about vision, head movement and body position, the result is a feeling of dizziness.

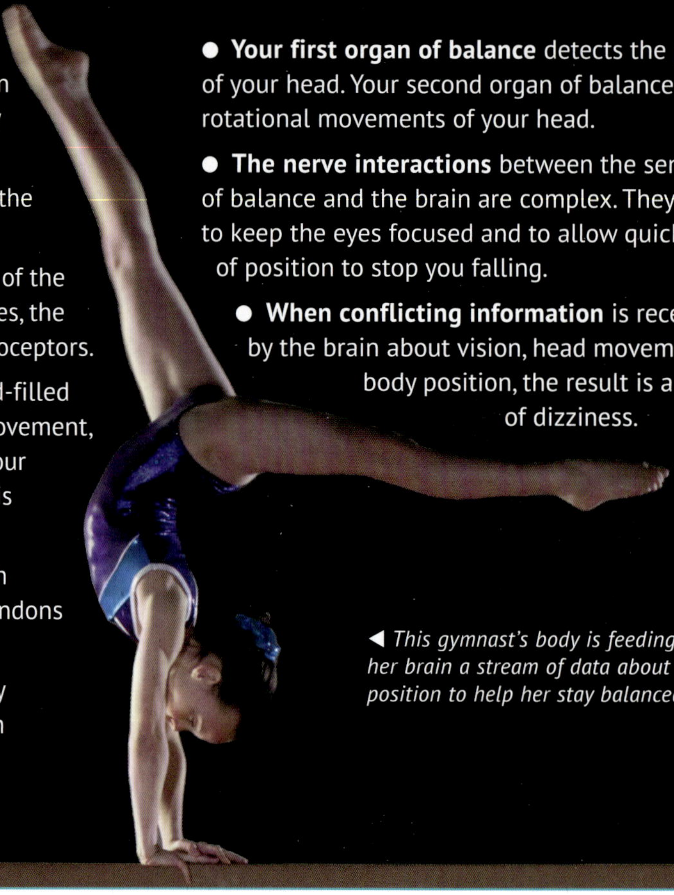

◀ *This gymnast's body is feeding her brain a stream of data about its position to help her stay balanced.*

Co-ordination

- **Co-ordination** means balanced or skilful movement.
- **To make you move**, the brain has to send signals out along nerves telling all the muscles involved what to do.
- **Co-ordination of the muscles** is handled by the cerebellum at the back of the brain.
- **The cerebellum** is told what to do by the brain's motor cortex.
- **The cerebellum sends** its commands via the basal ganglia in the middle of the brain.
- **Proprioceptor** means 'one's own sensors'. They are nerve cells that are sensitive to movement, pressure or stretching.

DID YOU KNOW?

Proprioceptors allow you to touch the exact tip of your nose, even with your eyes shut.

- **Proprioceptors are positioned** all over the body – in muscles, tendons and joints – and they all send signals to the brain telling it the position or posture of every body part.
- **The hair cells** in the balance organs of your ear are also proprioceptors.

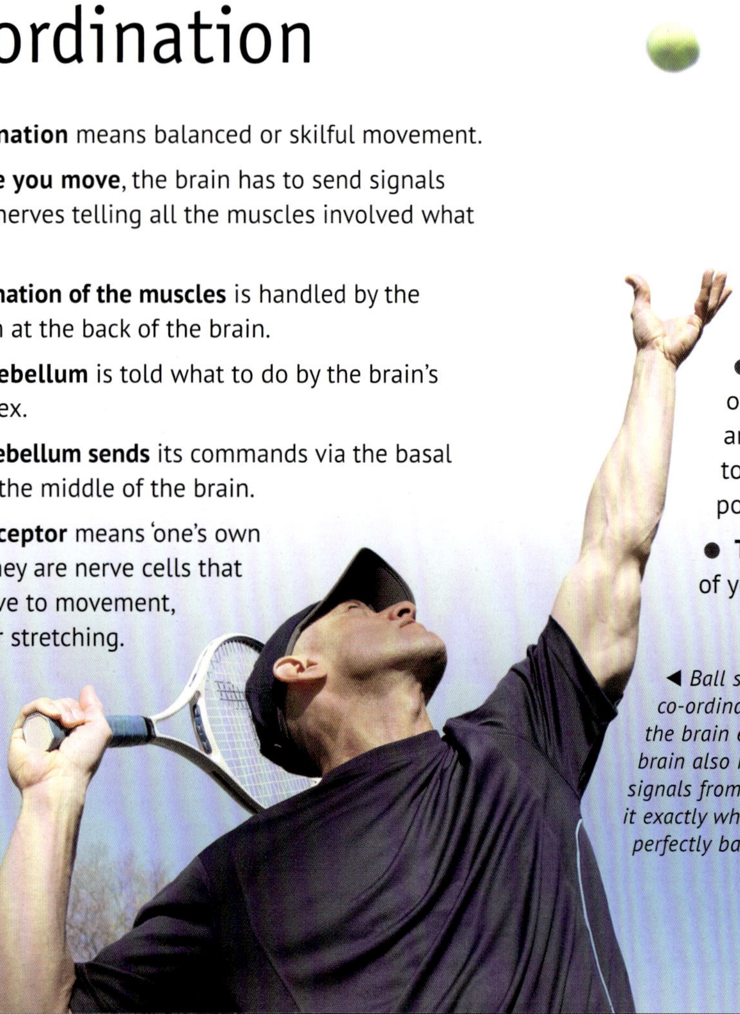

◀ *Ball skills demand incredible muscle co-ordination. The eyes follow the ball to tell the brain exactly where it is. At the same time, the brain also relies on a high-speed stream of sensory signals from the proprioceptor cells in order to tell it exactly where the leg is, and to keep the body perfectly balanced.*

Memory

- **When you remember something**, it is thought that the brain stores it by creating new nerve connections.
- **There are three types of memory** – sensory, short-term and long-term.
- **Sensory memory** is the impression that new information makes on the mind. It lasts for only a fraction of a second.

- **Short-term memory** is information that the brain stores for a few seconds, like a phone number remembered long enough to repeat it.
- **Long-term memory** is memory that can last for months or maybe even your whole life.
- **The brain** has two kinds of long-term memory, called declarative and non-declarative memories.
- **Non-declarative** memories are skills you teach yourself by practising, such as playing badminton or the flute.
- **Declarative memories** are either episodic or semantic.
- **Episodic memories** are memories of striking events in your life, such as breaking your leg or your first day at a new school. You not only recall facts, but sensations.
- **Semantic memories** are facts such as dates. The brain seems to store these in the left temporal lobe.

◀ *Learning to play the guitar involves non-declarative memory, in which nerve pathways become reinforced by repeated use. This is why practising is so important.*

Mood

- **Mood is your state of mind** – whether you are happy or sad, angry or afraid, overjoyed or depressed.
- **Moods and emotions** seem to be strongly linked to the structures in the centre of the brain, where unconscious activities are controlled.
- **Moods** have three elements – how you feel, what happens to your body, and what they make you do.
- **Scientists are only** just beginning to discover how moods and emotions are linked to particular parts of the brain.
- **Certain memories or experiences** are so strongly linked in your mind that they can trigger a certain mood.
- **It is possible that the bacteria** normally living in your intestines affect your mood. Substances made by these bacteria can affect nerves and the immune system, which in turn affect the brain.

▶ *Changes in the body can alter the way you feel – the act of smiling can make you feel more positive.*

DID YOU KNOW?

In one experiment, people injected with adrenaline found terrible jokes much funnier!

Sleeping

- **When you are asleep**, your body functions go on as normal. But your body may save energy and do routine repairs.
- **Lack of sleep** can be dangerous. A newborn baby needs 18–20 hours sleep a day.
- **As we grow**, we need less sleep. Toddlers and young children need around 11–15 hours a day. Adults need 7–8 hours.
- **Sleep is controlled** in the brainstem in the centre of the brain.
- **The activity of the brain** when awake and asleep can be investigated by placing electrodes on the skull that pick up the electrical activity inside the head. This investigation is called an electroencephalogram (EEG). Using this technique, wave patterns of electrical activity have been identified and named.
- **When you sleep**, the pattern to the electricity created by the firing of the brain's nerve cells becomes more regular.
- **For the first 90 minutes**, your sleep gets deeper and the brain waves become stronger.
- **After 90 minutes of sleep**, your eyes begin to flicker from side to side under their lids. This is called Rapid Eye Movement (REM) sleep. You are hard to wake up.
- **REM sleep** is thought to occur when you are dreaming.
- **While you sleep**, ordinary deeper sleep alternates with spells of REM lasting up to half an hour.

▼ *We all shut our eyes to sleep. When the body is asleep, the brain's activity pattern changes and the heartbeat slows.*

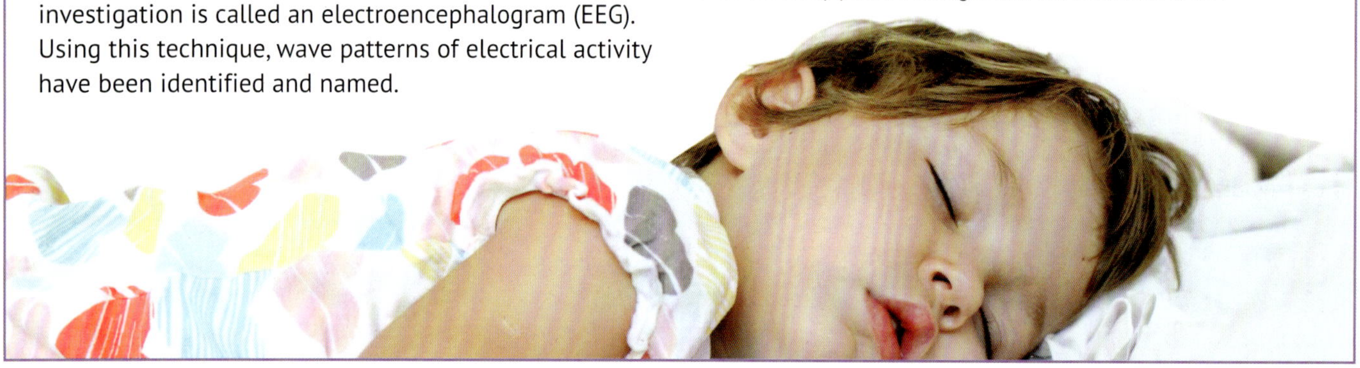

Temperature

- **The inside of your body** stays at a fairly constant temperature of 37°C (98°F), but can rise by a few degrees when you are ill.
- **The body creates heat** by burning food in its cells, especially the 'energy sugar' glucose.
- **Even when you are resting**, your body generates so much heat that you are comfortable only when the air is slightly cooler than you are.
- **Your body loses heat** as you breathe in cool air and breathe out warm air.
- **The body's temperature control** is the tiny hypothalamus in the brain.

DID YOU KNOW?

Your body temperature often changes during the course of a day – it drops a degree or two lower when you are sleeping compared to when you are awake.

- **Sensors in the skin**, in the body's core, and in the blood around the hypothalamus transmit signals to the hypothalamus about body temperature.

▲ *Sweat is made in the sweat glands. It cools the body by letting warm water out, and the moisture cools the skin as it evaporates.*

- **If it is too hot**, the hypothalamus sends signals to the skin telling it to sweat more. Signals also tell blood vessels in the skin to widen – this increases the blood flow, so the heat loss from your blood becomes greater.
- **If it is too cold**, the hypothalamus sends signals to the skin to cut back skin blood flow, as well as signals to tell the muscles to generate heat by shivering.
- **If it is too cold**, the hypothalamus may also stimulate the thyroid gland to send out hormones to make your cells burn energy faster and so make more heat.

Circulation

- **Circulation** is the system of tubes called blood vessels that carries blood from the heart to all body tissues and back again.
- **Blood circulation** was discovered in 1628 by the English physician William Harvey (1578–1657), who built on the ideas of Matteo Colombo.
- **Each of the body's** 600 billion cells gets fresh blood once every few minutes or less.
- **On the way out** from the heart, blood is pumped through vessels called arteries and arterioles.
- **On the way back** to the heart, blood flows through venules and veins.
- **Blood flows** from the arterioles to the venules through the tiniest tubes called capillaries.
- **The blood circulation** has two parts – the pulmonary and the systemic.
- **The pulmonary circulation** is the short section that carries blood that is low in oxygen from the right side of the heart to the lungs for 'refuelling'. It then returns oxygen-rich blood to the left side of the heart.
- **The systemic circulation** carries oxygen-rich blood from the left side of the heart all around the body, and returns blood that is low in oxygen to the right side of the heart.
- **In the blood**, oxygen is carried by the protein haemoglobin in red blood cells.
- **For each outward-going artery** there is usually an equivalent returning vein.

▼ Blood circulates continuously round and round the body through an intricate series of tubes called blood vessels. Bright red, oxygen-rich blood is pumped from the left side of the heart through vessels called arteries and arterioles. Blood that is low in oxygen returns to the right of the heart through veins and venules.

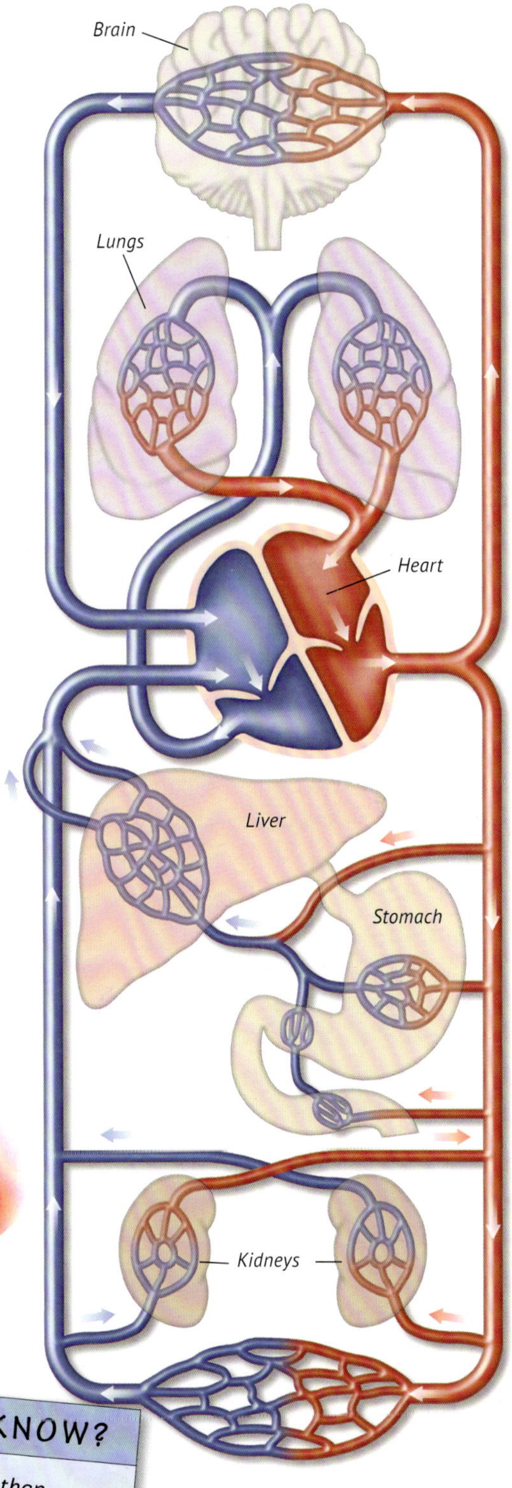

▼ A blood vessel wall has several layers, and blood itself contains different types of cells.

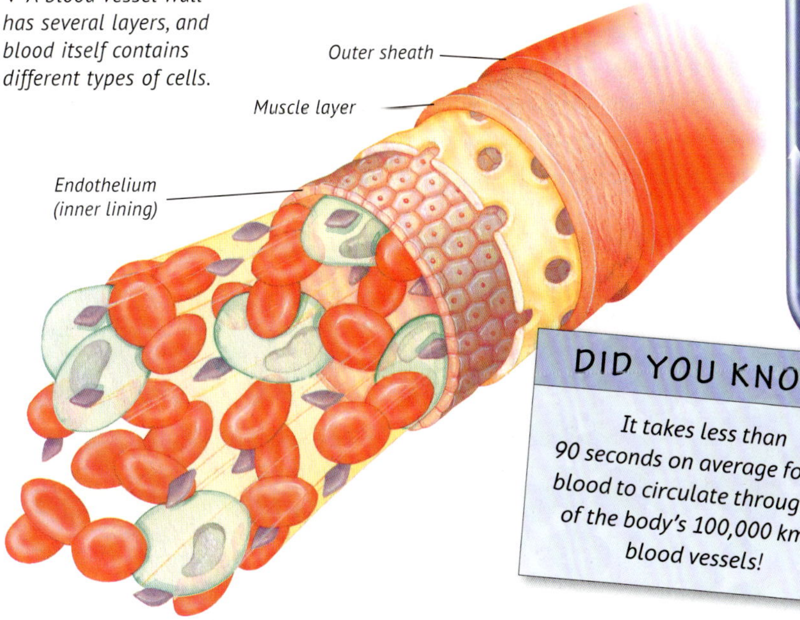

DID YOU KNOW?

It takes less than 90 seconds on average for the blood to circulate through all of the body's 100,000 km of blood vessels!

The heart

- **The heart** is the size of a clenched fist. It is inside the middle of the chest, and slightly to the left.
- **The heart** is a powerful pump made almost entirely of muscle.
- **To pump blood** out through your arteries, the heart contracts (tightens) and relaxes automatically about 70 times a minute.
- **The two sides** of the heart are separated by a muscle wall called the septum.
- **The right side** is smaller and weaker, and it pumps blood only to the lungs. The stronger left side pumps blood around the body.
- **Each side of the heart** has two chambers. There is an atrium at the top where blood accumulates (builds up) from the veins, and a ventricle below that contracts to pump blood out into the arteries.
- **Each of the heart's four chambers** ejects about 70 ml of blood with each beat.
- **There are two valves** in each side of the heart to make sure that blood flows only one way – a large one between the atrium and the ventricle, and a small one at the exit from the ventricle into the artery.
- **The coronary arteries** supply the heart. If they become clogged, the heart muscle may be short of blood and stop working. This is what happens in a heart attack.

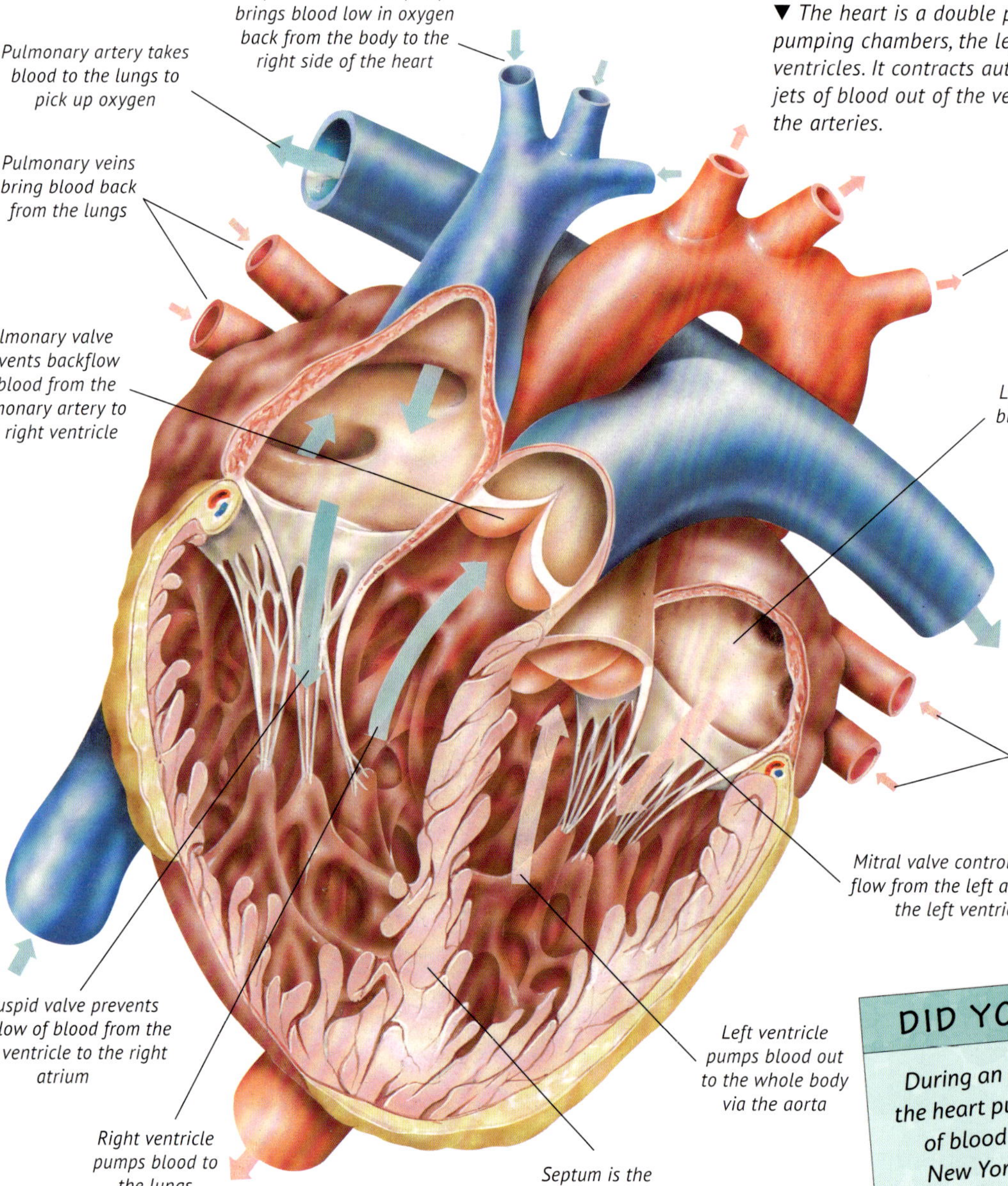

▼ *The heart is a double pump, with two pumping chambers, the left and the right ventricles. It contracts automatically to squeeze jets of blood out of the ventricles and through the arteries.*

DID YOU KNOW?

During an average lifetime, the heart pumps 200 million l of blood – enough to fill New York's Central Park to a depth of 15 m.

Heartbeat

- **The heartbeat** is the regular squeezing of the heart muscle to pump blood around the body.
- **The heartbeat has two phases** – systole (contraction) and diastole (resting).
- **Systole begins** when muscle contraction sweeps across the heart, squeezing blood from the atriums (blood receiving chambers) into the ventricles (pumping chambers).
- **When the contraction** reaches the ventricles, they squeeze blood into the arteries.
- **In diastole**, the heart muscle relaxes and the atriums fill with blood again.
- **The rate of beating** is controlled by a special group of nerve cells called a pacemaker. Nerve signals from the brain control the pacemaker, making it go faster or slower as required.
- **People with abnormal** heart rhythms can have an artificial pacemaker implanted in their body. These are small electrical devices that help to regulate the heart.

▼ **1** *Blood floods into the relaxed atriums.* **2** *The wave of muscle contraction squeezes blood into ventricles.* **3** *The ventricles fill with blood.* **4** *Blood is squeezed out of the ventricles into the arteries with oxygenated blood going to the body and deoxygenated blood to the lungs.*

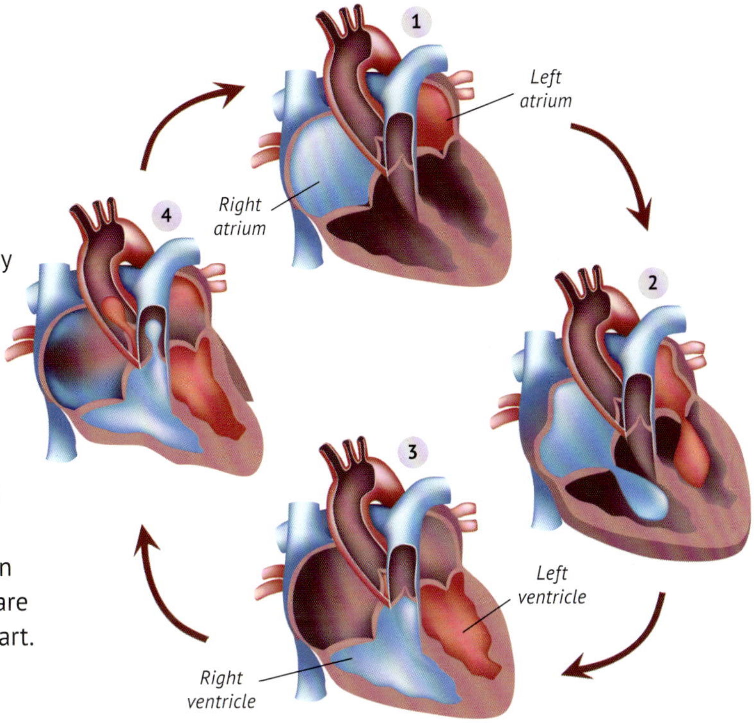

Pulse

- **Your pulse** is the powerful high-pressure surge or wave that runs through your blood and vessels as the heart contracts strongly with each beat.
- **You can feel your pulse** by pressing two fingertips on the inside of your wrist, where the radial artery nears the surface.

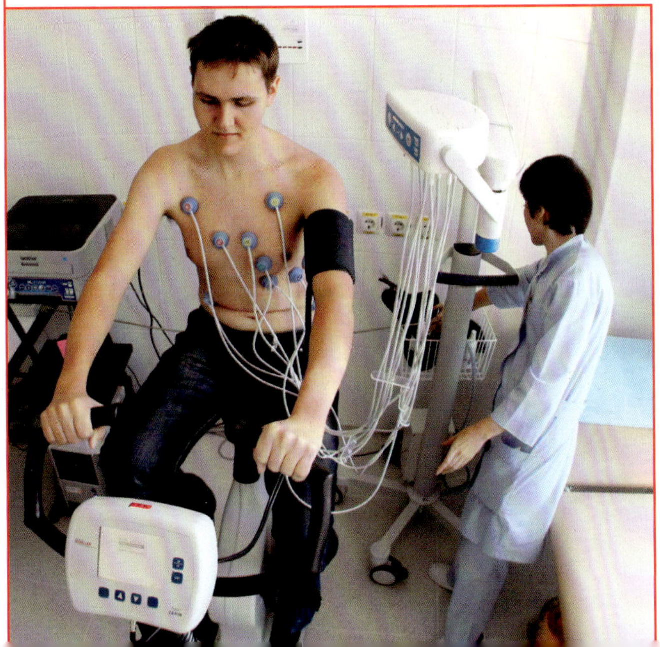

- **Other pulse points** include the carotid artery in the neck and the brachial artery inside the elbow.
- **Checking the speed of the pulse** is a good way of finding out how healthy someone is.
- **Normal pulse rates** vary between 50 and 100 beats a minute. The average for a man is about 71, for a woman it is 80, and for children it is about 85.
- **Tachycardia** is the medical word for an abnormally fast heartbeat rate.
- **Someone who has tachycardia** when sitting down may have drunk too much coffee or tea, or taken drugs, or be suffering from anxiety or a fever, or have heart disease.
- **Bradycardia** is an abnormally slow heart rate.
- **Arrhythmia** is an abnormality in a person's heart rhythm.
- **Anyone with a heart problem** may be connected to a machine called an electrocardiogram (ECG) to monitor their heartbeat.

◀ *By monitoring how much heart rate goes up and down during exercise, an ECG can show how healthy someone's heart is.*

Valves

- **Valves are crucial** in the circulation of your blood and lymph fluid, ensuring that liquids flow only one way.
- **The heart has four valves** to make sure blood flows only one way through it.
- **On each side of the heart** there is a large valve between the atrium and the ventricle, and a smaller one where the arteries leave the ventricle.
- **The mitral valve** is the large valve on the left. The tricuspid valve is the large valve on the right.
- **The aortic valve** is the smaller valve on the left. The pulmonary is the smaller valve on the right.
- **Heart valves** can sometimes get stiff and narrowed, or may start to leak. This makes the heart work harder and can cause heart failure.
- **A faulty heart valve** may be replaced with a valve from a human or pig heart, or a mechanical valve.
- **Valves in the arteries and veins** are simply flaps that open only when the blood is flowing one way.
- **The lymphatic system** also has its own small valves to ensure lymph fluid is squeezed only one way.

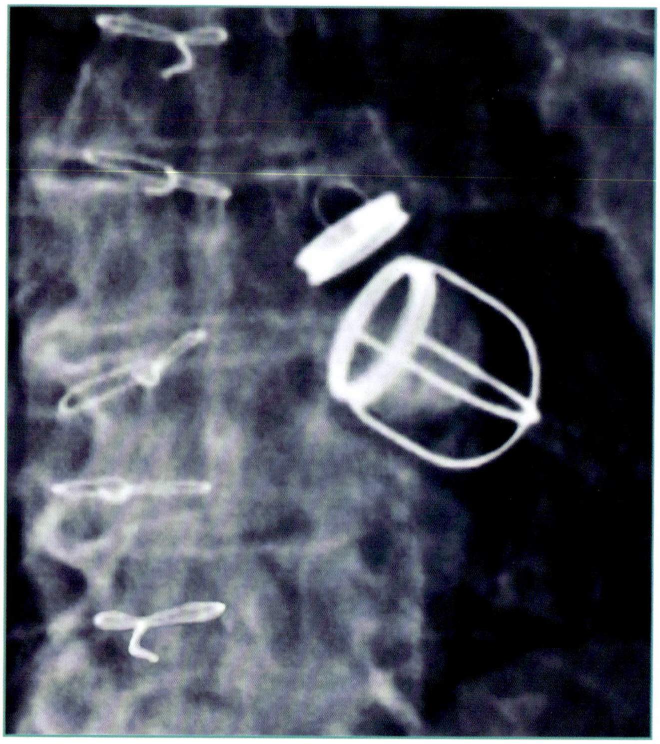

▲ *An X-ray of a patient who has had both the mitral and aortic valves of their heart replaced with artificial heart valves.*

Arteries and veins

- **An artery** is a tube-like blood vessel that carries blood away from the heart. Systemic arteries transport blood rich in oxygen around the body. Pulmonary arteries carry deoxygenated blood from the heart to the lungs.
- **An arteriole** is a smaller branch off an artery. Arterioles branch into microscopic capillaries.
- **Arteries run alongside** most of the veins that return blood to the heart.
- **Arteries have thicker, stronger walls** than veins, and can expand or relax to control the blood flow.

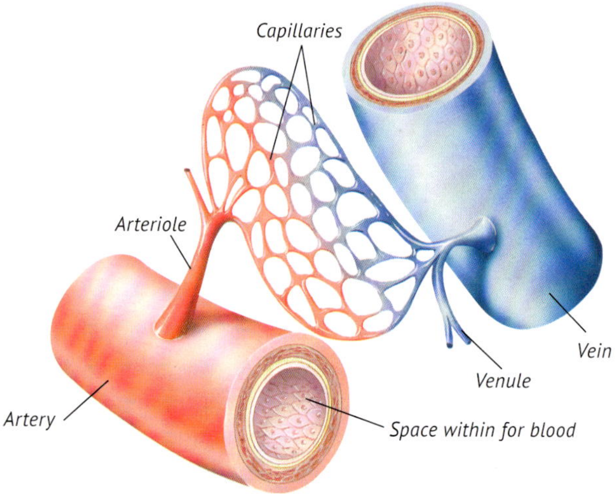

DID YOU KNOW?

At any moment, 75 percent of the body's blood is in the veins.

- **Veins are blood vessels** that carry blood back to the heart. The body cells have taken the oxygen they need from the blood, so it is low in oxygen.
- **When blood** is low in oxygen, it is red-brown in colour. Oxygenated blood, carried by the arteries, is bright red.
- **The only veins** that carry oxygenated blood are the four pulmonary veins – they carry blood from the lungs to the heart.
- **The two largest veins** in the body are the vena cavae that flow into the heart from above and below.
- **Most large veins** have flaps inside them that act as valves to make sure that the blood only flows one way.
- **Unlike arteries**, veins collapse when empty because their walls are thin.
- **Blood is helped** through the veins by surrounding muscles squeezing the vein walls.

◀ *This illustration shows how the main kinds of blood vessel in the body are connected. The artery (red) branches into tiny capillaries, which join up to supply the vein (blue).*

Capillaries

- **Capillaries** are the smallest of all the blood vessels, only visible under a microscope.
- **They link** the arterioles (small branch of an artery) to the venules (tiny vein).
- **Capillaries** were discovered by Italian biologist and physician Marcello Malphigi in 1661.
- **There are 10 billion** capillaries in the body, and the largest is just 0.2 mm wide.
- **Each capillary** is about 0.5–1 mm in length.
- **Capillary walls** are only one cell thick, which makes it easy for chemicals to pass through them.
- **Blood passes oxygen**, food and waste to and from each one of your body cells through the capillary walls.

DID YOU KNOW?

The average capillary is 0.001 mm in diameter – just wide enough for red blood cells to pass through one at a time.

- **Tissues which are very active**, such as muscles, liver and kidneys, have a particularly high number of capillaries.
- **Capillaries** allow more blood to reach the surface when you are warm, and less blood to reach the surface to save heat when you are cold.

◀ *You generate heat when exercising, which the body tries to lose by opening up capillaries in the skin, turning it red.*

Blood

- **Blood is the liquid** that circulates around the body. It carries oxygen and food to body cells, and takes carbon dioxide and waste away.
- **It also fights** infection, keeps you warm and distributes chemicals.
- **Blood is made up** of red cells, white cells and platelets, all carried in a liquid called plasma.
- **Plasma is** 90 percent water, but also contains hundreds of other substances, including nutrients and hormones.
- **Oxygen in the air turns blood bright red** when you bleed. In your veins it can be almost brown.
- **Platelets are tiny pieces of cells** that make blood clots form to stop bleeding.
- **Blood clots** also involve a lacy, fibrous network made from a protein called fibrin.
- **Most people's blood** belongs to one of four groups or types – A, O, B and AB. O is the most common.
- **Blood is also** either Rhesus positive (Rh+) or Rhesus negative (Rh–).
- **If your blood is Rh+ and your group is A**, your blood group is said to be A positive. If your blood is Rh– and your group is O, you are O negative, and so on.
- **When you are given blood** from another person's body it is called a transfusion. Your body will only accept blood from certain groups that match yours.
- **Blood transfusions** are given when someone has lost too much blood because of an injury or operation. It is also given to replace diseased blood.

▼ *When you are injured, red blood cells* **1** *and platelets* **2** *leak out into the surrounding tissues and a sticky substance called fibrin* **3** *is produced to help heal the wound.*

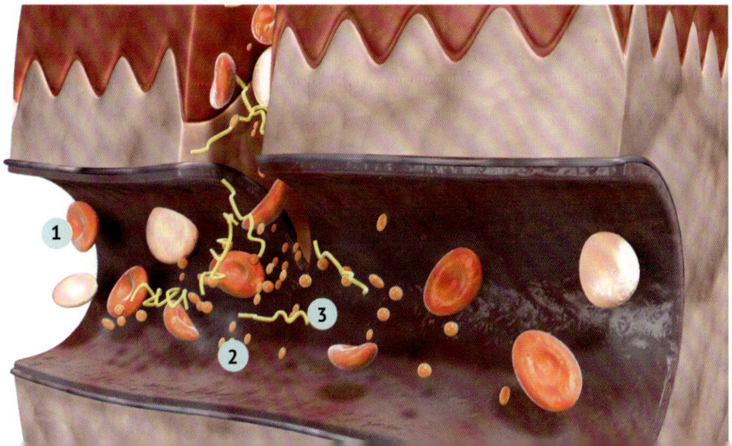

Blood cells

- **The blood has two main kinds of cell** – red cells and white cells – plus pieces of cell called platelets.
- **Red cells** are button-shaped and mainly contain red protein called haemoglobin.
- **Haemoglobin** allows red blood cells to transport oxygen around your body.
- **Red cells** also contain enzymes that the body uses to make certain chemical processes happen.
- **White blood cells** are big cells called leucocytes and most types are involved in fighting infections.
- **Most white blood cells** contain tiny little grains and are a type of leucocyte called a granulocyte.
- **Most granulocytes** are giant white cells called neutrophils. They are the blood's cleaners, and their task is to eat up invaders.
- **Eosinophils and basophils** are also types of granulocyte. They are involved in fighting disease and allergies. Some release antibodies that help fight infection.

▶ *Button-shaped red blood cells carry oxygen through the blood. Spiky ball-shaped white blood cells help your body fight infection.*

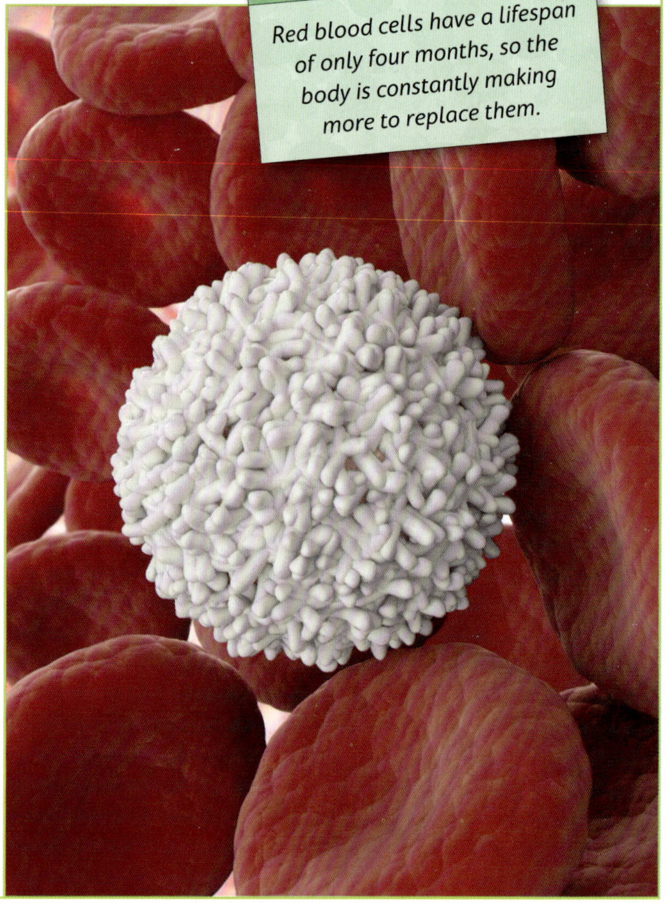

DID YOU KNOW?

Red blood cells have a lifespan of only four months, so the body is constantly making more to replace them.

Marrow

- **Some bones** contain a core of jelly-like substance called marrow.
- **Bone marrow** can be red or yellow, depending on whether it has more blood tissue or fat tissue.

▼ *Inside most bones is a core called marrow. The red marrow of some bones is the body's blood cell factory, making 5 million new cells a day.*

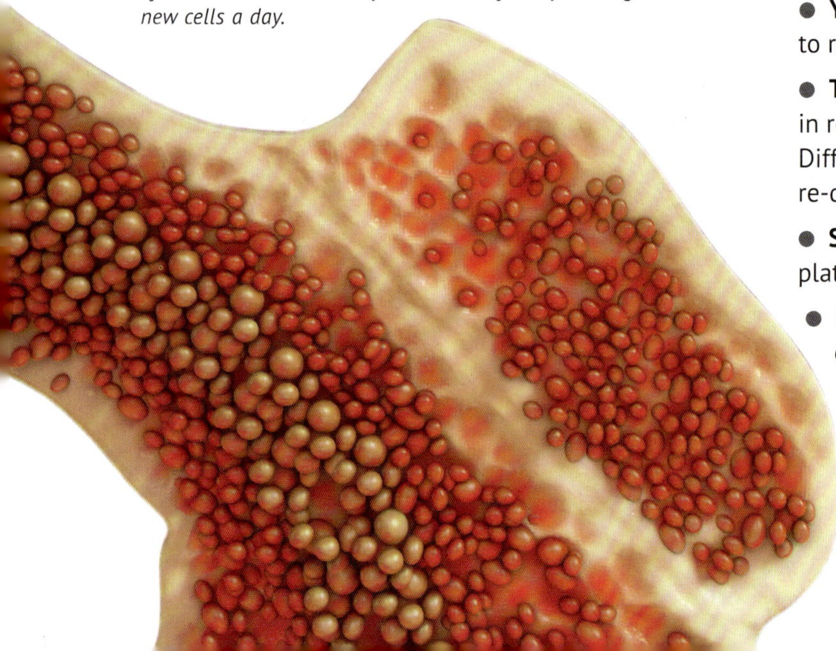

- **Red bone marrow** is where all blood cells, apart from some white cells, are made.
- **All bone marrow** is red when you are a baby, but as you grow older, more and more turns yellow.
- **In adults**, red marrow is only found in the spine, breastbone, ribs, shoulder blades, pelvis and the skull.
- **Yellow bone marrow** is a store for fat, but it may turn to red marrow when you are ill.
- **The many different** kinds of blood cell all start life in red marrow as one type of cell called a stem cell. Different blood cells develop as stem cells divide and re-divide.
- **Some stem cells** divide to form red blood cells and platelets.
- **Some stem cells** divide to form lymphoblasts. These divide in turn to form various different kinds of white cells – monocytes, granulocytes and lymphocytes.
- **The white cells** made in bone marrow play a key part in the body's immune system. This is why bone marrow transplants can help people with illnesses that affect their immune system.

The respiratory system

- **The respiratory system** includes the lungs and the airways. The airways allow the passage of air in and out of the nose and the lungs when breathing.
- **The airways are described** as upper and lower. The division between upper and lower is at the level of the voice box (larynx).
- **The upper airways** include the nose, throat (pharynx) and voice box (larynx).
- **The lower airways** include the windpipe (trachea), its branches and the airways of the lungs.
- **The mouth** is part of the airway only when vocalizing (speaking, shouting and singing) or when the nose is blocked.
- **The pharynx** allows the passage of food (to the stomach) as well as air (to the lungs). It is the tube at the back of the nose and mouth and below the back of the tongue.
- **The tonsils and adenoids** are swellings of lymph tissue that protect the airways from infection, especially in young children. They get smaller as you grow older.
- **The tonsils** are at the back of the mouth. You can see them on either side of the throat when you open your mouth wide. The adenoids are at the back of the nose.
- **The sinuses** are chambers containing air within the bones of the skull that form the face and forehead. If mucus blocks them when you get a cold, you may get pain in your face and teeth.

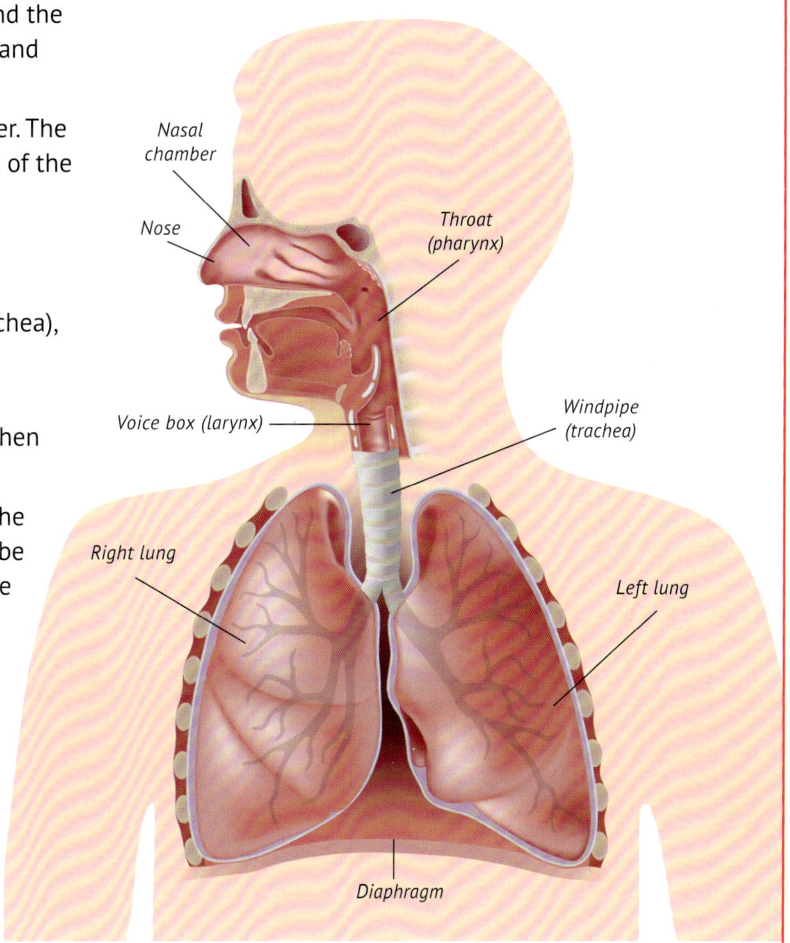

▲ *The respiratory system includes the upper and lower airways, which branch into the lungs.*

▼ *When you run fast, your muscles need extra oxygen, so your lungs must work hard to take in more air.*

DID YOU KNOW?

Your throat is linked to your ears by tubes, which open when you swallow to balance air pressure.

Breathing

- **You breathe** because every cell in your body needs a continuous supply of oxygen to burn glucose, the high-energy substance from digested food.
- **Scientists call breathing 'respiration'**. Breathing in is called 'inhalation' and breathing out is called 'exhalation'.
- **Oxygen is taken into the lungs**, and then carried in the blood to cells. Waste carbon dioxide from the cells is returned in the blood to the lungs, to be breathed out.
- **The diaphragm** is the sheet of muscle below your chest. It works with your chest muscles to make you breathe.
- **Speaking and singing** depend on the larynx (voice box) in the neck. This has bands of tissue called the vocal cords, which vibrate as air is breathed out over them.

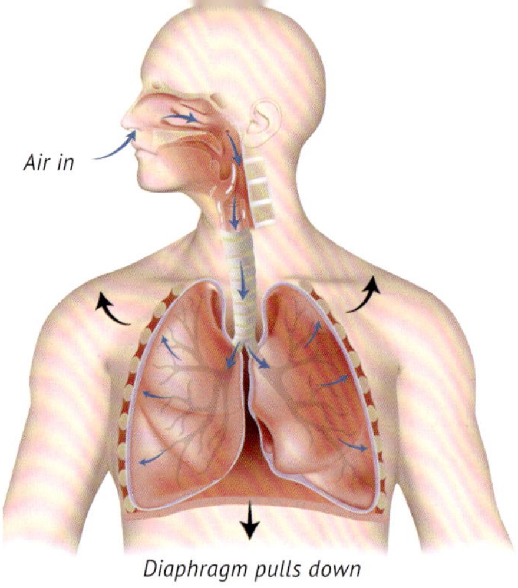

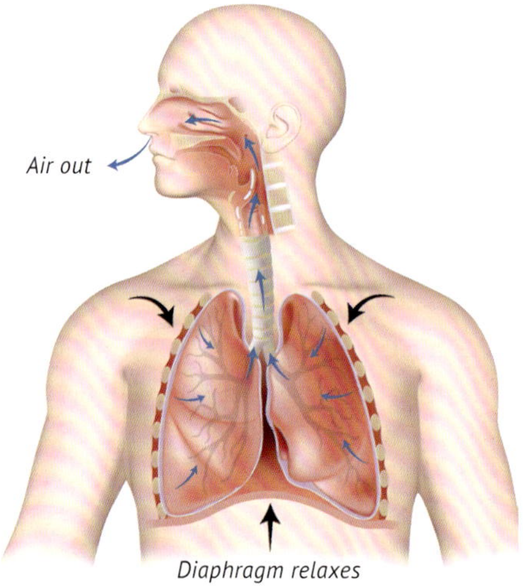

- **When you are silent**, the vocal cords are apart, and air passes between them freely. When you speak or sing, the cords tighten across the airway and vibrate to make sounds.
- **The tighter** the vocal cords are stretched, the more high-pitched the sounds you make will be.
- **The basic sound** produced by the vocal cords is 'aah'. By changing the shape of your mouth, lips and tongue, you can change this simple sound into letters and words.
- **Men's vocal cords** are longer than women's, so they vibrate more slowly and produce a deeper sound.

◀ *Breathing uses two main sets of muscles, the diaphragm and those between the ribs.*

The lungs

- **The lungs** are a pair of spongy organs inside your chest.
- **Each lung** is divided into lobes. The right lung has three, but the left lung has only two, to allow room for the heart.
- **Each lung** is surrounded by a double-layered membrane called the pleura. Fluid between the layers lubricates the movement of the lungs during breathing.
- **When you breathe in**, air rushes in through your nose or mouth, down your trachea (windpipe) and into the airways in your lungs.
- **The inner surface** of the airways is protected by a film of mucus. The lining cells have tiny hairs that waft the mucus towards the nose and mouth to clean the airways.
- **The two biggest airways** are called bronchi. They branch into smaller airways called bronchioles.

▶ *The two lungs lie in the chest, protected within the ribcage. Air enters the lungs through the trachea, which then branches into smaller and smaller air passages, taking air down into all parts of the lungs.*

- **The bronchioles** end at groups of tiny 'bubbles' called alveoli.
- **Alveoli** are covered by tiny blood vessels, and alveoli walls are just one cell thick – thin enough to let oxygen and carbon dioxide seep through.
- **Asthma** is a condition where the muscles around the airways tighten as a result of being irritated by something, such as house dust. This has the effect of narrowing the airways in the lungs and making it harder to breathe.

1 *Trachea (windpipe)*
2 *Superior vena cava*
3 *Aorta*
4 *Right atrium of heart*
5 *Ventricles of heart*
6 *Blood vessels in lung*
7 *Right lung*
8 *Left lung*

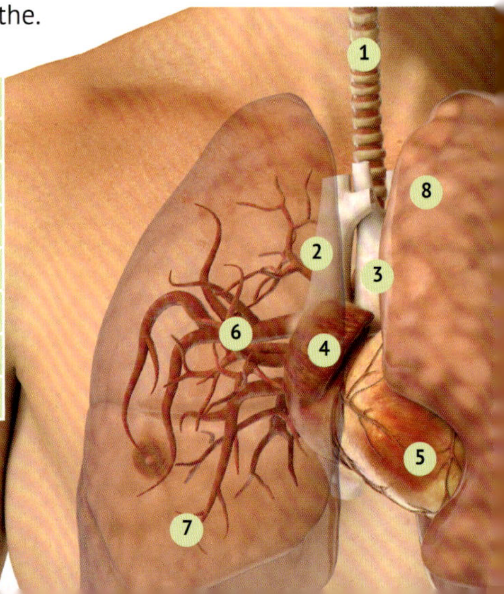

Alveoli

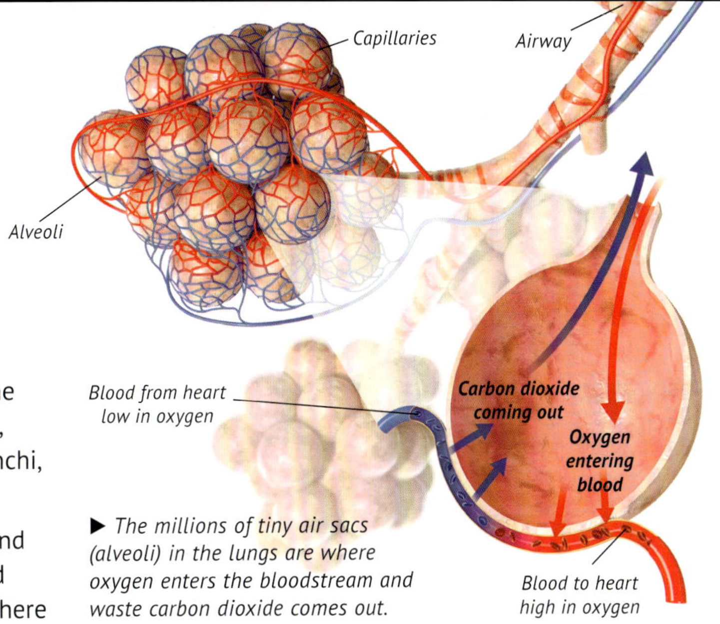

▶ *The millions of tiny air sacs (alveoli) in the lungs are where oxygen enters the bloodstream and waste carbon dioxide comes out.*

- **The heart and lungs** work together within the chest to get oxygen from the air and to send it out around the body in the bloodstream.
- **When a person breathes in**, air is sucked in through the nose and mouth, and carried down to the lungs through the trachea (windpipe). At the bottom, the trachea divides into two large air tubes, the bronchi, which each carry the air into a lung.
- **Within the lungs**, the air passages divide again and again until they end in tiny clusters of air sacs called alveoli. These look like tiny bunches of grapes, and there are millions of them in each lung.
- **Each single alveolus** is surrounded by very small capillary blood vessels. These bring blood from the heart, which has had a lot of its oxygen used up by the body.
- **The walls of the alveoli** and capillaries are very thin. This means that oxygen can pass through.
- **When a person breathes in**, the air inside of the alveolus has a lot of oxygen in it and this passes into the blood.
- **At the same time** that oxygen enters the blood, the waste gas carbon dioxide comes out and into the air in the alveolus. This swapping of oxygen and carbon dioxide is called gas exchange.
- **When a person breathes out**, the body gets rid of the waste carbon dioxide through the nose and mouth.
- **The newly oxygenated blood** in the capillaries around the alveoli travels back to the heart, which then pumps it to all parts of the body.

Bones

- **Bones** can cope with twice the squeezing pressure that granite can, or four times the stretching tension that concrete can, before breaking.
- **Weight for weight**, bone is at least five times as strong as steel.
- **Bones get their rigidity** from hard deposits of minerals such as calcium and phosphate in them.
- **Bones get their flexibility** from tough, elastic, rope-like fibres of collagen.
- **The hard outside of bones** (compact bone) is reinforced by strong rod-like structures called osteons.
- **Some bones** have a core of jelly-like bone marrow.

DID YOU KNOW?

The smallest bone in the body is only 3 mm long and is in the ear.

- **The inside (spongy bone)** is a light honeycomb made of thin supporting bars (trabeculae), which are angled to take stress.
- **Bones are living tissue** packed with cells called osteocytes. Each osteocyte is housed in its own hole, or lacuna.
- **In some parts of each bone**, there are special cells called osteoblasts that make new bone. In other parts, cells called osteoclasts break up old bone.
- **Bones grow** by getting longer near the end – at a region called the epiphyseal plate.

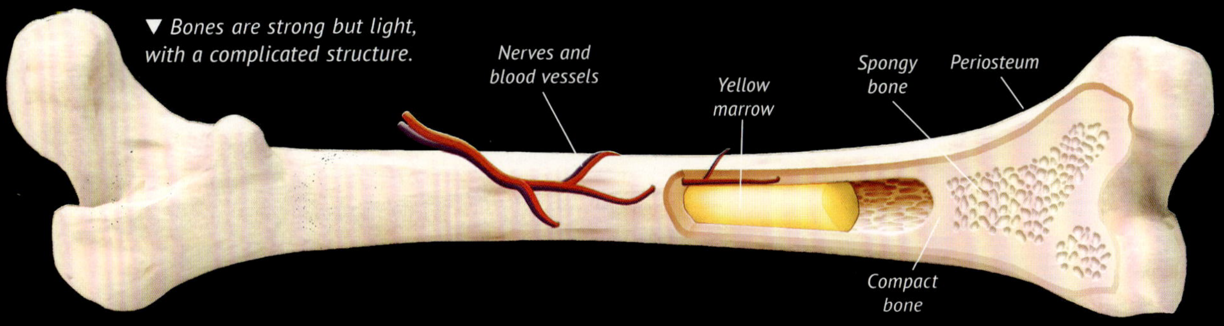

▼ *Bones are strong but light, with a complicated structure.*

The skeleton

- **The skeleton** is a rigid framework of bones, which provides an anchor for the muscles, supports the skin and other organs, and protects vital organs.
- **An adult's skeleton has 206 bones** joined together by ligaments.
- **A baby's skeleton has 300** or more bones, but some of these fuse (join) together as the baby grows older.
- **The parts of an adult skeleton** that have fused into one bone include the skull and the pelvis.

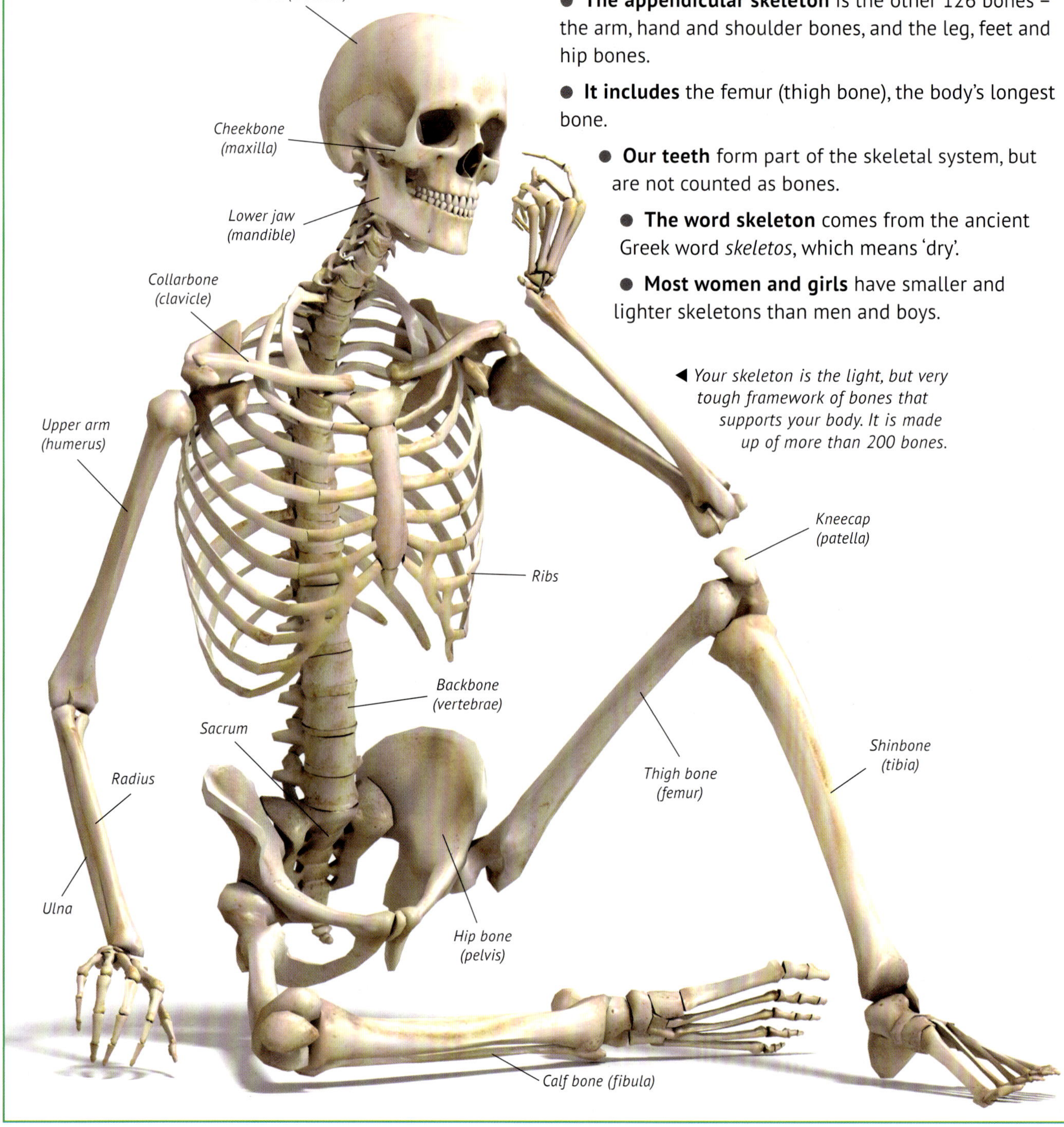

◀ *Your skeleton is the light, but very tough framework of bones that supports your body. It is made up of more than 200 bones.*

- **Your bones stop** growing when you are around 20, but they continue to constantly rebuild new bone cells.

DID YOU KNOW?

Bone is so light that it accounts for only 14 percent of your total body weight

- **The skeleton** has two main parts – the axial skeleton and the appendicular skeleton.
- **The axial skeleton** is the 80 bones of the upper body. It includes the skull, the vertebrae of the backbone, the ribs and the breastbone. The arm and shoulder bones are suspended from it.
- **The appendicular skeleton** is the other 126 bones – the arm, hand and shoulder bones, and the leg, feet and hip bones.
- **It includes** the femur (thigh bone), the body's longest bone.
- **Our teeth** form part of the skeletal system, but are not counted as bones.
- **The word skeleton** comes from the ancient Greek word *skeletos*, which means 'dry'.
- **Most women and girls** have smaller and lighter skeletons than men and boys.

Backbone

- **The backbone** (spine) extends from the base of the skull down to the hips.
- **It is a column** of drum-shaped bones called vertebrae (singular, vertebra). There are 33 altogether. Some of these fuse (join) together as the body grows.
- **Each vertebra** is linked to the next by facet joints, which are like tiny ball-and-socket joints.
- **The vertebrae are separated** by spinal discs of rubbery material.
- **The bones of the spine** are divided into five groups from top to bottom. These are the cervical spine (7 bones), the thoracic (12 bones), the lumbar (5 bones), the sacrum (5 fused bones), and the coccyx (4 fused bones).
- **The cervical spine** is the vertebrae of the neck. The thoracic spine is the back of the chest, and each bone has a pair of ribs attached to it. The lumbar spine is the small of the back.

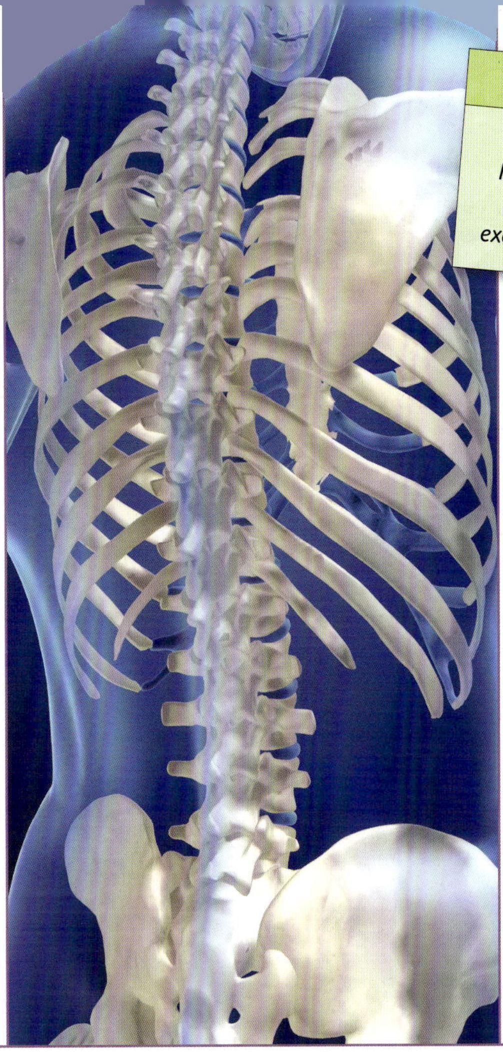

DID YOU KNOW?

The story character the Hunchback of Notre Dame suffered from kyphosis – excessive curving of the spine.

- **The sacrum** and coccyx are in the pelvic region.
- **A normal spine** curves in a slight S-shape – the cervical spine curves forwards, the thoracic backwards, the lumbar forwards, and the sacrum backwards.
- **On the back** of each vertebra is a bridge called the spinal process. The bridges on each bone link to form a tube that holds the spinal cord, the body's central bundle of nerves.

◀ *The 33 vertebrae of the backbone curve into an S-shape.*

Ribs

- **The ribs** are the thin, flattish bones that curve around your chest.
- **The rib bones**, the backbone and the breastbone combine to make up the rib cage.

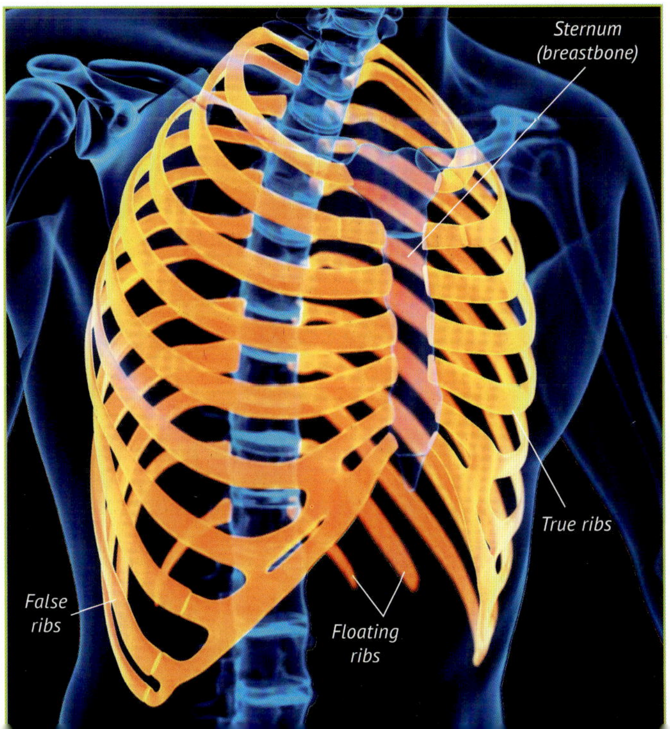

- **The rib cage** protects vital organs such as the heart, lungs, liver, kidneys and stomach.
- **You have 12 pairs** of ribs altogether.
- **Seven pairs** of your ribs are true ribs. Each of these pairs is attached to the sternum (breastbone) via a strip of costal cartilage, and curves around to join one of the vertebrae that make up the backbone.
- **There are three pairs** of false ribs. These are attached to vertebrae but are not linked to the breastbone. Instead, each rib is attached to the rib above it by cartilage.
- **There are two pairs** of floating ribs. These are attached only to the vertebrae of the backbone.
- **The gaps between the ribs** are called intercostal spaces. They hold sheets of muscle that expand and relax the chest during breathing.
- **The bones of the ribs** contain red marrow and are one of the body's major blood-cell factories.
- **Some people** don't have all of their ribs, whereas some people have an extra pair.

◀ *The ribs provide a framework for the chest and form a protective cage around the heart, lungs and other organs.*

The pelvis

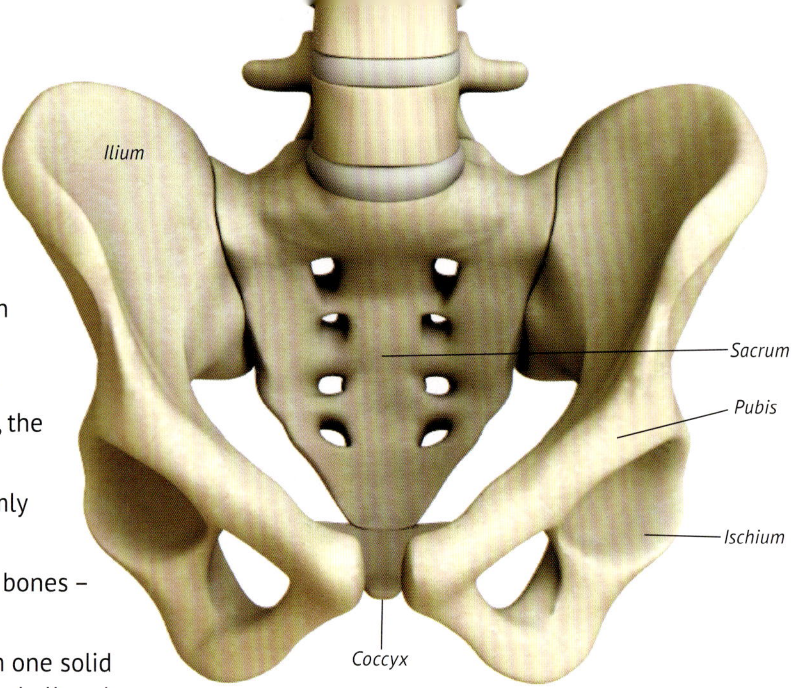

▲ *The pelvis is a strong ring made up of around 15 smaller bones, many of which are fused together.*

- **The pelvis** has two main functions. It allows movement of the body, such as walking and running, and it supports and protects the internal organs of the abdomen and pelvic cavity.
- **The pelvis** is a strong and sturdy ring of bone which is formed by the two hip bones, the sacrum and the coccyx.
- **The sacrum and the coccyx** are held firmly together by strong ligaments.
- **Each hip bone** is itself made up of three bones – the ilium, the ischium and the pubis.
- **These three bones** fuse together to form one solid structure that contains the socket half of the ball-and-socket hip joint.
- **The sacrum** is a wedge-shaped bone made up of five vertebrae that have become fused together. The back of the sacrum is roughened, where muscles attach to it.
- **The coccyx**, or tailbone, forms the lowest part of the spine. It is a small, triangular-shaped bone made up by the fusing of four tiny vertebrae.
- **A woman's pelvis** is much wider than a man's. This is because the opening has to be wide enough for a baby to pass through when it is born.
- **Experts can** usually tell the sex of a skeleton by looking at the pelvis.

Hands and feet

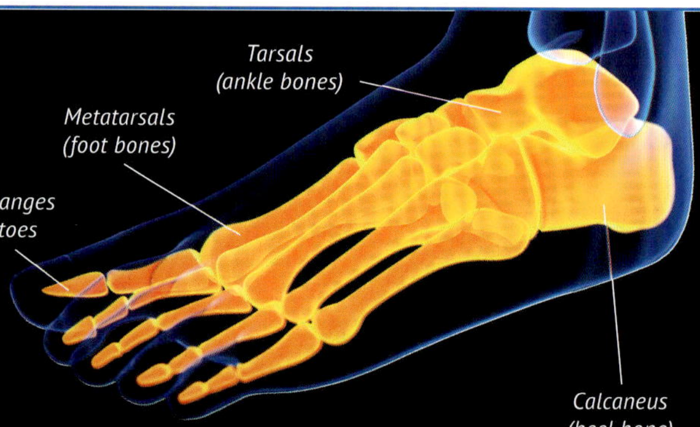

▲ *The 26 bones of the feet provide support for the weight of the body.*

- **Half of the bones** in the body are in the hands and the feet.
- **Each hand** has 27 bones, and each foot has 26.
- **The bones** in the hands and feet are arranged in a rather similar way. The first part is the wrist and ankle, then there is a longer middle part (the metacarpals and metatarsals), and finally the furthest part, the fingers and toes (phalanges).
- **The functions of the hands and feet** are very different, which is why the shape of the hand is different to the shape of the foot.
- **The wrist** is made up of eight carpal bones, which are all slightly different shapes.
- **The individual bones** are named for the shape they resemble – for example, the scaphoid bone is named from the Greek word for 'boat-shaped'.
- **There are five long metacarpals** in each hand, supporting the palm. Fourteen bones called phalanges make up the fingers and thumb.
- **Seven tarsal bones** make up the ankle and heel. Together with five long metatarsal bones and strong ligaments, they form the arches of the foot, which help carry the weight of the body. The toes contain 14 small phalanges.
- **There are many tiny joints** within the hands and feet, letting the bones move against each other. Muscles attach to the bones to allow the foot, and especially the hand, to move in many different ways.

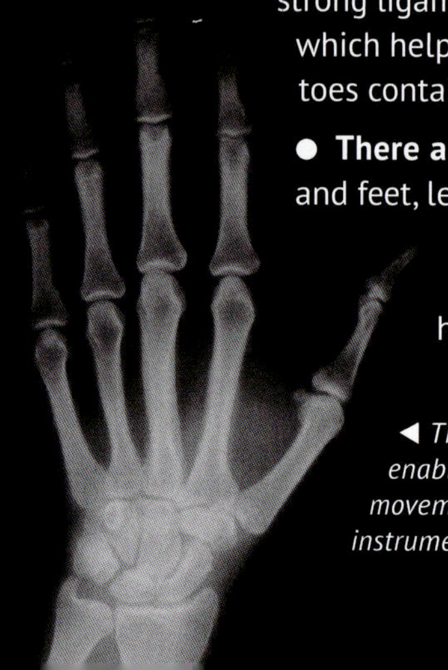

◀ *The intricate network of bones in your hands enables you to perform delicate and complex movements such as writing or playing a musical instrument.*

Teeth

● **Milk teeth** are the 20 teeth that start to appear when a baby is about six months old.

● **Around the age of six**, you start to grow your adult teeth – 16 in the top row and 16 in the bottom.

● **Molars** are the strong teeth with flattish tops (crowns) at the back of your mouth. Most people have three pairs on each side.

● **The third molars** at the back of the jaws are called wisdom teeth because they normally come through the gums (erupt) in early adulthood.

● **Incisors** are the four pairs of teeth at the front of your mouth. They have sharp edges for cutting food.

● **Canines** are the two pairs of pointed teeth behind the incisors. Their shape is good for piercing food.

● **The premolars** are the four pairs of teeth between the molars and the canines.

● **The enamel** on teeth is the body's hardest substance. Dentine inside teeth is softer but still hard as bone.

● **Teeth sit in sockets** in the jawbones and are held in place by the gums.

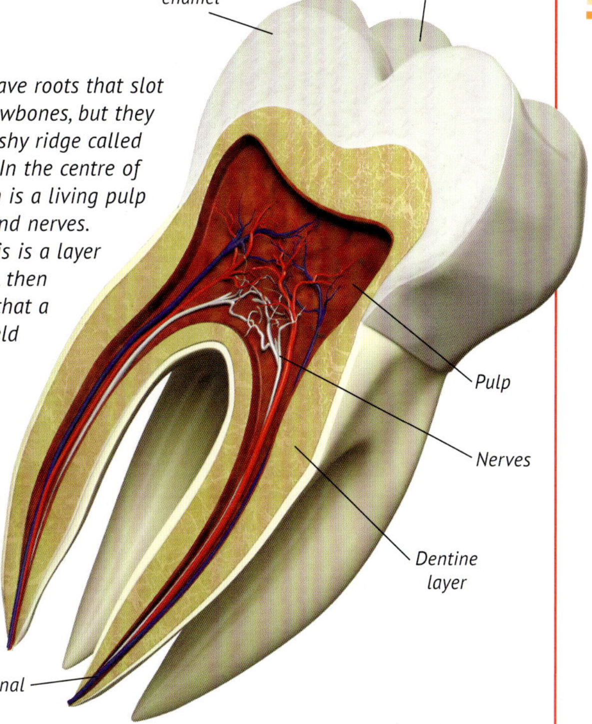

▶ *Teeth have roots that slot into the jawbones, but they sit in a fleshy ridge called the gums. In the centre of each tooth is a living pulp of blood and nerves. Around this is a layer of dentine, then on top of that a tough shield of enamel.*

● **The gums are layers** of connective tissue that surround each tooth and help to prevent it from damage by infection.

Cartilage

● **Cartilage is a rubbery substance** used in various places around the body. You can feel cartilage in your ear flap if you move it back and forward.

● **Cartilage is made from cells** called chondrocytes embedded in a jelly-like ground substance with fibres of collagen, all wrapped in an envelope of tough fibres.

● **The three types of cartilage** are hyaline, fibrous and elastic.

● **Hyaline cartilage** is the most widespread in your body. It is semi-transparent, pearly white and quite stiff.

● **Hyaline cartilage** is used in many of the joints between bones to cushion them against impacts.

● **Fibrous cartilage** is really tough. It is found between the bones of the spine and in the knee.

● **Cartilage in the knee** makes two dish shapes called menisci (single, meniscus) between the thigh and shin bones. Footballers often damage these cartilages.

● **Elastic cartilage** is very flexible and used in your airways, nose and ears.

● **Cartilage grows** more quickly than bone, and the skeletons of babies in the womb are mostly cartilage, which gradually ossifies (hardens to bone).

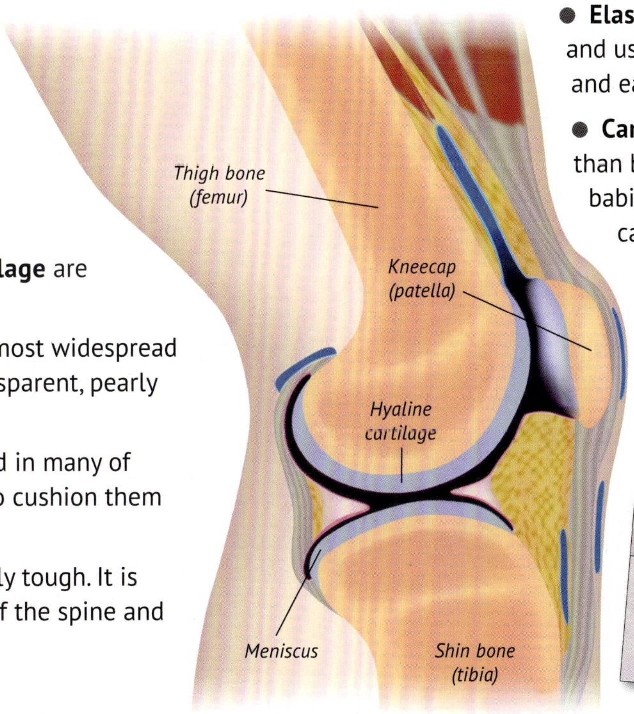

◀ *The knee is the body's biggest single joint.*

DID YOU KNOW?

Osteoarthritis is when joint cartilage breaks down, making movements painful.

Joints

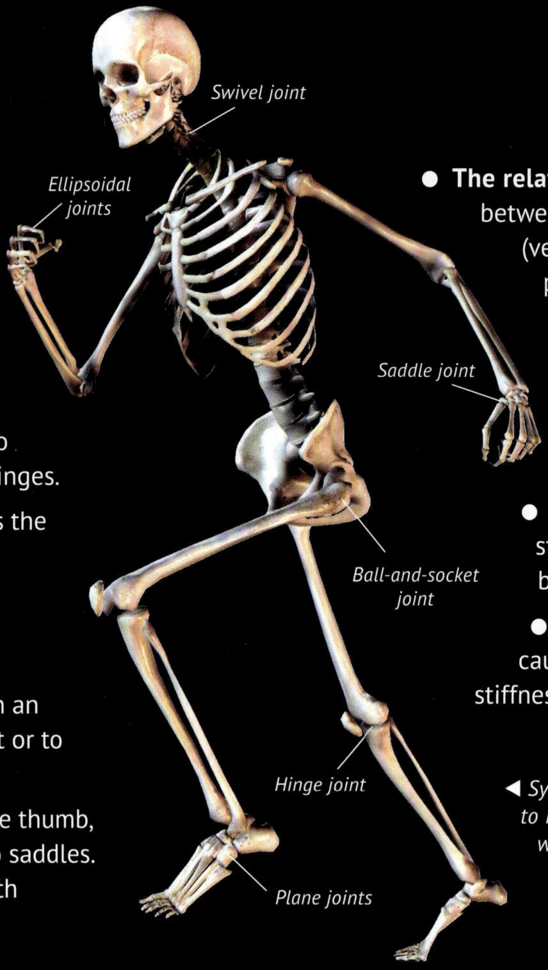

- **Body joints** are places where bones meet.
- **Most body joints** let bones move, but different kinds of joint let them move in different ways.
- **Hinge joints**, such as the elbow, let the bones swing to and fro in two directions in a similar way to door hinges.
- **In ball-and-socket joints**, such as the hip, the rounded end of one bone sits in the cup-shaped socket of the other and can move in almost any direction.
- **Swivel joints** turn like a wheel on an axle. Your head can swivel to the left or to the right on your spine.
- **Saddle joints**, such as those in the thumb, have the bones interlocking like two saddles. These joints allow great mobility with considerable strength.
- **The relatively inflexible joints** between the spine's bones (vertebrae) are cushioned by pads of cartilage.
- **Flexible synovial joints** such as the hip joint are lubricated with synovial fluid and cushioned by cartilage.
- **The knee joint can bend**, straighten and (when slightly bent) rotate.
- **Arthritis is** a disease that causes painful inflammation and stiffness of the joints.

◀ *Synovial joints allow the body to move in many ways so we can walk, run, play and work.*

Tendons and ligaments

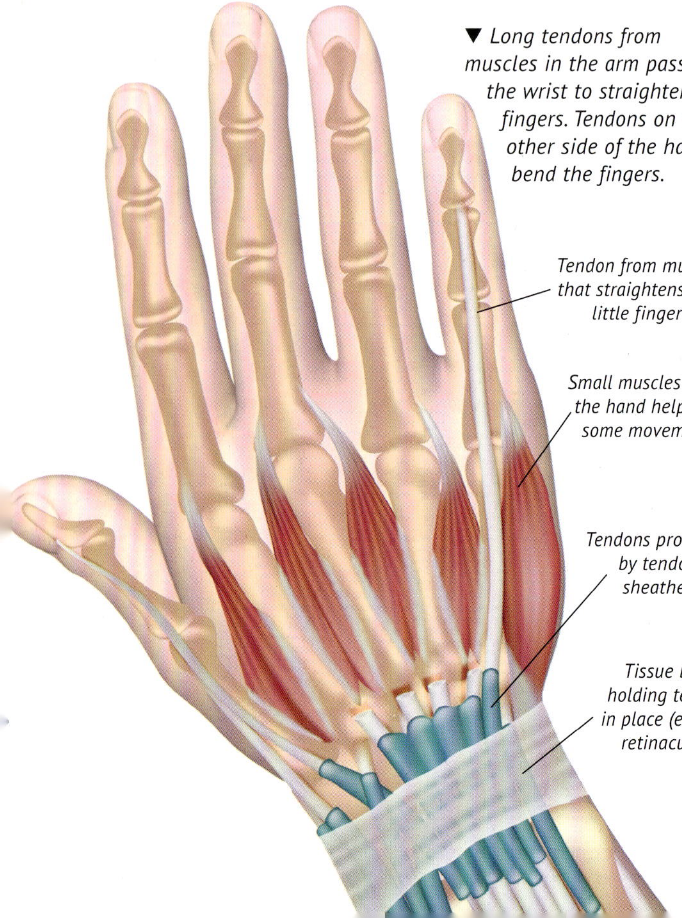

▼ *Long tendons from muscles in the arm pass over the wrist to straighten the fingers. Tendons on the other side of the hand bend the fingers.*

- **Tendons are cords** that tie a muscle to a bone or a muscle to another muscle.
- **Most tendons** are rope-like bundles of fibre. A few are flat sheets called aponeuroses.
- **Tendon fibres** are made from a rubbery substance called collagen.
- **Your fingers are mainly moved** by muscles in the forearm, connected to the fingers by long tendons.
- **The Achilles tendon** pulls up your heel at the back.
- **Tendons** can transmit a force of up to five times your body weight.
- **Ligaments are cords** attached to bones on either side of a joint to strengthen it.
- **Ligaments are made** up of bundles of collagen and a stretchy substance called elastin.
- **Ligaments also** support various organs, including the liver, bladder and uterus (womb).

DID YOU KNOW?

The Achilles tendon is named after the Greek hero Achilles whose only weakness was his heel.

Muscles

● **Muscles are special fibres** that contract (tighten) and relax to move parts of the body.

● **Voluntary muscles** are all the muscles you can control by thought, such as arm muscles.

● **Involuntary muscles** are those that work automatically, such as the muscles that move food through your intestine.

● **Most voluntary muscles** cover the skeleton and are called skeletal muscles.

● **Most involuntary muscles** form sacs or tubes such as the intestine.

● **Heart muscle** is a unique type of muscle. It has cells that work in a similar way to nerve cells, transmitting the signals for waves of muscle contraction to sweep through it.

● **Most skeletal muscles** are attached to two bones across a joint. Their job is to move those bones closer to each other.

● **The body's longest muscle** is the sartorius on the inner thigh. The widest muscle is the external oblique which runs around the side of the upper body.

DID YOU KNOW?

Your body's smallest muscle is the stapedius, inside the ear – it is about as big as this l.

▼ *Muscles let the body move, give it shape and provide support for internal body parts. Most muscles are attached to the skeleton, and there are over 600 of them.*

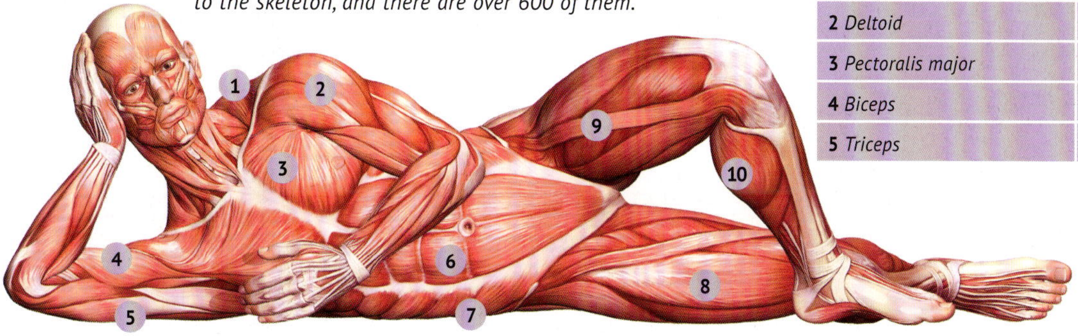

1 *Trapezius*	**6** *Rectus abdominis*
2 *Deltoid*	**7** *External oblique abdominal*
3 *Pectoralis major*	**8** *Quadriceps*
4 *Biceps*	**9** *Sartorius*
5 *Triceps*	**10** *Gastrocnemius*

Muscle movement

● **Most muscles** are long and thin and work by contracting (becoming shorter), sometimes by up to half their length.

● **Skeletal muscles** are made of cells that have many nuclei in a long fibre. Muscles are made from hundreds or thousands of these fibres.

● **These muscle fibres** are made up of strands called myofibrils, each marked with dark bands, making the muscle look stripy or 'striated'.

● **The stripes** in muscle are bands of two substances, actin and myosin, which interlock. When a signal comes from the brain, chemical 'hooks' found on the myosin pull the actin filaments along, shortening the muscle.

● **Skeletal muscles** have two types of fibres – fast twitch and slow twitch.

● **Fast twitch fibres** contract faster and more forcibly, while slow twitch fibres contract slowly but can maintain contraction for longer.

● **Muscles can only pull** and not push and are usually paired across joints.

● **When one muscle contracts** it pulls on the joint, causing movement. At the same time the muscle on the other side of the joint will be relaxed.

● **To move the joint** back to its original position, the contracted muscle relaxes and the opposing muscle contracts.

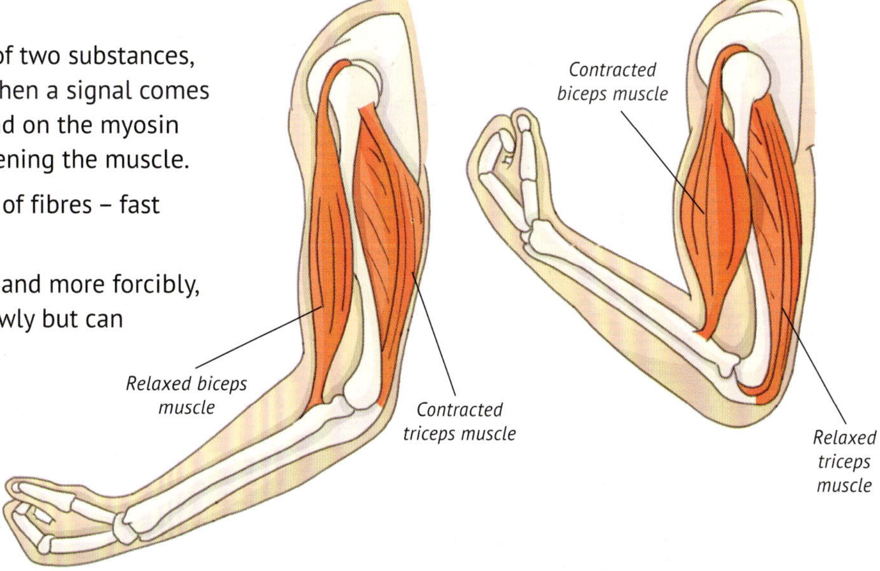

▶ *Muscles, such as the biceps and triceps in the upper arm, work in pairs, pulling in opposite directions to one another.*

Cells

● **Cells** are the basic building blocks of your body. Most are so tiny you would need 10,000 to cover a pinhead.

● **There are over 200 different kinds** of cell in your body, including nerve cells, skin cells, blood cells, bone cells, fat cells, muscle cells and many more.

● **A cell** is basically a little parcel of chemicals with a thin membrane (casing) of protein and fat.

● **The membrane** holds the cell together, but lets nutrients in and waste out.

● **Inside the cell** is a liquid called cytoplasm, and floating in this are various tiny structures called organelles.

● **At the centre** of the cell is the nucleus – this is the cell's control centre and it contains DNA.

● **Each cell** is a dynamic chemical factory, and the cell's team of organelles is continually busy – ferrying chemicals to and fro, breaking up unwanted chemicals, and putting together new ones.

DID YOU KNOW?

The human body contains more than 50 billion billion cells!

● **Some of the biggest cells** in the body are nerve cells. Although the main nucleus of a nerve cell is microscopic, the tails of some can extend for one metre or more through the body, and be seen even without a microscope.

● **Red blood cells** are among the smallest cells in the body. These are just 0.0075 mm across and have no nucleus.

● **Most body cells** are continually being replaced by new ones. The main exceptions are nerve cells – these are long-lived, but rarely replaced.

▶ This illustration shows a typical cell, cutaway to show some of the different organelles (special parts of a cell) that keep it working properly. The instructions come from the nucleus in the cell's 'control centre', but every kind of organelle has its own task.

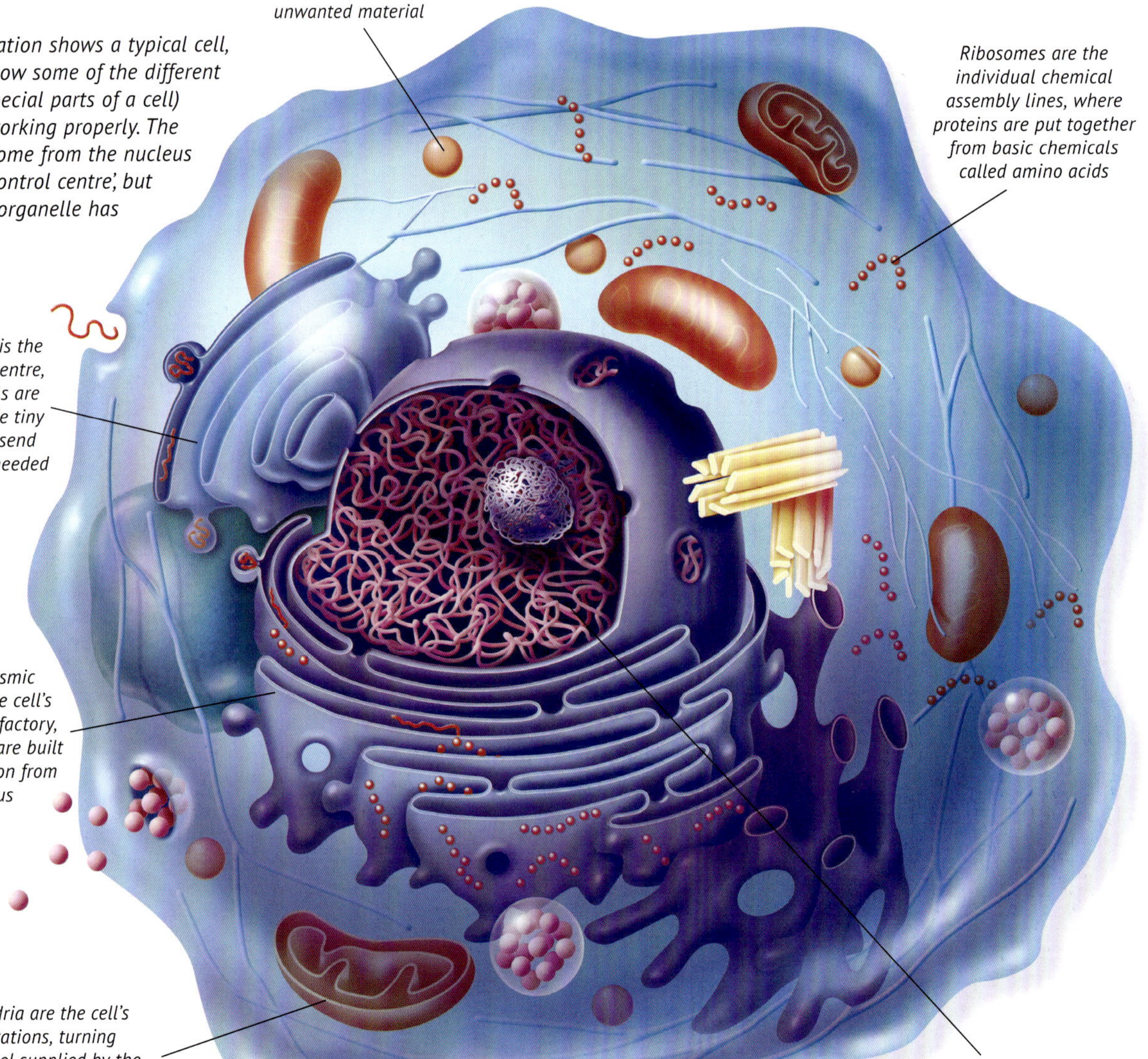

Tissues

- **A tissue** is a body substance made from many of the same type of cell. Muscle cells make muscle tissue, nerve cells form nerve tissue, and so on.
- **Your body** is entirely made up of tissues and fluid.
- **As well as cells**, some tissues include other materials.
- **Connective tissues** are made from particular cells (such as fibroblasts), plus two other materials – long fibres of protein (such as collagen) and a matrix.
- **A matrix is** a material in which the cells and fibres are set like the currants in a bun.
- **Connective tissue** holds all the other kinds of tissue together in various ways. The tissue that makes fat, tendons and cartilage is connective tissue.
- **Bone and blood** are both connective tissues.
- **Epithelial tissue** is good lining or covering material, making skin and other parts of the body.
- **Epithelial tissue** may combine three kinds of cell to make a thin waterproof layer – squamous (flat), cuboid (box-like) and columnar (pillar-like) cells.
- **Nerve tissue** is made mostly from neurons (nerve cells), plus the Schwann cells that coat them.
- **The heart** is made mostly of muscle tissue, but also includes epithelial and connective tissue.

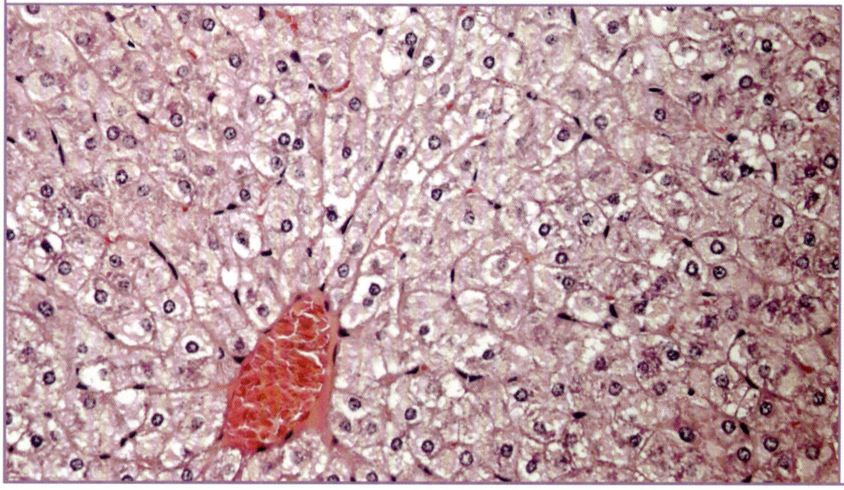

◀ *Liver tissue is made from densely packed liver cells, as shown in this highly magnified photograph.*

Organs

- **Organs are made** from combinations of tissues.
- **A collection** of related organs form a body system.
- **Body organs** include the brain, heart, lungs, kidneys and digestive organs. These all work together to keep the body functioning.
- **The largest organ** is the skin, which covers the whole body.
- **The smallest organ** is the pineal gland, a tiny organ in the brain that produces a substance that affects sleep.
- **The brain controls** the functions of many of the other body organs, making sure we keep breathing and our hearts keep beating.
- **We can survive** without some organs.
- **Some people** only have one kidney or lung or have had their appendix or spleen removed because of damage or disease.
- **Some organs**, such as the heart or liver, can be replaced by transplant surgery if they are damaged or diseased.

DID YOU KNOW?

The word 'organ' means instrument or tool in Greek.

ORGAN	WHAT IT DOES
Brain	*Controls the nervous system*
Heart	*Keeps blood flowing round the body*
Lungs	*Enable us to get oxygen from the air we breathe*
Voice box	*Produces sounds that we turn into speech*
Stomach	*Starts to break down food*
Liver	*Produces chemicals essential for survival and digestion*
Gall bladder	*Helps digestion of food*
Pancreas	*Helps to control sugar levels in the body*
Spleen	*Produces cells that help fight infections*
Small intestine	*Processes food and absorbs useful substances*
Appendix	*Has no known use in humans*
Large intestine	*Absorbs water from food and gets rid of unwanted material*
Kidneys	*Help control the body's fluid balance*
Bladder	*Stores urine*
Skin	*A protective covering over the body*

Inflammation

- **Inflammation** is the redness, swelling, heat and pain that occurs as the result of an injury or infection.
- **When the body** is damaged, nearby cells release histamines and other chemicals.
- **These chemicals** increase blood flow to the area, widening local blood vessels and causing redness and heat.
- **The chemicals** also attract white blood cells called leucocytes, which destroy any infections.
- **The leucocytes** also release chemicals that control the inflammation.
- **Additional fluid** at the injury causes swelling.
- **The area** may also become painful if nerve endings in the skin are affected.
- **In some people**, inflammation may occur when there has been no injury. In this case, the body will start attacking its own tissues. This is called an autoimmune disease.
- **Arthritis**, in which joints become swollen, painful, and stiff, is an autoimmune disease.
- **Acute inflammation** means a sudden reaction that lasts a few days; chronic inflammation means a slower reaction lasting weeks or months.

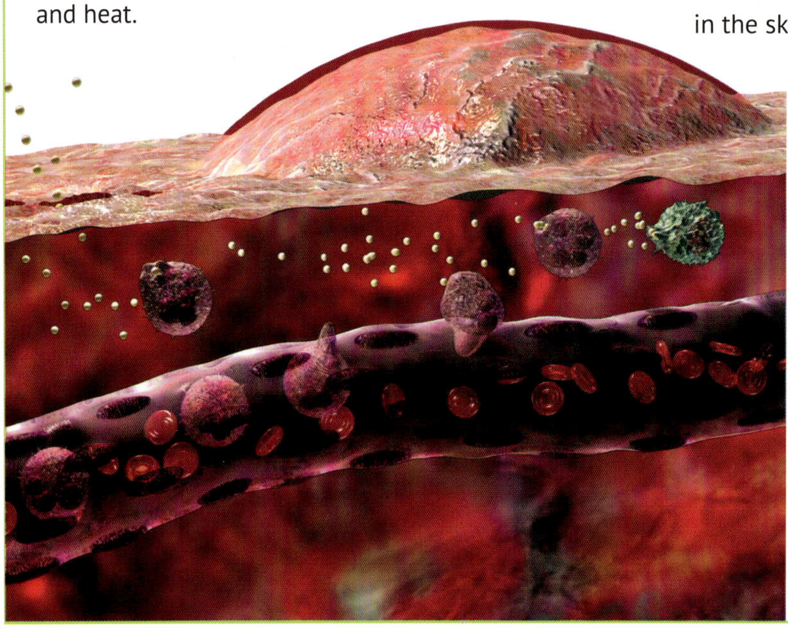

◀ *During an inflammatory response, blood vessels widen, causing swelling and redness, while special white blood cells (in purple and green) destroy any infection.*

Skin

- **Acting as a protective coat**, skin shields your body from the external environment and from infection, and helps to keep it at just the right temperature.
- **Skin is your largest sense receptor**, responding to touch, pressure, heat and cold.
- **Vitamin D is made** for your body by the skin from exposure to sunlight.
- **The epidermis** (the outer layer of skin) continually produces cells from underneath, which then pile up and gradually die.
- **This covering** of layers of dead cells contains a tough protein called keratin that protects the body.
- **Below the epidermis** is a thick layer of living cells called the dermis, which contains the sweat glands.
- **Hair roots** have tiny muscles that pull the hair upright when you are cold, giving you goose bumps.
- **This traps air** to create an extra layer of insulation.
- **Skin is 6 mm thick** on the soles of your feet, and just 0.5 mm thick on your eyelids.
- **The epidermis** contains cells that make the dark pigment melanin that determines skin colour.

DID YOU KNOW?

Even though its thickness averages just 2 mm, your skin gets one-eighth of all your blood supply.

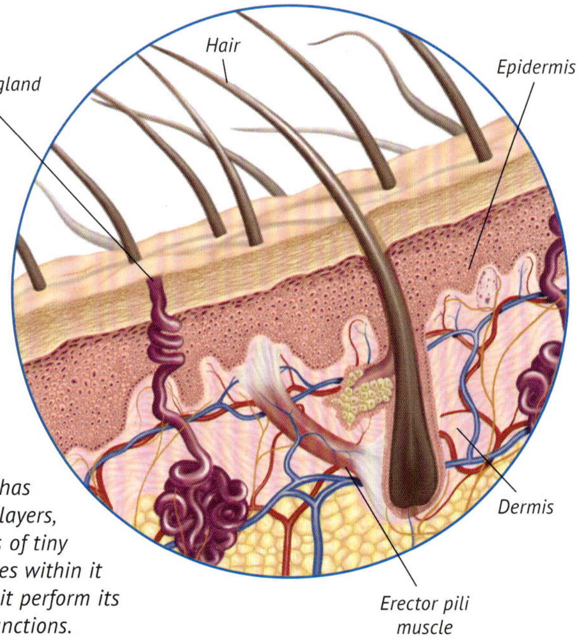

▶ *Skin has several layers, and lots of tiny structures within it to help it perform its many functions.*

Hair

● **Many mammals** have thick hair all over their skin, but human body hair is so short and fine that it gives the appearance of bare skin.

● **Lanugo** is the very fine hair babies are covered in when they are inside the womb, from the fourth month of pregnancy onwards.

● **Vellus hair** is fine, downy hair that grows all over your body until you reach puberty.

● **Terminal hair** is the coarser hair on your head, as well as the hair that grows on men's chins and around an adult's genitals.

● **The colour of your hair** depends on how much you have of pigments called melanin and carotene in the hairs.

● **Hair is red or auburn** if it contains carotene.

● **Black, brown and blonde hair** gets its colour from black melanin.

● **Each hair** is rooted in a pit called the hair follicle. The hair is held in place by its club-shaped tip, the bulb.

● **Hair grows** as cells fill with a material called keratin and die, and pile up inside the follicle.

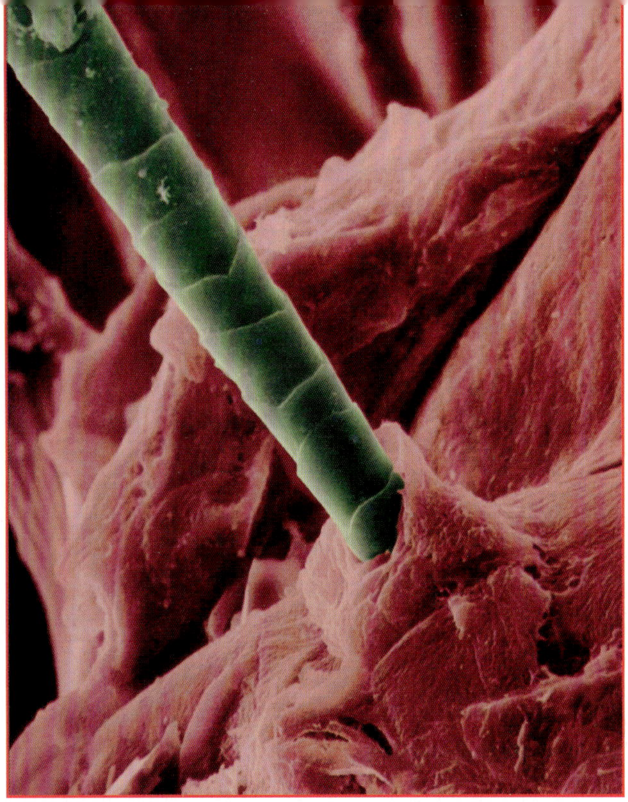

▲ *A microscopic view of a hair. It is only alive and growing at its root, in the base of the follicle. The shaft that sticks out of the skin is dead, and is made of flat cells stuck firmly together.*

● **The average person** has 120,000 head hairs and each grows about 3 mm per week.

Nails

● **A nail is a tough plate** that covers the surface of the end of each finger and toe.

● **Fingernails form a firm layer** at the back of the fingertip.

● **This layer** stops the flexible fingertip from bending too much, so we can feel, press and pick up small items more easily without damage.

● **Each nail** is a special growth of the epidermis (outer layer of the skin).

● **Nails are made** from the tough protein keratin.

● **A nail**, like a hair, grows at its root, which is under the skin at its base, and slides slowly along the finger. The root is the only living part of the nail.

● **The skin at the base of the nail** from which the nail grows is called the matrix.

● **The blood flow to the nail** is less visible at the nail base, leaving a paler, crescent-shaped area of nail visible. This is called the lunula.

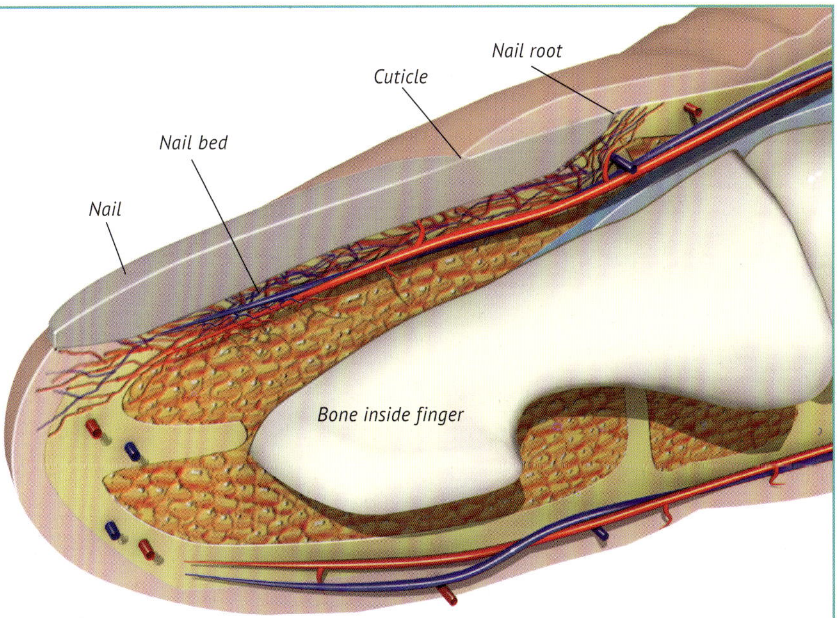

▲ *A nail has its root under the skin and grows along the nail bed – the skin underneath it.*

● **Nails grow faster** in summer than in winter, and faster by day than by night.

● **Nails lengthen** by about half a millimetre, on average, each week.

DID YOU KNOW?

Toenails require between 12 and 18 months to completely regrow.

Digestion

- **Digestion** is the process by which your body breaks down the food you eat into substances that it can absorb (take in) and use.
- **The digestive tract**, or passage, is basically a long, winding tube called the alimentary canal (gut). It starts at the mouth and ends at the anus.
- **If you could lay** your gut out straight, it would be nearly six times as long as you are tall.
- **The food you eat** is softened in your mouth by chewing and by chemicals in your saliva (spit).
- **When you swallow**, food travels down the oesophagus (a muscular tube) into the stomach.
- **The stomach** is a muscular-walled bag that mashes the food into a pulp, helped by chemicals called gastric juices.
- **When empty**, the stomach holds barely 0.5 l, but after a big meal it can stretch to more than 4 l. It works as a temporary storage facility, allowing you to consume a meal, and then digest it over a long period of time.
- **The half-digested food** that leaves the stomach is called chyme. It passes into the small intestine, usually within four hours of eating a meal.
- **The small intestine** is a 6 m-long-tube where chyme is broken down further, into molecules small enough to be absorbed through the intestine wall into the blood.
- **Food that cannot be digested** in the small intestine passes into the large intestine. It is then pushed out through the anus as faeces when you go to the toilet.
- **Digestive enzymes** play a vital part in breaking food down so it can be absorbed by the body.

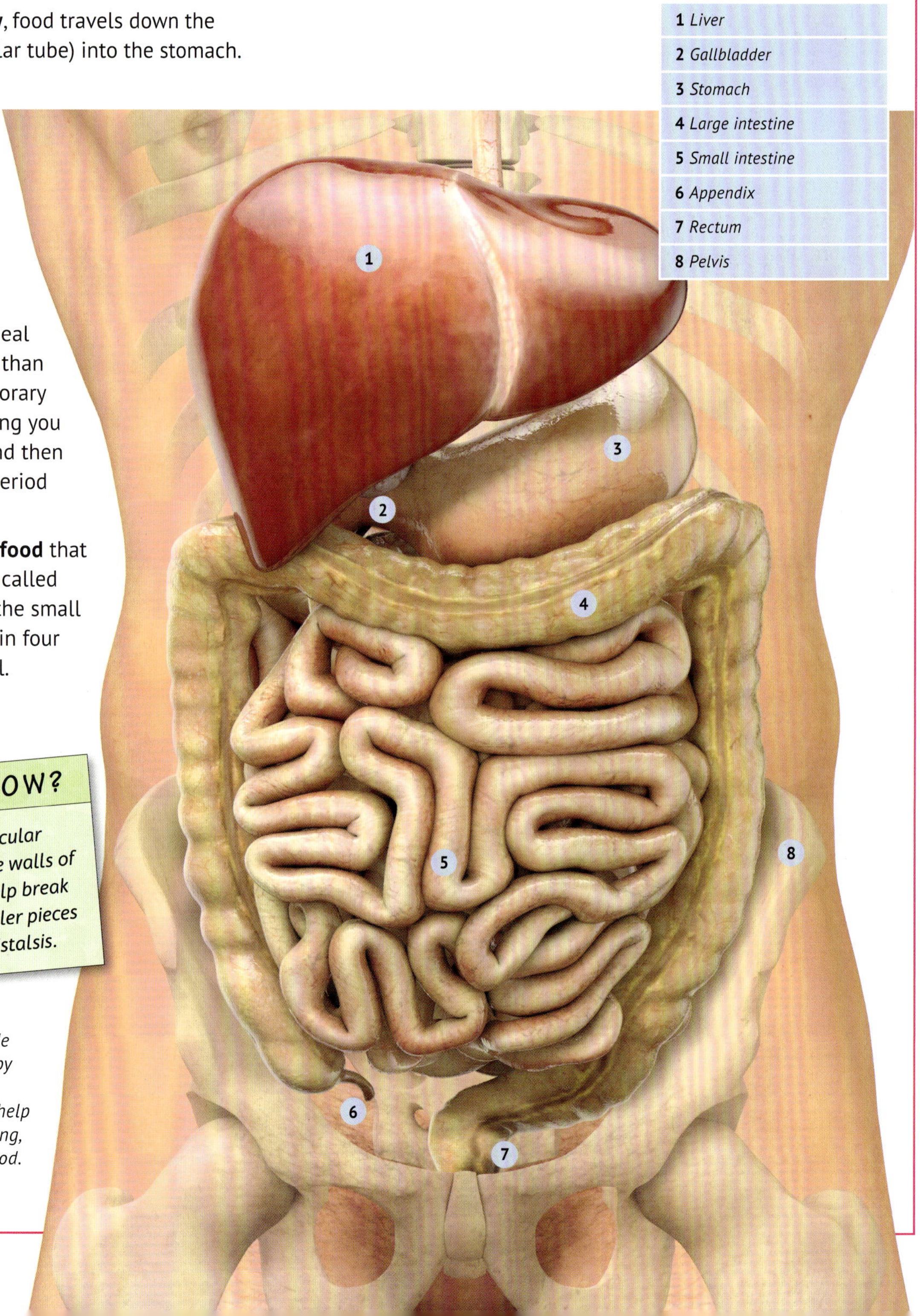

DID YOU KNOW?

The waves of muscular contraction along the walls of the stomach that help break food down into smaller pieces are known as peristalsis.

▶ *Much of the space inside the abdomen is taken up by the gastro-intestinal tract (gut) and the organs that help it do its work of transporting, digesting and expelling food.*

Diet

- **Your diet** is what you eat. A good diet includes the correct amount of proteins, carbohydrates, fats, vitamins, minerals, fibre and water.
- **Most of the food** you eat is fuel for the body, provided mostly by carbohydrates and fats.
- **Carbohydrates** are foods made from types of sugar, such as glucose and starch, and are found in foods such as bread, rice and potatoes.
- **Fats are greasy foods** that will not dissolve in water. Some, such as the fats in meat and cheese, are solid. Some, such as cooking oil, are in liquid form.
- **Proteins** are needed to build and repair cells, and are made from chemicals called amino acids.
- **Meat and fish** are very high in protein.
- **A correctly balanced** vegetarian diet can provide all the amino acids needed for health.
- **Fibre or roughage** is supplied by cellulose from plant cell walls.
- **Your body** cannot digest fibre, but needs it to keep the bowel muscles properly exercised.

▲ *This illustration shows the types and proportions of different foods in a healthy diet.*

Fats

- **Fats are an important source** of energy. Together with proteins and carbohydrates, they are the main components of the foods used by your body.
- **While carbohydrates** are generally used for energy immediately, your body often stores fat to use for energy in times of shortage.
- **Weight for weight**, fats contain twice as much energy as carbohydrates.
- **Fats (or lipids)** are important organic (life) substances, found in almost every living thing. They are made from substances called fatty acids and glycerol.
- **Food fats** are vegetable or animal fats that don't dissolve in water.
- **Most vegetable fats** are liquid, although some nut fats are solid. Most animal fats are solid. Milk is mainly water with some solid animal fats. Most solid fats melt when warmed.
- **Fats called triglycerides** are stored around the body as adipose tissue (body fat). These act as energy stores and also insulate the body against the cold.
- **Fats called phospholipids** are used to build body cells.
- **In your intestine**, bile from your liver and enzymes from your pancreas break fats down into fatty acids and glycerol. These are absorbed into your body's lymphatic system or enter the blood.

DID YOU KNOW?

Saturated fats are linked to high levels of cholesterol in the blood and may increase certain health risks, such as heart attack.

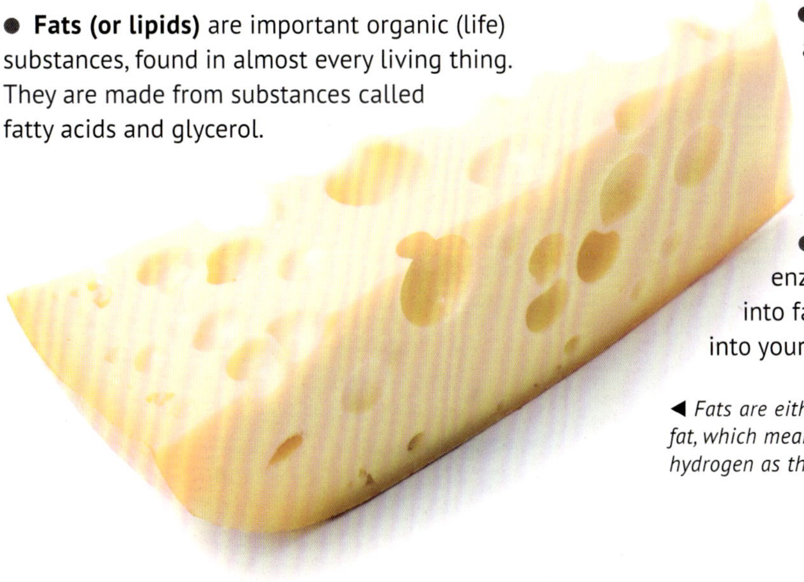

◀ *Fats are either saturated or unsaturated. Cheese is a saturated fat, which means its fatty acids are saturated with as much hydrogen as they can hold.*

Carbohydrates

> **DID YOU KNOW?**
> *Complex carbohydrates are a healthier source of energy in your diet than simple carbohydrates.*

- **Carbohydrates** are your body's main source of energy. They are plentiful in starchy food such as bread and cakes.
- **The body burns carbohydrates** to keep it warm and to provide energy for growth and muscle movement, as well as to maintain basic body processes.
- **Carbohydrates** are among the most common of all organic substances. Plants, for instance, make carbohydrates when they take energy from sunlight.
- **Carbohydrates are** made from chains of sugars and are classified as simple (having few chains) and complex (many chains).
- **Simple carbohydrates** such as glucose, fructose (the sugar in fruit) and sucrose (table sugar) are sweet and soluble (they dissolve in water).
- **Complex carbohydrates** (polysaccharides) are made when molecules of simple carbohydrates join together.
- **Dietary sources** of complex carbohydrates include whole cereal grains, potatoes, green vegetables, pulses and brown rice.
- **Your body** turns carbohydrates into glucose for use at once, or stores them in the liver as the sugar glycogen. More complex carbohydrates are converted into glucose more slowly.
- **Enzymes are used by the digestive system** to break down complex carbohydrates such as starch into simple sugars that can be absorbed into the blood. Saliva (spit) contains the enzyme amylase that converts starch into glucose.

◀ *Wholemeal bread is rich in complex carbohydrates, as well as simpler ones such as glucose and sucrose.*

Glucose

- **Glucose** is the body's energy chemical, used as the fuel in all cell activity.
- **Glucose is a kind of sugar** made by plants as they take energy from sunlight.
- **The body gets its glucose** from carbohydrates in food, broken down in stages in the intestine.
- **From the intestine**, glucose travels in the blood to the liver, where excess is stored in the form of glycogen.
- **For the body to work effectively**, levels of glucose in the blood (called blood sugar) must always be correct.
- **Blood sugar levels** are controlled by two hormones – glucagon and insulin – which are sent out by the pancreas.

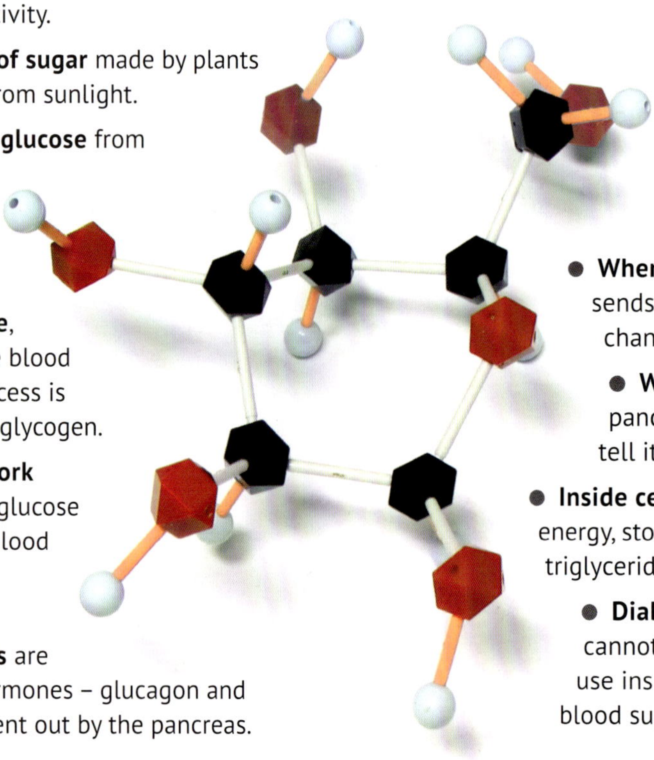

◀ *Glucose is built from six carbon, 12 hydrogen, and six oxygen atoms.*

- **When blood sugar is low**, the pancreas sends glucagon to the liver to tell it to change more glycogen to glucose.
- **When blood sugar is high**, the pancreas sends insulin to the liver to tell it to store more glucose as glycogen.
- **Inside cells**, glucose may be burned for energy, stored as glycogen, or used to make triglyceride fats.
- **Diabetes is an illness** where your body cannot produce enough insulin or cannot use insulin properly, causing they body's blood sugar level to become too high.

Protein

- **Proteins are essential** to the structure, function and regulation of the body.
- **Proteins are made** from strings of amino acids (molecules containing carbon, hydrogen, nitrogen, oxygen and sometimes sulphur).
- **There are 20 common types** of amino acid of which some must be eaten because they cannot be made in the body. These are called essential amino acids.
- **Protein in the diet** comes from meat, cheese, eggs, yoghurt, pulses, soya, nuts and seeds.
- **Protein in the diet** is broken down in the digestive system into amino acids that can be absorbed into the blood and then made into new proteins.
- **An adult man** needs to eat about 50 to 55 g of protein a day.
- **An adult woman** needs to eat about 45 g a day.
- **Women need more protein** when they are pregnant or breast feeding.
- **Animal sources of protein** contain all essential amino acids, while most plant proteins do not.

DID YOU KNOW?

Good sources of protein for vegetarians include nuts and seeds, pulses, cereals, eggs, milk, cheese and yoghurt.

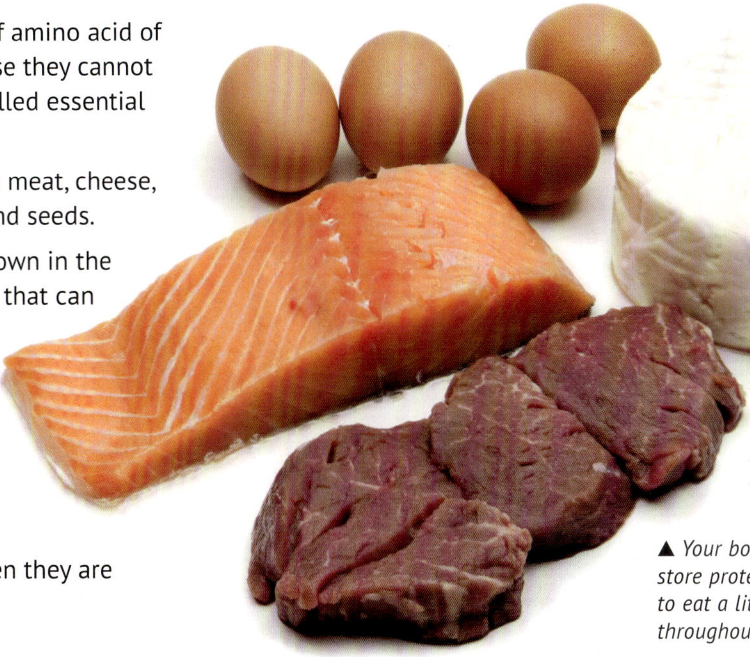

▲ *Your body is not able to store protein, so you need to eat a little every day throughout the day.*

Vitamins

DID YOU KNOW?

Lack of vitamin A affects night vision, because it is needed for the working of the retina.

- **Vitamins are special substances** the body needs to help maintain chemical processes inside cells.
- **Plants can make their own vitamins**, but humans must take most of their vitamins from food.
- **A lack of any vitamin** in the diet can cause illness.
- **The first vitamins** discovered were given letter names such as B. Later discoveries were given chemical names.
- **Before the 18th century**, sailors on long voyages used to suffer from the disease scurvy, caused by a lack of vitamin C from fresh fruit in their diet.
- **Some vitamins** such as A, D, E and K dissolve in fat and are found in animal fats and vegetable oils. They may be stored in the body for months.

- **Some vitamins** such as C and the Bs, dissolve in water and are found in green leaves, fruits and cereal grains. They are used by the body daily.
- **Vitamins D and K** are the only ones made in the body. Vitamin D is essential for healthy bones. It is made by the skin when exposed to sunlight – 15 minutes three times a week may be enough.
- **Vitamin K is essential** for your body's blood-clotting process. It is found mainly in green leafy vegetables.

◀ *Citrus fruit, such as oranges, lemons and limes, and green vegetables are full of vitamins, which is why they are so important in our diet.*

Enzymes

- **Enzymes** are molecules – mostly protein – which alter the speed of chemical reactions in living things.
- **There are thousands of enzymes** in your body – it could not function without them.
- **Some enzymes** need an extra substance, called a coenzyme, to work. Many coenzymes are vitamins.
- **Most enzymes** have names ending in 'ase', such as lygase, protease and lipase.
- **Pacemaker enzymes** help to control your metabolism – the rate at which your body uses energy.
- **The activity of an enzyme** is easily destroyed by heat. This is one reason why it is important that the body temperature is kept very steadily at 37°C (98°F).
- **Many enzymes** are essential for the digestion of food, including lipase, protease, amylase and the peptidases. Most of these are made in the pancreas.
- **Lipase** is released mainly from the pancreas into the alimentary canal (gut) to help break down fat.
- **Amylase** breaks down starches such as those in bread and fruit into simple sugars. There is amylase in saliva and in the stomach.
- **In the gut**, the sugars maltose, sucrose and lactose are broken down by the enzymes maltase, sucrase and lactase.

▼ *Saliva contains enzymes called amylase and lipase that start to break down food as soon as it enters your mouth.*

The liver

- **The liver** is the body's chemical processing centre, and the biggest internal organ.
- **The word hepatic** means 'to do with the liver'.
- **The prime task** of the liver is handling all the nutrients and substances digested from the food you eat and sending them out to your body cells when needed.
- **Carbohydrates**, the main energy-giving chemical for body cells, are turned into glucose in the liver.
- **The liver** also keeps levels of glucose in the blood steady. It releases more when levels drop, and stores it as glycogen, a type of starch, when levels rise.
- **Excess food energy** is sent off by the liver to be stored as fat around the body.
- **Proteins are broken down** and vitamins and minerals are stored in the liver.
- **The liver produces bile**, a yellowish or greenish bitter liquid that helps dissolve fat as food is digested.
- **Old red cells** and harmful substances, such as alcohol, are cleaned out of the body by the liver, and new plasma is made.
- **Thousands of hexagonal-shaped** units called lobules comprise the chemical processing units in the liver.
- **Lobules** take in unprocessed blood on the outside and dispatch it through a collecting vein in the centre of each one.

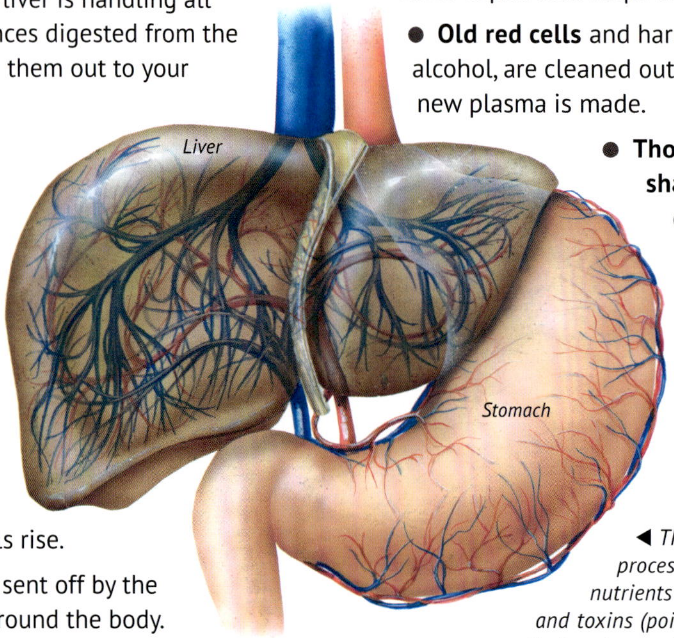

◀ *The liver is the body's cleaning and processing station for the blood, where nutrients are taken out for use by the body and toxins (poisons) are neutralized (made safe). It also stores vitamins, iron and carbohydrates.*

The pancreas

- **The pancreas** is a large gland that lies just below and behind the stomach.
- **The larger end** of the pancreas is on the right, lying against the gut. The tail end is on the left, just touching the spleen.
- **The pancreas** is made from a substance called exocrine tissue, embedded with hundreds of nests of hormone glands called the islets of Langerhans.
- **The exocrine tissue** secretes (releases) pancreatic enzymes such as amylase into the intestine to help digest food.
- **Amylase breaks down** carbohydrates into simple sugars such as maltose, lactose and sucrose.
- **The pancreatic enzymes** run into the intestine via a pipe called the pancreatic duct, which joins to the bile duct. This duct also carries bile – a fluid that aids digestion.
- **The pancreatic enzymes** only start working when they meet other kinds of enzyme in the intestine.
- **The pancreas** also secretes the body's own antacid, sodium bicarbonate, which helps settle an upset stomach.

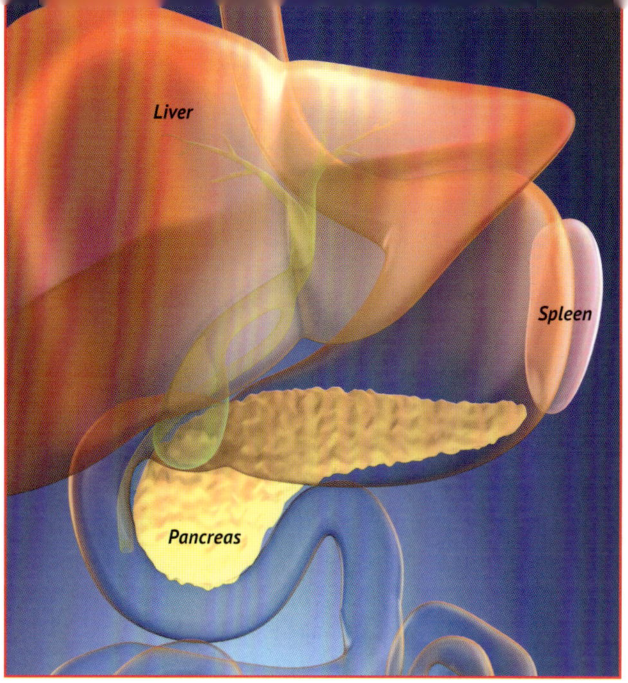

▲ *The pancreas is less than 20 cm long but produces one of the body's most important hormones – insulin.*

- **The islets of Langerhans** secrete two very important hormones – insulin and glucagon.
- **These are released** directly into the blood, not into the gut like the pancreatic enzymes.
- **Insulin and glucagon** regulate blood sugar levels.

Excretion

- **Digestive excretion** is the way your body gets rid of food that it cannot digest.
- **Undigested food** is prepared for excretion in the large intestine or bowel. The main part of the large intestine is the colon, which is almost as long as you are tall.
- **The colon** converts semi-liquid undigested food called chyme into solid waste by absorbing water – up to 1.5 l every day.
- **Sodium and chlorine** are absorbed, and bicarbonate and potassium are removed by the walls of the colon.
- **Billions of tiny bacteria** live inside the colon and help turn the chyme into faeces. These bacteria are harmless as long as they do not spread to the rest of the body.
- **Bacteria in the colon** make vitamins K and B – as well as gases such as methane and hydrogen sulphide.

DID YOU KNOW?

About two-thirds of the waste that our bodies produce is water.

- **The muscles of the colon** break the waste food down into segments ready for excretion.
- **About a third** of all faeces is not old food but 'friendly' gut bacteria and intestinal lining.

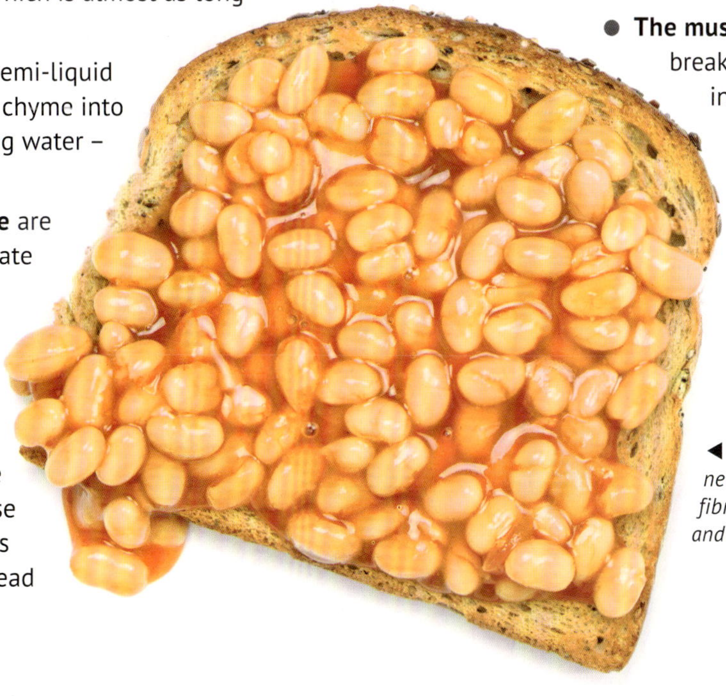

◀ *To function well, the bowel needs roughage – cellulose plant fibres found in food such as beans and wholewheat bread.*

Water

- **You can survive for weeks** without food, but no more than a few days without water.
- **You gain water** by drinking and eating, and as a by-product of cell activity.
- **You lose water** by sweating and breathing, and in your urine and faeces.
- **The average adult** takes in 2.2 litres of water a day – 1.4 l in drink and 0.8 l in food. Body cells add 0.3 l, bringing the total water intake to 2.5 l.
- **The average adult** loses 1.5 litres of water every day in urine, 0.5–0.6 l in sweat, 0.3–0.4 l as vapour in breath and 0.1–0.2 l in faeces.
- **The water balance** in the body is controlled mainly by the kidneys and adrenal glands.
- **The amount of water** the kidneys release as urine depends on the amount of salt in the blood.
- **If you drink lots**, the saltiness of the blood is diluted (watered down). To restore the balance, the kidneys let out water in the form of urine.
- **If you drink little** or sweat a lot, the blood becomes more salty, so the kidneys restore the balance by holding on to more water.

DID YOU KNOW?

Water accounts for around 60 percent of your body weight.

▶ *If you sweat a lot during heavy exercise, you need to make up for all the water you have lost by drinking. Your kidneys make sure that if you drink too much, you lose water as urine.*

Osmosis and diffusion

- **To survive**, every living cell must take in the chemicals it needs and let out the ones it does not through its thin membrane (casing).
- **Cells do this** in several ways, including osmosis, diffusion and active transport.
- **Osmosis** is the movement of water to even out the balance between a weak solution and a stronger one.
- **Osmosis occurs** when the molecules of a dissolved substance are too big to slip through the cell membrane – only the water can move.
- **Osmosis is vital** to many body processes, including the workings of the kidneys and the nerves.
- **Urine gets its water** from the kidneys by osmosis.
- **Diffusion is the movement** of substances dissolved in water, or mixed in air, to even out the balance.
- **In diffusion**, a substance such as oxygen moves in and out of cells, while the air or water it is mixed in stays put.
- **Diffusion is vital** to body processes such as cellular respiration, when cells take in oxygen and push out waste carbon dioxide.
- **Active transport** is the way a cell uses protein-based 'pumps' or 'gates' in its membrane to draw in and hold substances that might otherwise diffuse out.
- **Active transport** uses energy and is how cells draw in most of their food such as glucose.

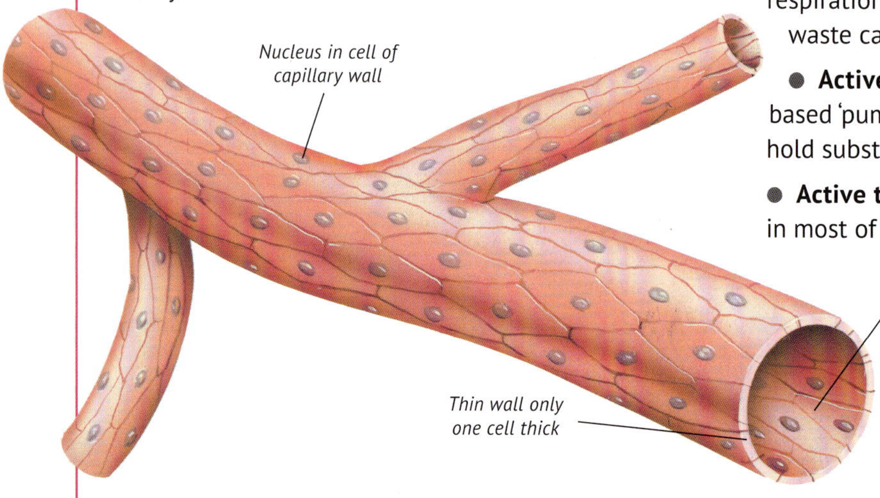

◀ *Oxygen diffuses from the air sacs in your lungs into your blood capillaries because the concentration of oxygen is higher in the air sacs and lower in the capillary.*

Body salts

- **Body salts** are an important group of chemicals that play a vital role in your body.
- **Examples of components** in body salts include potassium, sodium, chloride and manganese.
- **Body salts are important** in maintaining the balance of water in the body, and in body cells.
- **The body's thirst centre** is the hypothalamus in the brain. It tells you when you are thirsty and monitors salt levels in the blood and sends signals to the kidneys telling them keep water or let it go.
- **You gain salt** from the food you eat.
- **You can lose salt** if you sweat heavily. This can make muscles cramp, which is why people travelling in deserts sometimes take salt tablets or drink a weak salt solution.
- **Too much salt** in food may result in high blood pressure.

▲ *The body loses salt in sweat during exercise. Adequate hydration and sodium intake, either through sports drinks or food, is vitally important to keep the body going during long races.*

DID YOU KNOW?

A saline drip is salt solution dripped via a tube into the arm of a patient who has lost fluid.

- **When dissolved in water**, the chemical elements that salt is made from split into ions – atoms with either a positive or a negative electrical charge.

The kidneys

- **The kidneys** are a pair of bean-shaped organs inside the small of the back. They are the body's water control and blood-cleaning plants.
- **The kidneys are filters** that draw off water and important substances from the blood, and let unwanted water and waste substances go as urine.
- **All blood** flows through the kidneys every ten minutes, so it is filtered 150 times a day.
- **The kidneys** save nearly all the amino acids and glucose from the blood and 70 percent of the salt.
- **Blood entering each kidney** is filtered through filtration units called nephrons.
- **Each nephron** is an intricate network of pipes called convoluted tubules, wrapped around tiny capillaries. Useful blood substances are filtered into the tubules, then re-absorbed back into the blood.
- **The production of urine** is one of the body's ways of getting rid of waste. It is produced by your kidneys, which filter it from your blood.
- **Urine runs from each kidney** down a tube called the ureter, into the bladder. When your bladder is full, you feel the need to urinate.
- **Urine is mostly water**, but there are substances dissolved in it. These include urea – a substance that is left after the breakdown of amino acids, various salts, creatinine, ammonia and blood wastes.

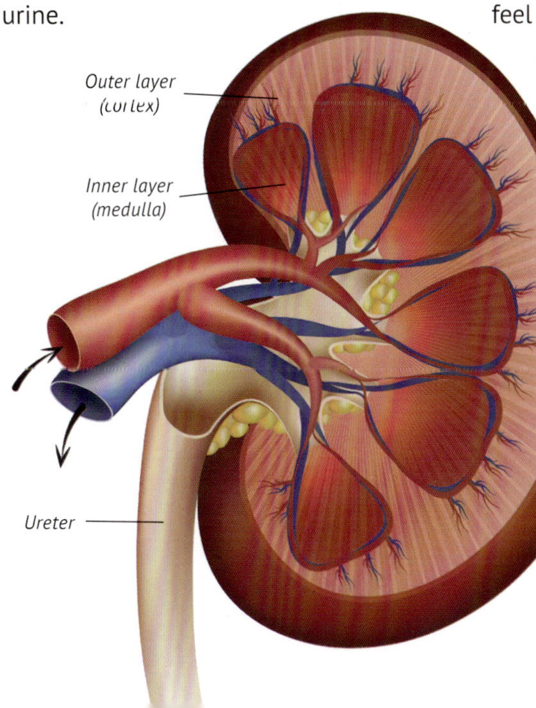

◀ *This cross-section of a kidney shows blood entering through arteries (red) and leaving through veins (blue). Waste fluid drains away through the ureter.*

The endocrine system

- **Many bodily functions** are controlled by special chemicals called hormones.
- **Hormones are produced** by a number of specialized glands called endocrine glands.
- **Endocrine glands** are also called ductless glands because they release secretions directly into the blood and not into a duct (tube) like other types of gland (the salivary glands for example).
- **The endocrine glands** include the thyroid gland, the pancreas, the pituitary gland, the adrenal glands, the testes, the ovaries and the parathyroid glands.

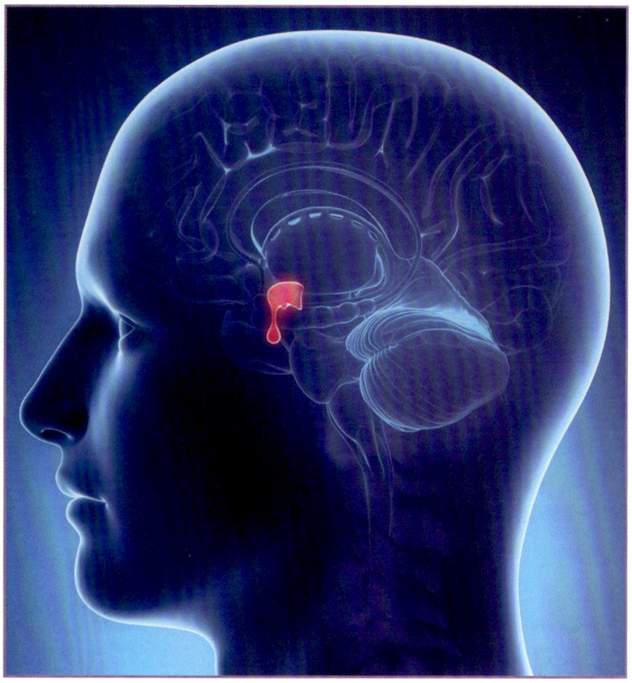

▲ The pituitary gland releases eight different hormones, and they control major developments in the body such as growth and reproduction.

- **Most hormones** are proteins but some are steroids (adrenal and sex hormones).
- **The effect of the hormones** produced by the endocrine system is usually far away from the site of release.
- **The pituitary gland** is located at the base of the brain sitting in a cup-shaped depression in the skull called the sella turcica.
- **The pituitary and hypothalamus** (a region of the brain situated just above the pituitary gland) produce the largest number of different hormones.
- **The parathyroid glands** are embedded in the back of the thyroid gland in the neck, which itself is an endocrine gland.
- **The pancreas** is unusual as it is both an endocrine gland (hormone producing) and an exocrine gland (manufactures chemicals that it secretes into a duct).
- **The thymus gland** is active only in childhood, and helps the immune system develop.

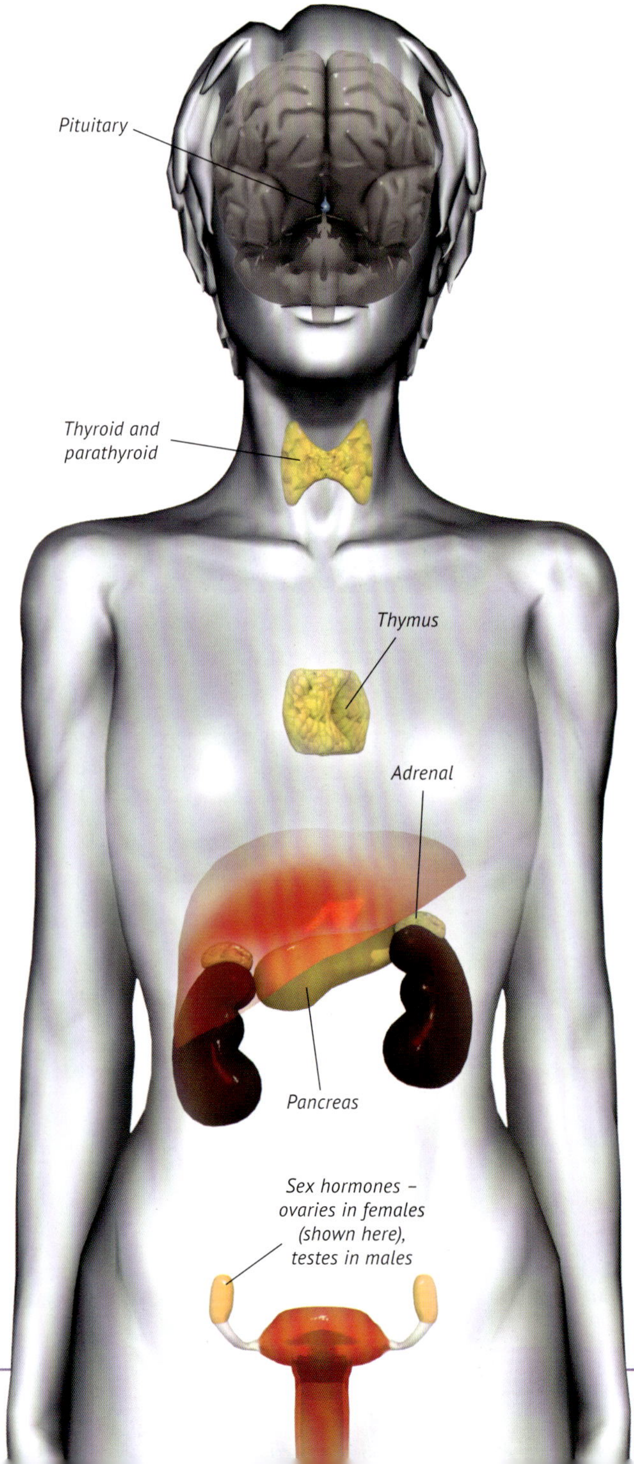

◀ Endocrine glands are situated all over the body, and each hormone affects only certain parts, known as target organs.

DID YOU KNOW?

The pineal gland (located in the brain) sets your body's clock by releasing melatonin, a hormone that makes you sleepy.

The thyroid gland

DID YOU KNOW?

Everyone has a different metabolic rate. It rises when you are afraid or if your body is working hard.

- **The thyroid gland** is shaped like a bow tie and sits at the front of the neck just below the voice box (larynx).
- **The thyroid** secretes (releases) three important hormones – triiodothyronine (T3), thyroxine (T4) and calcitonin.
- **The thyroid hormones** affect how energetic you are by controlling your metabolic rate.
- **Your metabolic rate** is the rate at which your cells use glucose and other energy substances.
- **T3 and T4** control metabolic rate by circulating in the blood and stimulating cells to convert more glucose.
- **If the thyroid** sends out too little T3 and T4, you get cold and tired, your skin gets dry and you put on weight. If it sends out too much T3 and T4, you get nervous, sweaty and overactive, and you lose weight.
- **The amount of T3 and T4** sent out by the thyroid depends on how much thyroid-stimulating hormone is sent to it from the pituitary gland.
- **If the levels of T3 and T4** in the blood drop, the pituitary gland sends out extra thyroid-stimulating hormone to tell the thyroid to produce more.
- **Calcitonin** helps to regulate levels of calcium in the blood.

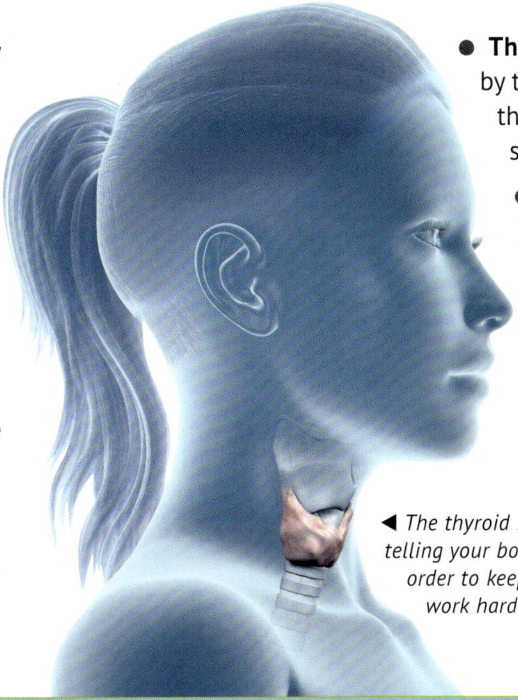

◀ *The thyroid is part of your energy control system, telling your body cells to work faster or slower in order to keep you warm or to make your muscles work harder.*

Hormones

- **Hormones** are the body's chemical messengers. They are released from stores to trigger certain reactions in different parts of the body.
- **Most hormones** are endocrine hormones that are spread around the body in the bloodstream.
- **Hormones are controlled** by feedback systems. This means they are only released when their store gets the right trigger – which may be a chemical in the blood or another hormone.
- **Major hormone sources** include the thyroid gland, the pituitary gland, the adrenal glands, the pancreas, a woman's ovaries and a man's testes.
- **The pituitary gland** is the source of many important hormones, including those that control growth and metabolism.
- **Adrenalin is released** by the adrenal glands to ready the body for action.
- **Insulin is a hormone** produced in the pancreas that helps control the level of glucose (sugar) in your bloodstream.
- **Oestrogen and progesterone** are female sex hormones that control a woman's monthly cycle.
- **Testosterone** is a male sex hormone that controls the workings of a man's sex organs.

◀ *When you are under pressure, adrenalin boosts your breathing and heartbeat, preparing your body for action.*

DNA

- **DNA** (deoxyribonucleic acid) is the molecule inside every cell in your body. It carries your genes.
- **Most of the time**, DNA is coiled up around tiny threads called chromosomes but, when needed, it unravels.
- **The structure** of DNA was first identified in 1953 by James Watson and Francis Crick, who announced that they had 'found the secret of life'.
- **DNA is shaped** in a double helix with linking bars, like a twisted rope ladder.
- **The bars** of DNA are four special chemicals called bases – guanine, adenine, cytosine and thymine.
- **Adenine** always pairs with thymine, and guanine always pairs with cytosine.
- **The bases** in DNA are arranged in groups of three, and the order of the bases in each group varies to provide a chemical code for the cell to make a particular amino acid.
- **When the cell** needs to make a new protein, the DNA 'unzips' and the groups of bases are matched by free bases, which make a copy of that part of the DNA.
- **The DNA copy** is then matched by amino acids in the cell, which join together to make a specific protein.
- **Because DNA** is responsible for making proteins, it is essential for growth, development and body function.
- **Each cell** contains about 2 m of DNA.

▼ *The sequence of bases along one strand of the DNA is a mirror image of the sequence on the other side. When the strand divides down the middle, each can be used like a template to make a copy.*

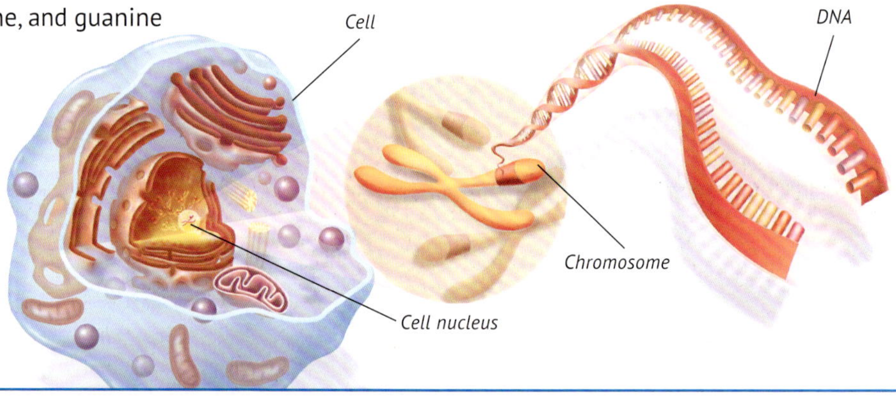

Chromosomes

- **Chromosomes** are the tiny threads inside every cell that carry your body's life instructions in chemical form.
- **There are 46 chromosomes** (in 23 pairs) in each of your body cells except red blood cells, which have no nucleus, and your sex cells (eggs or sperm), which have 23 chromosomes.
- **In human fertilization** a male and female sex cell join to make a fertilized egg that contains 46 chromosomes, 23 from the male and 23 from the female.
- **One chromosome from each pair** in your body cells came from your mother and the other from your father.
- **In a girl's 23 chromosome pairs**, each half matches the other (the set from the mother is equivalent to the set from the father). Boys have 22 matching chromosome pairs, but the 23rd pair consists of two odd chromosomes.
- **The 23rd chromosome pair** decides what sex you are, and the sex chromosomes are called X and Y. Girls have two X chromosomes, but boys have an X and a Y chromosome.
- **In every matching pair**, both chromosomes give your body life instructions for the same thing.

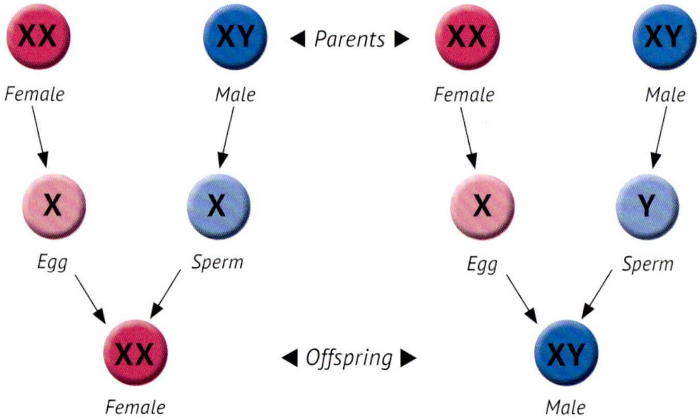

▲ *Offspring always inherit an X chromosome from their mother. If an X chromosome comes from the father, the offspring will be female (XX). If a Y chromosome comes from the father the offspring will be male (XY).*

- **The chemical instructions** on each chromosome come in thousands of different units called genes.
- **Genes for the same feature** appear in the same locus (place) on each matching pair of chromosomes in every human body cell. The entire pattern is called the genome.

DID YOU KNOW?

Different animals have different numbers of chromosomes. A dog has 78 and a horse has 64.

Genes

● **Genes are the body's chemical instructions** for your entire life – for growing up, surviving and having children.

● **Individual genes** are instructions to make particular proteins, the body's building-block molecules.

● **Small set of genes** control features such as the colour of your hair or your eyes, or create a particular body process such as digesting fat from food.

● **Each of your body cells** (apart from egg and sperm cells) carry identical sets of genes, because every one of your cells was made by other cells splitting in two, starting with the fertilized egg in your mother.

● **Your genes are a mixture**. Half come from your mother and half from your father, but none of your brothers or sisters will get the same combination, unless you are identical twins.

● **Genes instruct the human body** how to develop and carry out its life processes. It is our combination of genes that makes us unique.

▲ *The characteristics in this family group are clear to see, and have been passed on by DNA.*

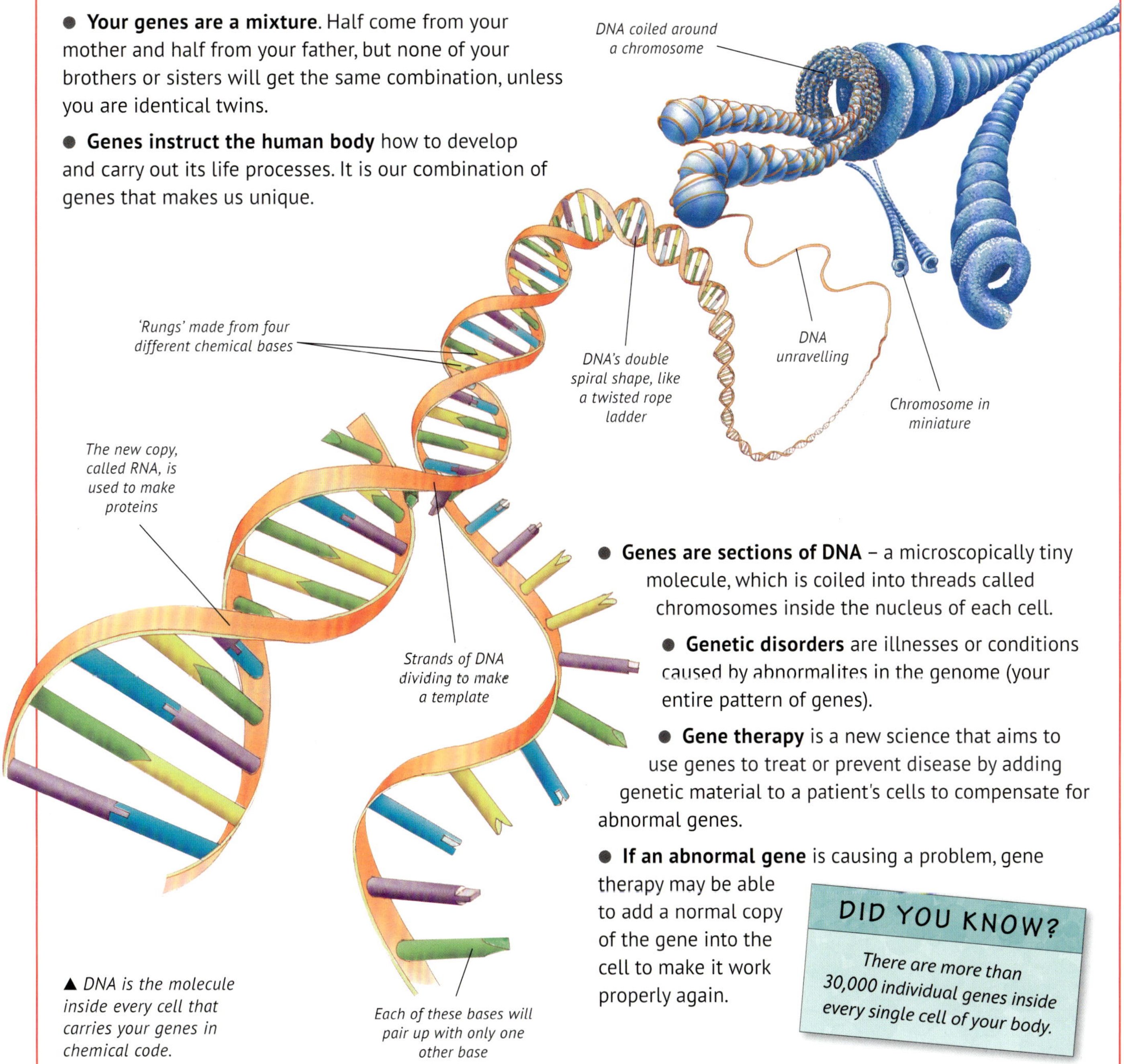

▲ *DNA is the molecule inside every cell that carries your genes in chemical code.*

● **Genes are sections of DNA** – a microscopically tiny molecule, which is coiled into threads called chromosomes inside the nucleus of each cell.

● **Genetic disorders** are illnesses or conditions caused by abnormalites in the genome (your entire pattern of genes).

● **Gene therapy** is a new science that aims to use genes to treat or prevent disease by adding genetic material to a patient's cells to compensate for abnormal genes.

● **If an abnormal gene** is causing a problem, gene therapy may be able to add a normal copy of the gene into the cell to make it work properly again.

DID YOU KNOW?

There are more than 30,000 individual genes inside every single cell of your body.

Heredity

- **Your heredity** is all the body characteristics you inherit from your parents – for example, your mother's hair colour.
- **Characteristics** are passed on by the genes carried on your chromosomes.
- **The basic laws** of heredity were discovered by the Austrian monk Gregor Mendel (1822–1884) around 150 years ago.
- **Your body characteristics** are a mix of two sets of instructions – one from your mother's chromosomes and the other from your father's.
- **Which genes** you have determine your characteristics such as hair colour, height, or shape of your nose.
- **Many characteristics** are determined not by a mixture of your parents' genes, but by one of the genes being stronger than the other, or 'dominant'. The dominant gene will affect your characteristic (be expressed), while the weaker 'recessive' gene won't.
- **A recessive gene** may be expressed when there is no competition – that is, when the genes from both of your parents are recessive.

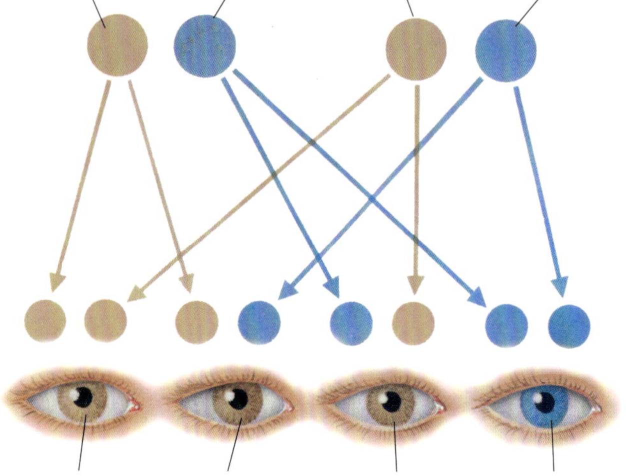

▲ *In this diagram, both parents have genes for brown and blue eyes. Brown eye genes are dominant.*

Puberty

- **Puberty is the stage** in life at which girls and boys mature sexually. The age of puberty varies, but on average it begins between 11 and 13 years.
- **Puberty begins** when two hormones – the follicle-stimulating hormone and the luteinizing hormone – are sent out by the pituitary gland.
- **Sexual development** concerns the development of primary and secondary sexual characteristics, and regulates all sex-related processes such as sperm and egg production.
- **There are three main types of sex hormones** – androgens, oestrogens and progesterones.
- **Androgens are male hormones** such as testosterone. Oestrogen is the female hormone made mainly in the ovaries.
- **Oestrogen** causes a girl's sexual organs to develop and controls her menstrual cycle.
- **Progesterone** is the female hormone that prepares a girl's uterus (womb) for pregnancy every month.

▶ *During puberty, glands in the skin produce extra sebum, a type of oil, that can block pores, causing spots.*

- **Primary sexual characteristics** are the internal organs that indicate whether someone is male or female – the ovaries and uterus in a girl and the testes and prostate gland in a boy.
- **Secondary sexual characteristics** are the external differences that develop during puberty that indicate whether someone is male or female. A girl's breasts develop, and hair grows under her arms and around her genitals. For a boy, hair grows on his face, under his arms and around his genitals.
- **A year or so after puberty begins**, a girl has her menarche (first menstrual period). When her periods are regular, she is able to have a baby.

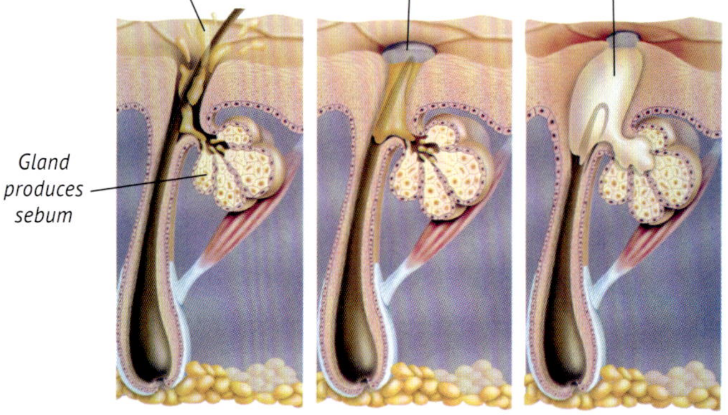

Ageing

● **Most people live** for between 60 and 100 years, although a few live even longer than this.

● **The longest officially confirmed** age is that of Frenchwoman Jeanne Calment, who died in 1997, aged 122 years and 164 days.

● **Life expectancy** is how long statistics suggest you are likely to live.

● **On average in Europe**, men can expect to live about 75 years and women about 80. However, because health is improving generally, people are living longer.

● **As adults grow older**, their bodies begin to deteriorate (fail). Senses such as hearing, sight and taste weaken.

● **Hair goes grey** as pigment (colour) cells stop working.

● **Muscles weaken** as fibres die.

● **Bones become more brittle** as calcium is lost. Cartilage shrinks between joints, causing stiffness.

● **Skin wrinkles** as the rubbery collagen fibres that support it start to sag. Exposure to sunlight speeds this process up, which is why the face and hands get wrinkles first.

▲ *Changes in health standards mean that more and more people than ever before are remaining fit in old age.*

DID YOU KNOW?

In the UK, there are more people aged over 60 than there are aged under 16.

● **With age**, circulation and breathing weaken. Blood vessels may become stiff and clogged, forcing the heart to work harder and raising blood pressure.

Male reproduction

● **A man's reproductive system** is where his body creates the sperm cells that combine with a female egg cell to create a new human life.

● **Sperm cells** look like tiny microscopic tadpoles.

● **They are made in the testes**, inside the scrotum, which hang outside the body where it is cooler, because this improves sperm production.

● **Sperm leave** the testes via the epididymis – a thin, coiled tube.

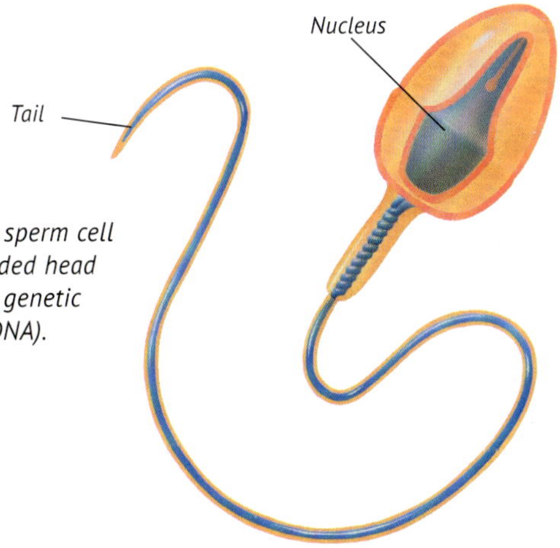

▶ *A single sperm cell has a rounded head containing genetic material (DNA).*

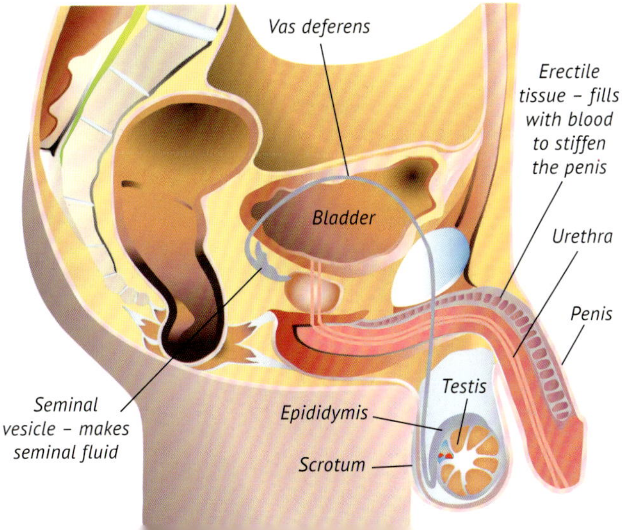

● **During sexual intercourse**, sperm are driven into a tube called the vas deferens and mix with a liquid called seminal fluid to make semen.

● **Semen** shoots through the urethra and is ejaculated into the woman's vagina.

● **The male sex hormone testosterone** is made in the testes. Testosterone stimulates bone and muscle growth, and the development of male characteristics such as facial hair and a deeper voice.

◀ *Side view showing the internal and external male reproductive organs.*

Female reproduction

● **A woman's reproductive system** is where her body stores, releases and nurtures the egg cells (ova) that create a new human life when joined with a male sperm cell.

● **All the egg cells** are stored from birth in the ovaries, which are two glands inside the pelvic region.

▼ *Side view of the female reproductive system, including the uterus (womb) which expands to accommodate a growing foetus.*

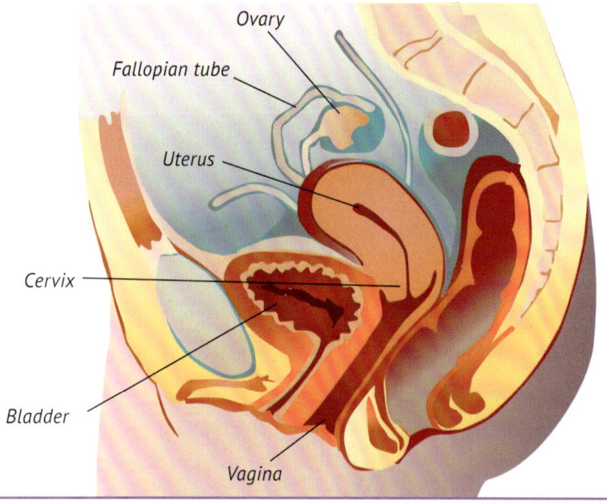

● **Each egg** is stored in a tiny sac called a follicle.

● **A monthly menstrual cycle** starts when the follicle-stimulating hormone (FSH) is sent by the pituitary gland in the brain to encourage follicles to grow.

● **As follicles grow**, they release the sex hormone oestrogen. Oestrogen makes the lining of the uterus (womb) thicken.

● **When an egg (ovum) is ripe**, it is released and moves down a duct called a fallopian tube.

● **One egg cell** is released every month by one of the ovaries.

● **If a woman** has sexual intercourse at this time, sperm from the man's penis may swim up her vagina, enter her womb and fertilize the egg in the fallopian tube.

● **If the egg is fertilized**, the womb lining continues to thicken ready for pregnancy, and the egg begins to develop into an embryo.

● **If the egg is not fertilized**, it is shed with the womb lining in a flow of blood from the vagina. This shedding is called a menstrual period.

Fertilization

● **Fertilization** – the beginning of a pregnancy – starts when an egg meets a sperm. They join together and implant in the uterus to grow into a new human being.

● **Every month**, an egg is released from a woman's ovary – this is called ovulation. The egg travels down the fallopian tube (part of the uterus).

● **If there are sperm** in the tube, following sexual intercourse, the egg may become fertilized by one of them. This usually leads to pregnancy and a baby being born nine months later.

● **A woman** can do a test to see if she is pregnant. It is usually done on a sample of her urine.

● **The pregnancy test** looks for a hormone called human gonadotrophin (HCG), which starts to be produced around six days after the egg is fertilized.

● **The new baby** gets genes from both its parents. The egg and sperm carry half the usual number of chromosomes, so that when they merge the new baby will have the right number.

● **The baby** will have some characteristics like its mother and some like its father.

● **If a woman** finds that she does not become pregnant it is called infertility. Doctors can often help to treat this.

● **One way to treat infertility** is with IVF (in vitro fertilization) – the doctor takes an egg out of the woman and fertilizes it with sperm in a laboratory.

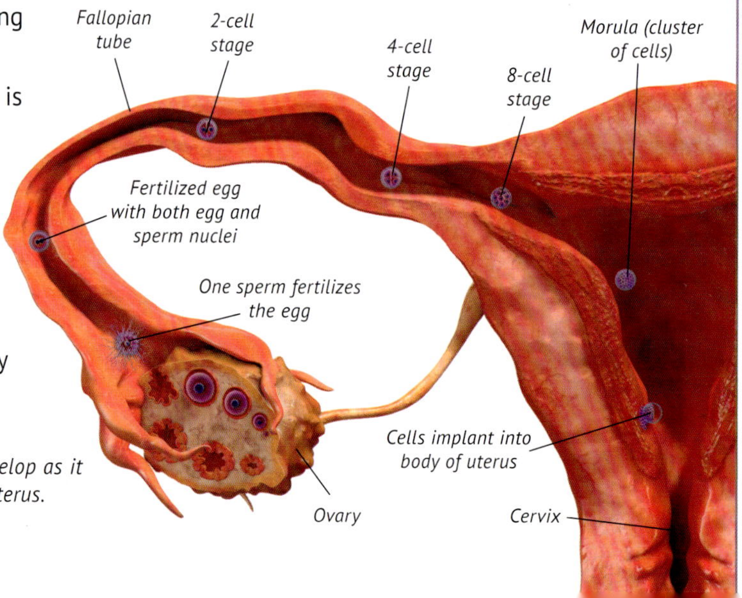

▶ *After fertilization the fertilized egg begins to divide and develop as it moves down the fallopian tube to implant in the body of the uterus.*

Pregnancy

● **Pregnancy begins** when a woman's ovum (egg cell) is fertilized by a man's sperm cell. Usually this happens after sexual intercourse, but it can begin in a laboratory.

● **When a woman becomes pregnant** her monthly menstrual periods stop. Tests on her urine show that she is pregnant.

● **During pregnancy**, the fertilized egg divides again and again to grow rapidly – first to an embryo (the first eight weeks), and then to a foetus (from eight weeks until birth).

● **By eight weeks** all the organs have formed in the developing baby.

● **Pregnancy lasts** nine months, and the time is divided into three trimesters (periods of about 12 weeks).

DID YOU KNOW?

An ultrasound scan uses a pen-like probe moved over the skin of the abdomen to show an image of the unborn baby on a screen.

● **The foetus** lies cushioned in its mother's uterus (womb) in a bag of fluid called the amniotic sac.

● **The mother's blood** passes food and oxygen to the foetus via the placenta, which is an organ attached to the lining of the womb during a pregnancy.

● **The umbilical cord** runs between the foetus and the placenta, carrying blood, oxygen and nutrients between them.

● **During pregnancy** a woman gains 30 percent more blood, and her heart rate goes up. Her breasts grow and develop milk glands.

At two months the main body parts are formed

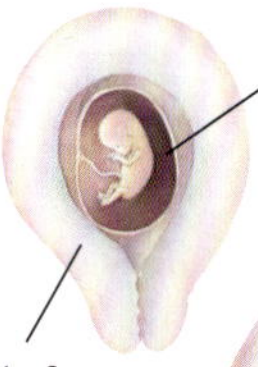

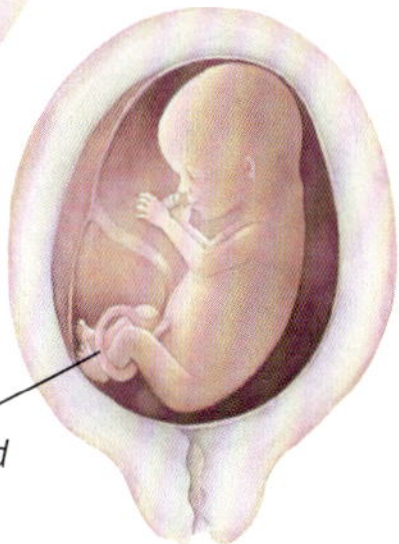

At three months the bones of the skeleton start to form

At five months the baby begins to move and kick

At seven months the baby can open its eyes

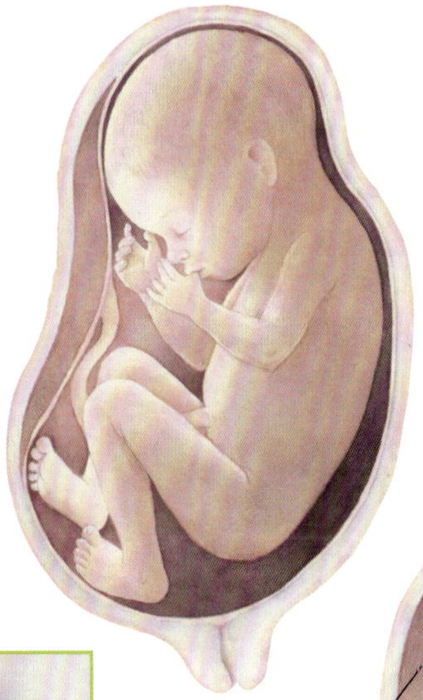

◀ *At first the tiny baby has plenty of room in the womb and can float about freely. But as it grows it becomes more cramped and has to bend its neck, back, arms and legs.*

At nine months the baby has usually 'turned' and is head down, ready to be born

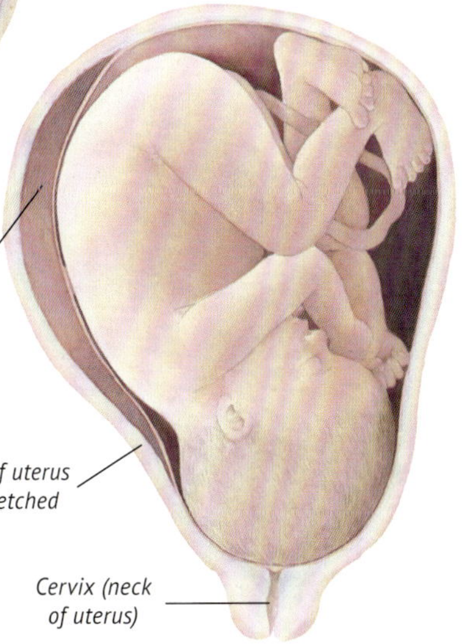

▼ *Being born can take an hour or two – or a whole day or two. It is very tiring for both the baby and its mother.*

Birth

- **Babies are usually born** 38 to 42 weeks after the mother becomes pregnant.
- **Usually a few days** or weeks before a baby is born, it turns in the uterus (womb) so its head is pointing down towards the mother's birth canal (her cervix and vagina).
- **Birth begins** as the mother goes into labour – when the womb muscles begin a rhythm of contracting (tightening) and relaxing in order to push the baby out through the birth canal.
- **There are three stages** of labour. In the first, the womb muscles begin to pull on the cervix to make it thinner and the opening wider in preparation for the second stage.
- **In the second stage** of labour, the baby is pushed out through the birth canal. Then the umbilical cord – its lifeline to its mother – is cut and the baby starts to breathe on its own.
- **In the third stage** of labour, the placenta comes out through the birth canal. It is often called the 'afterbirth'.
- **A premature baby** is one that is born more than three weeks early. It may not be fully developed and so will need to be carefully looked after for a while in hospital.
- **A miscarriage** occurs when the developing baby is born before it is old enough to survive.
- **A Caesarian section** is an operation that is carried out when a baby can't be born through the birth canal and emerges from the womb through a cut made in the mother's belly.

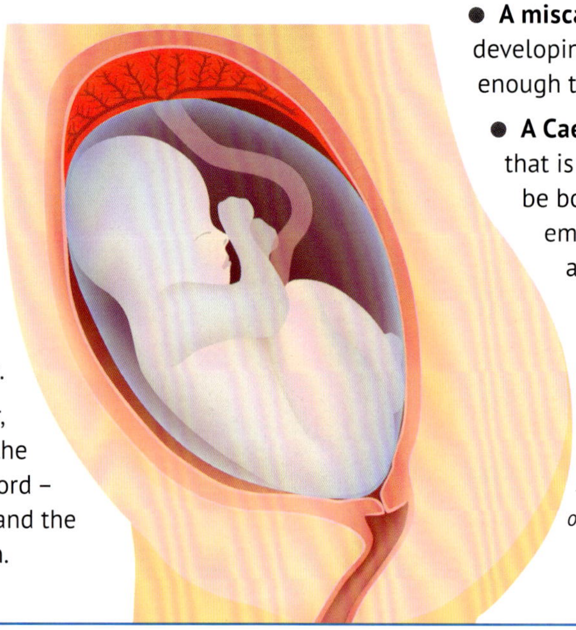

◀ *In a breech birth the baby comes out bottom first instead of head first.*

Babies

- **Newborn babies** usually weigh about 3–4 kg and are about 50 cm in length.
- **A baby's head** is three-quarters of the size it will be as an adult – and a quarter of its total body height.
- **The bones of a baby's skeleton** are made of cartilage when they first form and are gradually replaced by bone.
- **The order** in which the bones of the baby's body harden follows a set pattern.
- **Baby boys grow faster** than baby girls during the first seven months.
- **A baby** has a very developed sense of taste, with taste buds all over the inside of its mouth.
- **The sense of smell** is stronger in babies than adults – perhaps to help them identify their mother.

DID YOU KNOW?

A baby's brain is one of the fastest growing parts of its body.

- **A baby's body weight** will usually triple in its first year.
- **Primitive reflexes** are those that we are born with, such as grasping or sucking a finger.
- **A baby seems to learn** to control its body in stages, starting first with its head, then moving on to its arms and legs.

▶ *Babies learn to walk when their leg muscles grow strong enough, usually between nine and 15 months.*

The immune system

- **The immune system** is the complicated system of defences that your body uses to prevent or fight off attack from germs and other invaders.
- **Your body** has a variety of barriers, toxic chemicals and booby traps to stop germs entering it.
- **The skin is a barrier** that stops many germs getting in, as long as it is not broken.
- **Mucus is a thick, slimy fluid** that coats vulnerable internal parts of your body such as your stomach. It also acts as a lubricant (oil), making swallowing easier.
- **Mucus lines your airways and lungs** to protect them from smoke particles as well as from germs. Your airways may fill up with mucus when you have a cold, as your body tries to minimize the invasion of airborne germs.
- **Itching, sneezing, coughing** and vomiting are your body's ways of getting rid of unwelcome invaders. Small particles that get trapped in the mucus lining of your airways are wafted out by tiny hairs called cilia.
- **The body** has many specialized cells and chemicals that fight germs that get inside it.
- **Complement** is a mixture of liquid proteins in the blood that attacks bacteria.
- **Interferons** are proteins that help the body's cells to attack viruses and also stimulate killer cells (a type of lymphocyte).
- **Certain white blood cells** are cytotoxic, which means that they kill invaders.
- **Phagocytes** are big white blood cells that swallow up invaders and then use an enzyme to dissolve them. They are drawn to the site of an infection whenever there is inflammation.

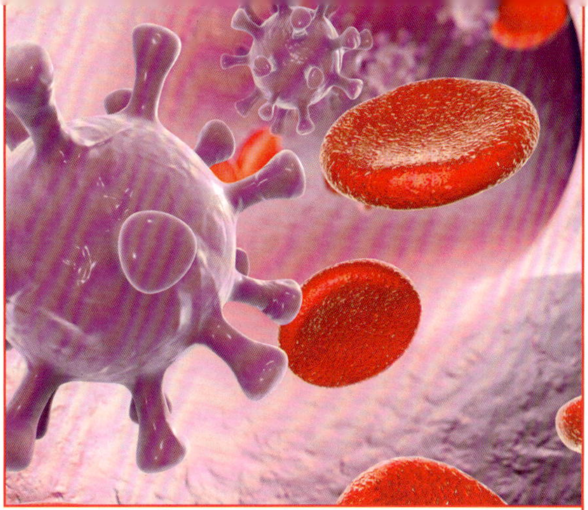

▲ *HIV, the AIDS virus, attacks the body's immune cells and prevents them dealing with infections.*

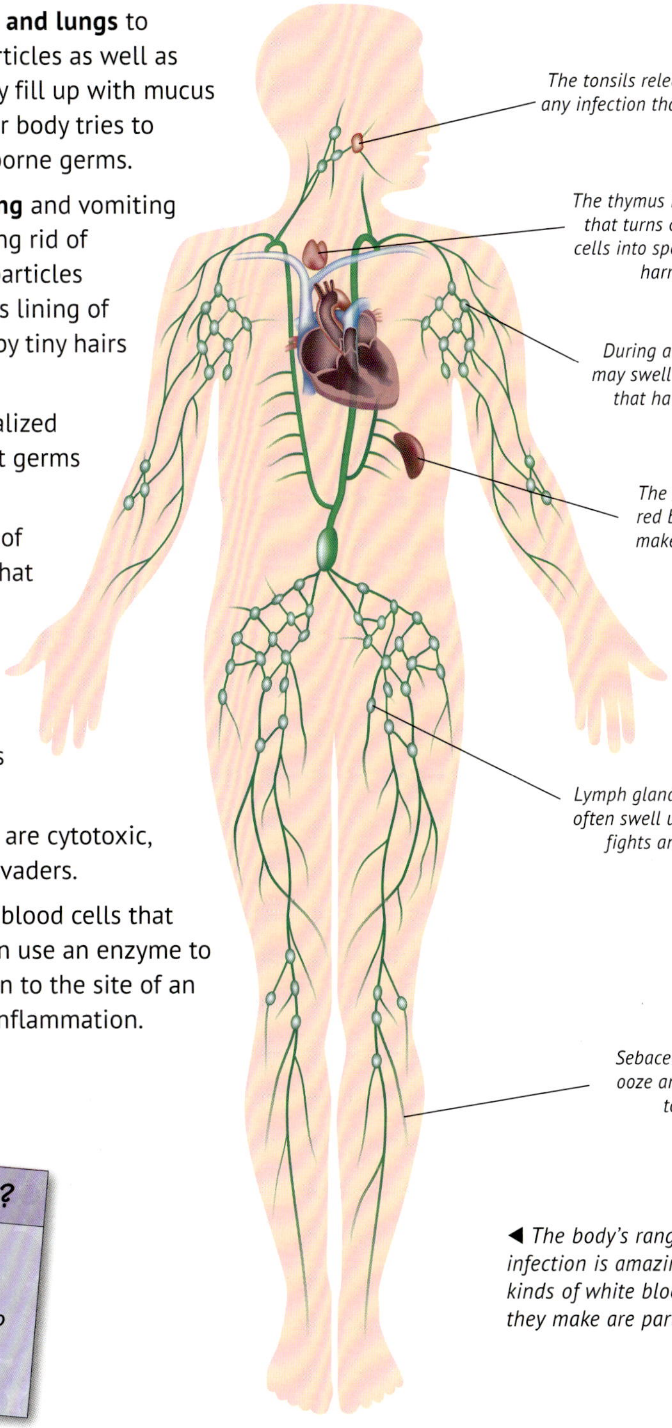

◀ *The body's range of interior defences against infection is amazingly complex. The various kinds of white blood cells and the antibodies they make are particularly important.*

DID YOU KNOW?

Your vulnerable eyes are protected by tears that wash away germs. Tears also contain an enzyme called lysozome that kills bacteria.

The lymphatic system

- **The lymphatic system** is a network of tubes that drains the fluid around the body's cells back into the bloodstream.
- **The 'pipes' of the lymphatic system** are called lymphatics or lymph vessels.
- **The lymph vessels** are filled with a liquid called lymph fluid that, along with bacteria and waste chemicals, drains from body tissues such as muscles.
- **The lymphatic system** has no pump to make it circulate. Instead, lymphatic fluid is circulated as a side effect of the heartbeat and muscle movement.
- **At places in the lymphatic system** there are tiny lumps called nodes. These are filters that trap germs that have got into the lymph fluid.
- **In the nodes**, armies of white blood cells called lymphocytes neutralize or destroy germs.
- **When you have a cold** or any other infection, the lymph nodes in your neck or groin, or under your arm, may swell, as lymphocytes fight germs.
- **Lymph fluid** drains back into the blood via the body's main vein, the superior vena cava.
- **The lymphatic system** is not only the lymphatics and lymph nodes, but includes the spleen, the thymus, the tonsils and the adenoids.
- **On average**, at any time about 1–2 l of lymph fluid circulates in the lymphatics and body tissues.

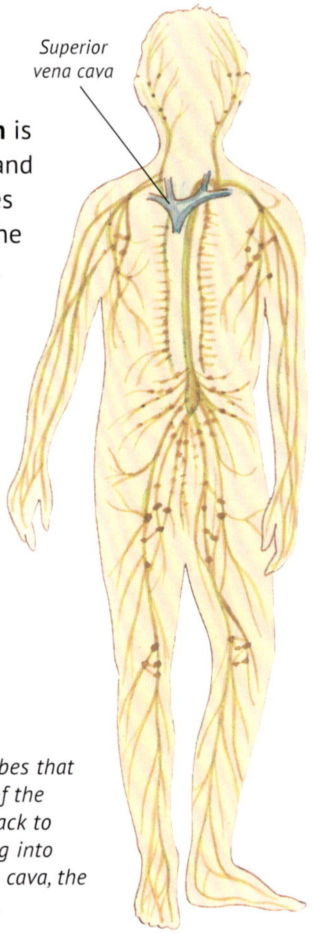

▶ The lymphatic system is a branching network of little tubes that extends to nearly every part of the body. It drains surplus fluid back to the centre of the body, running into branches of the superior vena cava, the body's main vein to the heart.

Lymphocytes

- **Lymphocytes are white blood cells** that are involved in the immune system. There are two kinds of lymphocyte – B lymphocytes (B-cells) and T lymphocytes (T-cells).
- **B-cells** develop into plasma cells that make antibodies to attack bacteria and some viruses.
- **T-cells** work against viruses and other micro-organisms that hide inside body cells, helping to identify and destroy these invaded cells or their products. They also attack certain bacteria.
- **There are two kinds of T-cell** – killer T-cells and helper T-cells.
- **Helper T-cells** identify invaded cells and send out chemicals called lymphokines as an alarm, telling killer T-cells to multiply.
- **Invaded cells** give themselves away by abnormal proteins on their surface.
- **Killer T-cells** lock on to the cells identified by the helpers, then move in and destroy them.
- **Some B-cells**, called memory B-cells, stay for a long time, ready for a further attack by the same organism.

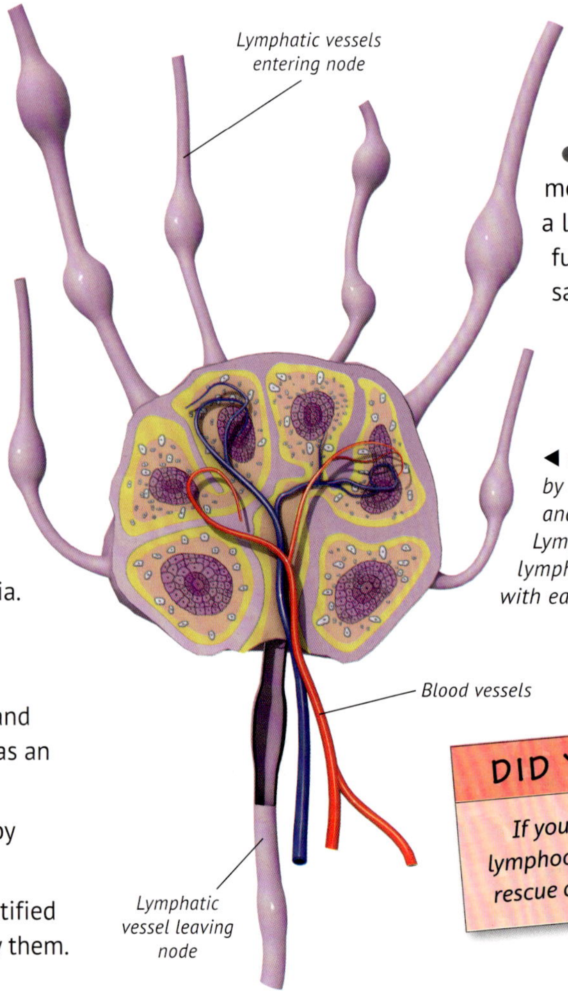

◀ Lymph nodes are supplied by both blood vessels and lymphatic vessels. Lymphocytes enter and leave lymph nodes, communicating with each other as they do so.

DID YOU KNOW?

If you get flu, it is your T lymphocytes that come to the rescue and fight off the virus.

Antibodies

- **Antibodies** are tiny proteins that make germs vulnerable to attack by white blood cells called phagocytes.
- **Human beings** each generate around ten billion different antibodies.
- **They are produced** by white blood cells derived from B lymphocytes.
- **There are thousands** of different kinds of B-cells in the blood, and each produces antibodies against a particular germ.

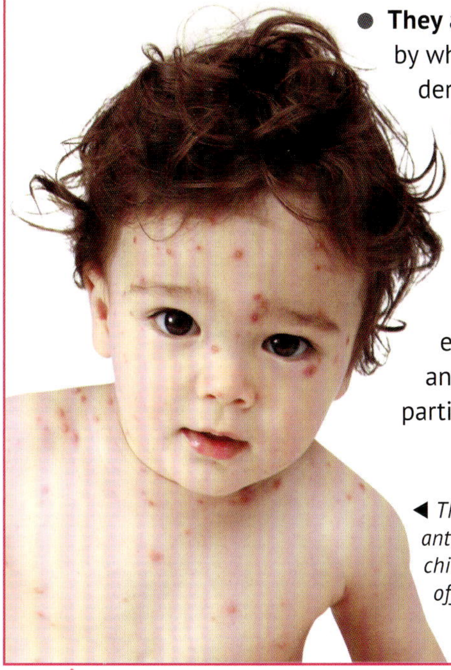

◀ *The body makes antibodies to the chickenpox virus to fight off the illness.*

- **Normally, only a few B-cells** carry a particular antibody. But when an invading germ is detected, the correct B-cell multiplies rapidly to release antibodies.
- **Invaders are identified** when your body's immune system recognizes proteins on their surface as foreign. Any foreign protein is called an antigen.
- **Your body was armed** from birth with antibodies for germs it had never met. This is called innate immunity.
- **If your body** comes across a germ it has no antibodies for, it makes some and leaves behind memory cells that can be activated if the germ invades again. This is known as acquired immunity.
- **Acquired immunity** means you only suffer once from some infections, such as chickenpox. This is also how vaccination works.
- **Allergies are sensitivity reactions** that happen in the body when too many antibodies are produced, or when they are produced to attack harmless antigens.
- **Autoimmune diseases** are ones in which the body forms antibodies against its own tissue cells.

Allergies

- **Allergies occur** when your body produces too many antibodies or produces antibodies against normally harmless antigens. They cause inflammation.
- **It is not known** why some people get allergies and some do not but they often occur in families. You are more likely to get an allergy if your parents, brothers or sisters have an allergy.
- **Hay fever** is an allergy to pollen and causes sneezing, watery and itchy eyes and a runny nose.
- **Trees, flowers and grasses** all produce pollen, and people with hay fever may be allergic to one or several types of pollen.

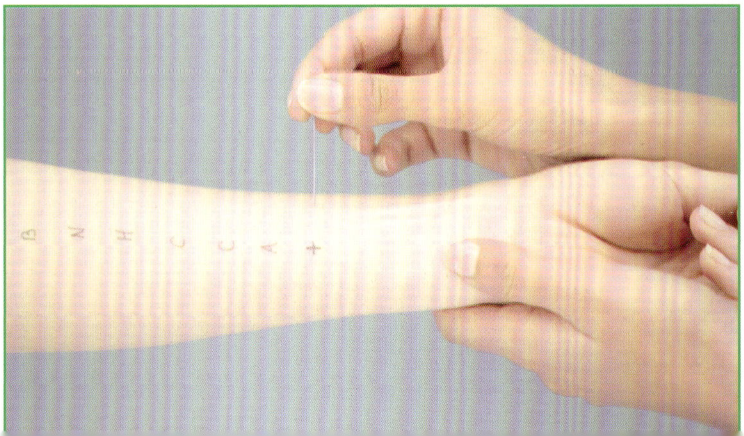

DID YOU KNOW?

Hay fever got its name because it was first noticed in farmworkers who were harvesting hay.

- **Some people** are allergic to dust. This can cause hay fever-like symptoms such as sneezing all year round.
- **Pet fur**, nickel in jewellery, chemicals in soaps or perfumes and some foods are all common causes of allergic reactions.
- **Most allergies** are minor but some are life threatening. A severe allergic reaction may cause the mouth and throat to swell up, causing problems with breathing. This is called an anaphylactic reaction.
- **An anaphylactic reaction** may be caused by any substance if someone is allergic to it. Insect stings, some antibiotics and some foods such as peanuts are common antigens.
- **Someone with a severe allergy** usually carries drugs that prevent or treat an anaphylactic reaction.

◀ *During a scratch test, substances that might cause allergies are scratched onto the skin. If a reaction occurs the patient is allergic to that substance.*

Vaccination

● **Vaccination** helps protect against infectious disease by exposing you to a mild or dead version of the germ in order to get your body to build up protection, in the form of antibodies.

● **Vaccination** is also called immunization, because it builds up your 'immunity' (resistance) to disease.

● **In passive immunization** you are injected with substances such as antibodies that have been made by someone exposed to the germ. This gives instant but short-term protection.

● **In active immunization** you are given a harmless version of the germ. Your body makes the antibodies itself for long-term protection.

● **Children in many countries** are given a series of vaccinations as they grow up, to protect them from serious diseases. Sometimes a number of different vaccines may be combined so that children do not have to have multiple injections.

● **If you travel abroad** you may have to have additional vaccinations against diseases that do not normally occur in your own country, such as yellow fever, rabies and typhoid.

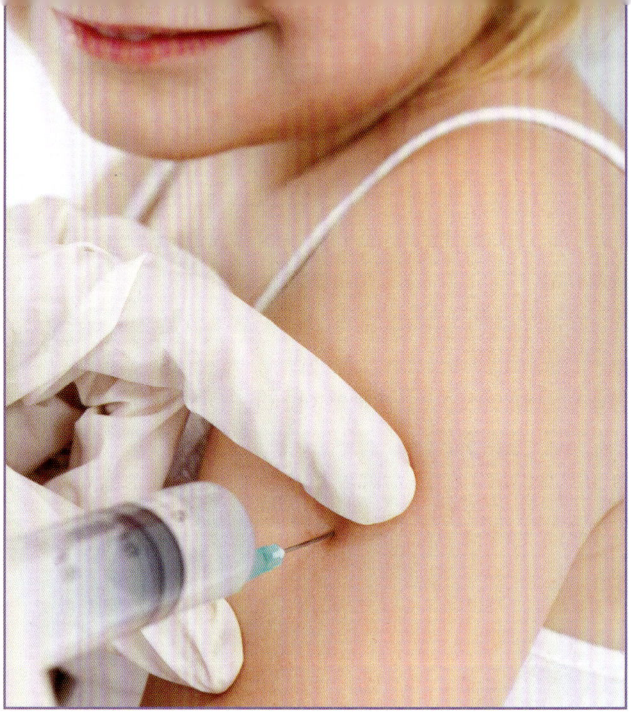

▲ *Diseases such as diphtheria and whooping cough are now rare in many countries thanks to vaccination.*

● **There is a small risk** of a serious reaction against a vaccine. The risks of not being vaccinated and getting the disease are usually much greater.

● **A new flu vaccine** is developed every year to protect against the current strain of the disease.

Types of disease

● **A disease** is something that upsets the normal working of any living thing.

● **It can be acute** (sudden, but short-lived), chronic (long-lasting), malignant (spreading) or benign (not spreading).

● **Some diseases** are classified by the body part they affect (such as heart disease), or by the body activity they affect (such as respiratory, or breathing, disease).

● **Heart disease** is the most common cause of death in the USA, Europe and also Australia.

● **Some diseases** are classified by their cause. These include the diseases caused by the staphylococcus bacteria – pneumonia is one such disease.

● **Contagious diseases** are caused by germs such as bacteria and viruses. They include the common cold, polio, flu and measles. Their spread can be controlled by good sanitation and hygiene, and also by vaccination programmes.

● **Non-contagious diseases** may be inherited or they may be caused by such things as eating harmful substances, poor nutrition or hygiene, or being injured.

DID YOU KNOW?

The most common disease in the world is tooth decay – so remember to brush your teeth!

● **Non-contagious diseases** may also be caused by body cells acting wrongly and attacking the body's own tissues. This type of disease is called an autoimmune disease.

● **Degenerative diseases** occur in older people as the body's tissues start to get older and either do not function normally or gradually disappear.

● **Endemic diseases** are diseases that occur in a particular area of the world, such as sleeping sickness in Africa.

● **Diseases can be** either contagious (passed on by contact) or non-contagious.

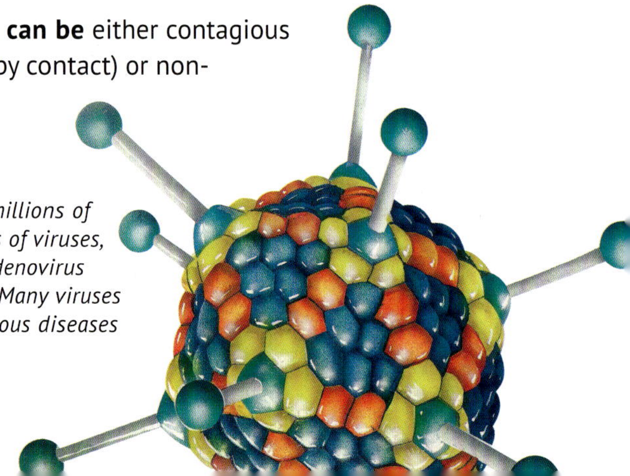

▶ *There are millions of different types of viruses, such as the adenovirus (shown here). Many viruses can cause serious diseases in humans.*

Bacteria

▲ *These rod-shaped bacteria have hairs so they can stick to other cells, and tail-like projections to help them move.*

- **Bacteria** are single-celled organisms. They are found almost everywhere in huge numbers, and multiply rapidly.
- **There are thousands** of different types of bacteria but most are harmless. Some even do us good.
- **Bacteria can be divided** into three groups – cocci are round cells, spirilla are coil-shaped, and bacilli are rod-shaped.
- **Bacteria usually cause disease** by producing harmful chemicals called toxins. The toxins enter cells in the body and destroy them.
- **Some types of bacteria** do not produce toxins but enter body cells instead.
- **Once the bacteria** are in the cells they multiply until they burst the cell. All the new bacteria then find new cells to enter.
- **Bacteria commonly cause infections** that affect the airways and lungs. Tuberculosis is caused by bacteria.
- **Bacteria also cause diseases** such as tetanus and typhoid. Bacteria that enter the bloodstream can cause blood poisoning.
- **The 'Black Death'** that killed millions of people in Europe in the 1340s was actually a bacterial infection called the bubonic plague.
- **Antibiotics** are drugs that are used to treat bacterial infections. These kill the bacteria in the body or stop then multiplying so that the body has a chance to destroy them.
- **However, over time** bacteria can fight back and develop resistance to some antibiotics. Scientists are constantly working hard to find new antibiotics to treat disease.

Viruses

DID YOU KNOW?

There are more than 200 types of virus that can cause a common cold.

- **Millions of viruses** can fit inside a single cell. They are the smallest living organisms in the world.
- **Viruses can only live** and multiply by taking over other cells – they cannot survive on their own.
- **They consist of** genetic material surrounded by a protective coat.
- **Viruses cause disease** by entering body cells. Once inside a cell they reproduce and leave the cell to go on and infect more cells.

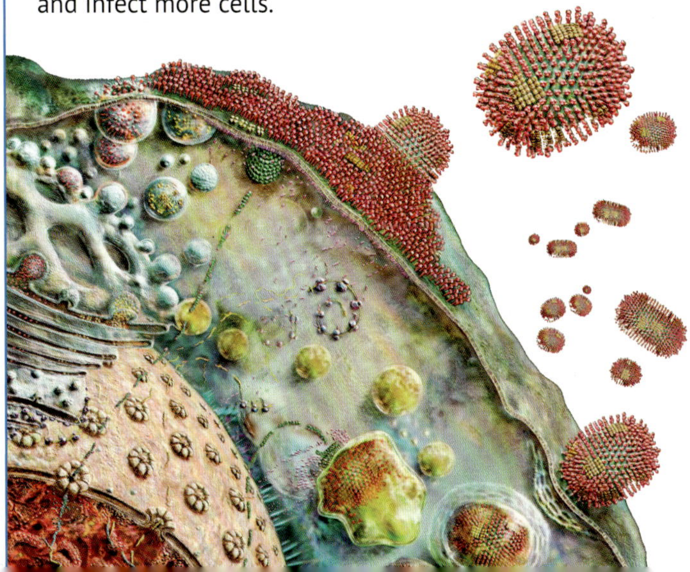

- **Common diseases** such as colds, flu, mumps, measles and chickenpox are all caused by viruses.
- **Viruses also cause** severe infections such as AIDS and fevers associated with bleeding.
- **Viral infections** can often be prevented by vaccinations.
- **An epidemic occurs** if many more people than usual get a viral infection. A pandemic occurs if the epidemic affects people around the world.
- **In 1918**, a flu virus infected about a third of the world's population and it is thought that about 50 million people died.
- **Doctors worry** that this might happen again with a different type of flu virus.
- **Antibiotics do not work against viruses** because viruses are much smaller than bacteria and work in a different way.

◀ *Once a virus has entered a body cell, it replicates and then leaves the cell to infect more cells.*

1000 PREHISTORIC LIFE FACTS

Beginnings of life

- **About 4600 million years ago (mya),** like the rest of the Solar System, the Earth formed from swirling gas, dust and rocks in space.
- **Early Earth had violent storms,** volcanoes and meteorite bombardments as the mountains, valleys, seas and oceans formed.
- **Gradually conditions calmed down** and the early atmosphere of air came into being, although it was poisonous to life as we know it today.
- **The first signs of preserved life-forms** – fossils – date from about 3500 mya, but they are only tiny specks in the rocks.
- **Experts debate** whether the remains are from small soft-bodied organisms or if they can be explained by natural features of rock formation.
- **The first living things** were probably simple single cells similar to today's bacteria and cyanobacteria (blue-green algae).
- **They would have appeared in the water,** as hostile atmospheric conditions and bare rock prevented life from forming on land.
- **Those early life-forms,** or organisms, probably gained energy from sunlight or from chemical sources in the sea.
- **Some idea of how they grew** can be gained from stromatolites that still form today.
- **Stromatolites are stony structures** in warm, shallow water made from small particles of rock cemented together by cyanobacteria and other microbes.

▼ Early life may have looked like today's stromatolites – low-domed or flat-topped stony mounds that grow in shallow coastal waters. They are formed by microbes mixed with fragments of rock minerals.

Earliest plants

- **Among the very first living things** on Earth were single-celled bacteria and cyanobacteria, also known as blue-green algae.
- **Blue-green algae emerged** as long ago as 3500 mya.
- **These algae** contain chlorophyll and were the first living organisms to photosynthesize (make energy from sunlight).

- **Photosynthesis** also produces oxygen. Over millions of years, the blue-green algae produced enough oxygen to enable more complex life forms to develop.

DID YOU KNOW?

Liverworts grew on mats of blue-green algae, which trapped nitrogen from the air. Liverworts used this nitrogen to grow.

- **True algae,** which are usually regarded as plants, developed more than 1500 mya.
- **By about 550 mya,** multi-celled plants had begun to appear, including simple seaweeds.
- **Algae and lichens** were the first plants to appear on land.
- **Bryophytes** (mosses and liverworts) emerged on land by around 400 mya. They are simple green seedless plants.
- **Unlike vascular plants,** which emerged later, bryophytes cannot grow high above the ground because they do not have strengthened stems.

◀ Lichens can survive in many places where other plants would die, such as the Arctic, on mountaintops and in deserts. Some Arctic lichens are over 4000 years old.

Prehistoric timescale

● **Earth's immense history is divided** into huge spans of time known as eras. These are drawn on a chart showing how long ago they occurred, in millions of years.

● **The main eras for living things** are Paleozoic or 'ancient life', Mesozoic or 'middle life', and Cenozoic or 'recent life'.

● **The eras are divided into periods**. For example the Mesozoic Era comprises the Triassic, Jurassic and Cretaceous Periods.

● **Each period is named after a feature** of the main rocks formed at that time. For example, the Jurassic Period is named after rocks from the Jura Mountains, part of the European Alps.

● **The last period**, the Quaternary, covers 2.6 mya to the present day.

● **The Quaternary Period** includes the most recent group of ice ages, the last one being at its coldest just 21,000 years ago.

● **Each period** is further divided into epochs. The Quaternary Period is made up of the Pleistocene and Holocene epochs.

● **We are still living in** the Holocene Epoch, which began approximately 11,700 years ago.

▲ *Dinosaurs roamed Earth during the Mesozoic Era. They were all extinct by the end of the Cretaceous Period.*

▶ *Periods in Earth's prehistory. The Cambrian to Permian make up the Paleozoic Era ('ancient life'), Triassic to Cretaceous make up the Mesozoic Era ('middle life'), and the Paleogene to Quaternary make up the Cenozoic Era ('recent/new life').*

Vascular plants

- **Vascular plants are more suited** to living on drier land than mosses and liverworts.
- **They have branching stems** with tube-like pipes (vascular bundles) that carry water and nutrients.
- **These stems and tubes** also mean the plants can stand tall. Early vascular plants had spores (reproductive cells, like seeds) – the taller the plant the more widely it could disperse its spores.
- **One of the first known** vascular plants was *Cooksonia*. It was about 5 cm tall, with a forked stem.
- **Scientists called palaeontologists** discovered fossil remains of *Cooksonia* in Wales. Palaeontologists study fossils of prehistoric plants and animals to see how they lived and evolved.
- **Rhynie in Scotland** is one site where lots of vascular plant fossils have been found.
- **The plants at Rhynie** would have grown on the sandy edges of pools in the Early Devonian Period (about 410 mya).
- **One plant fossil** found at Rhynie is *Aglaophyton*, which stood around 45 cm high.

▶ *The* Cooksonia *plant had forked stems ending in spore-filled caps. The earliest examples of* Cooksonia *have been found in Ireland, dating to around 430 mya.*

- ***Aglaophyton*** had underground roots and tissues that supported the plant stem. It also had water-carrying tubes and stomata (tiny openings) that allowed air and water to pass through.
- **Land-living plants** were essential for providing conditions for animals to make the transition from the seas to land. They created soil, food and ground cover for shelter.

Angiosperms

- **Angiosperms are flowering plants**. They produce seeds within an ovary, which is contained within a flower.
- **These plants** first appeared about 140 mya.
- **The earliest evidence** of flowering plants comes from the fossil remains of leaves and pollen grains.
- **Plant experts** used to think that magnolias were one of the first angiosperms, but they now think that an extinct plant called *Archaefructus* was older. It lived about 125 mya.

◀ *An* Archaefructus *plant, which is one of the earliest known examples of an angiosperm. The* Archaefructus *fossil, which may be around 125 million years old, has a number of angiosperm features including enclosed seeds and flowers.*

- **Fossil remains** of *Archaefructus* were discovered in northeast China in the mid to late 1990s.
- **By 100 mya**, angiosperms had developed into many dozens of families of flowering plants, most of which still survive today.
- **By 60 mya**, angiosperms had taken over from gymnosperms as the dominant plants on Earth.
- **The start of the Paleogene Period** (around 66 mya) saw a rise in temperatures that produced the right conditions for tropical rainforests.
- **It was in the rainforests** that angiosperms evolved into many different types of plants.
- **Angiosperms were successful** because they could grow very quickly, they had very extensive root systems to anchor them and take up water and nutrients, and they could grow in a greater range of environments than other plants, such as gymnosperms.

DID YOU KNOW?

The word angiosperm comes from the Greek terms angeion, meaning 'vessel', and sperma, meaning 'seed'.

Gymnosperms

- **Gymnosperms are plants** that produce exposed seeds on the surface of structures such as cones.
- **The word gymnosperm** comes from two Greek words: *gymnos*, meaning 'naked', and *sperma*, meaning 'seed'.
- **These plants** had appeared by 320 mya. They probably developed from early plants such as *Cooksonia*.
- **Gymnosperms** grew well in the damp, tropical forests of the Late Carboniferous Period (359–299 mya).

▲ *Conifer trees have needle-like leaves and make their seeds in cones rather than in flowers.*

◀ *Cycads have fern-like leaves growing in a circle around the end of the stem. New leaves sprout each year and last for several years.*

- **One extinct gymnosperm** is *Glossopteris*, which some palaeontologists believe was similar to the ancestors of later flowering plants.
- **Together with ferns** and horsetails (a type of herb), gymnosperms dominated landscapes during the Mesozoic Era (252–66 mya).
- **In the Jurassic Period** (201–145 mya), plant-eating dinosaurs ate their way through huge areas of coniferous forest.
- **Today, conifers are found** most often in cold or dry areas, to which they are well adapted.

- **Varieties of gymnosperms** include conifers, cycads and seed-ferns.
- **Cycads are palm-like plants** with feathery tops. They were more common in prehistoric times than they are today.
- **One type of cycad** is the maidenhair tree, *Ginkgo biloba*. It still grows in towns and cities, but is now very rare in the wild.

▶ *This* Araucaria, *or monkey puzzle tree, is a type of conifer that dates back to the Jurassic Period.*

▶ *Also known as maidenhair trees, ginkgos are an ancient type of plant with fan-shaped leaves and fleshy yellow seeds.*

The first invertebrates

DID YOU KNOW?

Spriggina has a curved, shield-like end to one part of its body. Some palaeontologists think this was its head, while others think it was an anchor that secured it to the seabed.

- **An invertebrate is an animal** that does not have a spinal column. Invertebrates were the first animals to live on Earth, in the prehistoric seas.
- **The very first animal-like** organisms that fed on other organisms or organic matter were single-celled and sometimes called protists.
- **Only prehistoric protists** with hard parts survive as fossils. The earliest fossils are more than 600 million years old.
- **One of the earliest known fossils** that could be a multi-celled animal is around 600 million years old. Called *Mawsonites*, it may have been a primitive jellyfish or worm – or the remains of a burrow or colony of microbes.
- **Some early invertebrate fossils** are from now-extinct groups of animals.
- **Some of these animals** had segmented bodies that looked a bit like quilts.
- **One such invertebrate** is *Spriggina*, named after geologist Reg Sprigg. In 1946, he discovered 550-million-year-old fossil remains near Ediacara in southern Australia.

- **Palaeontologists** have unearthed the fossils of many other invertebrates that resemble jellyfish from Ediacara.
- **Another famous invertebrate** discovery was made by Roger Mason, an English schoolboy, in 1957. This was the fossil of *Charnia*, an animal that was similar to a living sea pen.

◀ Charnia *was a prehistoric animal that grew in feather-like colonies attached to the seabed, like living sea pens.* Charnia *fossils date to more than 500 mya.*

Corals

- **Corals are the simplest living animals**. They have no brain, nerves, eyes or stomach.
- **Despite being so simple**, corals are very common in seas and oceans around the world, from warm tropical shallows to deep cold, water.
- **Most coral animals**, called polyps, look like tiny sea anemones, with a stalk topped by a ring of tentacles. They sting and catch tiny prey to pull into the opening at the top of the stalk.
- **Most corals also form** hard cup-like structures around themselves, from stony minerals they take from sea water. Over thousands of years these 'skeletons' build up into amazingly shaped formations we call coral reefs.

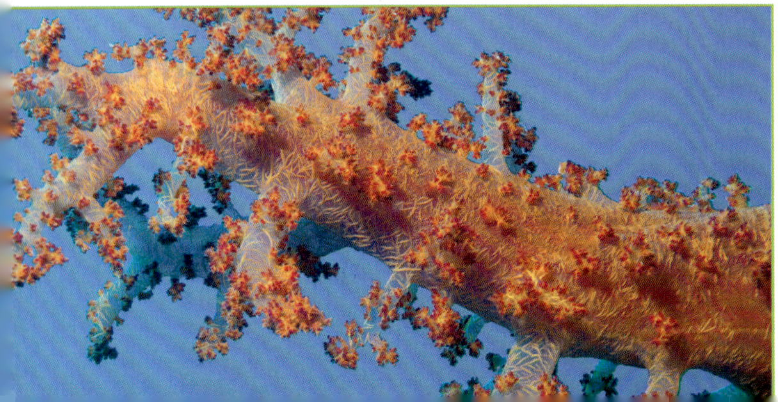

- **The rocky formations of ancient corals** have left many wonderful fossils, showing how these simple creatures lived in the seas millions of years ago.
- ***Halysites* was a type of tabulate coral**, whose rocky shapes look like layers and piles of six-sided bee honeycombs. It lived mainly during the Silurian Period, 443–419 mya.
- ***Halysites* is also called chain coral**, from the way its colony members grew next to each other – their fossils look like links in a chain.
- **Another tabulate coral was *Syringopora***, which survived to the Carboniferous Period, over 300 mya. Tabulate corals are now all extinct.
- **Rugose corals are also now extinct**. Some lived alone rather than in groups and made horn-shaped living chambers, such as *Caninia*.
- **The modern group of corals**, called scleractinians, appeared about 230 mya, in the Middle Triassic Period.

◀ *Corals live mainly in warm shallow seas, which were more common long ago.*

Arthropods

- **Arthropods form** the largest single group of animals. They include insects, crustaceans (crabs and lobsters), arachnids (spiders) and myriapods (millipedes) – any creature with a segmented body and jointed limbs.
- **Some of the earliest known remains** of arthropods come from the 505-million-year-old mudstone deposits of the Burgess Shale in Canada.
- ***Marrella* is one of the most common fossils** discovered at the Burgess Shale. It was about 2 cm long and had a head shield and two antennae.
- **Its body was divided** into segments, each of which had a jointed limb, probably for scurrying over the seabed.
- **At first**, palaeontologists thought *Marrella* was a trilobite, but they now regard it as an entirely different type of arthropod.
- **One of the first** – if not the first – groups of animals to emerge from the sea and colonize the land were arthropods, some time between 500 and 400 mya.
- **Arthropods were well suited** for living on land. Many had exoskeletons (outer skeletons) that prevented them from drying out. Their jointed limbs meant they could move over the ground.
- **Woodlice-like creatures** may have been among the first arthropods on land. They fed on rotting plant material, which they would have found on seashores.
- **The largest-ever land arthropod** was a millipede-like creature called *Arthropleura*, which was 1.8 m long.
- ***Arthropleura* lived on forest floors** during the Carboniferous Period (359–299 mya). Like woodlice, it ate rotting plants.

◀ Arthropleura *was as long as a human. It was the biggest-ever land arthropod – a group of creatures that were the first to colonize the land.*

Trilobites

- **Trilobites belonged** to the invertebrate group called arthropods – animals with segmented bodies and hard outer skeletons.
- **The name trilobite** means 'three lobes'. Trilobites' hard outer shells were divided into three parts.
- **The first trilobites** appeared by about 520 mya. By 500 mya, they had developed into many different types.
- **These invertebrates** had compound eyes, like insects' eyes, which could see in many different directions at once.
- **Some trilobites could roll up** into a ball, like some woodlice do today. This was a useful means of protection.
- **Long, thin, jointed legs** enabled trilobites to move quickly over the seabed or sediment covering it.
- **Trilobites moulted** by shedding their outer skeletons. Most trilobite fossils are the remains of these shed skeletons.
- **One of the largest known trilobites** was *Isotelus*, which grew more than 70 cm long.
- **Other trilobites** were much smaller, such as *Conocoryphe*, which was about 2–5 cm long.
- **Trilobites became extinct** around 250 mya – along with huge numbers of other marine animals.

▼ *This* Conocoryphe *trilobite lived in the seas of the Mid Cambrian Period, about 510 mya. It was one of the smaller trilobites.*

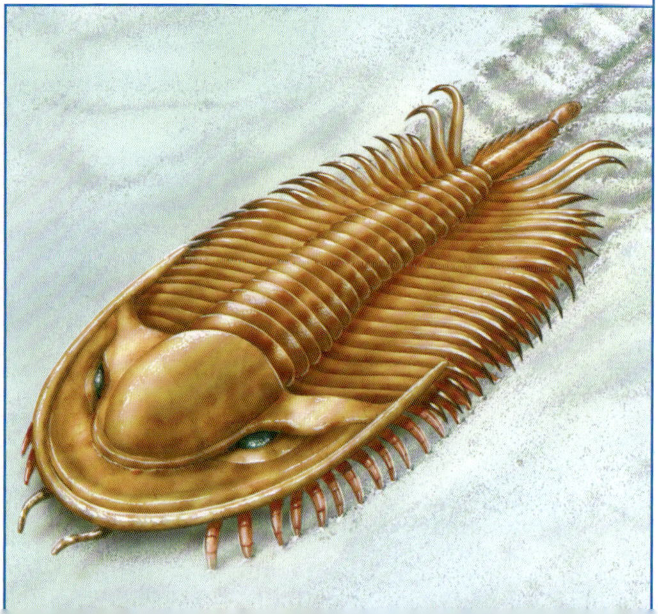

Insects

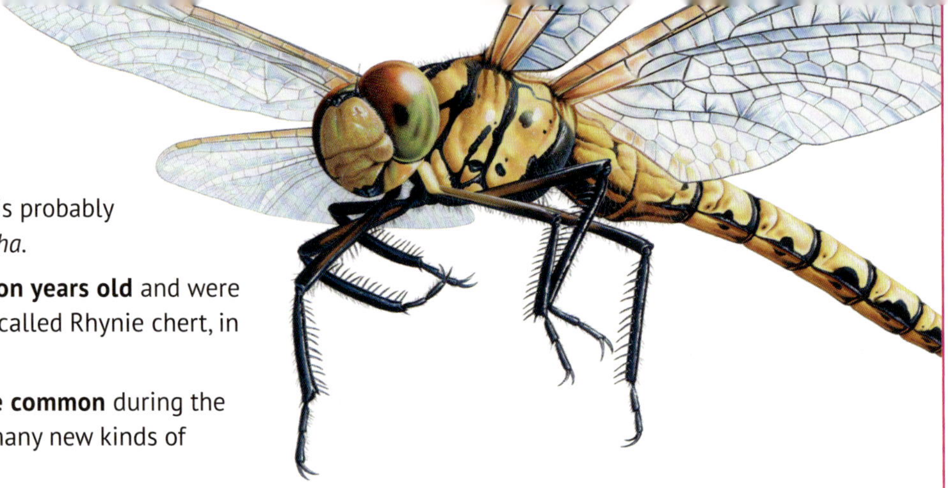

▲ Meganeura *was another enormous griffinfly from the late Carboniferous Period. With a wingspan of 60 cm, it swooped on other, smaller flying insects of the time.*

- **One of the oldest fossils** that is probably a true insect is named *Rhyniognatha*.
- **Its fossils are about 400 million years old** and were preserved in a formation of rocks called Rhynie chert, in Scotland.
- **As land habitats became more common** during the Devonian Period, 419–359 mya, many new kinds of insects started to appear.
- **These early insects included cockroaches**, the grasshopper and cricket group known as odonatans, and the first flying insects similar to today's mayflies and dragonflies.
- **The biggest-ever flying insect** was *Meganeuropsis*, a dragonfly-like griffinfly that lived in Late Carboniferous and Early Permian forests, around 300–290 mya.
- ***Meganeuropsis* lived in North America** and had wings spanning 70 cm, compared to the largest dragonflies today, at 20 cm.
- **The most numerous insects today** – beetles – probably first appeared during the Early Permian Period, around 290 mya.
- **An amazing insect fossil** was found in China and named in 2008 as *Ororaphidia*.
- **It was a type of snakefly**, from the insect group Rhaphidioptera.
- ***Ororaphidia* was only 12 mm long** but the details of the fossil show many tiny parts such as the veins on its wings.

DID YOU KNOW?

The early insects were smaller than this 'o', yet they evolved into today's most numerous creatures with more than one million different species.

Starfish and sea urchins

▲ *Today's starfish are mostly predators, levering open shellfish with their powerful arms and dissolving the soft flesh inside.*

- **The animal group called echinoderms**, meaning 'spiny skins', includes starfish, brittlestars, sea urchins, sea cucumbers, and sea lilies and feather stars, or crinoids.
- **All echinoderms live in the sea** and have a radial or 'circular' body design.
- **Echinoderms have one of the longest fossil histories** of any large animal group, stretching back to the Early Cambrian Period more than 530 mya.
- **There are about 7000 kinds** of living echinoderms – but twice this number are known only from fossils.
- **A fossil find from 2012 in Morocco**, North Africa, was *Helicocystis* – one of the first known echinoderms, from 520 mya.
- **The *Helicocystis* fossils show** it had five grooves in a spiral shape around its body, which probably trapped small bits of food.

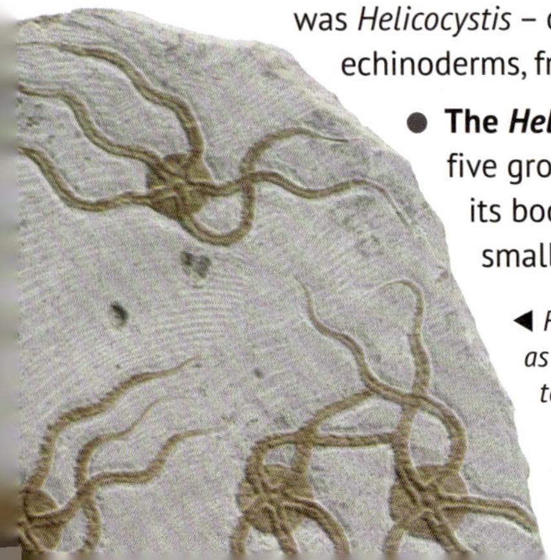

◀ *Fossil brittlestars from as long as 500 mya are very similar to today's versions, scavenging on the deep seafloor.*

- **Many modern starfish and brittlestars** have arms in multiples of five, linking *Helicocystis* to this group.
- ***Geocoma* was a brittlestar from Europe** that lived about 170 mya in the Middle Jurassic Period. Its fossils are very similar to living brittlestars.
- ***Pentacrinites* was a sea lily** that was widespread in the oceans from 220 to 40 mya, a huge time span of survival.
- ***Pentacrinites* remains** were so common in some rocks that they are known as 'penta beds'.

Brachiopods

● **Brachiopods are filter-feeding shellfish** that were once hugely diverse and common in all seas and oceans, but are now much more limited.

● **More than 12,000** kinds of brachiopods are known from fossilized remains, compared to about 320 living species.

● **Brachiopods resemble** mollusc shellfish such as mussels and clams, with a two-part shell, and each part is known as a valve.

● **However, in a brachiopod** the valves cover the top and bottom of the animal inside, while in molluscs, the valves are on the left and right sides.

● **Some brachiopods are known as lampshells**, since the shell shape resembles that of an old oil lamp.

● **Brachiopods first evolved** in the Cambrian Period, more than 500 mya, and dominated the seas of the Paleozoic Era.

● **One of the first known from fossils** was *Aldanotreta*, which lived in what is now Siberia, 525 mya.

● **Many brachiopods died out** in the greatest mass extinction known, which occured at the end of the Permian Period, 252 mya and is called the 'Great Dying'.

● **The living brachiopod *Lingula*** is very similar to its relatives from 450–400 mya.

● **Most living brachiopods** are less than 5 cm long, while some fossil kinds were over 20 cm in length.

◀ *The living brachiopod* Lingula *has a long fleshy stalk at its rear end that anchors it into the mud or sand of the seabed.*

Molluscs and graptolites

● **Modern molluscs** include gastropods (slugs, snails and limpets), bivalves (clams, oysters, mussels and cockles) and cephalopods (octopuses, squids and cuttlefish).

● **Modern and prehistoric molluscs** represent one of the most diverse animal groups ever to have lived.

● **The first molluscs** were the size of a pinhead. They appeared early in the Cambrian Period, about 540 mya, or even before.

● **The first cephalopod molluscs** emerged towards the end of the Cambrian Period, around 490 mya.

● **One early cephalopod** was *Plectronoceras*, which had a horn-shaped shell divided into different chambers.

● **Gastropod molluscs** (snails and slugs) were one of the first groups of animals to live on land.

● **Snails and slugs** are limited to where they can live on land as they require moist conditions.

● **Cephalopods** are the most highly developed of all molluscs. Squids and octopuses evolved big brains, good eyesight, tentacles and beak-like jaws.

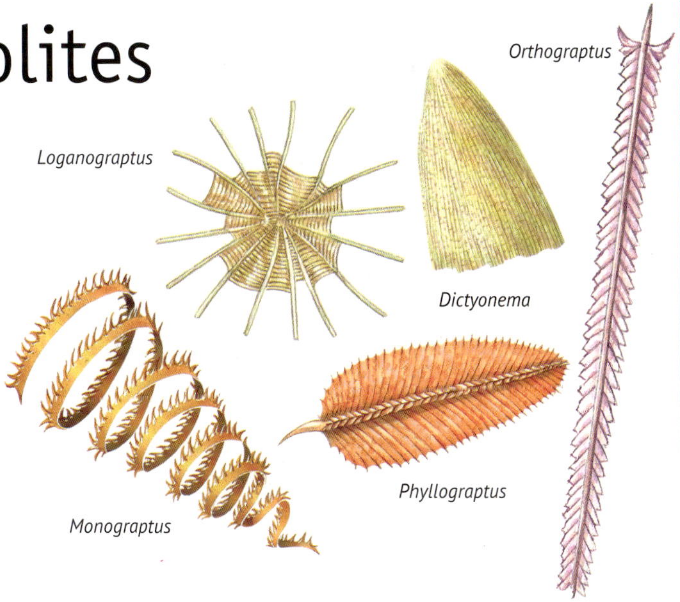

▲ *Graptolites have left an extraordinary range of fossil shapes that range from sawblade-like marks to coils, spirals and stars.*

● **Graptolites are an extinct group** of simple animals that lived in string-like communities. Graptolite means 'written stone' because the fossils of these creatures resemble scrawled handwriting.

● **Graptolites had tentacles** that they may have used to sieve food particles from the water or the seabed.

Ammonites

● **Ammonites belong to** the cephalopod group of molluscs. They were once widespread in the oceans, but they died out at the end of the Cretaceous Period (about 66 mya).

● **The number of ammonite fossils** that have been found shows how plentiful these animals once were.

● **Ammonites were predators** and scavengers. They had very good vision, long seizing tentacles and powerful mouths.

● **Their mouths consisted** of sharp beaks, perhaps venom glands, and a tooth-covered tongue.

▶ *An ammonite swims through the sea in search of food. The animal swam backwards, with its tentacles trailing behind.*

● **Ammonites had multi-chambered shells** that contained gas and worked like flotation tanks, keeping the creatures afloat.

● ***Stephanoceras* was an ammonite** with a spiral, disc-shaped shell, 20 cm across. It was very common in the seas of the Mesozoic Era.

● **A living relative** of ammonites is *Nautilus*, a cephalopod that lives near the seabed and feeds on small creatures and carrion.

● **People once thought** that ammonite fossils were the fossils of curled-up snakes.

● **In some places**, builders have traditionally set ammonite fossils into the walls of buildings for decoration.

Pikaia

● **A small, worm-like creature** called *Pikaia* is thought to be similar to the ancestors of backboned animals.

● **Its fossil remains** were found in the 505-million-year-old mudstone deposits of the Burgess Shale in Canada.

● ***Pikaia* may have been** an early chordate, a group of animals with a stiff supporting rod, called a notochord, along their back.

● **All vertebrates** are chordates, as well as marine animals called tunicates and acraniates.

▼ Pikaia *looked a little like an eel with tail fins. The stiff rod that ran along its body developed into the backbone in later animals.*

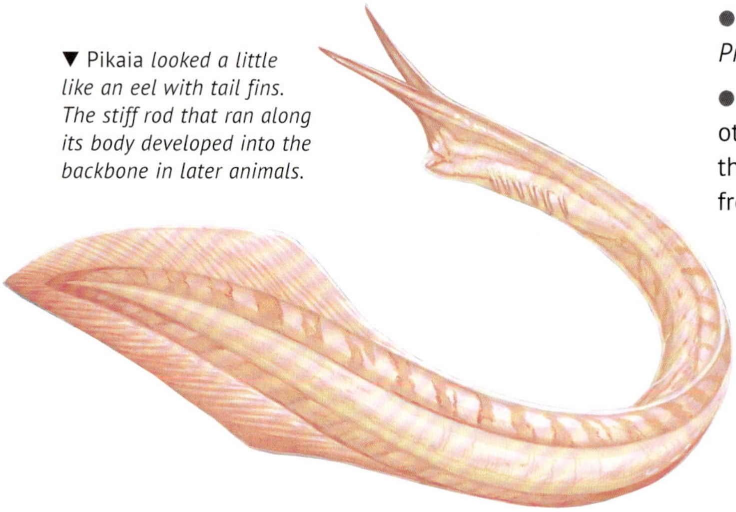

● ***Pikaia* was 5 cm long** with what could be a notochord (stiffening rod) running along its body – a kind of primitive spine that gave its body flexibility.

● **The notochord** also allowed the animal's simple muscles to work against it, and the body organs to hang from it.

● ***Pikaia* was very similar** to *Branchiostoma*, a small, transparent modern-day creature that lives in sand at the bottom of the sea.

● **As it lacked a bony skeleton**, paired fins and jaws, *Pikaia* was not really a fish.

● ***Pikaia* was a more complex creature** than many other animals found in the Burgess Shale. It suggests that other complex creatures must have lived before it, from which it evolved.

● **The head of *Pikaia*** was very primitive with a pair of tentacles, a mouth and a simple brain (a swelling of the nerve cord) for processing information.

● ***Pikaia* swam** in a zigzag fashion, similar to a sea snake.

Jawless fish

- **The first fish probably appeared** during the Late Cambrian Period, about 500 mya.
- **These fish had** permanently gaping mouths – as they had no jaws they could not open and close their mouths.
- **Early fish** were called agnathans, which means 'jawless'.
- **Agnathans ate** by sieving plankton through their simple mouth opening, also perhaps scooping up small items such as algae, tiny animals and rotting flesh on the seabed.
- **Among the oldest** complete agnathan fossils are *Arandaspis*, which comes from Australia and was found in 1959, and *Sacabambaspis* found in South America in the 1980s.

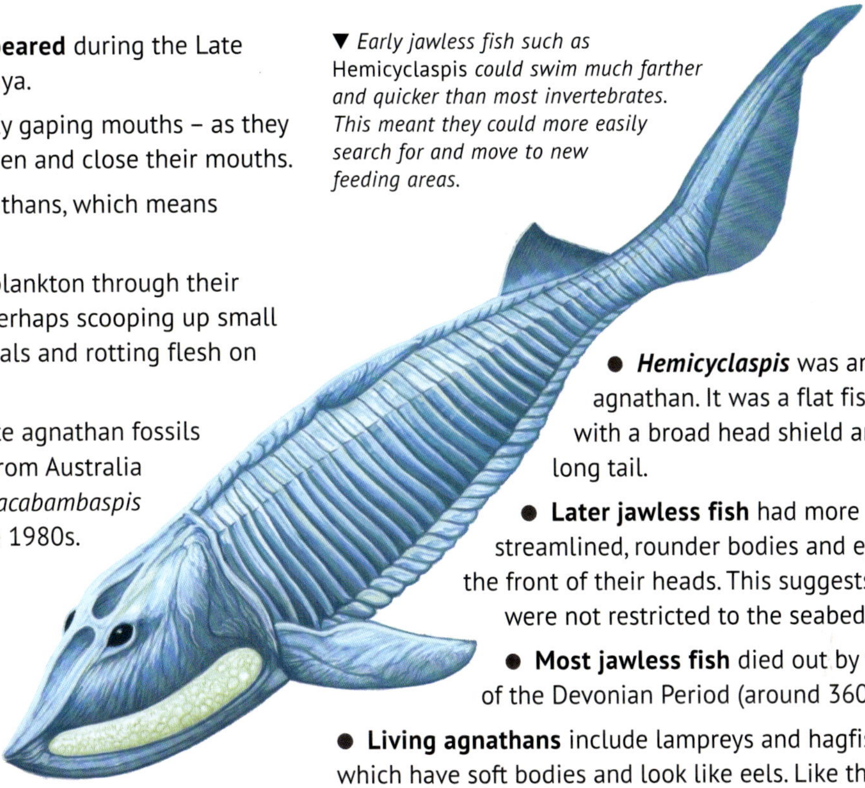

▼ *Early jawless fish such as* Hemicyclaspis *could swim much farther and quicker than most invertebrates. This meant they could more easily search for and move to new feeding areas.*

DID YOU KNOW?

Hemicyclaspis had eyes on top of its head. This suggests it lived on the seabed and used its eyes to keep a lookout for predators above.

- ***Hemicyclaspis*** was another agnathan. It was a flat fish with a broad head shield and a long tail.
- **Later jawless fish** had more streamlined, rounder bodies and eyes at the front of their heads. This suggests they were not restricted to the seabed.
- **Most jawless fish** died out by the end of the Devonian Period (around 360 mya).
- **Living agnathans** include lampreys and hagfish, which have soft bodies and look like eels. Like their ancient relatives, they do not have jaws.

Jawed fish

- **The first jawed fish probably** emerged during the Silurian Period (443–419 mya).
- **An early group of jawed fish** were acanthodians, from the Greek word *akantha*, meaning 'thorn' or 'spine'.
- **Jaws and teeth** gave acanthodians a huge advantage over jawless fish – they could eat a greater variety of food and defend themselves more effectively.
- **Jaws and teeth allowed** acanthodians to become predators.
- **Acanthodians' jaws** evolved from structures called gill arches in the pharynx (throat), the tube from the mouth to the stomach.
- **Gill arches are bony rods** and muscles that support the gills, the breathing organs of a fish.
- **As acanthodians developed jaws**, they also developed teeth.
- **The earliest fish teeth** were cone-like shapes along the jaw, made out of bone and coated with hard enamel.

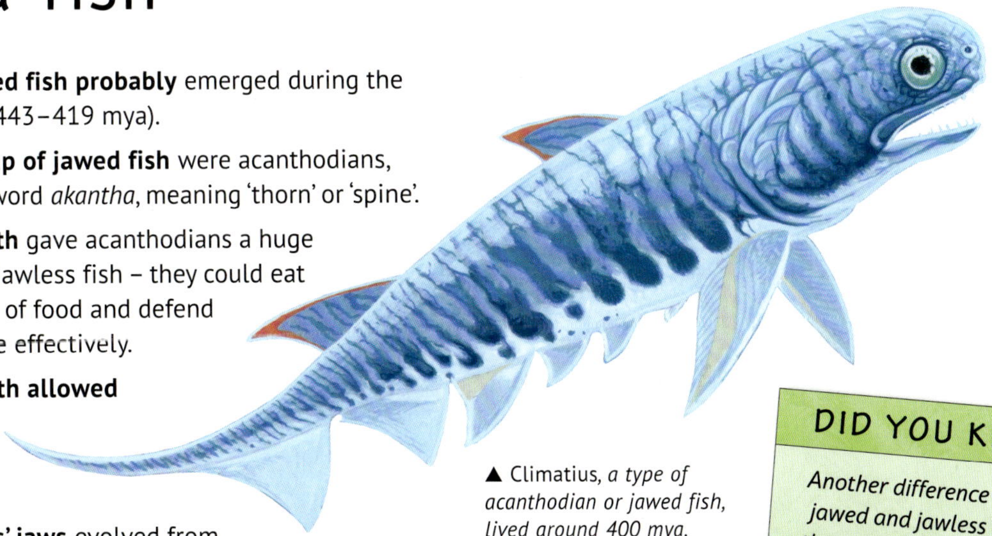

▲ Climatius, *a type of acanthodian or jawed fish, lived around 400 mya. Acanthodians are also called 'spiny sharks' – although they were not sharks, many had spines on the edges of their fins.*

DID YOU KNOW?

Another difference between jawed and jawless fish was that jawed fish had a pair of nostrils, while jawless fish only had one.

- **The teeth** of early acanthodians varied greatly. In some species they were sharp and spiky, in others they were like blades, while in others they resembled flat plates.

Sharks

▲ *This modern Caribbean reef shark is a fast swimmer and a fierce hunter. The main features of sharks – from their tightly packed, needle-sharp teeth to their streamlined shape – have changed little over 400 million years.*

DID YOU KNOW?

Prehistoric sharks' jaws were fixed to the side of their skull, while modern sharks' jaws hang beneath their braincase, which gives them a more powerful bite.

- **The earliest known shark fossils** are scales from rock layers of the late Silurian Period, about 420 mya.
- **Sharks belong to the group** known as cartilaginous fish, which also includes rays and skates. Their skeletons are made from cartilage, not bone.
- ***Cladoselache* was a prehistoric shark**, which could grow up to 2 m long.
- ***Cladoselache* appears** to have been quite similar to a modern shark – it had a streamlined body, a pair of dorsal (back) fins and triangular-shaped pectoral (front side) fins.
- **Early sharks hunted squid**, small fish and crustaceans.
- ***Stethacanthus* was a prehistoric shark** that looked nothing like a modern one. It had an anvil-shaped head projection covered in teeth.
- ***Stethacanthus* lived** in the Carboniferous Period (359–299 mya).
- **Sharks are at the top** of the food chain in modern seas, but this was not the case during the Devonian Period.
- **Other Devonian fish** were much larger than sharks. For example, *Dunkleosteus* grew to be up to 3.7 m long and would have been able to snap up any contemporary shark in a flash.

▼ Hybodus *was a blunt-headed prehistoric shark that lived between 250 and 100 mya in the time of the dinosaurs. It grew to about 2 m and looked quite similar to modern sharks, but had very different jaw.*

Bony fish

- **Bony fish have internal skeletons** and external scales made of bone.
- **Fossil evidence shows** they first appeared during the Late Silurian Period, around 420 mya.
- **Bony fish evolved** into the most abundant and varied fish in the seas.
- **There are two types** of bony fish – ray-finned fish and lobe-finned fish.
- **There were plenty** of prehistoric lobe-finned fish, but only a few species survive today. They belong to one of two groups – lungfish or coelacanths.
- **Amphibians** – and ultimately reptiles and mammals – evolved from lobe-finned fish.
- **Ray-finned fish** were so-called because of the bony struts (rays) that supported their fins.
- **Most early ray-finned** fish were small, ranging in size from about 5–20 cm long.
- ***Rhadinichthys* and *Cheirolepis*** were two early ray-finned fish. They were small predators equipped with good swimming ability and snapping jaws.
- **Around 250 mya**, ray-finned fish lost many of the bony rays from their fins. The fins became more flexible and the fish became better swimmers.
- **New types of ray-finned fish**, called teleosts, also developed more symmetrical tails and thinner scales.

◀ *This modern-day coelacanth is a direct descendant of the lobe-finned bony fish that lived 350 mya. Coelacanths were thought to be extinct until a fisherman caught one off the coast of South Africa in 1938.*

Dunkleosteus

- **The now-extinct fish group** known as placoderms lived during the Silurian and Devonian Periods, 443 to 359 mya.
- **The name placoderm** means 'plated skin' and these fish had large shields of bone over the head and front of the body for protection.
- **The biggest placoderm** was *Dunkleosteus*, from around 370 mya, the Late Devonian.
- **Its fossils come** from North America, North Africa and Europe.
- ***Dunkleosteus*** was 10 m or more in length and weighed up to 5 tonnes.
- **It did not have teeth**, but curved plates or blades of bone that formed a sharp edge for biting and slicing.
- **The estimated closing force** of these 'blades' was greater than almost any other living or fossil creature, including *Tyrannosaurus*.
- ***Dunkleosteus* was named** in 1956 after fossil expert David Dunkle of Cleveland, USA.
- **A very similar giant placoderm** called *Dinichthys* is known from few fossils and may actually be the same creature as *Dunkleosteus*.

▶ Dunkleosteus *had a rigid, armour-plated head and front body, but its rear body and fins were flexible for fast swimming.*

From fins to limbs

● **The first land-dwelling**, backboned animals were called tetrapods. They needed legs to hold up their bodies so they could move around in search of water and food.

● **Tetrapods evolved** from lobe-finned fish, which had all the right body parts to develop arms and legs.

● **The fossil skeleton** of the lobe-finned fish *Eusthenopteron* shows that the organization of bones in its front and rear fins was similar to the arrangement of limbs in tetrapods.

● ***Eusthenopteron* lived in** shallow waters. It could use its fins as primitive legs and move over land if the waters dried out.

▼ Eusthenopteron, *which means 'good strong fin', used its fins to move out of the water.*

● **Recent research suggests** that another lobe-finned fish, *Panderichthys*, could use its fins more effectively as limbs than *Eusthenopteron*. According to scientists, *Panderichthys* was more like a tetrapod than a fish.

● **The front fins** in lobe-finned fish connected to a shoulder girdle, while the rear fins connected to a hip girdle. These girdles connected to the backbone.

● **These hip and shoulder** connections meant that the limbs of future tetrapods were connected to a skeleton, which prevented the limbs from pressing against the inside of the body and damaging it.

● **The shoulder girdle** of lobe-finned fish also connected to their heads. Tetrapods, however, developed heads that were separated from their shoulders and joined instead by a neck.

● **Necks were a great advantage** to land-living animals. They could use them to bend down, to reach up, and to turn around to see in other directions.

DID YOU KNOW?

Suitable fins were not the only feature that meant lobe-finned fish could evolve into land-dwelling animals. They also had lungs for breathing air.

Breathing air

● **Fish breathe oxygen** in water through their gills. When a fish is out of the water, these gills collapse.

● **For creatures to adapt** to living on land, they had to develop air-breathing lungs.

● **Tetrapods were not** the first creatures to develop lungs – this step was taken by lobe-finned fish.

● **Lungfish are lobe-fins** that still exist today. They live in hot places and when rivers dry out, they bury themselves in mud and breathe through lungs.

● **Early tetrapods**, such as *Ichthyostega* and *Acanthostega*, had both gills and lungs, suggesting they could breathe in both air and water.

DID YOU KNOW?

Animals could only evolve to live on land due to plants producing oxygen over millions of years, which became part of Earth's atmosphere.

● **Later tetrapods** breathed through gills when they were first born, but, like modern frogs and newts, their gills became smaller as they got older and were replaced by lungs.

● **Modern amphibians** also take in oxygen through their skin, which is soft and moist.

● **Early tetrapods** had tougher skin, so were unable to breathe through it.

● **Breathing through skin** limits an animal's size, which is why modern amphibians are much smaller than many of their prehistoric ancestors.

▼ *Like this modern lungfish, prehistoric lungfish had lungs as well as gills. They were able to breathe air if the pools or rivers they lived in dried out.*

Acanthostega

● ***Acanthostega* was an early tetrapod**. It had a fish-like body, which suggests it spent most of its life in water.

● **It had fish-like gills** for breathing water as well as lungs for breathing air.

● **Fossil remains** of *Acanthostega* were found in rock strata dating from the Late Devonian Period (around 365 mya).

● ***Acanthostega's* body** was about one metre in length.

● **This tetrapod had** a wide tail that would have been useful for swimming but inconvenient for moving on land.

● ***Acanthostega's* legs** were well-developed, with eight toes on the front feet and perhaps seven on the rear ones.

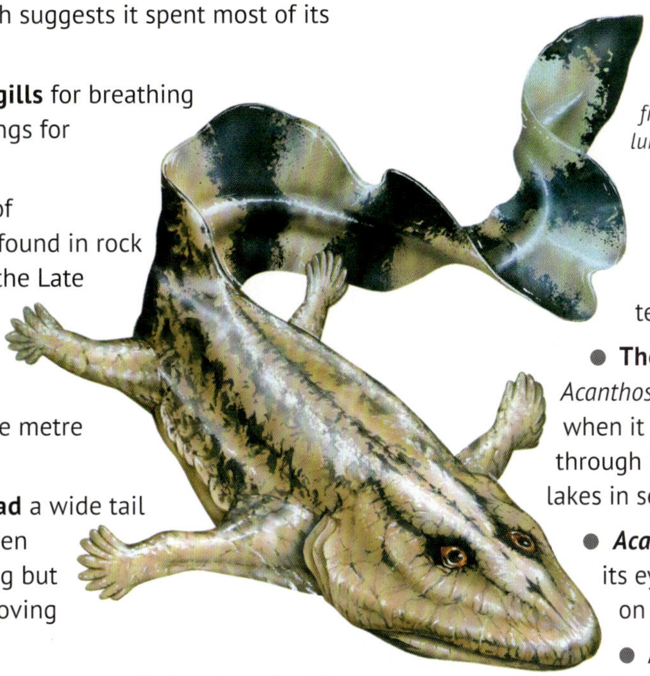

◀ Acanthostega *may have evolved from lobe-finned fish similar to* Eusthenopteron *and* Panderichthys. *It shared a number of features with these fish, including a similar set of gills and lungs, as well as a tail fin and braincase.*

● **The number of toes** on its feet was surprising to palaeontologists – they had previously thought all tetrapods had five toes.

● **The legs and toes** would have helped *Acanthostega* give its body a thrusting motion when it swam. They would also aid movement through plants at the bottom of rivers and lakes in search of prey.

● ***Acanthostega* had a flattened skull** and its eye sockets were placed close together on the top of its head.

● **A complete but jumbled-up** *Acanthostega* fossil was discovered in hard rock in Greenland. Palaeontologists had to work very carefully to prise the fossil from the rock.

Great amphibians

● **The Carboniferous** and Early Permian Periods, from around 350–270 mya, are sometimes called the 'Age of Amphibians'.

● **At this time** the main large land animals were amphibian tetrapods, which evolved to become plant-eaters and carnivores.

● **Some of these amphibians** looked similar to later creatures such as crocodiles.

● **From the Middle Permian Period** the reptiles began to take over as the dominant land animals, and the tetrapod amphibians were restricted to more specialized habitats.

● **One of the strangest was *Diplocaulus***, which had a wide, curved head shaped like a boomerang.

● ***Diplocaulus* was about one metre long** and lived during the Late Permian Period in North America and North Africa.

● **One of the last great amphibians** was *Koolasuchus*, which lived about 120 mya in the Early Cretaceous Period.

● **Its fossils come from the state of Victoria**, Australia. Other fossils found with them suggest there was a cool climate with plenty of streams and rivers at that time.

● ***Koolasuchus* was similar** to crocodiles and very large, up to 5 m long and weighing half a tonne.

▼ Diplocaulus' *strange head may have worked like a hydrofoil or 'water-wing' to give front-end lift while swimming forwards.*

Eryops

DID YOU KNOW?

The bulky body and sprawling limbs of Eryops suggest it waddled with effort on land, dragging its tail behind.

▲ *The skull of* Eryops *was relatively huge, more than 60 cm long, and the jaws were able to swallow large prey whole.*

- **One of the toughest-looking** amphibian tetrapods was *Eryops*, whose name means 'long face'.
- ***Eryops* lived in the Early Permian Period** some 295 mya, and was one of the biggest animals on land at that time.
- **Fossils of *Eryops*** have been found in various sites across North America, especially in the southwest.
- **In particular the thick, heavy skull** bones have left many well-preserved fossils.
- ***Eryops* looked like** a combination of a salamander and a crocodile, and grew to about 2 m long and 100 kg in weight.
- **Eyes towards the top of its head** suggest *Eryops* lay on a river or lake bed, looking upwards for prey swimming past.
- **It would then lunge up** and bite the victim with its huge gaping mouth, armed with many sharp teeth.
- **In water it was probably** a powerful swimmer but not very speedy, due to its relatively short tail.

Frogs and salamanders

◀ Triadobatrachus *was one of the earliest known frogs. Frogs and salamanders may be descendants of a group of amphibious temnospondyls known as dissorophids.*

- **Modern amphibians**, such as frogs, toads, newt and salamanders, all belong to the group called the lissamphibians.
- **Lissamphibians evolved later** than the early tetrapods, probably during the Late Permian Period (260 mya).
- ***Triadobatrachus* lived** in the Early Triassic Period in Madagascar, was 10 cm long and had a frog-like skull.
- **Compared to earlier amphibians,** *Triadobatrachus* had a shortened back with fewer spinal bones and a shortened tail.
- **Evolution did not stop** with *Triadobatrachus* – modern frogs have even fewer spinal bones and no tail.
- ***Triadobatrachus*' hind legs** were roughly the same size as its front legs. Again, this is different to modern frogs, which have longer hind legs for hopping.
- **The first known salamanders** lived in the Middle Jurassic Period (174–163 mya) in China, Mongolia and Kazakhstan. They were about 20 cm long with a broad skull.
- **More modern-looking frog** and salamander fossils have been discovered in Messel, Germany. They date from the Early Eocene Epoch (around 50 mya).
- **Some Messel frog fossils** have their legs bent as if they were in mid-hop. There are even tadpole fossils from Messel.

DID YOU KNOW?

Andrias scheuchzeri *was a salamander from the Miocene Epoch (23–5 mya). It was named after the Swiss scientist Johannes Scheuchzer, who discovered it in 1726.*

First reptiles

● **Reptiles evolved** from amphibians during the Carboniferous Period (359–299 mya).

● **Unlike amphibians**, which usually live near and lay their eggs in water, reptiles are much more adapted for living on land.

● **Compared to amphibians**, reptiles had better limbs for walking, a more effective circulatory system for moving blood around their bodies, and bigger brains.

▲ Hylonomus, *meaning 'forest dweller', was one of the earliest reptiles. Fossil hunters discovered its remains in fossilized tree stumps at Joggins in Nova Scotia, Canada.*

● **They also had more powerful** jaw muscles than amphibians and would have been better predators. Early reptiles ate millipedes, spiders and insects.

● **One of the earliest reptiles** was *Hylonomus*, a small creature that lived in the Late Carboniferous Period, 315–310 mya.

● ***Hylonomus* lived in forests** on the edges of lakes and rivers. Fossil remains of this reptile have been found inside the stumps of clubmoss trees.

● **Another early reptile** was *Paleothyris*. Like *Hylonomus*, it was about 20 cm long and had a smaller head than amphibians.

● **One animal that may represent** a staging post between reptiles and amphibians is *Westlothiana lizziae*, which was discovered in Scotland in the 1980s.

● ***Westlothiana lizziae*** lived in the Early Carboniferous Period (about 335 mya).

● **At first, palaeontologists thought** that *Westlothiana lizziae* was the oldest reptile. However, its backbone, head and legs more closely resemble those of an amphibian.

Eggs

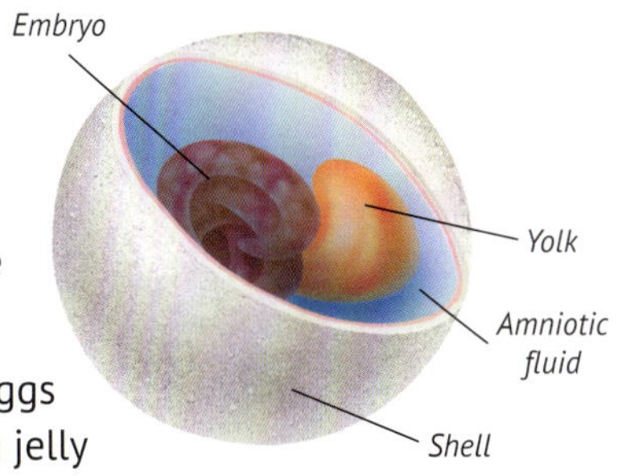

◀ *Reptiles broke the link between reproduction and water by laying hard-shelled eggs on land. This snake shell contains the developing young (embryo), a food store (yolk) and a protective liquid (amniotic fluid).*

● **Reptile eggs** were a major evolutionary advance over amphibian eggs.

● **Early amphibians**, like modern ones, laid their eggs in water. This is because their eggs were covered in jelly (like modern frogspawn) and would dry out on land.

● **Reptiles evolved eggs** that were covered by a protective shell. This meant they could lay them on land and they would not dry out.

● **One advantage** of shelled eggs was that reptiles did not have to return to water to lay them.

● **Another advantage** was that reptiles could hide their eggs on land. Eggs laid in water are easy pickings for hungry animals.

● **Reptile embryos** complete all their growth phases inside eggs. When they hatch they look like miniature adults.

● **In contrast**, baby amphibians hatch out of their eggs as larvae, such as tadpoles. They live in water and breathe through gills before they develop lungs and can live on land.

● **Reptile shells are hard** and protect the growing embryos. The eggs also provide the embryos with food while they develop.

● **During the evolution** from amphibians to reptiles, some tetrapods laid jelly-covered eggs on land.

● **A number of today's amphibians** lay jelly-covered eggs on land, including some tropical frogs and mountain salamanders.

◀ *Frogs lay their eggs in water in jelly-like clumps called spawn.*

Skulls

● **The jaws of reptiles** are another feature that shows their evolutionary progression from amphibians.

● **Amphibian jaws** are designed to snap but not to bite together tightly.

● **In contrast**, reptiles had more jaw muscles and could press their jaws together more firmly. This meant they could break insect body casings and chew through tough plant stems.

● **By the Late Carboniferous Period** (about 300 mya), reptiles developed openings in their skulls behind the eye socket. These openings allowed room for more jaw muscles.

● **Four types of reptile skull** developed. Each belonged to a different type of reptile.

● **Anapsids had no openings** in their skull other than the eye sockets. Turtles and tortoises are anapsids.

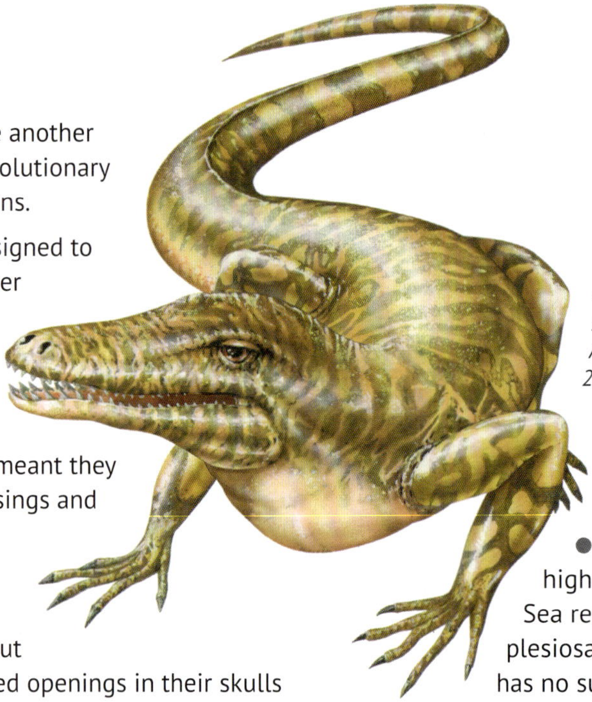

◀ Varanosaurus *was a one metre-long synapsid reptile that lived in North America in the Permian Period, about 280–260 mya. There are important similarities between the skulls of synapsid reptiles and mammals.*

DID YOU KNOW?

Plants developed tough stems and leaves, spines and poisons to protect themselves from hungry reptiles.

● **Euryapsids had one opening** high up on either side of the skull. Sea reptiles such as ichthyosaurs and plesiosaurs were euryapsids, but this group has no surviving relatives.

● **Synapsids had one opening** low down on either side of the skull. Mammal-like reptiles and mammals are descended from this group.

● **Diapsids had two openings** on each side of the skull. Dinosaurs and pterosaurs were diapsids – so too are crocodiles, lizards, snakes and birds.

Synapsids

● **Synapsids were tetrapods** that had one opening on each side of the lower skull behind the eye socket, onto which their jaw muscles attached.

● **They appeared** in the Late Carboniferous Period (about 310 mya), and became the dominant land animals in the Permian Period (299–252 mya).

● **Synapsids are the ancestors** of mammals, which explains why they are sometimes described as 'mammal-like reptiles'.

▼ Diictodon *was a small mammal-like reptile that lived about 255 mya. A plant-eater and a burrower,* Diictodon *was an advanced form of a synapsid known as a dicynodont.*

● **The first synapsids** are called pelycosaurs. They were large, heavy-bodied animals that walked a bit like modern-day crocodiles.

● **The fierce meat-eater** *Dimetrodon* and the plant-eating *Edaphosaurus* – both of which had long, fan-like spines on their backs – were pelycosaurs.

● **Later synapsids** are called therapsids. The earliest therapsids had bigger skulls and jaws than pelycosaurs, as well as longer legs and shorter tails.

● **Later therapsids** are divided into two subgroups – dicynodonts and cynodonts. Dicynodont means 'two dog teeth' – cynodont means 'dog tooth'.

● **Dicynodonts were herbivores**. Most had round, hippopotamus-shaped bodies, and beaks that they used to cut plant stems.

● **Cynodonts were carnivores**. They used different teeth in their mouth for different tasks – for stabbing, nipping and chewing.

● **Some cynodonts** had whiskers and may even have been warm-blooded, like mammals.

Dimetrodon

● **Although dinosaur-like in appearance**, *Dimetrodon* was not a dinosaur – although it is often classed as a reptile.

● ***Dimetrodon* lived** in the Early–Middle Permian Period, 290–270 mya, and was one of the largest land animals of that time.

● **It is known from plentiful fossils** in the Permian 'Red Beds' of Texas, USA, which are mainly reddish sandstone.

● ***Dimetrodon* grew to 3 m long** and was a fierce predator with a large mouth lined with sharp teeth.

● **One of the strangest features** of *Dimetrodon* was its tall back sail, probably made of skin and muscle.

● **The back sail extended** to a height of 2 m and would have had a very large surface area.

● **It was held up by** tall, thin rods of bone extending from the backbones or vertebrae, called neural spines.

● **The sail may have helped** *Dimetrodon* to warm up quickly by absorbing the sun's heat early in the morning as the reptile stood side-on to the rays.

● **It may also have had** colours and patterns, to scare enemies or attract mates for breeding.

● ***Dimetrodon* was a reptile** that belonged to the group known as synapsids – from which mammals eventually evolved.

▶ *Dimetrodon belonged to the pelycosaur subgroup of synapsids. Although dinosaur-like, it lived 40 million years before dinosaurs appeared.*

Crocodilians

● **The broad group** containing living and extinct crocodiles, Crocodylomorpha, appeared in the Late Permian Period, about 260–255 mya.

● **The first true crocodiles** appeared during the Late Triassic Period (220–201 mya). They were called protosuchians and lived in pools and rivers.

● **As its name suggests**, *Protosuchus* was a protosuchian. It had a short skull and sharp teeth, and would have looked quite like a modern crocodile.

● **Other early crocodiles**, such as *Terrestrisuchus*, looked less like modern crocodiles.

● ***Terrestrisuchus* had a short body** and long legs. Its name means 'land crocodile' because palaeontologists think it may have been more at home on land than in water.

● **The next group** of crocodilians to evolve were the mesoeucrocodylians, which lived in the sea.

◀ *Fossils of* Protosuchus, *meaning 'first crocodile', have been discovered in Arizona, dating to around 200 mya. Although* Protosuchus *was similar to living crocodiles in many ways, its legs were much longer.*

● ***Metriorhynchus*** was a marine mesoeucrocodylian. It had flippers instead of limbs and very sharp teeth for stabbing fish. It lived in the Late Jurassic Period (around 160 mya).

● **The subgroup called eusuchians** includes all modern crocodiles, alligators, gharials and caimans.

● ***Deinosuchus*, from 80–75 mya**, was thought to be the largest-ever crocodile at 11 m in length, until a recent discovery of more *Sarcosuchus* fossils.

DID YOU KNOW?

Modern crocodiles are living fossils. They look similar to the crocodiles that were alive 100 mya.

Turtles and tortoises

▶ Proganochelys, *an early relation of modern turtles and tortoises, had a 60-cm-long shell, but it was unable to pull its head or legs inside.*

- **Turtles and tortoises** both have shells that cover and protect their bodies. They belong to a group of reptiles called chelonians.
- **Chelonian shells** evolved from belly ribs that grew outside of the body.
- **The earliest chelonian fossils** come from the Mid Triassic Period (220 mya). They have been found in Germany and Thailand.
- **One very early chelonian** was *Proganochelys*.
- ***Proganochelys* had a well-developed**, heavily-armoured shell, but palaeontologists think that it could not pull its head, legs or tail inside it.
- **The ability to pull the head**, legs and tail inside the shell is important for turtles and tortoises because it provides them with maximum protection.
- **The protective shells** of turtles and tortoises may have helped them survive at the end of the Cretaceous Period, 66 mya, when so many other reptiles became extinct.
- **Tortoises have bigger shells** than turtles. This is because they are very slow-moving land creatures – unlike the swimming turtles – and need more protection.
- **A huge number and variety** of turtle fossils have been discovered at Riversleigh in Australia, dating from the Miocene Epoch (23–5 mya) in the Neogene Period.

▼ Archelon *fossils show that, at 4 m long, it was similar to, but much bigger than, modern leatherback turtles. Its front limbs were thinner and longer than its hind ones and were more useful in the water.*

DID YOU KNOW?

Turtles and tortoises evolved a toothless beak for slicing flesh or plants.

Placodonts

- **After adapting so well** to life on land, some groups of reptiles evolved into water-dwelling creatures.
- **Placodonts were early aquatic** (water-living) reptiles. They lived during the Triassic Period (about 252–201 mya).
- **The name placodont** means 'plate tooth'. These reptiles had large cheek teeth that worked like crushing plates.
- **Placodonts appeared** at about the same time as another group of aquatic reptiles called nothosaurs.
- **They had shorter**, sturdier bodies than the nothosaurs but, like them, they did not survive as a group for long.
- ***Placodus* was a placodont**. It had a stocky body, stumpy limbs and webbed toes for paddling. It may have had a fin on its tail.
- ***Placodus* probably used** its wide, flat teeth, which pointed outwards from its mouth, to prise shellfish off rocks or the seabed.
- ***Psephoderma*** was a turtle-like placodont. Its body was covered by a bony shell, which was in turn covered by hard horny plates.
- ***Psephoderma* also had** a horny beak, like a turtle's, and paddle-shaped limbs.
- ***Henodus* was another** turtle-like placodont. It also had a beak, which it probably used to grab molluscs from the seabed.

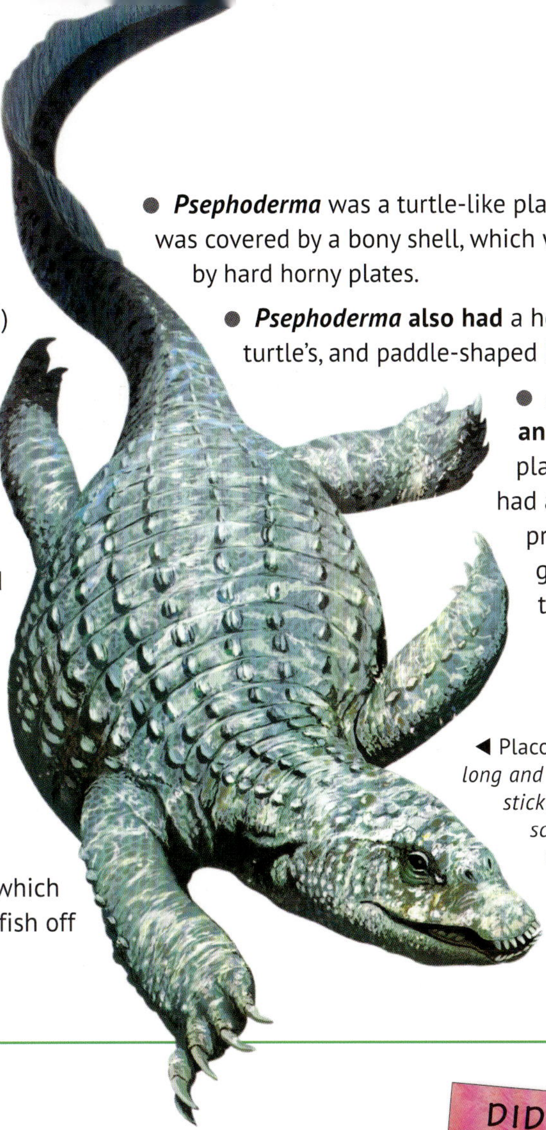

◀ Placodus *grew up to 2 m long and probably used its sticking-out front teeth to scrape up molluscs from the seabed. Its plate-like side teeth would then make short work of crunching the molluscs.*

Snakes

- **Snakes probably first appeared** 120–110 mya. *Dinilysia*, found in Argentina and from the Late Cretaceous Period, lived about 80 mya.
- **Earlier snake-like fossils** do exist, but palaeontologists generally think that these were snake-like lizards and not true snakes.
- **The ancestors of snakes were lizards.** Palaeontologists think these ancestors would have been a type of lizard called a varanid lizard. The modern monitor lizard is an example of this.
- **Snakes are an evolutionary triumph**. They are one of the few land-living animals to survive and flourish without limbs.
- **Compared to other reptiles**, snake fossils are rare. This is because snake bones are delicate and do not fossilize well.
- **Snakes evolved** into a huge variety of types from the Paleogene Period (66–23 mya).

▶ Titanoboa *was the biggest known snake, up to 14 m long and weighing perhaps 1.2 tonnes. It lived in tropical forests around 60 mya in Colombia, South America, and may have hunted in water like today's bulkiest snake, the anaconda.*

- **Today, there are more than 3400** snake species living in nearly every type of habitat.

DID YOU KNOW?

Snakes are one of the few reptile groups that had their main evolutionary development after the time of the dinosaurs.

- **Fossils from 50 mya** found in Messel, Germany, include the well-preserved remains of a 2-m-long early python called *Palaeopython*.
- **Early snakes killed their prey** by squeezing it to death. Modern boas and pythons also use this method to kill.
- **Poisonous snakes**, such as vipers, adders and cobras, did not evolve until the Miocene Epoch (23–5 mya).

Nothosaurs

● **Another group of reptiles** that returned to live in the sea were the nothosaurs.

● **As its name implies,** *Nothosaurus* was a nothosaur. Its neck, tail and body were long and flexible.

● ***Nothosaurus* was about** 4 m long and its approximate weight was 250 kg.

● **Impressions left** in some *Nothosaurus* fossils show that it had webs between its toes.

● ***Nothosaurus*' jaw** had many sharp, interlocking teeth, which would have crunched up the fish and shrimps on which it fed.

▲ Nothosaurus *was an aquatic reptile that could use its webbed feet to move over land. The long-necked nothosaurs were probably the ancestors of plesiosaurs, many of which also had long necks.*

DID YOU KNOW?

Nothosaurus had nostrils on the top of its snout, which suggests that it came to the water's surface to breathe, like crocodiles.

● ***Ceresiosaurus*** was another nothosaur. Palaeontologists think it swam by swaying its body and tail from side to side, like a fish.

● ***Ceresiosaurus*** means 'lizard of Ceresio'. It was as long as *Nothosaurus* but slimmer, only 120 kg in weight.

● **Nothosaurs emerged** near the start of the Triassic Period about 250 mya, but were extinct by the end of it.

● **The place left** by the extinct nothosaurs was taken by the plesiosaurs – another group of marine reptiles that were better adapted to life in the seas.

Plesiosaurs

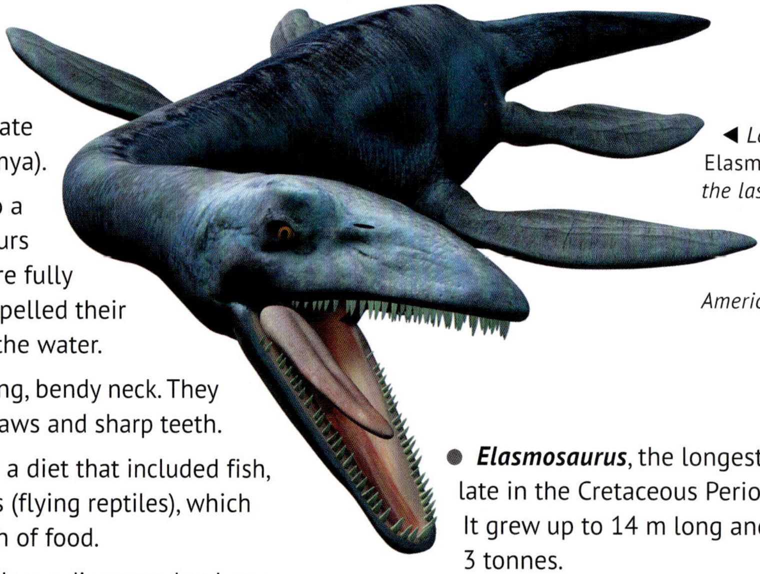

◀ *Long-necked* Elasmosaurus *was one of the last of the plesiosaurs. It lived in a shallow sea that covered much of North America about 80 mya.*

● **Plesiosaurs were marine reptiles** that were plentiful from the Late Triassic to the Late Cretaceous Periods (210–66 mya).

● **They were better suited** to a marine lifestyle than nothosaurs or placodonts. Their limbs were fully developed paddles, which propelled their short bodies quickly through the water.

● **Many plesiosaurs** had a long, bendy neck. They had small heads with strong jaws and sharp teeth.

● **These marine reptiles** had a diet that included fish, squid and probably pterosaurs (flying reptiles), which flew above the water in search of food.

● **The first *Plesiosaurus*** fossil was discovered at Lyme Regis on the south coast of England by Mary Anning in the early 19th century. The fossil, which is in the Natural History Museum, London, is 2.3 m long.

● ***Plesiosaurus* was not** a fast swimmer. It used its flipper-like limbs to move through the water but it had a weak tail that could not propel it forward very powerfully.

● ***Elasmosaurus***, the longest plesiosaur, lived late in the Cretaceous Period, about 80 mya. It grew up to 14 m long and weighed up to 3 tonnes.

● **One group of plesiosaurs** were known as pliosaurs. They had much shorter necks and much larger heads, with huge jaws and enormous teeth.

● **Research suggests** that plesiosaurs may have caught their prey with quick, darting head movements.

● **The huge pliosaur *Liopleurodon*** grew 10–12 m long and was one of the biggest sea animals of its time.

Ichthyosaurs

- **Ichthyosaurs looked similar** to both sharks, which are fish, and to later dolphins, which are mammals.
- **When one type** of animal comes to look like another, scientists call it convergent evolution.
- **Unlike plesiosaurs**, which relied on their paddles to propel them forwards, ichthyosaurs swayed their tails from side to side like fish.
- **Hundreds of complete skeletons** of the ichthyosaur *Ichthyosaurus* have been discovered. This reptile could grow up to 2 m long and weighed around 90 kg.

▼ *Fossil marine reptiles such as* Ichthyosaurus *created a sensation in the early 19th century, before dinosaurs were discovered. Ichthyosaurs had long, slim jaws to snap up fish and squid.*

DID YOU KNOW?

The first Ichthyosaurus fossil was found in 1811 by the English fossil hunter Mary Anning. It took seven years before scientists identified the skeleton as that of a reptile.

- ***Ichthyosaurus* had very large ear bones.** It may have been able to pick up underwater vibrations caused by prey.
- **Some fossilized skeletons** of *Ichthyosaurus* and other ichthyosaurs were found with embryos inside. This shows that ichthyosaurs gave birth to live young, as opposed to laying eggs.
- **One of the largest ichthyosaurs** was *Shastasaurus*, which was over 20 m long and may have weighed as much as 25 tonnes.
- **Ichthyosaurs were plentiful** in the Triassic and Jurassic Periods (252–145 mya), but became rarer in the Late Jurassic and Cretaceous Periods, dying out 66 mya.
- **Ichthyosaur means** 'fish lizard'.
- **Fossil hunters have found** ichthyosaur remains all over the world – in North and South America, Europe, Russia, India and Australia.

Mosasaurs

◀ Mosasaurus *was a fast swimmer. It had an enormous tail and paddle-shaped limbs, which it probably used as rudders.*

- **Another group of large sea reptiles** were the mosasaurs. They appeared from about 140 mya at the time when ichthyosaurs were becoming less common.
- **Mosasaurs were diapsid reptiles** – a group that included dinosaurs and pterosaurs. Most other large sea reptiles belonged to another group – the euryapsids.
- **Unlike other** giant prehistoric sea reptiles, mosasaurs have living relatives. These include monitor lizards, such as the Komodo dragon.
- **The best known mosasaur** is *Mosasaurus*, which could grow up to 16 m long and 20 tonnes in weight.
- **The huge jaws of *Mosasaurus*** were lined with cone-shaped teeth, each of which had different cutting and crushing edges. They were the most advanced teeth of any marine reptile.
- **So distinctive** are *Mosasaurus* teeth that palaeontologists have identified its tooth marks on the fossils of other animals, in particular the giant turtle *Allopleuron*.
- **The jaws of a *Mosasaurus*** were discovered in a limestone mine in Maastricht, in the Netherlands, in the 1770s. The fossil disappeared in 1795 when the French invaded Maastricht, but later turned up in Paris.
- **At first, scientists thought** the jaws belonged either to a prehistoric whale or a crocodile, until they decided they were a giant lizard's.
- ***Mosasaurus* means** 'lizard from the River Meuse' because it was discovered in Maastricht in the Netherlands, through which the River Meuse flows.
- **In 1998**, more than 200 years after the discovery of the first *Mosasaurus* fossil, palaeontologists discovered the remains of another *Mosasaurus* in the same location – the St Pietersburg quarry in Maastricht.

Reptile gliders

- **Only four groups of animals** have developed true powered, sustained, controlled flight – insects, pterosaurs, birds and bats.
- **But many kinds of animals** can swoop or glide in an effective way, although they cannot stay airborne for long.
- **The living lizard *Draco*** is called the 'flying dragon' although it glides rather than truly flies.
- **Some prehistoric reptiles** could glide and swoop in a similar way, including *Kuehneosaurus* and *Icarosaurus*.
- ***Kuehneosaurus* lived** in what is now England during the Late Triassic Period, some 210 mya.
- **It had bony ribs** sticking out from the sides of its body, which probably held out flaps of skin to work as a parachute.
- ***Kuehneosaurus* was about 70 cm long** and each 'wing' was up to 15 cm wide.
- ***Icarosaurus* was a similar** lizard-like reptile, but not a true lizard, from about 230 mya in North America.
- ***Icarosaurus* had much wider wings** in proportion to its smaller body, with a total length of 30 cm and wingspan of 25 cm.
- **Both of these gliders** probably leapt from trees to avoid enemies, landing some distance away.

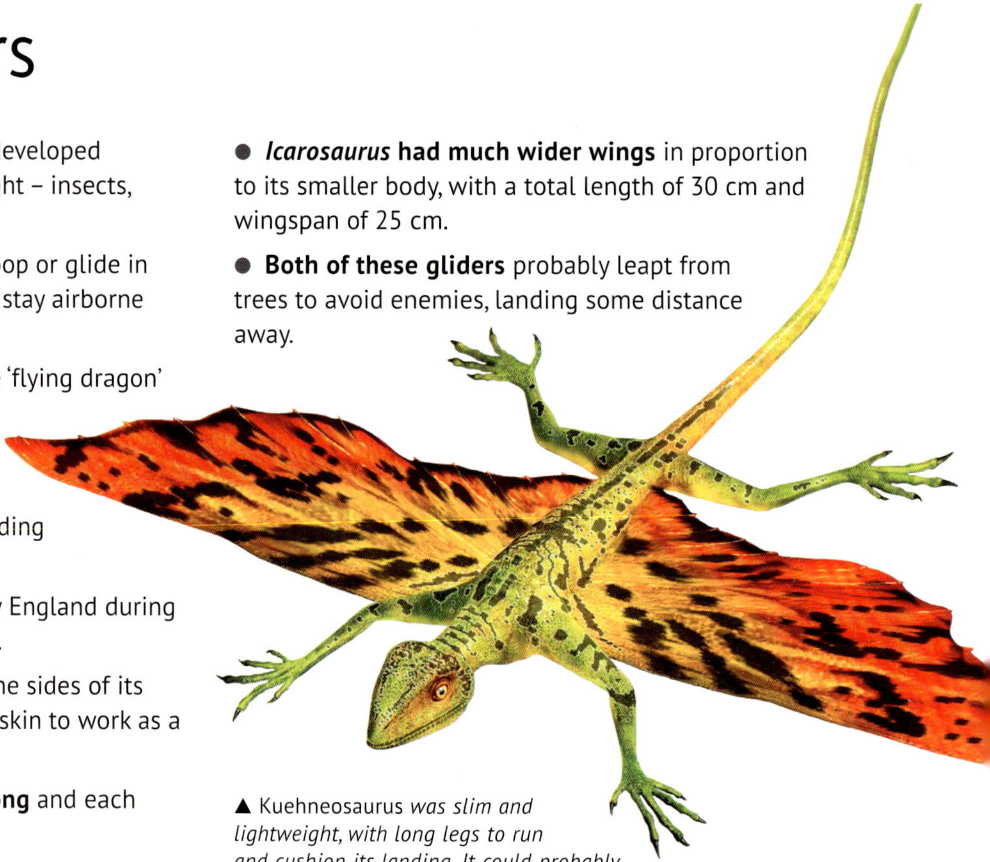

▲ Kuehneosaurus *was slim and lightweight, with long legs to run and cushion its landing. It could probably change direction in the air and land on a tree trunk or branch as well as the ground.*

Rhamphorhynchoids

- **The earliest pterosaurs** (flying reptiles) were the rhamphorhynchoids.
- **These creatures** first appeared in the Mid–Late Triassic Period (around 230–220 mya).
- **Rhamphorhynchoids had long tails** that ended in a diamond-shaped vane, like a rudder.
- **Their tails** gave them stability in flight, which meant they could soar and swoop effectively.
- **One of the first rhamphorhynchoids** – and first flying vertebrates – was *Peteinosaurus*.
- **Well-preserved fossils** of *Peteinosaurus* have been found near Cene, Bergamo, in Italy.
- **These fossils reveal *Peteinosaurus*'** sharp, cone-like teeth and suggest it ate insects that it caught in the air.

DID YOU KNOW?

Fossil hunters have found Rhamphorhynchus fossils alongside those of the early bird Archaeopteryx in Solnhofen, Germany.

◀ Dimorphodon *had a wingspan of about 1.5 m and a body length of 1 m. Palaeontologists think that it lived and hunted along seashores and rivers.*

- **In contrast**, another early rhamphorhynchoid, *Eudimorphodon*, had fangs at the front of its mouth and smaller spiked ones behind. This suggests it ate fish.
- ***Dimorphodon*** was a later rhamphorhynchoid from the Early Jurassic Period (201–174 mya). It had a huge head that looked a bit like a puffin's.
- ***Rhamphorhynchus*** was a later rhamphorhynchoid, appearing in the Late Jurassic Period (about 160 mya).

Giant pterosaurs

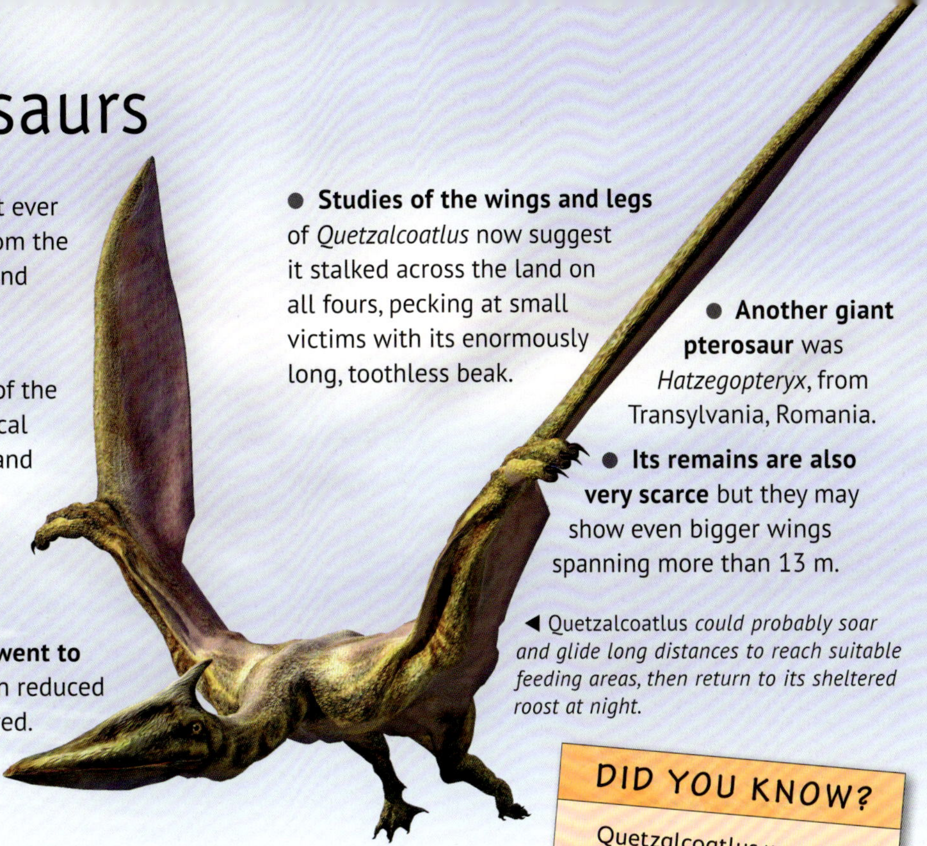

● **The largest flying animals** that ever lived were the great pterosaurs from the end of the Cretaceous Period, around 80–66 mya.

● **One of the largest was *Quetzalcoatlus***, named in honour of the feathered serpent god from mythical times in Southern North America and Central America.

● ***Quetzalcoatlus* is estimated** to have a wingspan of at least 10 m, and perhaps more than 12 m.

● **Previous wingspan estimates went to 20 m** or more, but these have been reduced as more fossils have been uncovered.

● ***Quetzalcoatlus* dates** from the very end of the Cretaceous Period, about 72–66 mya.

● **Its fossils come from North America**, but because pterosaurs had such light, fragile bones, the fossils are scarce and fragmentary.

● **Studies of the wings and legs** of *Quetzalcoatlus* now suggest it stalked across the land on all fours, pecking at small victims with its enormously long, toothless beak.

● **Another giant pterosaur** was *Hatzegopteryx*, from Transylvania, Romania.

● **Its remains are also very scarce** but they may show even bigger wings spanning more than 13 m.

◀ Quetzalcoatlus *could probably soar and glide long distances to reach suitable feeding areas, then return to its sheltered roost at night.*

DID YOU KNOW?

Quetzalcoatlus was once thought to swoop down like a vast vulture to feed on the carcasses of dead dinosaurs and other big animals.

Later pterosaurs

◀ *The largest type of* Pteranodon *had a wingspan of more than 6 m. It lived about 88–80 mya, feeding on fish that lived in the shallow seas that then covered much of North America.*

● **Pterodactyls are a later group** of pterosaurs (flying reptiles) than the rhamphorhynchoids.

● **They lived in the Late Jurassic** through to the Late Cretaceous Periods (about 160–66 mya).

● **Although pterodactyls** lacked the long, stabilizing tail of rhamphorhynchoids, they were probably more effective fliers and able to make quicker turns in the air.

● **These later pterosaurs** were also much lighter than rhamphorhynchoids because their bones were hollow.

● **The pterodactyl** *Pterodactylus* and the rhamphorhynchoid *Rhamphorhynchus* were roughly the same size, but *Pterodactylus* weighed between 1–5 kg, while *Rhamphorhynchus* was heavier at about 10 kg.

● **Some of the largest pterodactyls**, such as *Pteranodon*, appeared in the Late Cretaceous Period and had wingspans of over 5 m.

● **Unlike earlier flying reptiles**, *Pteranodon* had no teeth. Instead, it used its long, thin beak to scoop up fish.

● **At the bottom** of its mouth *Pteranodon* had a pelican-like pouch – it probably used this to store fish before swallowing them.

● ***Pteranodon* weighed** over 20 kg. This was heavier than earlier pterodactyls and suggests it was probably a glider rather than an active flyer.

● **A long crest** on *Pteranodon's* head may have worked as a rudder during flight.

Birds and dinosaurs

- **In 1868 Thomas Henry Huxley**, English biologist and supporter of Charles Darwin's theory of evolution, examined newly discovered fossils of the early bird *Archaeopteryx*.
- **Huxley saw how similar** these fossils were to those of small meat-eating dinosaurs such as *Compsognathus*.
- **However, his suggestion that birds evolved** from small dinosaur meat-eaters gradually fell out of favour for almost a century.
- **Since the 1970s, however**, new fossil discoveries of small meat-eating dinosaurs and early birds have shown that the two are closely related.
- **The common features shared by both groups** include hollow lightweight bones, the arrangement of bones in the chest, shoulder, arm and wrist, feathers, and also behaviours such as nest-building and care of young.
- **Today, most experts accept** that birds evolved from the small meat-eating dinosaur group known as maniraptorans, meaning 'hand snatchers'.
- **The maniraptoran group includes** the dromaeosaurs or raptor dinosaurs, and the troodontids.
- **However, feathers are not unique** to maniraptorans and birds – they are known from several other groups of dinosaurs.

DID YOU KNOW?

The most likely direct ancestors of birds were the troodontids, a group that includes Troodon, Anchiornis, Mei *and* Saurornithoides.

▼ *Creatures like* Anchiornis *show how difficult it is to separate birds from other groups of dinosaurs, which is why the main modern view is that birds are a subgroup of dinosaurs.*

Archaeopteryx

- **The earliest known bird** for which there is good fossil evidence, and which lived during the Age of Dinosaurs, is known as *Archaeopteryx*, meaning 'ancient wing'.
- ***Archaeopteryx* lived** in Europe during the Late Jurassic Period, about 150–147 mya.
- **At about 50–60 cm** from nose to tail, *Archaeopteryx* was about the size of a large crow.
- ***Archaeopteryx* resembled** a small, meat-eating dinosaur in many of its features, such as the teeth in its long, beak-like mouth, and its long, bony tail.
- **In 1951**, a fossilized part-skeleton was identified as a small dinosaur similar to *Compsognathus*, but in the 1970s it was re-studied and named *Archaeopteryx* – showing how similar the two creatures were.
- **Three clawed fingers** grew halfway along the front of each of *Archaeopteryx's* wing-shaped front limbs.
- **The flying muscles** were anchored to its large breastbone.
- ***Archaeopteryx* probably flew**, but not as fast or as skilfully as today's birds.
- ***Archaeopteryx* was covered** with feathers that had the same detailed designs found in those covering flying birds today.

▶ *Some reconstructions of* Archaeopteryx *show feathers only on the limbs and tail, where they formed air-proof flying surfaces. This bird could probably glide, swoop and turn as it pursued flying prey such as dragonflies.*

Confuciusornis

- ***Confuciusornis* is one of the earliest birds** known to have a horny beak with no teeth, like modern birds, and a very short bony tail, rather than the long trailing tail of vertebrae or backbones.
- ***Confuciusornis* lived** during the Early Cretaceous Period, 125–120 million years ago.
- **It was named in 1995** after the famous Chinese philosopher Confucius, who lived about 2500 years ago.
- **Hundreds of detailed fossils** of *Confuciusornis* have been collected from the rocks known as the Jiufotang and Yixian Formations in China.
- ***Confuciusornis* weighed** about 0.5–1.5 kg and its wings measured up to 80 cm from tip to tip.
- **It had feathers** on its head, body, wings and upper legs.
- **The wing feathers were shaped** like those of a modern flying bird and were more than 20 cm long. They probably allowed for good gliding, and perhaps short bursts of powered flight.
- **Some specimens of *Confuciusornis*** had very long tail feathers called streamers, shaped like narrow flat tape, although most did not.
- **These tail streamers may show** that the specimen was a certain sex, for example, male rather than female.
- **Possibly the streamers may show** it was an adult rather than a youngster.
- **Lack of streamers could mean** they had just been shed or moulted with the seasons.

◀ *Studies of the micro-details of* Confuciusornis *feather fossils suggest it was coloured in patches of brown, white and black.*

Terror birds

- **After the large dinosaurs** became extinct (about 66 mya), huge flightless birds – known as terror birds – seized the opportunity to become the dominant predators of their day.
- ***Gastornis* was one** such terror bird, standing around 2 m tall.
- **It had a huge** head and powerful legs, like those of its dinosaur ancestors, so it could outrun its prey.
- **Some experts believe** that *Gastornis* is a close cousin of ducks, geese and other related birds.

▲ Gastornis *attacks a small mammal of its time,* Leptictidium.

DID YOU KNOW?

Gastornis was named in 1855 after Gaston Planté, a fossil-hunter who turned to physics, and four years later invented the lead-acid battery used in cars and trucks.

- **Even though these birds** were huge, they were also light-footed, fast runners. This is because, like all birds, they had hollow bones.
- **The diets of terror birds** included small and medium-sized mammals, such as prehistoric rodents and horses.
- **During the Late Eocene** and Oligocene Epochs (40–23 mya), the big carnivorous mammals became more powerful and better hunters. They became dominant, and took over.
- **However, in South America**, which was cut off from North America and the rest of the world for much of the past 66 million years, terror birds managed to stay dominant for a longer period of time.
- **One South American terror bird** was *Phorusrhacus*, which grew to be 2.5 m tall.
- ***Titanis* was one** of the few North American terror birds, and one of the biggest of all – it was 2.5 m tall and weighed 150 kg.

Other flightless birds

● **Most prehistoric flightless birds** were giants, but not all of them were terror birds.

● **Much later giant birds** grew to incredible sizes. *Dinornis*, for instance, was the tallest flightless bird ever at 3.5 m tall.

● ***Dinornis* lived** in New Zealand. It first appeared about 2 mya and survived until perhaps as recently as 500 years ago.

● ***Dinornis* was one of a group** of birds known as moas.

● **At various times** there were probably about eight or nine different kinds of moas living on the two main islands of New Zealand.

● **The largest kinds of *Dinornis*** were the giant moas, which were extremely heavy, weighing over 200 kg.

● **The disappearance of the moas** came soon after humans reached New Zealand, and all moas were probably extinct by the end of the 15th century.

● **Another group** of enormous flightless birds lived on the island of Madagascar, and were called elephant birds.

● **At 450 kg**, the giant elephant bird *Aepyornis* was probably the heaviest bird ever to have lived. Like moas, the elephant birds became extinct within the last 500 years.

● **Both *Dinornis* and *Aepyornis*** were herbivores. Their diet consisted of seeds and fruit.

DID YOU KNOW?

Genetic studies show the closest living relative of moas is probably the ostrich of Africa.

◀ *On Madagascar, in the absence of large mammal grazers and browsers, elephant birds evolved to become the biggest land herbivores.*

Water birds

● ***Ichthyornis* was a prehistoric seagull**, which first appeared in the Late Cretaceous Period (100–66 mya).

● **It was similar in size** to a modern seagull, but had a much larger head and a beak full of very sharp teeth.

● ***Presbyornis* was related** to modern ducks. Like *Ichthyornis*, it evolved in the Late Cretaceous Period and was abundant in the Early Paleogene Period (66–40 mya).

● ***Presbyornis* was much bigger** than a modern duck – it stood between 0.5 m and one metre tall.

● **It had much longer legs** than its modern relative and so may have been a wading bird rather than a diving bird.

● ***Presbyornis* lived in large flocks** on lake shores, like modern flamingos.

● ***Osteodontornis* was a huge flying bird**, with a wingspan up to 6 m across.

● **It lived in the Miocene Epoch** (23–5 mya) and would have flown over the North Pacific Ocean.

● ***Osteodontornis* had a long bill**, lined with tooth-like bony spikes. Its diet probably included squid, seized from the surface of the sea.

◀ Osteodontornis *was in the bird group called pseudotooths, where the 'teeth' were small bony points or spikes growing from the jaw bones, rather than true teeth.*

DID YOU KNOW?

The skull of Presbyornis most closely resembles that of the living Australian duck Stictonetta.

Land birds

- **Land birds are flying birds** that fly in the skies over land and hunt or feed on the ground, unlike water birds.
- **Fossils of prehistoric land birds** are rare because their bones were light and would not have fossilized well.
- **As a result**, there are big gaps in palaeontologists' knowledge of the evolution of many species of birds. However, they do know about some early land birds.
- ***Archaeopsittacus* was an early parrot** of the Late Oligocene Epoch (28–23 mya) that lived in what is now France.
- ***Ogygoptynx* was one** of the first known owls. It lived in the Palaeocene Epoch (66–56 mya).
- ***Aegialornis* was an early** swift-like bird, which lived in the Eocene and Oligocene Epochs (56–23 mya). It may be the ancestor of swifts and hummingbirds.
- ***Gallinuloides* was an early member** of the chicken family. Its fossils have been found in Wyoming, USA, in rock strata of the Eocene Epoch (56–33 mya).
- **The earliest known hawks**, cranes, bustards, cuckoos and songbirds also lived in the Eocene Epoch.
- **The earliest known vultures** lived in the Palaeocene Epoch (66–56 mya).
- ***Neocathartes*** was an early vulture-like bird. There are similarities between its skeleton and those of storks, which suggests vultures and storks are closely related.

▶ *Vultures have been following the same scavenging way of life for more than 50 million years.*

Argentavis

- ***Argentavis magnificens*** is the biggest known flying bird of all time, with wings measuring up to 7 m from tip to tip.
- **Its name means** 'magnificent Argentine bird' after the place where several sets of its fossils were found in Argentina.
- ***Argentavis* lived** in the late Miocene Epoch, about seven million years ago.
- **In overall shape** it resembled the vultures and condors of today, with wide wings for soaring.
- ***Argentavis* may have weighed** up to 75 kg – as much as an adult human.
- **It probably stood up to 2 m high**, had a head-body length of 1.3 m, and main flight feathers that were over 1.3 m long.
- **Like modern vultures**, *Argentavis* probably soared high on uprising air currents called thermals, so it rarely had to flap its enormous wings.
- **One idea is that *Argentavis* swooped** down to scavenge on sick, dying or dead large animals, tearing off pieces of flesh with its hooked beak.

▲ Argentavis, *also called the giant teratorn, could spot faraway food as it circled at height, then glided down to feast.*

- **However, a newer idea** is that its head, jaws and beak were not fully adapted to scavenging. Rather, it may have pecked up small creatures like mice, young birds and lizards, and swallowed them whole.

Mammal fossils

● **Fossil finds** of prehistoric mammals include skulls, teeth, jawbones, ear bones, horns, tusks and antlers.

● **There are few fossils** of the earliest mammals because scavengers would usually have eaten their bodies.

● **However, coprolites** (fossilized dung) of predators and scavengers sometimes contain undigested parts of the early mammals themselves, such as their teeth.

● **Palaeontologists can tell** a lot from a mammal's molars (cheek teeth). They can work out its species and the period it lived in from the pattern of ridges and furrows on their surface.

● **Palaeontologists can also estimate** the age of a mammal when it died by looking at the wear and tear on its teeth.

● **Some mammal fossils** are preserved in tar pits – natural pools of thick, sticky tar, which ooze up from the ground in some places, such as forests and scrublands.

● **Tar pits at Rancho La Brea**, near present-day downtown Los Angeles, USA, contained a perfectly preserved skeleton of the sabre-tooth carnivore *Smilodon*.

▲ *This enormous mammoth skull was found in South Dakota, USA. In Siberia, palaeontologists have also discovered the remains of mammoth skin, hair and other body parts.*

● **Freezing is another very effective way** of preserving animals. Remains of frozen mammoths have been discovered in near-perfect condition in Siberia.

● **Explorers using dog sledges** discovered some of the first frozen mammoths. Their remains were so well preserved that the dogs were able to eat the meat on the bones.

● **In 2007, a fantastically well-preserved** frozen baby mammoth was discovered in northern Russia. Named Lyuba, she died around 42,000 years ago.

Mammal offspring

● **Mammals developed a very different way** of producing young, compared to reptiles and birds, which both lay eggs.

● **Instead, most mammals** are viviparous, which means they give birth to live young.

● **One unusual group of mammals**, the monotremes, defy this rule by laying eggs. There are five surviving monotremes – the duck-billed platypus and four species of echidna.

▼ *Mammal mothers care for their young, as with* Toxodon, *which lived in South America as recently as 20,000 years ago.*

DID YOU KNOW?

The word 'mammal' comes from the name for the mammary glands – the part of female mammals' bodies that secretes milk.

● **After the young of mammals are born**, their mothers feed them milk that is produced in their mammary glands.

● **Early mammals**, such as *Megazostrodon*, *Eozostrodon* and *Morganucodon*, grew one set of milk teeth, which suggests that the young fed on milk.

● **Milk teeth** are temporary teeth that grow with the nutrients provided by milk, and prepare the jaw for later teeth.

● **Mammals can be divided** into three groups depending on how they rear their young – placentals, marsupials and monotremes.

● **In placental mammals**, the offspring grows inside its mother's body, in the womb, until it is a fully developed baby – at which point it is born.

● **Marsupial mammals** give birth to their offspring at a much earlier stage. The tiny infants then develop fully in their mothers' pouch, called a marsupium.

Early mammals

- ***Megazostrodon*** was one of the first true mammals. It appeared at the start of the Early Jurassic Period (about 200 mya).
- **This shrew-like insectivore** (insect-eater) was about 12 cm long. It had a long body that was low to the ground, and long limbs that it held out to the side in a squatting position.

▲ *Among the best-preserved fossil mammals is the shrew-like* Leptictidium *dating from around 50 mya.*

- ***Eozostrodon*** was another very early mammal, which emerged about the same time as *Megazostrodon*.
- **It had true mammalian teeth**, including two different sorts of cheek teeth – premolars and molars – which were replaced only once during its lifetime.
- **Its sharp teeth** suggest it was a meat-eater, and its large eyes suggest that it hunted at night.
- **Another early mammal** was *Morganucodon*. It also had premolars and molars and chewed its food in a circular motion, rather than the up-down motion of reptiles.
- ***Sinoconodon*** was yet another early mammal that lived in the Early Jurassic Period, about 190 mya. It was probably covered in fur.
- **These early mammals** had three middle ear bones, which made their hearing more sensitive than that of reptiles.
- **They also had whiskers**, which suggests they had fur. This in turn suggests that they were warm-blooded.
- **All true mammals** are warm-blooded, which means they maintain a constant body temperature. Fur helps mammals keep warm in cold conditions.

Juramaia

▲ Juramaia *was probably small and quick-moving, darting among rocks and undergrowth in search of small creatures to eat.*

- ***Juramaia* was a small, rat-shaped mammal** about 10–12 cm long. It lived towards the end of the Jurassic Period, 160 mya.
- **Fossils of *Juramaia*** were found in China, in rocks known as the Tiaojishan Formation.
- **These rocks**, in the area of Liaoning, northwest China, have provided many other beautifully preserved, highly detailed remains of mammals, dinosaurs, birds, insects and plants.
- **The main single specimen** of *Juramaia* has an almost complete set of fossil bones for the front of the skeleton, including the skull, teeth, upper backbone, ribs and front legs.
- ***Juramaia* probably lived** like a shrew of today, eating worms, bugs and other small prey.
- **Its feet show it was well adapted** to climbing and so it may have lived mainly in trees.
- **Clues from the jaws**, teeth, front legs and other parts show that *Juramaia* was in the mammal group called eutherians.
- **This group includes** placental mammals – those whose young develop in the womb, nourished by the placenta (unlike the marsupial or egg-laying mammals).
- ***Juramaia* is the earliest known** placental mammal, living more than 30 million years before the previous first-known, *Eomaia*.
- **The full name *Juramaia sinensis*** was given in 2011 and translates as 'Jurassic mother from China'.
- **This means that *Juramaia*** was the first of the eutherian mammals and it lived in the Jurassic Period.

Repenomamus

▲ Repenomamus *fossil bones show it was a powerful, muscular mammal that relied on strength rather than speed and agility.*

- **Before the discovery** of *Repenomamus*, 'reptile mammal', it was thought all mammals from the Age of Dinosaurs were smaller than today's pet cats or even brown rats.
- **Two different kinds of *Repenomamus*** have been discovered in the famous fossil-rich Yixian rocks in the province of Liaoning, northwest China.
- **Their fossils date back** to the Early Cretaceous Period, 130–125 mya.
- **The larger of the two kinds**, *Repenomamus giganticus*, was described and named in 2005.
- ***Repenomamus giganticus*** had a total length of over one metre and probably weighed more than 12 kg.
- **It had a build similar** to today's badger, with a stocky body and strong legs, but with a longer tail.
- **The second kind**, *Repenomamus robustus*, was described and named in 2000. It was similar to its larger cousin but around half the length, at 50–60 cm, and weighed about 5 kg.
- **One fossil specimen** of *Repenomamus robustus* had some bones of a small dinosaur preserved with it, in the place where its stomach would have been.
- **This small dinosaur** was *Psittacosaurus*, a young 'parrot-beak', that *Repenomamus* had probably eaten.
- **Both kinds of *Repenomamus*** belonged to an early mammal group called eutriconodonts. The name of this group means 'true three-pointed tooth', and they died out by 70 mya.

Fruitafossor

- **This prehistoric mammal dated back** to the Late Jurassic Period, around 155–150 mya.
- ***Fruitafossor* was quite small**, around 15 cm long from head to tail, and weighed less than 40 g.
- ***Fruitafossor* was thought to be** quite unusual when its fossils were dug up, studied and named in 2005.
- **Experts were surprised** by its several specialized features, which would have allowed it to dig and probably live in burrows, and feed on ants and termites.
- **Until the discovery of *Fruitafossor***, most mammals from the Age of Dinosaurs were thought to be shrew-like with a diet of creatures such as worms and bugs.
- **However *Fruitafossor* showed** that mammals of that time could be as specialized for different ways of life as modern mammals.
- **The teeth of *Fruitafossor*** were small and shaped like short pegs, very similar to the teeth of modern termite-eaters such as anteaters and aardvarks.
- **The front legs of *Fruitafossor*** were relatively large and strong, and used for digging up and scratching out its tiny prey. This gave it the nickname 'Popeye', after the strong cartoon sailor.
- ***Fruitafossor* means** 'Fruita's digger', from its digging and tunnelling adaptations.

DID YOU KNOW?

Fruitafossor was not named from any direct connection with fruits, but from the town where its fossils were discovered – Fruita, Colorado, USA.

▼ Fruitafossor *may have dug into termite and ant nests, and perhaps dug a burrow for its home.*

Marsupials

◀ *Thylacoleo, the 'marsupial lion', was similar to a modern small puma (mountain lion), but with huge slashing thumb claws. Its remains have been discovered in Australia.*

- **Marsupials are mammals** that give birth to their offspring at a very early stage in their development – when they are still tiny.
- **After being born**, the infant crawls through its mother's fur to a pouch called the marsupium, where it stays, feeding on milk, until it is big enough to leave.
- **Palaeontologists think** that the first marsupials evolved in Asia and then spread to the Americas and Australia.
- **An early marsupial** called *Alphadon*, meaning 'first tooth', emerged around 70 mya. It lived in North America.
- ***Alphadon* was 30 cm long** and weighed 300 g. It would have lived in trees, using its feet to climb, and fed on insects, fruit and small vertebrates.
- **When Australia became isolated** from the rest of the world and became an island, about 40 mya, its marsupials continued to evolve – unlike most other regions of the world, where they fell into decline.
- **Marsupials continued** to exist in South America, which was also isolated from the rest of the world during much of the last 66 million years, in the Paleogene and Neogene Periods.
- **When South America** became reconnected with North America, from about 4 mya, the arrival of placental mammals from the north led many marsupials to extinction.
- **Today, there are only two surviving groups** of marsupials in the Americas – the opossums found throughout North America and the rat opossums found in South America.
- **Australia has many living marsupials**, such as kangaroos and koalas. However it had a much greater marsupial population in the Paleogene and Neogene Periods – we know this from fossil sites such as Riversleigh in northwest Queensland.

Australian mammals

- **Australia has a unique natural history** because it became isolated from the rest of the world around 40 mya.
- **Australia's native mammals**, living and extinct, are mostly marsupials – mammals that give birth to tiny young, which then develop in their mother's outside pouch.
- **The earliest Australian marsupials** date from the Oligocene Epoch (34–23 mya). Many fossils come from the Miocene Epoch (23–5 mya) or later.
- **These fossils show** that there were giant kangaroos, called *Procoptodon*, as well as giant wombats, called *Diprotodon*.

▶ *At 3 m long, the giant wombat* Diprotodon *was probably the largest marsupial ever to have lived. It had tusks for its front teeth, but its cheek teeth were like a kangaroo's.*

- **Two marsupial carnivores** preyed on these giant herbivores. One was the lion-like *Thylacoleo*, the other was the smaller, wolf-like *Thylacinus*.
- **Palaeontologists** are very interested in *Thylacoleo* and *Thylacinus* because they demonstrate how different species can evolve to look very similar – the process known as evolutionary convergence.
- **Although they had different ancestors** and lived on different continents, *Thylacoleo* came to look like a placental lion, while *Thylacinus* came to look like a placental wolf.
- **The Miocene fossil site** in Riversleigh, northern Queensland, has revealed the extent and variety of prehistoric marsupials in Australia.
- **Among the fossils** are many long-extinct marsupials. One of these was so unusual that at first palaeontologists called it a 'thingodont', although now it is known as *Yalkaparidon*.
- ***Thylacinus* continued** to exist in Australia into the 20th century, as the thylacine. The last one died in a zoo in Tasmania in 1936.

South American mammals

- **South America was separated** from the rest of the world for much of the last 60 million years.
- **Like Australia**, South America's isolation meant that certain mammals only evolved there.
- **The main difference** between them was that South America had placental mammals as well as marsupials.
- **Placental mammals** included the giant ground sloths, such as *Megatherium*, and huge rodents the size of bears.
- **Marsupial mammals** included the marsupial carnivores, such as *Thylacosmilus*.
- **Evolutionary convergence**, when different species develop to look very similar, happened in South America just as in Australia. One example was *Thoatherium*, which looked very much like the small horses that were evolving in other parts of the world.
- **The formation** of the Panama isthmus (a strip of land) reconnected South America to North America from about 4 mya.
- **Many South American mammals** journeyed north. Some, such as armadillos, porcupines and guinea pigs, were very successful in their new homes.
- **Others, like the glyptodonts**, eventually died out. This might be because of climate change – or because humans hunted them to extinction.

◀ *The South American hoofed mammal known as* Macrauchenia *used its short trunk to gather vegetation. It lived from about 6 million to 30,000 years ago.*

DID YOU KNOW?

A good example of evolutionary convergence was Pyrotherium, which had the trunk, cheek teeth and tusks of an early elephant – but it belonged to a different group.

Megatherium

- **Also called the giant ground sloth**, *Megatherium* was one of the largest-ever land mammals not belonging to the elephant group.
- **It was up to 6 m long** and weighed over 4 tonnes.
- ***Megatherium* had long, curved claws** on its front feet, and so it probably walked on its knuckles when moving on all fours.
- **It could also sit upright** or even stand on two legs, using its tail as a support.
- **In this position**, *Megatherium* could reach up with its front legs to a height of perhaps 5 m.
- **It could then hook high branches** with its claws and pull them down towards its mouth to chop up with its sharp-edged teeth.
- ***Megatherium* lived in South America** from about 5 million to 10,000 years ago.
- **It may have died out** when humans spread through its range and hunted it to extinction with spears and other weapons.
- ***Megatherium* was named** more than 200 years ago, in 1796, by French animal and fossil expert Baron Georges Cuvier.
- **Its fossils were also collected** and studied in 1832 by English naturalist Charles Darwin, on his round-the-world voyage in the ship HMS *Beagle*.

▶ *Elephant-sized* Megatherium *was well armed with its long hand and toe claws – similar to its relatives, the tree sloths of today.*

Creodonts

▲ Hyaenodon *fossils are known from many regions around the world including Europe, Asia, Africa and North America.*

- **Creodonts** were the first big flesh-eating mammals. They lived from the Paleocene to the Miocene Epochs (about 50–10 mya).
- **These mammals came** in many different shapes and sizes. Some were as small as weasels, others were bigger than bears.
- **Many creodonts** were flat-footed and walked on short, heavy limbs tipped with claws.
- **They hunted early herbivores** that, like these early carnivores, had not yet evolved into quick runners.
- **Creodonts had smaller**, more primitive brains than later carnivores – these were cleverer, faster hunters than the creodonts, and forced them into decline.

DID YOU KNOW?

Hyaenodon species ranged in size from 30 cm high at the shoulders to 1.2 m high – the size of a small rhinoceros.

- **Another way** in which creodonts were less successful than later carnivores was their teeth, which were less effective at stabbing or slicing.
- **Creodonts were**, however, the top predators of their day. The wolf-sized *Hyaenodon* was particularly successful.
- **Fossils of *Hyaenodon* skulls** show that they had a very highly developed sense of smell, as well as powerful, bone-crushing jaws.
- **Fossils of male *Hyaenodon* teeth** reveal grinding marks, which palaeontologists think means that they ground their teeth to ward off rivals, like some modern animals do.

Carnivores

- **The first carnivorous mammals** were the creodonts, which ranged in size from the cat-like *Oxyaena* to the wolf-like *Mesonyx*.
- **In the Late Eocene Epoch** (around 40 mya) large hoofed carnivores, such as *Andrewsarchus*, began to appear.
- **Modern carnivores** are descended from a separate group called miacids.
- **Modern carnivores** belong to the order Carnivora. This order has two subgroups – the feliforms, which include the cats, and the caniforms, which are the dog families and the pinnipeds (seals, sea lions and walruses).
- **Some classification** schemes put pinnipeds in their own mammal group, separate from the other carnivores.
- **In the Oligocene Epoch** (34–23 mya), carnivorans began to replace creodonts as the dominant carnivores.
- **Carnivorans were smarter**, faster, and deadlier than creodonts.
- **Faster mammals** evolved in the Oligocene Epoch as thick forests changed into open woodlands, with more space to run after, and run from, other creatures.
- **As carnivorans evolved** they developed bigger brains, more alert senses, sharper claws and teeth, and stronger jaws and limbs.
- **The pinnipeds** are carnivorous mammals that, like whales and dolphins, reinvaded the seas.
- **The pinniped *Allodesmus*** was a prehistoric seal. It had flippers, large eyes and spiky teeth, which it used to impale fish.

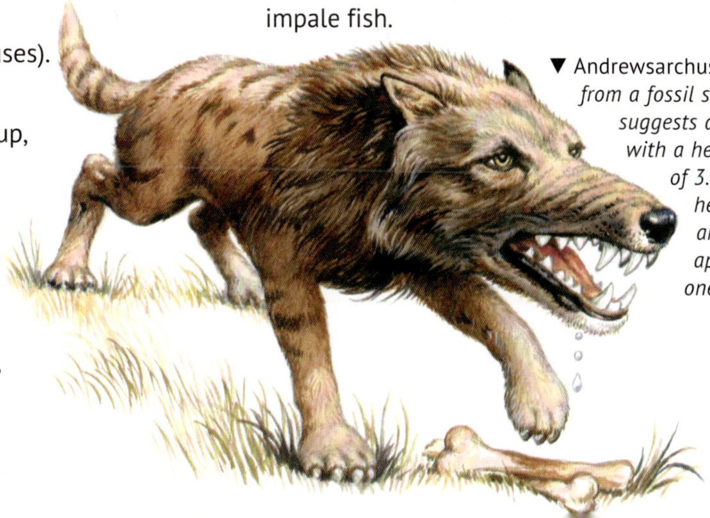

▼ Andrewsarchus *is known only from a fossil skull, which suggests a huge beast with a head-body length of 3.5 m, a shoulder height of 1.7 m and a weight approaching one tonne.*

Cats

- **The most highly developed** carnivores are cats. They are the fastest hunters, with the greatest agility, and have the sharpest claws and teeth.
- **Cats evolved** along two lines. One group included the various kinds of sabre-tooths, of which *Smilodon* was one. This group is extinct today.
- **Sabre-tooths** probably specialized in killing large, heavily built animals with thick hides, which explains their long canine teeth.
- **The other group** of cats is the felines, which are the ancestors of all modern cats, from lions and cheetahs to pet cats.

▼ Dinofelis *was a muscular, heavily built predator with relatively short canines for a sabre-tooth cat.*

DID YOU KNOW?

Prehistoric cats' ability to unsheathe and retract their claws provided them with one of their deadliest weapons – and it's one that cats still have.

- **The felines were faster** and more agile than the sabre-tooths, which may have become extinct because their prey became faster and more able to outrun them. The felines, however, continued to be successful hunters.
- **One prehistoric feline** was *Dinictis*, a puma-sized cat that lived in the Oligocene Epoch (37–23 mya).
- **Later felines** were various types of *Dinofelis*, which lived between 5 and 1.3 mya across North America, Europe, Africa and Asia.
- **The name *Dinofelis*** means 'terrible cat'. It looked like a modern jaguar, but had stronger front legs that it used to press down on its victims before stabbing them with its teeth.
- ***Dinofelis*' diet** included baboons, antelope and perhaps australopithecines – our prehistoric human relatives.

Smilodon

- ***Smilodon* is often called** a sabre-tooth 'tiger', but it was not an especially close relative of today's tigers.
- **A better name is sabre-toothed cat**, since *Smilodon* was in the general cat group, felids, along with lions, tigers, cheetahs and wildcats.
- ***Smilodon* belonged** to the cat subgroup known as machairodonts, which have all died out.

▲ *Snarling* Smilodon *tracks a victim by scent, its huge canine teeth ready to deliver a deadly strike.*

- **Several kinds of *Smilodon*** lived in North and South America from around 2.6 million to 11,000 years ago.
- **The largest kind had** a head-to-tail length of 3.5 m, stood 1.2 m at the shoulder, and was heavily built, weighing over 350 kg.
- **The 'sabres' were canine teeth** in the upper jaw of *Smilodon* – up to 30 cm long, curved, very sharp and pointed, but not particularly strong.
- ***Smilodon* could open its mouth** very wide, so the teeth almost pointed forwards.
- ***Smilodon* probably used these long teeth** to slash and stab at its prey's throat very quickly, then it backed away and waited until the victim bled to death, before starting to feed.
- **Hundreds of *Smilodon***, along with many other animals such as bison, wolves and mammoths, were trapped and preserved in the La Brea natural tar pits in modern-day Los Angeles, USA.

Dogs

- **Early dogs probably hunted** in a similar way to most modern wild dogs – in packs.
- **Dogs developed** long snouts, which gave them a keen sense of smell, and forward-pointing eyes, which gave them good vision.
- **Dogs also developed** a mixture of teeth – sharp canines for stabbing, narrow cheek teeth for slicing, and, farther along the jaw at the back, flatter teeth for crushing.
- **These different teeth** meant that dogs could eat a variety of different foods, including plants, which they might have had to eat if meat was in short supply.
- **One of the ancestors** of dogs, as well as bears, was the bear-dog *Amphicyon*. Its name means 'in-between dog'.
- ***Amphicyon* lived** between 20 and 10 mya.
- **Trace fossils** of *Amphicyon's* footprints show that it walked like a bear, with its feet flat on the ground.
- ***Hesperocyon*** was one of the earliest dogs, living between about 40 and 30 mya.

▲ *In North America a pack-leading, or alpha-male,* Hesperocyon *tackles a now extinct relative of deer,* Synthetoceras.

- ***Hesperocyon*** was the size of a small fox. It had long legs and jaws, forward-pointing eyes and a supple, slender body.

DID YOU KNOW?

Hunting in packs allowed Hesperocyon to catch large animals that it would not have been able to kill on its own.

Herbivores

- **The first specialist herbivores** (plant-eaters) appeared in the Late Palaeocene Epoch (around 60 mya).
- **They ranged in size** from the equivalent of modern badgers to pigs.
- **These early herbivores** were rooters or browsers – they foraged for food on the floor or among branches in their forest homes.

▶ Elasmotherium *was a huge rhinoceros, about the size of modern elephants, that lived 2–1 mya in Europe and Asia.*

- **It was not until** the very end of the Palaeocene Epoch (56 mya) that the first large herbivores evolved.
- **Large herbivores** emerged before large carnivores. They must have had a peaceful life – for a while.
- ***Uintatherium* was one** of the large early herbivores. It was the size of a large rhinoceros, with thick limbs to support its heavy body.
- ***Uintatherium* had three pairs** of bony knobs protruding from its head. Males had very long, strong canine teeth, which they would have used if attacked by creodont carnivores.
- **The growth of grasslands** and the decline of forests in the Miocene Epoch (23–5 mya) sped up changes to herbivores' bodies.
- **Herbivores developed** faster legs to outrun carnivores in open spaces.
- **They also developed** better digestive systems to cope with the new, tough grasses.
- **The most important** requirements for a herbivore are complex teeth and digestive systems to break down tough plant food and release its energy.

Rodents

- **In terms of their numbers**, variety and distribution, rodents are the most successful mammals that have ever lived.
- **Squirrels, rats, guinea pigs**, beavers, porcupines, voles, gophers and mice are all types of rodent.
- **Rodents have been** – and still are – so successful because they are small, fast-breeding and able to digest all kinds of foods, including substances as hard as wood.
- **One of the first known** rodents was *Paramys*, which appeared more than 50 mya.
- ***Paramys* was a squirrel-like rodent** that could climb trees. It was 60 cm long, and had a long, slightly bushy tail.
- **Modern squirrels evolved** around 40 mya. These mammals have one of the longest known ancestries for any living mammal group.
- **Another early rodent** was *Epigaulus*, which was a gopher with two horns. The horns were side by side on the top of its snout, pointing upward.
- ***Epigaulus* was 30 cm long** and lived in North America in the Miocene Epoch (23–5 mya). It probably used its horns for defence or digging up roots.
- **Prehistoric rodents** could be massive. *Castoroides* was an early beaver that was over 2 m long – almost the size of a black bear.

DID YOU KNOW?

Rabbits and hares are descended from rodents. Modern hares first appeared around 5 mya.

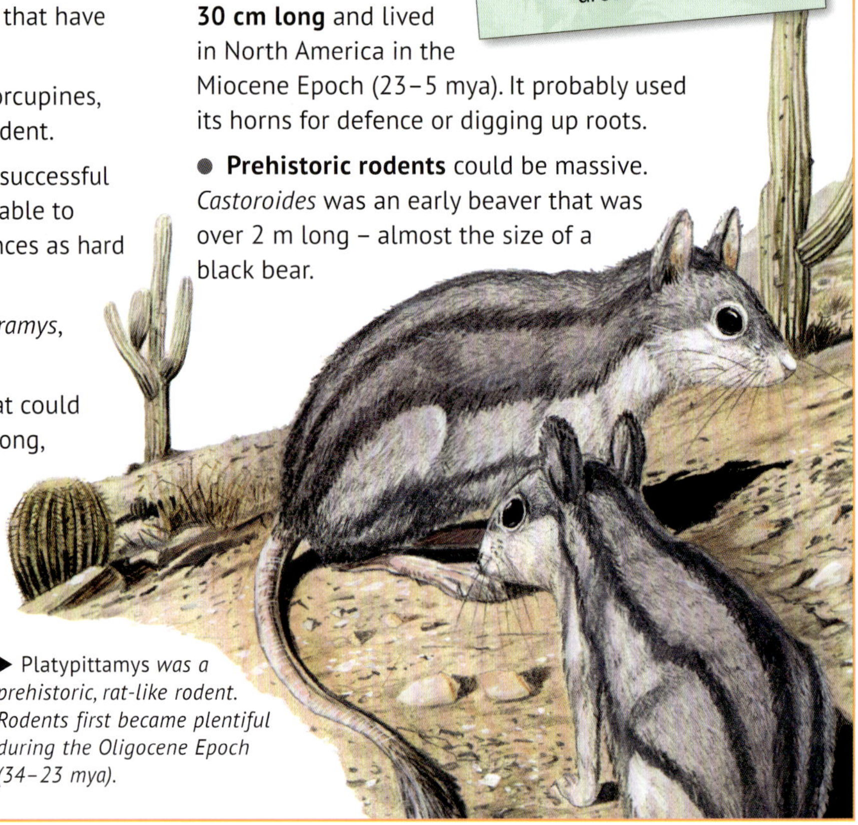

▶ Platypittamys *was a prehistoric, rat-like rodent. Rodents first became plentiful during the Oligocene Epoch (34–23 mya).*

Condylarths

- **Condylarths were among** the first hoofed mammals.
- **They lived in** the Paleogene Period, 66–23 mya.
- **Early condylarths** were rabbit-sized. Later ones, however, were as big as bears.
- **All later hoofed mammals**, from horses to pigs, are probably descended from condylarths or similar animals.
- **The earliest condylarths** had claws as opposed to hooves.
- **Later species evolved** longer limbs, tipped with nails or hooves, for running away quickly from carnivores.
- **The first known condylarth** was *Protungulatum*, a rabbit-sized plant-eater, living 64–63 mya.
- **A slightly later condylarth** was *Phenacodus*, which palaeontologists think was an insectivore (an insect-eater).
- ***Phenacodus* was the size** of a small sheep, and had clearly developed hooves.
- **Condylarths spread** over most of the world, including Europe, Asia, South America and Africa.

◀ Arctocyon, *from about 50 mya, was probably 2 m long from head to tail. Muscle marks on fossils suggest it could climb trees.*

Perissodactyls

- **Perissodactyls are plant-eating**, hoofed mammals with an odd number of toes (either three or one) on their feet.
- **The three living groups** of perissodactyls are horses, tapirs and rhinoceroses.
- **Two extinct groups** of perissodactyls are brontotheres and chalicotheres.
- **Brontotheres included** massive beasts, such as *Brontotherium*, which had elephant-like limbs and a blunt, bony prong jutting from its nose. It ate only soft-leaved plants.
- **Chalicotheres had long front legs** and long curved claws, which they could not place flat on the ground. Instead, they walked on their knuckles, like apes.
- ***Chalicotherium*** was a chalicothere. It lacked front teeth, and ate by placing soft plant shoots in the back of its mouth, like a modern panda.
- **The earliest ancestors** of modern horses, tapirs and rhinos, appeared before 50 mya, probably as the Paleocene Epoch gave way to the Eocene, 56 mya.
- ***Miotapirus* was an early type** of tapir. It lived in North America about 20 mya and was similar in size to living tapirs, 1.5–2 m long.
- **Perissodactyls' feet** carried the weight of the animal on the middle toe, either in a single hoof, as in horses, or a big toe with one on each side, as in tapirs and rhinos.
- **For much of the Paleogene Period** (66–23 mya), perissodactyls were the most abundant form of hoofed mammals. They then declined, however, and artiodactyls (even-toed mammals) became dominant.

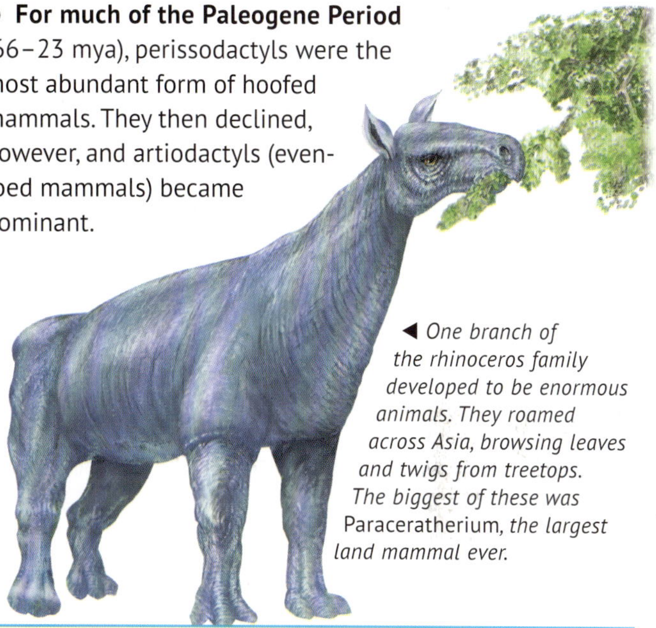

◀ *One branch of the rhinoceros family developed to be enormous animals. They roamed across Asia, browsing leaves and twigs from treetops. The biggest of these was* Paraceratherium, *the largest land mammal ever.*

Artiodactyls

- **Artiodactyls are hoofed mammals** with an even number (either two or four) of toes on their feet.
- **Pigs, camels, giraffes**, sheep, goats, cattle, hippopotamuses, deer, antelopes and their ancestors are all artiodactyls.
- **Like the perissodactyls**, artiodactyls first appeared about 55–50 mya.
- ***Dichobune* was an early artiodactyl**, which lived between 40 and 30 mya. It had short limbs and four-toed feet.
- **In smaller artiodactyls**, such as sheep and goats, the foot is often divided into two parts (toes).
- **In very heavy artiodactyls**, such as hippopotamuses, there are four toes to carry the animal's weight.
- **At least two** of the middle toes on artiodactyls' feet carry an equal weight.
- **During the Miocene Epoch** (23–5 mya), artiodactyls became the most successful hoofed mammals.
- **Artiodactyls' success** lay more in their stomachs than in their feet.
- **They evolved** more advanced digestive systems, which allowed them to process the tough grasses that had replaced the earlier, softer, forest plants.
- **Another difference** between artiodactyls and perissodactyls is their ankle bones. Artiodactyls' ankle bones have more rounded joints at both ends, which means they provide more thrust when they run.

▶ Synthetoceras *had a long, forked nose horn, unlike any modern artiodactyl. However, this horn was probably present only in males.*

Entelodonts

- **Entelodonts were large** pig-like mammals that lived in Asia and North America in the Eocene and Miocene Epochs (56–5 mya).
- **These mammals are also known as** 'terminator pigs' or 'hell pigs' because of their fearsome appearance.
- **One of the largest** entelodonts was *Daeodon* (*Dinohyus*). It stood almost 2 m tall at the shoulder with a skull that was around one metre long.
- ***Daeodon* probably fed** off plant roots or scavenged for prey.
- ***Daeodon* had** very distinctive teeth. Its incisors (front teeth) were blunt, but the teeth next to them, the canines, were sturdy and substantial, and could have been used for defence.

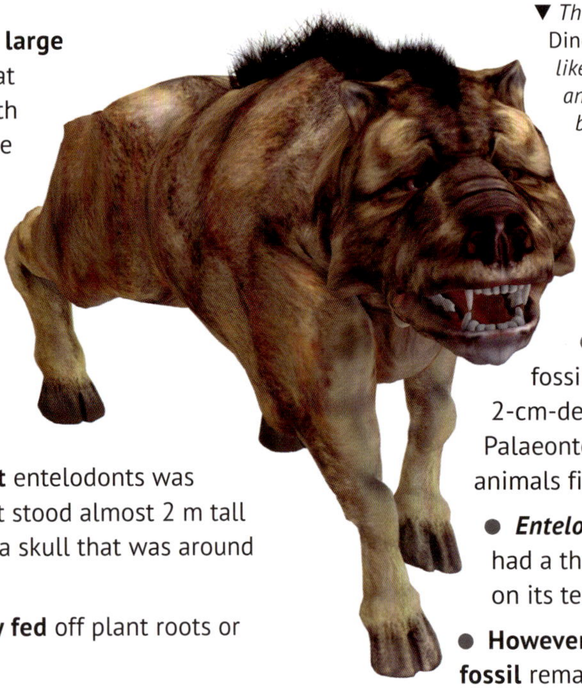

▼ *The fierce-looking* Daeodon, *formerly known as* Dinohyus, *may well have scavenged for its food like modern hyenas. Its powerful neck muscles and large canine teeth suggest it could have broken bones and eaten flesh.*

- **Another entelodont** was the scavenger *Entelodon*, the largest of which was about the same size as *Daeodon*.
- **There are severe wounds** in the fossils of some *Entelodon* skulls, such as a 2-cm-deep gash in the bone between its eyes. Palaeontologists think these were caused by the animals fighting among themselves.
- ***Entelodon* means** 'perfect-toothed'. This mammal had a thick layer of enamel on its teeth.
- **However, many fossil** remains of *Entelodon* have broken teeth – a result of the tough, varied diet of this scavenger.

DID YOU KNOW?

Entelodon's face had bony lumps all over it. One reason could be that they protected its eyes and nose during clashes with rivals.

Bats

- ***Icaronycteris* is one of** the earliest known bats. Its fossil remains are about 52 million years old.
- **Despite its age**, *Icaronycteris* looks very similar to a modern bat. It has a bat's typically large ears, which it probably used as a sonar, like modern bats.
- **One difference** from modern bats was that *Icaronycteris*' tail was not joined to its legs by flaps of skin.
- **Palaeontologists think** that there must have been earlier, more primitive-looking bats from which *Icaronycteris* evolved.
- **The chance of finding** earlier prehistoric bat fossils is very small – like birds, bats have fragile skeletons that do not fossilize well.

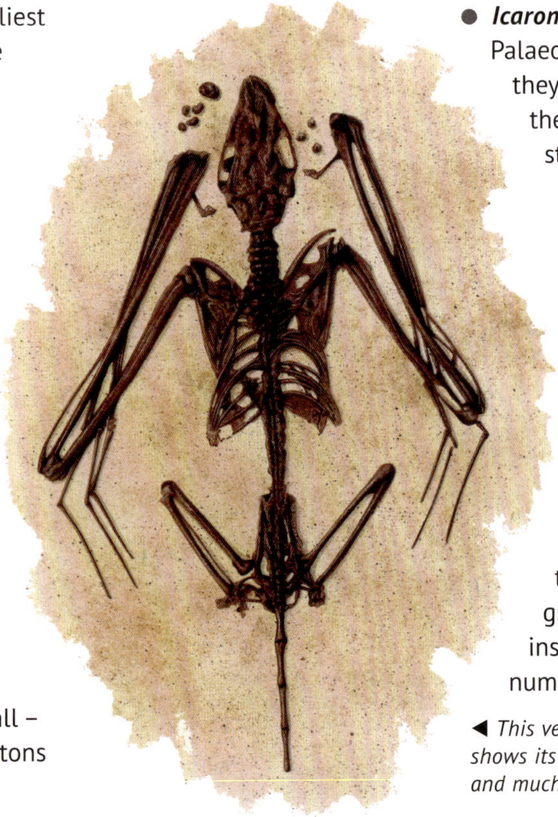

- ***Icaronycteris* ate insects**. Palaeontologists know this because they have found insect remains in the part of the fossil where its stomach would have been.
- ***Icaronycteris* fossils** have been found in North America.
- **The fossil remains** of another prehistoric bat, *Palaeochiropteryx*, have been found in Europe.
- **Like *Icaronycteris***, this bat seems to have been an insectivore (insect-eater).
- **The earliest bats** belong to the Microchiroptera mammal group. These are the smaller, insect-eating bats that are most numerous today.

◄ *This very rare fossil of* Icaronycteris *shows its long, strong arm or wing bones and much smaller leg bones.*

Elephant evolution

● **Elephants and their ancestors** belong to an order of animals called Proboscidea, meaning 'long-snouted'. Another word for the elephant group is proboscideans.

● **The first elephants** appeared around 40 mya. They didn't have trunks and looked a bit like large pigs.

● ***Moeritherium* is one of the earliest** known animals in the elephant group.

● **Its name comes** from Lake Moeris in Egypt, where fossil-hunters discovered its remains.

● **The American palaeontologist** Henry Fairfield Osborn (1857–1935) described *Moeritherium* as 'a missing link' between elephants and other mammals.

● ***Moeritherium* was 3 m long**, weighed 200 kg, lived around 37 mya, and probably spent much of its life wallowing in rivers or shallow lakes, like a hippopotamus.

● **Another stage** in the development of elephants was *Phiomia*, which lived about 35 mya.

● ***Phiomia* had a shoulder height** of about 2.5 m. Its fossils come from North Africa and other remains found with them show it lived in swampy areas.

● **The deinotheres** were members of the elephant group, with one pair of enormous downward curving tusks in the lower jaw.

● **The other groups** of the Proboscidea were the true elephants (which resembled elephants living today) and the mammoths. These animals appeared in the Pliocene Epoch (5–2.5 mya).

▼ *Most elephants through time had a long trunk and enlarged teeth known as tusks.*

Moeritherium
37 mya

Palaeomastodon
35 mya

Primelephas
7 mya

DID YOU KNOW?

Mammoths were giant elephants. The steppe mammoth stood up to 4 m tall at the shoulder and probably weighed more than 15 tonnes.

Woolly mammoths

- **Woolly mammoths** (scientific name *Mammuthus primigenius*) first evolved over 200,000 years ago, probably in Asia.
- **They lived on the cold grasslands** of Asia, Europe and North America, and some survived to as recently as 4000 years ago.
- **To survive** in these cold places, woolly mammoths were designed for warmth and insulation.
- **Their woolly coats** were made up of two layers of hair – an outside layer of long, coarse hairs, and a second layer of densely packed bristles.
- **Woolly mammoths also had** very tough skins, up to 2.5 cm thick, beneath which was a deep layer of fat.
- **Male woolly mammoths** could grow up to 3.5 m long and 2.9 m high at the shoulder, and weigh up to 6 tonnes.
- **They had long tusks** that curved forward, up and then back.
- **Mammoths used** their tusks to defend themselves against attackers and probably to clear snow and ice to reach low-lying plants.
- **Some cave paintings** by ice-age humans clearly depict woolly mammoths.
- **Many excellently preserved** woolly mammoth remains have been discovered in the permanently frozen ground of Siberia.

DID YOU KNOW?

People often think the woolly mammoth had red hair, but in fact this colour was a chemical reaction that happened after the animal died.

◀ *Woolly mammoths had thick, shaggy fur to keep them warm, small ears and enormous tusks.*

Rhinoceroses

- **Rhinoceroses were a very important group** of mammals in the Paleogene and Neogene Periods (66–2.6 mya).
- ***Hyracodon* was an early rhino-like mammal** that lived in North America about 30 mya.
- **Long, slender legs** meant that *Hyracodon* would have been a fast runner. It grew to about 1.5 m long.
- **Amynodonts were a group** of prehistoric rhinos that experts believed evolved from *Hyracodon*.

▼ *The woolly rhino of the last great ice age died out less than 10,000 years ago.*

- ***Metamynodon* was** an amynodont rhino-like creature. It was as large as a hippopotamus and may have had a similar lifestyle to one, wading in rivers and lakes.
- **True rhinoceroses**, the ancestors of modern rhinos, were probably descended from early versions such as *Hyracodon*.
- **One of the first true rhinos** was *Trigonias*, which had four developed toes on its front feet but three on its hind feet. It lived about 35 mya in the Late Eocene or Early Oligocene Epoch.
- ***Caenopus*, another true rhino**, had three toes on all four feet. This was the pattern for all later rhinos.
- **The largest rhinoceros** horn of all time may have belonged to *Elasmotherium*, which lived in Europe possibly up to 50,000 years ago. The horn could have been a massive 2 m long.
- **Rhinos became extinct** in North America between 5 and 2 mya, and later in Europe. But they survived in Asia and Africa and continue to do so today, although they are severely threatened by extinction.

Paraceratherium

- ***Paraceratherium* was the biggest** known land mammal ever.
- **Several kinds of *Paraceratherium*** lived around 35–20 mya across Asia.
- **The biggest *Paraceratherium*** stood almost 5 m tall at the shoulder, with long, powerful legs and a long neck.
- **Its head and body were 8 m long**, and the total weight was over 15 tonnes, perhaps even 20 tonnes – heavier than the biggest-ever mammoth.
- **However *Paraceratherium* was not a mammoth** or other member of the elephant group – it was a kind of rhino, without a horn.
- **The head of *Paraceratherium*** was at a similar height to today's giraffe, around 6 m.
- ***Paraceratherium* probably fed** in a similar way to a giraffe, among trees at a height that no other ground-based animal could reach.
- ***Paraceratherium* had tusk-like front teeth** to pull and strip leaves, fruits and twigs from trees.

▲ *A mother and calf* Paraceratherium *cross a plain to reach woodland where they can feed.*

- ***Paraceratherium* was named** in 1911, from fossils discovered in present-day Pakistan.
- **Similar huge fossils** have been given various names over the years, such as *Baluchitherium*, *Indricotherium* and *Thaumastotherium*, but many experts suggest these should now all be called *Paraceratherium*.

The first whales

- **The very first whales** looked nothing like the enormous creatures that swim in our oceans today.
- ***Ambulocetus***, one of the first members of the whale family, looked more like a giant otter. It lived about 50 mya.
- ***Ambulocetus* means** 'walking whale', and it may have spent more time on land than in water.
- **Fossil remains show** that *Ambulocetus* had webbed feet and hands, so it would have been a good swimmer.
- **An even earlier whale** ancestor than *Ambulocetus* was *Pakicetus*, which lived about 52 mya.
- ***Pakicetus* is named** after the country Pakistan, where a fossil of its skull was found in 1979.
- ***Pakicetus* was around** 1.8 m long. *Ambulocetus*, at 3 m, was bigger.
- **Palaeontologists used to think** that the whale and dolphin group, Ceracea, evolved from carnivorous hoofed mammals called mesonychids. A modern view is that the cetaceans are more closely related to the even-toed ungulates of hoofed mammals, the artiodactyls.
- **Around 40 mya**, the first true whales evolved from their half-walking, half-swimming ancestors. They stayed in the ocean waters and didn't come onto land.

DID YOU KNOW?

Only the back of Pakicetus' skull and part of its lower jaw have been found. However, from this palaeontologists can tell it was not able to dive very deeply.

◀ Pakicetus *could run fast and swim well. It probably lived alongside water and hunted animals both in and out of the water.*

Horses

- **Horses have one of** the best fossil records of any animal.
- **Palaeontologists** have been able to trace horse evolution from the earliest horse-like mammals to the modern horse.
- ***Hyracotherium* was an early horse**. It lived in forests in Europe in the Late Palaeocene and Early Eocene Epochs (58–50 mya).
- **Another name** for *Hyracotherium* used to be *Eohippus*, which means 'dawn horse', but *Eohippus* has now been given its own status as another type of early horse.
- ***Hyracotherium* was the size** of a small fox, with its head and body about 60 cm long. It had a short neck, a long tail and slender limbs. It also had three toes on its hind feet and four toes on its front feet.
- ***Mesohippus* was one of the horses** to evolve after *Hyracotherium*, between 40 and 30 mya. Its name means 'middle horse'.
- ***Mesohippus* had longer legs** than *Hyracotherium* and would have been a faster runner.
- **It would also have been better** at chewing food, because its teeth had a larger surface area.

▲ Hyracotherium *is the earliest known horse. Over time, horses became the best adapted of all hoofed animals for life on the open plains.*

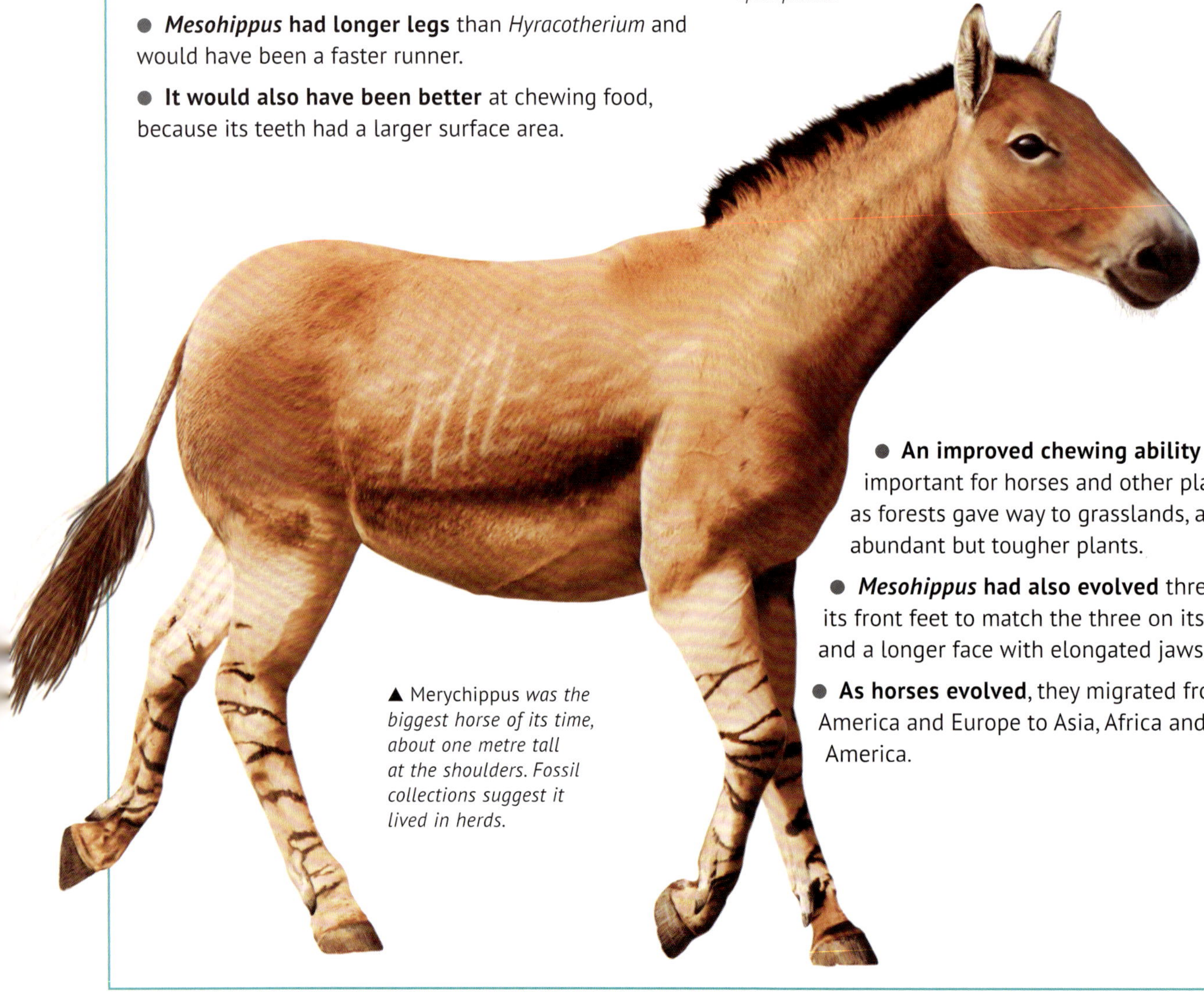

▲ Merychippus *was the biggest horse of its time, about one metre tall at the shoulders. Fossil collections suggest it lived in herds.*

- **An improved chewing ability** was important for horses and other plant-eaters as forests gave way to grasslands, and more abundant but tougher plants.
- ***Mesohippus* had also evolved** three toes on its front feet to match the three on its hind feet, and a longer face with elongated jaws.
- **As horses evolved**, they migrated from North America and Europe to Asia, Africa and South America.

Early primates

● **The primates** are a group of mammals that include lemurs, bushbabies, tarsiers and monkeys, and apes such as gorillas, chimps and humans.

● **Primates have** a much greater range of movement in their arms, legs, fingers and toes than other mammals.

● **They also have** a more acute sense of touch because their fingers and toes end in flat nails, not curved claws, so the skin underneath evolved into a sensitive pad.

● **The ancestors of primates** were small insectivorous (insect-eating) mammals that looked like shrews.

● **One of the first known** primates was *Plesiadapis*, which lived about 57 mya in Europe and North America. It was a squirrel-like tree climber.

● **More advanced primates** developed about 5–10 million years later. They looked a bit like modern lemurs.

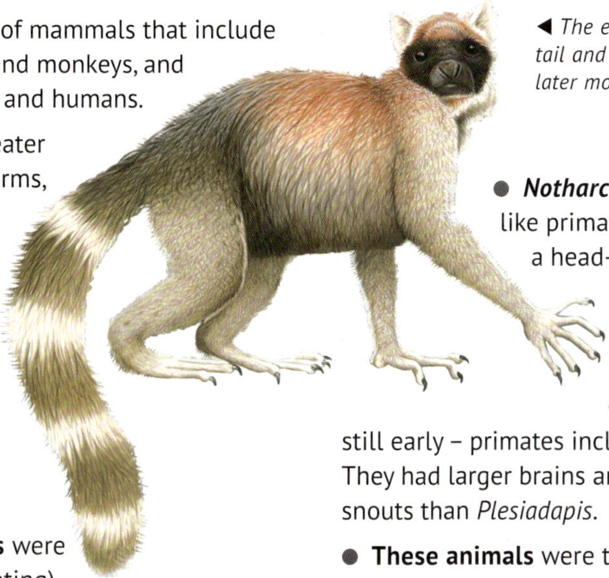

◀ *The early primate* Plesiadapis *had a long tail and claws on its fingers and toes – unlike later monkeys and apes, which had nails.*

● ***Notharctus* was one** of these lemur-like primates. It ate leaves and fruit, had a head-body length of 40 cm, and a grasping thumb that would have gripped well around branches.

● **Other more advanced** – but still early – primates include *Smilodectes* and *Cantius*. They had larger brains and eyes, longer tails and smaller snouts than *Plesiadapis*.

● **These animals** were the early relatives of lemurs and lorises, but probably not of the higher primates – the monkeys, apes and humans. Palaeontologists believe that this role belongs to a different branch of primate evolution.

● **One early monkey** was *Mesopithecus*, which lived about 6 mya in Greece and Turkey. It was similar to modern monkeys in many ways, but had a longer tail.

Apes

● **Apes are primates** that have more complex brains than monkeys and no tails. They include lesser and great apes and humans.

● ***Aegyptopithecus*** was one of the early pre-apes. It lived in Egypt in the Oligocene Epoch (34–23 mya). It was small and had a short tail.

● **An early ape** that lived between 25 and 23 mya was *Proconsul*. Its body size varied from that of a small monkey to that of a female gorilla, and it had a larger brain than *Aegyptopithecus*.

● ***Proconsul* was a fruit-eater**. It probably walked on four limbs with part of its weight supported by the knuckles of its hands, like modern chimps and gorillas.

● **Several lines of apes** developed after *Proconsul*. They led to lesser apes or gibbons, the Asian great apes and the African great apes.

● ***Dryopithecus* was a chimp-like ape** that evolved after *Proconsul* and lived in the Late Miocene Epoch (15–5 mya).

▶ *The early ape* Dryopithecus *stood about one metre tall. It had the largest brain for its size of any mammal at the time.*

DID YOU KNOW?

Proconsul was named in 1927 after Consul, a performing chimpanzee that appeared on stage smoking a pipe and riding a bicycle.

● ***Sivapithecus* was an ape** that lived from about 12 to 8 mya. It is now thought to be part of the chain of evolution of Asian apes and is possibly an ancestor of the orang-utan.

● **Australopithecines were a further step** in the evolution from apes to humans. Australopithecines (meaning 'southern apes') were found in Africa and some walked on two legs.

● **The biggest ape** was *Gigantopithecus*, which lived in China from about 8 to less than 1 mya. It may have been up to 2.5 m tall and weighed 300 kg.

Sahelanthropus

- ***Sahelanthropus* was an ape-like creature** whose fossils have been found in Chad, central North Africa.
- **The region where the remains were found** is called The Sahel, leading to the name *Sahelanthropus*, 'Sahel ape'.
- **Fossils of *Sahelanthropus***, found in 2001–2002 and named in 2008, consist of parts of the skull, including bits of jaws and teeth.
- **These fossils** have been given the nickname 'Toumai', meaning 'Hope of Life' in the local language.
- **These remains are enough** to know that *Sahelanthropus* was a member of the ape group – gorillas, chimps, humans and orang-utans.
- **However the fossils are not complete** or detailed enough to show the relationship between *Sahelanthropus*, gorillas, chimps and humans.
- ***Sahelanthropus* lived at least 6 mya** and probably about 7 mya, although possibly even earlier.
- **Some fossil experts** say this is the time when the human line of evolution was separating from our closest living relatives, the chimpanzee line.

▲ *Fossils of* Sahelanthropus *are not complete enough to know whether it lived mainly in trees or on the ground.*

- ***Sahelanthropus* may have lived** just before this split, as the last common ancestor of chimps and humans.
- **Or *Sahelanthropus* may have existed** just after the split, as the earliest human-line ancestor, or, less likely, on the other side of the split as an early chimp ancestor.

Orrorin

- **The name *Orrorin*** means 'Original Man' in the local language of the Tugen Hills in Kenya.
- **Several *Orrorin* fossils** have been unearthed here since 2000, giving them the nickname 'Millennium Human'. It received its official name in 2001.
- ***Orrorin* fossils include** bits of thigh and upper arm bones, fingers, lower jaw and teeth.
- **Comparing these remains** to similar parts of other fossil and also living apes, *Orrorin* was probably about 1.4–1.5 m tall and weighed around 40–50 kg.
- **Dating *Orrorin* fossils** by various means gives an age of around 6 million years, that is, after *Sahelanthropus* but before *Ardipithecus*.
- **The shape of the thigh bones** found suggests *Orrorin* could stand and walk upright.
- **The teeth are also more similar** to modern humans, compared to certain other fossil apes.
- **These features have led** some experts to propose that *Orrorin* is a direct ancestor of modern humans.
- **If so, this could place** the extinct *Australopithecus* on a side branch of human evolution, rather than as our ancestor, as described later.
- **However, other bones** of *Orrorin* are shaped more for tree-climbing than for upright walking.

DID YOU KNOW?

Features of Orrorin fossils show it is more similar to modern humans than some later human-type primates causing a real puzzle for experts.

◀ *About 20 fossils of* Orrorin *have been found in Kenya, East Africa.*

Ardipithecus

● **A possible early hominin** (humans and close relatives) was *Ardipithecus ramidus,* which lived about 4.5 mya.

● **It would have looked similar** to a chimpanzee in many ways, except for one major difference – *Ardipithecus ramidus* could walk on two legs.

● **It probably lived** in woods and forests, sleeping in trees at night, but foraging on the ground for roots during the day.

● **A full-grown** *Ardipithecus ramidus* was about 1.3 m tall and weighed up to 50 kg.

● **Archaeologists discovered** the teeth, skull and arm bone fossils of *Ardipithecus ramidus* in Ethiopia and it was named in 1994.

● **In 2001**, archaeologists in Ethiopia found the remains of an even older hominid, *Ardipithecus kadabba*, which lived between 5.6 and 5.8 mya.

● **The fossils** of *Ardipithecus kadabba* are similar to those of *Ardipithecus ramidus*, so it is possible they are very closely related.

● **The name** ***kadabba*** comes from the local language version of 'basal family ancestor'.

● ***Australopithecus anamensis*** is a later hominin than *Ardipithecus ramidus*. Its fossils date to between 4.2 and 3.9 million years old.

● **A fossil** of one of *Australopithecus anamensis*' knee-joints shows that it shifted its weight from one leg to the other when it moved – a sure sign that it walked on two legs.

◄ Ardipithecus ramidus. *Scientists chose its name from the Afar language of Ethiopia –* ardi *means 'ground' while* ramid *means 'root' – words that express its position at the base of human history.*

Australopithecus africanus

● ***Australopithecus africanus***, which means 'the southern ape of Africa', was an early hominin that emerged between 3 and 2 mya.

● **This species** was the first australopithecine to be discovered.

● **The Australian-born** scientist Raymond Dart discovered this important fossil in South Africa in 1924.

● **The fossil** was found in a quarry near the village of Taung, on the edge of the Kalahari Desert.

● **It was the fossil** of a skull, belonging to a child around two or three years old. The fossil became known as the Taung child.

● **Many people** did not believe in Dart's discovery – they thought it was an ape, not a hominin. But one person did believe it – the archaeologist Robert Broom.

DID YOU KNOW?

'Hominid' is used to refer to modern and extinct Great Apes and all their immediate ancestors. 'Hominin' is used to refer to modern and extinct humans and all their immediate ancestors.

● **In 1947**, Broom himself found a skull of an adult *Australopithecus africanus*.

● **The adult skull** became known as 'Mrs Ples' because Broom first thought it belonged to a different species, *Plesianthropus transvaalensis*.

● **By the 1950s** other parts of *Australopithecus africanus*' skeleton had been unearthed, including a pelvis and a femur.

● **These fossils proved** beyond doubt that *Australopithecus africanus* was an upright-walking hominin.

◄ *This reconstruction of* Australopithecus africanus *shows a projecting ape-like jaw but also a forehead that does not slope back so much as in modern apes.*

Australopithecus afarensis

● **One of the most famous** of all hominin fossils is 'Lucy'.

● **'Lucy' was a female** young adult *Australopithecus afarensis*, which means 'Southern Ape from Afar'.

● **Her remains** were excavated near Hadar in the Afar region of Ethiopia, northeast Africa, in 1974, and named in 1978.

● **About two-fifths of the skeleton** of 'Lucy' were preserved – a very large amount compared to other human fossils from such a long time ago. The hip bones show she was female.

● **Many other fossils** of *Australopithecus afarensis* have also been found in East Africa.

● **These include parts** of a group of 13 individuals of various sizes known as the 'First Family', which were found at Hadar in 1975.

● **The fossil of a young girl** about three years old, 'Selam', was also found near Hadar in 2000.

● ***Australopithecus afarensis*** lived between 4 and 3 mya.

● **Its spine, hips, legs and feet** show it could walk quite well, upright on two legs, while the shoulders, arms and hands were adapted to grasping, as when climbing in trees.

● **The typical height** of an adult *Australopithecus afarensis* was 1.1 m for females and 1.5 m for males, with a weight of 40 kg for males and 30 kg for females. Brain size was small, usually less than 400 cubic cm.

● ***Australopithecus afarensis*** may have been our direct ancestor, on the evolutionary line to modern humans, or a close relation of this ancestor.

◀ *Fossils found with those of 'Lucy' and her kin indicate these creatures lived in a mixed habitat with water, trees and grasses.*

Homo erectus

● **About 1.8 million years ago** a new form of human appeared in Africa – *Homo erectus*.

● **The body of *Homo erectus*** was very similar to that of a modern human, and was also tall, with some specimens standing 1.8 m in height.

● **The head was different** to that of modern humans, having a heavy ridge of bone over the eyes and protruding jaws that made it look more ape-like.

● **Some remains indicate** that *Homo erectus* was capable of building huts out of wood and brushwood.

● ***Homo erectus*** spread beyond Africa and settled in Europe and Asia.

● **In the late 19th century**, Eugène Dubois discovered *Homo erectus* fossils on the Indonesian island of Java. At the time he named them *Pithecanthropus erectus*, which later changed to *Homo erectus*.

DID YOU KNOW?

The 'Peking Man' fossils disappeared at the beginning of World War II and have never been found. They were confiscated by Japanese troops just when they were about to be shipped to the USA.

● **In the 1930s**, archaeologists found over 40 *Homo erectus* skeletons in China, naming them *Sinanthropus pekinensis*.

● **For a long time**, people called the human to which the Chinese fossils belonged 'Peking Man'. It was much later that palaeoanthropologists realized it was in fact *Homo erectus*.

● **Archaeologists have also found** evidence that *Homo erectus* used fire and practised cannibalism.

◀ *Stone hearths that were used by* Homo erectus *prove that it had mastered fire. Fire provided warmth, light, protection and the means to cook food and make tools and weapons.*

Homo habilis

- ***Homo habilis*** is one of the earliest known members of the genus Homo, to which we also belong. It lived between 2.3 and 1.4 mya.
- **The archaeologists** Louis and Mary Leakey first discovered its remains at Olduvai Gorge in Tanzania, in 1960–1961.
- **Fossils of *Homo habilis*** skulls have since been found around Lake Turkana in Kenya, one of the richest sites for hominid and hominin fossils in the world.
- **The skulls show** that *Homo habilis* had a flat face with prominent cheekbones, similar to the australopithecines, which it would have lived alongside.
- ***Homo habilis*** was much more ape-like than its successors, such as *Homo ergaster*.
- **It probably** had body fur and lacked any form of language.

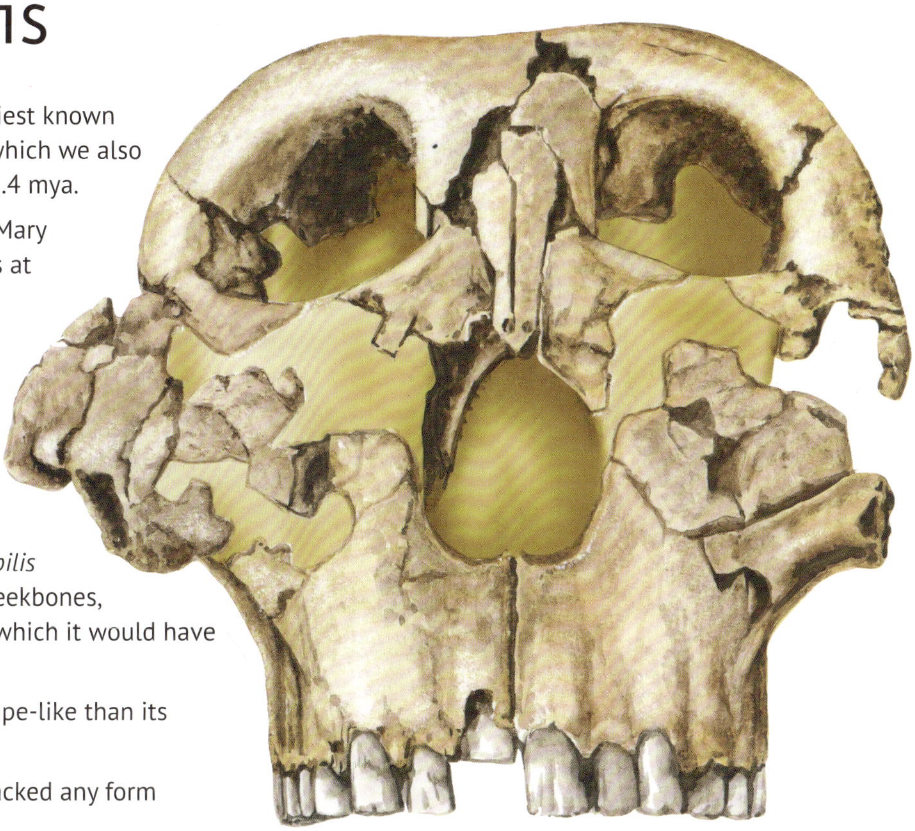

▲ *The first* Homo habilis *skull found by Louis and Mary Leakey in Tanzania. It had a bigger brain than any previous hominin.*

◀ Homo habilis *showed the trend of jaws that protruded less compared to earlier relatives.*

DID YOU KNOW?

Homo habilis used stone tools to crack open animal bones so it could eat the nutritious marrow inside.

- **But it did have a bigger brain** than any australopithecine. It also had more flexible hands and straighter, more sensitive fingers.
- ***Homo habilis*** means 'handy man'. It could use its hands to gather fruit and it also created stone tools, known as Oldowan.
- **A fully grown** *Homo habilis* male was around 1.4 m tall and weighed about 50 kg.

Homo heidelbergensis

- ***Homo heidelbergensis*** may well be the direct ancestor of our own species, *Homo sapiens*, and perhaps the Neanderthals as well.
- **This species is named** after a bone called the Heidelberg jaw, found in Germany in 1907 and officially described in 1908.
- **Thousands of similar fossils** have been found since then, across Europe, Western Asia and Africa, from Boxgrove in England to South Africa.
- ***Homo heidelbergensis*** probably appeared in Africa, perhaps evolving from *Homo erectus*, some 1,100,000 to 750,000 years ago, and then spread to other regions.
- **Although it was about as tall** and heavy as modern humans, *Homo heidelbergensis* had a slightly smaller brain size, around 1200–1300 cubic cm.
- **Many stone tools** are associated with *Homo heidelbergensis*, including hand axes, scrapers and spear points.
- **From the details** of preserved skull, ear and throat (hyoid) bones, *Homo heidelbergensis* may well have had some form of language.
- ***Homo heidelbergensis*** may be the same species as another fossil, *Homo rhodesiensis*, found only in Africa.
- **It seems that** *Homo heidelbergensis* had died out by 200,000 years ago, as Neanderthals appeared in Europe and modern humans appeared in Africa.

▶ Homo heidelbergensis *may well have hunted in cooperative groups using spears, clubs and similar simple weapons.*

Homo neanderthalensis

- ***Homo neanderthalensis*** – or Neanderthals – lived between around 300,000 and perhaps 30,000 years ago across Europe, West Asia and parts of the Middle East.
- **The name *Homo neanderthalensis*** means 'man from the Neander Valley', which is the site in Germany where the first of its fossil remains were found in 1865.
- **Neanderthals are our extinct cousins** rather than our direct ancestors – they are from a different branch of the human family.

DID YOU KNOW?

Many people think that Neanderthals were slow and stupid, but in fact their brains were at least as big as modern humans' brains.

- **They were about 30 percent heavier** than modern humans. Their bodies were more sturdy and they had shorter legs.
- **Neanderthals' shorter, stockier bodies** were better suited than modern humans to life in Europe, West Asia and parts of the Middle East during the ice ages of the Pleistocene Epoch (2.6 million to 12,000 years ago).
- **Their faces** were also different, with sloping foreheads and heavy brow ridges.
- **They buried their dead**, cooked meat and made various tools and weapons.
- **Neanderthals made** the first ever spears tipped with stone blades.

◀ *Neanderthals showed great skills in hunting, collecting plants and cooking foods.*

Towards Homo sapiens

● **All people alive today** belong to the species *Homo sapiens*, 'Wise Human'.

● **More accurately**, we belong to a subgroup or subspecies known as *Homo sapiens sapiens*, (*H. s. sapiens*), which are anatomically modern humans or simply 'modern humans'.

● **Before the appearance** of the *Homo sapiens sapiens* subgroup around 200,000 years ago, fossils show there were several other kinds of *Homo sapiens* with more ancient or primitive features. These are known by the general name of archaic *Homo sapiens*.

● **These primitive or archaic features** included slightly different brain size, thicker skull bones, a sloped-back forehead, bony eyebrow ridges, a projecting face and less protruding cheek bones.

● **Other archaic features** compared to modern humans were bigger teeth, a sloped-back or rounded chin, and a skeleton that had a generally heavier or more robust build.

● **Some kinds of archaic *Homo sapiens*** have one or a few modern features mixed with the primitive ones, which makes it difficult to put them into precise, well-defined groups.

● **One version of the evolutionary line** leading to us goes from *Australopithecus* (probably *A. afarensis*), perhaps to *Homo habilis*, then *H. erectus*, on to *H. heidelbergensis* (*H. rhodesiensis*), then archaic *H. sapiens*, and finally modern humans, *H. s. sapiens*.

● **In this version**, the whole evolution of the *Homo* group occurred in Africa.

● **However, this sequence** is only one of many suggestions. Different experts have very different opinions and debate them with great passion.

DID YOU KNOW?

Homo sapiens sapiens probably originated in Africa around 200,000 years ago.

▼ *These are model reconstructions of hominins in chronological order:* Australopithecus, *early* Homo erectus *(Java Man), late* Homo erectus *(Peking Man),* Homo heidelbergensis *(Rhodesian Man),* Homo neanderthalensis *(Neanderthals) and early* Homo sapiens *(Cro-Magnons).*

1 *Australopithecus*

2 *Early Homo erectus* (Java Man)

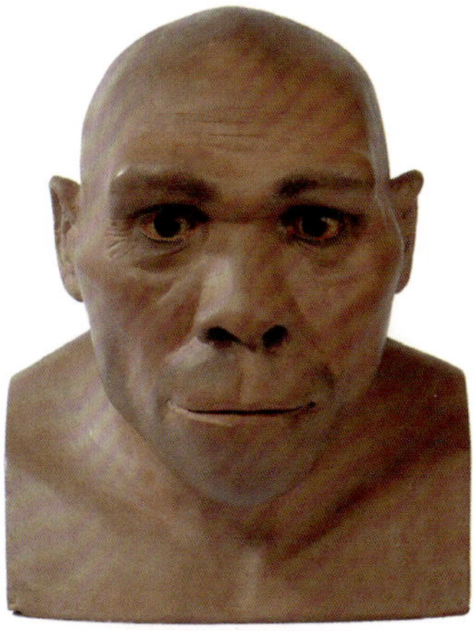

3 *Late Homo erectus* (Peking Man)

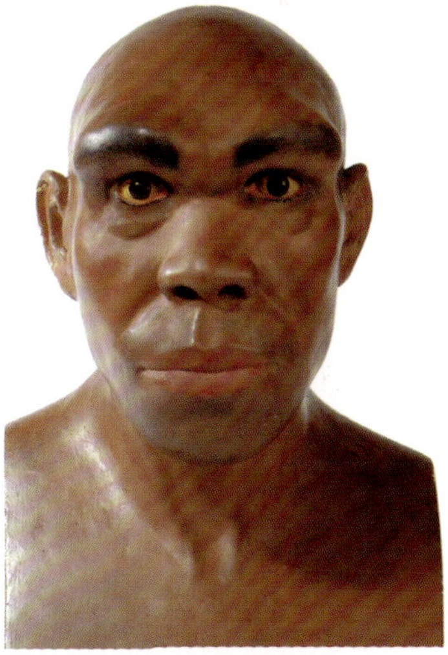

4 *Homo heidelbergensis* (Rhodesian Man)

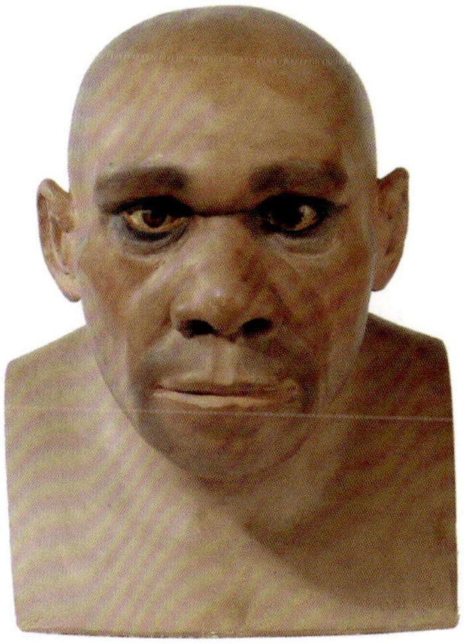

5 *Homo neanderthalensis* (Neanderthals)

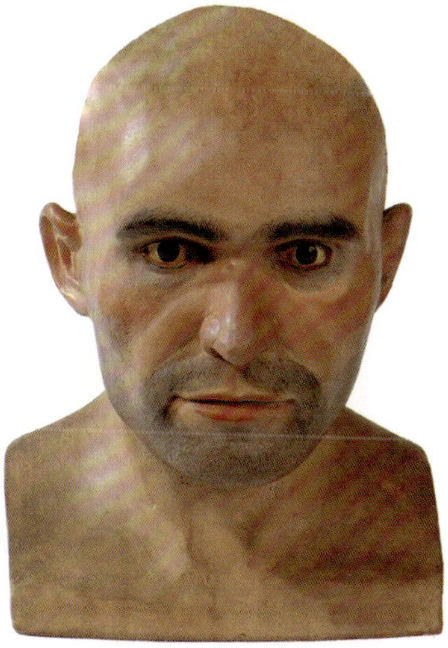

6 *Early Homo sapiens* (Cro-Magnons)

Modern humans

- **All people alive today** are (anatomically) modern humans, subspecies *Homo sapiens sapiens*.
- **Various evidence suggests** when and where modern humans appeared, including tools, fossil bones and teeth, genetic material (DNA) extracted from them, and genes from living people.
- **Most evidence shows** that modern humans appeared around 200,000 years ago in East Africa.
- **The oldest fossils recognized** as modern humans come from Omo, Ethiopia, dated to 195,000 years ago.
- **By 90,000 years ago**, modern humans had become established in Africa and started to spread into the Middle East. This migration is known as 'Out of Africa'.
- **From the Middle East**, modern humans spread into Europe by 40,000 years ago as 'Cro-Magnon People'.
- **They also spread east** into Asia, South East Asia and then Australia by 45,000 years ago.
- **Other modern humans** spread north-east through Asia into north-west North America by 15,000 years ago, and then south through the Americas.
- **As modern humans spread**, they replaced archaic *Homo sapiens* and other humans living in each region.
- **However modern humans** may have interbred with some of these other groups, such as the Neanderthals in Europe.
- **Modern humans gradually** adapted to the climate and other conditions in each region, producing the variety of people around the world today.

▲ *Neanderthals are not our direct ancestors but may well have interbred with modern humans around 40,000 years ago.*

DID YOU KNOW?

About 100,000 years ago there were probably fewer than half a million humans in the world. Today there are over 7600 million.

▼ *Improved climate (green area) enabled humans to migrate into Europe and Asia from Africa. Changes in the sea level (orange area) opened up the route to Australia. Ice age glaciations (blue areas) limited migration north and east, but once established, the Americas were swiftly populated.*

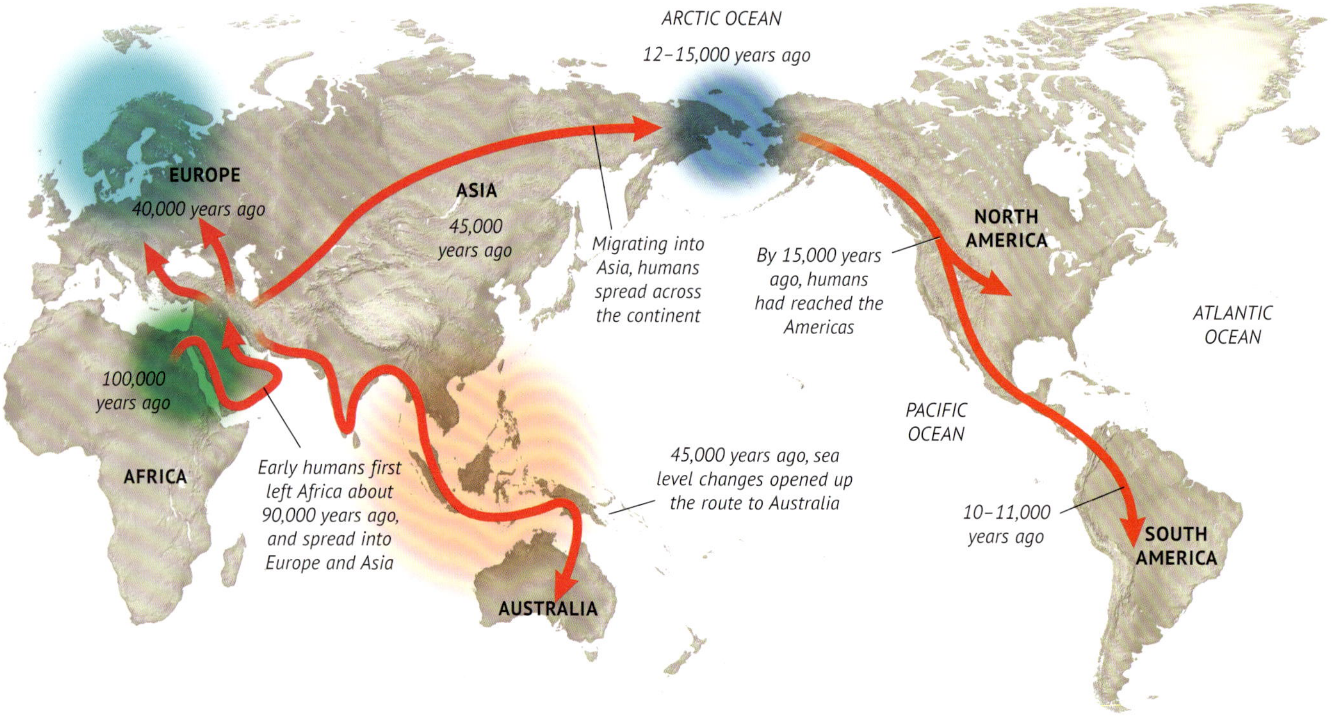

Denisovan and Red Deer people

● **Denisovan humans** are named after Denisova Cave in the Altai Mountains of Central Asia.

● **Numerous kinds of fossils** were found here of three distinct kinds – Neanderthals, anatomically modern humans (*Homo sapiens sapiens*), and Denisovan people.

● **The Denisovan fossils** include teeth and pieces of finger and toe bones, from around 40,000 years ago.

● **Denisovan people** may have evolved separately from the line leading to modern humans around 800,000 years ago. They probably separated from the Neanderthal line 650,000 years ago.

● **However studies of genetic material** from fossils and living people show these three groups bred with each other at certain times, so that some modern humans from Asia and Australia have inherited certain Denisovan genes.

● **Red Deer Cave people** are known from preserved bones and teeth found in the cave of that name, in Yunnan, South China.

● **These fossils** have some differences from those of modern humans, yet the most recent date from only 11,500 years ago.

● **It is unclear** whether Red Deer people were a different species from modern humans, a result of interbreeding, or a regional variation of modern humans.

◀ *Palaeontologists carefully sift this cave for fossils of Denisovan humans, along with other animals and plants of their time, 40,000 years ago.*

DID YOU KNOW?

Discoveries such as Denisovans and Red Deer people show that in the last 50,000 years there were more kinds of humans than was once believed.

Brains and intelligence

● **Primates, including all the various** kinds of humans, had bigger brains in relation to their body size than other mammals.

● **Primates developed** larger brains – and more intelligence – because living in and moving between trees required a high degree of balance, coordination and the skilful use of hands and feet.

● **Once hominids' brains** started getting bigger, so their skulls began to change.

● **Bigger brains** led to the development of foreheads.

● ***Homo habilis'* brain** was 50 percent bigger than its australopithecine predecessors. It had a brain capacity of 750 cubic cm.

● **The structure of its brain** was different to that of earlier hominids. It had much bigger frontal lobes – the parts of the brain associated with planning and problem-solving.

● ***Homo habilis*** put its greater intelligence to use in the quest to find meat, which it scavenged from other animals' kills to supplement its diet.

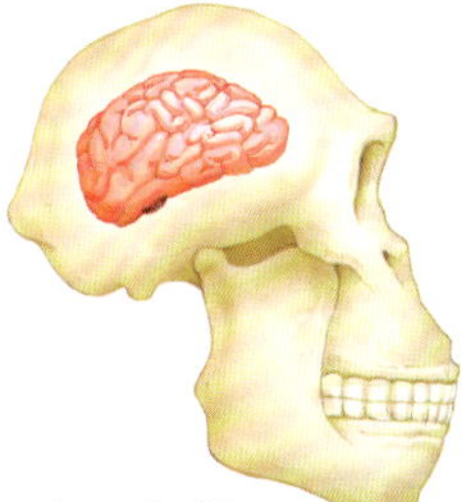

Australopithecus afarensis

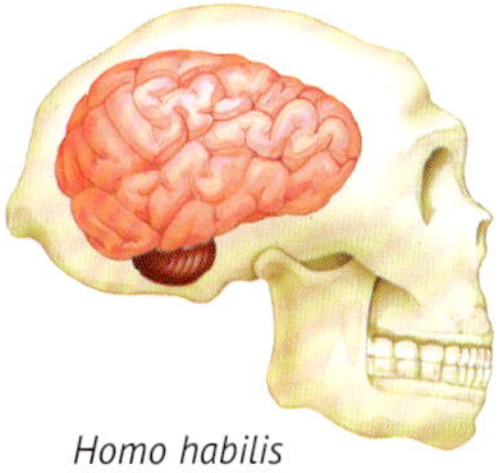

Homo habilis

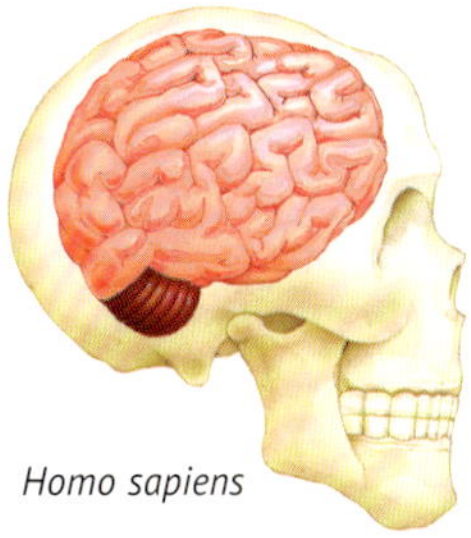

Homo sapiens

● **Eating more meat** allowed hominids' brains to get even bigger. Breaking down plant food uses up a huge amount of energy, so the fewer plants hominids ate, the more energy was available for their brains.

● ***Homo ergaster*** was a type of hominid with an even bigger brain, with a capacity of around 1000 cubic cm. It could use this intelligence to read tracks left by animals – a major development in hunting.

● **The brain** of *Homo erectus* became larger during its existence. About one million years ago its brain capacity was 1000 cubic cm, and 500,000 years later it was 1300 cubic cm.

● **The average human brain** capacity today is 1350–1450 cubic cm.

◀ *Brain size is linked to intelligence, but size isn't everything. What makes humans and our ancestors intelligent is our brain's complex structure.*

Tools

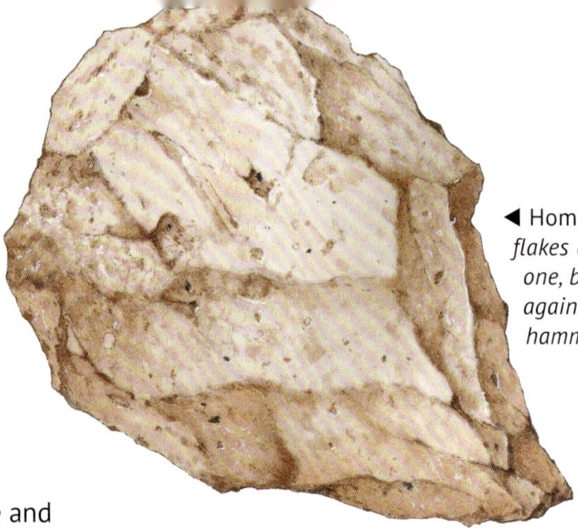

◀ Homo habilis *produced flakes of stone, such as this one, by striking one stone against another, called a hammerstone.*

- **The greatest number** of *Homo habilis* tools has been found in the Olduvai Gorge in Tanzania.
- **They include rocks** that were used as hammers, flakers, choppers and scrapers.
- ***Homo habilis*** used these tools to cut meat and, especially, to scrape open animal bones to eat the marrow inside.
- **The stone tools** used by *Homo habilis* are crude and basic. This hominin was one of the the first tool-makers, but not a skilled one as yet.
- **Making these early stone tools** was still a challenging task – the tool-maker needed to strike one rock with another so that it would produce a single, sharp flake rather than shattering into many pieces.
- **Tool-making requires** considerable intelligence. It involves the use of memory, as well as the ability to plan ahead and to solve abstract problems.
- ***Homo erectcus'* tools** were more advanced. This hominin made tear-drop shaped, symmetrical hand axes called Acheulean axes, after the place in France where similar axes have been discovered from a later period.
- **Neanderthals developed** a method for producing razor-sharp flakes of stone, called Levallois flakes, which could be placed on the end of spears.
- **This method** required great precision and dexterity. While modern humans have a much broader range of skills, most would be very hard pushed to produce such tools themselves.
- **Modern humans** developed the greatest variety of tools. Cro-Magnon tools include knives, spearpoints and engraving tools.
- **Cro-Magnon humans** also began to make tools from materials other than stone, including wood, bones, antlers and ivory.

Hobbit people

- **In 2003**, the bones of some very small people, hardly one metre tall yet living within the past 15,000 years, were found on the island of Flores, Southeast Asia.
- **Bones from several individuals** were found, including one partially complete skull. They showed a brain size of 400–450 cubic cm – one-third that of modern humans.
- **These remains were described** in 2004 as the species *Homo floresiensis*, or 'Flores Human'.
- **The movie series *Lord of the Rings***, featuring small human-like hobbits, was released around this time, leading to the nickname 'Hobbit people' for *Homo floresiensis*.
- ***Homo floresiensis* bones** date from around 40,000 to 13,000 years ago. Stone tools found at the site are between 95,000 and 13,000 years old.
- **Experts argue** about whether *Homo floresiensis* was a separate species from modern humans, or a group of modern humans who were extra-small, perhaps because of genetic changes called mutations, or some form of disease.

▲ *Flores humans may have used their tools to kill and cut up pygmy elephants that also lived on their island.*

- **Puzzling was the presence of stone tools** presumably made by *Homo floresiensis* when it had the brain size of a chimpanzee.
- **Recent studies show** *Homo floresiensis* had a curious mix of modern and primitive features which cannot easily be explained.
- ***Homo floresiensis* may have lived** on Flores alongside modern humans, perhaps in just the past few thousand years.

Hunting

- **One of the earliest** human hunters was *Homo erectus*. Other hominins that came before it, like *Homo habilis*, may have hunted small or lame animals, but probably they mostly scavenged other animals' kills.
- ***Homo erectus*** used fire to drive animals into traps. They also developed handaxes, which they used to kill animals or butcher them once they were dead.
- **In the 1990s**, finds of *Homo heidelbergensis* weapons in Boxgrove, England, included axes, slicing knives, and blades for cutting and slashing.
- **A site at Schöningen, Germany**, preserved the remains of several polished wooden spears of spruce wood, probably made by *Homo heidelbergensis*.
- **Each of these spears** was over 2 m long, and was designed to be thrown like a javelin.
- **Hunting developed** into a way of providing not only food, but also clothing (animal skins) and materials for tools (bones, horns and hooves).
- **It was the Neanderthals** that excelled in hunting – a skill they developed during the icce ages of the Pleistocene Epoch (2.6–0.01 mya).

▲ *Various kinds of evidence show Neanderthal people hunted animals, lived in rock shelters, and held ceremonies to bury their dead.*

- **Neanderthals used nets** or spears to catch spawning fish. They also hunted seals by spearing them through holes in the ice or by throwing spears at them.
- **As well as hunting** for meat, hominins also gathered wild fruits, vegetables and nuts.
- ***Homo sapiens*** developed new weapons for hunting, including the bow and arrow, the blowpipe and the boomerang.

Cave art

- **Cro-Magnon people** produced many cave paintings.
- **One of the best examples** is the Grotte de Chauvet in the Ardeche, France, which was discovered in 1994.
- **The Grotte de Chauvet** caves contain more than 300 drawings of animals, from lions and deer to buffalos and woolly rhinoceroses.
- **People used to be very sceptical** that early humans could have produced cave paintings and thought they were hoaxes.

DID YOU KNOW?

Cro-Magnon people made hand outlines by blowing a sooty pigment over their hand as they pressed it against the cave wall.

- **Another magnificent example** of cave painting is that of the Altamira cave in northern Spain, which has an 18-m-long ceiling covered with red, violet and black coloured paintings of bison.
- **Most cave paintings** date from around 30,000 to 15,000 years ago, when Cro-Magnon man lived in Europe and elsewhere.

- **Other cave paintings** may be much older. Some archaeologists think that the Cave of El Castillo paintings in Spain are 40,000 years old.
- **Many cave pictures** appear to represent hunting scenes, but there are also many symbols in caves, including patterns of squares and dots.
- **Another very common** image in caves is that of a human hand.

◀ *The Lascaux Cave in southwest France has more than 600 wall paintings that are around 17,000 years old. They depict animals, human figures and abstract signs.*

1000 MAMMAL FACTS

What are mammals?

- **All mammals have** at least some hair on their bodies, a large brain and special mammary glands for feeding their young with milk.
- **There are about 5500 species of mammal** in the world (and at least one million insect species!).
- **About 90 species of mammal** are marine mammals. This group is called cetaceans and is made up of whales, dolphins and porpoises.
- **All mammals** give birth to live young except the duckbilled platypus and spiny anteater. These two species are called monotremes and they lay eggs.
- **Mammals** are warm blooded.
- **The two main mammal groups** are the marsupials (whose young develop in the mother's pouch) and the placentals.
- **All mammals** have three little bones in their ears that transfer sound vibrations to the inner ear from the eardrum.
- **Mammals** give a level of maternal care beyond that of other animals.

▶ Young mammals mature more slowly than other animal young, so they are looked after for longer.

- **Mammals** have a variety of teeth shapes: chisels for gnawing, long fangs for fighting and killing prey, sharp-edged slicers and flat-topped crushers.
- **Land mammals** have a palate that enables them to breathe through their noses while chewing.

Bison

- **Bison are the largest** land animals in North America. Males can grow nearly 2 m tall, 3.5 m long and weigh more than 1000 kg.
- **The American plains bison** helped preserve the open prairies by eating the tree seedlings.
- **In the 1800s**, the US Government approved the policy of killing bison in order to starve the Native Americans into submission.
- **Hunting and loss of** habitat (as the plains were taken over for farming) reduced the number of bison from 50 million to a just a few hundred between 1800 and 1900.
- **Saved by conservationists**, the American bison survives in small, managed herds in national parks and reservations.
- **The European bison**, or wisent, grazes on forest leaves of oak, willow and elm, unlike its American relations, which graze on grass.
- **Standing up to 2 m high** at the shoulder, the European bison is the continent's largest wild animal.
- **The last truly wild** European bison was killed in 1927.
- **New European bison herds** – bred from zoo animals – have been established in reserves, in particular in the Bialowieza Forest in Poland.
- **Bison groom themselves** by rubbing their heads and bodies against tree trunks, and rolling in the dust.

◀ Male bison compete for herd leadership by charging at each other, and have developed very thick skulls to withstand the blows.

Sea otters

● **Sea otters** live in the northeastern Pacific. They rarely come ashore, and sleep floating on their backs, sometimes wrapping themselves in kelp seaweed to stop them drifting away.

● **The sea otter's thick fur** – the densest of any mammal in the world – keeps it warm in cold waters.

● **The heaviest** of all otters, the sea otter weighs up to 45 kg and reaches up to 1.4 m from nose to tail.

● **To maintain warmth and energy**, the sea otter eats up to 25 percent of its total weight each day, diving repeatedly for shellfish, sea urchins and squid.

● **The sea otter** was the most recent mammal to evolve from a life on land to one in the sea.

● **In the 1700s and 1800s**, sea otters were hunted almost to extinction for their valuable fur, which was known as 'soft gold'.

● **To crack open shells**, the sea otter lies on its back and balances a rock on its stomach, and then smashes the shells on it.

● **Sea otters** sleep, socialize and give birth on kelp beds.

● **Unique among otters**, sea otters can extend and contract the claws of their front feet, like a cat.

● **They have pockets** of skin under their arms, which they use to store food they catch when diving, leaving their hands free to catch more.

◀ *The sea otter uses both its front paws to hold food while floating on its back.*

Porcupines

● **When threatened**, some African porcupines erect their detachable quills and run backwards at their enemy.

● **African crested porcupines** warn off would-be predators by vigorously shaking their tail quills to produce a warning rattling sound.

● **The North American porcupine** has very poor eyesight.

● **Crested porcupines** are the longest lived of all rodents, the record being over 27 years.

● **American porcupines** are particularly vulnerable to attacks by fisher martens, which bite the porcupine's face – thus avoiding the quills – to weaken it before turning it on its back to kill it.

● **New World (the Americas) porcupines** climb trees but Old World (Europe, Africa and Asia) porcupines don't.

▶ *A porcupine's quills are soft when it is born, but harden within a few hours.*

DID YOU KNOW?

Some porcupines collect bones, which they gnaw on to sharpen their teeth. The bones provide them with phosphate.

● **Some prehensile-tailed porcupines** of South America move to a new tree every 24 hours.

● **The North American porcupine** can have as many as 30,000 quills on its body.

● **Some North American porcupines** have a craving for salt, and have been known to gnaw gloves, boots and saddles that are salty with sweat.

The first mammals

● **Before true mammals emerged**, some mammal-like reptiles, such as the doglike Cynodonts, had developed mammalian characteristics such as hair and specialized teeth.

● **The mammary glands** with which mammals suckle their young evolved from sweat glands.

▲ *The tiny* Megazostrodon *kept well-hidden from predatory reptiles, and was active at night.*

● **Some** mammal-like reptiles may have exuded a type of milk from sweat glands for their young.

DID YOU KNOW?

Within 10 million years of the extinction of the dinosaurs, most modern mammal orders, including horses and primates, had appeared.

● **The earliest true mammals** appeared more than 210 million years ago and were only 15 cm long.

● **One of the best-known** of the earliest fossil mammals was an insect eater named *Megazostrodon*.

● **A major difference** between mammals and reptiles was the development of the little bones linking the eardrum and inner ear, found only in mammals.

● **During the Age of the Dinosaurs**, which lasted 160 million years, mammals were small.

● **By the time the dinosaurs became extinct** about 65 million years ago, marsupials, placentals and monotremes had all evolved.

● **Fossils of very early mammals** have been found in Europe, South Africa and China.

Sloths

● **The sloths of South America** have a variable body temperature, and each morning need to bask in the sun above the forest canopy.

● **The three-toed sloth** has the most neck vertebrae of any mammal, and can look forwards when upside down.

● **Sloths even mate** and give birth while hanging upside down by their powerful, curved claws.

● **The mother sloth** carries her infant for up to 9 months on her belly, where it feeds on the leaves it can reach.

● **A sloth's large stomach** is divided into many compartments; the food inside can account for up to two thirds of the animal's weight.

● **It can take** up to a month for a meal of leaves to be fully digested by a sloth.

● **The main predator** of the sloth is the harpy eagle.

● **Algae** grows in the grooves on a sloth's fur, helping to camouflage it in the forest greenery.

● **Sloths** have an amazing ability to heal themselves, and their wounds rarely become infected.

● **On land**, sloths can only move in an awkward, spread-eagled crawl, impeded by their curved claws.

▼ *Sloths' fur grows in the opposite direction to that of most mammals, pointing towards the ground so the rain runs off the body.*

Walruses

- **A single walrus tusk** can measure up to one metre long and weigh 5.4 kg.
- **Walruses swim** by moving their entire bodies and sweeping their huge rear flippers from side to side, each one opening in turn like a one metre wide fan.
- **The walrus is protected from the cold** by a thick layer of blubber – up to a third of its total weight.

▼ *Walruses are very sociable, and like to gather in groups on coastal ice or rocks*

- **In the summer**, basking walruses turn deep pink in colour as their blood vessels dilate to radiate heat away from the body.
- **Walruses** manage to excavate shellfish from seabed mud by squirting a high-pressure blast of water from their mouths.
- **The walrus has 300 whiskers** on each side of its moustache, which it uses to help it find food in murky waters.
- **A walrus uses its long tusks** to help it clamber onto ice floes – its scientific name, *Odobenus*, means 'tooth walker'.
- **In water**, a walrus turns a pale grey colour as blood leaves its skin to maintain the temperature of its body core.
- **A walrus can eat** up to 4000 clams in a single day.

DID YOU KNOW?

Walrus pups are born 15 months after the parents have mated – 4–5 months pass before the egg starts to grow in the mother's womb.

Wild pigs and peccaries

- **To obtain fruit** that is out of reach, African bush pigs will lean against fruit trees, making them topple over.
- **The warthog** uses its huge tusks for fighting and impressing other warthogs, and sometimes for digging for food – it feeds mostly on grass.
- **The fleshy 'warts'** on a male warthog's face protect its eyes from tusk blows when it is fighting.
- **The largest wild pig**, at over 2 m long, is the African giant forest hog, which weighs in at 275 kg or more.
- **Pigs** were first domesticated at least 9000 years ago in southwest Asia.
- **The babirusa**, or pig-deer, of the Indonesian islands has four tusks, two of which can pierce its flesh and grow through the top of its muzzle.
- **Peccaries**, the wild pigs of South America, have complex stomachs for digesting tough plant fibres.
- **Unlike other wild pigs**, peccaries live in herds which include the adult males.
- **When a herd of peccaries** is attacked by a predator, a single peccary may confront the attacker, allowing the rest of the herd to escape.

◀ *Agile and powerful, the warthog forages across African woodlands and grasslands, often in family groups.*

DID YOU KNOW?

In 1971, the Chacoan peccary, which was previously known only from old fossils, was found surviving in the forests of western Paraguay.

Tigers

- **Five species** of tiger exist in the wild – Siberian, Bengal, Indochinese, Malayan and Sumatran tigers – and all of these are endangered.
- **In the early 1900s** there were probably around 100,000 tigers. Now numbers have fallen to 4000 or less, with half of these living in India.
- **At over 3 m long** and weighing up to 300 kg, the rare Siberian tiger is the largest living member of the cat family. Tigers originated in Siberia.
- **Tigers need a very large hunting area**. If prey is scarce, they may patrol an area of 500 sq km or more.
- **After feeding**, tigers sometimes save the remains of a kill for a later meal, burying it under branches to hide it from scavengers or other tigers.
- **In 1945** there were only 50 Siberian tigers left in the wild. Now there are 500 surviving in eastern Russia.
- **In India and Bangaladesh**, in the Sunderbans mangrove swamps, tigers keep cool in the water and ambush pigs, deer and monkeys.

▲ *The tiger uses its long canine teeth to bite the throat or neck of its prey as it brings it to the ground. Its sharp-edged rear teeth cut through the flesh by sliding against each other like scissor blades.*

- **A tiger's stripes** camouflage it as it hunts in the tall grasses by day. But tigers mostly hunt at night, and their night vision is at least 6 times more acute than a human's.
- **Tiger cubs** depend entirely on their mothers for food until they are about 18 months old, when they begin to make their own first kills.

DID YOU KNOW?

Tigers eat a variety of foods, ranging from fish and turtles during times of flood to locusts during locust swarms.

▲ *To keep out the cold, the Siberian tiger has an outer coat of long, pale fur over a thick undercoat.*

Orang-utans

- **Orang-utans** spend much more time in trees than the other great apes, and are the largest tree-dwelling mammals in the world.
- **Insatiable eaters**, orang-utans can spend up to seven hours a day feeding. Their favourite food is fruit.
- **The name 'orang-utan'** means 'man of the forest' in the language of the local tribespeople of Southeast Asia.
- **A mature male orang-utan** makes his presence known to other orang-utans by breaking branches, bellowing and groaning. Local legends explain this as a sign of the ape's grief over losing a human bride.
- **In Sumatra**, the major predators of orang-utans are tigers at ground level, and clouded leopards in trees.
- **Once found all over Southeast Asia**, orang-utans now live only in tropical Borneo and Sumatra.
- **Like chimpanzees**, orang-utans use sticks as tools to retrieve food from crevices and to scratch themselves.
- **Male orang-utans** have large air sacs that extend from their throats to their neck and upper chest. These increase the loudness and range of their calls.
- **To help her young** move from tree to tree, a mother orang-utan pulls the branches of two trees closer together and makes a bridge with her body.
- **Orang-utans make a nest** at night, building a roof to keep off the rain.

◀ *Orang-utans are slow breeders, and may only give birth to three or four babies in a lifetime.*

Beavers

DID YOU KNOW?

European beavers took to living in burrows to avoid predators and, later, human hunters. They are now protected by law.

- **Beavers** are born with innate dam-building instincts. In zoos, they regularly 'repair' concrete dams with twigs.
- **It takes two adult beavers** about 15 minutes to gnaw their way through a tree trunk with a 10 cm diameter.

- **Mother beavers** push tired youngsters ahead of them through the water, like swimming floats.
- **Storing extra oxygen** in its lungs and body tissues, a beaver can remain under water for up to 15 minutes.
- **Beavers use the split claws** on their hind feet for grooming and spreading waterproof oil.
- **A beaver signals danger** by smacking the water with its tail. The noise carries over one km.
- **The territory-marking secretion** of the beaver contains salicyclic acid, the main ingredient in aspirin, which is found in willow bark, part of the beavers' diet.
- **Beavers' dams** and lodges can help create environments for fish.
- **In the 1940s and 50s**, in some parts of the USA, beavers were parachute-dropped into areas where remote rivers needed damming to reduce erosion.

◀ *The beaver uses its huge incisor teeth to gnaw through branches and tree trunks.*

Aardvarks

- **When in danger**, the aardvark can dig at great speed, and can outpace a team of men armed with spades.
- **An aardvark** has several burrows on its territory, often many kilometres apart.
- **Termites and ants** form the main food of the aardvark, which digs through concrete-hard termite mounds to reach them.
- **To stop termites and dust** entering its nose, the aardvark has stiff bristles on its muzzle, and can close its nostrils.
- **A moderate blow to the head** can kill an aardvark, which depends on its acute senses and digging abilities for survival.

▲ *The aardvark usually feeds at night, eating termites in the wet season and ants in the dry season.*

- **If attacked**, the aardvark may roll onto its back and lash out with its feet.
- **The aardvark swallows** food without chewing, grinding it up in its stomach.
- **Baby aardvarks** depend on their mothers for about 6 months, when they leave to live independently.
- **Some African peoples** who also eat termites keep an aardvark claw as a charm to increase the harvest.

DID YOU KNOW?

'Aardvark' is Afrikaans for 'earth-pig' (but in fact aardvarks do not belong to the pig family).

Giraffes and okapis

- **The giraffe's black tongue** is almost 0.5 m long. It uses it to grip vegetation and pull it into its mouth.
- **The giraffe is the world's tallest animal** – some males reach up to 6 m in height.
- **Male giraffes stretch** up to reach leaves high in the trees, while females bend their necks to take lower leaves, thus reducing food competition.
- **Bony growths** on a male giraffe's skull continue to grow all its life, making its skull up to three times heavier than a female's.
- **The extraordinarily long necks** of giraffes have only seven neck vertebrae, just like other mammals, but they are greatly elongated.
- **From a few weeks old**, young giraffes spend much of their time in a 'crèche', looked after by a pair of adults.

◄ *A giraffe's front legs are longer than its rear legs.*

- **Female giraffes with calves** have been seen to beat severely and drive off attacking lions, using their hoofs, necks and heads as weapons.
- **To reach water**, giraffes have to spread their front legs wide apart. Special valves stop the blood rushing to and from their heads as they raise and lower them.
- **Okapis**, which are related to giraffes, closely resemble fossils of the giraffe's most recent ancestor, *Paleotragus*, from about 12 million years ago.
- **Okapis live so deep in the forests** of the Congo that they were not discovered by Europeans until 1901.

Wild dogs

- **The South American bush dog** pursues prey into the water, and, unlike most dogs, can swim underwater.
- **African Cape hunting dogs** live in packs in which only the dominant female has young.
- **Cape hunting dog cubs** are left in the den, protected by adult guardians, while the pack hunts, and are fed with disgorged meat when it returns.

- **Cape hunting dogs** do not creep up on prey, but approach a herd openly, selecting a single target to chase.
- **Cape hunting dogs** can run at speds of 60 km/h for 5 km or more.
- **They may travel** up to 50 km a day while hunting, and patrol a range of 1500 to 2000 sq km.
- **Indian wild dogs**, or dholes, hunt in packs of up to 30, and can drive tigers and leopards from their kills.
- **Dholes** hunt in thick undergrowth, advancing in an extended line until they have flushed out their prey.
- **The raccoon dog** of east Asia eats insects, shellfish and fruit.
- **Australian dingoes** are probably descended from Indian wolves that were domesticated in Asia and taken by Aboriginal settlers to Australia, where they reverted to the wild.

◀ *Cape hunting dogs are well camouflaged – no two individuals have the same markings.*

Reindeer and caribou

- **Reindeer** (Europe and Asia) and caribou (North America) are basically the same animal.
- **Reindeer** were probably first tamed in the 5th century by hunters, who used them as decoys when hunting wild reindeer.
- **The broad hoofs** of reindeer and caribou help them to walk on snow.
- **In 1984**, 10,000 migrating caribou drowned in Canada when dam sluices were opened.
- **Reindeer** have a well developed homing instinct, and can find their way even in blinding snowstorms.
- **Reindeer bulls fight with their feet** and rarely with their antlers, which could become locked together, leading to the starvation of both animals.
- **Reindeer are the best swimmers** of the deer family, due to the buoyancy of the hollow hairs of their coats.
- **Unlike other deer**, a reindeer's muzzle is covered in hair. This keeps its nose warm while it forages in the snow.
- **Reindeer dig** through the snow with their feet to find food.

▶ *Caribou bulls rarely fight with their antlers, preferring to use their feet.*

DID YOU KNOW?

The name 'caribou' means 'shoveller' in the language of one group of Canadian indigenous people.

Desert life

- **The American kangaroo rat** derives water from its food and by recycling its breath.
- **Prairie dogs** have air-conditioned homes. The air in their tunnels is renewed every 10 minutes by the suction effect of the entrances being at different heights.

- **Desert ground squirrels** have hairy feet to protect them from hot sand.
- **Desert bighorn sheep** let their body temperatures rise from 36.8°C to 40°C, re-radiating the excess heat at night.
- **Some desert-dwelling badgers and sheep** have a fatty layer that insulates their internal organs from heat.
- **The Australian fat-tailed dunnart** is a marsupial that looks a bit like a mouse. It has a carrot-shaped tail that stores fat, which it lives off when food is scarce.
- **Most desert mammals** rest in shade or burrows by day, emerging to seek food in the cool of night.
- **Collared peccaries**, or javelinas, are American desert pigs. In times of drought they eat cacti, spines and all.
- **The burrowing Australian bilby** licks seeds from the desert surface, and its dung pellets are 90 percent sand.
- **The long legs** of the Arabian camel raise its body to a height where air temperatures are up to 25°C cooler than ground temperatures.

◀ *Living on dry plains, prairie dogs may inhabit extensive tunnel-and-nest 'towns' that cover up to 65 hectares.*

Sheep and goats

- **Despite their massive curled horns**, American bighorn rams fight predators with their feet.
- **The musk ox** of the Arctic tundra is more closely related to sheep and goats than to bison or oxen.
- **Sheep and goats** were domesticated as early as 7500 BC.
- **When young sheep and goats play**, they often leap onto their mothers' backs, practising for mountain life among the rocks.
- **Goats and sheep** have scent glands on their feet that mark mountain trails, helping herds stay together.

▼ *Most domestic sheep have adapted to a life of migratory grazing, moving on as the grass is cropped.*

▲ *Both wild and domestic male goats sport distinctive beards.*

- **Bighorn rams** only fight with one another if their horns are of a similar size, ignoring larger or smaller rivals.
- **Avalanches** are the main threat to Rocky Mountain goats.
- **Of the two**, only sheep have scent glands on their faces, and only male goats have beards and a strong odour.
- **Central Asian argalis** are the largest Eurasian wild sheep, weighing up to 200 kg.
- **In a fight**, a European chamois may fake death to avoid being killed, lying flat with its neck outstretched.

Horses and asses

- **The earliest-known ancestor** of the horse, *Hyracotherium*, lived 50 million years ago, and was a forest dweller the size of a small dog.
- **A mule** is the offspring of a male ass and a female horse, while the rarer offspring of a male horse and female ass is called a hinny.
- **Both mules and hinnies** are unable to produce young.
- **Horses have very strong homing instincts**, and have been known to wander hundreds of kilometres to return to the place of their birth.
- **The domestic horse** is the only member of the horse family in which the mane falls to the side – in all others, including asses and zebras, it stands erect.
- **Horses' eyes** are set high in the head and far apart, giving almost all-round vision. They can focus on near and far objects at the same time.

▲ *By nature horses are herd animals. In the wild, a herd usually consists of one dominant stallion, accompanied by a number of mares and their young.*

- **The horse's large eyes** give it excellent night vision – almost as good as that of owls.
- **Most horses sleep standing up** during the day, and at night sleep on the ground with their legs gathered under their bodies.
- **The earliest horses** had four toes per foot. These reduced as the horse moved from a forest to a plains life, and the modern horse has just a single toe.

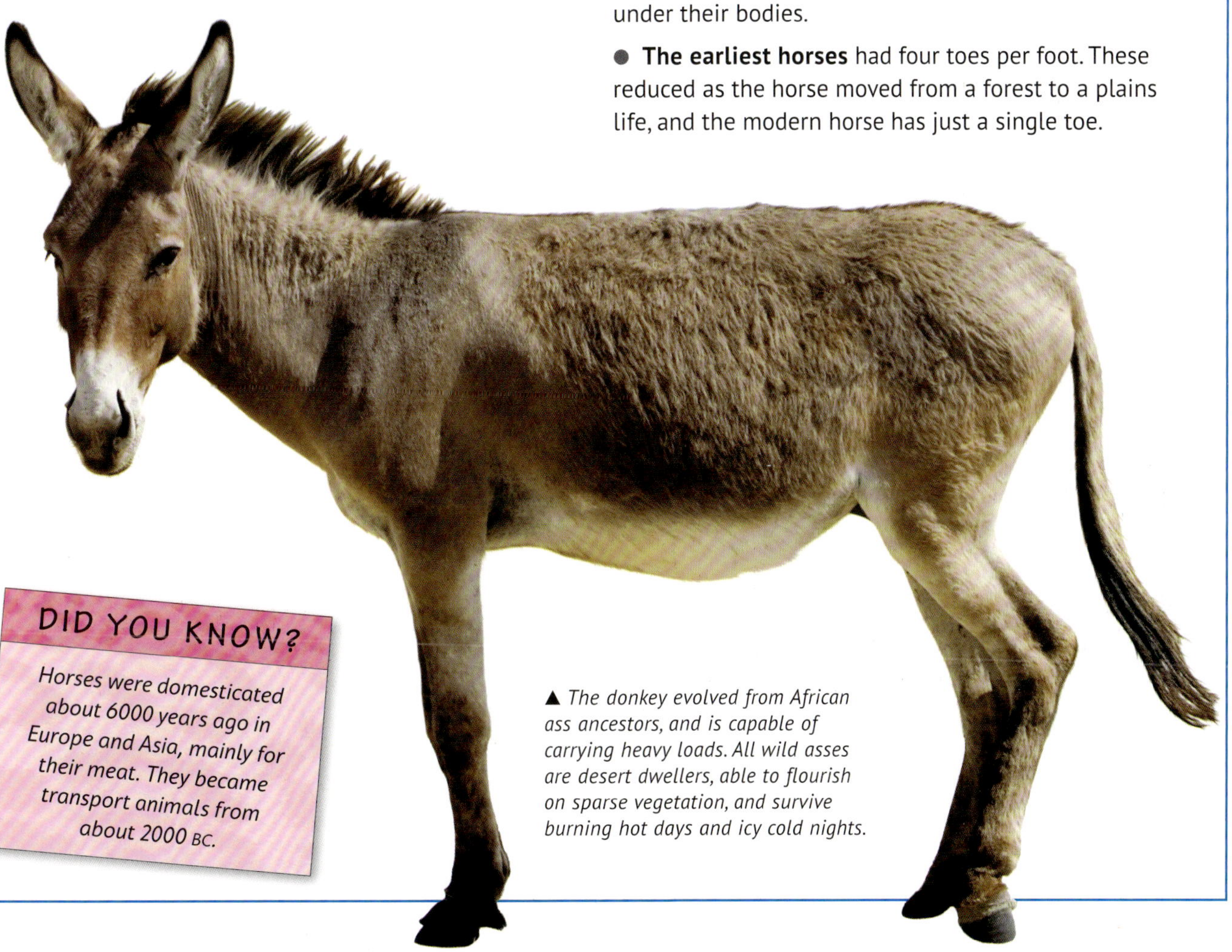

▲ *The donkey evolved from African ass ancestors, and is capable of carrying heavy loads. All wild asses are desert dwellers, able to flourish on sparse vegetation, and survive burning hot days and icy cold nights.*

DID YOU KNOW?

Horses were domesticated about 6000 years ago in Europe and Asia, mainly for their meat. They became transport animals from about 2000 BC.

Tasmanian wolf

- **The Tasmanian wolf** was a meat-eating Australian marsupial that is thought to have become extinct in 1936.
- **Tasmanian wolves** may survive in the dense forest of Tasmania, but this remains to be proved.
- **Once common** throughout Australia and New Guinea, the Tasmanian wolf retreated to Tasmania some 3000 years ago, driven out by dingoes.
- **The Tasmanian wolf** had a pouch that opened to the rear, where the young spent their first 3 months.
- **Also called the Tasmanian tiger**, because of its stripes, the Tasmanian wolf was in fact neither a wolf nor a tiger.
- **The Tasmanian wolf** had a thick-based tail and hopped on its back legs if chased.
- **The jaws** of the Tasmanian wolf opened almost 180 degrees, allowing it to kill an animal by crushing its skull.
- **With its powerful jaws**, the Tasmanian wolf could kill a pursuing hunting dog with one bite.
- **Fossil remains** of an animal almost identical to the Tasmanian wolf were discovered in America.

DID YOU KNOW?

Thousands of Tasmanian wolves were killed in the late 1800s, because they preyed on sheep.

▼ *Some people claim to have seen Tasmanian wolves still surviving in remote parts of Tasmania.*

What are rodents?

- **Rodents**, which include mice, squirrels, beavers, porcupines and guinea pigs, have two incisor teeth in each jaw that never stop growing. The name 'rodent' means 'gnawer'.
- **If a rodent's teeth** are not constantly worn down by gnawing, they can curve round into the animal's skull and kill it.
- **Forty percent of mammal species are rodents**. They range in size from the 1.4 m-long capybara to the Baluchistan pygmy jerboa, at 4.7 cm (body length).
- **The earliest-known rodents** appeared in 57-million-year-old fossil beds in both Asia and North America.
- **The house mouse** and the brown rat occur more widely than any land mammal except humans, and are found on all continents, including Antartica.
- **Guinea pigs** in South America and edible dormice in Europe have both been bred to be eaten by humans.
- **Female Norway lemmings** can begin to breed when only 14 days old.
- **The fastest rodents** over the ground may be kangaroo mice and jerboas, which can bound along on their hind legs at speeds of up to 48 km/h.
- **Around 3–4 million years ago**, some South American rodents were the size of cattle.
- **A female house mouse** can produce 14 litters a year.

◀ *The Arctic ground squirrel is a rodent that hibernates for up to seven months every year.*

Hippopotami

- **The mouths of hippos** can open up to 1.5 m wide, and contain strong muscles for grazing on short grasses.
- **Hippos feed** for 5 hours a night, and spend the next 19 hours resting in the water.

- **Hippos suckle** their young underwater and often sleep submerged, surfacing regularly to breathe while still unconscious.
- **A pygmy hippo** is born on land in just 2 minutes, and has to be taught how to swim.
- **In dry air** the pygmy hippo loses water by evaporation at about five times the rate of human water loss.
- **Hippos travel** up to 30 km at night in search of food, but if frightened will run back to water to hide.
- **Hippos** are probably Africa's most dangerous animal. They kill a large number of humans each year.
- **Bull hippos** mark their territory by whisking their tails back and forth to scatter their dung over a large area.
- **Aggressive hippos** warn off other hippos by opening their jaws to display their formidable tusks. They regularly fight to the death.
- **Male hippos** can weigh as much as 3200 kg.

◀ *The male hippo can be extremely aggressive, opening its huge mouth wide and displaying its tusks as a warning to other males.*

Rabbits and hares

- **Hares are born with fur** and have their eyes open. Rabbits are born naked, with their eyes shut.
- **Mother hares** visit their young in their underground nest for just 5 minutes a day to feed them on their milk.
- **Snowshoe hares** have broad, hairy hind feet for moving over snow.
- **If a hare** sees it is being stalked by a fox, it stands up to put the fox off a chase (which the hare would win).
- **The pikas** of Asia and western America 'sing' loudly.
- **Rabbits' incisors** grow constantly.
- **Both sexes of hares 'box'** as part of the mating ritual, punching at each other with their front feet.
- **Hares can reach speeds** of up to 60 km/h when running flat out.
- **The large-eared pika** is one of the highest-living mammals in the world, inhabiting mountain ranges in Asia at altitudes up to 6130 m.

DID YOU KNOW?

Numbers of American snowshoe hares rise and fall in an 8–11 year cycle, affecting the numbers of lynxes, which depend on them as food.

▲ *The snowshoe hare's large eyes help it see during dusk and after dark, when it is most active.*

Elephants

● **The name 'elephant'** means 'visible from afar'.

● **Elephants communicate** over great distances by making low frequency sounds (too low for humans to hear).

● **War elephants** were used by the Carthaginian general Hannibal against the Romans in the 3rd century BC, and by the Romans invading Britain in the 1st century AD.

● **Elephants sometimes enter caves** to excavate minerals such as sodium, which is needed as a supplement to their diet.

● **Elephants** spend up to 18 hours a day feeding.

● **Elephants are good swimmers** – some Asian elephants have been seen to swim non-stop for as much as 10 km.

● **Asian elephants** are the world's longest-lived mammals after humans, and can live for over 70 years.

● **An African elephant** needs to eat up to 6 percent of its bodyweight each day – 300 kg for a 5000 kg bull.

● **An adult elephant** uses eight of its 24 grinding teeth to eat with at any one time, with others moving into position when the used ones fall out.

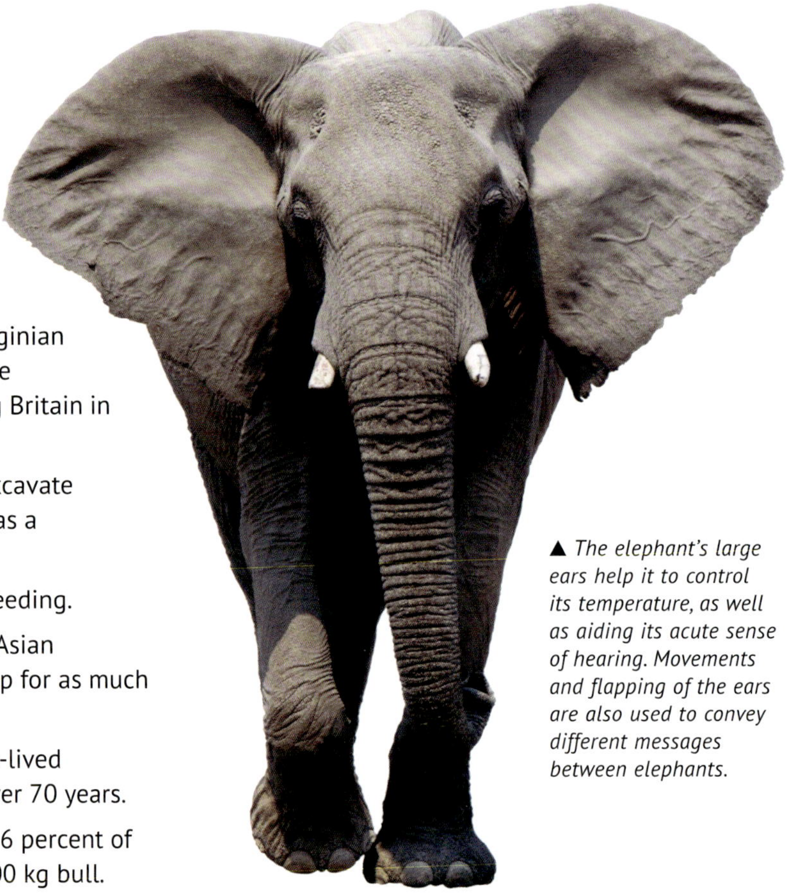

▲ *The elephant's large ears help it to control its temperature, as well as aiding its acute sense of hearing. Movements and flapping of the ears are also used to convey different messages between elephants.*

▼ *An elephant's trunk is a combination of upper lip and nose, and is used to place food into its mouth. It also doubles as a hose, squirting water down its throat and acting as a shower spray.*

DID YOU KNOW?

Stone Age rock paintings in North Africa show that elephants once lived in the Sahara region, before it became desert.

Cheetahs

- **The cheetah is the world's fastest** land animal. It can accelerate from 0 to 72 km/h in 2 seconds, and can reach a top speed of 120 km/h.
- **Cheetahs cannot** retract their claws. They grip the ground, like spikes on a sprinter's shoes.
- **A silver vase** (*c.*2300 BC), found in the Caucasus, shows a cheetah in a collar, which suggests people used cheetahs then as hunting animals.
- **The 16th-century Mogul emperor Akbar** kept 1000 cheetahs, which he used to hunt gazelles.
- **Cheetahs** have the same body length as leopards, but stand a good 35 cm taller on their long legs.
- **In the Kalahari Desert**, cheetahs can survive for 10 days without water by eating wild melons.
- **Young male cheetahs** often hunt in small groups (called coalitions), and are healthier than solitary males.
- **Cheetahs avoid lions**, which will kill them.
- **A cheetah will chase a warthog** that runs, but will usually leave one that stands its ground.
- **If a cheetah does not catch its prey** in the first 300–400 m of the chase, it gives up and tries again later.

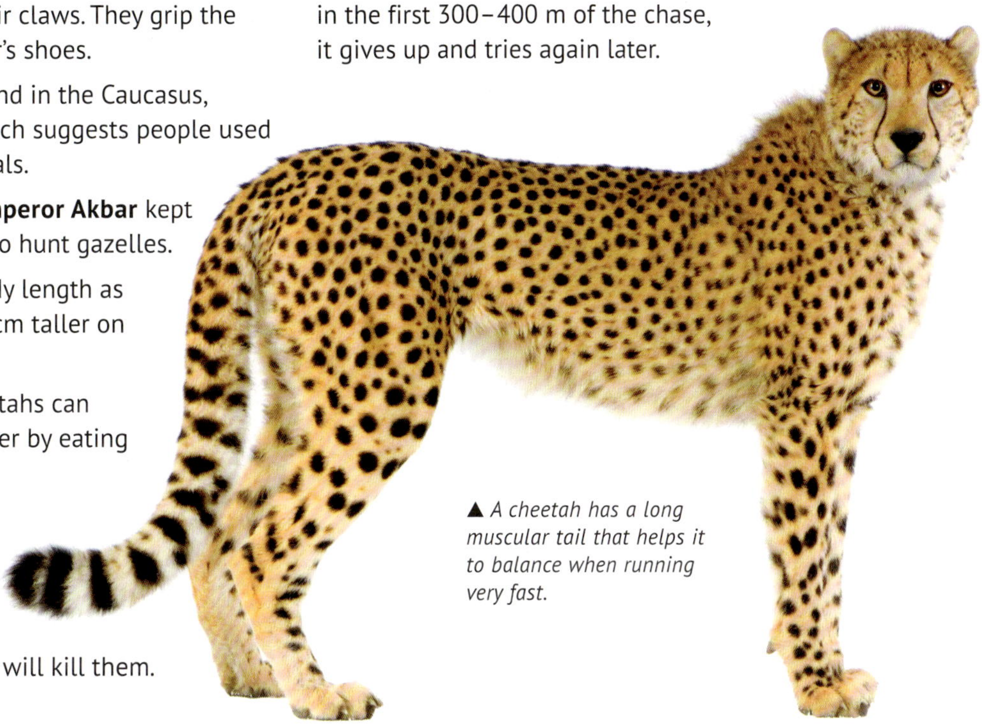

▲ *A cheetah has a long muscular tail that helps it to balance when running very fast.*

Gorillas

DID YOU KNOW?

The 'nose-prints' of gorillas are as distinctive as human fingerprints – no two are identical.

- **Male gorillas mostly walk on four limbs**, but will run on two legs, beating their chests, when showing off.
- **Adult gorillas** sleep in a new nest every night.
- **The mature male leader** of a gorilla group is called a 'silverback', after the saddle of white hair on its back.

- **Young male gorillas** form their own groups by kidnapping females from other groups.
- **Mountain gorillas** spend almost all their lives at 2800–3400 m above sea level, in damp, cloudy conditions.
- **Some gorillas supplement their plant diet** by eating handfuls of potassium- and calcium-rich soil.
- **If a gorilla cannot keep up** with the group because of a wound, the silverback slows down so it is not left behind.
- **When aggressive male gorillas** beat their chests and mock-charge one another, they give off an armpit odour powerful enough to be detected 25 m away by humans.
- **Despite their huge strength**, silverbacks are gentle with their offspring, allowing them to play on their backs.

◀ *The male gorilla is far larger than the female, and is the largest of all the primates – big silverbacks can weigh as much as 200 kg.*

Squirrels

● **Grey squirrels** have been known to kill and eat rabbits, rats, cockerels and stoats.

● **Flying squirrels** are nocturnal, and when gliding may emit high-pitched squeaks that help them to locate a landing place.

● **North American red squirrels** tap birch and maple trees for their sweet sap in spring.

● **Many squirrel species** spread woodland trees by burying nuts and then forgetting where they put them.

● **The North American red squirrel**, or chicaree, buries green pine cones in damp soil to delay their ripening until they are needed.

● **An adult red squirrel** can sniff out a pine cone buried 30 cm deep.

◀ *The squirrel's bushy tail is a good balancing aid and rudder when climbing and leaping.*

● **The largest member of the squirrel family** is the alpine marmot, at 73 cm long not including the tail.

● **Southeast Asian giant squirrels** prefer to hang upside down by their hind feet while eating.

● **Chipmunks**, or ground squirrels, store huge quantities of nuts in a single cache.

● **To prevent it slipping backwards** down a tree trunk, the scaly-tailed flying squirrel presses the horny scales of its tail against the trunk.

Mammal senses

● **Cheetahs** have dark 'tear' marks beneath their eyes, which reduce glare from the sun, enabling them to hunt better in bright light.

● **Desert mammals** such as the long-eared kit fox find sharp hearing more useful than a keen sense of smell as fewer scents are carried in the dry desert air.

● **Polar bears can smell** seals up to 60 km away across the ice.

● **Cats have glands** between their toes that leave an identifying scent when they scratch trees.

● **Blue whales and fin whales** communicate by means of the loudest sounds produced by any living creature (up to 188 dB).

● **Baby wood mice** emit ultrasonic distress calls in their first 10 days to summon their mother.

● **Many nocturnal mammals** have reflective areas in their eyes that help night vision.

● **The unusually large ears** of fennec foxes can detect the sound of termites chewing beneath the ground.

● **Migrating whales** can sense the Earth's magnetic field, due to particles of the mineral magnetite in their bodies.

● **Skunks use a powerful scent weapon** to deter their enemies.

▶ *Big cats have eyes on the front of their heads rather than at the sides, helping them to focus on their prey as they hunt.*

Rhinoceroses

- **The Sumatran rhino** is a relative of the woolly rhinoceros of the last Ice Age, and has reddish fur.
- **When black rhinos** are fleeing, the calf follows the mother, but when white rhinos are in flight, the mother runs behind the calf.
- **African ox-birds** ride aboard rhinos, cleaning out ticks from the folds in their hides.
- **Despite weighing 2 tonnes** or more, the rhino can run at 50 km/h, and make a 180 degree turn within its own body length.
- **If two rhinos feel threatened**, they stand back to back, confronting their enemies from different directions.
- **Rhinos can be heard** munching on plants from a distance of 400 m.
- **The upper lips** of the African white rhino are square, for grazing on grass. Those of the African black rhino are pointed, for plucking leaves.
- **Rhinos have poor eyesight**, and cannot locate a motionless object further than 30 m away.
- **A prehistoric relative** of the rhinoceros, *Indricotherium*, stood 5.4 m tall and weighed 20 tonnes.
- **Thicker skin** on a rhino's flanks protect it from horn wounds from rivals.

◀ *The rhino has excellent hearing but poor eyesight.*

Seals

- **When chasing penguins**, the leopard seal can leap 2 m high from the sea onto an ice floe.
- **Male southern elephant seals**, which weigh up to 3500 kg, have inflatable snouts that they use to impress females during mating displays.

▼ *The spotted seal frequents the icy waters of the North Pacific and Arctic Ocean.*

- **In the four days after birth**, hooded seal pups double their weight from 25 kg–50 kg.
- **The elephant seal** can dive 1500 m, and stay under water for 1–2 hours.
- **Leopard seals** are the only seals known to make unprovoked attacks on humans, lunging through ice to get at their feet.
- **Seals sleep** floating vertically in the water just beneath the surface, rising to breathe through their nostrils.
- **When a seal dives deep**, its heartbeat slows from 55–120 beats per minute to 4–15 beats per minute.
- **Despite their name**, crab-eater seals feed almost exclusively on shrimp-like krill. They have special teeth that they use like strainers to catch their food.
- **The fur seals** of the North Pacific spend up to 8 months of the year continuously at sea, feeding.

DID YOU KNOW?

The world's largest mammal herd consists of up to 1.5 million northern fur seals, which breed on two islands in the Pacific sub-Arctic region.

Old World camels

- **Single-humped dromedaries** and twin-humped Bactrian camels can go for months without food and water, living on the fat in their humps.
- **A female dromedary** can produce 6 litres of milk a day for 9 to 18 months – the staple food for some camel-herding peoples.
- **After not drinking for many months**, a camel can drink up to 130 litres in just a few minutes.
- **Unlike other mammals**, camels have oval instead of round blood-cells. These prevent their blood thickening as their body temperature rises.
- **Evolving originally in North America**, some camel ancestors crossed land bridges to Asia to become today's Bactrian camels and dromedaries.
- **Introduced to Australia** as desert transport animals in the 1860s, dromedaries reverted to the wild there.
- **Domesticated in Arabia** some 6000 years ago, the dromedary, or Arabian camel, ceased to exist in the wild (except in Australia) about 2000 years ago.
- **Camels do sweat**, but not until their body temperature has reached 40.5°C.
- **In the annual King's Camel Race** in Saudi Arabia, some 3000 camels are raced over a 23 km course.
- **Only about 1000** wild Bactrian camels survive, in Mongolia's Gobi Desert.

◀ *A camel's average laden speed is 3–8 km/h, which it can maintain for up to 18 hours without rest.*

Otters

- **Otters enjoy playing** games, such as dropping pebbles into water and catching them on their heads.
- **The African clawless otter** can move its thumb across the other fingers to hold onto objects.
- **Clawless otters** gather freshwater mussels and then smash them on rocks.
- **When hunted by hounds**, otters have been known to drag their pursuers under water and drown them.

DID YOU KNOW?

The giant otter of Brazil is the longest of the otter family, at almost 2 m long.

- **Otters have special whiskers** on their muzzles and elbows that are sensitive to water disturbances and help them to locate prey.
- **Giant otters** clear a series of 7-m-wide areas around their territories before scent-marking them.
- **Male Eurasian otters** patrol a territory of up to 50 km of river bank. Females' territory is 10 km.
- **The marine otter** of the west coast of South America is the smallest sea mammal in the world, weighing no more than 4.5 kg.
- **Some otters**, including the Cape clawless otter and the Oriental short-clawed otter, catch their prey in their paws rather than in their mouths.

◀ *The otter's coat is made up of a dense layer of underfur, with an outer layer of long guard hairs.*

Hibernation

- **The hibernating dormouse** does not attract the attention of predators because its body temperature is so low that it gives off no body odour.
- **The core body temperature** of some hibernating bats falls below freezing – in some cases as low as –5°C – without harming them.
- **Bears are not true hibernators**, but have a moderately reduced body temperature during their winter sleep, offset by the huge amounts of food that they eat before going to sleep.
- **The raccoon dog** is the only member of the dog family to hibernate.
- **Brown fat**, found in high levels in hibernating mammals, creates heat as the temperature falls.

▼ *Many bat* (1) *species are true hibernators, as is the dormouse* (2), *which may hibernate for up to 9 months, and the hedgehog* (3), *which usually sleeps through the winter. The grey squirrel* (4) *is not a true hibernator, but is only active briefly on cold winter days. Eurasian badgers* (5) *also become lethargic during cold spells.*

- **The Eastern European dormouse** and the Canadian woodchuck may spend as much as 9 months of the year in hibernation.
- **Hibernators** such as ground squirrels have internal clocks that cause them to go into hibernation at the usual time of year, even if they are kept in warm conditions with plenty of food.
- **A hibernating bat's breathing rate** falls from about 200 breaths per minute to between 25 and 30 breaths a minute for 3 minutes, followed by an 8 minute no-breathing break.
- **Alaskan ground squirrels**, born at the end of June, start to dig burrows 22 days later, and feed, fatten up and begin to hibernate by the end of August.

DID YOU KNOW?

Hibernating mammals wake up by shivering violently, creating heat that passes to the brain, the vital organs and the rest of the body.

Monotremes

DID YOU KNOW?

The duckbilled platypus lives almost all its life either underwater or underground.

- **Monotremes** are egg-laying mammals. There are only two groups: the duckbilled platypus of Australia and the echidna, or spiny anteater, of Australia and New Guinea.
- **If harassed** on soft ground by a predator, the echidna digs down until only an area of spines is showing.
- **The platypus** can detect the electric fields of its underwater prey by means of electro-receptors in its muzzle.
- **Hunting underwater** with eyes and ears closed, the platypus eats up to a third of its own weight each day.
- **The female echidna** has a pouch in which the young develop after hatching from their soft-shelled egg.

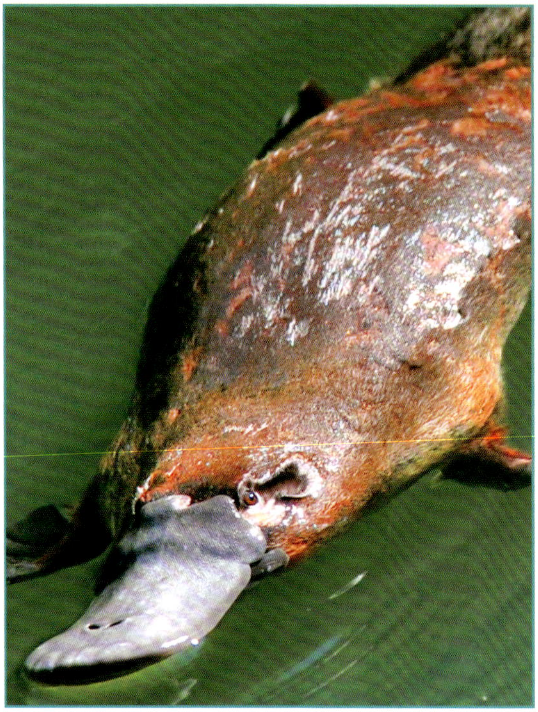

▲ *The duckbilled platypus swims mainly with its front legs, trailing its rear legs as a rudder.*

- **Poison** from the spurs on the male platypus's hind ankles can kill a dog within minutes.
- **Before the discovery** of fossil platypus teeth in Argentina, the animal was believed only to have existed in Australia and New Guinea.
- **The platypus loses its teeth** a few weeks after birth, and thereafter grinds its food using gravel it scoops up in its mouth.
- **The platypus's burrow** can extend 30 m from the water's edge to the nest. It blocks the burrow entrance to deter snakes.

Badgers

- **Successive generations** of Eurasian badgers use the same den or sett, sometimes for over a century.
- **The ferret badger** is the smallest member of the badger family, and the only badger to climb trees.
- **The honey badger** is led to bees' nests by the greater honey-guide bird, which attracts it with special calls. It feeds on beeswax once the badger has opened the nest.
- **The American badger** can burrow fast enough to catch a ground squirrel that is burrowing in the ground ahead of it trying to escape.
- **A female European badger** sometimes has female helpers that babysit her cubs, often in their own nests, while she forages for food.
- **Despite a bear-like appearance**, badgers belong to the mammal group known as mustelids, and are related to otters and weasels.
- **The honey badger's** extremely tough skin protects it from all kinds of dangers, ranging from bee stings and porcupine quills to snake bites.
- **Earthworms** are one of the badger's favourite foods, and females suckling their young feed on little else.
- **Badgers are enthusiastic housekeepers** – they regularly change their bedding, and also dig latrines some distance from their setts.
- **Eurasian badgers** will enlarge their favourite setts over many generations. One ancient den consisted of 879 m of tunnels, with 178 entrances and 50 subterranean chambers.

▼ *A Eurasian badger may eat several hundred earthworms a night.*

Hedgehogs

DID YOU KNOW?
The hedgehog keeps up a ceaseless whistling sound while hunting for food.

- **The Eurasian hedgehog** has between 5000 and 7000 spines on its back and sides, each erected by its own muscle, creating a defence difficult for predators to penetrate.
- **When a hedgehog rolls into a ball** at the approach of danger, a special muscle draws its loose skin together (like a drawstring on a bag) over its head and rump.
- **From Roman to medieval times** in Europe, it was believed that hedgehogs carried fruit to their nests, impaled on their spines.
- **Over 50,000 hedgehogs** are killed every year on the roads of the UK alone.
- **The moonrats** of Southeast Asia and China are closely related to hedgehogs, but have no spines.
- **The long-eared and desert hedgehogs** of Asia and North Africa dig short burrows.
- **Hedgehogs can go without water** for long periods, and if dehydrated will drink half their bodyweight in one go.
- **A western European male hedgehog** has a foraging territory of up to 35 hectares.
- **Lack of food** rather than cooling temperatures causes a hedgehog to hibernate.

◀ *Scent is important to hedgehogs, as they communicate and track food by smell.*

Domestic dogs

- **All modern domestic dogs**, from Chihuahuas to Great Danes, are direct descendants of grey wolves.
- **Grey wolves** were first domesticated over 12,000 years ago in Europe and Asia, for use as guards and herders.
- **Female domestic dogs** can have two litters of puppies a year; wild members of the dog family have only one.
- **Some dogs can sense** when their owner is about to have an epileptic fit, and others can detect some cancers before the recognized symptoms appear.
- **Native Americans** used dogs to drag a type of sledge.
- **The Portuguese water dog** can be trained to dive and retrieve fishing equipment in fresh or salt water.
- **Bloodhounds** can pick up a trail over two weeks old, and follow it for over 200 km.
- **The caffeine compounds** in a bar of dark chocolate can kill a small dog (weighing up to 5 kg).
- **St Bernard rescue dogs** work in teams of three – two to keep the victim warm, one to fetch their handler.
- **During World War II**, over 50,000 dogs were enlisted in the US forces, performing tasks from sentry duty to stealing enemy documents.

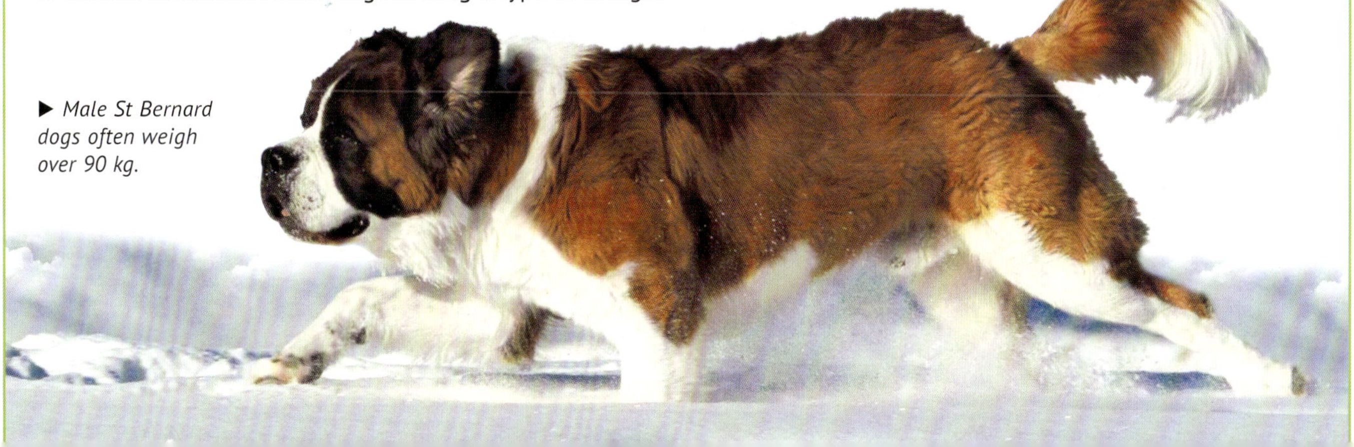

▶ *Male St Bernard dogs often weigh over 90 kg.*

Polar bears

DID YOU KNOW?

Female polar bears may go without eating for up to 8 months – existing solely on their body fat – while overwintering and feeding their newly born young.

◀ *Apart from pregnant females, which spend the winter in dens where they give birth, polar bears are active all through the winter months, often travelling great distances in search of food.*

The heavy forelimbs are ideal for breaking through ice to get at seals' lairs beneath

- **The polar bear** is the only bear which is almost exclusively a meat eater, other bears eat plants too.
- **Adult males** can measure more than 2.5 m in length and weigh up to 700 kg.
- **While stalking a seal**, a polar bear will sometimes lie on its chest with its front legs trailing at its sides and its rump in the air, pushing itself forward with its rear legs.
- **Polar bears** can detect the scent of seal pups in dens buried one metre deep in snow.
- **Polar bears** have a number of tiny protrusions and suction pads on the soles of their feet to give them a firm grip on the ice.
- **The most southerly place** that polar bears regularly visit is James Bay in Canada, which is on the same line of latitude as London, England.
- **Female polar bears** can put on as much as 400 kg in weight in the course of their summer feeding binge on seal cubs.
- **The polar bear** is a powerful swimmer, even though it uses only its front paws as paddles, letting its rear legs trail behind.
- **Beneath its thick white fur**, a polar bear's skin is black. Translucent hairs channel heat from the sun to the animal's skin, which absorbs the heat.

▼ *The huge feet are used as paddles for swimming and snow shoes for crossing ice.*

Manatees and dugongs

- **Manatees and dugongs**, known as sirenians, are the only vegetarian sea mammals in the world.
- **In the days of sail**, sailors sometimes mistook manatees, which can float upright in the water, for mermaids.
- **About 90 percent of Florida's manatees** carry scars on their bodies caused by power-boat propellers.
- **Manatees** are slow breeders, and currently more die each year than are born.
- **They have been used** successfully to clear waterways of the fast-growing water hyacinth.
- **Stella's seacow** was a massive North Pacific sirenian, up to 9 m long and weighing 6400 kg. It was hunted to extinction in the 18th century.
- **Fossil evidence** shows that manatees and dugongs have existed for about 50 million years. They are probably related to elephants.
- **The teeth of manatees** are regularly replaced, being shed at the front as they wear out, and replaced by new ones moving forward.
- **Amazonian manatees**, found only in the Amazon River and its tributaries, don't eat during the 6-month dry season.
- **The dugong** of the Indian Ocean and South Pacific feeds on eel grass, the only flowering marine plant.

▶ *Manatees have rounded tails – dugongs' tails are more whale-like.*

Tapirs

DID YOU KNOW?

The Malayan tapir walks along the bottom of rivers and lakes like a hippopotamus.

- **The forest-dwelling tapirs** of Asia and America are related to horses and rhinos, and probably resemble early horses.
- **Tapirs** moved across land bridges from North America to South America and Asia over 5 million years ago.
- **The Malayan tapir** has black-and-white colouring that breaks up its body outline in moonlit forests.
- **Tapirs use** their long snouts as snorkels, staying under water for several minutes to elude predators.
- **Newborn tapirs** have stripes and spots.
- **The South American mountain tapir** grazes at altitudes of over 5000 m.
- **The earliest-known tapir** lived some 55 million years ago.
- **Tapirs belong to** the Perissodactyla order of mammals, with an odd number of toes per foot.
- **In South America**, engineers have built roads along ancient tapir trails, which accurately follow land contours.

▼ *The Malayan tapir eats the young shoots of rubber trees.*

Llamas and their relatives

- **First domesticated some** 5000 years ago, tame llamas and alpacas were especially important to the Inca empire (1433–1533 AD). The vicuña remained untameable.
- **Vicuña herds** defend two permanent territories, one where they feed, and a smaller one at a higher altitude where they sleep at night.
- **The Incas** used llamas to carry secret messages tied into their fur.
- **Vicuñas** can live at altitudes of up to 5000 m, where the air is too thin for most mammals.
- **Unlike** in other hoofed mammals, vicuñas' incisor teeth never stop growing.
- **Fine vicuña wool** was reserved for the robes of the Inca royal family and their nobles.
- **When annoyed**, llamas spit at their opponents, sometimes including a pebble as a missile in with their saliva.
- **Llama herders** use the animals' fur for rugs and ropes, their hides for shoe leather, their fat for candles, their dung for fuel, and their milk and flesh for food.

DID YOU KNOW?

A llama can carry a 60 kg load up to 30 km a day across high mountainous terrain.

- **Baby llamas** can get up and follow their mothers just 15–30 minutes after being born.

▶ *Tame domestic llamas are usually mild-mannered, but still spit to show their ill-temper.*

Migration

- **Florida manatees** usually migrate south in winter, but recently they have moved instead into the warm water outlets of hydroelectric generating plants.
- **Hooded seals** usually migrate south from Greenland in the Atlantic Ocean, but in 1990 one seal ended up off California in the Pacific, having taken a wrong turn.
- **Migrating noctule bats** established themselves in Hawaii, after being blown 3000 km off course.

- **Migrating whales** travel huge distances with the aid of internal magnetic navigation.

DID YOU KNOW?

Each year, grey whales migrate 20,000 km in all, going to and from their breeding grounds.

- **Oil pipe-lines** are serious obstacles to caribou, which follow traditional migratory routes every year.
- **Straw-coloured fruit bats** migrate up to 2000 km from the rainforests of the Democratic Republic of Congo to Zambia, following seasonal patterns of food availability.
- **American grey squirrels** sometimes travel in their thousands, crossing roads, rivers and towns in their search for food.
- **Beluga whales** return to the estuaries where they were born to give birth.
- **Over one million wildebeest** take part in a circular seasonal migration in east Africa's Serengeti region.

◀ *When winter arrives, large herds of reindeer migrate south from their summer homes in the Arctic tundra, travelling as much as 2500 km in a year.*

Rats

- **New World wood rats**, or pack rats, continually gather twigs and build them into mounds near their nests.
- **Polynesian voyagers** carried rats on their boats as a form of live meat.
- **One species** of the Southeast Asian bandicoot rat has a body and tail length of almost one m.
- **To stop the black rat** stowing away on ships, mooring ropes are sometimes fitted with metal cones, which the rats cannot get past.
- **Baby Norwegian rats** signal to playmates that their play-fights are not serious by occasionally flipping over onto their backs.
- **Rats** constantly investigate their environment, which makes them good problem-solvers in laboratories.
- **Observers** have seen rats kick traps until they are sprung, before eating the bait in safety.
- **Norwegian or brown rats** are natural burrowers, and expert at colonizing human buildings.
- **Following heavy rains** in drought regions, 19th-century Australian settlers were subjected to plagues of long-haired rats.

◀ *Rats are among the world's most successful mammals.*

DID YOU KNOW?

The black rat was indirectly responsible, via its fleas, for the death of 50 percent of the entire human population of Europe by bubonic plague between 1347 and 1352.

Anteaters

- **To protect their long, curved digging claws**, giant anteaters have to walk awkwardly on the knuckles of their front feet.
- **Anteaters have no teeth.** They use their extremely long, sticky tongues to gather up ants and termites after breaking into their concrete-hard mounds.
- **The tamandua and pygmy anteaters** of South and Central America use their prehensile tails to climb trees, in search of termite and ant nests.
- **The Australian numbat** is the only marsupial adapted to feed exclusively on ants and termites. It has a long, sticky tongue but short, weak claws.
- **Giant anteaters**, over 2 m long from nose to tail tip, cover themselves with their bushy tails when sleeping.
- **Baby anteaters** ride clinging to their mother's backs until they are half her size.
- **Even jaguars are deterred** by the sharp, slashing claws of a giant anteater reared up on its hind legs.
- **The 15 cm long pygmy anteater** has jointed soles to its feet that help it to climb the trees in which it lives.
- **The mouth** of the giant anteater is so small that you could not insert a finger into it.
- **Fossils** found in Germany show that anteaters lived there over 50 million years ago.

▼ *The giant anteater sleeps up to 15 hours a day, and has one of the lowest mammal body temperatures at 32.7°C.*

Pandas

- **In the late 1900s**, many pandas starved to death because the fountain bamboo they ate came to the end of its 100-year growth cycle and died back.
- **Giant pandas** often give birth to twins, but in the wild one cub is always left to die.
- **Pandas** have an inefficient digestive system – up to 50 percent of the plant material they eat passes out of the body intact within 10 hours.
- **Although bamboo** forms the bulk of its diet, the giant panda also eats fish, small birds and rodents.
- **In ancient China**, pandas were believed to have magical powers, and people wore panda masks to ward off evil spirits.
- **Reduced in number** by hunting and deforestation, there are probably fewer than 1000 giant pandas left in the wild, in forest reserves in southeast China.

DID YOU KNOW?

Giant and red pandas have an extra 'thumb' that enables them to grasp their food.

- **Panda babies** are born blind, pink and nearly hairless, and measuring around 18 cm in length.

▲ *The giant panda eats sitting up, pushing bamboo canes into its mouth for 16 hours a day.*

- **Much livelier** than the giant panda, the red panda is a nimble climber. It uses its long tail for balance, and when threatened rears up and hisses.
- **Giant pandas** reach a weight of up to 150 kg, but when newborn weigh only 100–150 g.

Moles and shrews

- **Shrews** have to forage and eat almost continuously, day and night, to avoid dying of starvation.
- **The Namib golden mole** 'swims' through the desert sand, using its hypersensitive hearing to locate its insect prey.
- **The pygmy white-toothed shrew**, weighing about 2 g, is the smallest living land-based mammal on the planet.
- **European desmans** are aquatic members of the mole family, with long, flat tails, waterproof fur and webbed toes.
- **The African armoured shrew** has such strong vertebrae that it can survive being stood on by a full-grown man.
- **After their milk teeth have gone**, shrews usually only have one set of teeth. When these wear out, the shrews die.
- **Some European water shrews** have stiff hairs on their feet and tail that trap air bubbles, enabling them to scurry across the surface of water.
- **Baby shrews** may follow their mother in a line, each one holding a mouthful of the rump of the one in front.

- **The star-nosed mole** has 22 mobile, pink tentacles around the end of its snout, which help it locate prey underground.
- **The American short-tailed shrew** has enough venom in its bite to kill 200 mice.

◀ *Most of a mole's food comes from the creatures that fall into its tunnels.*

Grizzly bears

● **Originating in China**, the ancestors of the modern grizzly crossed land bridges from Asia to North America some 40,000 years ago.

● **Grizzlies once ranged** across the USA, with numbers as high as 50,000–100,000. But as their terrain has been taken over by humans, their numbers have fallen to 6000–8000.

● **The great hump** behind a grizzly's head is solid muscle, which enables it to overturn 50 kg rocks with its front paws, or kill an elk with a single blow.

● **During its winter sleep** the grizzly loses about 1 kg of bodyweight each day. Some grizzlies emerge from their sleep 50 percent lighter.

● **Grizzlies sometimes dig** huge holes to excavate food, using their powerful shoulder muscles and long, non-retractable claws.

● **Native Americans** had great respect for the grizzly, and apologized before killing it, sometimes laying out ceremonial clothes for it to wear in the spirit world.

● **Grizzlies are immensely strong**. They have been known to bite through cast iron, bend rifle barrels, and open up cars like tin cans in search of food.

▲ *Grizzly mothers give birth to their cubs in their dens in winter, and go on to look after them for anything up to a further 4–5 years, teaching them to forage and hunt, and protecting them from predators.*

● **Despite their size**, grizzlies are nimble enough to catch squirrels and mice, and can reach a speed of over 55 km/h when charging.

● **Grizzlies** often enter their winter dens just ahead of a snowstorm, so that the snow covers up their fresh tracks and seals them in for their long winter sleep.

DID YOU KNOW?

The huge Kodiak grizzly bear of the Alaskan coastal islands can reach a height of 3 m on its hind legs, and weigh up to one tonne.

▼ *Most grizzlies are dark brown in colour, but regional colouring varies from black to very pale yellow.*

Arctic life

● **White fur** helps creatures such as Arctic hares and foxes to hide from predators in the snow, but also camouflages predators such as polar bears as they hunt.

● **The ringed seal**, the most northerly of the seals, has been reported at the North Pole itself.

● **Polar bears** and Arctic foxes have tiny ears to reduce the loss of body heat in the icy Arctic.

● **In winter and spring**, Arctic foxes depend on scavenging from polar bear seal-kills – but can end up on the menu themselves!

● **Narwhals and belugas** migrate from the Arctic to warm estuaries and fjords to give birth, returning to the pack ice in late summer.

● **The bulky Arctic musk ox** has a double coat of dense wool overlaid with thick hair, and can stay in the Arctic all year, surviving temperatures of –70°C.

● **During blizzards**, musk oxen form a circle with the calves protected in the centre from the wind and snow.

● **The walrus** is a permanent inhabitant of the Arctic region, spending much of its life on the pack ice.

● **The ringed seal** gives birth in a snow cave, entered from the water through a hole in the ice.

● **Inuit hunters** fear a female walrus defending her calf more than they fear a polar bear.

◀ *The coat of the Arctic fox changes colour with the seasons. It is white during the winter and brown in summertime.*

Lemurs

● **All lemurs** live on the island of Madagascar, where they evolved in isolation, separated from the African mainland by the 300 km wide Mozambique Channel.

● **In lemur groups** the females are the more aggressive protectors of territory than the males.

● **Early European travellers** to Madagascar described a giant lemur, now extinct, that was as large as a calf.

● **Contesting male lemurs** transfer scent from their wrist glands onto their tails, then use their tails to hurl scent 'bombs' over their heads at their rivals.

● **Lemurs were able to evolve** into their many species on Madagascar mainly because they had no competition from monkeys or other primates.

● **Long after Madagascar broke away** from Africa 65–50 million years ago, the lemurs' ancestors crossed the widening channel on rafts of floating vegetation.

● **The aye-aye**, a close relative of the lemurs, has huge ears and can hear grubs chewing wood beneath bark. It extracts them with an elongated middle finger.

● **The indri** is the largest lemur, at up to one m from its nose tip to its almost tail-less rump.

● **Fat-tailed dwarf lemurs** sleep through the dry season in July and August, living on the fat stored in the thick bases of their tails.

● **Lemurs groom** using a special claw on one finger, and their front teeth, which resemble a comb.

▼ *The ring-tailed lemur uses its distinctive tail to signal to others of its species. It may live in groups of up to 30 individuals.*

Capybaras and coypus

- **The South American capybara** is the world's largest rodent, a water-loving giant up to 134 cm long and 64 kg in weight.
- **Capybaras graze** in large groups on river banks. At the first sign of danger they dash into the water and the adults surround the babies.
- **South American coypu females** suckle their young while swimming, from rows of teats high on their sides.
- **Like capybaras, coypu** are also semiaquatic rodents but are much smaller – up to 60 cm long and 9 kg in weight.
- **They were hunted** almost to extinction in the 1800s for their thick, soft fur, overlain with coarse hairs.
- **Captive farming of coypu** for what was called 'nutria' fur began in the 1920s. Many countries now have feral populations established by escaped captives.
- **The male capybara** has a hairless scent gland on its snout called the morillo (Spanish for 'small hill').

▲ *The capybara spends much of its life in the water, and has webbed feet.*

- **Some extinct capybara** weighed as much as a grizzly.
- **Capybaras mate in the water**, but give birth on land. All the females in a group will feed the young if they have milk.
- **Capybaras can stay underwater** for up to 5 minutes. They also sleep underwater with their nose sticking out.

The weasel family

- **Weasels, polecats, otters**, mink, wolverine and badgers are all members of the weasel family.
- **Ferrets**, traditionally used in Europe to catch rabbits, are a domesticated form of the European polecat.
- **Male weasels** are often twice the size of females.
- **Pest control** of American prairie dogs, the main prey of the black-footed ferret, has led to the extinction of this ferret in much of its range.
- **A mink's broad diet** includes fish, bringing it into direct competition with otters.

DID YOU KNOW?

The American least weasel, at 15 cm long and weighing 30 g, is the world's smallest carnivore.

- **The 25-kg wolverine**, the largest weasel close relative, has large feet for hunting reindeer in deep snow.
- **Bred for the fur trade**, many American mink escaped into the European countryside, replacing European mink and depleting water vole populations.
- **Black-footed ferret young** are cared for by their mother in a separate burrow until they are self-sufficient.
- **In New Zealand**, introduced weasels have almost wiped out some native birds by eating their eggs.

◀ *Weasels are the smallest mammal carnivore. Fearsome hunters, they mostly prey upon mice and voles and need to kill and eat about half their body weight each day.*

Toothed whales

- **Toothed whales** are whales that have teeth rather than the baleen plates (a row of bristles that act as a filter-feeding system) of baleen whales.
- **Sperm whales** will form a defensive circle, heads to the centre, around young or wounded group members, and beat off predators with their tails.
- **Beaked whales** feed mainly on cuttlefish and squid – one bottle-nosed whale was found to have the remains of 10,000 cuttlefish in its stomach.
- **All dolphins are toothed whales**. The orca – the largest member of the dolphin family – sometimes half-beaches itself to catch seals at the water's edge.
- **Beaked whales will dive to 500 m** or more to escape orcas, staying in the depths for an hour or more until the danger has passed.
- **Spending 85 percent of the day** under the sea's surface, bottle-nosed whales have been recorded diving to well over 1500 m in their search for their squid prey.
- **Beluga whales** are frequently stranded in coastal shallows as the tide retreats, and wait patiently for the next tide to refloat them.
- **The massive sperm whale**, which weighs up to 70 tonnes, has the largest brain of any mammal on Earth. Fat deposits in its brain case help to focus the sounds the whale produces by echolocation.
- **Toothed whales** cooperate with one another far more than baleen whales do, often working together to herd prey into a tight mass for easy feeding.

▲ *Beluga whales are the only white whales. They were once called 'sea canaries' by seamen, because their bird-like calls can be heard above the water's surface.*

DID YOU KNOW?

The male strap-toothed whale has two teeth in its lower jaw that grow to wrap around its upper jaw, severely restricting its ability to open its beak-like mouth.

▼ *Orcas are found throughout the world's oceans. They travel in close-knit social groups of up to 40 individuals, and hunt cooperatively, herding prey fish such as salmon into a close-packed mass before attacking them.*

What are marsupials?

- **Marsupials** are born in a tiny, undeveloped form, and many spend months in a protective pouch that is part of their mother's body, constantly sucking on a teat.
- **They originated** in South America some 100 million years ago, but are now most commonly associated with Australia.
- **Australia's red kangaroo** is the largest living marsupial today.
- **Marsupials range in size** from tiny shrew-like creatures to large kangaroos weighing 90 kg.

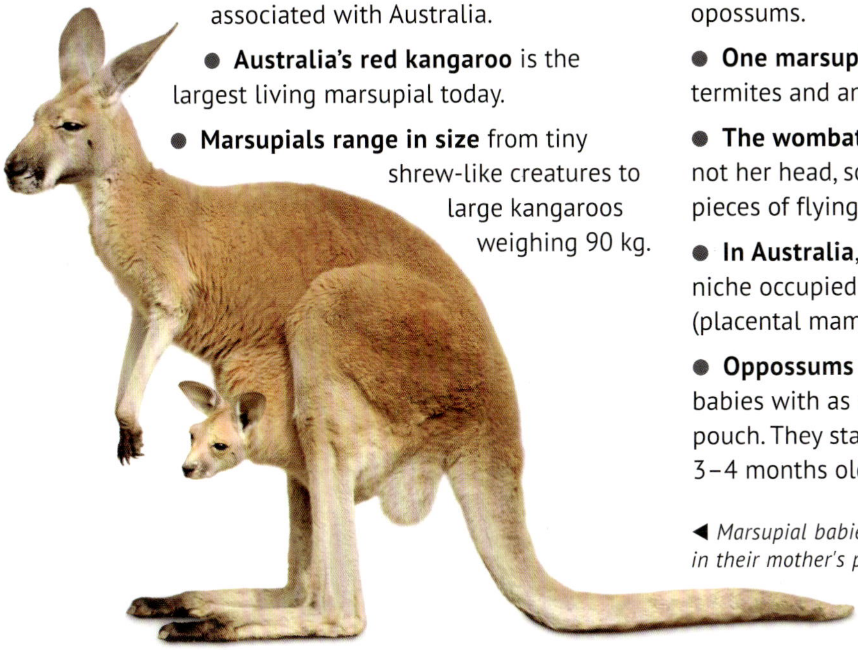

- **Marsupials** have lower body temperatures than most other mammals, and have smaller brains than placentals of a similar size.
- **Two-thirds of all marsupials** live in Australia and New Guinea. One-third are mainly South American opossums.
- **One marsupial**, the Australian numbat, eats only termites and ants.
- **The wombat's pouch** faces the mother's tail end, not her head, so that the young are protected from pieces of flying earth when she is digging.
- **In Australia**, kangaroos fill the plains-grazing niche occupied elsewhere by antelopes and gazelles (placental mammals).
- **Oppossums often give birth** to large numbers of babies with as many as 13 attaching to teats in the pouch. They stay there until they are weaned at 3–4 months old.

◀ *Marsupial babies, such as this kangaroo, are called joeys and live in their mother's pouch until they are able to fend for themselves.*

Leopards and jaguars

- **A leopard** can carry a prey animal three times its own weight up a tree, out of reach of scavengers.
- **Black panthers** are leopards with black pigmentation. Any leopard litter may include a black cub.
- **The South American jaguar** is America's only big cat.
- **A frozen leopard** carcass was found on Mount Kilimanjaro, Africa, at an altitude of 5692 m.
- **The jaguar** catches not only fish, but also otters, turtles, alligators and frogs.
- **Snow leopards**, which inhabit the mountains of Central Asia, have never been known to roar.
- **The snow leopard** has paws cushioned with hair to act as snow shoes. In the Himalayas it seldom goes below 2000 m, and sometimes goes as high as 5500 m.
- **Leopards** have survived successfully partly because they will eat almost anything, from crabs to baboons.
- **By far the best climber** of the big cats, the leopard sometimes drops straight out of a tree onto its victim.
- **The jaguar** was worshipped as a god by early South American cultures.

▲ *The leopard is by far the best climber of the big cats, and often sleeps in the branches, as well as storing food there and mounting a look-out.*

Armadillos and pangolins

- **Armadillos are nocturnal** insect-eating mammals found mostly in Central and South America. There are around 20 species.
- **Although they look a bit like armadillos, pangolins** are not related. There are eight pangolin species and they live in Africa and Asia.
- **The giant armadillo** has up to 100 small teeth.
- **The South American three-banded armadillo** can roll itself up into an impenetrable ball.

DID YOU KNOW?

Stone Age people used the 1.5 m high shell of the Glyptodon, an armadillo, as a shelter.

- **The African giant pangolin** has a long tongue that extends internally as far as its pelvis.

- **The nine-banded armadillo** has four identical, same-sex young per litter, all developed from one egg.
- **The armadillo's armour** is made up of small bone plates covered in heavy skin. The pangolin's consists of overlapping plates of horn.
- **Pangolins** often use only their back legs when running.
- **The long-tailed tree pangolin** has 37–46 tail vertebrae – a mammal record for the most tail bones.

◀ *Armadillos walk mainly on their hind legs, with their forelegs just brushing the ground.*

Domestic cattle

- **European domestic cattle** are descended from the aurochs, a large wild ox seen in ancient cave drawings.
- **The wild auroch** was domesticated about 6500 BC.
- **Humped zebu** are the main domestic cattle of Asia.
- **In India**, zebu are considered holy by Hindus, and are allowed to roam free, eat fruit off market stalls, and sleep in the roads.
- **Domesticated water buffalo** in Egypt, India and southeast Asia are powerful draught animals, and are also regularly milked.
- **India** is the country with the most domestic cattle: more than 270 million.
- **A large feral population** of domesticated water buffalo lives in northern Australia.
- **Masai cattle herders** in Kenya regularly take blood from the throats of their cattle and drink it.
- **In Tibet**, domesticated yaks thrive at altitudes well over 6000 m, providing meat, milk and transport.
- **Domestic cattle** usually sleep for just 1–5 minutes at a time, for a total of around 4 hours a day. But they do spend up to 14 hours a day lying down, dozing.

▼ *The world's largest domestic cattle are Italian Chianina, descended from the oxen used by the ancient Romans to pull carts.*

Kangaroos

- **Kangaroos are** the world's largest marsupials and are found only in Australia and New Guinea. A large adult male can reach up to 2 m in height and weigh 90 kg.
- **Flat out**, some kangaroos can reach speeds of almost 65 km/h, making huge hops of over 8 m in length.
- **Hopping** is a good way to travel fast, but to go slowly a kangaroo has to use its tail as a fifth supporting leg.
- **Some tree kangaroos** can leap to the ground from as high as 30 m without coming to harm.
- **New-born kangaroos** are called joeys and are deaf as well as naked and blind. They stay inside their mother's pouch for around 8 months.
- **Female kangaroos** suckling young of different ages at the same time are able to produce milk of different concentrations for the individual youngsters.
- **Wallabies** are smaller members of the kangaroo family, with hare wallabies weighing only 1–4.5 kg.
- **Rock wallabies** live on rocky outcrops. Their rough-soled feet are fringed with stiff hairs, enabling them to climb steep rock faces.
- **When male kangaroos fight**, they support themselves on their tails and deliver slashing kicks with their hind legs.

▲ *A kangaroo uses its large, muscular tail as a counter-balance.*

DID YOU KNOW?

Prehistoric kangaroos in Australia included a giant that stood 2.4 m tall and weighed 270 kg, and at least one meat-eating species.

Voles and lemmings

- **Voles are small, mouse-like rodents** that live in grasslands. There are more than 150 vole species.
- **Related to voles, lemmings** are small, short-tailed thickset rodents that live in the Arctic tundra.

▼ *The European water vole stores food for the winter.*

- **Some species of voles and lemmings** have their first litters when they are only 5 weeks old themselves.
- **Every 3 or 4 years** some vole and lemming species undergo population explosions, followed by high numbers of deaths from stress and food shortages.
- **At the peak** of a lemming population explosion, lemmings devastate the local vegetation – and the next summer predators can find them more easily.
- **Eurasian water voles** live in riverbank burrows with entrances below the level of the water's surface.
- **The mole-lemming** of the Central Asian steppes digs tunnels using its protruding incisor teeth.
- **At one metre below the snow's surface**, a lemming's winter nest can be 10°C, while outside it is below freezing.
- **The collared lemming** is the only rodent to change the colour of its coat to white in winter.
- **Lemmings** will swim across any water in their path as they migrate in search of new food sources. If the water is too wide to cross, they drown – hence the myth of lemmings committing mass suicide.

Communication

- **Whales' low frequency** calls travel thousands of km through the water.
- **Some whales** communicate with complex 'songs'. All of the individuals in one ocean region sing the same song.
- **Some of the puppies** from the litter of a poodle bred with a jackal had the poodle's 'language'. Others had the jackal's. But the two groups could not communicate with one another.
- **Male chimps** establish their status by seeing who can make the most noise.
- **One chimp** learned to use 130 gestures of American Sign Language.
- **Cats and dogs** erect the hair on parts of their bodies to impress rivals and mates, or frighten off predators.

▶ *Chimps communicate with a wide range of facial expressions.*

- **In gorilla groups** over 90 percent of all vocal signals and calls are made by the males.
- **A well-fed lion** can walk head-up through a herd of antelope without panicking them, but if its head is low, the antelope run, knowing it is hunting.
- **The sifaka lemur** has one alarm call to warn of birds of prey, and another to warn of snakes.
- **Many young mammals** have a 'play' body language just for mock fights.

Old World monkeys

- **The Old World monkeys** of Africa and Asia rest by sitting down, and have tough pads on their bottoms to prevent sores developing.
- **Unlike New World monkeys**, Old World monkeys generally do not have prehensile (grasping) tails.
- **Some female red colobus monkeys** in Gambia gang up to attack, and even kill, strange males.

DID YOU KNOW?

The Barbary macaque is the only primate, apart from humans, living in the wild in Europe.

- **Some colobus monkeys** gnaw on the charcoal of burned trees to help neutralize the toxins in some leaves.
- **Red colobus monkeys** often travel in mixed groups with diana monkeys, as the diana monkeys are better at spotting the chimps that prey on colobus monkeys.
- **Talapoin monkeys** in Central Africa live in forests that are frequently flooded. Excellent swimmers, they often sleep on branches overhanging the water.
- **In Japan**, in areas where humans regularly feed macaques, the birth-rate of the animals rockets, leading to groups of up to 1000.
- **The Hanuman grey langur** of India is protected by religious law, in honour of Hanuman, the monkey god.
- **Some Japanese macaques** have learned to dip food in the sea to clean and salt it, and have become good swimmers in the process.

◀ *Japanese macaques sit in hot springs in winter to keep warm.*

Lions

- **Lions** are the only big cats that lead social lives, cooperating in hunting and sharing their prey.
- **The average male lion weighs** 150–190 kg, but the largest-known wild lion was an African male man-eater, shot in 1936, that weighed 313 kg.
- **Male lions** have the job of protecting the pride, leaving the hunting to the females most of the time. However, the males insist on eating first from any kills.
- **Lions usually kill large prey** such as zebra by suffocating them, biting their throats and holding them around the neck with their paws.
- **When a new male** takes over a pride of lions by driving off its leading male, he kills cubs under about 6 months old and mates with their mothers.
- **Once widespread** throughout Southwest Asia and India, the only lions now surviving outside Africa are a few Asiatic lions found in the Indian Gir Forest wildlife reserve.
- **A male lion** will not usually allow other pride members to share a kill until he has had enough, though he may make an exception for small cubs.
- **Lion cubs** suckle from their mother for the first six months of their lives, but begin to eat meat at three months old.

▲ *Only male lions have a mane, which shows off their size, and also protects them during fights. The females are the main hunters in the pride.*

- **The roar** of a male lion, used to intimidate rivals and locate pride members, is audible 8 km away.

DID YOU KNOW?

A male lion can eat up to 40 kg of meat at one sitting, and then will not need to eat again for several days.

▼ *Lions spend most of their time sleeping, usually dozing for up to 20 hours of the day.*

Parental care

● **Many mammals carry** their young around with them. Some bats even go hunting with a youngster aboard.

● **Mother whales** have to nudge and encourage newborn young up to the surface to take their first breath, often aided by 'aunts' from the same pod.

● **In wild dog packs**, several females may take turns to suckle and guard all the young in the group.

● **Sperm whale** offspring have sometimes been known to suckle for up to 15 years, although the mother's milk has usually stopped after 2–4 years.

● **Elephant young** are born after 22 months.

● **Mother cheetahs** teach their young how to hunt by bringing small live prey back for them to practise on.

● **A female big cat** carries her young by holding the back of the neck in her mouth, in a gap behind her teeth.

● **Young kangaroos** leave the pouch at 5–11 months, but continue to stick their head in to suckle for 6 months.

● **Many cats**, large and small, start to train their young by allowing them to attack their twitching tails.

DID YOU KNOW?

Baby gorillas may only climb on the silverback while they still have a white rump tuft.

▼ *Baby baboons depend on their mother for food and transport, but are also protected from danger by certain males in the group.*

Dolphins

● **Groups of common dolphins**, travelling and feeding together, may number up to 2000 individuals.

● **Orcas, or killer whales**, are actually the largest species of dolphin. They sometimes feed on other dolphin species.

● **There are five species** of freshwater dolphin living in Asian and South American rivers. Most catch fish by sound rather than sight.

● **Dolphins** have been known to aid humans by keeping them afloat and driving off attacking sharks.

● **Spinner dolphins** are named for the acrobatic leaps they perform, spinning up to 7 times in mid-air.

● **The Atlantic hump-backed dolphin** helps fishermen in West Africa by driving shoals of mullet into their nets.

● **In Mexico's Baja California**, bottle-nosed dolphins chase fish up onto the shore, then roll up onto the beach, completely out of the water, to grab them.

● **Military observers** once recorded a group of dolphins swimming at 64 km/h in the bow wave of a warship.

● **The striped dolphin**, seen in ancient Greek art, leaps up to 7 m to perform somersaults and spins.

● **The Yangtse dolphin**, or baiji, is one of the world's rarest mammals – probably less than 300 survive.

◄ *Many dolphin species 'spy-hop', holding their heads out of the water as they check on their surroundings for predators and potential food.*

Moose and elk

- **The world's largest deer** – called moose in North America and elk in Europe – stand up to 2 m tall at the shoulder.
- **Moose escape from wolves** by retreating to marshes and lakes.
- **The prehistoric Irish elk**, which became extinct 10,000 years ago, had massive antlers up to 3.6 m across. It also stood 2.1 m tall to the shoulders.
- **Moose** have reached Isle Royale in Lake Superior, USA, by swimming across 32 km of water.
- **To protect her calf** from wolves, the mother moose shepherds it into shallow water and stands between it and the wolves, which usually give up.
- **A moose will use its** great weight to push over young trees to get at twigs and shoots.
- **A moose eats** the equivalent of 20,000 leaves a day.
- **The antlers** of a moose are 'palmate', which means they have broad areas like hands.
- **A young moose** stays with its mother for almost a year, but she chases it away just before she is about to give birth to a new calf.

DID YOU KNOW?

The moose has been known to dive to 5.5 m, staying under water for 30 seconds, to reach water plants and roots.

◀ *Two male elk spar with their antlers, which they lose and regain every year.*

Australasian marsupials

- **The brush-tailed possum** is Australia's most common marsupial. It often moves into the lofts of houses.
- **Kangaroos** are not restricted to Australia – several tree-kangaroo species live in Papua New Guinea.
- **Australian marsupial moles** strongly resemble true moles, but have different ancestors.
- **Wombats live in burrows** and weigh up to 40 kg (but one fossil wombat weighed in at a hefty 100 kg).
- **The Tasmanian devil** is the largest surviving marsupial carnivore, eating mainly carrion.
- **The Australian pygmy possum** sleeps so soundly that you can pick it up without it waking.
- **The muscular tail** of the long-tailed dunnart is up to 21 cm long (twice its body length).
- **Some bandicoots** (nocturnal, rat-like marsupials) have a gestation period of just 12.5 days – a mammal record.
- **The striped possum** digs for grubs in tree bark with an elongated finger.

▲ *The stocky wombat is related to the koala, but cannot climb trees and digs large burrows.*

DID YOU KNOW?

Kangaroos are serious competitors with sheep for grass, because with front teeth in both jaws instead of just one, they crop it much closer.

Nocturnal mammals

- **Animals that are most active** at night are called nocturnal. It is estimated that around 70 percent of mammals are nocturnal.
- **Many have highly** developed senses of sight, hearing or smell to help them navigate the world at night.
- **For some mammals** the darkness offers protection from predators while for others it helps to hide them as they sneak up on prey.
- **Lions prefer to hunt** at night when it is much cooler than daytime in their habitat.
- **A harvest mouse uses** its super-sensitive long whiskers to feel its way around in the dark.
- **The owl monkeys** (also known as night monkeys) of the Americas are the only truly nocturnal monkeys. They have large, owl-like eyes for good night vision, and they hoot and holler to one another to communicate in the darkness.
- **Some of the world's** commonest mammals are the nocturnal rodents, such as mice, rats, voles and lemmings.

▲ *The ocelot of Central and South America comes out at night to look for food. It hunts birds, rodents, lizards and bats.*

- **Rhinos prefer to feed** at night when it's cool. These huge plant eaters have poor eyesight so depend on their excellent sense of smell to find food and detect predators.
- **Sloth bears** hunt for termites using their highly developed sense of smell. Once they pick up the scent of an ant or termite nest they rip it open using their long claws and then suck up the insects.

DID YOU KNOW?

Aardvarks live alone and come out at sunset to forage for food. They can eat up to 50,000 insects a night.

▼ *Hippos have sensitive skin that can burn easily in the sun, so they spend their days wallowing and napping in water. They come out after dark to feed, grazing on as much as 40 kg of plants and grass every night.*

Mongooses, civets and genets

- **Mongooses, civets and genets** are small, cat-like carnivorous mammals. Civets and genets are nocturnal while mongooses are active during the day.
- **African banded mongooses** gang up together to repel and attack predators such as jackals.
- **A mongoose will tire out a cobra** by making quick movements, then kill it.

- **The Malaysian binturong** is related to civets, and is the only Old World mammal with a prehensile tail, which it uses as a brake when descending trees.
- **The palm civet** of Asia is known as the toddy cat, because it has a taste for a fermented alcoholic drink.
- **Civets** were once kept captive in Ethiopia and 'milked' of their strong-smelling musk, which was used in the perfume industry.
- **The dwarf mongoose** marks its territory by doing a handstand to deposit a scent mark as high as possible on a rock or bush.
- **Common genets** are found in France and Spain. They may have been introduced in medieval times as pets and rat-catchers by the Moors of North Africa.
- **Otter civets**, like true otters, have webbed feet and closable nostrils. They catch fish and can climb trees.
- **Largest of the civet-mongoose family**, the fossa of Madagascar has a cat-like head and retractable claws.

◄ *The banded mongoose lives and forages in large groups, leaving a babysitting adult back in the den to guard the young.*

Camouflage

- **The simplest camouflage** makes an animal a similar colour to its surroundings, such as the white of a polar bear in snow.
- **Some whales and dolphins** are dark on top and light underneath, camouflaging them against the dark of deep water or the light of the sky.
- **Some camouflage** mimics the broken shapes of light shining through trees, as can be seen in the dappled markings of giraffes.
- **The young** of many mammal species, such as lions and pigs, have early camouflage markings that disappear as the animals grow older.
- **Stripes** benefit both predators and prey by breaking up the body shape, for example in tigers and zebras.
- **The coats of Arctic foxes** and hares change from dark in summer to white in winter.

DID YOU KNOW?

Not all camouflage is visual – some mammals roll in dung to disguise their own scents.

- **Bold markings**, such as the contrasting shapes of the oryx, camouflage by breaking up body outline.
- **The bobcat's spots** camouflage it in rocks, while the similar-shaped plain lynx merges with forest.
- **Even the elephant's huge grey form** disappears as it stands still in the shadows.

▼ *A cheetah's colouring and its irregular pattern of spots act as an effective camouflage, enabling it to sneak up on prey in its grassland habitat.*

New World marsupials

DID YOU KNOW?

The Maya civilization of Central America believed the opossum to be a magical animal.

- **American marsupials** are nearly all from the opossum family, which has lived in America for 70 million years.
- **Opossums** are around the size of a domestic cat. They have spread successfully northwards as far as Canada, but are vulnerable to frostbitten ears and tails.
- **When attacked**, the opossum goes into a death-like trance, called 'playing possum'.
- **The Virginia opossum** usually has 13 teats in its pouch, but often gives birth to a higher number of young. Those that are not able to attach to a teat soon die.
- **The newly born mouse opossum** is barely larger than a grain of rice – the smallest newborn mammal.
- **Once a baby opossum** has attached itself to a teat, it cannot let go until it is fully developed.
- **Some opossum species** have prehensile tails which they wind round those of their young when carrying them.
- **The yapok**, or water opossum, is the only mainly aquatic marsupial. It has webbed rear feet.
- **The monito del monte** is a rat-sized marsupial unrelated to opossums, and found in Chile's cool forests.

▶ *As marsupials, oppossum babies start life in their mother's pouch. As they get larger they continue to hang onto their mother until old enough to look after themselves.*

Mountain lions

- **The mountain lion**, or puma, is the widest-ranging American mammal, occurring from Canada in the north to southern Chile in the south.
- **Mountain lions** are the largest American desert carnivores.
- **The Patagonian puma** has a hunting territory of up to 100 sq km. Its main prey is the llama-like guanaco.

- **As a form of territorial marking**, pumas build little piles of soil or vegetation called scrapes.
- **Although the size of a leopard**, the mountain lion is classified as a small cat because it can purr.
- **In the Sierra Nevada**, the main prey of mountain lions is the mule deer, which can be twice the lion's weight.
- **High altitude varieties** of mountain lion may be much larger (113 kg) than those living lower down (45 kg).
- **Below the tree line**, the mountain lion hunts by night. At higher altitudes it may have to hunt by day.
- **There are few reports** of mountain lion attacks on humans, but attacks have increased as humans have taken over more of the mountain lion's territories.
- **Mountain lions** are solitary, avoiding one another except to mate. When the young leave their mother, they relocate at least 45 km away.

◀ *The puma is the largest of the so-called small cats, and its prey ranges from mice to full-grown deer.*

Black bears

- **American black bears** vary in colour from black, brown, cinnamon, honey and grey, to white.
- **Beavers are a favourite food** of some black bears.
- **In autumn**, feeding up for the winter sleep, black bears put on up to 1.5 kg per day.
- **Black bears mate** in the summer, but the fertilized egg does not begin to develop until the autumn. The cubs are born in January.
- **'Nuisance' bears** that have learned to scavenge garbage in US national parks have to be tranquillized and moved to new areas.
- **The most northerly** Canadian black bears have a varied diet ranging from caribou and seals to birds' eggs and tiny shrimp.

DID YOU KNOW?

Asiatic black bears are constipated when they awake from their winter hibernation, and drink birch tree sap as a laxative.

- **The sun bear** of Southeast Asia is the world's smallest bear, at 27–65 kg. It specializes in gathering honey and insects with its long tongue.

▲ *Black bears occasionally raid people's beehives and orchards, as well as city dumps.*

- **South America's only bear** is the spectacled bear, which builds feeding and sleeping platforms in the branches of fruit trees.
- **The black sloth bear** of India has a mobile snout and closable nostrils so it doesn't inhale a lot of soil when sucking up ants.

Mole rats

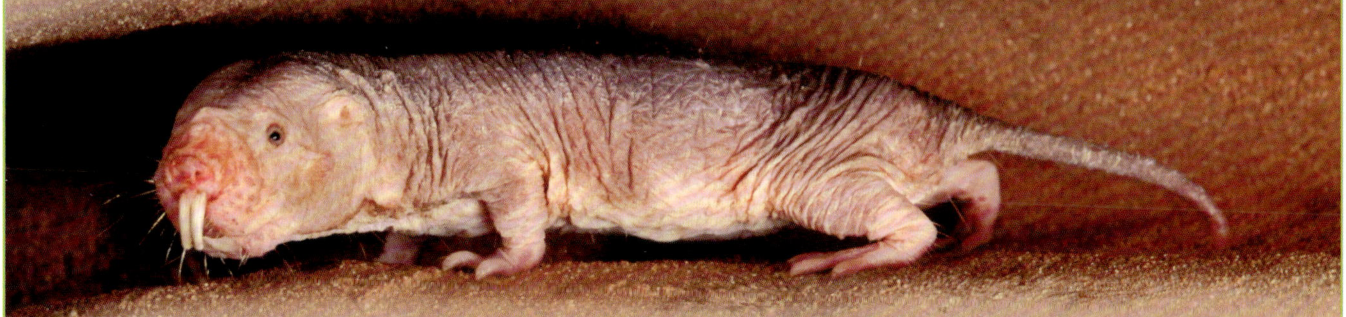

- **Unlike most rodents**, mole rats live for several years.
- **Mole rats** have extremely loose skin, which enables them to turn around in the tightest of tunnels.
- **Naked mole rats** have no fur. They live in colonies, like some insects, with a queen that bears all the young, and workers that dig the tunnels.
- **Mole rats**, unlike moles, dig with their protruding front teeth. Lip folds prevent them swallowing earth.
- **Mole rats** have poor vision, but they may use the eye surface to detect air currents in the burrow.
- **They have been observed** biting off the growing sprouts of roots and tubers before storing them, preventing them losing nutritional value before use.

▲ *Naked mole rats enjoy stable temperatures of around 29°C in their humid burrows, when outside surface temperatures can be as high as 60°C.*

- **Blind mole rats** of the eastern Mediterranean have skin-covered eyes. Despite this, they dig individual tunnel systems up to 350 m long.
- **Naked mole rats** cooperate to dig tunnels, several moving the soil to the surface and one kicking it out of the hole.
- **The 'queen'** of a naked mole rat colony suppresses the breeding ability of other females by means of chemical signals.
- **The Cape dune mole rat** can move up to half a tonne of soil in just one month.

Bushbabies, tarsiers and lorises

● **Bushbabies, tarsiers and lorises** are all small, tree-dwelling nocturnal primates with large eyes for good night vision.

● **They belong to** the prosimian group of primitive primates.

● **Bushbabies, also called galagos**, live in the forests of east and central Africa where they run through trees at night hunting for insects, flowers, seeds and eggs to eat.

● **During the day**, bushbabies huddle together in hollow trees or sleep in old birds' nests.

● **Once found widely** around the world, tarsiers now live only on islands in Southeast Asia.

● **Tarsiers are the only** entirely carnivorous primates, feeding on insects, lizards, small birds, frogs and bats.

● **They use their long** fingers and toes to grip branches tightly as they jump from tree to tree. They can jump up to 5 m, which is more than 40 times their body length.

● **Tarsiers can't move** their eyes but can swivel their heads 180 degrees in each direction, which helps them to hunt insects at night.

● **Lorises live** in India and Sri Lanka and use their nimble fingers to grab insects for food.

● **Unusually for mammals**, slow lorises have a toxic bite that they use to defend themselves, and loris mothers lick their young with toxic saliva to protect them from predators.

◀ *Each one of a tarsier's eyeballs is actually bigger than its brain.*

The mating game

● **In some species** of Australian marsupial mouse, the male dies after a two-week mating period.

● **A beaver** stays with its mate for many years, producing a new litter each year.

● **A male hedgehog** courts a female by circling her, sometimes wearing a deep groove in the soil, until she accepts him.

DID YOU KNOW?

The hooded seal impresses females by inflating a nostril lining into a red balloon.

● **Male Californian sea-lions** bark to guard their mating territory. Underwater, the barks produce bursts of bubbles.

● **The red markings** on a male mandrill's blue and red face become brighter during the mating season.

● **To attract potential mates**, orang-utan males emit a series of loud roars that tail off into groans.

● **Narwhal males** compete for mates by 'fencing' with their long, spiral tusks.

● **Hippos prefer to mate in the water**, with the female often completely submerged, and having to raise her head to breathe every so often.

● **Naked mole rats** live in colonies organized around a single breeding queen. She secretes hormones that stops other females being fertile so that she is the only one that breeds.

◀ *White rhino males have strict territorial boundaries. They try to keep receptive females within the territory, but if a female strays outside, he will not follow her.*

Bats

- **Bat species** form 22 percent of the world's mammals, and are the most common rainforest mammal.
- **The Mexican free-tailed bat** can fly at speeds of up to 95 km/h.
- **The bumblebee bat** of Thailand is the world's smallest mammal. Its body is just 3 cm long, and it weighs only 2 g.
- **In one North American cave**, 10 million Mexican free-tailed bats give birth each year to 10 million young over a period of about a week.
- **In some bat species**, males are known sometimes to produce milk, but it is not known if they ever suckle the young.
- **A resting bat** emits 10 sound pulses per second, rising to 30 per second as it flies, 60 per second when approaching an object, and 200 per second when approaching an insect.
- **Australia's ghost bat** is the continent's only meat-eating bat. It hunts and devours frogs, birds, lizards, small mammals, and even other bats.

▲ *The only mammals capable of powered flight, bats come in a diverse range of shapes and sizes – but all have excellent hearing. Shown here are:* (1) *the red bat,* (2) *the Mexican fishing bat,* (3) *the African yellow-winged bat,* (4) *the noctule bat,* (5) *the long-eared bat,* (6) *the hoary bat,* (7) *the horse or hammer-headed bat,* (8) *the lesser horseshoe bat and* (9) *the spotted bat.*

▼ *Vampire bats feed solely on the blood of other animals. Chemicals in their saliva prevent the blood of their victims from clotting.*

- **Many tropical nectar- and pollen-eating bats** are important pollinators of plants, including some trees. They transfer the pollen from one plant to another as they feed inside the flowers.
- **The bulldog bat** feeds on fish, grabbing them from the surface of the water with its specially elongated toes.

DID YOU KNOW?

The vampire bat uses razor-sharp teeth to make tiny cuts in the neck, flank or back of a sleeping mammal, and then laps up the blood.

Baleen whales

- **Baleen whales** have rows of bristles called baleen plates in their mouths that trap the tiny creatures that the whales feed on.
- **The baleen plates** of modern baleen whales evolved about 30 million years ago.
- **Women's corsets** were once made using baleen, which is also known as whalebone.
- **Baleen whales** include blue whales, the planet's largest animals. They grow up to 27 m long and the heaviest known weighed over 190 tonnes.
- **Blue whale calves** grow about 1000 times faster in the womb than human babies.

▶ *Humback whales have been seen to leap out of the water as many as 100 times in quick succession.*

- **Right whales** were so-named because they were the 'right' ones to hunt – heavy with oil, meat and baleen.
- **Right whales** force water through their baleen plates to trap their food, which is mostly the tiny crustaceans called krill.
- **Despite being protected** since the 1940s, there are less than 450 northern right whales surving.
- **Bowhead whales** are estimated to eat up to 100,000 kg of krill a year.

DID YOU KNOW?

Humpback whales produce columns of air bubbles that force their prey into clusters.

Buffaloes

- **The African buffalo** will stalk and attack a human even if unprovoked, and will mob lions and kill their cubs if it gets the chance.
- **The wild Asiatic buffalo** can weigh up to 1200 kg, and has the longest horns of any living animal, sometimes exceeding a 4-m spread.
- **African buffaloes** have a wide range of vocal communications, including signals for moving off, direction-changing, danger and aggressive intent.
- **In Australia in the dry season**, female feral water buffaloes leave their calves with a 'nursemaid' on the edge of the plains where they graze.
- **The African savannah buffalo** can weigh up to 875 kg, and herds can number several thousand.
- **A wounded African buffalo** will ambush its hunter, exploding out of cover in an unstoppable charge.
- **Needing to drink every day**, African buffaloes never stray more than 15 km from water.
- **Buffaloes rarely fight**. Contests consist of tossing the head, pawing the ground and circling, before one bull walks away.
- **Blind or crippled buffaloes** are sometimes observed living healthily in a herd, whereas loners would soon die.
- **In the rinderpest cattle epidemic** of the 1890s, nine African buffaloes died for every one animal that survived.

◀ *Swamp mud helps protect a water buffalo's skin from heat and insects.*

Lynxes and bobcats

DID YOU KNOW?

Snow hares provide 70 percent of the North American lynx's diet. Lynx numbers fluctuate with the 10-year population cycle of the snow hare.

- **Bobcats and lynxes** are closely related, but the lynx inhabits northern conifer forests and swamps, and the bobcat prefers rocky regions with dense undergrowth.
- **Lynxes have shorter tails** than bobcats, and their longer legs help them to move through deep snow.

- **Chased by dogs**, the bobcat often takes to water, where it is a superior swimmer to its pursuers.
- **In experiments**, bobcats with clipped ear-tufts heard less well, suggesting the tufts aid their hearing.
- **Lynxes have thick fur** on the soles of their feet to keep them warm and help prevent slipping on icy surfaces.
- **The bobcat** is only found in America, but the lynx has populations across Europe and Asia.
- **Bobcats** are taught to hunt by the age of 7 months. At 12 months the mother drives them away.
- **Unlike the lynx**, the bobcat flourishes in deserts.
- **The bobcat may live up to 20 years**, eating rabbits, prairie dogs, rattlesnakes and crayfish.

◀ *Its long ear tufts help the lynx to hear its main prey, the snow hare, and long legs enable it to chase its prey through deep snow.*

Koalas

- **Koalas are** bear-like tree-dwelling marsupials native to Australia. They can reach 85 cm in length and weigh up to 15 kg.
- **Male koalas mark their territories** by rubbing their large chest gland, which females lack, onto tree trunks.
- **The koala feeds** mainly on eucalyptus leaves.
- **Koalas** are the sole living representatives of their family, but are distantly related to wombats.
- **The koala grips** branches with its sharp-clawed hands by opposing the first two fingers to the other three.
- **Koalas spend 80 percent** of their day asleep in trees.
- **When its body temperature** nears 37°C, the koala licks its paws and rubs cooling saliva onto its face.
- **The name 'koala'** comes from an Aboriginal word meaning 'no drink' – it gets most of the moisture it needs from the leaves it eats.
- **A giant koala**, weighing twice as much as today's animals, existed over 40,000 years ago.

▶ *Although resembling a bear, koalas are not related to the bear family.*

DID YOU KNOW?

A koala weighs less than 0.5 g at birth, and remains in its mother's pouch for 7 months.

Chimpanzees

● **Chimps have a strict social ladder**, with dominant males at the top. These top males recognize property rights, and never steal food from their inferiors.

● **Grooming is a very important** activity among chimps. It helps to create strong bonds between individuals, and to establish the group's pecking order.

● **Observers** have noted chimpanzees carefully lifting a fellow chimp's eyelid to remove a speck of grit.

● **Chimpanzees** actively hunt for meat, especially when plant food is scarce, and collaborate to catch colobus monkeys, young baboons, birds and rodents.

● **If a chimpanzee** finds a tree laden with fruit, it drums on a tree trunk and makes loud panting cries to summon other chimps from many kilometres away for a share of the feast.

● **Bands of male chimpanzees** have been observed attacking and killing all the males in a neighbouring band. Up to a third of adult male chimp deaths result from territorial disputes.

● **Bonobos**, or pygmy chimpanzees, are found in the dense forests along the Congo River. They are darker than other chimps, with longer legs and smaller heads, and walk upright more often.

▲ *Chimps eat a range of plants as medicines, to get rid of conditions such as stomach aches and parasitic worms.*

● **A bonobo named Kanzi**, a very successful participant in language experiments, also learned how to light a barbecue and cook his own sausages.

● **With a large brain** and intense curiosity, chimps can absorb considerable amounts of information, and are also able to learn by imitation.

▼ *Chimps are some of the best tool-users after humans. They use grass stems to fish for termites in their mounds, stones and anvils to crack nuts, and chewed leaves as sponges for gathering water.*

DID YOU KNOW?

Chimpanzees reach puberty at about 10 years, give birth every four to five years, and may live into their 50s.

Life on the plains

- **In the 1800s**, a vast springbok herd, 25 km wide and 160 km long, crossed the plains of southern Africa.
- **The Argentine maned wolf** has extremely long legs for hunting in the tall pampas grasses.
- **The African springhare** resembles a miniature kangaroo.
- **The world's biggest** grouping of large land mammals takes place every year on Africa's Serengeti plains, with the migration of 1.5 million wildebeest and one million other hoofed animals.
- **Savannah buffalo** graze on tall grasses, reducing them to the height preferred by other grazers.
- **Newborn wildebeest** have a strong instinct to approach anything that moves – even, fatally, hyenas or lions.
- **As herds of wildebeest** trample and manure the ground, they stimulate the rapid regrowth of grasses.
- **If young wild dogs tire** while hunting on Africa's Okavango flood plain, the adults hide them and return for them later.

▲ *During migration, herds of wildebeest travel hundreds of miles.*

- **The American pronghorn antelope** can see the white warning patches on the rump of another pronghorn from several kilometres away.
- **The Bactrian camel** of Central Asia eats salty plants avoided by other grazers.

New World monkeys

- **New World monkeys** have broad noses with sideways-pointing nostrils. Old World monkeys' noses are narrow, with downward-pointing nostrils.
- **Unlike Old World monkeys**, most New World monkeys also have prehensile tails, and can suspend their whole bodies from them when travelling or feeding.
- **The howler monkey** has a special throat bone that enables it to produce its distinctive deep roar.
- **The pygmy marmoset** is the world's smallest monkey, weighing just 125 g.
- **The pygmy marmoset** uses its teeth to gouge holes in tree bark so that it can extract the gum – a major part of its diet.

◀ *The howler monkey makes ear-shattering calls to warn off rivals.*

- **The South American night monkey** is the only truly nocturnal monkey.
- **The capuchin** is the brainiest New World monkey. In captivity, it soon learns to use tools to obtain food.
- **Marmosets and tamarins** always give birth to twins, carried mainly by the father.
- **Titi monkeys** live in small family groups, and all sleep together with their tails entwined.

DID YOU KNOW?

Spider monkeys hang by their tails from low branches over rivers to drink.

Heat regulation

- **Fruit bats** are susceptible to heat stroke, so to keep themselves cool, some lick themselves all over and fan cool air at their bodies with their wings.
- **The oryx** has special blood vessels in its nose to keep its blood temperature low in the desert heat.
- **Dogs can only sweat** through their paws, so they get rid of excess heat by panting.

- **The desert bighorn sheep** draws air over a thickly veined area of its throat to cool its blood.
- **Wallowing in mud** keeps pigs cool and protects their skin from the sun.
- **A hippos' skin** exudes a red, lacquer-like substance to protect it from sunburn.
- **During hot spells**, kangaroos lick their wrists a lot, so that the evaporation of the saliva causes cooling.
- **Indian zebu cattle** have more sweat glands than western cattle, and maintain a lower body temperature, making them common in China, Africa and South America as well as India.
- **The eland's temperature** can rise several degrees without causing sweating, allowing it to conserve 5 litres of water daily.
- **After feeding their young**, mother bats often leave them in the heat of the cave and perch near the cooler entrance.

◀ *Large-eared desert species, such as this fennec fox, use their ears as radiators to get rid of body heat.*

Fruit bats

- **Fruit bats eat their weight** in fruit each day, and are key seed-dispersers, spitting out seeds as they eat.
- **In Southwest Asia**, some date farmers protect their fruit from fruit bat raiders by covering the dates with bags of woven palm leaves.
- **Island fruit bats** are vulnerable to tropical storms that can blow them far out to sea. This is how some species reached islands in the first place.
- **Fruit bats** enjoy eating fruit in mangrove forests, where seawater minerals supplement their diet.
- **Large fruit bats** strip the leaves from the trees in which they roost to give them a clearer view.
- **Male hammer-headed bats** gather together in riverside trees called leks, so that the females can choose a mate from among them. As they hang, the males flap their wings and call out.
- **The Queensland tube-nosed bat** has tube-like nostrils projecting 5–6 mm from its face. These may act as snorkels as it feeds on pulpy fruit.

▶ *Unlike echolocating bats, fruit bats, such as this large flying fox, have well-developed eyesight and navigate visually.*

- **Some fruit bats** chew leaves to get protein, but spit them out after swallowing the juice as they can't digest leaf fibres.

DID YOU KNOW?

The largest fruit bat is the Indian flying fox, which has a wingspan of up to 150 cm.

- **Spectacled flying foxes**, a type of large fruit bat, sometimes drink seawater as they skim by, and have been snapped up by saltwater crocodiles.

Wolves

● **Wolves** migrated into Europe, Asia and Africa from North America some 7 million years ago.

● **In wolf packs**, only the dominant female normally mates and has cubs. The female wolves sometimes fight to establish who is to be the pack mother.

● **Forest wolves stay all year** in their own territory, while tundra wolves are nomadic, following the migrations of prey such as caribou.

● **Wolves howl** to avoid territorial fights – if they know where another pack is, they usually steer clear of it.

● **Grey wolves** often go for a week without food. They only average one kill in every ten hunting expeditions.

● **Although they normally hunt large prey** such as deer, wolves will also eat carrion, berries and even fish.

● **Wolf packs** may number 20 or so where moose are plentiful, but only six or seven where deer are the main prey.

● **Tundra wolves** hunt larger prey than wolves further south, and tend to be larger themselves.

● **A pack's dominant pair** scent mark their home range (up to 1000 sq km) by urinating about every 3 minutes.

● **Wolves cull the old and weak** members in a herd of prey animals, improving the herd's overall health.

◀ *The grey wolf is the ancestor of the domestic dog, and still occasionally mates with dogs such as huskies.*

Racoons

DID YOU KNOW?

At one time raccoon skins were used as currency in parts of Tennessee, USA.

● **Raccoons** belong to a family that includes long-tailed kinkajous, coatis and cacomistles in the Americas, and the red pandas in Asia.

● **Hunting raccoons** with coonhounds at night is popular in parts of the USA, but raccoons have been known to lure dogs into water and then drown them.

● **In many suburban areas** of the USA, raccoons have moved into sheds and roof spaces, emerging at night to raid garbage cans.

● **Raccoons** use their slender-fingered front paws to capture frogs and crayfish.

● **Raccoons have a weakness** for sweetcorn, raiding crops just ahead of the farmer.

● **The crab-eating raccoon** of South America leads a semi-aquatic life, and is also a good tree climber.

● **In the northern part of their range**, raccoons may retire to their nests in winter for a month or two.

● **Captive raccoons** appear to wash food before eating it, but in the wild a raccoon's underwater manipulations are to locate food rather than to wash it.

● **In urban areas**, raccoons sometimes carry off garbage cans, even untying rope knots to remove lids.

◀ *The raccoon's distinctive 'mask' fits its reputation as a night-time bandit, thief and garbage raider.*

Gibbons

- **The gibbons of Southeast Asia** are the smallest and most agile of the apes. They pair for life, and each couple has its own song of whoops and wails.
- **Swinging by their long arms**, gibbons hurtle through the forest, flying up to 15 m between hand-holds.
- **With the longest arms** relative to body size of all the primates, gibbons often hang by just one arm.
- **Noone** has been able to keep up with gibbons to time how fast they swing arm over arm (brachiation).
- **Siamangs** are the largest gibbons, at up to 15 kg.
- **About 2 million years ago** there was only one gibbon species, but ice age changes in sea levels created forest islands, where separate species developed.
- **A gibbon sleeps** sitting up on a branch with its head between its bent knees, not in a nest like great apes.
- **Gibbons are more closely related** to orang-utans than to the chimps and gorillas of Africa.
- **Gibbons have highly flexible** shoulder joints, and can rotate through 360 degrees while hanging from one arm.

▲ *From earliest infancy the gibbon spends nearly all of its life above ground in the trees.*

DID YOU KNOW?

In the black gibbon species, the male is all black, whereas the female is light cream with a black face.

Hyenas

- **After making a successful kill**, the spotted ('laughing') hyena emits a blood-curdling, laugh-like cry.
- **Hyenas** are more closely related to mongooses than to members of the dog family.
- **The spotted hyena** can chase a wildebeest for 5 km at speeds of up to 60 km/h.
- **The hyena's powerful jaws** can crush large bones, which its digestive system dissolves in a few hours.
- **Hyenas may suckle** their young for more than a year, compared to 2 months in the dog family.
- **All hyenas hide surplus food** for later – sometimes even underwater in the case of the spotted hyena.
- **In South Africa**, brown hyenas, or 'beach wolves', beachcomb for dead crabs, fish and sea mammals.
- **The aardwolf** is a small, insect-eating member of the hyena family. One specimen was found to have over 40,000 termites in its stomach.
- **A female brown hyena** was once seen to take a springbok carcass from a leopard, and drive the leopard up a tree.
- **Brown and striped hyenas** erect their long manes to make them look larger when displaying aggression.

◀ *Often portrayed as a skulking scavenger, the spotted hyena is in fact an aggressive hunter. However, it is also capable of driving lions from their kills at times.*

Gazelles and antelopes

DID YOU KNOW?

The pronghorn is not a true antelope, and is more closely related to the deer family.

◀ *A fleeing springbok may leap vertically in an activity known as 'pronking', confusing predators and giving the springbok a better view.*

- **The smallest antelope**, the West African royal antelope, is only the size of a brown hare, and weighs between 1.5 and 3 kg.
- **When the Indian blackbuck antelope** runs flat out, it reaches 80 km/h, making 8-m long strides. The Indian aristocracy once used trained cheetahs to hunt them.
- **When a dominant greater kudu bull lies down**, he suddenly loses all authority, and female and young bull kudus often harass and annoy him with impunity.
- **The giant eland** of West and Central Africa is the largest of all antelopes, reaching 3.5 m in length, 1.85 m at the shoulder, and weighing up to 940 kg.
- **The American pronghorn antelope** has been timed running at 56 km/h for 6 km, and up to 88.5 km/h over short distances less than one km.
- **When migrating** to new grazing grounds, herds of wildebeest sometimes number up to 1.5 million individuals, and the herd may measure as much as 40 km in length.
- **The Arabian oryx** is a desert specialist, with a pale, heat-reflecting coat and splayed hoofs for walking in soft sand. Its small size enables it to shelter in the shade of shrubby trees.
- **The spiral-horned antelopes**, which include elands, kudus and bongos, are found only in Africa, and are an offshoot of the ancestors of domestic cattle.
- **The springbok** is famous for its spectacular leaps while running – a display activity known as 'pronking'.

▲ *The Indian blackbuck is one of the world's fastest animals, with herds travelling at up to 80 km/h for one km at a time.*

▲ *The male pronghorn has several scent glands for marking territory, including glands beneath the ears, on the rump, above the tail and between the toes.*

Coyotes and jackals

DID YOU KNOW?

Young coyotes may spend a year helping to raise their younger brothers and sisters.

- **Coyotes and jackals are wolf-like** wild dogs that often hunt in pairs or small packs. Coyotes are native to North America and jackals live in Africa, southern Asia and southeast Europe.
- **Black-backed jackals** lived in Africa's Olduvai Gorge some 1.7 million years ago, and still live in the region.

- **Hunting at dawn and dusk**, their prey includes small mammals, birds, reptiles and carrion (dead animals).
- **The golden jackal** of Eurasia and Africa is fond of fruit, eating figs and berries as well as animal prey.
- **The coyote** is probably the only predator whose range is increasing across North America.
- **Coyotes can live to be over 14 years old** in the wild, and over 21 years old in captivity.
- **Jackals are fearless defenders** of their family groups – a single jackal will attack a hyena five times its weight.
- **Native Americans** celebrated the cunning 'trickster' coyote, and told myths about its cleverness.
- **When fighting a predator** or stealing a kill, pairs of jackals employ a 'yo-yo' technique, dashing in from each side alternately.

◀ *A keen hunter, the coyote's prey ranges from mice to sheep.*

Gliders

- **Gliding mammals** include the flying squirrels of America and Asia, the scaly-tailed squirrels of Africa, and the marsupial gliding possums of Australia.
- **The Australian feather-tailed glider** is the smallest gliding mammal, weighing just 12 g.
- **Gliding mammals** glide by means of a membrane called a patagium that joins the fore and hind limbs.
- **The Southeast Asian flying lemur's** glide membrane stretches from its neck to its fingers, toes and tail-tip.
- **When flying squirrels** come to land on a tree, they brake by turning their tail and body under.

▲ *The southern flying squirrel fluffs out its tail and uses it as a rudder in mid-air.*

DID YOU KNOW?

The longest glide by a gliding mammal ever recorded was 450 m by a giant flying squirrel.

- **Africa's scaly-tailed flying squirrels** live in colonies of up to 100, and glide from tree to tree after dark.
- **Australia's gliders** feed on sap and gum, biting through tree bark and lapping up the sweet liquids.
- **Some flying squirrels**, when they land, quickly move to the opposite side of the tree trunk to avoid predators.
- **The flying lemur** is virtually helpless on the ground.

Tenrecs and otter shrews

- **Tenrecs live** on the island of Madagascar. Their physical appearance ranges from hedgehog lookalikes to shrews and web-footed otters.
- **Otter shrews**, close relatives to tenrecs, evolved separately on the African mainland.
- **The body temperature** of tenrecs and otter shrews falls close to the surrounding air temperature while they are resting, enabling them to save energy.
- **The common tenrec** rears more young than any other mammal on the planet, with litters of up to 24.
- **Some tenrecs** find their way around at night by using a form of echolocation, based on a series of fast clicking noises made with the tongue.
- **The web-footed tenrec** was thought to be extinct, but was recently re-discovered in Madagascar.
- **The insect-eating rice tenrec** resembles a mole, with large front feet for digging and small eyes and ears.
- **The common tenrec**, weighing up to 1.5 kg, is the world's largest insectivore, and a ferocious fighter. It uses sharp neck spines to spike its attackers.
- **When alarmed**, baby common tenrecs rub the quills on their backs together to make a vibrating noise.
- **The aquatic otter shrews** of Africa use touch-sensitive whiskers to locate crabs and other prey.

▼ *The strange-looking lowland streaked tenrec lives in the forests of Madagascar.*

Deer and chevrotains

- **Chevrotains, or mouse-deer**, are in a separate family from true deer. They eat fish and meat as well as plants.
- **Reindeer are** the only deer species where the females have antlers, using them to find moss under the snow.

- **Most deer** have large, mobile ears that are constantly alert.

DID YOU KNOW?

In the Middle Ages, the kings of Europe planted royal forests specially for deer-hunting.

- **The tiny Chinese water deer** is unique in the deer family in giving birth to as many as seven fawns at a time.
- **Male musk deer** use their long, down-curved canine teeth when fighting rival males in the mating season.
- **Indian chital deer** seek out langur monkeys, feeding on the leafy stems thrown down by the monkeys above.
- **When competing for females**, red deer stags prefer to roar at each other rather than fight and risk an injury.
- **Newly grown antlers** are covered with a protective skin known as 'velvet', which stags rub off against trees.
- **On the Scottish island of Rhum**, red deer supplement their plant diet by snacking on Manx shearwater chicks.

◀ *The antlers that male deer use for fighting are shed each year, regrowing the following spring.*

The smaller cats

- **The caracal** is a lynx-like African cat weighing up to 20 kg. It can kill antelopes twice its own weight.
- **The fishing cat** of Southeast Asia and India inhabits marshes and swamps, and has slightly webbed paws. It preys on fish, crayfish, birds and small mammals.
- **The Iriomote cat** is probably the world's rarest cat. Less than 100 exist, on a remote, mountainous island off southern Japan.
- **The serval** is a cat of tall grasses, with very long legs and neck. It locates prey with its prominent ears, catching it with a high, fox-like pounce.
- **The black-footed cat** of South Africa is the smallest wild cat. It spends the day in disused burrows, and eats spiders and beetles as well as small rodents.
- **The secretive Andean mountain cat** lives at altitudes of up to 5000 m, protected from the cold by its fine fur and long, bushy tail.
- **The Central American margay** specializes in hunting birds high in the treetops, and is the best of all cat climbers, with flexible legs and ankles.
- **The sand cat** of Africa and Asia does not need to drink, and has hairy foot-pads for walking in hot sand.
- **Unlike most small cats**, the ocelot runs down its prey instead of ambushing it, and is an excellent swimmer.
- **The smaller cats** purr but, unlike larger cats, cannot roar.

◀ The long-legged caracal is a good jumper and climber, and even takes sleeping birds, including eagles.

Baboons

- **Baboons are large** ground-dwelling Old World monkeys with long snouts and large teeth.
- **Baboons' feet** are better suited to walking than grabbing branches.

DID YOU KNOW?

Olive baboon males fighting over females will enlist the help of a third male.

- **Some East African baboons** cooperate in hunting small antelopes, but are unwilling to share the catch.
- **Male Hamadryas baboons** herd their females to keep them from other males.
- **The olive baboons** of the East African highlands live in troops of up to 140 individuals.
- **When old male Hamadryas baboons** are defeated by younger males, they lose weight, and their distinctive grey mantle changes to the colour of the females' hair.
- **Chacma baboons**, found in the far south of Africa, often enter water to feed on water plants or shellfish.
- **For their first few weeks**, baby baboons hang upside down from their mother's chest, but by 4 or 5 months they are riding on her back.
- **The ancient Egyptians** sometimes trained Hamadryas baboons to harvest figs.

◀ The male mandrill has a bright blue and red face for attracting females.

Domestic cats

- **Domestic cats** probably evolved from African wild cats, which were domesticated as early as 4000 BC in Egypt.
- **The ancient Egyptians** revered cats, and believed they held the daylight in their eyes and gave it out again at night.

- **Clay tiles in a Roman temple** in Britain bear the imprint of cats' paws. It is likely that the Romans introduced domestic cats to the British Isles.
- **The long-haired Turkish Van cat** is sometimes called the swimming cat, and is known for its love of water.
- **Some 98 percent of the patched cats** known as tortoiseshells, or calico cats, are females.
- **The Maine Coon**, the oldest breed of domestic cat in the USA, may have Viking origins.
- **In 1950**, a 4-month-old kitten followed some climbers to the summit of the Matterhorn in the Swiss Alps.
- **Siamese cats** were once found only in Thailand's temples and palaces. One king's favourite cat was entombed with him, but it later escaped.
- **In November 1939**, in Devon, UK, a tabby cat called Puss celebrated its 36th birthday, and died the next day.
- **In the 10th-century**, a kitten was worth 2 pence before it caught its first mouse, and 4 pence afterwards.

◀ *Domestic cats have retained their wild hunting instincts, and are major predators of garden birds.*

Skunks

- **There are 11 species** in the skunk family, including hog-nosed skunks, hooded, striped and spotted skunks.
- **They are found** throughout North America and in large parts of South America.
- **Skunks were thought** to belong to the same family as weasels and polecats, all of which have smelly sprays, but now it is thought that they are unrelated.
- **Skunks are great diggers**. They use their long, straight claws to rip apart rotten logs for grubs, and to dig in sand and mud for eggs.
- **Skunks sleep in communal dens** when temperatures reach freezing, with up to 20 skunks in a den.

- **The skunk squirts a sticky spray** at its enemy from glands under its tail. It can reach a target up to 6 m away, and is accurate up to 2 m.
- **The skunk's spray** can cause temporary blindness.
- **Before spraying**, a skunk stamps its feet as warning. The spotted skunk does a handstand and walks with its hind legs in the air.
- **Most predators avoid skunks**, but it is a favourite prey of the great horned owl, which has a poor sense of smell.
- **In the USA**, skunks are major carriers of rabies.

◀ *The skunk eats mainly live prey, such as insects and small mammals, and also enjoys fruit and birds' eggs.*

Meerkats

- **Meerkats live in cooperative groups** of up to 30 individuals in a complex warren system.
- **Young meerkats** care for their younger brothers and sisters while their mother forages for food to maintain her milk supply.
- **Meerkats dig** for many food items, such as beetles, moth pupae, termites and spiders.
- **They enthusiastically attack** and eat scorpions, first rendering them harmless by biting off their tail stings.
- **If surprised in open ground** by a hawk, the adults in a meerkat pack will cover the young with their bodies.
- **Living in the arid regions** of southern Africa, the meerkat sometimes obtains moisture by chewing Tsama melons and digging up plant roots.
- **Grey meerkats** attack intruders without warning or threats, and kill with an energetic shaking, followed by a neck bite.
- **Faced with attack**, the normally slim meerkat becomes almost spherical in shape with its hair bristling, tail up and back arched as it growls, spits and rocks to and fro.
- **Grey meerkats** often share their burrow systems with ground squirrels.

DID YOU KNOW?

Meerkat warrens can cover an area of up to 25 m by 32 m, with 90 separate entrances.

▶ *Meerkats warm themselves up in the morning sun, standing tall on their hind feet and tails, while constantly on the lookout for enermies.*

Mice

- **Mice are small rodents** that typically have long tails and relatively large ears. Common species include the field mouse, harvest mouse and house mouse.
- **In the early 1940s**, a huge population of house mice in California had a density of about 200,000 per hectare.
- **The Andes fishing mouse** – only discovered in 1994 – fishes in streams at an altitude of at least 3600 m.
- **The Australian pebble mound mouse** builds large piles of rounded stones, and then takes up residence in them.
- **The Oldfield mouse** has an escape tunnel leading from its nest near to the surface, so it can escape intruders by breaking through the apparent 'dead end'.
- **The water mice** of Central America have webbed, hairy feet that help them dive for water snails and fish.
- **American grasshopper mice** defend their territory by standing on their hind legs, shrieking at rival mice.
- **Grasshopper mice** are sometimes kept as pets to clear a house of insect pests such as cockroaches.
- **The Old World harvest mouse** climbs through tall grasses using its grasping tail and flexible feet.
- **American kangaroo mice** have long, hairy hind feet and a long tail, and often travel in a series of leaps.

◀ (1) *House mouse,* (2) *field mouse,* (3) *harvest mouse.*

Foxes

- **There are 37 species** of fox found throughout the world.
- **The larder of one Arctic fox** was found to contain 50 lemmings and 40 little auks, all lined up with their heads bitten off.
- **African bat-eared foxes** have huge ears for radiating heat away from the body.
- **Arctic foxes** live only 480 km from the North Pole.
- **The grey fox** of North and Central America is the oldest surviving member of the dog family, first appearing up to 9 million years ago.
- **When locating insects** under the ground, the bat-eared fox cups its large ears, gradually pinpointing the exact position of the prey before digging.

◀ *Although basically a night hunter, the red fox is often seen during the day, and shows up sharply against winter snow.*

- **The African fennec fox's** 15-cm long ears are the largest of any carnivore.
- **The American grey fox** leaps with ease between tree branches.
- **Some foxes roll about** and chase their tails to 'charm' rabbits, which are lured closer, allowing the fox to make a grab.
- **The red fox** has adapted with great success to urban life, even moving into houses via cat flaps.

Zebras

- **A zebra's stripes** are as individual as human fingerprints – no two zebras are exactly the same.
- **The quagga** was a South African zebra that only had stripes on the front part of its body.
- **It once existed** in very large herds, but became extinct through over-hunting in the 1870s.
- **Grevy's zebra** is a large species with narrowly spaced stripes and very large, mule-like ears.
- **The home range** of Grevy's zebra, which roams desert and savannah terrains in northeastern Kenya, sometimes exceeds 10,000 sq km.
- **The zebra** can be a formidable foe, driving off lions, and even killing humans to defend its foals.
- **The plains zebra** lived north of the Sahara, in Algeria and Tunisia, up until 10,000 years ago, when it was replaced by the African wild ass.
- **A plains zebra stallion** will challenge any potential rival coming within 50–100 m of his herd.
- **Mountain zebras** follow ancient trails to mountain springs and pools in the dry season, and dig for subsurface water in dried-up stream beds.
- **Chapman's zebra** has shadow stripes – light, greyish stripes that alternate with the dark main stripes.

▼ *Zebras are sociable animals that like physical contact and mutual grooming.*

1000 BIRD FACTS

The world of birds

● **There are more than 10,000** species of birds.

● **Scientists estimate** that there are about 300 billion individual birds in the world – that's 50 birds for every person on the planet.

● **More than a third** of all known bird species live and breed in South and Central America.

▼ *Many birds are highly sociable, flocking together to feed and raise their young.*

● **All birds** lay hard-shelled eggs, in which their young develop. If a mother bird had young that developed inside her body instead, she would be too heavy to fly.

● **One of the most widespread** of all birds is the osprey, which is found nearly all over the world.

● **The marsh warbler** is one of the greatest mimics of the bird world, able to imitate the songs of more than 70 different species.

● **The world's heaviest flying birds** are the kori bustard and the great bustard, which weigh up to 18 kg.

● **The wandering albatross** is one of the longest-lived birds. Individuals may live as long as 60 years or more.

● **The red-billed quelea** is probably the most common wild bird. There are thought to be at least 1.5 billion.

● **The largest bird**, the ostrich, weighs almost 80,000 times more than the smallest, the bee hummingbird.

Cormorants and relatives

● **The biggest species of cormorant**, the great cormorant, is up to one metre long.

● **A great cormorant** eats about 15 percent of its body weight in fish a day. That's like an adult human eating more than 80 hamburgers a day.

● **The feathers of cormorants** and darters lack waterproofing and quickly get soaked through. This makes the birds heavier in water and better able to dive for fish.

● **Cormorants migrate** in large, V-shaped flocks, like migrating geese.

● **In parts of Asia**, fishermen use cormorants to catch fish – the birds dive for the fish but do not swallow them.

▲ *After diving for food, cormorants stand on rocks with their wings outstretched to dry.*

● **The pirates of the bird world** are frigatebirds, which often chase other seabirds in the air and harass them into giving up their catches.

● **Frigatebird chicks** depend on their parents for longer than most birds. They start to fly at about six months, but continue to be fed until they are one year old.

▲ *The male frigatebird has a bright-red throat pouch that he inflates during courtship to attract females.*

● **The four species of anhinga**, or darter, all live in freshwater in tropical parts of the world. They are all expert underwater hunters.

● **The American darter**, or snake bird, swims with its neck held in a snake-like curve above the water's surface.

DID YOU KNOW?

Some shags dive to an incredible depth of over 100 m to hunt for fish.

Ducks

◀ *In the breeding season, the male teal has a chestnut head with a green eye patch. In flight, the black and yellow feathers under the tail show up well.*

● **There are more than 100 duck species.** They live all over the world, except Antarctica.

● **Most ducks** are good at flying. They take off almost vertically when alarmed and fly off with fast-beating wings.

● **Teal are typical 'dabbling' ducks**, nibbling food (such as plant seeds or insects) from the surface of the water while swimming, or walking in shallow water.

● **In deeper water**, dabbling ducks often 'upend' to reach food beneath the surface.

● **Diving ducks**, such as pochard, scaup and tufted ducks, dive underwater to collect food, such as shellfish, water plants and insects.

● **Tufted ducks** dive down to depths of up to 6 m and can stay underwater for up to 30 seconds.

● **The goldeneye** nests in tree holes and the chicks often tumble a long distance down to the ground when they leave the nest. They take eight weeks to grow their flight feathers.

● **The courtship display** of the male long-tailed duck includes a far-carrying yodelling call that sounds rather like someone playing the bagpipes.

● **The female eider duck** lines her nest with soft down feathers that she pulls from her breast. Humans use the feathers too, to make quilts and sleeping bags.

● **Like cuckoos**, the black-headed duck lays its eggs in the nests of other birds, such as coots. Just one day after hatching, the ducklings leave the nest to fend for themselves.

◀ *Long-tailed ducks have an unusual flying style, with shallow upstrokes but deep downstrokes of their wings. They are named for the long tail feathers of the male.*

Hoopoes and relatives

● **The hoopoe** is named after its characteristic 'hoo-poo-poo' call, which carries over long distances. Hoopoes often live near people and hunt for worms and grubs in gardens.

● **The hoopoe** lines its nest with animal excrement, perhaps so that the smell will keep enemies away.

● **The eight noisy, insect-eating wood hoopoe** species live in forests in central and southern Africa.

● **Groups of wood hoopoes** make loud calls and rocking movements, and pass bark to each other, in a display of territorial ownership.

● **If threatened by a bird of prey**, the hoopoe hides by flattening itself on the ground with its wings and tail spread out.

● **The 16 or so species of roller** and ground roller live in southern Europe, Asia, Africa and Australia.

● **Rollers** have spectacular courtship flights, rolling and somersaulting as they dive towards land.

● **A light, coin-shaped mark** on each wing of the broad-billed roller is the reason for its other common name – 'dollar bird'.

● **The cuckoo-roller** lives only in Madagascar and the Comoros Islands, where it catches chameleons and insects.

● **The broad-billed roller** catches winged termites in the air. A roller will eat as many as 800 termites in a single evening.

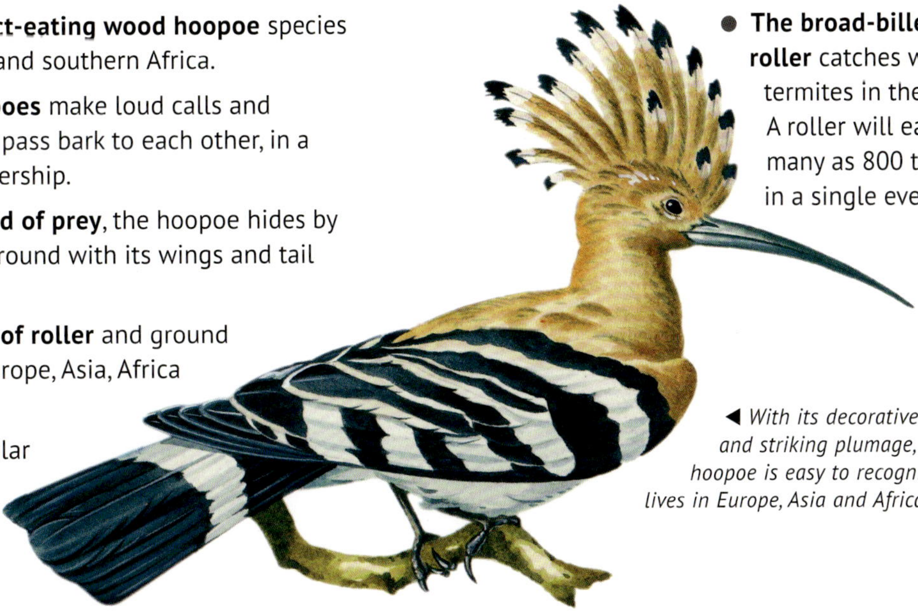

◀ *With its decorative crest and striking plumage, the hoopoe is easy to recognize. It lives in Europe, Asia and Africa.*

Starlings

- **There are about 113 species** of starling in Europe, Africa and Asia. Starlings have also been introduced into Australasia and North America.
- **The largest starlings** are over 30 cm long and weigh over 225 g.
- **Male starlings** bring fresh green leaves to the nest while the eggs are incubating. The leaves help the nestlings to cope with bird parasites, such as lice.

- **The male European** or common starling has glossy, iridescent plumage whereas the female is much plainer, with brownish feathers.
- **The male wattled starling** loses his head feathers in the breeding season. Scientists investigating cures for human baldness are researching the bird's ability to regrow its head feathers each year.
- **When kept in captivity**, hill mynahs mimic human speech, but in the wild they do not imitate the calls of other bird species, only the calls of other hill mynahs.
- **The Brahminy starling** has a brush-like tip on its tongue, used for collecting pollen and nectar.
- **One hundred starlings** were released in New York in the 1890s. Today more than 200 million starlings live in North America.
- **Locusts are the favourite food** of the rose-coloured starling. Large flocks fly to wherever they are plentiful.

◀ *European starlings feed their young on a range of insects and insect larvae, and may make up to 400 feeding trips a day.*

The structure of birds

- **Birds are the only animals** with feathers. These keep them warm and, in most species, allow them to fly.
- **Like mammals, fish and reptiles**, birds are vertebrates – this means they have backbones.
- **Birds have a body temperature** of between 40°C and 44°C.
- **Birds have a lightweight beak**, or bill, which is made of bone that is covered by layers of a substance called keratin.
- **Birds do not have teeth**, so cannot chew their food. Some birds, such as birds of prey, use their bills to tear up their food.
- **A bird's feathers** and claws are also made of keratin.

DID YOU KNOW?
A bird looks as if its knees bend backwards, but this joint is in fact the ankle joint, so birds walk on their toes. A bird's knees are higher up its legs, hidden under its feathers.

- **Birds do not have true tails** with bones down the middle. Their tail feathers are attached to a bony stump called the pygostyle.
- **Birds have** a very high metabolic rate, which is the rate at which they can burn up food and release the energy it contains. This creates the energy they need for flight.
- **Birds have mobile necks**, so they can look all around for danger or food.

▶ *The main external parts of a bird are shown on this mistle thrush.*

Swifts

● **There are about 100 species of swift** found all over the world, except in the far north and far south.

● **Swifts do almost everything** in the air. They eat, drink, court and sometimes even sleep on the wing.

● **They can stay airborne** for up to an incredible 10 months at a time.

● **Trials with ringed birds** have shown that a young common swift that has only just left the nest can fly from London to Madrid in three days.

● **A swift's legs and feet** are so small and weak that it cannot move on the ground. It must land on a cliff ledge or building in order to launch itself into the air again.

● **Swifts regurgitate** mouthfuls of food for their young to eat. Each mouthful may contain hundreds or thousands of tiny insects and spiders.

▼ *The common or Eurasian swift is often seen in Europe in the summer, swooping overhead as it hunts for insects. It flies to tropical Africa for the winter.*

● **The largest swift**, the white-naped swift, is about 25 cm long and weighs 175 g – about the weight of a lemon.

● **The African palm swift** glues its nest to the underneath of a palm leaf with its own spit, and glues its eggs to the nest. The parents cling on with their claws while incubating the clutch.

● **The edible-nest swiftlet** makes a nest of its own spit and a few feathers on a cave wall. Soup made from these nests is considered a great delicacy in Asia.

● **The cave swiftlet** finds its way in totally dark caves by using a form of echolocation.

Partridges and relatives

● **The partridge family** includes more than 90 species of partridges and francolins. They feed mainly on seeds.

● **In parts of Europe and North America**, partridges are reared in captivity and then released and shot for sport.

● **A group of partridges** is called a 'covey'. A covey usually contains a family of male, female and young, plus a few other birds.

● **The long-billed wood partridge** lives at altitudes of up to 1200 m in the upland forests of Asia, particularly in areas of bamboo forest.

● **The female red-legged partridge** lays one clutch of eggs for her mate to incubate, and another to incubate herself.

● **The common quail** spends the winter in Africa, but migrates to Europe and parts of western Asia to breed in the summer months.

● **Tiny quail chicks** are born with their eyes open and their bodies covered in warm, downy feathers. They are able to follow their mother within one hour of hatching.

● **A mother quail** helps her chicks learn how to find food by pointing at food items with her beak.

● **At about 50 cm long**, the vulturine guineafowl is the largest of the six species of guineafowl. It lives in Africa and eats fallen fruit.

● **Francolins** are large, powerful gamebirds of Africa and Asia, which have patches of bare skin on their heads or necks.

▶ *The crested wood partridge (1) lives in the tropical rainforests of Southeast Asia. The male has a red, brush-like crest on his head. The Barbary partridge (2) lives in dry, open, often hilly country in North Africa, Gibraltar and the Canary Islands. The Chinese painted quail (3) is the smallest of all the quails, reaching an average length of only 13 cm. The male (shown here) is more colourful than the female.*

Birds of paradise

- **Birds of paradise**, of which there are about 44 species, live only in New Guinea and northeastern Australia.
- **The king of Saxony bird of paradise** has two 50-cm-long head plumes decorated with small, sky-blue squares. They look so unusual that they were first thought to be fake.
- **The magnificent riflebird** gets its name from its loud whistling call, which sounds like a passing bullet.
- **Most female birds of paradise** make a cup or dome-shaped nest, and lay one or two eggs.
- **During courtship**, the blue bird of paradise hangs upside-down from a branch, with its splendid blue feathers and tail plumes spread over its head.

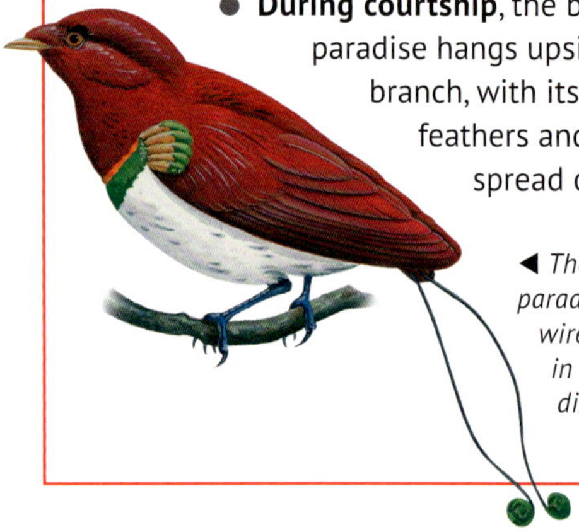

◀ *The male king bird of paradise uses its long, wire-like tail feathers in its courtship display.*

◀ *The blue bird of paradise is a rare member of this exotic family. It is threatened by the destruction of its forest habitat.*

- **Fruit and insects** are the main foods of the birds of paradise. Some also eat leaves and buds.
- **New Guinea tribesmen** traditionally wear bird of paradise feathers in their head-dresses.
- **During the early 19th century**, 100,000 bird of paradise skins were sold each year in Europe for hat and dress decorations.
- **The first bird of paradise skins** brought to Europe from New Guinea did not have feet, so some people thought the birds never landed.

DID YOU KNOW?

The tail feathers of the male ribbon-tailed bird of paradise are up to one metre long.

Geese and swans

- **Geese feed mostly on leaves**, and can eat as many as 100 blades of grass in one minute.
- **Snow geese** breed in the Arctic tundra, but fly south to spend the winter months around the Gulf of Mexico – a journey of some 5000 km. In the winter, snow geese gather in huge flocks that may contain tens of thousands of birds.
- **Red-breasted geese** often make their nests near those of peregrines and buzzards. This gives them protection, and they do not seem to get attacked by the birds of prey.
- **Canada geese** can live for up to 30 years in the wild and even longer in captivity.
- **Whooper, trumpeter and mute swans** are among the heaviest flying birds, weighing up to 16 kg.
- **The black swan** makes a nest of sticks and other plant material in shallow water and lays up to six eggs. Both parents help to incubate the eggs.

DID YOU KNOW?

Most birds fly at altitudes of up to 900 m, but bar-headed geese are able to fly over the Himalayas at altitudes of up to 9000 m.

- **Tundra swans mate for life**, returning year after year to the same nesting site. They usually make their nests on marshland and lay three to five eggs.
- **Although quieter than other swans**, the mute swan is not really mute, as it makes many snorting and hissing calls.
- **Male swans** are known as cobs, females as pens and baby swans are called cygnets.

▼ *The red-breasted goose breeds on the Arctic tundra of Russia but migrates mainly to Bulgaria and Romania for the winter months. This rare goose is threatened by hunting, industrial development and the loss of its tundra habitat due to climate change.*

Tyrant flycatchers

● **The tyrant flycatcher family** is the largest family of birds with more than 400 species. They range from northern Canada to the bottom tip of South America.

● **Not all flycatchers** feed only on insects. The great kiskadee dives into water for fish and tadpoles, as well as catching flying insects in the air.

● **The boat-billed flycatcher** has a larger beak than other flycatchers. It eats frogs and other small animals, as well as insects.

● **The vermilion flycatcher** is one of the few brightly coloured flycatchers. The male has bright red plumage, which he shows off in his courtship display.

● **In 1976, ornithologists** (scientists who study birds) found a previously unknown flycatcher, which they named the cinnamon-breasted tody-tyrant. It lives only in cloud forests on a few mountain peaks in Ecuador and Peru.

▼ *The vermilion flycatcher brings a flash of colour to the desert and dry scrub of southwestern USA, Central America and tropical South America.*

DID YOU KNOW?

In the Galápagos Islands, vermilion flycatchers often perch on the backs of giant tortoises, so they can snap up the insects disturbed by the tortoises' huge feet.

◀ *The tyrant flycatchers are the largest bird family in North and South America. Shown here are: (1) buff-breasted flycatcher, (2) lesser flycatcher and (3) great-crested flycatcher.*

▼ *The common tody-flycatcher is around 10 cm in length with bright yellow underparts. It is found from southern Mexico to southern Brazil.*

● **The royal flycatcher** is a plain, brownish bird, but it has an amazing crest of feathers on its head that it sometimes unfurls and shows off. Males have red crests and females have yellow or orange crests.

● **Smallest of all the tyrant flycatchers** is the short-tailed pygmy tyrant, at only 6.5 cm long. It lives in northern South America.

● **The eastern phoebe** makes a nest of mud mixed with grass and plant stems. The female lays three to seven eggs, and incubates them for 14–16 days. The young leave the nest when they are about 17 days old.

● **Some flycatchers**, including the great crested flycatcher, line their nests with snakeskins that have been cast off.

Nightjars and relatives

DID YOU KNOW?

Potoos can squirt their faeces away from their perches, so they do not mark their hiding places for a predator to find.

- **There are about 70 species** of nightjar, which live in most parts of the world, especially in the tropics.
- **An old name for nightjars** is goatsuckers, because people mistakenly thought they saw the birds feeding on goats' milk, when in fact they were snapping up insects disturbed by the animals.
- **The bristle-fringed beak** of the nightjar opens very wide to help it snap up moths and beetles at night.

- **After hunting for insects** at night, the common potoo rests by day in a tree, where its colouration makes it look like a broken branch.
- **The 12 species of frogmouth** live in the rainforests of Southeast Asia and Australia.
- **The common poorwill** is one of the few birds known to hibernate. It sleeps in a rock crevice.
- **The oilbird** is the only bird to feed on fruit at night. Its excellent sense of smell helps it find the oily fruits of palms and laurels in the dark.
- **Oilbird chicks** put on so much weight from their rich diet that they may weigh much more than their parents when they are only a couple of months old.
- **The oilbird nests** in dark caves and uses echolocation to aid navigation.

◀ *Nightjars are active fliers but rest on the ground during the day, where they are well camouflaged.*

Oystercatchers and relatives

- **The oystercatcher** uses its strong, blade-like beak to prise mussels off rocks and open their shells.
- **Oystercatcher chicks** stay with their parents for up to one year while they learn how to find and open shellfish.
- **The 17 species** in the courser and pratincole family live in southern Europe, Asia, Africa and Australia.
- **The Egyptian plover** (courser family) buries its eggs in sand and leaves them to be incubated by the warmth of the Sun. The parents sit on the eggs at night, and if the weather is cool.
- **If the Egyptian plover's** chicks get too hot, the parent birds soak their own belly feathers with water and give their young a cooling shower.
- **The cream-coloured courser** has pale, sandy feathers that help to keep it hidden in its desert home.
- **The common pratincole** nests on sand or rocks, and lays two to four mottled, well-camouflaged eggs. The parents take turns to incubate the eggs for 17–18 days.
- **The nine species** in the thick-knee family include the stone curlew and the dikkop. These long-legged birds usually feed at night on insects, worms and shellfish.
- **The thick-knees** get their common name from the knobbly joints on their legs – actually between the ankle and shin bones.
- **The pygmy seed-snipe** of southern South America blends in with the plains landscape so well that it is almost invisible when it crouches on the ground.

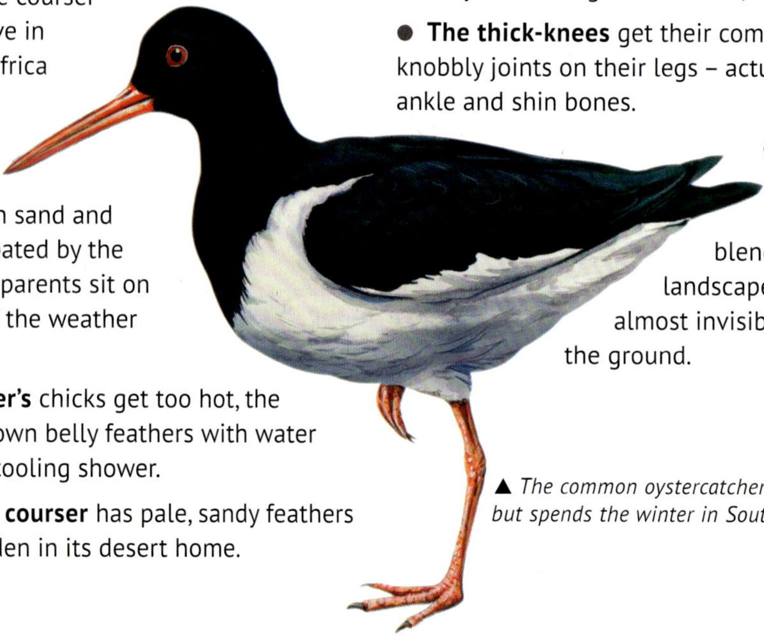

▲ *The common oystercatcher breeds in Europe and Asia, but spends the winter in South Africa and southern Asia.*

Fairy-wrens and relatives

● **The 26 species of fairy-wrens** live in Australia and New Guinea, where they forage for insects on the ground.

● **Young fairy-wrens** often stay with their parents and help them raise the next brood of young. Pairs with helpers can raise more young than those without.

● **During its courtship display**, the male superb fairy-wren may present his mate with a yellow flower petal.

● **If a predator** comes too close to a fairy-wren's nest, the parent birds make a special 'rodent run' away from the nest, squeaking and trailing their tails to confuse and distract the enemy.

● **The rockwarbler** makes its nest in a dark cave or mineshaft and attaches it to the walls with spider webs.

▶ *The white-throated gerygone belongs to the Australasian warbler family, found in Australia, New Zealand and adjacent islands.*

▶ *Male splendid fairy wrens have shiny, bright blue feathers in the breeding season. Females are duller in colour all year round.*

● **The 50 or so species of thickhead** live in rainforests and scrub in Southeast Asia and Australasia and have a whistling call.

● **The white-throated gerygone's nest** hangs from a eucalyptus branch and is made from bark strips and plant fibres woven together with spider webs.

● **The hooded pitohui** (thickhead family) is one of the very few poisonous birds known. Its feathers and skin contain a poison that protects it from predators. The poison comes from beetles that the bird eats.

● **The Australasian warbler family** includes 65 species of gerygone, thornbills and scrubwrens.

● **The golden whistler** is probably the most variable of birds – the 70 or more species all have slightly different feather patterns or beak shapes.

Beaks and feet

● **A beak** is made up of a bird's projecting jaw bones, covered in a hard horny material called keratin.

● **The hyacinth macaw** has one of the most powerful beaks of any bird, strong enough to crack open Brazil nuts.

● **The puffin** has special spines on the upper part of its beak and its tongue. This enables it to carry 50 or more sand eels in its bill at the same time.

● **A pelican** uses its huge, baggy bill pouch to scoop up fish from the water, rather like a fishing net.

● **Birds that feed on insects**, such as bee-eaters, have thin, pointed bills to probe under bark and stones.

● **A bird's legs and feet** are covered in scales, a link to the ancient ancestors of birds, the dinosaurs.

DID YOU KNOW?

A baby bird has a spike called an 'egg-tooth' on its beak for breaking its way out of its egg.

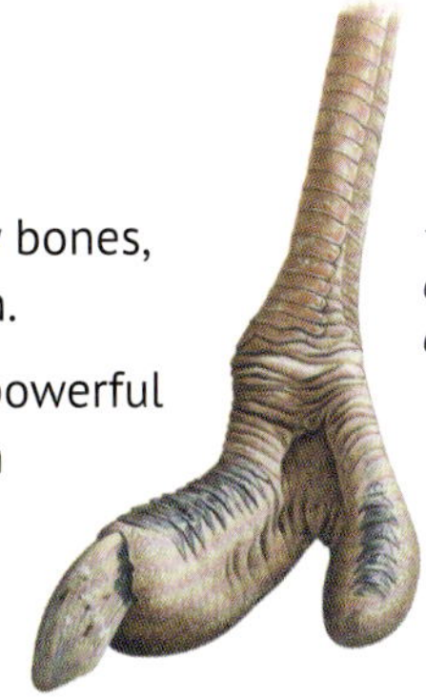

◀ *The ostrich is the only bird to have just two toes on each foot. Emu, rheas and cassowaries have three toes and most other birds have four toes.*

● **Birds of prey** have long, curved talons on their toes for catching and killing their prey. Most birds of prey find it difficult to walk on their talons.

● **On land**, small birds use their legs to hop, while larger birds use their legs for walking.

● **Webbed feet** make all waterbirds very efficient paddlers.

▶ *The crossbill is so-called because the upper and lower portions of its beak cross over one another.*

Divers and grebes

- **Diver birds feed only on fish**, which they catch underwater. The great northern diver can dive to depths of 20 m or more.
- **Divers are so well-adapted** for diving and swimming that adult birds cannot walk upright on land.
- **At 90 cm long**, the white-billed diver is the largest of the four species of diver.
- **The chicks** of great northern divers leave the nest a day or so after hatching. They spend the next two or three months with their parents, often riding on their backs to keep warm.
- **There are about 20 species of grebe**, three of them flightless. They live near freshwater lakes and marshes.
- **Grebes feed on fish**, insects and shellfish. They swallow moulted feathers, which may help them regurgitate waste such as fish bones and keep their guts free of parasites.
- **Grebes** have up to 20,000 feathers to keep their bodies warm and dry as they dive for food.

▶ The red-necked grebe builds a floating nest of water plants, anchored to other vegetation. Most of the nest is below the water. The female lays four or five eggs, which both parents incubate.

- **The short-winged grebe** lives on lakes high in the mountains of Peru and Bolivia, and cannot fly. It basks in the sun to warm its body up after a cold night.
- **The great crested grebe** makes a nest of water plants floating near the water's edge. It lays three to six eggs, which both the male and female incubate.
- **Little grebes** chase rivals away from their territories, rushing low over the water while splashing, diving and calling loudly.

Falcons and caracas

- **The peregrine falcon's** hunting technique is so demanding that only one in ten attacks is successful.
- **At up to 60 cm long**, the gyrfalcon is the largest species in the falcon family, and can catch ducks and hares.
- **The common kestrel** hovers above the ground on fast-beating wings while it searches for small mammals.
- **In winter**, both male and female kestrels spend about a quarter of their day hunting. But when the female is incubating eggs, the male hunts for longer.

- **Eleonora's falcon** is named after a 14th-century Sardinian princess, who brought in laws to protect it.

DID YOU KNOW?

Kestrels can see ultraviolet light, which reflects off the urine that a rodent uses to mark its tracks.

- **Falconets and pygmy falcons** are the smallest birds of prey. The Philippine falconet is only 15 cm long.
- **Caracaras are chicken-sized** birds of prey, related to falcons. They have long legs and can move quickly to avoid danger. They often join vultures to feed on animal carcasses, but they also feed on a variety of live prey, such as birds, fish, frogs, small mammals and insects.
- **The yellow-headed caracara** sometimes perches on the backs of farm animals to feed on the ticks on their skin.
- **The tiny black-thighed falconet** is only 16 cm long and is one of the smallest birds of prey. It flies out from a perch in the forests to catch insects and small birds.

◀ Peregrines use their wings and body to 'cloak' or hide their prey. A peregrine can eat a meal weighing as much as a quarter of its own weight in one sitting.

Parrots

● **There are over 370 species** in the parrot group, including birds such as macaws, budgerigars, lories and cockatoos. They live in Central and South America, Africa, southern Asia and Australasia.

● **Parrots lay white eggs** and their young are helpless when they hatch out.

● **The only flightless parrot** is the New Zealand kakapo or owl parrot, which is now extremely rare.

● **Unlike most parrots**, the kea of New Zealand eats meat as well as fruit and insects. It feasts on carrion (animals that are already dead) and also hunts young shearwaters in their burrows.

● **The little blue-crowned hanging parrot** gets its name from its strange habit of hanging upside down from a branch when at rest.

◀ *Cockatoos are parrots that have a crest on their head, such as this palm cockatoo, also known as the goliath cockatoo or great black cockatoo.*

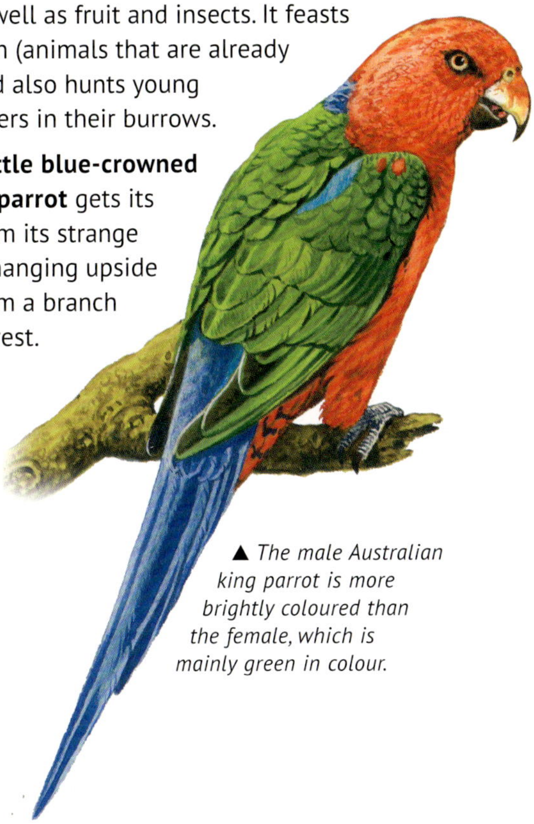

▲ *The male Australian king parrot is more brightly coloured than the female, which is mainly green in colour.*

● **At about 85 cm long**, the scarlet macaw of South and Central America is one of the largest members of the parrot family.

● **Macaws nest** in tree holes high in rainforest trees. The female lays two eggs, which her mate helps to incubate. The young macaws stay with their parents for up to one year.

● **Macaws swallow** beakfuls of clay from riverbanks. The clay may help to protect the birds from the effects of some plants and seeds that they eat, many of which are poisonous to other creatures.

● **The largest cockatoo**, and the largest Australian parrot, is the palm cockatoo. As part of his courtship display, the male holds a stick in his foot and drums it loudly against a tree trunk.

▶ *With its bright red feathers, the scarlet macaw is one of the most beautiful of all the parrots. It can fly at up to 56 km/h as it searches the rainforest for fruit, nuts and seeds to eat.*

DID YOU KNOW?

The average lifespan of a scarlet macaw is 30–50 years, but they have been known to live for up to 75 years in captivity.

Bird senses

- **Almost all birds** have excellent sight and most depend on their eyes for finding food.
- **A bird's outer ear** consists of a short tube leading from the eardrum to the outside. In most birds the ear openings are just behind the jaw.
- **A barn owl's hearing** is so good that it can detect and catch prey in complete darkness without using its eyes at all.
- **A chicken** has only 24 taste buds and a starling has about 200 – a human has 9000.
- **An eagle** can spot prey from as much as 1.6 km above the ground.
- **A starling's eye** is as much as 15 percent of the total weight of its head. A human's eye is only one percent of the head weight.
- **An ostrich's eye** is 5 cm in diameter. This is larger than any other land animal's eye.
- **Birds are ten times** more sensitive to changes of pitch and intensity in sounds than humans.
- **A bird's nostrils** are usually at the base of the beak, but in the kiwi, which has a better sense of smell than most birds, they are at the tip of the beak.
- **Albatrosses** have a good sense of smell. In experiments, they have been attracted to food from a distance of 30 km away.

▼ *The tip of the snipe's bill is flexible and very sensitive, which allows it to detect and identify worms and other small creatures.*

Terns and skimmers

- **The 42 or so species of terns** are found all over the world, mostly along coasts.
- **The noddy**, a species of tern, gets its name from its habit of nodding its head during its courtship display.
- **The black skimmer's beak** has a flattened lower part that is longer than the upper part. The bird flies over water with the lower part of its beak just below the surface, ready to snap up prey.
- **Arctic terns** are long-lived birds, known to survive to 27 – and sometimes even 34 – years of age.
- **Most terns** eat fish, squid and shellfish, but marshland terns also eat insects and frogs.
- **At up to 59 cm long**, the Caspian tern is the largest of the terns, and one of the most widespread.
- **The fairy tern** does not make a nest. Instead, it balances its one egg on a tree branch and manages to sit on it without knocking it off.
- **Most terns** mate for life. Even if they don't stay together all year round, pairs meet up when they return to breeding sites.
- **There are only three species** of skimmers. All live in areas of tropical Africa, Southeast Asia and North and South America.

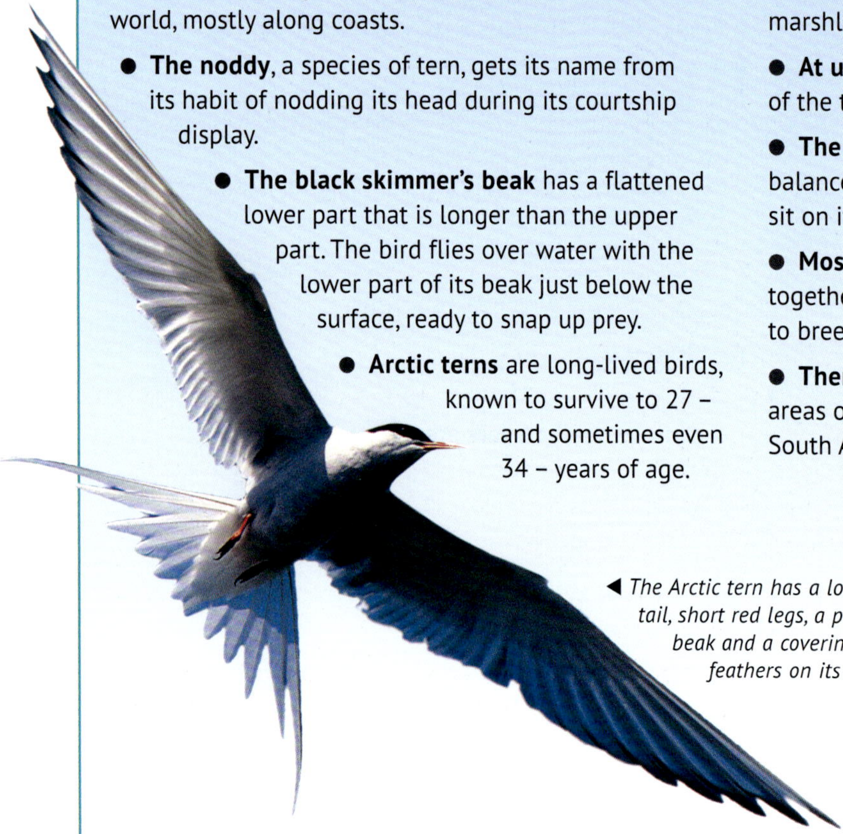

◀ *The Arctic tern has a long, forked tail, short red legs, a pointed beak and a covering of black feathers on its head.*

DID YOU KNOW?

Over a lifetime of migration journeys, an Arctic tern travels the equivalent distance of three trips to the Moon and back.

Weavers and relatives

- **The cuckoo weaver** is a small, yellow bird that lays its eggs in the nests of grass warblers, leaving the warblers to raise its young.
- **Desert-living sociable weavers** use their nests all year round to shelter from sun, wind and cold. At night, when temperatures drop, the nest holes stay 20°C warmer than the outside.
- **Most weavers** have short, strong beaks that they use for feeding on seeds and insects.
- **The baya weaver** makes a beautiful nest of woven grass and leaves, which it hangs from a tree or roof.
- **The red-vented malimbe** (a weaver) feeds mainly on the husks of oil palm nuts.
- **Whydah birds** do not make their own nests, but lay their eggs in the nests of other birds, usually waxbills.
- **Young whydahs** make the same sounds and have the same mouth markings as their foster parents' own young, and because of this they get fed.
- **In the breeding season**, the male paradise whydah grows 28-cm-long tail feathers – almost twice the length of its body – for display in flight.
- **The red bishop** mates with three or four females, who all nest in his territory.
- **The male bishop bird** has bright red and black plumage in the breeding season. For the rest of the year, his feathers are a streaky brown colour.

◀ *When a male cape weaver has finished making a nest, he calls to a female.*

Plovers and lapwings

DID YOU KNOW?

Many plovers pat the ground with their feet to imitate the sound of rain. This draws worms to the surface, where they are snapped up.

- **There are 60 or so species** of plovers and lapwings (also known as peewits) around the world.
- **The wrybill**, a New Zealand plover, has a unique beak that curves to the right. The bird sweeps its beak over sand to pick up insects.

▼ *The lapwing is sometimes called the green plover, after the greenish, iridescent plumage on its back. When it flies, its white underparts are very obvious and its broad, rounded wings are different from those of other waders.*

- **The markings** of Kentish plover chicks look like the stones and pebbles of their nest site. If danger threatens, the chicks flatten themselves on the ground and are almost impossible to see.
- **Female dotterels** lay clutches of eggs for several males, who then incubate the eggs.
- **To attract females**, the male lapwing performs a spectacular rolling, tumbling display flight.
- **Spur-winged plovers** are often seen close to crocodiles in Africa and Asia – they may feed on small creatures that the crocodiles disturb.
- **Most plovers** feed on insects, shellfish and worms.
- **Golden plovers** have been recorded flying at speeds of more than 113 km/h.
- **The blacksmith plover** is named after its harsh call, which sounds like a blacksmith striking an anvil with a hammer.

Penguins

● **Not all of the 18 species** of penguin live in Antarctica. A few species live around Australia and South Africa, and there is even one species resident in the Galápagos Islands on the Equator.

● **Penguins have wings**, but cannot fly. They spend as much as 85 percent of their time in water, where they use their wings like flippers to help push themselves through the water.

● **The king penguin** has been known to dive down to 250 m in search of prey.

● **An emperor penguin** may travel at least 900 km on a single feeding expedition.

● **Like many other penguins**, gentoos nest in a simple hollow in the ground, but they surround it with a ring of pebbles. A courting gentoo shows its mate an example of the sort of pebbles it will provide.

● **The emperor penguin** keeps its egg warm on its feet, where it is covered by a fold of skin. The temperature there stays at a constant 36°C, despite the freezing surroundings.

▲ *A king penguin incubates its egg by holding it on its feet against a bare, warm patch of skin called a brood patch. Both parents take it in turns to keep their egg warm.*

● **Penguins** eat fish, squid and shellfish. They have spiny tongues to help them hold on to slippery prey.

● **A dense covering** of three layers of feathers keeps penguins warm. An emperor penguin has about 12 feathers in each square centimetre of its skin.

● **Penguins** usually swim at 5–10 km/h, but can reach speeds of up to 24 km/h.

◀ *A chinstrap penguin chick waits for its parent to regurgitate (cough up) a meal of fishy food from its stomach. Penguin chicks grow fast and are always hungry.*

DID YOU KNOW?

The male emperor penguin incubates its mate's egg for 60 days, eating nothing and losing as much as 45 percent of his body weight in the process.

Bird songs and sounds

- **Birds make two main sorts of sounds** – simple calls, giving a warning or a threat, and the more complicated songs sung by some males at breeding time.
- **Birds' songs** have regional accents. The songs of a group of chaffinches in one area will sound slightly different from those of a group somewhere else.

- **A songbird** reared in captivity away from its family produces a weak version of its parents' song, but cannot perform the whole range.

DID YOU KNOW?

A baby songbird starts to learn to sing about ten days after it hatches, and continues to learn for about 40 days.

- **Gulls and parrots** do not sing, but they do make various calls to attract mates or warn off enemies.
- **A bird sings** by vibrating the thin muscles in its syrinx – a special organ in its throat.
- **A sedge warbler** may use at least 50 different sounds in its songs.
- **Male and female boubou shrikes** sing a duet together, performing alternate parts of the song.
- **Songbirds** may make as many as 20 calls; gulls make only about ten.
- **Birds make** other sounds too. During courtship flights, male wood pigeons make a loud clapping noise with their wings.

◀ *Male nightingales sing to attract a mate and defend their territory. They sing more loudly in urban areas to make themselves heard above all the loud noise around them.*

Shrikes and vangas

- **There are about 70 species** of shrikes found in Africa, Europe, Asia and North America, as well as 84 species of cuckoo shrikes and 14 species of helmet shrikes.
- **All shrikes** have powerful hooked beaks that they use for killing insects, lizards and frogs.
- **Shrikes** often hunt from a perch, swooping down to catch insects or other prey in their strong bills.
- **The yellow-billed shrike** lives in noisy groups of up to 15 individuals. All members of the group help to defend their territory and feed the female that lays the eggs, as well as her young when they hatch.
- **The fiscal shrike** is very aggressive – it sometimes kills other birds.
- **During its courtship display**, the male puffback (a shrike) fluffs up the long feathers on its lower back like a powder puff.

◀ *The sickle-billed vanga is named after its long, curved beak.*

▲ *Shrikes are also known as 'butcher birds', because of their habit of storing prey on the thorns and barbs of trees and bushes.*

- **The call of the brubru shrike** sounds just like a phone ringing.
- **The loggerhead shrike** makes a nest of twigs and grass in a thorny bush or tree, where the female incubates between five and seven eggs.
- **The sickle-billed vanga** uses its long, curved beak to probe bark for insects. It hangs upside down by its claws while it feeds.
- **Most of the vanga shrikes** live in groups out of the breeding season, feeding and moving in loose flocks of up to 12 individuals.

Pigeons and sandgrouse

- **There are more than 300 species** of pigeon, found all over the world, except in the far north and Antarctica.
- **Pigeons and doves** can suck up water when they drink. This is unique among birds – all other birds have to tip their heads back to drink.
- **Both male and female pigeons** can make a milky substance in their crops (a pouch in their throat), which they feed to their young.
- **Wood pigeons** feed on leaves, seeds, nuts, berries and some insects. Those living near humans also eat bread and food scraps.
- **The dark green feathers** of the African green pigeon provide good camouflage in its forest home, especially when it keeps very still.
- **At 70–75 cm long** (nearly as big as a turkey), the Victoria crowned pigeon of New Guinea is the largest member of its family.
- **Pigeon 'races'** are held in which birds return to their homes from as much as 1000 km away.

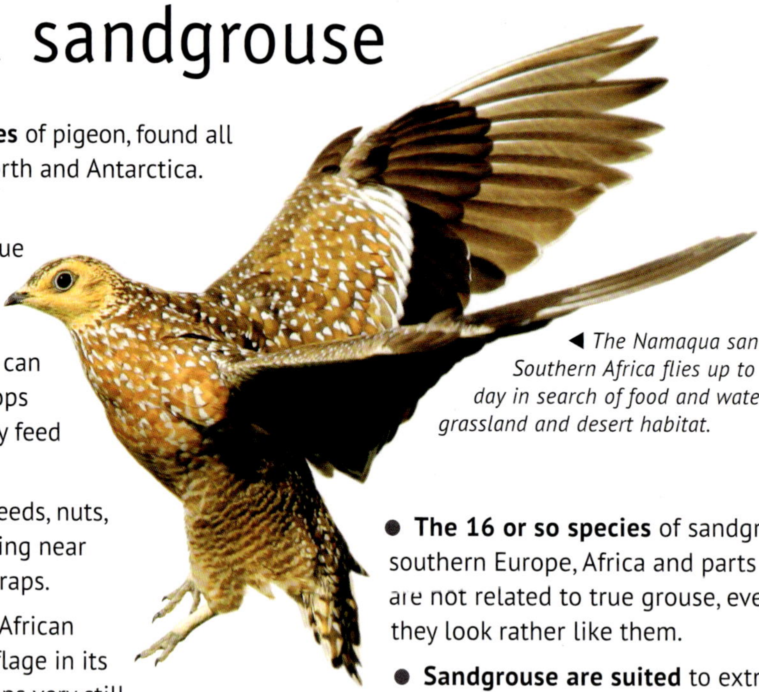

◀ *The Namaqua sandgrouse of Southern Africa flies up to 80 km a day in search of food and water in its dry grassland and desert habitat.*

- **The 16 or so species** of sandgrouse live in southern Europe, Africa and parts of Asia. They are not related to true grouse, even though they look rather like them.
- **Sandgrouse are suited** to extreme desert conditions, withstanding soaring temperatures with little need for water. They are strong fliers and travel long distances to find water.
- **Domesticated pigeons** are descended from the wild rock dove. These pigeons were first domesticated in Iraq over 6000 years ago.

Tits and chickadees

DID YOU KNOW?

The willow tit may bury up to 1000 nuts and seeds a day, to eat later when food is scarce.

- **There are about 50 species of true tits** found in Europe, Africa, Asia and North America. In addition, there are seven species of long-tailed tits and ten species of penduline tits.
- **The largest of the tits** is the Asian sultan tit, at about 22 cm long and 30 g in weight. It is twice the size of most other tits.
- **The blue tit** is only 10–11 cm long, but lays as many as 15 eggs – more than any other bird that feeds its young.
- **The penduline tit** makes an amazing nest woven from plant fibres suspended from the end of a twig. The walls of the nest may be 2.5 cm thick.
- **The black-capped chickadee** gets its name from its call, which sounds like a 'chick-a-dee-dee', and is one of the most complex of any bird songs.
- **The female great tit** lays seven to 12 eggs, each of which is about 10 percent of her body weight.
- **Great tits** hatch blind and helpless, and are fed by their parents for about three weeks. The parents may make 1000 feeding trips a day to the young.
- **The long-tailed tit** makes its nest from feathers and moss that it collects – one nest may contain as many as 2000 feathers.
- **The long-tailed tit** is only about 14 cm long, and more than half of its length is its tail feathers.

▶ *Both male and female penduline tits weave their purse-like nest from grass, leaves, lichens and moss. It takes about two weeks for them to build the nest, which keeps the chicks warm for two to three weeks while they grow their feathers.*

Hawks and harriers

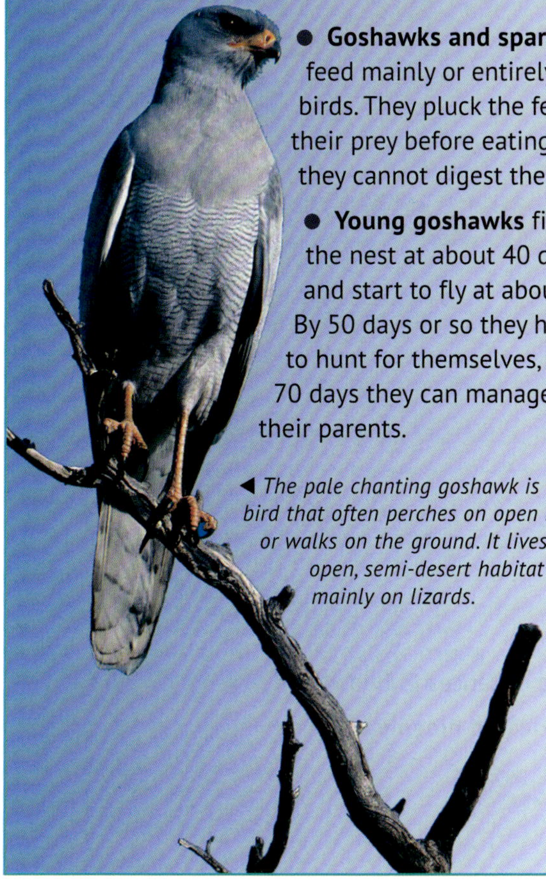

◀ *The pale chanting goshawk is an African bird that often perches on open branches or walks on the ground. It lives in a dry, open, semi-desert habitat and feeds mainly on lizards.*

- **Goshawks and sparrowhawks** feed mainly or entirely on other birds. They pluck the feathers off their prey before eating them, as they cannot digest the feathers.
- **Young goshawks** first leave the nest at about 40 days old and start to fly at about 45 days. By 50 days or so they have learnt to hunt for themselves, and by 70 days they can manage without their parents.
- **The largest hawk** is the northern goshawk, which is up to 60 cm long and weighs as much as 2 kg.
- **Northern goshawks** are powerful birds. The females can catch prey as large as pheasants, wood pigeons or hares.
- **The female sparrowhawk** is up to 25 percent larger than the male. At breeding time she defends the nest, while the more agile male brings the family food.
- **Harriers are slender** birds of prey with long wings and long legs. They usually nest on the ground, which is unusual for birds of prey.
- **Hen harriers** (also called northern harriers or marsh hawks) hunt by flying slowly above the ground, taking their prey, such as small rodents, by surprise. These harriers are the only ones that live in North America.
- **Female hen harriers** and marsh harriers fly up from the nest to catch food dropped by the male. They turn upside down and catch the food in mid-air with their feet.
- **The African harrier hawk** likes to feed on baby birds. It has long, double-jointed legs that allow it to reach into other birds' nests and grab the chicks.

Rails and bustards

- **There are more than 130 species** of rails found all over the world, including on many small islands. The family includes moorhens, coots and crakes, as well as rails.
- **The takahe**, a large flightless rail, is now extremely rare and lives only on South Island, New Zealand.
- **Coots are the most aquatic** of all rail species. They dive in search of plants and water insects to eat.
- **Moorhen chicks** leave the nest when they are only two or three days old. They can already swim well at this very young age.
- **The water rail** makes loud groans and often sounds like a grunting or squealing pig.
- **The 22 species** of bustard live in Africa, southern Europe, Asia and Australia.
- **Bustards are large birds** with long legs. They live on the ground in deserts and open, grassy places.
- **These heavy birds** mainly rely on hiding or running away from predators instead of flying. Their mottled brown feathers provide good camouflage.
- **Male crested bustards** perform spectacular 'rocket flights', during which they fly vertically into the air for about 30 m, then puff out their breast feathers, turn upside down, and drop vertically back down to the ground again.
- **Little bustards** are short, chunky birds, which weigh less than one kilogram.

▼ *A great bustard taking off from a field shows its enormous wingspan of up to 2.5 m. This is probably the world's heaviest flying bird.*

Early birds

● **The oldest-known feathers** of any creature belong to a small feathered dinosaur called *Anchiornis huxleyi*, which lived in China between 150 and 160 million years ago.

● **Scientists believe** that birds evolved from lightly built dinosaurs, such as *Compsognathus*, which ran on two legs.

● **The earliest-known bird** is *Archaeopteryx*, which lived 155 to 150 million years ago. It had feathers like a modern bird, but teeth like a reptile.

● **Although it could fly**, *Archaeopteryx* could not take off from the ground, and probably had to climb a tree before launching itself into the air.

● ***Ichthyornis*** was a seabird with long, toothed jaws. It lived alongside dinosaurs in the Late Cretaceous period.

● ***Hesperornis*** was a large, flightless seabird that lived about 70 million years ago. It was a strong swimmer that dived underwater to catch fish.

● **The ancient flightless bird** *Diatryma* lived in North America and Europe about 50 million years ago. It stood about 2 m tall on its long legs and probably used its powerful, hooked beak to catch mammals.

▲ Archaeopteryx *was about the size of a crow, with a wingspan of 60 cm. Its name means 'ancient wing'.*

● **The largest-known** predatory bird to have ever lived is a terror bird, *Titanis walleri*. It died out from two to one million years ago. This flightless bird could run after prey at speeds of up to 64 km/h and used its large claws and axe-like bill to make the kill.

● **An early member** of the vulture family, *Argentavix* of South America had an amazing 7.3 m wingspan.

DID YOU KNOW?

Dinosaurs probably used feathers for display for millions of years, before some evolved into birds and used them for flying.

Waxwings and relatives

● **The waxwing** gets its name from the red markings on its wing feathers, which look like drops of wax.

● **Adult waxwings** eat mainly berries, but feed their young on insects for the first two weeks of their lives.

● **There are three species** of waxwings. They are all sociable, tree-dwelling birds.

● **The bohemian waxwing** makes a nest of twigs, moss and grass, usually in a conifer tree. The female incubates four to six eggs, while the male keeps her fed.

● **Adult cedar waxwings** store berries in their crops, or throat pouches, and regurgitate them for their young.

● **The single species of palmchat** is found on the islands of Hispaniola, Saona and Gonâve in the Caribbean.

● **Palmchats** nest in palm trees. One nest may house 30 pairs of birds, each with its own tunnel entrance.

● **The silky flycatcher** feeds mostly on mistletoe berries, passing out the seeds.

● **Long-tailed silky flycatchers** build a nest of lichens. Both adults incubate the eggs and feed the young.

● **Courting waxwings** pass small objects, such as berries, flower petals or insects, back and forth.

◀ *Bohemian waxwings will strip a bush clean of its berries before moving on to find more food.*

True and harpy eagles

- **The golden eagle** makes a bulky nest of sticks and branches (an eyrie) that may measure as much as 2 m high and 1.5 m across.
- **The harpy eagle** flies through the treetops of the South American rainforests at speeds of up to 80 km/h. It uses its powerful hooked beak to tear the flesh from its prey.
- **Golden eagles** usually have a hunting territory of about 260 sq km.
- **The most powerful of all eagles**, the South American harpy eagle hunts prey that may weigh more than itself, such as large monkeys and sloths.
- **A harpy eagle** weighs over 8 kg, has a wingspan of more than 2 m, and talons the size of a bear's claws.
- **The male crowned eagle** of Africa shows off its chestnut underwings to its mate during its courtship display.
- **True eagles** are also known as booted eagles, because their legs are covered with feathers down to their toes.
- **At up to 96 cm long**, the martial eagle is the largest African eagle. It feeds on mammals such as hyraxes and young antelope, and on other birds, including guineafowl and even storks.
- **A young martial eagle** is fed by its parents for about 60 days, by which time it has a full covering of feathers and is able to tear up prey for itself.

DID YOU KNOW?

Verreaux's eagle lays two eggs, but the first chick to hatch usually kills the younger chick.

▼ *Golden eagles lay two eggs, but one of the chicks usually dies. At first the mother keeps the surviving chick warm while the male finds food, but as the chick grows larger, both parents are kept busy supplying it with food.*

Mockingbirds and relatives

- **Mockingbirds** are so-called because they imitate the calls of as many as 36 other bird species.
- **As well as mockingbirds**, the 32 species in the family include catbirds, thrashers and tremblers. They live in North and South America.
- **'Mimic of many tongues'** is the meaning of the northern mockingbird's scientific name, *Mimus polyglottus*.

▲ *The northern mockingbird is the best mimic in its family, usually copying the sounds made by other bird species.*

- **Some birds in the mockingbird family** and several other distantly related families are called catbirds because of their strange, cat-like calls.
- **The grey catbird** migrates at night, arriving in southern USA in spring after spending the winter in Central America.
- **The grey catbird** lines its cup-shaped nest of sticks, leaves and grasses with pine needles and down. The female lays three to five eggs, and incubates them for 12–13 days.
- **The brown trembler**, a resident of some Caribbean islands, gets its name from its habit of shaking its body from time to time.
- **The 13 accentor species** live in mountainous parts of northern Africa, Europe and Asia.
- **The dunnock** (accentor family) is a small brown bird. Its name comes from the Old English word dunn, meaning 'dark or dull'.

DID YOU KNOW?

The northern mockingbird can sing 200 songs, as well as mimicking pianos, frogs and humans.

Turkeys and grouse

- **Male wild turkeys** of the USA, Mexico and Central America can weigh up to 8 kg.
- **An adult turkey** has approximately 3500 feathers.
- **Wild turkeys** are not fussy eaters. They feed on a variety of seeds, nuts, berries, leaves, insects and other small creatures.
- **The 17 species of grouse** live in North America, Europe and northern Asia.
- **At 87 cm long**, the western capercaillie is the biggest of the 17 species of grouse.

DID YOU KNOW?

The heaviest ever domestic turkey weighed 39 kg – as much as a 12-year-old child.

- **In winter**, the spruce grouse feeds mainly on the buds and needles of pine trees.
- **To attract females** and challenge rival males, the ruffed grouse makes a drumming sound with its wings.
- **The ruffed grouse lays nine to 12 eggs.** When the young hatch, the female shows them where to find food.
- **At the start of the breeding season**, foot-stamping dances are performed by groups of male prairie chickens (a type of grouse) at their traditional display areas.

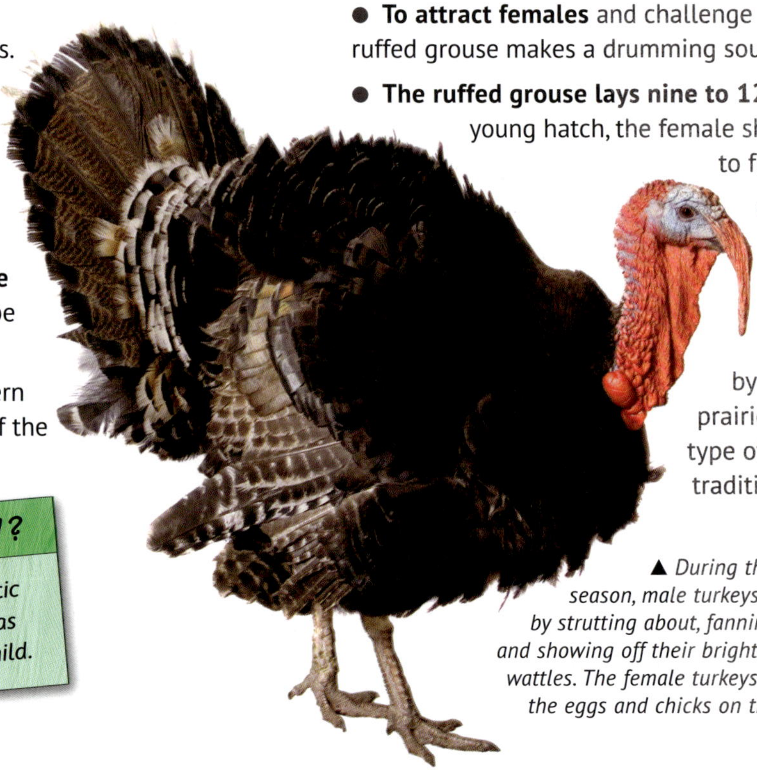

▲ *During the breeding season, male turkeys attract females by strutting about, fanning out their tails and showing off their brightly coloured throat wattles. The female turkeys (hens) look after the eggs and chicks on their own.*

Wrens

◀ *The cactus wren is the largest wren in North America, reaching lengths of 18–22 cm. These active and curious wrens get almost all their water from their food, which includes insects, seeds, fruit and some lizards and frogs.*

- **The cactus wren** builds its dome-shaped nest among the spines of cacti in the deserts of North America. Few enemies will brave the spines to steal the wren's eggs or young.
- **At about 23 cm long**, the black-capped donacobious of South America is the largest of the wren family.
- **A male wren** courts a mate by building up to 12 nests. The female chooses one in which to lay her eggs.
- **The northern (or winter) wren** usually lays between five and eight eggs, and incubates them for 14–17 days. The young stay in the nest for 20 days.
- **Most wrens** live in North and South America. Only the northern wren lives in Europe, Asia and Africa.
- **The rock wren** survives in a harsh, rocky environment by eating small insects and worms. It has a brown rump.
- **Cactus wrens** produce up to four broods of young every year.
- **The tiny northern wren** can fly well but spends most of its time hopping and flitting over the ground or through bushes, probing for insects and spiders with its needle-sharp bill.
- **The song of the flutist wren** consists of a series of high-pitched whistling notes and may last up to 30 seconds.
- **Male long-billed marsh wrens** build clusters of 25–35 nests over a breeding season of three months. Males sing near their nests and show them off to the females. However, the females breed in another nest away from the courtship area.

Baby birds

- **Many baby birds** are blind, naked (without feathers) and helpless when they hatch. They have to be cared for by their parents.
- **Helpless baby birds** are called 'altricial young'. The word altricial comes from the Latin word *alere*, meaning 'to rear or nourish'.
- **Birds such as herons**, hawks, woodpeckers, crows, cardinals, owls, magpies, lorikeets, wrens, pigeons and sparrows all have altricial young.
- **Altricial birds** lay smaller eggs and build strong nests to protect them, usually in trees, bushes or shrubs. One or both of the parents incubates (sits on) the eggs to keep them warm.
- **Altricial young**, or nestlings, grow quickly, develop feathers and usually leave the nest within two to four weeks. Most nestlings grow to the same size as their parents in this short space of time.
- **Precocial baby birds** are much more developed than altricial baby birds when they hatch out of their eggs.
- **Birds with precocial chicks** include emus, ducks, lapwings, gulls, geese, swans, brush turkeys, terns and many wading shorebirds.

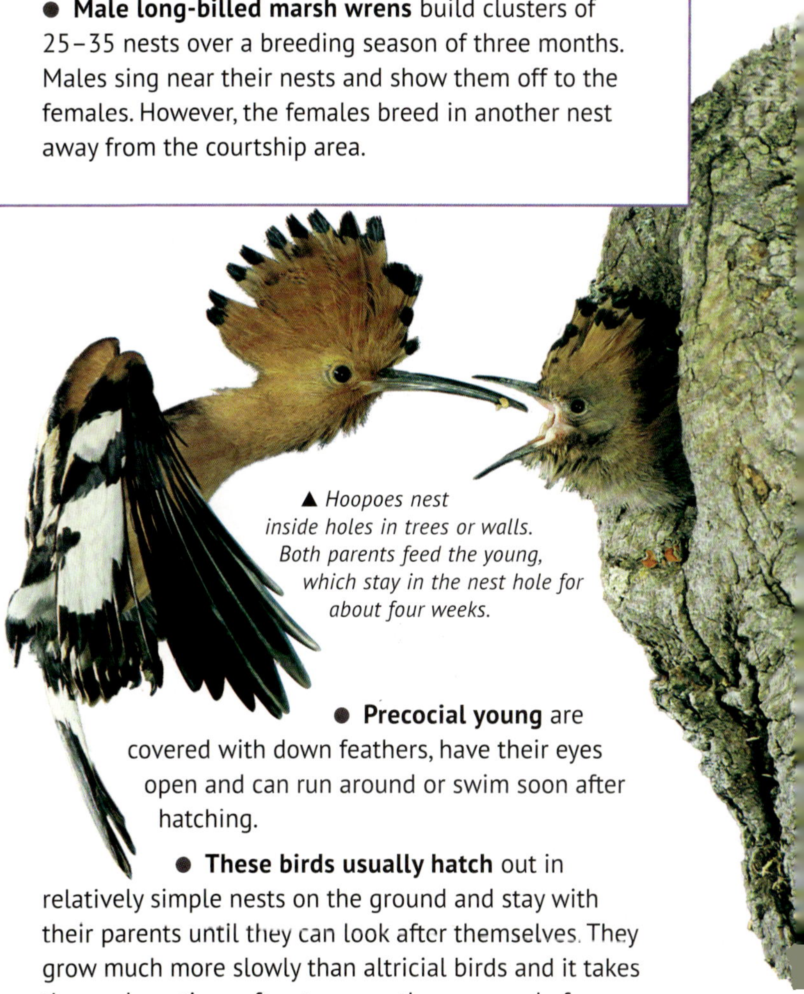

▲ *Hoopoes nest inside holes in trees or walls. Both parents feed the young, which stay in the nest hole for about four weeks.*

- **Precocial young** are covered with down feathers, have their eyes open and can run around or swim soon after hatching.
- **These birds usually hatch** out in relatively simple nests on the ground and stay with their parents until they can look after themselves. They grow much more slowly than altricial birds and it takes them a long time, often two months or more, before they are able to fly.
- **Parents of precocial chicks** spend a lot of time watching out for predators, since their small, flightless chicks are vulnerable to attack until they grow their flight feathers.

Ostriches and emus

● **The ostrich** is the largest of all birds alive today. It stands 2.5 m tall and weighs around 130 kg – about twice as much as an average human.

● **The male ostrich** makes a shallow nest on the ground and mates with several females, all of whom lay their eggs in the nest. The chief female incubates the eggs during the day, and the male takes over at night.

● **Ostriches** don't really bury their heads in the sand. But if a female is approached by an enemy while sitting on the nest, she will press her long neck flat on the ground to appear less obvious.

● **Ostrich chicks** have many enemies, including jackals and hyenas. Only 15 percent are likely to survive until they are one year old.

● **In Southwest Asia**, the shells of ostrich eggs are believed to have magical powers. They are sometimes placed on the roofs of houses as protection from evil.

● **The largest bird** in Australia is the emu, which measures 2 m tall and weighs as much as 45 kg. Like the ostrich, it cannot fly.

DID YOU KNOW?

Emus can sprint at speeds of up to 50 km/h and make long leaps over distances of up to 2.7 m.

● **Seeds, fruits, flowers and plant shoots** are an emu's main sources of food, but it also eats some insects and small animals.

● **The male emu** incubates its mate's clutch of eggs for eight weeks, during which time it does not eat or drink. It lives on the stores of body fat that it has built up during the previous months.

● **An emu's feathers** are each made up of two quills, which are the same length.

▲ *Ostriches live in Africa, in dry grassland areas. They often have to run long distances in search of food.*

Migration

- **Migration is the journey** made by many animals twice a year between a summer breeding area, where food is plentiful, and a wintering area with a good climate.
- **Many migrating birds** have to build up fat stores to allow them to fly non-stop for days without food.
- **Some small birds** double their weight before migrating to provide them with enough energy stores for travelling long distances.
- **Most birds** that migrate long distances fly at night, when they are safer from predators.
- **Nearly half** of all the world's birds migrate.
- **Birds find their way** by observing landmarks, the patterns of stars and the position of the setting Sun. They also use their sense of smell and monitor the Earth's magnetic field.
- **Some birds** migrate short distances. The Himalayan monal pheasant migrates up and down the mountains with the seasons, moving down to the warmer lower slopes in winter.
- **In the Northern Hemisphere**, birds tend to move south to warmer places in winter, while in the Southern Hemisphere, they fly north.
- **Many birds** migrate to the Arctic to nest during the brief summer months when there is plenty of food available there.
- **Before migration was studied**, some people thought swallows simply spent the winter asleep in mud.

▼ *Geese migrate in huge flocks, but pairs stay together within the flock.*

Finches and relatives

- **The crossbill** gets its name from its crossed beak, which is specially shaped for extracting seeds from pine cones.
- **The male American goldfinch** brings the female food while she incubates the four to six eggs.
- **The kernels** of cherry stones and olive stones are a favourite food of the strong-beaked hawfinch.
- **The goldfinch** uses its slender tweezer-like beak to take seeds from between the spines of a teasel head.
- **Young chaffinches** can fly just 12 days after hatching.

▲ *The goldfinch has a red face, beige body and a broad yellow bar on its black wings. A flock of goldfinches is called a 'charm'.*

▶ *The distinctive, pink-breasted male bullfinch.*

- **The oriole finch** is named after its colours, which are similar to those of true orioles. It lives in the mountain forests of Africa.
- **In winter**, when food becomes scarce, large flocks of different species of finches and tits search for food together.
- **Redpolls are named** after their red forehead, or 'poll'. Young birds have no red colouring and also have yellower bills than the adults.
- **The blue chaffinch** is a rare species, which lives only in the Canary Islands. Adults eat mainly seeds, but the young are fed on insects.

DID YOU KNOW?

Although the hawfinch weighs only 50 g, its beak can exert a pressure of 45 kg.

Cranes and trumpeters

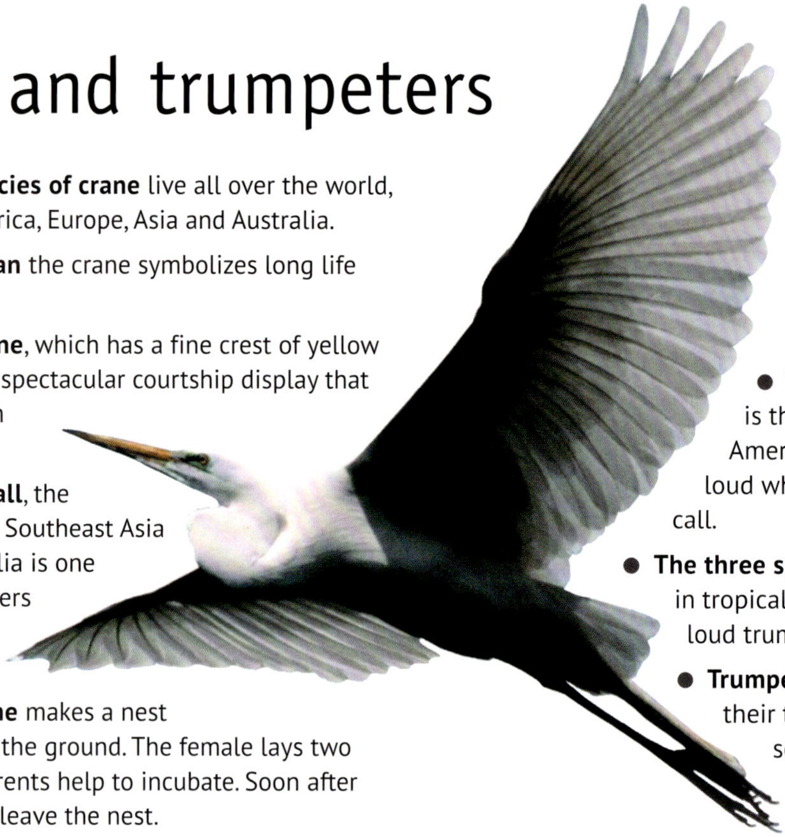

◀ *Cranes fly with their necks stretched forwards and their legs held straight out beyond their short tails.*

- **The 15 or so species of crane** live all over the world, in North America, Africa, Europe, Asia and Australia.
- **In China and Japan** the crane symbolizes long life and good luck.
- **The crowned crane**, which has a fine crest of yellow feathers, performs a spectacular courtship display that involves leaping 2 m into the air.
- **At about 1.8 m tall**, the Sarus crane of India, Southeast Asia and northern Australia is one of the largest members of the crane family.
- **The sandhill crane** makes a nest of plant material on the ground. The female lays two eggs, which both parents help to incubate. Soon after hatching, the young leave the nest.
- **Siberian cranes** have been known to live for more than 80 years. One captive male even fathered chicks at the age of 78!
- **The whooping crane** is the rarest crane in North America. It is named after its loud whooping or trumpeting call.
- **The three species of trumpeter** live in tropical rainforests. All make loud trumpeting calls.
- **Trumpeters** spend most of their time on the ground searching for fruit, nuts and insects, but they roost in trees.
- **The limpkin** is a relative of the cranes and the only member of its family. It has a long, curved beak, which it uses to remove snails from their shells.

Bowerbirds

- **Male bowerbirds** build bowers of twigs and other plant material to attract females. They decorate their creations with berries and shells, and some even perform dances in front of their bowers.
- **The spotted bowerbird** decorates his bower with piles of white and green objects, while the fawn-breasted bowerbird uses green berries.
- **Male bowerbirds' bowers** are not built as places for the female to lay eggs and rear young. The females build their own, more practical nests.
- **Bowerbirds** feed on fruit, berries, seeds, insects and other small creatures.
- **A female bowerbird** has between one and three chicks and cares for them alone.
- **The Vogelkop gardener bowerbird** builds a hut-like structure big enough for a person to crawl into.
- **The forests of New Guinea** and northern and eastern Australia are home to the 18 or so species of bowerbird.
- **At about 36 cm long**, the great grey bowerbird of northern Australia is the largest of the family.
- **The male regent bowerbird** paints its bower yellow using a mix of spit and the juice of crushed leaves.
- **The spotted catbird** is a member of the bowerbird family but the males do not build bowers and males and females look alike.

▼ *A male satin bowerbird builds his bower from two walls of sticks, forming an 'avenue' to attract a female, and has decorated the area around it with blue objects.*

Feathers

- **Feathers evolved** from reptile scales and they grow out of little pits, or follicles, in a bird's skin, just as the hairs on human skin grow from hair follicles.
- **Feathers grow** at a rate of 1–13 mm a day.
- **The ruby-throated hummingbird** has an average of just 940 feathers, while the whistling swan has 25,000.
- **A bird's feathers** are replaced once or twice a year in a process known as moulting.
- **Feathers keep a bird warm**, protect its skin, provide a flight surface, and may also help attract a mate.
- **In most birds**, a third of the feathers are on the head.
- **The longest feathers** ever known were 10.59 m long and belonged to an ornamental chicken.
- **The feathers** that cover a bird's body are called contour feathers. Down feathers underneath provide extra warmth.
- **A bald eagle** has around 7000 feathers weighing over 650 g, more than twice as much as its skeleton.
- **Birds spend time** every day preening – cleaning and rearranging their feathers with their beaks.

◀ Flight feathers on a bird's wings and tail provide a large continuous surface area to push the bird through the air. Their aerofoil shape helps to lift the bird into the air as well as twist and turn in flight.

▶ Soft down feathers trap warm air next to a bird's body. The side branches (barbs) are long and soft. There are few hooks (barbules) to hold the barbs together, so the feather stays fluffy.

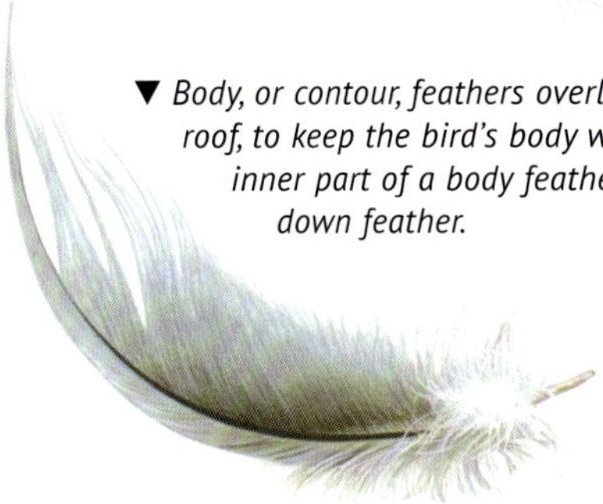

▼ Body, or contour, feathers overlap like tiles on a roof, to keep the bird's body warm and dry. The inner part of a body feather is fluffy, like a down feather.

Antbirds and tapaculos

- **Antbirds** follow columns of army ants as they march over the forest floor, perching just above the ground to seize other insects as they flee from the ants' path.
- **The 230 or so species of antbird** live in Mexico, Central and South America.
- **Antbirds** mate for life.
- **During the courtship ritual** of the ocellated antbird, the male presents the female with an item of food.
- **Antbirds have white spots** on their back feathers, which they use to signal warnings to each other. They show the spots in particular patterns according to the message – like a sort of Morse code.
- **Antbird species** range from 10–38 cm long, and have differently shaped beaks to suit their food.
- **Some larger species of antbirds** have a special 'tooth' inside the beak that helps them chew food.
- **Most antbirds** do not fly much and have poorly developed wings, but their legs are strong for running and perching.
- **The 30 species of tapaculos** are insect-eating birds that live in the cool mountain forests of South America or in dry scrubland.

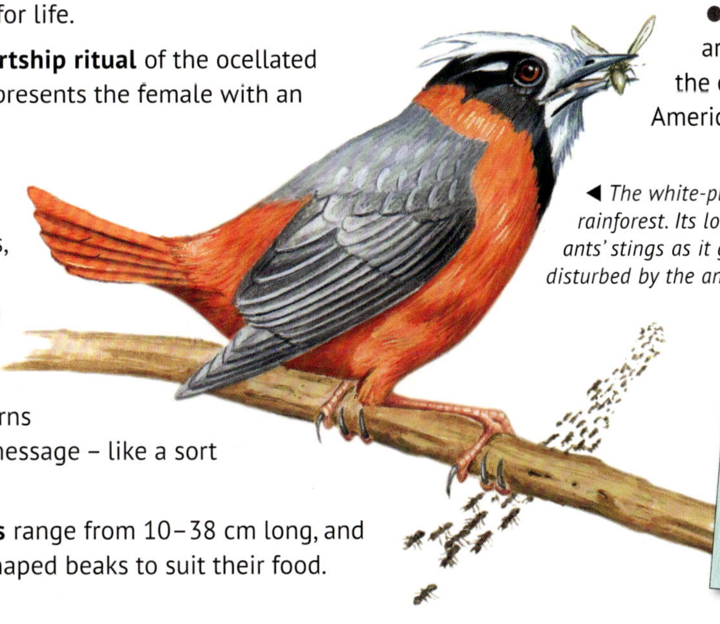

◀ The white-plumed antbird lives in the Amazon rainforest. Its long legs help to protect it from the ants' stings as it gathers up the other insects or spiders disturbed by the ants.

DID YOU KNOW?

An antbird rubs a mouthful of ants over its feathers to clean them. The formic acid from the ants kills any lice and mites in the feathers.

Swallows and martins

● **There are about 80 species** of swallows and martins found all over the world. Most of these migrate between breeding grounds and wintering areas.

● **In most swallow species**, males and females are alike, but in the rare blue swallow, the female has a short tail, while the male's is long and forked.

● **Swallows** catch their insect food in the air as they fly.

● **There is an old saying** that the weather will be good when swallows fly high, but bad when swallows fly low. This is based on fact – in wet weather, insects stay nearer the ground, so the swallows do the same.

● **An adult swallow** will carry a mass of crushed insects, squashed into a ball in its throat, back to its young. A barn swallow may take 400 meals a day to its chicks.

◀ *Swallows may lay up to eight eggs at a time, often in 'mud cups' attached to buildings.*

● **The sand martin** digs a 120-cm-long nesting burrow in riverbanks.

● **Only discovered in 1968**, the white-eyed river martin spends the winter in reedbeds on Lake Boraphet in Thailand.

● **Purple martins** often nest in old woodpecker holes or in nest-boxes. The female incubates the four to five eggs alone, but the male helps feed the young.

● **Sand martins** breed in the Northern Hemisphere, migrating south in the winter in flocks of thousands.

● **The house martin** often lives near people, making its nest under the eaves of buildings, bridges or other structures.

Snake and sea eagles

● **The bald eagle** performs an amazing courtship display, in which the male and female lock their claws together and tumble through the air to the ground.

● **Bald eagles** are not really bald. They have white feathers on their heads, which may make them appear bald from a distance.

● **The bald eagle** is able to catch a salmon that weighs as much as its own body weight.

● **In 1782** the bald eagle was chosen as the national emblem of the USA, and it appears on most of the gold and silver coins in the USA.

● **The white-tailed sea eagle** snatches fish from the water using its sharp, powerful talons.

● **Spikes** on the underside of its toes help the African fish eagle hold onto its fish prey. It also catches birds, terrapins and baby crocodiles.

● **Snake eagles** eat snakes and have short, strong toes ideal for tackling their writhing victims.

● **The short-toed eagle** kills a snake with a bite to the back of the head, instantly severing the backbone.

● **The bateleur**, a snake eagle, may fly as much as 300 km a day in search of food.

● **The word** bateleur means 'tumbler' or 'tightrope walker', so the bateleur eagle is named for the rocking, acrobatic movements that it makes in flight.

◀ *The bald eagle catches a lot of fish, snatching them from the water with its lethally sharp talons.*

Rainforest birds

- **With its abundance** of flowers, leaves, fruits and insects, a rainforest is the ideal home for many different kinds of birds.
- **Flocks of brightly coloured macaws** sometimes feed on soil because it is rich in minerals and keeps them healthy.
- **Quetzals** feed on avocado trees and help to spread the trees' seeds through the forest in their droppings. The trees and the birds help each other to survive.
- **The king vulture** of South America is the only vulture to live in rainforests. As well as feeding on carrion, it also kills mammals and reptiles.
- **The muscovy duck** is now familiar in farmyards and parks in many parts of the world. However, it originally came from the rainforests of Central and South America.
- **The crowned eagle** lives in African rainforests, where it feeds on monkeys and other mammals, such as mongooses and rats.
- **Large, flightless cassowaries** live in the rainforests of New Guinea, where people hunt them to eat.
- **The male argus pheasant** clears a patch of forest floor in the breeding season so it can strut up and down, calling loudly to attract females.
- **The hornbills of Africa** and the toucans of South America look similar because they live, feed and survive in a similar way. This is called convergent evolution.

DID YOU KNOW?

One-fifth of all bird species live in the Amazon rainforest.

▶ *The tropical rainforest has more types of bird than anywhere else. Many of the birds in the canopy are amazingly colourful. Game birds and little insect-eaters patrol the forest floor.*

Larks and wagtails

- **There are over 90 species** of lark, which live mainly in Africa, Europe and Asia. More than half of all lark species are found in Africa.
- **Larks have more elaborate calls** than most birds and are famous for their complex, beautiful songs, which males use to defend their breeding territories and attract mates.
- **The skylark** performs a beautiful song as it flutters up to a great height, hovers and descends again.

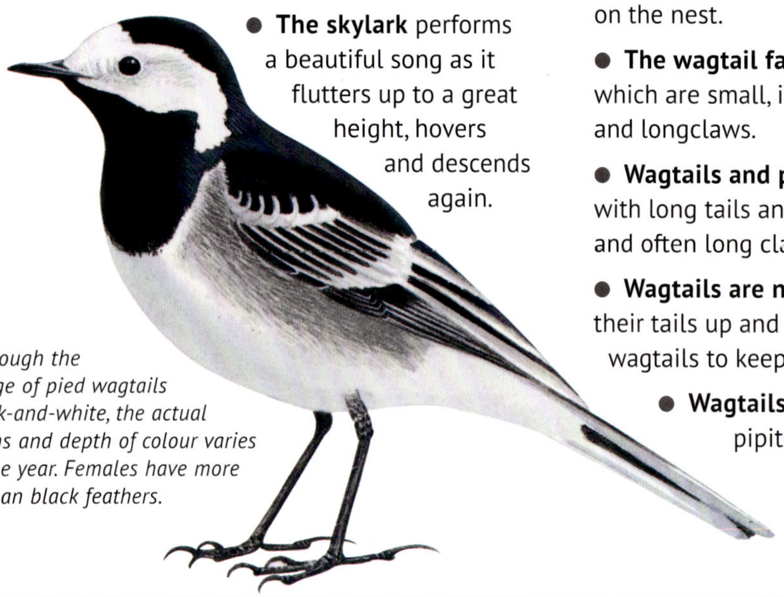

▶ *Although the plumage of pied wagtails is black-and-white, the actual patterns and depth of colour varies over the year. Females have more grey than black feathers.*

DID YOU KNOW?

Pied wagtails are often mistaken for young magpies, but they can be distinguished by their bouncing tails.

- **Larks spend most of their time** hopping along the ground and most species have long back claws, which help them to balance.
- **Most larks** have dull, streaked-brown feathers, which gives them good camouflage on the ground, especially on the nest.
- **The wagtail family** has about 60 species, most of which are small, insect-eating birds. They include pipits and longclaws.
- **Wagtails and pipits** are mostly small, slender birds, with long tails and long legs. All species have long toes and often long claws, particularly the back toe.
- **Wagtails are named** after their habit of flicking their tails up and down, which may tell neighbouring wagtails to keep out of their territory.
- **Wagtails have more striking colours** than pipits, but their songs are mostly quiet, whereas pipits have loud songs.

Kingfishers

- **The 90 or so species of kingfisher** are found all over the world, except in parts of the far north and Antarctica.
- **The giant kingfisher** of Africa and the Australian laughing kookaburra (a kingfisher) are the largest of the family, at about 45 cm long.
- **The common kingfisher** nests at the end of a one-metre-long tunnel that it excavates in a riverbank. The female lays four to eight eggs.
- **Common kingfishers** incubate their eggs for 19–21 days and feed the young for up to four weeks.
- **A flash of iridescent** turquoise feathers streaking at high speed along a quiet riverbank indicates the presence of a common or European kingfisher.

◀ *The tiny pygmy kingfisher is only 12 cm long. It lives in the woodlands and forests of Africa.*

- **The African pygmy kingfisher** feeds mainly on dry land, diving down from a perch to catch insects, spiders, millipedes and even small frogs and lizards.
- **The shovel-billed kingfisher** is armed with its own spade for digging in mud – it uses its large, heavy bill to dig up worms, shellfish and small reptiles.
- **In the forests of New Guinea**, the male paradise kingfisher shows off its long tail feathers to females as part of its courtship display.
- **The laughing kookaburra** is named for its call, which sounds like noisy laughter. It makes its call to claim territory. Once one starts, others tend to join in.
- **In northern Australia**, termite mounds are adopted as nest sites by the buff-breasted kingfisher.

Thrushes

- **There are about 173 species** of 'true thrushes', which include the American robin, Eurasian blackbird, fieldfare, redwing, ring ouzel and ground thrush.
- **Thrushes** are plump birds with soft plumage (feathers). They often feed on the ground.
- **Thrushes** have slender bills and feed primarily on insects, but most species also eat worms, snails and fruit.
- **The songs** of some thrush species are very beautiful.
- **The lower legs** of thrushes are covered in front with one long scale instead of many short ones.
- **Most species of thrush** are grey or brown in colour, often with speckled underparts. The young are usually spotted in their first plumage.

◀ *The song thrush is named after its magnificent song. It is also known for its habit of using a large stone as an anvil to smash open snail shells.*

- **The American robin** – the largest of the North American thrushes – lives both in cities and mountains.
- **The female blackbird** makes a cup-shaped nest of plant stems, grass, twigs and roots. The four to five eggs she lays hatch after 11–17 days.
- **Blackbirds** were taken to Australia and New Zealand in the 19th century. Their songs are now clearly different to blackbirds living in Europe.
- **A number of unrelated birds**, such as ant-thrushes, babbling thrushes and laughing thrushes, are called thrushes because they look similar to true thrushes.

▶ *Fieldfares are noisy thrushes that eat insects, spiders and centipedes, as well as seeds and fruit, such as apples and hawthorn berries. Parents will squirt droppings at predators to defend their young.*

Sandpipers and snipes

- **Sandpipers** are the largest family of wading birds, with about 90 species.
- **The sandpiper and snipe family** also includes curlews, dowitchers, dunlins, godwits, redshanks, sanderlings and turnstones.
- **During migration**, bar-tailed godwits sometimes fly for 10,000 km without stopping to rest or feed.
- **Sandpipers incubate their eggs** for 18–30 days and the young are quite independent as soon as they hatch.
- **The western curlew** plunges its long, curved beak into soft coastal mud to find worms and clams.
- **As it dives towards Earth**, air rushing through the outermost tail feathers of the European snipe makes a sound called 'drumming'.
- **Unusually for birds**, female phalaropes are more brightly coloured than males. The female lays several clutches of eggs, leaving the male parent of each clutch to care for the young.
- **The turnstone** is so-called because it turns over stones on the beach when searching for shellfish and worms.
- **In the breeding season**, male ruffs grow amazing feathers around their heads and necks, and dance in groups to attract females.

DID YOU KNOW?

Red knots travel up to 30,000 km twice a year as they migrate between their breeding grounds in Canada and their wintering grounds in South America.

▶ *The curlew's long legs are ideal for wading over marshland.*

◀ *Red legs are the most obvious identifying feature of a redshank. If danger threatens, redshanks fly up into the air, making a series of harsh, piping alarm calls.*

Seabirds

- **The white-tailed tropicbird** is noted for its amazing tail streamers, which can measure up to 40 cm in length.
- **The three species of tropicbird** are all expert in the air and can dive into the sea to find prey, but cannot walk on land. With their legs set far back on their bodies, they are only able to drag themselves along.
- **An albatross** may fly over 16 million km in a lifetime, soaring over the ocean waves on its long, powerful wings.
- **Manx shearwaters** nest in colonies, usually in burrows on remote islands. They come ashore at night to tend to their chicks, in order to avoid attacks from great black-backed gulls.
- **Diving petrels** have small wings, which they use to 'fly' underwater to catch food.

▶ *The red-billed tropicbird's narrow tail streamers are almost the same length as its body. They may help to stabilize the bird in flight and are also used during the courtship display.*

- **In the 19th century**, the droppings (guano) in seabird colonies off the coast of Peru reached depths of 46 m. Today, people have harvested most of the guano for fertiliser and it is only about 0.3 m deep.

DID YOU KNOW?

Fulmars defend themselves by squirting predators with a horrible smelly oil, produced from their stomachs. Even a young fulmar chick can defend itself in this way.

- **Shags can be distinguished from cormorants** by the lack of a white patch on their face.
- **Great skuas** dive-bomb intruders to their nest site, kicking them with their webbed feet and pecking them with their powerful bill.
- **The courtship flight** of the sandwich tern includes a 'fish flight', which involves the male offering the female a fish in mid-air.

Sunbirds and relatives

- **The 132 or so species of sunbird** live in tropical parts of Africa, Asia and Australia.
- **Sunbirds use** their long, slender beaks and tubular tongues to extract sweet liquid nectar from flowers.
- **Female sunbirds** make purse-shaped nests for their two to three eggs, which hatch after 13–15 days.
- **The male pygmy sunbird** has long tail spikes and metallic feathers during the breeding season, but has a short tail and dull plumage at other times.
- **In order to attract a mate**, both male and female scarlet-tufted malachite sunbirds puff out red tufts of feathers on the front of their wings.
- **At about 23 cm long**, the Sao Tomé giant sunbird is the largest of its family. It uses its hooked beak to dig into the bark of trees for insects.
- **The flowerpecker family** contains about 44 species living in parts of Asia, Southeast Asia and Australia.
- **Flowerpeckers** are small, stout, dumpy birds with short necks, legs and tails. They range in size from the 10 cm pygmy flowerpecker to the 18 cm mottled flowerpecker.
- **The crested berrypecker** (flowerpecker family) has a habit of rubbing its plumage with crushed flower petals.
- **Flower nectar** is important in the diet of many flowerpeckers. They have short, thick, curved bills and tubular tongues to help them feed on nectar.

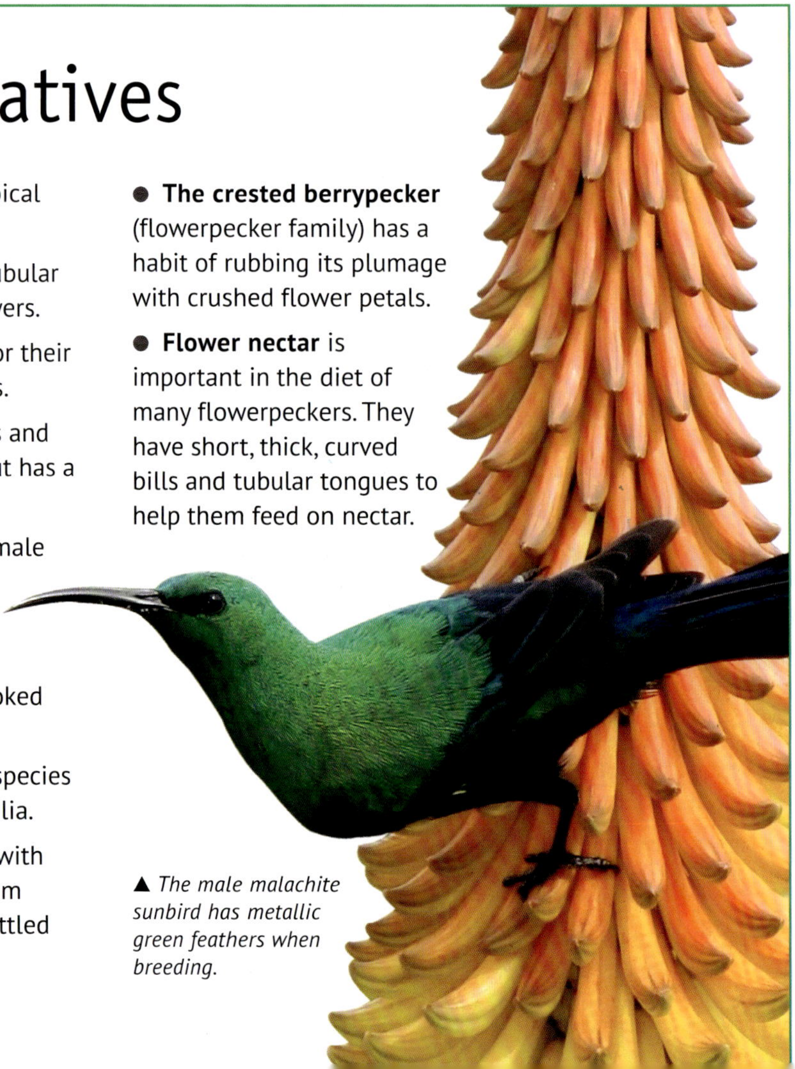

▲ *The male malachite sunbird has metallic green feathers when breeding.*

Nests

▲ *Weaverbirds loop, knot and twist grass stems together with their beaks to make complex woven nests. Narrow entrance tunnels face downwards, making it difficult for predators to get inside.*

- **The bald eagle's nest** can be as large as 2.5 m across and 3.5 m deep – big enough for several people to hide inside.
- **The bee hummingbird's nest** is the smallest – only the size of a thimble.
- **Hummingbirds** and honeyeaters use spiders' webs to hold their nests together.
- **The European bee-eater** nests underground to keep cool. While the surface temperature may reach 50°C, the bee-eater's nest remains a pleasant 25°C.
- **The horned coot** of the Andes builds a huge pile of stones under the water. It then builds its nest at the water's surface, on top of the artificial island of stones.
- **Australian brush turkeys** build large mounds of leaves and soil up to 1.5 m high and 4 m across. The eggs develop in the warmth of these giant compost heaps.
- **About one in eight** bird species worldwide nest in colonies (large groups). Nesting colonies are common amongst seabirds and waterbirds, such as herons and storks.

▲ *The black-shouldered kite builds a large, untidy stick nest, about one metre wide, high in a tree or on a telegraph pole. The male usually collects the nest material and the female builds the nest.*

- **There is safety in numbers**, and birds in a colony also help each other to locate food sources. The disadvantages of colonial living include competition for space, food and mates, as well as the danger of diseases spreading quickly.
- **Many seabirds** nest in colonies on steep cliffs, where it is difficult for predators to reach their eggs and young. Different species share out the available nesting sites by nesting at different levels.
- **Cormorants nest** in such large colonies that huge deposits of their droppings, known as guano, build up. People sometimes collect this guano to use as fertiliser.

▶ *The eggs of the ringed plover are laid in a shallow hollow, scraped in sand or shingle along the shoreline. The eggs are well camouflaged against the background since the nest gives them little protection.*

Old World flycatchers

▶ *The male Japanese blue flycatcher attracts a mate using his brilliant blue feathers and complex, trilling song. These flycatchers migrate to Japan for the warmer spring and summer months, nesting and feeding in woodlands, gardens and parks.*

- **There are 147 species of Old World flycatchers**. Some live in wooded parts of Europe, but they are more common in Asia, Africa and Australasia.
- **The spotted flycatcher** sits on a branch watching for insect prey, then darts out to catch it in mid-air. It has been seen catching one insect every 18 seconds.
- **Male spotted flycatchers** provide all the food for their brood when they first hatch. Later, both parents feed the chicks.
- **The rufous-bellied niltava** lives and breeds in the Himalayas at altitudes of up to 2300 m.
- **Pied flycatchers** usually nest in holes in old trees, but will also nest in nest boxes put up by people. Their nest hole is between one and 15 m above the ground.
- **In autumn and winter**, the pied flycatcher eats worms and berries as well as insects.

▶ *The spotted flycatcher lives in woodland, parks and gardens in Europe and parts of Asia and Africa.*

- **After a summer in Europe**, the red-breasted flycatcher flies to India and Southeast Asia for the winter.
- **The female red-breasted flycatcher** makes a cup-shaped nest of moss, leaves, spiders' webs and plant down, in which to lay her five to six eggs.
- **The white-throated jungle flycatcher** is now very rare and lives only on two islands in the Philippines.
- **Instead of catching all its food in the air**, the Australian flame robin often pounces onto its prey from a low perch.

Ovenbirds and relatives

- **Ovenbirds** live in the forests, mountains and semideserts of Mexico, Central and South America.
- **The nest of the firewood-gatherer** (ovenbird family) looks like a bonfire. A group of birds make the nest together and sleep in it during the winter.
- **The common miner** (an ovenbird) digs a 3-m-long burrow with a nest chamber at the end, where it raises its chicks and roosts for the rest of the year.
- **Des Murs' wiretail** (an ovenbird) has only six tail feathers, four of which may be three times the length of its own body.
- **The campo miner** (an ovenbird) nests in a very particular place – an old armadillo burrow.

▲ *The rufous hornero is the national bird of Argentina.*

▶ *The red-billed scythebill is easily distinguished by its long, downwards-curving beak.*

DID YOU KNOW?

The barred woodcreeper of Central and South America follows army ants as they march across the rainforest floor, snatching up insects that are trying to escape from the advancing army.

- **The 50 or so species of woodcreeper** live in forests and woodland in Mexico, Central and South America.
- **Woodcreepers** often nest in old woodpecker nests.
- **The red-billed scythebill** (a woodcreeper) has a long, curved beak for delving deep into rainforest plants, such as ferns and bromeliads, to search for insects.
- **Red-billed scythebills** use their stiff tail feathers for support on tree trunks, rather like woodpeckers. They also cling onto the bark with their strong feet.

Polar and tundra birds

- **The willow ptarmigan** lives on the Arctic tundra. In winter, it has white feathers that help to keep it hidden in the snow, but in summer it grows darker feathers again.
- **Snowy owls** are among the fiercest Arctic birds. They soar over the tundra preying on other birds and small mammals, such as lemmings.
- **The Laysan albatross** breeds on central Pacific islands, but spends most of the year flying over the Arctic hunting for schools of fish to eat.
- **The auks** of the Arctic look similar to the penguins of the Antarctic because they have similar lifestyles. Unlike penguins, auks can fly, as well as using their wings to swim underwater as they chase prey.
- **Tundra swans** nest on the treeless land around the Arctic, which is called the tundra. They migrate south for the winter.
- **Penguins** huddle together to keep warm in the icy cold Antarctic. A tightly packed group of penguins can reduce heat loss by up to 50 percent.
- **The great skua** is the biggest flying bird in Antarctica, weighing up to 5 kg.
- **Only two species** of penguin, the emperor and the Adélie, breed on the continent of Antarctica, but gentoo, macaroni, chinstrap, rockhopper and king penguins all breed within Antarctic waters.
- **The emperor penguin** breeds in colder temperatures than any other bird. It can survive temperatures of −40°C as it incubates its egg.
- **Most birds leave Antarctica in winter**, but the southern black-backed gull stays all year round. It feeds on fish and birds' eggs as well as some carrion.

▼ *Adélie penguins may have to travel up to 100 km from the sea to reach their breeding colonies in the Antarctic. More than two million pairs of these penguins nest in the Antarctic each year.*

Avocets and relatives

DID YOU KNOW?

Jacanas have extremely long toes and claws that spread their weight, allowing them to walk on floating water-lily leaves.

- **The seven species of stilts** and avocets are all long-legged wading birds with long, slender beaks.
- **Avocets lay about four eggs** in a hollow in open ground. The female avocet spreads her wings to shelter her eggs from the Sun.
- **Avocets nest in a hollow** in the ground, lined with dead leaves. Both partners incubate the eggs.
- **Young avocets** can run soon after hatching, and can fend for themselves after six weeks.
- **Jacanas** (tropical wading birds) range in size from 16–53 cm in length.
- **Female pheasant-tailed jacanas** mate with up to ten males in one breeding season. The males incubate the eggs and care for the young.
- **If a male pheasant-tailed jacana** thinks its eggs are in danger, it may move them one at a time, holding them between its breast and throat.
- **Northern jacanas** are quarrelsome birds. They often fight each other using the sharp spurs on their wings as weapons.
- **The black-winged stilt** has extremely long, bright-pink legs that allow it to wade in deeper water than other stilts as it searches for worms and shellfish.

▶ *The long, curved beak of the pied avocet turns up at the end. The bird sweeps this strange tool through mud or shallow water to find worms and shrimps.*

Lyrebirds and relatives

- **The two species of lyrebird** live in dense mountain forest in southeastern Australia.
- **In its loud song**, the lyrebird may imitate other birds, barking dogs, chainsaws and even passing trains.
- **The female lyrebird** builds a domed nest, usually close to the ground. Her single chick stays with her for eight months or more.
- **One of the biggest of all the songbirds**, the superb lyrebird has an extraordinary lyre-shaped tail, with feathers more than 50 cm long.
- **Young male superb lyrebirds** do not grow their lyre-shaped tails until they are three or four years old.

- **The two species of scrub-bird** live in Australia, where they feed on insects, lizards and frogs.
- **Male scrub birds** have powerful, ringing calls, which can be heard from a long distance away in dense scrub.
- **The rufous scrub-bird** spends most of its time on the ground and rarely flies.
- **A full-grown rufous scrub-bird** is 16–18 cm long and weighs about 30 g.
- **The female rifleman**, one of the three species of New Zealand wrens, lays eggs that are about 20 percent of her body weight. She and the male recruit helpers to bring food to their young.

◀ *During his courtship display, the male superb lyrebird fans out his long tail and arches it forwards over his head to form a shimmering curtain. He does not build a nest or take care of the young.*

Eggs

- **All bird species** lay eggs.
- **The biggest egg** is the ostrich egg. At 1.5 kg, it is 30 times heavier than an average hen's egg.
- **Incubation is the process** of keeping eggs warm while they develop. It can take between ten and 80 days.
- **The yolk** in an egg provides nourishment for the embryo (developing young). The white provides food and moisture and protects the yolk.
- **Egg yolks** are not always yellow. The common tern's yolk is deep red and the gentoo penguin's is a pinky red.

▼ *When a chick is ready to hatch, it makes a tiny hole in the shell with its 'egg-tooth' – a process called 'pipping' – and then struggles out.*

- **Gannets stand on their eggs** to keep them warm.
- **The shell of an egg** contains 50–100 tiny pores per sq cm. This means that oxygen can pass through the shell to the baby bird inside and carbon dioxide can pass out.
- **Eggshells vary in thickness** from 0.2 mm in the night heron's egg, to 0.75 mm in the common murre's.
- **Not all eggs are oval** – those of owls and toucans are round, and auks lay pear-shaped eggs.

DID YOU KNOW?

The bee hummingbird lays the smallest egg, at 0.3 g. You could fit 4700 of them into a single ostrich egg.

First tiny hole · *Egg cracks* · *Chick appears* · *Chick breaks free of egg*

Crows, rooks and ravens

● **Members of the crow family** live on all continents of the world, except Antarctica.

● **There are about** 117 species, including jackdaws, rooks, ravens, nutcrackers, choughs and jays, as well as common crows.

● **Bold and aggressive**, a typical crow is a big bird with a strong body, strong legs, and a powerful beak that can deal with nuts, seeds and even small prey.

● **Crows are thought to be** among the most intelligent of all birds. Studies on ravens have shown that they are able to count up to five or six.

● **A species of crow** that lives on the Pacific island of New Caledonia uses tools, such as hooked twigs and sharp-ended stems, to extract grubs from the crowns of palm trees.

● **At 66 cm long**, the raven is the largest member of the crow family, with a wingspan of nearly 1.5 m.

● **In spring**, jackdaws collect soft fibres for their nests and they may even pluck wool from sheeps' backs.

● **Famous for their acrobatic skills** in the air, choughs (pronounced 'chuffs') swoop and soar on their broad, rounded wings, with their wingtips spread out like fingers. Courting choughs take part in a display flight before nesting.

● **Choughs are mainly** mountain birds. They live at altitudes of nearly 9000 m in the Himalayas.

● **Breeding pairs** of Australian white-winged choughs use a team of up to eight other choughs to help them find food for their young.

● **Great spotted cuckoos** often lay their eggs in the nests of pied crows, causing some of the pied crow chicks to starve.

▼ *The secret of the crow's success is its adaptability. Crows eat a wide range of foods and are intelligent enough to learn how to make use of new food sources.*

Old World sparrows

- **Most sparrows** are about 14–18 cm long and have brownish or grey plumage.
- **The 40 or so** species of Old World sparrow live in Europe, Africa and parts of Asia, though some have been introduced elsewhere.
- **Chestnut sparrows** drive other birds from their nests and use the nests themselves, instead of making their own.

▼ *The male house sparrow has a grey crown and black bib. The female is a duller brown colour with less distinct white wing bars. House sparrows have a conical bill for eating seeds, but are adaptable and intelligent birds that will feed on almost any food in towns and cities.*

- **The snow finch** lives high in mountain ranges and makes its nest on mountain ledges at altitudes of 5000 m.
- **The desert sparrow** makes a nest of grass and twigs, often in a wall, and lays between two and five eggs.
- **The house sparrow** originally came from Southwest Asia, but has spread throughout the world. It feeds mainly on seeds, but also eats some insects and scraps put out on bird tables.
- **House sparrows** rarely nest away from human habitation.
- **The house sparrow** was introduced into Brooklyn, New York, in 1851, and San Francisco and Salt Lake City in the 1870s. It is now common across all of North America except Alaska and far northern Canada.
- **One pair of house sparrows** may raise an average of 20 chicks in a breeding season. They have a very short incubation period of between ten and 12 days.

DID YOU KNOW?

Sparrows like to bathe and splash in water, and will even bathe in snow in winter.

Auks

- **The auk family** includes 22 species of diving birds, including auks, guillemots, puffins and razorbills. They live in and around the North Pacific, Atlantic and Arctic Oceans.
- **The common guillemot** is the largest of the auks, at about 45 cm long and one kilogram in weight. The least auklet is the smallest auk, at 16 cm long and 90 g.
- **Common guillemots** nest in colonies of thousands, with as many as 70 pairs occupying one square metre.
- **The common guillemot nests** on narrow cliff ledges. Its eggs are pointed, so that if they get knocked, they roll in a circle and do not fall off.
- **The ancient murrelet** is so-called because it develops fine white feathers on its head in the breeding season. These are said to look like the white hairs of an elderly person.
- **The guillemot** can dive to a depth of 100 m as it hunts.

▼ *The red, yellow and blue bill of the puffin fades after the breeding season when the colourful outer scales are shed.*

- **The little auk** nests in cliff crevices and lays one or two eggs, which both parents then incubate.
- **The razorbill** is named after its very sharp bill, which helps it to hold slippery fish and other sea creatures, as well as being a useful means of defence against predators.
- **Razorbill chicks** are only 10–18 days old when they flutter down to the sea from their nests on the cliffs.

DID YOU KNOW?

The puffin flies at up to 88 km/h, with its wings beating 300–400 times a minute.

Bee-eaters and relatives

- **The 27 species of bee-eater** are colourful birds that live in southern Europe, Africa, Asia and Australia.
- **Bee-eaters** catch bees or wasps and kill them by striking them against branches. The birds rub the insects against the branches to get rid of their stings.
- **The European bee-eater** flies some 16,000 km between Europe, where it breeds, and Africa, where it spends the winters.
- **A European bee-eater** eats about 200 bees a day. Its summer diet is mainly bumblebees, and in winter it eats honeybees and dragonflies.
- **The ten species of motmot** live only in forests stretching from Mexico to northern Argentina.
- **Motmots range in size** from the 19-cm-long tody motmot to the 53-cm-long upland motmot.
- **Motmots lay their eggs** in chambers at the ends of burrows dug in earth banks. Both parents incubate the eggs and feed the chicks.
- **The blue-crowned motmot** has two long tail feathers with racquet-shaped tips. The bird swings its tail like a clock's pendulum as it watches for prey.
- **Todies** nest in 30-cm-long tunnels, which they dig with their beaks.
- **The five species of tody** are all insect-eating birds that live in the tropical Caribbean islands.

◀ *Bee-eaters feed mainly on bees, but also catch other flying insects, such as dragonflies.*

Warblers

- **The warbler family** has more than 380 species. Most live in Europe, Africa, Asia and Australasia, but there are a few species in North and South America.
- **Typical warblers** are small birds, with fine, narrowly pointed bills. They have strong feet, which are well-suited to perching.
- **Most warblers** are 9–16 cm long, but the two largest – the South African grassbird and the Australian songlark – are up to 23 cm long.
- **Insects** are the main food of most warblers, but they also eat some fruits, berries and seeds.
- **Chiffchaffs and willow warblers** look almost exactly alike, but their songs are quite different.
- **The willow warbler** is only 11 cm long, but it flies all the way from northern Europe and Siberia to Africa to spend the winter. This is a distance of some 12,000 km.
- **The Aldabra brush warbler**, discovered in 1967, used to live on the Aladabra coral atoll in the Indian Ocean. It became extinct in 1986, possibly because cats, rats and goats were introduced to the island.
- **Sedge warblers** nest in hedges, reeds, coarse grass or even cereal crops. They bind their cup-shaped nests firmly to plant stems.
- **If a willow warbler is disturbed** on her nest, she may pretend to be injured, fluttering away from the nest to lure predators away.

DID YOU KNOW?

The goldcrest and the firecrest are only about 9 cm long, and are Europe's smallest birds. The females make finely woven nests of lichen and cobwebs.

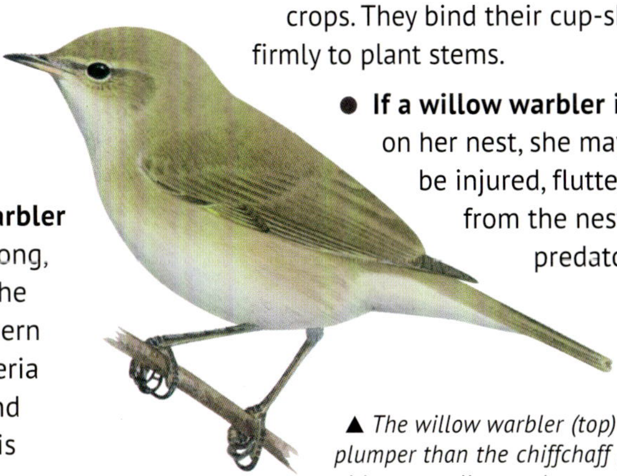

▲ *The willow warbler (top) is generally plumper than the chiffchaff (bottom), with more yellow underparts and paler legs. The chiffchaff has dark legs.*

Pheasants and relatives

▲ *The peafowl is a native of India, Sri Lanka and Pakistan, but it has been introduced in many areas throughout the world. Only the male (the peacock) has the spectacular tail, which does not reach its full glory until the bird is about three years old. It may continue to grow for another two to three years.*

● **All 49 species of wild pheasant** are from Asia, except the Congo peafowl, which lives in the rainforests of central Africa.

● **To attract females**, the male great argus pheasant dances and spreads out its enormously long wing feathers.

● **The male great argus pheasant** plays no part in building a nest or raising the young.

● **The peacock's** wonderful train contains about 200 shimmering feathers, each one decorated with eye-like markings. When courting, the peacock spreads its train and makes it 'shiver' to attract a female.

● **The male pheasant** mates with several females, each of which lays up to 15 eggs in a shallow scrape on the ground. The females incubate the eggs for 23–27 days and the chicks are covered with downy feathers when they hatch out.

● **Most pheasants** nest on the ground, but the five species of tragopan, which live in tropical forests in Asia, nest in trees. They often take over the abandoned nests of other birds.

DID YOU KNOW?

Pheasant chicks begin growing their flight feathers as soon as they hatch out and can fly short distances when they are two weeks old.

● **The satyr tragopan** lives high up on Asian mountains in the summer, but moves down to the lower slopes in winter.

● **The common pheasant** comes from Asia, but is now common in Australia, North America and Europe, where it is shot for sport.

● **Male pheasants** have folds of red skin called wattles, hanging from the sides of their faces. The bright colour helps them attract females.

▶ *The male common pheasant has iridescent plumage on its head, bright red wattles on its face and may have a white neck ring. Originally from Asia, this pheasant has been introduced in Europe and North America, where it is very common.*

Manakins and cotingas

● **Manakins are small birds** that live in Central and South America. There are about 57 species.

● **In his courtship display**, the male wire-tailed manakin brushes the female's chin with his long, wire-like tail feathers.

● **Female manakins** do all the nesting work alone – they build the nest, incubate the eggs and care for the young.

● **Fruit and insects** are the main foods of both manakins and cotingas.

● **The 65 or so cotinga species** live in the forests of Mexico, some Caribbean islands and Central and South America.

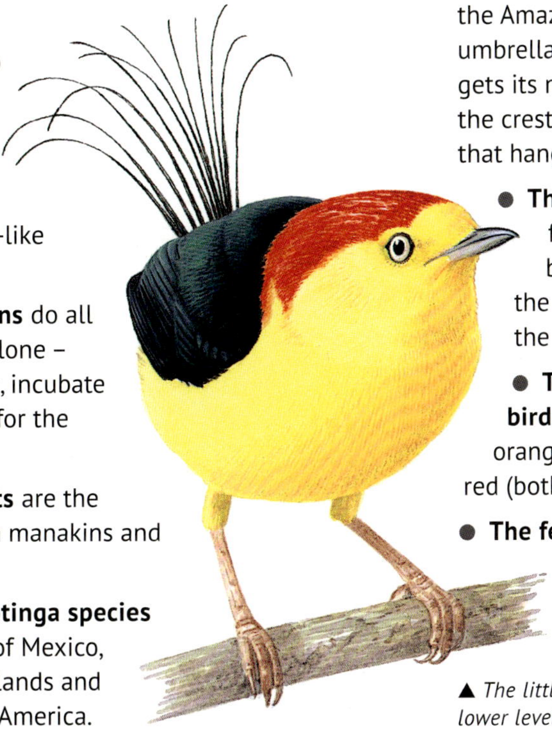

● **The largest of the cotingas** is the Amazonian umbrellabird, which gets its name from the crest of feathers that hangs over its head.

DID YOU KNOW?

The female lovely cotinga destroys her nest after the young leave. This may help to stop predators finding the nest site, which is used year after year.

● **The three-wattled bellbird** (cotinga family) is famous for its loud, explosive calls, which can be heard up to 800 m away. It is named after the three black, worm-like wattles that hang from the sides of its mouth.

● **Two of the most colourful South American birds** are the Guianan cock-of-the-rock, which is orange, and the Andean cock-of-the-rock, which is red (both cotinga family).

● **The female cock-of-the-rock** makes a nest of mud and plants attached to a rock or cave wall, and incubates her eggs alone.

▲ *The little wire-tailed manakin lives in the lower levels of the Amazonian rainforest.*

New World vultures

● **There are seven species of New World vultures** in North and South America. Like Old World vultures (that live in Europe, Asia and Africa), their diet includes carrion, but they have weaker, thinner beaks than Old World vultures.

● **New World vultures** do not build nests, but simply lay their eggs on the ground or on cliff ledges. The parent birds feed their young on regurgitated food.

● **New World** vultures have weak feet, rather like those of chickens. They cannot lift and carry food with their feet, but they do step on their food to hold it in place.

● **The king vulture** has an excellent sense of smell and can find carrion even in dense rainforests.

▲ *The Andean condor is one metre or more in length, with black-and-white plumage and distinctive wing feathers, which are splayed out like fingers during flight.*

▶ *Unusually colourful for a bird of prey, the king vulture has bright red, orange and yellow bare skin and wattles (loose folds of skin) on its head.*

● **King vultures** have stronger beaks than other New World vultures and are able to tear apart large animals.

● **Pairs of turkey vultures** raise their young together. The female usually lays up to three eggs, and both parents help to incubate them for up to 41 days.

● **Black vulture chicks** are looked after by both parents. They do not fly until they are 11 weeks old.

● **Vultures can go for weeks** without food. When they do find carrion, they eat as much as possible.

● **The largest of all birds of prey** is the Andean condor, with a wingspan of more than 3 m.

● **The Andean condor** soars high in the sky on its outstretched wings, sometimes rising to heights of 7000 m over the mountains. It has very keen eyesight and can spot dead animals from great heights.

Shearwaters and petrels

- **The 70 or more species** in the shearwater family include petrels, fulmars and prions. They range from the Antarctic to the Arctic.
- **Unlike most birds**, shearwaters and petrels have a good sense of smell. They have long, tube-shaped nostrils on the tops of their beaks.
- **Shearwaters and petrels** are not tuneful birds, and at night the colonies make a very loud, harsh noise.
- **Shearwaters' legs** are placed far back on their bodies, making them expert swimmers, but preventing them from standing up properly. They move awkwardly on land and have to launch themselves into the air from trees.
- **Largest of the shearwater family** are the giant petrels. At 90 cm long, they are bigger than some albatrosses.
- **Fish and squid** are the main food of shearwaters, but giant petrels also feed on carrion, and can rip apart whales and seals with their powerful beaks.
- **The manx shearwater** lays one egg in a burrow. The male and female take turns incubating it and feeding one another.
- **Young shearwaters** are fed on a rich mixture of regurgitated fish and squid, and may put on weight so quickly that they are soon heavier than their parents.
- **Prions feed on tiny plankton**, which they filter from the water through comblike structures at the sides of their beaks.

DID YOU KNOW?

To defend themselves, shearwaters can spit out food and fish oil to a distance of one metre.

▶ *Storm petrels often patter their feet over the water's surface when hunting for fish.*

Cassowaries and kiwis

- **There are three species of kiwi**, all found only in New Zealand. All are flightless birds that live in burrows.
- **Largest of its family is the brown kiwi**, which is about 55 cm long and weighs up to 3.5 kg.
- **Among all birds**, only the kiwi has nostrils at the end of its beak.
- **The kiwi** is the national symbol of New Zealand, appearing on stamps, coins and bank notes.
- **About 94 percent** of the chicks of the northern brown kiwi die before they are able to breed. Major threats include introduced predators, such as stoats and cats.
- **Cassowaries** in Australia are known to eat the fruits of 75 different types of tree.
- **The female cassowary** mates with several males, laying six to eight eggs each time. The males care for the young.
- **The female dwarf cassowary**, or moruk, is an extremely dangerous bird and will attack anything that comes near the nest with her 10-cm-long claws.
- **During his courtship display**, the male double-wattled cassowary circles the female, using his inflated throat pouch to make booming sounds.

DID YOU KNOW?

A kiwi lays the largest eggs for its size of any bird – each egg weighs 25 percent of its body weight. Females lay up to 100 in a lifetime.

◀ *Cassowaries use the tall, horny casques on their heads to push aside the tangled undergrowth in their rainforest home. Their long, hair-like feathers protect their skin from scratches.*

Storks

- **The 19 species of stork** live in North and South America, Europe, Africa, Asia and Australia.
- **In tropical areas**, storks' nests perched high on buildings can get very warm, so parents cool their young by regurgitating a shower of water over them.
- **The white stork** has long been a symbol of fertility in Europe. Parents used to tell their children that new babies were brought by a stork.
- **Marabou storks** often scavenge on rubbish tips.
- **The tail feathers of marabou storks** were once used to trim hats and dresses.
- **The upper and lower parts** of the openbill stork's beak meet only at the tip. This helps it to hold its favourite food of large snails.
- **When the wood stork's** partly open beak touches a fish under water, it snaps shut in 25 milliseconds – this is one of the fastest reactions of any animal.
- **Male and female white storks** take it in turns to incubate their clutch of three to five eggs. When the partners change shifts, they perform a special bill-clattering display.
- **The adjutant stork** is named after the adjutant army officer, because of its stiff, military-style walk.
- **The rooftop nests** of some European white storks have been used continuously for hundreds of years.

▶ *White storks build huge, bulky nests of branches and sticks, which may be up to 3 m deep. Parent birds add to the nest each year, with the male bringing most of the extra materials.*

Gulls and relatives

- **There are about 50 species** of gull found on shores and islands all over the world.
- **The great skua** is a pirate – it chases other birds and forces them to give up their prey in mid-air.
- **The snowy sheathbill** scavenges for food on Antarctic research bases, and also steals eggs and chicks from penguin colonies.
- **Arctic glaucous and ivory gulls** sometimes feed on the faeces of marine mammals.
- **At up to 79 cm long**, the great black-backed gull is the giant of the gull group. The little gull is one of the smallest, at 28 cm long.
- **The Arctic explorer** James Clark Ross discovered Ross's gull in the 19th century.
- **Skuas, also called jaegers**, usually lay two eggs in a shallow, moss-lined nest on the ground. Both parents incubate the eggs and feed the young, which can fend for themselves after about seven weeks.

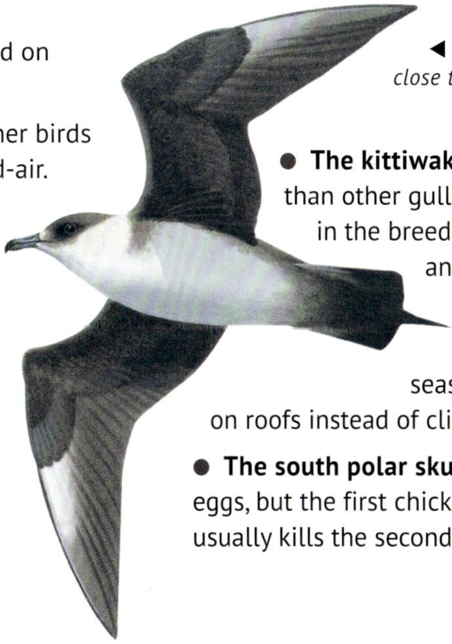

◀ *Skuas are found in marine habitats close to Antarctica and the Arctic.*

- **The kittiwake** spends much more time at sea than other gulls, and usually only comes to land in the breeding season. It has very short legs and rarely walks.
- **Herring gulls** have learned that they can find food in seaside towns, and many now nest on roofs instead of cliff ledges.
- **The south polar skua** lays two eggs, but the first chick to hatch usually kills the second.

▶ *The kittiwake builds a nest of seaweed lined with grass. Both parents sit on the nest for about four weeks to incubate the eggs.*

Jacamars and relatives

- **Jacamars live** in Central and South America.
- **They nest in tunnels** made in the ground or in termite mounds, and lay two to four eggs, which they incubate for 20–23 days.

- **A jacamar** snaps up an insect in the air, then returns to its perch and bangs the insect against a branch to kill it before eating it.
- **Brightly coloured barbets** live in tropical forests and woodlands in Africa, Asia and South America.
- **Biggest of the 83 species of barbet** is the toucan barbet, at 20 cm long. It lives in mountain forests in the northern part of South America.
- **The double-toothed barbet** is named after the two sharp points on the top part of its bill.

◀ *The crested barbet of southern Africa usually searches for food on the ground. It roosts in holes in trees.*

▶ *At 30 cm long, the great jacamar is the largest of the 17 species of jacamar. Its beak alone is almost 5 cm long.*

- **Many barbet** pairs sing together to keep their relationship close. One bird starts to sing, then stops, and the other bird continues the song within a fraction of a second.
- **There are about 35 species of puffbird** living in Mexico and Central and South America.
- **The white-fronted nunbird** (puffbird family) digs a nesting burrow about one metre long. The bird lays its eggs in a chamber at the end of the burrow.

DID YOU KNOW?

At night, the white-whiskered puffbird seals the entrance to its nest burrow with green leaves.

Drongos and relatives

- **The greater racquet-tailed drongo** has two long, wire-like tail feathers with twisted tips that make a humming noise as the bird flies.
- **The pied currawong** (Australian butcherbird family) attacks other birds and takes their young from their nests.
- **The 25 species of Old World oriole** live in Europe and parts of Asia, Africa and Australia. They are mainly tree-dwellers, feeding on insects, seeds and fruit.
- **The golden oriole** makes a neat, cup-shaped nest that it binds to two supporting twigs. It lays three to four eggs.
- **The figbird** (oriole family) is a forest fruit-eater, but is now also common in towns.
- **There are two surviving species** of New Zealand wattlebirds – the kokako and the saddleback. The saddleback lives only on offshore islands that have been cleared of predators.
- **The huia**, a species of wattlebird from New Zealand, is now extinct.
- **Australia and New Guinea** are home to the ten species of insect-eating bell-magpies.
- **Australian mud-nesters** work together to build nests of mud on the branches of trees.
- **Wood swallows**, found in Australasia and Southeast Asia, feed mostly on insects, but also drink nectar.

▶ *The black-headed oriole builds a hanging nest in a tree, woven partly from fresh green grass. This shy American bird travels in pairs, even out of the nesting season.*

Ibises and relatives

- **Ibises and spoonbills** are an ancient group of birds – fossils of their ancestors have been found that date back 60 million years.
- **The spoonbill's beak** has a spoon-shaped tip that it uses to search shallow water for fish and small creatures.
- **At 1.4 m in height** and weighing about 4 kg, the greater flamingo is the largest of the five species of flamingo.
- **The greater flamingo** has a huge wingspan of 140–165 cm.
- **The flamingo** feeds by forcing mud and water through bristly plates at each side of its beak with its tongue. Tiny creatures, algae and other food particles are trapped and swallowed.
- **Until their beaks have developed fully**, young flamingos feed on a milky substance from their parents' throats.
- **The glossy ibis** makes its nest in a reedbed or tree, and lays three or four eggs. The female does most of the incubation, but the male helps to rear the young.
- **Flamingos sleep** standing on one leg, with the other leg folded up and tucked underneath the body and the head laid over the back.
- **When young flamingos** are able to walk around, they gather into small flocks, or crèches, which the adults take turn to guard from predators.

▲ *The scarlet ibis is one of the most striking birds in the world with its deep red plumage and black tail feathers.*

DID YOU KNOW?

Young flamingos have grey feathers at first. Adult birds get their pink colour from pigments in the algae that they eat.

▼ *The greater flamingo lives in huge flocks around lakes and deltas in Europe, Asia, parts of Africa, the Caribbean and Central America. It may live to be at least 50 years old.*

Rheas and tinamous

- **The largest bird in South America** is the greater rhea, which stands 1.5 m tall and weighs up to 25 kg.
- **Rheas feed mostly on plants**, but will also eat insects and even lizards when they can.
- **Flocks of rheas** can number between five and 50 birds.
- **If threatened**, a rhea lies flat on the ground with its head stretched out in an attempt to hide.
- **Rhea feathers** are used to make feather dusters, for sale mainly in the USA and Japan.

▶ *Flocks of rheas live on the pampas grasslands and in open woodland in southeastern South America.*

- **Tinamous are small grassland birds.** The 45 or so species of tinamou all live in Central and South America.
- **Most tinamous** can fly, if only for short distances, but they tend to run or hide rather than take to the air.
- **Tinamous** generally eat fruit, seeds and other plant matter, but some species also eat insects.
- **Female tinamous** lay eggs in the nests of more than one male. Males incubate the eggs and feed the chicks.

DID YOU KNOW?

Male rheas mate with as many as 15 females, all of which lay eggs in the male's large nest.

Gannets and boobies

- **There are three species of gannet** and six species of booby. Boobies generally live in tropical and subtropical areas, while gannets live in cooler, temperate parts of the world.
- **A seabird, the gannet** plunges 30 m or so through the air and dives into the water to catch prey such as herring and mackerel.

▼ *Cape gannets reinforce their pair bond by 'fencing' with their bills. Both birds then help each other to build a nest and defend their territory.*

- **A specially strengthened skull** helps cushion the impact of the gannet's high-speed dive into water.
- **Gannets usually** lay just one egg, which both parents help to incubate for 43–45 days. They feed their chick with regurgitated food for up to 13 weeks.
- **When one gannet parent** arrives at the nest to take over incubating the egg, it presents its mate with a piece of seaweed, which is then added to the nest.
- **Young gannets** and boobies are kept warm on their mother's feet for their first few weeks.
- **Boobies were given** their common name because they were so easy for sailors to catch and kill.
- **The male blue-footed booby** attracts a mate by dancing and holding up his brightly coloured feet as it struts about.
- **Boobies spend** the majority of their time at sea, only landing to breed and rear their young.
- **At up to 86 cm long** and with a wingspan of 152 cm, the masked booby is the largest of the boobies.

Pelicans

▲ *Pelicans are often found in large colonies, particularly during the breeding season.*

- **All four of a pelican's toes** are joined together by a web of skin, which helps the birds to paddle along when swimming.
- **There are two main groups** of pelicans: white pelicans, which nest on the ground, and grey or brown pelicans, which nest in trees. The Peruvian pelican nests on rocks by the sea.
- **The great white pelican** catches about 1.2 kg of fish a day in its large throat pouch.
- **The brown pelican** dives from a height of 15 m above the water to catch fish below the surface.
- **There are seven species** of pelican. Most live and feed around fresh water, but the brown pelican is a coastal seabird.
- **One of the largest pelicans** is the Australian pelican, which is up to 180 cm long and weighs about 15 kg.
- **The white pelican** lays one or two eggs in a nest mound on the ground. Both parents incubate the eggs and care for the young.
- **Pelican chicks** are able to stand at three weeks old and can fly at 10–12 weeks old.
- **White pelicans** work as a group to herd fish into a shoal by swimming around them in a horseshoe formation. Then they scoop up pouchfuls of fish with their large beaks.
- **In flight**, a pelican flaps its wings 1.3 times a second. This is one of the slowest wingbeat speeds of any bird.

Buzzards and kites

- **One of the most common** of all birds of prey is the black kite, which lives throughout most of Europe, Africa, Asia and Australia.
- **The black kite** is a scavenger as well as a hunter. It will take food from dustbins and even market stalls.
- **The red kite** often takes over the old nest of a raven.
- **Hundreds of years ago**, red kites were commonly seen on the Tudor streets of London, England, where they scavenged from the city's rubbish heaps. Nowadays, the red kite lives only in the countryside in the UK and is a rare bird.
- **Kites have** distinctive forked tails. This shape works like a rudder, helping the kite to change direction quickly and allowing it to move around obstacles with ease.
- **The American swallow-tailed kite** has a tail shaped like that of a real swallow. It often behaves in a similar way, catching flying insects and skimming the water's surface to drink and bathe.
- **A buzzard** can spot a rabbit popping up out of its burrow from more than 3 km away.
- **The rough-legged buzzard** is common over open tundra in the far north. It preys on rodents and rabbits.
- **In spring**, the Eurasian buzzard has a spectacular courtship display. Males and females pass sticks to each other in mid-air and sometimes lock their feet together as they tumble down to the ground.
- **Jackal buzzards** often feed on carrion by the roadside in Africa, even flying between the cars.

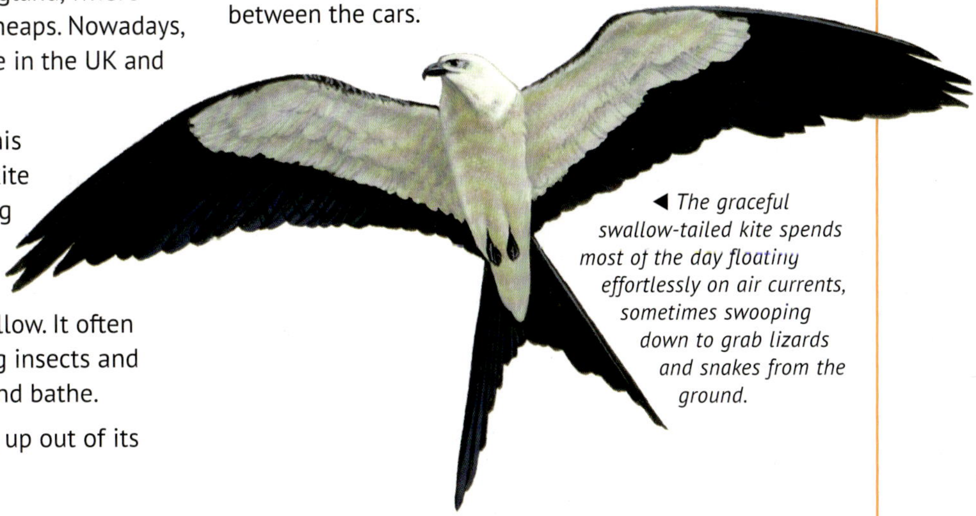
◀ *The graceful swallow-tailed kite spends most of the day floating effortlessly on air currents, sometimes swooping down to grab lizards and snakes from the ground.*

Toucans and honeyguides

● **There are about 40 species of toucan**. They live in Mexico and Central and South America.

● **Toucans feed** mostly on fruit, which they pluck from branches with their long beaks. They also eat some insects and small animals, such as lizards.

● **Although a toucan's beak is large**, it is not heavy. The beak is made of a lightweight material with a honeycomb structure.

● **They usually nest** in tree holes. The female lays two to four eggs and the male helps to incubate them, which takes about 15 days.

● **When toucans first hatch**, they have spiky ankle pads, which help to protect their feet from the rough wood and piles of discarded seeds inside their nesting hole.

● **At 61 cm in length**, the toco toucan is the largest toucan. Its colourful beak alone is up to 20 cm long.

● **There are about 15 species of honeyguide**. Most live in forests and woodlands in Africa, but there are a few species resident in Asia.

● **Honeyguides are the only birds** that are able to feed on the wax from bees' nests, as well as on the insects themselves.

▲ *The pallid honeyguide – seen here feasting on beeswax – is a small bird, on average just 13 cm in length and weighing less than 20 g.*

● **The black-throated honeyguide** likes to feed on bees and their larvae. When it finds a bees' nest, it leads another creature, such as a honey badger, to the nest and waits while the animal breaks into the nest to feed on the honey. The honeyguide then has its share.

DID YOU KNOW?

Toucans are noisy creatures – their loud squawks can be heard nearly one kilometre away.

▼ *The toco toucan of Brazil is the best-known of the toucans. As well as eating fruit, insects, frogs and small reptiles, it will sometimes perch on a branch near another bird's nest to steal the eggs or chicks.*

Woodpeckers

● **The 200 or so species** of woodpecker live all over the world, except in Antarctica, Madagascar and Australia.

● **Woodpeckers feed** by drilling into tree bark with their sharp beaks, and then inserting their long tongues into the holes to pick out insects living beneath the bark.

● **A woodpecker's tongue** is well-adapted for catching insects. It is so long that the woodpecker can stick it out beyond the tip of its beak. The tongue's sticky coating easily mops up prey.

● **Woodpeckers drum on tree trunks** with their beaks to signal their ownership of territory or their readiness to mate. The great spotted woodpecker has been timed making 20 strikes a second.

● **Woodpeckers nest** in holes in trees. They may use a hole from a previous year, or dig out a new one for their two to 12 eggs.

◀ *The great spotted woodpecker has red feathers under its tail and white shoulder patches. The male also has a red patch on the back of its head (nape).*

● **A woodpecker** may eat as many as 1000 ants in one feeding session.

● **The imperial woodpecker** is thought to be critically endangered and may be extinct. At 55 cm long, it is the biggest of its family, while the little scaled piculet is only 8 cm long.

● **The sapsucker** (woodpecker family) feeds on sweet, sugary sap. It bores a hole in a tree and laps up the sap that oozes out.

● **As well as insects**, the great spotted woodpecker eats the eggs and young of other birds.

● **During autumn**, the acorn woodpecker of North America bores as many as 400 holes in tree trunks and puts an acorn in each one, to store for the winter.

Grassland birds

● **A variety** of seed and insect-eating birds live in grasslands. Some of them follow herds of grazing animals and catch the insects disturbed by their feet.

● **One of the biggest creatures** on the South American pampas is the flightless rhea, which feeds mainly on grass. Their long legs help them see over tall grasses and watch for predators.

● **The mottled patterns** on the crested tinamou's feathers help to camouflage it from predators. It is not good at flying, but can run fast for short distances.

● **The burrowing owl** nests in burrows in the ground, either digging its own with its claws, or taking over the burrows of other animals, such as prairie dogs.

● **The South American grasslands** are home to the red-legged seriema, a fast-running bird that eats virtually anything it can find, including snakes.

● **The yellow-billed oxpecker** of the African grasslands sits on buffaloes' backs, pulling ticks from their skin.

▶ *Marabou storks are the only storks to eat carrion (dead animals). They often gather with vultures at animal carcasses, where the vultures give way to these aggressive storks, letting them eat first.*

● **Flocks of one million or more red-billed quelea** are seen moving like vast clouds over southern Africa.

● **Cattle egrets** accompany large grassland mammals, feeding on the insects that live on or around them.

● **Many honeyguides** lay their eggs in the nests of other birds, such as woodpeckers. When they hatch, the young honeyguides kill the chicks of the host bird.

● **Vultures feed** on grassland animals when they die. Their bare heads and necks allow them to feed inside animal carcasses without getting their feathers dirty.

Monarchs and relatives

- **Monarch flycatchers** feed mainly on insects, darting out to catch them in the air and then taking them back to a perch to eat.
- **The male** African paradise flycatcher's tail feathers are up to 20 cm long – much longer than its body.
- **The yellow-breasted boatbill**, a monarch flycatcher, has a broad beak with a hooked tip, which it uses to pick small insects off leaves.
- **The male yellow-breasted boatbill** builds most of the nest, using vine tendrils to hang it from a fork in a tree branch.
- **During the breeding season**, willie wagtails are very aggressive and will attack much larger predators.
- **The pied fantail's beak** is ringed with bristles that may help the bird to trap insect prey.
- **The white-browed fantail** flicks its wings and tail to disturb insects from crevices in old tree bark.
- **The paradise flycatcher** makes a neat nest of lichens and plant roots, held together with spiders' webs, on a slender branch or twig.
- **Black-naped blue monarchs** take insect prey back to a perch and hold it under one foot as they break it in pieces.

DID YOU KNOW?

According to Aboriginal folklore, the willie wagtail (a fantail), is a gossipy bird that spreads secrets.

▶ *Black-naped blue monarchs lay three to four eggs in a nest of grass and bark, bound together with spiders' webs. The nest is usually built on a forked branch.*

Megapodes and guans

- **There are more than 20 species of megapodes** – ground-living birds found in Australia and some Pacific islands. Megapode means 'large foot'.
- **The mallee fowl** (a megapode) lays its eggs in a huge mound of rotting leaves and sand, which acts as an incubator. The mound can be up to 11 m across and 5 m high.
- **One megapode in Tonga** makes a nest of warm volcanic sands and soil, which keeps its eggs warm.
- **The male mallee fowl** checks the temperature of its nest mounds with its beak and keeps it a constant 33°C by adding or removing material.
- **Mallee fowl chicks** must dig their way out of their nest mound, and are able to fly a few hours later.
- **To attract females**, the male crested guan flaps its wings briefly at over twice the normal speed, making a whirring sound as it flies.
- **Now rare**, the white-winged guan lives in the Andean foothills, feeding on fruit, berries, leaves and insects.
- **The 45 species of guan and curassow** live from the southern USA to northern Argentina.
- **The great curassow** is 95 cm long and weighs 4.8 kg.
- **True to its name**, the nocturnal curassow comes out at night to sing and feed on fruit.

◀ *The crested guan lives in the forests of Central America. It lives mainly in trees and walks or runs along the branches to look for wild figs, berries and leaves to eat.*

Owls

● **There are more** than 200 species of owl and they live in most parts of the world except the far north and Antarctica.

● **Owls range** in size from the elf owl, at only 12–14 cm long, to the Eurasian eagle owl, at 71 cm long.

● **The soft, fluffy edges** of an owl's feathers help to reduce flight noise, so it can hunt almost silently.

● **The 'disc' of feathers** on an owl's face helps to focus sounds, enabling it to hear the noises made by its prey in the dark.

● **Owls swallow their prey**, such as mice and insects, whole.

● **Owls cannot digest** the bones, fur and feathers of their prey, so they cough them up in the form of large pellets.

◀ *The huge great grey owl has a wingspan of about 1.5 m. It feeds largely on tiny voles. This owl defends its nest hole fiercely and will even attack people if it feels threatened.*

● **Owls are divided** into two main groups – the 18 species of barn owls, grass owls and the bay owl, and the nearly 200 species of typical owls.

● **Barn owls, grass owls and the bay owl** have a heart-shaped disc on their faces, rather than the round disc of typical owls.

● **Grass owls** come from Africa, Southeast Asia and Australia. They are very similar to barn owls but have longer legs.

● **Eagle owls** (a typical owl) have a wingspan of about 2 m and are twice the size of barn owls. They live for up to 40 years in the wild.

▶ *A barn owl swoops silently down onto its unsuspecting prey, holding out its sharp talons to seize its meal.*

Buntings and tanagers

- **More than three-quarters** of all bunting species live in the Americas. There are about 60 species in North America alone.
- **Buntings have a stout**, cone-shaped bill for crushing seeds and removing the husks around the outside. The top and bottom parts of the bill can be moved sideways in some species, such as juncos.
- **The little snow bunting** breeds in northern Greenland, further north than any other bird.
- **The Galápagos finches** (bunting family) are a group of closely related species. The similarities and differences between them were important evidence for Charles Darwin's theory of evolution.
- **The Lapland bunting** migrates to the Arctic tundra to nest in the summer months. These buntings often nest in small groups so they can warn each other of danger.
- **The 240 species in the tanager family** include flowerpiercers, honeycreepers and euphonias. All live in North and South America.
- **One tanager**, the glossy flowerpiercer, has a hooked, upwards-curving beak that it uses to pierce the bases of tubular flowers so it can feed on the nectar inside.
- **The western tanager** lines its nest of twigs and moss with fine roots and animal hair. The female incubates three to five eggs.
- **Some tanagers follow columns of army ants** in forests, and snap up the insects that flee the ants' path.
- **Groups of hooded mountain tanagers** feed together, calling loudly at dawn to tell other groups of tanagers where they are.

◀ *Adult male snow buntings have black-and-white feathers in summer, but turn brown and white in winter.*

Hornbills

- **There are about** 57 species of hornbill – 23 in Africa and 34 in Southeast Asia. Most live among trees.
- **Most hornbills** feed mainly on fruit, but the two ground hornbills catch and eat small animals.
- **All hornbills** have large beaks. In many species the beak is topped with a casque (a kind of helmet) made of keratin and bone.
- **The helmeted hornbill** has a dense, ivory-like casque, which makes up about 10 percent of the bird's weight.
- **Hornbills are the only birds** in which two neck vertebrae are fused, possibly to help support the weight of the beak.

▶ *The great Indian hornbill has a big yellow casque and a loud, roaring call. When it flies, its large wings make a whooshing sound.*

- **Hornbills range** from 30–120 cm in size. The largest of the family is the southern ground hornbill and the smallest is the black dwarf hornbill.
- **Hornbills live** for 35–40 years in the wild and up to 50 years in captivity in zoos.
- **The eastern yellow-billed hornbill** and the dwarf mongoose have an unusual relationship – they help each other find food and watch out for predators.
- **In parts of South Africa**, the southern ground hornbill is traditionally considered sacred and is protected.
- **A male hornbill** may carry more than 60 small fruits at a time to its nest to regurgitate for its young.

◀ *The yellow-billed hornbill is 50 cm long and lives in southern Africa.*

Bulbuls and relatives

- **There are about 120 species of bulbul** found in Africa and southern Asia, usually in forests, although some bulbuls have adapted to built-up areas.
- **Bulbuls** range in size from 14–23 cm, and eat mainly insects and fruit.
- **The bearded greenbul** lives in African rainforests and has a beautiful whistling call, that it uses to keep in touch with others of its species in the dense jungle.
- **Despite its small size**, the red-vented bulbul is an aggressive bird. In Asia, people sometimes bet on a male bird to win a fight against another male.

DID YOU KNOW?

When courting, the male common iora fluffs up its feathers, leaps into the air and tumbles back to its perch again.

- **The yellow-vented bulbul** makes a nest of twigs, leaves and vine stems, often in a garden or on a balcony. Both parents incubate the two to five eggs and care for the young.

▼ *The red-whiskered bulbul is a common sight in gardens and cultivated land in India, south China and Southeast Asia.*

- **The two species of fairy bluebirds** live in Asia, feeding on fruit, nectar and some insects.
- **Male fairy bluebirds** have bright-blue upperparts. Females are a dull greenish-blue with dark markings.
- **Leafbirds** lay two to three eggs in a cup-shaped nest made in the trees.
- **The common iora** (a leafbird) scurries through trees searching for insects. It sometimes eats mistletoe and other berries.

▶ *The fairy bluebird spends most of its time in trees, feeding on nectar and ripe fruit, especially figs.*

Old World vultures

- **There are about** 15 species of Old World vulture living in southern Europe, Africa and Asia. (These continents are known as the 'Old World', while North and South America are known as the 'New World'.)
- **Most vultures** are scavengers rather than hunters – they feed on the carcasses of dead animals.
- **The lack of feathers** on a vulture's head means it does not have to do lots of preening after it has plunged its beak deep into a carcass to feed.

▼ *The lappet-faced vulture has a bigger beak than any other bird of prey.*

DID YOU KNOW?

The bearded vulture drops bones from a great height to smash them. It then swallows the bone fragments, which are broken down by powerful acids in its stomach.

- **Different species** of vulture eat different parts of a body – bearded vultures (lammergeiers) even eat the bones of their prey.
- **In hot weather**, some vultures cool down by squirting urine onto their legs.
- **Unlike most birds of prey**, the palm-nut vulture is mostly vegetarian. Its main food is the husk of the oil palm fruit, although it also eats fish, frogs and other small creatures.
- **The European black vulture** is the biggest of all the Old World vultures. It weighs up to 12 kg and has a wingspan of over 2.75 m.
- **The female white-backed vulture** lays one egg in a large stick nest made high in a tree. She incubates the egg for 56 days, being fed by the male.
- **The lappet-faced vulture** is the largest vulture in Africa – it measures about one metre long and has a huge 2.8 m wingspan.

Herons and bitterns

- **There are about 60 species** of heron and bittern.
- **The great blue heron** makes a platform nest of twigs, often high in a tree. The four eggs take 25–29 days to hatch.
- **Like most herons**, the grey heron feeds on fish and frogs, which it catches with swift stabs of its beak.

▼ *Herons are efficient hunters, using their long, sharp beaks to stab at fish.*

- **When hunting**, the black heron holds its wings over its head like a sunshade. This may help the bird spot fish, or the patch of shade may attract fish to the area.

DID YOU KNOW?

The green-backed heron of Japan tempts fish with bits of 'bait' such as bread or feathers.

- **Purple herons** have extra-long toes, which help them to walk over floating plants without sinking into the water.
- **The loud booming call** made by the male bittern in the breeding season can be heard up to 5 km away.
- **The brown mottled plumage** of bitterns blends in with the reeds in the marshes where they live. When threatened, bitterns often point their bills to the sky and even sway to and fro like reeds in the wind.
- **Cattle egrets** (a type of heron) nest in colonies – there may be more than 100 nests close together in one tree.
- **Cattle egrets** often gather around large grazing animals to feed on the insects and other small animals disturbed by their feet.

Hummingbirds

- **The 320 or so species of hummingbird** live in North, Central and South America. Largest is the giant hummingbird, at about 20 cm long and weighing 20 g.
- **A hummingbird** hovers in front of flowers to collect nectar with its tongue, which has a brush-like tip.
- **Hummingbirds** are the only birds able to fly backwards as well as forwards while they are hovering.
- **To fuel its energy needs**, a hummingbird must eat at least half its weight in food each day.

▶ *The sword-billed hummingbird uses its extraordinary bill to reach deep inside trumpet-shaped flowers and feed on the insects and nectar.*

▼ *The crimson topaz hummingbird feeds on flowers high up in the canopy of the Amazon rainforest. The male (shown here) is more colourful than the female and has long tail feathers that cross over half way down.*

- **Hummingbirds are so active** that their hearts beat more than 1200 times a minute.
- **The bee hummingbird** is not much bigger than a bumblebee and, at 6 cm long, is probably the world's smallest bird.
- **Tiny ruby-throated hummingbirds** migrate each autumn from the USA, across the Gulf of Mexico, to Central America. Although only 9 cm long, the bird flies at a speed of about 44 km/h.
- **Hummingbirds** have the fewest feathers of any birds with about 1000–1500 in total.
- **A hummingbird's flight muscles** make up a total of 25–30 percent of its overall weight.
- **Despite their size**, hummingbirds will chase away rivals or attack large predators, such as crows, hawks and jays.

Nuthatches

● **The 24 or so species of nuthatch** live in North America, Europe, north Africa, Asia and Australasia.

● **Nuthatches make the entrance** to their nest hole smaller by plastering it in with mud, which dries to create a rock-hard surface.

● **Insects and spiders** are the main food of nuthatches, but in autumn the birds store nuts and seeds for the winter.

● **A nuthatch** wedges nuts, such as acorns, into crevices in tree bark and then hammers them open with its chisel-like bill.

● **The largest nuthatch** is the giant nuthatch, which is up to 20 cm in length.

● **The red-breasted nuthatch** paints the entrance of its tree hole nest with sticky pine resin. This may stop insects and other creatures getting into the nest, but the birds also have to take care not to get their own feathers stuck.

● **Red-breasted nuthatches** sometimes store the seeds from conifer tree cones as a food supply to last them through the winter.

▶ *A Eurasian nuthatch takes a nut from a garden bird feeder.*

● **The Eurasian nuthatch's** six to nine eggs hatch after 14–18 days.

● **Eurasian nuthatches** usually nest in old woodpecker holes near the tops of tall trees. They line the nest hole with flakes of bark and lichens.

● **The Kabylie nuthatch** digs its own nest holes in soft and rotten wood.

Finfoots and relatives

● **The sunbittern** gets its name from the rich, red-orange markings on its wings, which look like the colours of the sky at sunset.

● **The only species in its family**, the sunbittern lives in jungles and swamps in Central and South America.

● **The sunbittern** lays two eggs in a tree nest made of leaves and plant stems. Both parents take turns to incubate the eggs and care for the chicks.

● **Finfoots are aquatic birds** that feed in the water on fish, frogs and shellfish. There is one species each in Africa, Southeast Asia and Central and South America.

● **The sungrebe** (finfoot family) has an unusual way of caring for its young. The male bird carries its chicks in two skin pouches beneath its wings while they complete their development. It can even carry them while flying.

● **The two species of seriema** live in South America. They eat snakes, banging the snakes' heads on the ground to kill them.

● **Seriemas can fly**, but prefer to escape danger by running fast over the grassy plains where they live.

● **Sungrebes and finfoots** have lobed feet, which help them swim.

● **The rare kagu** lives only in the forests and shrubland of the Pacific island of New Caledonia. It has structures covering its nostrils, which are not found in any other bird.

● **The kagu** is almost flightless, but can use its wings to glide away from danger or move quickly through the forest. It also uses its wings for display.

▼ *A sunbittern spreads its wings, showing off its beautiful plumage.*

Desert birds

▲ *Elf owls shelter from the heat of the day in giant cacti, inside holes that are dug out by other birds, such as the gila woodpecker.*

- **With few trees and bushes to sit in**, desert birds spend most of their lives on the ground.
- **The mourning dove** is a desert bird of the southwestern USA. A fast flier, it often travels great distances to find food and water.
- **Water is precious** in the desert. The roadrunner, a member of the cuckoo family, reabsorbs water from its faeces before excretion.
- **The gila woodpecker** digs out a nesting hole in the stem of a desert cactus. It is much cooler inside the cactus and the spines help to protect the woodpecker's young from predators.
- **The smallest owl** in the world, the elf owl, comes out at night to escape the heat of the day.
- **The elf owl** feeds mainly on insects, but will also eat desert scorpions, taking out the sting before eating its meal.
- **Insects are a favourite food** of many desert birds, but some catch small mammals and others eat seeds.
- **Most desert birds** are active at dawn and towards sunset, resting in shade for much of the day.
- **The sandgrouse** travels up to 50 km a day to fetch water for its young chicks in the nest. A male sandgrouse soaks its belly feathers at a desert waterhole, then flies back to its nest so the chicks can drink from its plumage.
- **Budgerigars roam** the deserts of the Australian outback in flocks of thousands. They fly hundreds of kilometres in search of water.

Mesites and relatives

▲ *The secretive white-breasted mesite searches for insects among the leaves on the forest floor. It lives in family groups, resting in the shade during the day and perching on low branches at night.*

- **Mesites are thrushlike birds** that search for insects on the forest floor. They do have wings, but rarely fly.
- **Three species of mesite** live on the island of Madagascar, but they are all rare and threatened by habitat destruction.
- **The 15 species of buttonquail** live in parts of Europe, Africa, Asia, Australia and some Pacific islands, usually on grassland. Although they look like quails, they are not related.
- **Shy little birds**, buttonquails lurk among low-growing plants feeding on seeds and insects.
- **The female buttonquail** is larger than the male. It mates with several males and leaves each to incubate the clutch of eggs and rear the young.
- **Buttonquail young** can fly two weeks after hatching, and start to breed when only four to five months old.

◀ *The little buttonquail lives in southern Europe, Africa and parts of Asia. It is 13–15 cm long.*

- **Buttonquails** are sometimes known as hemipode, or half-footed, quails, because they lack rear toes.
- **The plains-wanderer** lives on the dry plains of central Australia. If in danger, it stays very still.
- **Plains-wanderers** are now rare because so much of the grassland where they live and feed has been cleared for agriculture. There may be fewer than 8000 left in the wild.
- **The female plains-wanderer** lays four eggs, usually in a nest made in a hollow on the ground, but it is the male that incubates the eggs and rears the young.

Cuckoos and relatives

- **The Eurasian cuckoo** is a 'brood parasite' – it lays its eggs in the nests of other birds.
- **A female Eurasian cuckoo** removes an egg from another bird's nest before laying her own.
- **Most birds** take several minutes to lay an egg, but the cuckoo lays one in just ten seconds, so it can quickly take advantage of any brief absence of the host bird.
- **The eggs of brood parasite cuckoos** vary in colour and markings according to the host they use. A Eurasian cuckoo's eggs may resemble those of reed warblers, garden warblers or redstarts.

▶ The hoatzin, from northern South America, has a large plume on its head and, unlike other birds, feeds almost entirely on leaves.

- **Of the 140 or so species of cuckoo**, only about 59 lay their eggs in other birds' nests.
- **The hoatzin** is 60 cm in length and lives deep in South America's rainforest.
- **Hoatzin chicks** leave the nest soon after hatching. Two little claws on each of their wings help them clamber about.
- **The 22 species** of turaco live only in Africa. Largest is the 75-cm-long great blue turaco, weighing one kilogram.
- **Turacos feed mostly** on fruit, leaves and flowers, but also catch some insects in the breeding season.
- **The Australian koel** prefers fruit to the creatures, such as caterpillars, eaten by other cuckoos.

◀ A redstart flycatcher busy feeding a cuckoo chick in its nest.

Pittas and relatives

- **The brightly coloured pittas** live in Africa, Southeast Asia and Australia. Pitta is an Indian word meaning 'bird' and was first used in the 1700s.
- **The 26 or so species of pitta** range in size from 15–25 cm. They are known for their use of tools, such as using a stone or a log to break open snail shells.
- **Pittas are said to have the best sense of smell** of any songbird. This may help them find worms and snails in the dim light of the forest floor.
- **The Indian pitta** makes a nest of moss and twigs. Both parents incubate the four to six eggs.
- **The four species of asity** are found only in Madagascar.

▶ Giant pittas are shy birds that live in the forests of Southeast Asia. They are threatened by the destruction of their forest habitat.

- **The wattled false sunbird** (asity family) gets its name from its long, sunbird-like beak. Like the sunbirds, it takes nectar from flowers.
- **The broadbills** of tropical Africa and Southeast Asia are named after their flat bills, which have a very wide gape.
- **Most broadbills** feed on insects, which they catch in the air. Some also eat lizards and frogs.
- **The green broadbill** hangs its nest from a vine and covers it with lichen and spiders' webs.

DID YOU KNOW?

Rainbow pittas put wallaby droppings in and around their nests to disguise their own smell and keep tree snakes away from their eggs.

Mousebirds and trogons

● **The six species of mousebird** are all small, dull-coloured birds that are not related to trogons. They live in Africa to the south of the Sahara.

● **Mousebirds** are named for their habit of scurrying around on the ground like mice, as they search for seeds and leaves to eat.

● **Mousebirds** are plant eaters, feeding on a variety of leaves, buds, flowers and fruits.

● **There are about 37 species of trogon** living in the forests and woodlands of Central America, the Caribbean islands and parts of Africa and Asia.

● **Trogons range in size** from the black-throated trogon, at 23 cm long, to the resplendent quetzal, which measures 33 cm in length.

◀ *Trogons have a wide, hooked bill, which is surrounded by bristles that help them to catch flying insects.*

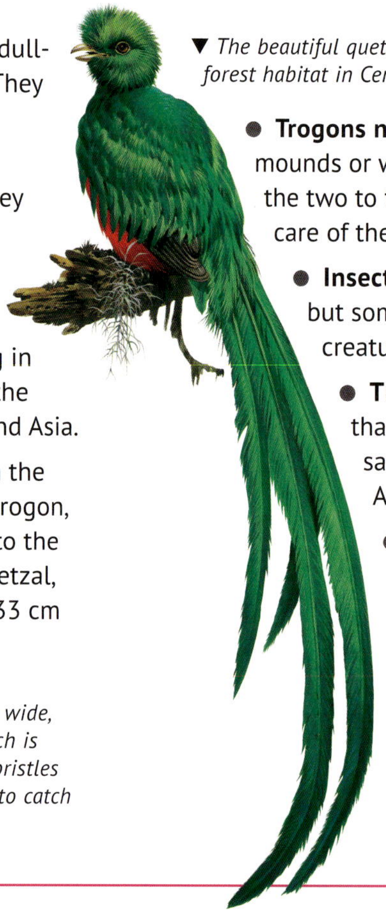

▼ *The beautiful quetzal is becoming rare because much of its forest habitat in Central America has been destroyed.*

● **Trogons nest in tree holes**, old termite mounds or wasps' nests. Both parents incubate the two to four eggs for 17–19 days and take care of the young.

● **Insects are the main food** of trogons, but some also eat fruit and catch creatures, such as lizards.

● **The quetzal** is a species of trogon that lives in Central America. It was sacred to the ancient Maya and Aztec civilizations.

● **The male quetzal's** tail feathers are up to one metre long.

DID YOU KNOW?

The monetary unit of Guatemala is known as the quetzal, after the stunning quetzal – the country's national bird.

Wood warblers and icterids

● **The 118 species of wood warbler** live in North, Central and South America. They are also called New World warblers.

● **All the wood warblers** are fairly small birds. The smallest species is the Lucy's warbler, which is about 11 cm long.

● **Most wood warblers** live and feed in trees, where they use their delicate bills to catch insects.

▼ *Common grackles have highly iridescent plumage. They may seem to have black, blue, purple, green or bronze feathers, depending on the light. They are common near houses, and form large, noisy roosts containing thousands of birds.*

● **Male cerulean warblers** are very aggressive in the breeding season. They attack each other with their feet and bills, while falling through the trees with their wings and tail spread out.

● **Cowbirds** lay their eggs in magnolia warbler nests and the young cowbirds may push the warbler eggs and young out of the nest.

● **The icterid family** contains nearly 100 species of American birds, including blackbirds, the bobolink, meadowlarks, oropendolas, grackles, orioles and cowbirds.

● **The male red-winged blackbird** sings and flashes its brightly coloured 'shoulder pads' to defend its breeding territory.

● **The largest of the 92 species** of icterid is the olive oropendola, which measures 52 cm in length.

● **Male icterids** are generally much larger than females. The male great-tailed grackle is as much as 60 percent heavier than the female.

● **Great-tailed grackles** are big, noisy birds that scavenge on rubbish as well as feeding on insects, grain and fruit. They are common in towns and villages.

Vireos and relatives

▲ *The red-eyed vireo breeds in North America in the summer.*

- **The 43 species of vireo** live in North, Central and South America, and range in size from 10–16 cm.
- **Insects** such as caterpillars and aphids are the main foods of vireos, but some species also eat fruit.
- **When vireos were first named** in the 1800s, people thought they heard the word 'vireo', meaning 'I am green', in the birds' song. In fact most vireos are green.
- **Vireos take about a week** to make their nests. The female makes a cup-shape of spiders' webs and silkworm threads around her body, and then adds plant material such as grass and moss.
- **The black-capped vireo** usually attaches its nest to a forked twig. Both parents incubate the three to five eggs and feed the young.
- **Red-eyed vireo chicks** are naked and helpless when they hatch, but open their eyes after four to five days, and leave the nest after 12 days.
- **Plantcutters get their name** from their large, serrated beaks, used to chop leaves from plants.
- **The three species of plantcutter** live in southern South America. The birds are 17–20 cm long.

◀ *Different species of vireo often live alongside each other in their forest habitats by feeding at different levels.*

- **The sharpbill** of Central and South America picks tiny insects and spiders from leaves.
- **The brown-headed cowbird** often lays its eggs in the nests of vireos, which sometimes throw out the cowbird's eggs.

Endangered birds

- **Over 1200 (one in eight)** bird species are threatened with extinction and 190 species are critically endangered, which means they face a very high risk of extinction in the near future.
- **Some bird families** are especially endangered, such as albatrosses, cranes and parrots.
- **Endangered birds** live all over the world, many in tropical areas, especially in forests and on islands. Island birds are very specialized and not well adapted to deal with human threats.
- **The population of Algerian nuthatches** is less than 2000 pairs. This species is threatened by habitat destruction.
- **Five vultures** that were common across India now face extinction, mainly as a result of being poisoned by a drug in the livestock carcasses they feed on.

▶ *The Indian, or long-billed, vulture is one of the world's 20 most endangered birds. It may be saved from extinction by being bred in captivity and released into the wild.*

- **The only wild population** of whooping cranes exists in Wood Buffalo National Park in Canada.
- **Yellow-eyed penguins** live only in New Zealand and may be the rarest penguins in the world. Their numbers have been dramatically reduced by the destruction of their habitat, as well as introduced predators.
- **White-headed ducks** are one of the rarest birds in the world. A population of 100,000 birds in the early 20th century has been reduced to only 15,000 today.
- **The gorgeted puffleg** (a hummingbird) lives only in a small area of cloud forest in Columbia, but about 8 percent of its habitat is being destroyed every year for farming.
- **Less than 100 breeding pairs** of Madagascar fish eagles are left in the wild. Its habitat has been destroyed and it is persecuted because it competes for fish with people and is hunted for its body parts, which are used in traditional medicines.

1000 SHARK FACTS

All about sharks

◀ *Blue sharks have long, slender bodies and pointed snouts, which slide easily through the water, helping them to swim fast.*

● **Sharks are a type of fish.** They live and breathe underwater and most of them are brilliant swimmers.

● **Sharks have lived** on our planet for over 400 million years, long before dinosaurs or people appeared on Earth.

● **All sharks are carnivores.** This means that they eat meat. Many kinds are fierce hunters and chase after their prey.

● **Most sharks are not dangerous to people.** Only a few types attack people, including the great white shark, tiger shark and bull shark.

● **Sharks are mostly found in seas** and oceans, although a few rare sharks live in rivers.

● **A species** is the name for a particular type of living thing. Sharks of the same species can mate and have offspring (young).

● **There are more than 500** different species of shark, and more than 550 types of batoids (rays, skates, sawfish and guitarfish), which are their close relatives.

● **Many shark species** look similar, with long bodies, triangular fins and lots of sharp teeth. They can range greatly in size – from about the length of a banana to bigger than a bus.

● **Some sharks lay eggs**, but many sharks give birth to live young, which are called pups.

● **Many sharks** and rays are very rare and over 30 percent are in danger of dying out soon, especially river sharks.

Records and statistics

● **The most widespread shark** is the blue shark, found in most of the world's seas and oceans.

● **The brightest luminescent shark** is the cookie-cutter. Its glow is as bright as a reading lamp.

● **The sharks with the flattest bodies** are wobbegong sharks and angelsharks.

● **The bigeye thresher shark** has the biggest eyes in relation to its body size.

● **Shortfin makos** make the highest leaps. They can jump more than 5 m out of the water.

● **The fussiest eaters** of the shark world are bullhead sharks. The diet of some bullheads consists of sea urchins and nothing else.

● **The common thresher shark** has the longest tail compared to its body size. The tail can be up to half of the shark's body length.

● **The fastest shark** is the shortfin mako shark, which reaches speeds of over 50 km/h.

● **The shark with the most poisonous** flesh is the Greenland shark.

● **The longest lifespans** for sharks range from 75 years for the spiny dogfish to perhaps over 100 years for the whale shark and over 300 years for the Greenland shark.

▼ *A thresher shark's tail is up to 1.5 m long. When flicked from side to side, the tail makes a powerful weapon for catching prey.*

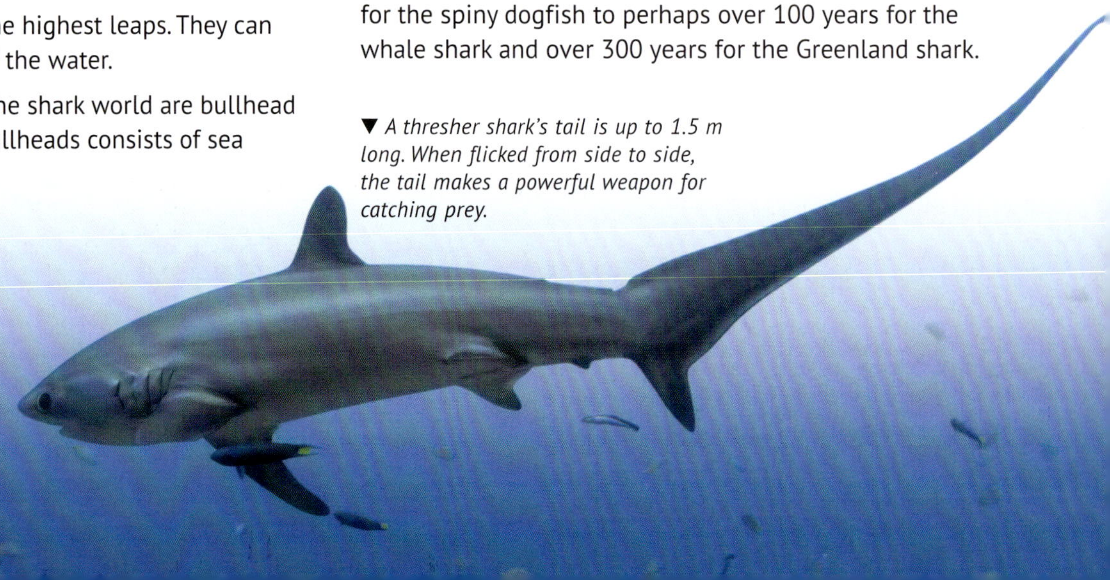

DID YOU KNOW?

Thresher sharks are the second most threatened shark family, after angelsharks.

Big and small

- **The biggest shark** ever, *Megalodon*, is now extinct. This means the species has completely died out. Scientists think *Megalodon* may have weighed almost twice as much as a whale shark.
- **The whale shark** is the biggest living shark. It can measure over 12 m in length – that's as long as a bus! Whale sharks are gentle fish that feed by filtering tiny food particles from the water.
- **The biggest hunting shark** is the great white. Its mouth can measure up to 1.2 m wide – big enough to swallow a seal whole.

DID YOU KNOW?
The smallest sharks would fit into a human hand.

▼ *The gigantic whale shark is the biggest fish in the world.*

- **Most sharks** are medium-sized, measuring 1–3 m in length.
- **The average size** for a shark is very similar to the average size of a human.
- **Although some types** are small, most sharks are still bigger than other kinds of fish.
- **The smallest types** are the spined pygmy shark and the dwarf lanternshark. The dwarf lanternshark is only about 16–19 cm long.
- **The giant lanternshark** is four times longer than these tiny sharks. It grows up to 86 cm long.
- **Smaller sharks** usually feed near the ocean floor, while larger sharks feed in the middle of the ocean and near the surface, where they can hunt larger prey, such as seals.
- **The hammerhead shark** with the biggest 'hammer' is the winghead shark. The width of its hammer is about 50 percent of its body length.
- **The biggest ray** is the oceanic manta ray, which is usually about 7 m wide and 7 m long (including the tail). The biggest mantas are nearly 9 m wide.

▼ *Pygmy sharks are no more than 27 cm long.*

Around the world

- **Sharks are found** in seas and oceans around the world. They are almost all marine fish, which means they live in the salty seas rather than in fresh water.
- **They are most common** around coasts. Many species live in shallow sandy bays, near coral reefs or in the medium-deep water a few kilometres from the shore.
- **Coral reefs** and seaweed forests are good homes for young sharks. They provide them with food and shelter.
- **Species that live** in the open ocean, such as blue sharks and great whites, are known as pelagic sharks.
- **Lots of species live** in warm waters, but a few, such as the Greenland shark, inhabit cold water around the Arctic.
- **Sharks are hardly ever found** in the Southern Ocean around Antarctica – probably because it is too cold.
- **Epaulette sharks** are often found in rockpools. They can move from one pool to another across land by dragging themselves with their strong pectoral fins.
- **Cold water sharks**, such as the frilled shark and goblin shark, often live in very deep water.
- **Some sharks are warm-blooded**. This means they can control their body temperature, so they are able to live in a greater variety of water temperatures than other sharks. The great white shark is warm-blooded.

DID YOU KNOW?

A few sharks, such as bull sharks and river sharks, can survive in fresh (not salty) water. They are able to swim in rivers and lakes.

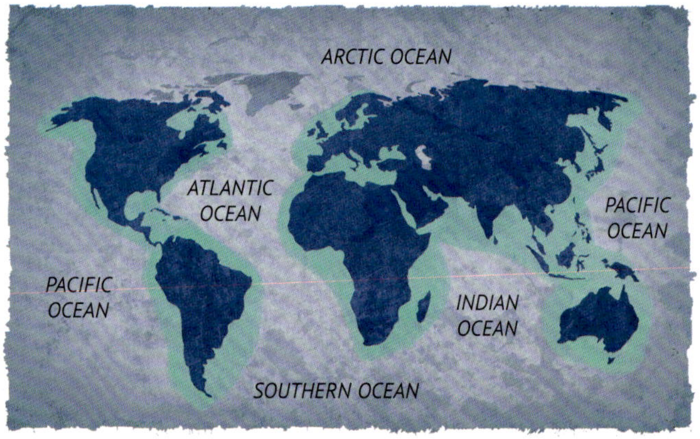

▲ *The green areas on this world map show the parts of the oceans where sharks are most common.*

Tropics to Poles

- **More species of sharks** live in warm or hot tropical oceans than in cold polar waters.
- **Most of the top shark hunters**, such as blue sharks or oceanic whitetip sharks, thrive in tropical oceans where the water is warmer than 21°C.
- **Other tropical species** that prefer to swim and hunt in warm waters include reef sharks, nurse sharks and whale sharks.
- **Temperate water sharks**, such as mako sharks, basking sharks and horn sharks, live in cooler waters, where temperatures range from 10–20°C.
- **The great white shark** lives in temperate waters, but also swims in tropical oceans and warm seas, such as the Mediterranean Sea.
- **Where water temperatures** are lower than 10°C, fewer sharks are able to survive and they move more slowly.
- **Cold water sharks** include the smoothhound shark, spiny dogfish, porbeagle shark and sleeper sharks.
- **The porbeagle shark** lives in waters with temperatures as low as 2°C, but is still able to chase fish at the surface of the sea.
- **The Greenland shark** is the only shark that survives under the polar ice in the North Atlantic Ocean.

▼ *Greenland sharks live in the cold waters of the North Atlantic Ocean – further north than almost any other shark.*

► *Scalloped hammerhead sharks swim in warm temperate and tropical oceans all over the world. They migrate northwards in summer, but return to warmer tropical waters in the winter.*

Shallows to the deep

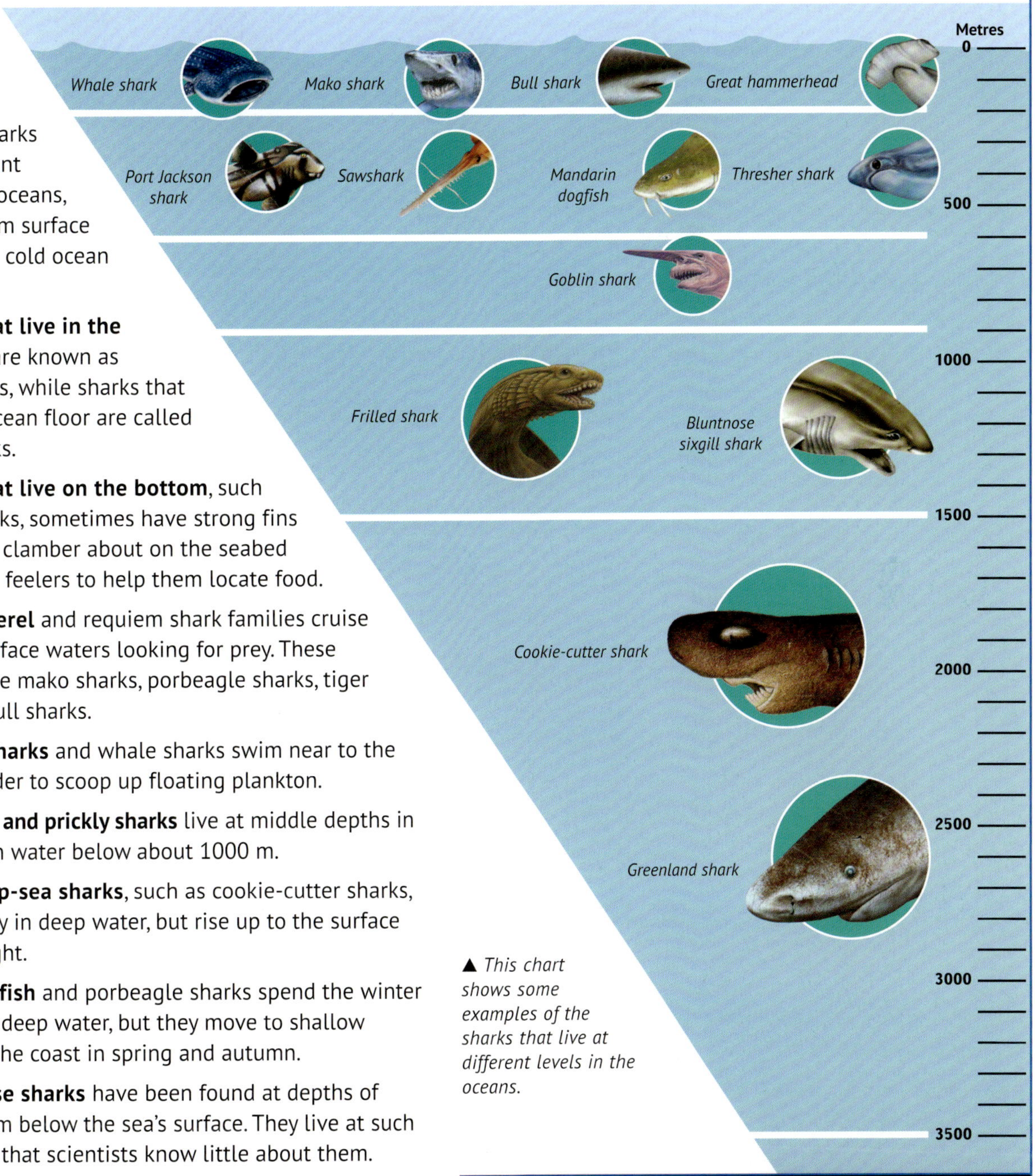

▲ *This chart shows some examples of the sharks that live at different levels in the oceans.*

● **Different species** of sharks live at different levels in the oceans, from the warm surface waters to the cold ocean depths.

● **Sharks that live in the open ocean** are known as pelagic sharks, while sharks that live on the ocean floor are called benthic sharks.

● **Sharks that live on the bottom**, such as nurse sharks, sometimes have strong fins to help them clamber about on the seabed and sensitive feelers to help them locate food.

● **The mackerel** and requiem shark families cruise the sunlit surface waters looking for prey. These sharks include mako sharks, porbeagle sharks, tiger sharks and bull sharks.

● **Basking sharks** and whale sharks swim near to the surface in order to scoop up floating plankton.

● **Catsharks and prickly sharks** live at middle depths in the oceans, in water below about 1000 m.

● **A few deep-sea sharks**, such as cookie-cutter sharks, spend the day in deep water, but rise up to the surface to feed at night.

● **Spiny dogfish** and porbeagle sharks spend the winter sheltering in deep water, but they move to shallow waters near the coast in spring and autumn.

● **Portuguese sharks** have been found at depths of nearly 3700 m below the sea's surface. They live at such great depths that scientists know little about them.

● **Cold water sharks**, such as the frilled shark and the goblin shark, often live in very deep water.

● **Many deep-sea sharks**, such as the dwarf shark and the velvet belly lantern shark, glow in the dark to help them find food in deep, dark water.

● **Gulper sharks** and other deep-sea sharks have huge green eyes to help them see in dark and gloomy waters.

● **Living on the deep-sea floor** are sixgill, sevengill and sleeper sharks. They eat food that sinks down from the surface of the sea.

▲ *Sixgill sharks have large eyes to help them capture as much light as possible in deep, dark waters. This shark is only a pup.*

Life on the bottom

- **Many sharks live** near the seabed. These sharks usually swim slowly, and spend time resting on the bottom or in sea caves.
- **Some of these sharks**, such as nurse sharks, swellsharks or catsharks, rest during the day and come out at night to hunt.
- **Angelsharks** have flat bodies that help them to lie close to the sea floor.
- **Their colours and patterns** give them good camouflage while they lie in wait for their prey.
- **Wobbegong sharks** look just like the rock, coral and seaweed on the seabed, which enables them to make surprise attacks on fish and other sea creatures.
- **Sharks that hide** on the sea bed may take in water through a breathing hole (spiracle) behind their eyes to stop their gills becoming clogged up with sand or mud.
- **Sharks that live** on the bottom, such as nurse sharks, bamboo sharks and bullhead sharks, often have strong fins to help them clamber about on the seabed or lift themselves up above the sea floor.
- **Sawsharks use** their long, barbed snouts to dig up food from the seabed.
- **Bottom-dwelling sharks** sometimes have sensitive feelers, called barbels, to help them locate food.
- **Leopard sharks** survive in very shallow water. They even follow the tide in and out to feed on shellfish and worms.

▼ *The two barbels on the snout of a nurse shark sense touch, water currents and chemicals in the water. They help the sharks to find prey hidden in the sand or mud on the seabed.*

Reef sharks

- **Many species of shark** live on or around coral reefs because of the warm waters, and the variety of food and places to shelter.
- **Reef sharks** often patrol along the edge of the reef, ready to catch fish that are out hunting by day when they return to the safety of the reef at night.
- **The names of some sharks**, such as grey reef sharks and blacktip reef sharks reflect their habitat.
- **Many reef sharks** are very curious. They will swim close to divers, or steal fish from the spears of fishermen hunting underwater.

▼ *Caribbean reef sharks are the most common sharks on the reefs in the Caribbean Sea. They are large, reaching lengths of 2–3 m.*

- **Silvertip sharks** are bold and aggressive reef sharks. Adults often have a lot of scars from fights with other sharks and they sometimes attack human divers.
- **Whitetip reef sharks** rest during the day in caves or under rocks, and hunt for fish in packs at night. Their tough skin helps to protect them from the sharp coral.
- **Like many sharks**, reef sharks have dark backs and paler undersides. This helps to camouflage them from predators or prey, either looking down at the dark water below them, or up towards the lighter water at the sea's surface.
- **The blacknose shark** is a small reef shark, which often swims with other blacknose sharks in large schools. This shark is a fast swimmer and feeds on small fish, such as anchovies.
- **Reef sharks** do not usually make long migration journeys as they have a plentiful supply of food, and places to mate and rear their young all year round.
- **Grey reef sharks** use body language, such as arching their backs and pointing their front fins down, to warn rivals to keep away from their patch of coral reef.

Skeleton and muscles

- **A shark's skeleton is made of cartilage**, a tough, gristly, rubbery substance that is lighter and more flexible than bone.
- **The cartilage skeleton** supports the shark's body, protects its organs and provides a strong framework for muscles to pull against to move the body.
- **Joints at different parts** of a shark's skeleton allow a complex range of movement.
- **A shark's body is held together** by muscle. There are two giant bands of muscle along the length of the body, one on either side of the spine.

▲ *With incredibly powerful muscles, a great white shark can explode right out of the water when hunting its prey. The great white can reach speeds of up to 56 km/h.*

▼ *Some sharks are so flexible that they can bend their body right round into a horseshoe shape to completely change direction. Less flexible sharks tilt their front fins and curve their bodies slightly to make more gradual turns.*

- **For its size**, a shark's body contains twice as much muscle as the human body. This makes sharks powerful swimmers and helps some sharks to travel long distances through the oceans.
- **Sharks have two types** of muscle for moving their skeleton – red muscle and white muscle.
- **About 10 percent** of a shark's muscle is red, which means it has a good blood supply and can work for a long time without tiring.
- **About 90 percent** is white muscle, which enables a shark to achieve short bursts of speed. However, white muscle quickly becomes tired and needs time to recover.

▼ *A great white shark's muscles work so efficiently that it can swim strongly without using a lot of energy.*

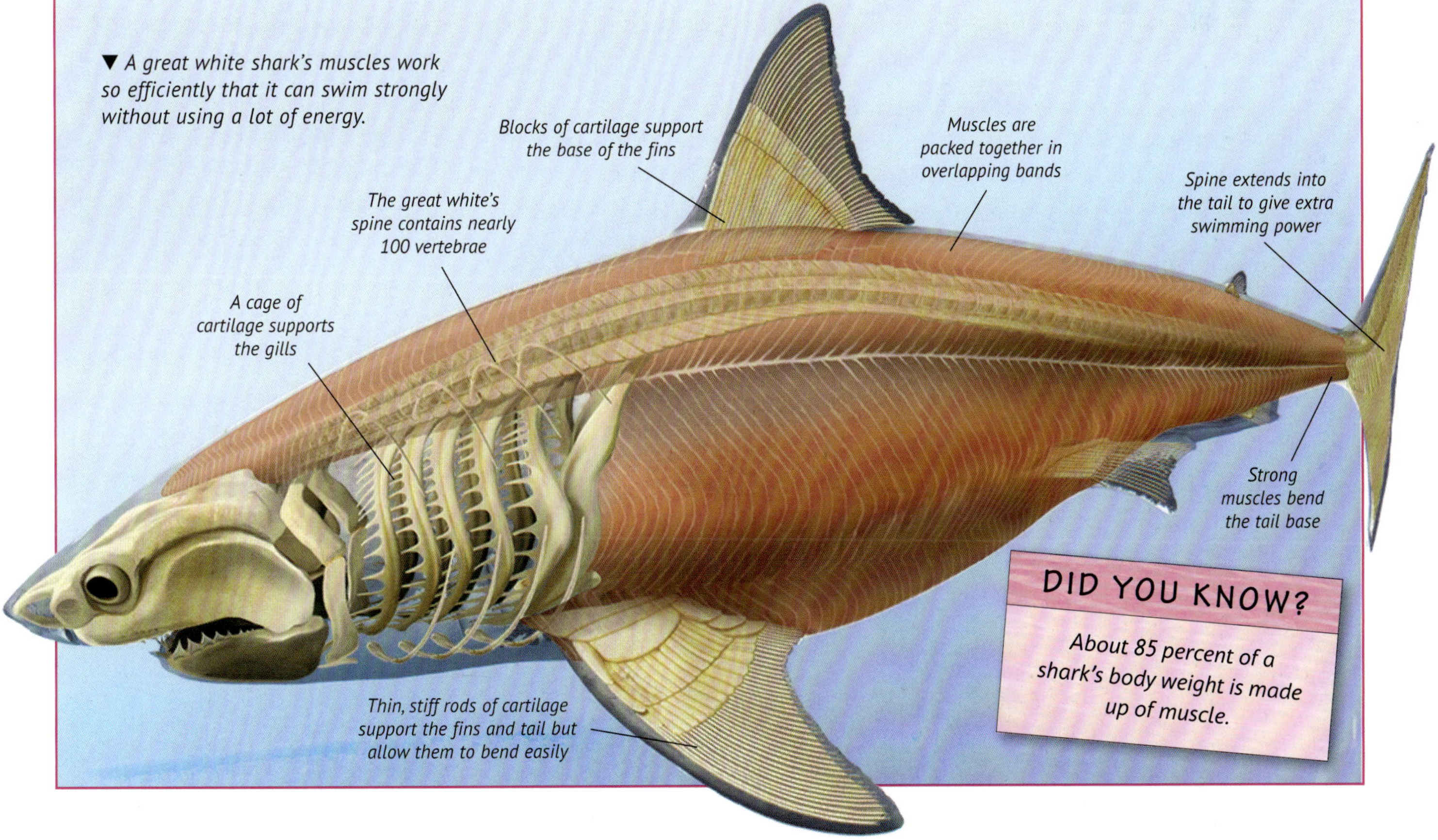

DID YOU KNOW?

About 85 percent of a shark's body weight is made up of muscle.

On the move

- **Most sharks** don't have a fixed home. They are constantly swimming, looking for food or a mate.
- **Some species** appear to have a territory, or special area of their own, that they patrol and guard.
- **Whitetip reef sharks** stay in the same area for several months, or even years, although they don't defend it like a true territory.

- **Some sharks**, such as horn sharks, pick a special nursery area in which to lay their eggs.
- **Underwater sea caves** are used by some species as a place to rest during the day.
- **Certain species** of sharks have preferences about where they live. The Galapagos shark is only found around groups of small, tropical oceanic islands.
- **Some sharks** have a daily routine, spending the day in deep waters, but moving to shallow waters near the shore to feed at night.
- **Blacktip reef sharks** seem to prefer their own space. As they swim up and down the edge of a coral reef, individuals will move their jaws or open their mouths to tell other blacktip reef sharks to keep their distance.
- **Some sharks** need to keep moving all the time in order to breathe. These sharks sleep with their eyes open, allowing parts of their brain to rest while they continue swimming.

◀ *Whitetip reef sharks rest during the day on the seabed, and inside underwater caves or rock crevices. At night, they hunt for fish and octopuses among the coral.*

Swimming skills

- **To propel itself** through water, a shark moves its tail from side to side.
- **A shark's fins** help it to balance, to change direction in the water and also to slow down.
- **Sharks normally swim** with a regular rhythm. They don't dart around like most bony fish do.
- **As a shark swims**, its body moves from side to side, forming S-shaped curves.
- **Many species** swim in a figure-of-eight pattern if they feel threatened.
- **Sharks swim silently** through the water and sneak up on prey.
- **Some types**, such as sand tiger sharks, swallow air to help them float better.
- **A shark may use** warm water currents to help it rise higher above the seabed, rather like birds use hot air currents to soar high in the sky.
- **To slow down**, sharks change the angle of their front fins and push against the water. The fins work rather like brakes.
- **A shark's oily liver** helps it to float, because oil is lighter than water. The basking shark's giant liver makes up about one quarter of its body weight and helps it to float at the surface of the sea, where it feeds.
- **Many sharks** don't need to float in the water because they spend a lot of time on the seabed. Some bullhead sharks spend as much time using their fins to 'walk' on the seabed as they do swimming.

▼ *With its slim, streamlined body and long, wing-like front fins, the blue shark is well suited to both cruising near the surface or diving to deeper waters.*

Fast sharks

● **Large sharks** swim at an average speed of about 2.4 km/h, but the most active hunters can speed along much faster when they need to catch prey.

● **It is difficult** for scientists to measure the speed of sharks accurately in the wild because they don't swim in a straight line over a measured course, like a human swimmer.

● **The fastest shark** is the shortfin mako, which can reach speeds of over 50 km/h and possibly over 75 km/h.

● **The mako** has a streamlined body and a pointed snout to cut through the water easily, as well as powerful swimming muscles.

● **The mako needs** to swim fast to catch its speedy prey, such as swordfish and sailfish, which are two of the world's fastest fish.

● **Smaller and chunkier** than its cousin the great white, the salmon shark's top swimming speed rivals that of mako sharks.

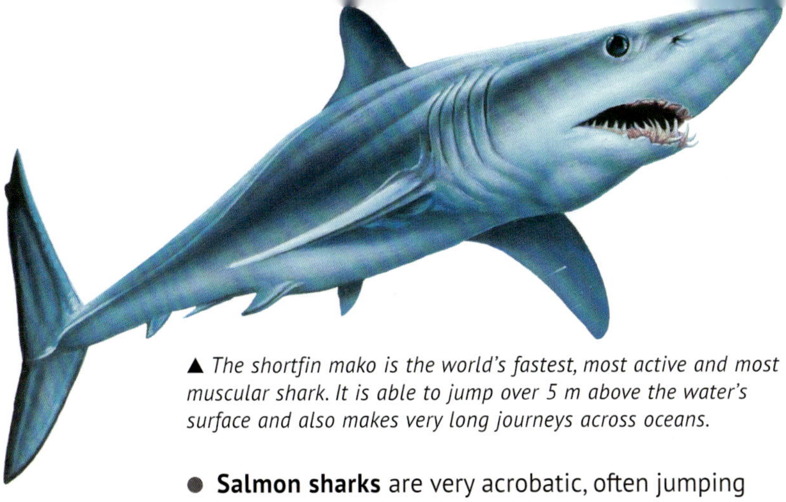

▲ *The shortfin mako is the world's fastest, most active and most muscular shark. It is able to jump over 5 m above the water's surface and also makes very long journeys across oceans.*

● **Salmon sharks** are very acrobatic, often jumping about 6 m above the water as they chase after schools of salmon migrating through the oceans.

● **The blue shark** is like an underwater glider plane, with long front fins and a flat belly. It can reach speeds of up to 40 km/h, gliding down to the ocean depths and then swimming back to the surface again.

● **Compared with a submarine**, a blue shark needs six times less driving power. This is partly due to its rough skin, which reduces the drag of the water.

DID YOU KNOW?

The great white shark can swim seven times faster than the best Olympic swimmers.

Long-distance travel

● **Many shark species** travel long distances over the course of their lives. As all the seas and oceans are connected, it is easy for them to cover huge distances.

● **Dogfish sharks** that have been tagged and released back into the sea have been located more than 8000 km away from where they were first caught.

▼ *This map shows the blue shark's route around the Atlantic Ocean. It travels huge distances after mating to have its pups.*

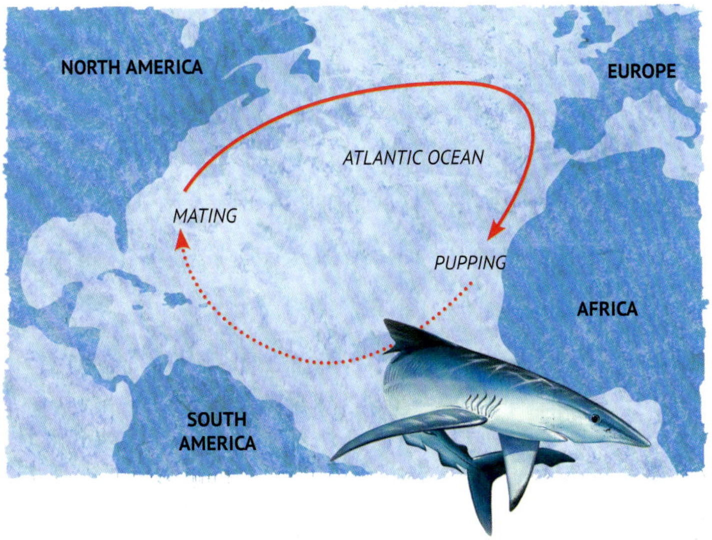

● **Migrating means moving around**, usually from season to season, according to a regular pattern.

● **The longest migrations** are made by blue sharks. They swim around the Atlantic Ocean in a huge circle and can cover more than 15,000 km in just one year.

● **Sharks sometimes mate** in one place, then swim far away to another area to lay their eggs or have their pups.

● **They also migrate** to find food, following shoals of fish as they move around the oceans.

● **Scientists think** sharks may be able to detect the Earth's magnetic field, helping them to navigate and find their way over long distances.

● **Many species** spend the day in deep water, but swim up to the surface at night. This is called vertical migration.

● **Migrating mako sharks** travel to the middle of the Atlantic Ocean, then turn around and swim back to the shores of the USA, where the water is the temperature they prefer to swim in.

Shark fins

● **A typical shark** has up to seven fins, not including its tail.

● **Most sharks** have five different types of fins: dorsal, pectoral, pelvic, anal and caudal (tail) fins. Sharks usually have two dorsal fins, but some species only have one.

● **The large fin** on the back is called the first dorsal fin. It stops a shark's body swinging from side to side while swimming, and sometimes sticks out of the water.

● **Two large pectoral fins** near the front of the body help a shark to steer and stop it from sinking.

● **A shark's two pelvic fins** are beneath its body, by the tail. Like the pectoral fins, they also help to lift the shark up in the water and stop it sinking.

● **A shark has one anal fin**, which is under its body, closer to the tail than the pelvic fins. The anal fin helps to stop the shark from rolling sideways.

● **Megamouth sharks** have soft, rounded fins for swimming slowly in the deep ocean.

● **The wing-like fins** of angelsharks help them to accelerate quickly when they are chasing prey.

● **Epaulette sharks** use their pectoral fins like legs to 'crawl' along the seabed.

● **A whale shark's** pectoral fins are up to 2 m long.

▼ *The grey reef shark has a typical shark shape with seven fins. The tail powers the body through water.*

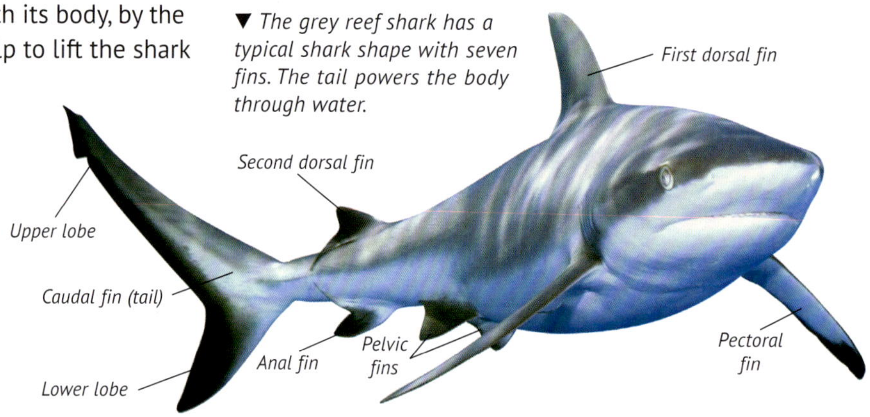

DID YOU KNOW?

Without their fins, sharks wouldn't be able to stay the right way up – they would roll over in the water.

Shark tails

● **The tail** is also known as the caudal fin. The anal fin is just in front of the tail.

● **A shark's flattened tail** helps to push it through the water.

● **Sharks that live** at the bottom of the sea, such as the nurse shark, usually have large, flat tails, with a large upper lobe to the tail.

● **Sharks that swim** in the open ocean tend to have slimmer, more curved tails, but still have a larger upper lobe to the tail.

● **The two tail lobes** are an equal size in the fastest sharks, such as the mako shark. This makes the tail a curved shape and produces a powerful thrust, propelling the shark forwards at high speed.

● **The keel**, or ridge, on the tail of some sharks, such as the porbeagle, mako or great white, provides stability while swimming and probably helps them to turn more easily in the water.

● **Some sharks** smack the surface of the water with their tails to frighten their prey.

● **Thresher sharks** are known for their very long upper tail lobes, which they use to stun prey.

● **Sharks can also** use their tails to sweep across the seabed in order to reveal prey hiding in the sand or mud.

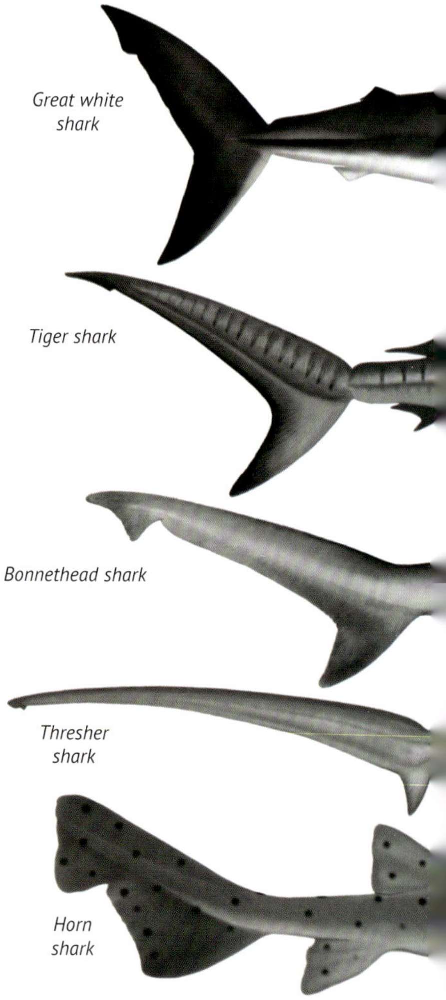

▶ *The shape of a shark's tail usually indicates its swimming speed. High-speed swimmers (great white shark) have equal upper and lower lobes; cruisers (tiger shark) have a larger upper lobe; slow swimmers (horn shark) have large, flat tails.*

Shark shapes

● **All sharks** have the same basic body plan – a head with eyes, nostrils and a mouth, and a body with a tail and fins.

● **A typical shark** has a long, narrow, torpedo-shaped body. This helps it move quickly through the water.

● **Most sharks** are built for speed and are streamlined in shape. This means water can move past them easily with very little resistance or 'drag'.

● **The tip of a shark's nose** is called the snout. Most are pointed, like the tip of a bullet.

● **Some sharks** have snouts with unusual shapes. Sawsharks have very long, saw-like snouts and the goblin shark has a horn-shaped snout.

● **Frilled sharks** live in the deep sea. Their long, thin bodies are shaped more like those of eels than those of typical sharks.

● **Carpet sharks**, such as wobbegongs, have a flat body shape, which helps them to hide from predators and prey on the seabed.

● **Angelsharks** have wide, spread-out fins that look like wings.

● **Hammerhead sharks** get their name because their heads are shaped like wide, flat hammers.

● **Engineers** sometimes study sharks to determine the best shapes for plane wings or boat hulls.

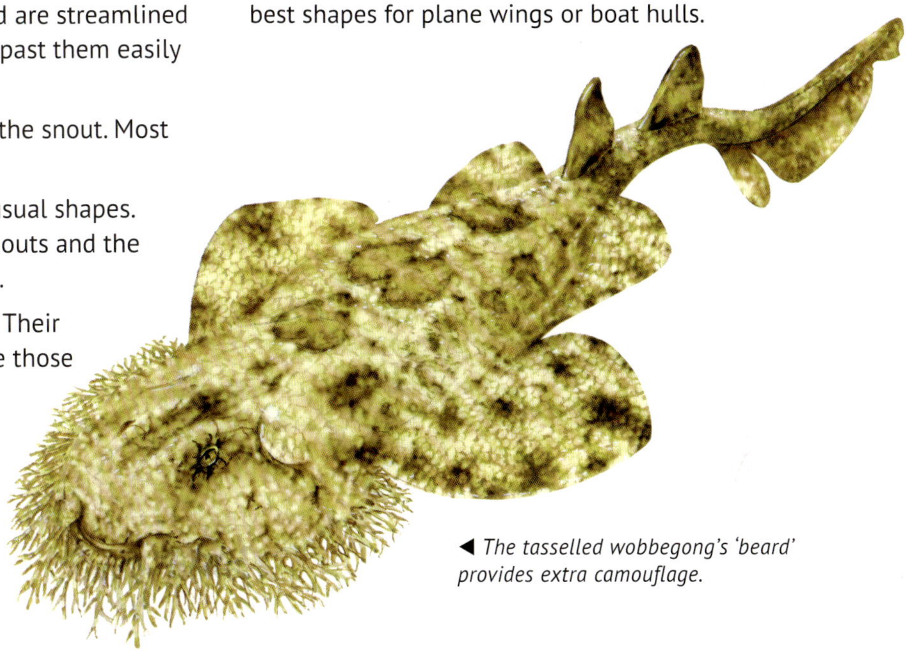

◀ *The tasselled wobbegong's 'beard' provides extra camouflage.*

Sandpaper skin

● **Unlike other fish**, sharks don't have scales. Instead their skin is covered with tiny, hard points called denticles.

● **The word denticle** means 'little tooth'. Denticles range from microscopic in size to about 5 mm across.

● **Denticles** provide protection from enemies, and help sharks to swim more easily through the water.

● **If you were to touch** a shark's skin, it would feel very rough. Some swimmers have been badly scratched just from brushing against a shark.

● **The denticles** on the side of a shark's body are the sharpest to ensure fast movement through the water.

● **Many sharks** release a slimy substance from their skin to make their bodies move faster through water.

● **A shark's denticles** overlap like tiles on a roof, which allows the shark's skin to bend.

● **Denticles are very different** from the scales of bony fish, such as salmon. They have the same composition as teeth and are on little stalks.

● **A shark's denticles** eventually fall out and are replaced, just like their teeth.

● **The bramble shark** has large, thorn-like denticles, whereas the silky shark has tiny denticles and a smoother skin than most other sharks.

▼ *A shark's denticles channel the water flowing across its body so as to reduce the energy needed for swimming. They also help sharks to swim quietly, enabling them to sneak up on their prey.*

Staying safe

● **Smaller sharks** make a tasty snack for other animals, so they need to defend themselves against predators, such as dolphins and porpoises.

● **The biggest species** are rarely eaten by other sea creatures, but they can still be hunted by humans.

● **Some sharks** are good at hiding. They slip between rocks or into caves to escape from predators.

● **When in danger**, some species swim in a jerky, random manner to confuse their attacker.

● **Thresher sharks** use their tails to fight off predators, as well as for attacking prey.

● **Shark skin** acts like armour, making it hard for predators to bite them.

● **Species** with spines can often put a predator off by giving it a sharp stab.

▶ *A swellshark can puff up its body when it is in a small space in-between rocks. A predator can't pull the shark out because it is wedged in so tightly.*

● **The sharp spines** of spiny dogfish and Port Jackson sharks inject poison into an attacker.

● **Roughsharks** have large spines on their back but they also have very rough skin, which scratches predators if they try to attack – their skin is rather like barbed wire.

● **Saw sharks** may use their saw-like snouts to defend themselves against predators.

In disguise

● **Many sharks** can disguise themselves to look like their surroundings. This is called camouflage.

● **Camouflage is a good way** to hide from enemies, but it can also be used to help sharks sneak up on their prey without being seen. Many small species, such as zebra sharks, epaulette sharks and wobbegongs, have brown or grey patterns to help them blend in with coral and seaweed.

● **The marbled catshark** is named after the camouflage patterns on its skin, which look like the patterns in marble rock.

● **Sharks are often darker** on their top half and paler underneath. This is called countershading. A shark with countershading viewed from below will blend with the brightly lit sea surface. Seen from above, it will blend with the murky depths.

● **Some wobbegong sharks** have barbels that look like seaweed around their mouths. Fish and other prey think the wobbegong is a harmless piece of seaweed and swim right into the shark's open mouth.

● **Angelsharks** have flat, smooth bodies. When they lie on the sandy seabed they become almost invisible.

● **The shovelnose shark** or guitarfish, a type of ray, disguises itself by burying its body in the sand or mud on the sea floor, with only its eyes sticking out.

● **The cookie-cutter shark** uses patches of light on its skin to attract hunting fish, seals or whales to come close – then the cookie-cutter takes a bite out of them.

● **When leopard sharks** are young, they have spots for camouflage. As they get older and bigger, they don't need as much protection, so the spots fade.

◀ *The spots on a young leopard shark's body help to break up its body shape and make it hard to see against a rocky background.*

A look inside

● **Sharks are vertebrates** – they have a skeleton with a backbone. Many animals, including all fish, reptiles, birds and mammals, are vertebrates.

● **The cartilage** that makes up a shark's skeleton is usually white or pale blue in colour. Because cartilage is flexible, sharks can twist and turn easily in the water.

● **A shark's backbone**, or spine, is made of a string of hourglass-shaped vertebrae under an arch that protects the spinal cord (the main nerve leading from the brain along the spine).

● **A shark's jaws** probably developed from the first arch of cartilage supporting the gills, so are not attached to the shark's skull.

● **Most of the vital organs** are in a cavity in the middle of the body. A shark has many of the same organs as other animals.

● **A shark's heart** pumps blood around its body, delivering oxygen and food nutrients and taking away waste.

● **One-way valves** in each chamber of the heart keep blood flowing in the same direction and prevent it from flowing backwards.

● **The liver** contains lots of oil. Oil is lighter than water, so it helps the shark to float.

● **The stomach** is stretchy. It expands to allow the shark to consume large amounts of food quickly.

● **Sharks have short intestines**, or guts, where nutrients from the shark's food are absorbed into the body.

● **Most sharks** are cold-blooded, which means their blood is the same temperature as the water around them.

● **A shark's brain** controls and co-ordinates its whole body. Networks of nerves carry coded electrical signals to and from the brain.

● **The sense of smell** is the most important sense for many sharks. About two thirds of a shark's brain processes information about smells in the shark's environment.

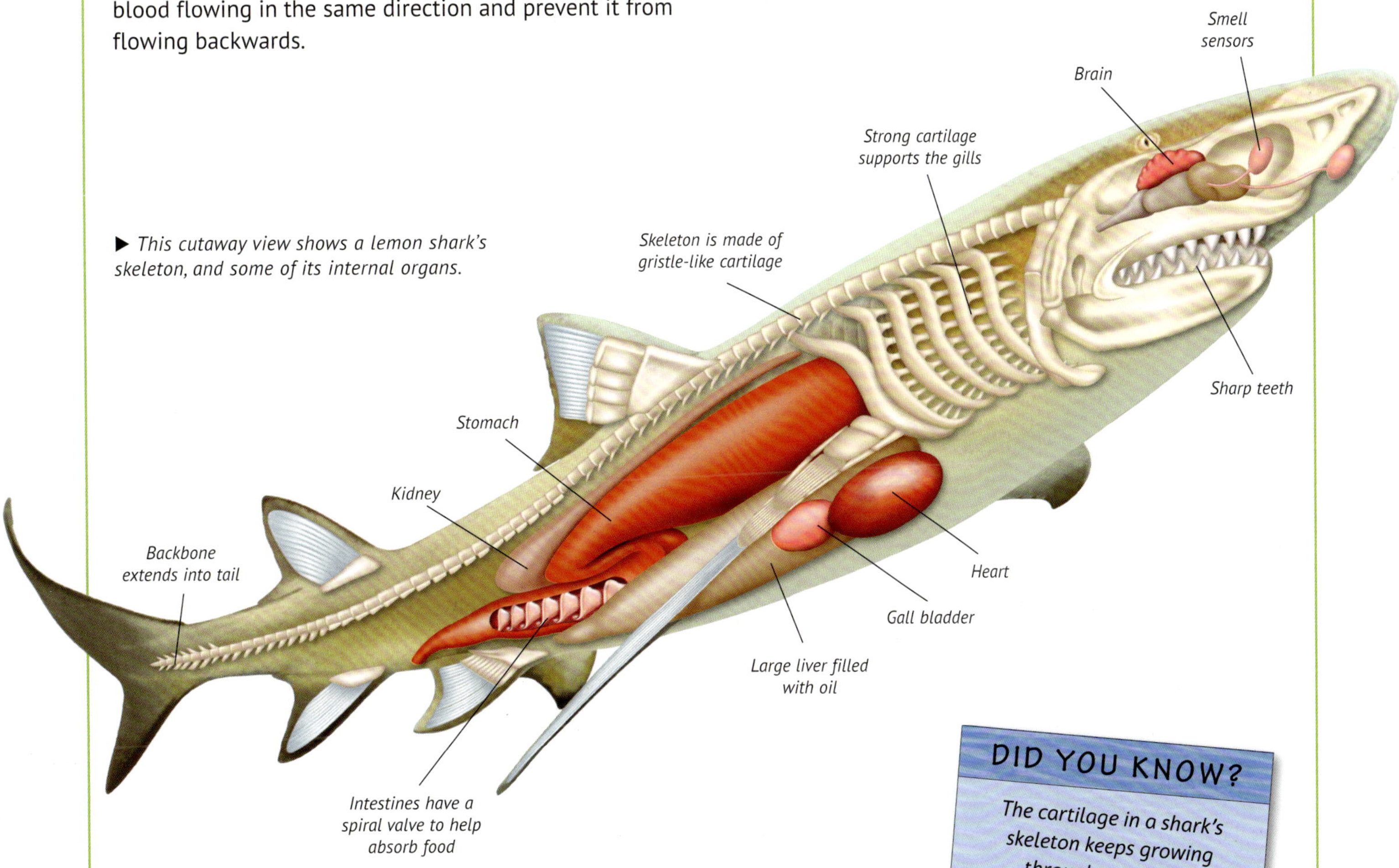

▶ *This cutaway view shows a lemon shark's skeleton, and some of its internal organs.*

DID YOU KNOW?

The cartilage in a shark's skeleton keeps growing throughout its life.

Gills and breathing

- **Like all animals, sharks need oxygen to survive**. Oxygen helps to convert food into energy, and sharks take in oxygen from the water using their gills.
- **The gills are beneath the slits in the shark's skin** on either side of the head. Gills contain tiny blood vessels, which absorb oxygen from the water as it passes over them.
- **Water contains less oxygen than air**, so sharks need plenty of water flowing over their gills to allow them to breathe.
- **Fast-moving sharks** have to keep swimming in order to breathe. Water flows into a shark's body through its mouth and out through the gill slits.
- **The gills absorb oxygen** from the water and pass it into the blood. They also get rid of carbon dioxide, the waste gas from breathing, by passing it from the blood back into the water.
- **Slow-moving sharks**, or those resting on the seabed, may use muscles to pump water over their gills.
- **Sharks that live on the seafloor** often rely on extra breathing holes called spiracles. These are located on the shark's head, behind its eyes. The shark sucks water into its spiracles and the water flows out through the gill slits.

▲ A basking shark uses its gills for feeding as well as for breathing. Its huge gill slits go almost right around its head. Slimy bristles called gill rakers, which are in front of the gills, trap small particles of food such as plankton, from the water. A basking shark has more than 5000 gill rakers. To feed, it simply swims with its mouth wide open.

- **A shark's gills consist of** a set of hair-like filaments full of blood vessels, which is why the gills are red. These blood vessels have very thin walls to allow oxygen to pass quickly from the water into the blood.
- **The blood is pumped** around a shark's body by its heart. The blood travels to the gills to pick up oxygen, then flows around the body to deliver the oxygen, before returning to the heart.
- **The filaments in a shark's gills** are divided into tiny, leaf-like branches, called lamellae. These provide a large surface area for absorbing as much oxygen as possible from the water.

▼ Blue sharks are one of the fastest sharks in the ocean, reaching speeds of almost 30 km/h. As a blue shark speeds along, it keeps its mouth and gills open so that oxygen-rich water rushes past its gills all the time. If a blue shark is trapped, or forced to stop swimming, it can suffocate through lack of oxygen.

Eyes and vision

● **Sharks have well developed eyes**, which work in a range of light levels but sharks probably can't see in colour.

● **Sharks need** to be able to see well in the dark as there is limited light underwater.

● **Some species** have a special eyelid called the nictitating membrane. This closes over the eye when the shark is about to bite, to protect it from damage.

● **White sharks** and whale sharks don't have nictitating membranes. Instead, they swivel their eyes back into their eye sockets to protect them. This means they can't see their prey as they bite.

● **Many sharks** have a layer of shiny plates called the *tapetum lucidum* (Latin for 'bright carpet') at the back of their eyes. These collect and reflect light, helping them to see, even in the gloomy darkness.

● **The *tapetum lucidum*** makes shark eyes appear to glow in the dark. In very bright light, the *tapetum* can be covered with dark coloured cells, which work rather like sunglasses to protect the sensitive layer at the back of the eye.

● **Deepwater and nocturnal** sharks have huge, glowing, green eyes to capture as much light as possible in the darkness.

● **Some sharks** have a third eye, called a pineal eye, under the skin in their foreheads. It can't see as well as a normal eye, but it can sense daylight.

● **The shy-eye shark** gets its name because when it is caught, it covers its eyes with its tail to shield them from the light.

● **A shark's eyes** are ten times more sensitive to light than our eyes. However, sharks can't judge distances as well as we can.

▼ *Some species, such as blacktip reef sharks, have cat-like, slit-shaped pupils.*

Sensing smells

DID YOU KNOW?

Great white sharks can smell tiny amounts of blood in water up to 5 km away!

● **As a shark swims**, water constantly flows into the nostrils on its snout. It then travels over the scent-detecting cells inside the nostrils. A shark uses its nostrils purely for detecting scents in the water.

● **The sense of smell** is the most important sense for many sharks.

● **Sharks can smell blood** in water, even if it's diluted to one part in ten million. That's like one pinhead-sized drop of blood in a bathtub of water.

● **Swimmers** have been known to attract sharks just by having a tiny scratch on their skin.

● **Sharks use their sense of smell** to detect prey, but probably also to detect mates and to help them find their way on long migration journeys.

● **Some sharks** can detect smells in the air. Oceanic whitetip sharks sometimes point their noses up through the water's surface to see if there is any smelly food nearby, such as a rotting whale carcass.

● **The biggest parts** of a shark's brain are the olfactory lobes – the area used for processing smells.

● **The great white** has the biggest olfactory lobes of all sharks, which means it probably has the best sense of smell.

● **A shark homes in** on a scent by zigzagging its snout from side to side and then moving towards the side where the smell is strongest.

◀ *The nostrils of hammerhead sharks are at the tips of their 'hammers', so they smell in stereo, which helps these sharks to track down the source of a smell.*

Touch and taste

DID YOU KNOW?

A shark's lateral line can pick up the movements of prey in the water from distances of 100 m or more.

- **Like us**, sharks can feel things that touch their skin. They have millions of nerve endings that can feel pressure, temperature and pain.
- **They also have** an extra sense organ called the lateral line. This is a long tube running down each side of a shark's body, under its skin. All fish, not just sharks, have lateral lines.
- **As a shark swims**, ripples in the water pass into the lateral line through tiny holes in the skin. Hairs inside sense the ripples, and send signals to the brain.
- **The shark's brain** interprets the signals from its lateral line as possible prey, predators or other sharks.
- **The lateral line** also helps a shark to keep its balance and avoid bumping into objects in its surroundings.

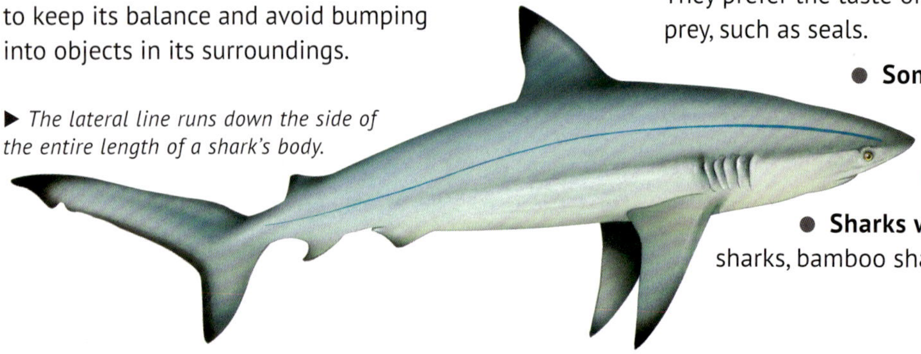

▶ *The lateral line runs down the side of the entire length of a shark's body.*

- **As it is most effective** for picking up vibrations close to the shark's body, the lateral line helps sharks to find their way in murky or dark water, when their other senses are not much use.
- **Sharks taste the animals** or objects they bite with the tastebuds inside their mouths. They can also taste chemicals dissolved in the water. This helps them to find prey and avoid pollution.
- **Sharks use** their sense of taste to help them decide whether to swallow or spit out an object or piece of food. Great white sharks tend to spit out human flesh. They prefer the taste of fatty blubber from their usual prey, such as seals.
- **Some species** have fleshy whiskers on their snouts called barbels, which help them to sense the location of food on the seabed.
- **Sharks with barbels** include nurse sharks, bamboo sharks, sawsharks and wobbegongs.

Hearing sounds

- **Sharks have ears**, but they're hard to spot. The openings are tiny holes, just behind the eyes. People sometimes mistake the spiracles, which are used for breathing, for ears.
- **In the sea**, sound travels in the form of vibrations rippling through the water. Sharks hear by sensing these vibrations.

▼ *Sharks can also detect the sounds of air bubbles coming from scuba-diving tanks, so this blue shark can hear the diver breathing.*

- **Inside the ear** is a set of looping, fluid-filled tubes called the labyrinth. Inside the labyrinth are microscopic hairs. Vibrations travel through the fluid, moving the hairs, which send signals to the shark's brain.
- **Sharks hear** low sounds best, such as the noise made by an injured animal underwater.
- **Sharks can pick up** these sounds from around 200 m away.
- **Ears also help sharks** to keep their balance. The movement of fluid inside their ears tells them which way up they are.
- **The grey reef shark** has a very well-developed balance system in its inner ear. This helps it to keep its balance when swimming in a large group of reef sharks.
- **The sound of research submersibles** can easily be detected by sharks and may frighten deep-sea sharks, making it difficult for scientists to study them.
- **Sharks gather** at popular shark feeding sites when they hear the sounds of boat engines, which they learn to associate with food.

The sixth sense

- **A shark has six senses.** Besides vision, hearing, touch, taste and smell, it can sense the tiny amounts of electricity given off by other animals.
- **To detect electricity**, a shark has tiny holes in the skin around its head and snout. They are called the ampullae of Lorenzini.
- **The ampullae of Lorenzini** are named after Stefano Lorenzini (born *c.*1652). He was an Italian scientist who studied the anatomy of sharks.
- **Ampullae** are a type of Roman bottle. The ampullae of Lorenzini have a narrow-necked bottle shape. Each ampulla contains a jelly-like substance, which collects electrical signals.
- **All animals** give off tiny amounts of electricity when their muscles move. Electricity doesn't travel well through air, but it does through water.

DID YOU KNOW?

Some other animals, such as the duck-billed platypus, can detect electricity too.

- **The ampullae of Lorenzini** can sense animals within a range of about one metre.
- **Some sharks** use their electrical sense to find prey that is buried in the seabed.
- **A fierce hunting species**, such as the tiger shark, has up to 1500 ampullae of Lorenzini.
- **Slow-moving sharks** that live on the seabed have only a few hundred ampullae of Lorenzini.
- **Sharks sometimes bite** on seabed cables because these objects produce electric signals.

◀ *The dots on this tiger shark's snout are the ampullae of Lorenzini.*

Smart sharks

DID YOU KNOW?

Captive lemon sharks learn how to perform scientific tests 80 times faster than cats or rabbits.

- **Most shark species** have big brains for their body size and are probably smarter than many bony fish.
- **Almost all of the brain** is used for processing information from the senses. The parts used for learning and thinking are small.
- **In relation to their body size**, hammerhead sharks have the biggest brains.
- **Scalloped hammerheads** are one of the smartest sharks. They are fast, fierce hunters.
- **Hammerheads** spend time in groups and scientists think they have simple social systems.
- **In captivity**, some sharks have learned to do simple tasks in exchange for rewards.
- **Captive lemon sharks** have been taught to ring bells, press targets, swim through mazes and recover rings in order to receive rewards of food.

- **Sharks are curious** and inquisitive animals. They are able to solve problems, as well as to learn and remember things. All these qualities are signs of intelligence.
- **Some species** are brighter than others. Fast hunters such as great whites are the most intelligent. Slow-moving bottom-feeders such as carpet sharks are less smart.

◀ *A scientist releasing a young lemon shark during a study of how lemon sharks avoid predators in the wild. Studying the behaviour of young sharks helps scientists to understand more about how sharks learn to survive.*

Food and feeding

- **Large, fast, hunting sharks**, such as great whites and bull sharks, feed on large fish (including other sharks), as well as seals, turtles, octopuses, squid, seabirds and other sea creatures.
- **Smaller sharks**, such as dogfish sharks, hunt smaller fish, octopuses and squid.
- **Slow-moving species**, such as nurse sharks, angelsharks and carpet sharks, crunch up crabs, shrimps and shellfish that they find on the seabed.
- **Filter-feeders** feed on plankton – tiny floating animals and plants – which they filter from the water.
- **There are hardly** any animal species in the sea that aren't part of the diet of one shark species or another.
- **Tiger sharks** will eat anything they can find, even objects that aren't food, such as tin cans.
- **Most sharks** don't eat every day. Some large hunters can go without food for months.
- **Some sharks prefer** to eat just a few types of food. Giant hammerhead sharks like to eat stingrays, and the sicklefin weasel shark prefers a diet of octopus.
- **Big sharks** often feed on smaller sharks. Some sharks are cannibals, eating sharks of their own species. Tiger sharks are cannibals.
- **A big shark** can eat more than half its own body weight in one meal.

▼ *When small fish are in danger from sharks, they often cluster together in a tight sphere called a bait ball. These bronze whaler sharks have disturbed the cluster to make the fish easier to catch.*

Teeth and jaws

- **A hunting species**, such as the great white or the tiger shark, has several rows of teeth.
- **Only the two front rows** of teeth are used for biting. The rest are lining up to replace them when they wear out or break.
- **In a lifetime**, some sharks will get through 30,000 teeth. You can sometimes find shark teeth washed up on beaches.
- **Some shark teeth**, such as those of bull sharks, have serrated edges (like a saw) and are as sharp as razors. This allows them to slice through meat easily.
- **The biggest teeth** belong to the great white shark. Its teeth can grow to more than 6 cm in length.
- **Some species**, such as smooth-hound sharks, don't have sharp biting teeth. Instead they have hard, flat plates in their mouths for grinding up crabs and shellfish.
- **The outside of a shark's teeth** is made up of fluoride – an ingredient in most toothpastes – as it prevents tooth decay. This means that sharks don't get holes in their teeth.

DID YOU KNOW?

A great white shark uses about 80 teeth in every bite it takes from its prey.

◀ *The tiger shark has large, saw-edged, hooked teeth in both jaws. It has a varied diet, from fish, sea snakes, sea turtles and seabirds, to jellyfish, rotting meat and rubbish.*

▶ *Port Jackson sharks have small, sharp, pointed teeth at the front of their jaws and large flattened teeth at the back, for crushing sea urchins, starfish and shellfish.*

Going hunting

- **Most sharks are nocturnal** – they hunt at night – or crepuscular – they hunt at dusk.
- **Sharks use several senses** to track down and home in on prey. They locate it from a distance by smell, and use their electric sense, sight and hearing to close in on it. Sharks can also feel ripples in the water made by the movement of other animals.
- **Before attacking**, some sharks 'bump' their prey with their snouts, probably to see if it's edible.
- **When it is about to bite**, a shark raises its snout and thrusts its jaws forwards, so that its teeth stick out.
- **Sometimes lots of sharks** are attracted to a source of food, and they all rush to eat it at the same time. This is known as a feeding frenzy.
- **Most hunters** prefer prey that's weak or helpless because it's easier to catch. Sharks are good at smelling blood – it tells them when an animal is injured.
- **Many species** give their prey a fatal bite, then move away while it bleeds to death. They return later to feed on the body.
- **A great white shark** usually attacks from behind or below so its prey does not see it coming. It moves so fast, it may leap right out of the water with its victim in its jaws.
- **Some sharks**, such as whitetip reef sharks, silky sharks, spiny dogfish and tiny pygmy sharks work together to catch prey. They catch more food by working as a team.
- **Groups of silky sharks** or sandtiger sharks sometimes herd fish into a ball by swimming at them from all directions. The sharks then pick off the fish that are swimming on the outer edges of the ball.

DID YOU KNOW?

Sharks have very strong jaws. Some can bite other animals in half – even those with tough shells, such as turtles.

▲ *A school of lemon sharks stirs up clouds of white sand as individuals compete for their share of food.*

Filter feeding

- **The biggest shark species** of all – whale sharks, basking sharks and megamouths – eat plankton, which is the smallest prey. These sharks are called filter-feeders.
- **Plankton** is made up of small sea creatures such as shrimps, baby crabs and squid, little fish and tiny, free-floating plants. It drifts along with the currents.
- **Filter-feeding sharks** have gill rakers. These are comb-like bristles in their throats that sieve plankton out of the water.
- **Gill rakers are coated** in mucus to help plankton stick to them.
- **Filter-feeders swallow** the plankton they have collected, while water they have sieved escapes from their gills.
- **These sharks have massive mouths**, so they can suck in as much water as possible.
- **To collect a kilogram of plankton**, a shark has to filter one million litres of water.
- **In one hour**, a whale shark filters around 2 million litres of water, and collects 2 kg of food.

▲ *Whale sharks open their big mouths wide to take in lots of water. Then they filter plankton from the water as it flows over their comb-like gills and back out of the body.*

- **Whale sharks** sometimes suck in shoals of little fish, such as sardines, that are also busy feeding on plankton.
- **The blue whale**, the world's biggest animal, is also a filter-feeder.

Scavenging food

- **Scavenging** means feeding on other hunters' leftovers, or on animals that are dying or already dead.
- **Almost all sharks** will scavenge if they cannot find other food.
- **Some species**, such as the Greenland shark and the smooth dogfish, get a lot of their food by scavenging.
- **In deep water**, sharks often feed on dead sea creatures that sink down from higher levels.
- **Sharks scavenge** human food too, especially waste food that's thrown overboard from ships.
- **Sometimes sharks eat fish** caught in fishing nets before the nets are pulled to the surface.
- **Scavenging is natural recycling**. It cleans the oceans, and ensures leftovers and dead animals are rapidly removed rather than left to slowly decompose.
- **The tiger shark** is famous for its scavenging habits and will eat almost any dead meat, from fish, squid and sea snakes to seals, dolphins and whales.
- **Tiger sharks** will also eat the carcasses of land animals, such as chickens, dogs, horses and cows that are washed into the sea.

▼ *It can take up to 100 years for a whale carcass to be eaten by scavengers. More than 30,000 different types of animal feed and live off the carcass at different stages.*

DID YOU KNOW?

Old, rotting meat is bad for humans to eat, but many wild animals such as sharks can eat it safely.

Pack hunters

● **Some shark species work together** to catch prey as it is a more efficient way for them to hunt.

● **Tiny pygmy sharks** hunt together so they can catch and kill fish much bigger than themselves.

● **Blacktip reef sharks** co-operate to drive fish into shallow water and onto the beach. Then they wriggle onto the beach, grab the fish and slide back into the sea.

● **A group of sharks** will often herd fish into a tight ball by swimming towards them from different directions. The sharks then grab the fish from the outside of the ball.

● **Sharks that herd fish** like this include silky, dusky, bronze whaler, whitetip reef and sandtiger sharks.

● **Thresher sharks work in pairs**, using their long tails to push fish into swirling balls of bite-sized mouthfuls.

● **Two or three great white sharks** may sometimes hunt together and share each other's catches.

● **When many young seabirds** or seals enter the water for the first time, groups of sharks, such as tiger sharks, gather to eat as much as they can.

● **Whitetip reef sharks** hunt in groups on coral reefs, working together to find and capture prey.

◀ *Spiny dogfish sometimes gather in huge groups and swim along the seabed, forcing prey to swim away. Any animal that cannot escape is eaten by the sharks.*

Spikes and spines

● **Many prehistoric sharks** had sharp spines in front of their dorsal fins. Scientists think they may have helped hold the fins up.

● **Today only a few species** have spines, spikes or sharp horns on their bodies. They are usually used for defence against attackers.

● **Spines are made** of modified, extra-large denticles.

● **Some dogfish sharks** and horn sharks have two sharp fin spines in front of their dorsal fins.

● **The spined pygmy shark** is the only species that has just one fin spine, which can inflict a painful wound. Other kinds have two spines, or none at all.

● **Smaller species are more likely to have spines.** They are most at risk of being eaten by other animals, so they need defences to deter their enemies.

● **Spiny dogfish coil themselves** right around their enemies to stab them with their spines.

● **The sharp spines** of the spiny dogfish and Port Jackson sharks inject poison into an attacker.

● **Velvet belly lanternsharks** have glowing spines, which are visible from above and the side. These 'light sabres' warn predators to keep away because these spiny sharks would be hard to swallow.

● **Stingrays** have poisonous stings in the middle of their tails.

▶ *The piked dogfish has a spine in front of each of the dorsal fins on its back. The spines inject a mild poison into an attacker.*

Teeth and digestion

▼ *A shark has short intestines and a special valve structure that slows down the movement of food. A silky shark has a spiral-shaped valve, which curves round and round, rather like a spiral staircase. This increases the surface area of the intestine and allows it to absorb more nutrients from the food passing through.*

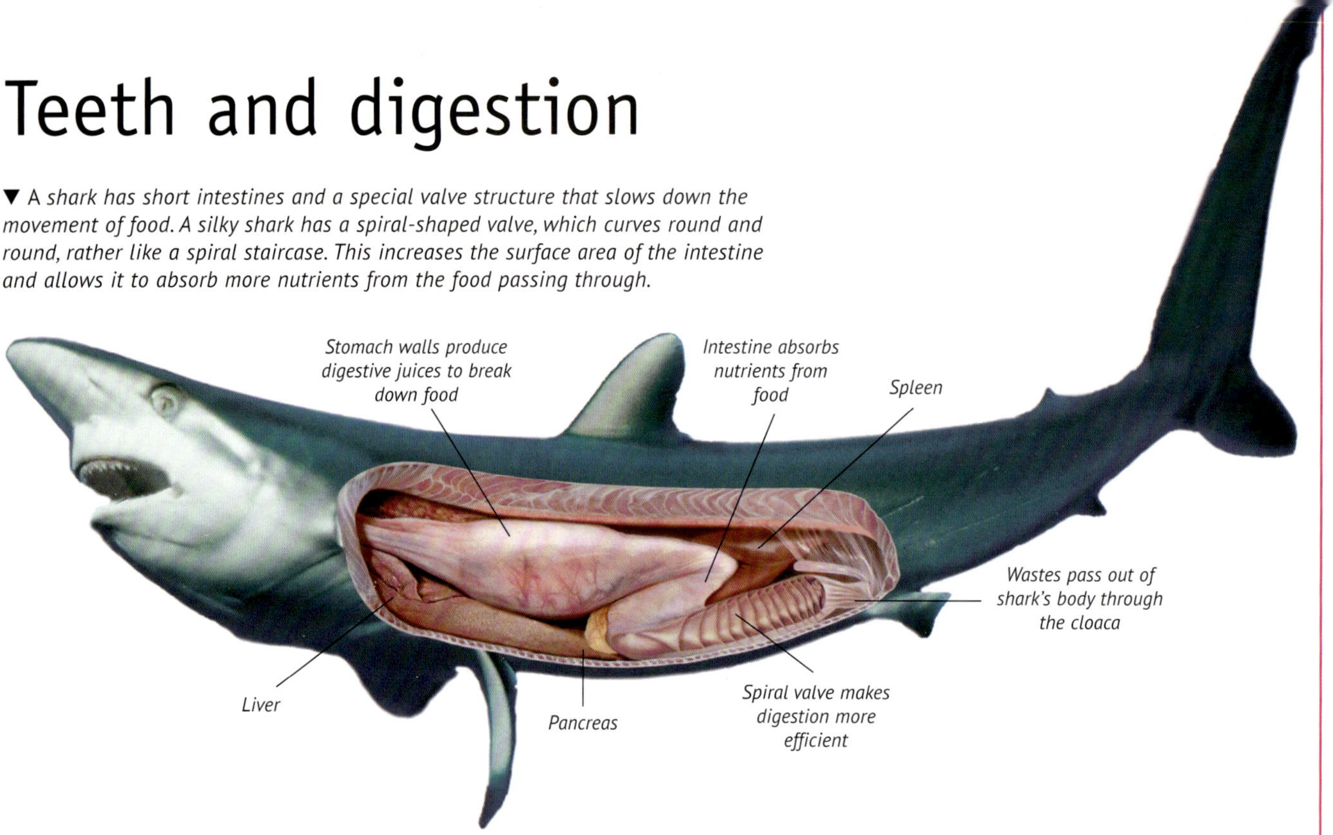

● **Most sharks use their teeth for catching and killing prey**. They don't usually chew their food. Instead, prey is torn into chunks, or swallowed whole.

● **So the process of breaking down**, or digesting, food does not start until it enters the shark's digestive system. Digesting a meal can take up to four hours.

● **A shark's digestive system** consists of a long tube, with an entry point (the mouth) at one end and an exit hole (the cloaca) at the other end. Food that cannot be digested leaves the shark's body through the cloaca, which is between its pelvic fins, near the tail.

Spiked sand tiger shark teeth for gripping

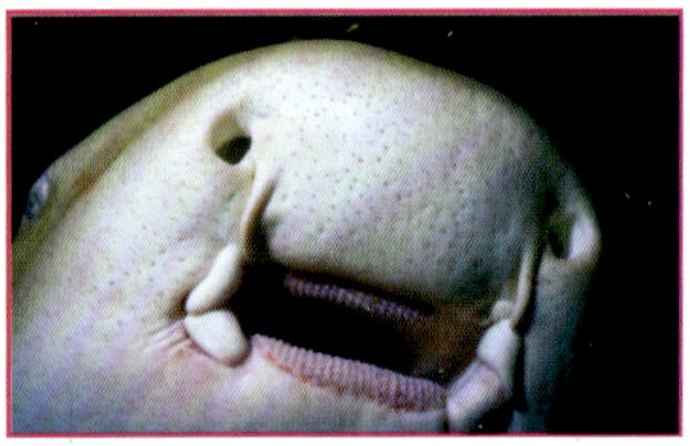
Flat zebra shark teeth for crushing

Ring of cookie-cutter shark teeth for biting

▲ *The shape of a shark's teeth depends on its diet. The long, pointy teeth of great white, mako and tiger sharks ar good for gripping slippery prey, such as fish and squid. The flat, blunt back teeth of zebra sharks are shaped to crush shellfish. Cookie-cutter sharks have a ring of teeth for slicing circles of flesh from their prey, rather like a person cutting circles of cookie dough.*

● **A shark's stomach** is like a stretchy bag, which can hold large meals.

● **When a shark swallows food**, it slides down into its stomach. The muscular walls of the stomach churn up the food and strong digestive juices and acids break the food down into a soupy paste.

● **From the stomach**, the partly digested food passes into the shark's intestine. Muscular waves in the walls of the intestine move the food along. Further digestive juices then break the food down, and nutrients are absorbed through the walls of the intestine.

● **Some sharks**, such as the lemon, tiger and mako sharks, can project their stomach right out of the mouth to get rid of indigestible items they have swallowed. In just a few seconds, they push their stomach out into the water, shake it to rinse it clean and swallow it back into place again.

● **The sliding jaws** of a great white shark are normally tucked away under its snout. However, before the shark take a bite, its jaws slide forward very fast and its snout lifts up. This allows the shark to take very big bites out of its prey.

● **A shark's teeth** are only loosely joined to the skin inside its mouth and new teeth form in rows behind the old ones.

● **When the front teeth** break off or wear down, teeth from the row behind move forward to fill the gap. The teeth move forward as if they are on a conveyor belt.

● **The new teeth** are bigger than the ones they replace, so older sharks have bigger teeth.

Loners and groups

- **Many shark species**, such as bull sharks, are solitary. This means that they live alone.
- **Sharks don't live** in families. They meet up to mate, but do not stay together afterwards. Once born, young sharks do not live with their parents either.
- **Some sharks form groups** with other members of their species. Whitetip reef sharks often rest together in small groups of about ten individuals.

▼ *During the day, hammerhead sharks hunt together in schools. At night, they separate to hunt alone.*

- **Sharks may form** groups because there is safety in numbers. A group is less likely to be attacked than a single shark.

DID YOU KNOW?

Groups of nurse sharks sometimes relax by lying in a heap on the seabed.

- **Being in a group** may also help sharks to find a mate.
- **Some species**, such as lemon sharks, blue sharks and spiny dogfish, form single-sex groups of just males or females outside the breeding season. Scientists are not sure why.
- **Basking sharks** have been seen in groups of 50 or more, in places where there is lots of plankton floating on the sea for them to eat.
- **Great white sharks** sometimes travel in pairs or small groups.
- **Two or three great white sharks** may sometimes hunt together and share each other's meals.
- **Shark pups** often stay together in shallow water 'nurseries', well away from larger adult sharks, which might eat them.

Sending messages

- **Animals don't have** complicated languages like humans – but they can still communicate.
- **Sharks can 'talk'** using body language. They make different postures, just as humans show their feelings using different expressions.
- **Sharks also release** special scents called pheromones to send messages to other sharks. These can indicate if a shark is looking for a mate or feeling agitated.
- **When they live in a group**, the strongest sharks usually become the leaders. They will sometimes fight with the other sharks to show their dominance.
- **When a shark is aggressive** or frightened, it arches its back, raises its snout, and points its pectoral fins down.
- **A few species** can make sounds. Swellsharks can make a barking noise, but experts are not sure if it is a way of communicating.
- **A threatened sand tiger shark** makes a sound rather like a gunshot when it slaps its tail loudly on the water's surface.
- **Great white sharks** warn rivals to keep away by showing their sharp teeth, splashing their tail at the surface, or even hitting a rival with their strong tail.
- **If a rival does not back off**, the great white will give it a small bite and hope that it swims away without the need for a fight, which may injure both sharks.

◀ *This shark is displaying aggression. Its raised snout, arched back and lowered fins mean it is ready to attack.*

DID YOU KNOW?

Bioluminescence (lighting up) helps some species to communicate. It can enable a shark to recognize another of the same species in the dark.

Meeting and mating

- **During mating**, a male and female shark of the same species join together. Sperm cells from the male fertilize the egg cells inside the female to begin the development of a new shark.
- **Sometimes females** store sperm from a male shark for fertilization in the future, perhaps in a year or more.
- **When they mate**, the male shark uses his claspers to place sperm into an opening in the female's body, called the cloaca.
- **A small, flexible male shark**, such as a dogfish, wraps its body tightly around the female to get in the right position for mating.
- **Larger sharks**, such as whitetip reef sharks, with more rigid bodies, mate swimming side by side or with their heads down and their undersides together.
- **Many species**, including nurse sharks and blue sharks, have special mating areas in shallow parts of the sea.
- **In other species**, such as whitetip reef sharks, females release chemicals called pheromones to help males locate them.
- **Males sometimes bite** females to show that they want to mate with them.
- **Females often have thicker skin** than males (up to three times as thick) so that being bitten during courtship doesn't harm them.
- **Sharks don't mate very often**. Most species only reproduce once every two years.

▶ *Male whitetip reef sharks sometimes spend time resting in shallow water during the day. If they smell a pheromone scent from a female, they will try to find her.*

Male and female sharks

● **In most species of sharks**, the females are larger than the males. This may help them to produce large eggs, or look after the developing pups inside their bodies.

● **Female sharks** may weigh up to a quarter more than male sharks of the same species.

● **Male and female sharks** look similar on the outside. The main difference is that males have two claspers for delivering sperm to the females.

● **The claspers** of a male shark are folds of skin with grooves. They are formed from the inner sides of the pelvic fins, which are rolled around like a scroll.

● **Each clasper** has a mechanism for pumping the sperm through the channel in the middle of the scroll.

● **Claspers vary** in different species. They may be flat, round, smooth or covered with denticles (skin scales) shaped like hooks or spurs.

● **Inside a female shark** there are usually two ovaries, which make eggs, and two egg tubes, called oviducts.

● **Sperm from a male shark** fertilizes the eggs inside the oviducts of the female shark.

● **After fertilization**, the eggs are covered with a tough, protective covering and move into the female's womb, or uterus, which has two chambers.

◀ *Male blacktip reef sharks are smaller than females. Males are 91–100 cm long, whereas females are 96–112 cm long.*

Laying eggs

● **Many sharks** have young by laying eggs. Most bony fish also reproduce this way.

● **Sharks that lay eggs** are called oviparous sharks. They typically lay between 10 and 20 eggs at a time.

● **About 40 percent** of sharks lay eggs that hatch outside the female's body.

▼ *A baby catshark develops slowly in its protective case. At 50 days it is smaller than the yolk, its store of food.*

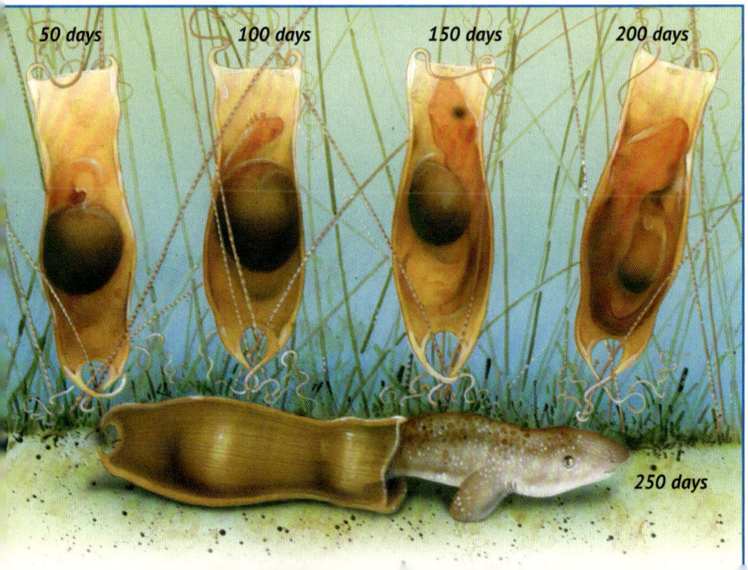

● **A mother shark** doesn't guard her eggs. She lays them in a safe place, such as between two rocks or under a clump of seaweed, then leaves them to hatch.

DID YOU KNOW?

Female skates and chimaeras also lay eggs with leathery egg cases to protect their developing young.

● **The eggs are enclosed** in cases, which allow oxygen to pass in and body wastes to pass out.

● **Inside the egg**, the baby shark grows for between six and 12 months before hatching.

● **When the baby shark** hatches out of the egg, it looks like its parents.

● **Female sharks** lay relatively large eggs compared to their body size. For instance, a female shark about 1.8 m long lays egg cases 5–10 cm long.

● **A huge female whale shark** lays eggs cases up to 30 cm long.

● **Oviparous species** include bullhead sharks, dogfish sharks, horn sharks, zebra sharks, swellsharks, bamboo sharks, wobbegong sharks and many catsharks.

Eggs and babies

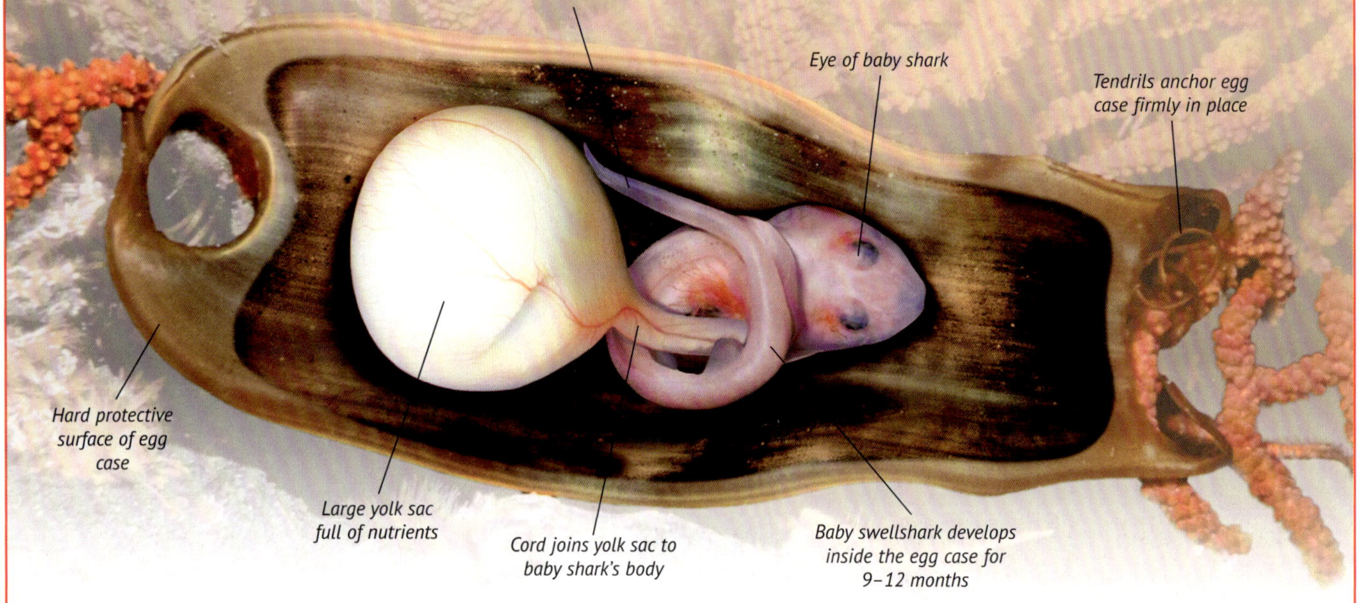

▲ *While inside its egg case, a baby shark gets food from a large yolk sac that is joined to its belly by a cord. Oxygen in the surrounding water passes through the egg case so that the shark can breathe. As it develops, the baby sprouts fins and begins to wriggle about. This shark is about three months into its development.*

- **Most sharks give birth to pups** after pregnancies lasting from three months in some species to as long as two years or more in others.
- **The number of pups born** at any one time also varies with the species of shark, from two pups at once to hundreds of babies for the whale shark.
- **Other sharks**, such as dogfish and swellsharks, lay eggs, which are protected inside strong cases.
- **Shark egg cases** come in many shapes, such as tubes, spirals and pillows. Many of them are rather like purses or pouches, with the eggs safely hidden inside.
- **Female sharks lay their eggs** in places where there is a good supply of food for the baby sharks.
- **The females may take hours** to push the egg cases out of their bodies. The cases are soft and flexible at first, but they harden when they come into contact with the seawater.
- **Sharks don't look after their egg cases** and many baby sharks do not survive long enough to hatch out.

▶ *Empty shark egg cases are sometimes washed up on beaches. Before people understood what these were, they were nicknamed 'mermaids' purses' because they looked as if they could be purses belonging to mythical mermaids.*

- **The eggs may be eaten** by predators, such as sea snails, or the egg cases may be washed up on beaches, where they dry out so the baby sharks inside them die.

Giving birth

● **Not all sharks lay eggs**. Some give birth to live young. These sharks are known as viviparous or ovoviviparous.

● **In ovoviviparous species**, such as basking sharks, the young, called pups, grow inside eggs. They hatch out while inside the mother's body, before being born.

● **About 40 percent** of all sharks are ovoviviparous, including frilled sharks, sand sharks, thresher sharks, tiger sharks, nurse sharks and mako sharks.

● **In viviparous sharks**, such as hammerheads, the pups grow inside the mother's body, but not in eggs.

● **Viviparous sharks** develop inside the mother's uterus, or womb, where they receive food through a structure called a placenta, which develops from the pup's yolk sac. The placenta is attached to the wall of the mother's uterus.

● **Mother sharks** with pups developing inside them like this are 'pregnant'. Most shark pregnancies last up to about one year.

● **Some shark pregnancies** are much longer. In the spiny dogfish, pregnancy lasts up to two years.

▲ *A newborn lemon shark swims away from its mother. Lemon shark pups are 60–65 cm long at birth.*

● **In sand tiger sharks** and several other species, the strongest pups eat the others while they are still inside the mother's body.

● **Baby hammerhead sharks** are born head-first, but have their 'hammer-heads' folded back to avoid harming their mother.

DID YOU KNOW?

Viviparous young are attached to their mothers in the womb by an umbilical cord, just like human babies.

Newborn sharks

● **Most shark pups** look like smaller versions of their parents. They often have a narrower body shape and stronger colours.

● **Some species**, such as sand tiger sharks, give birth to just two pups in a single litter.

● **The pups of some species** are born with the yolk still attached. The yolk continues to nourish the shark as it grows.

● **The long, thin shape** of newborn sharks makes them look more like water snakes, which means that predators are less likely to attack them.

● **Mako sharks** produce large, strong pups, which are ready to swim in the open ocean and begin hunting as soon as they are born.

DID YOU KNOW?

Whale sharks are thought to be able to give birth to up to 300 pups at a time.

● **Lemon sharks** hide among seaweed in shallow water for the first two years after they are born, before moving to deeper water.

► *The egg sac full of yolk is still attached to the body of this blue shark pup.*

● **Newborn dusky sharks** have a huge liver, which helps them to survive until they catch their first meal. The liver quickly reduces in size, from 20 percent of the pup's body weight at birth to only 6 percent after a few days.

● **Blue sharks** give birth to up to 135 pups at a time. The pups are about 51 cm long when they are born.

● **Some female sharks**, such as bonnethead sharks, zebra sharks, blacktip sharks and whitespotted bamboo sharks, are able to give birth to pups without mating with a male shark.

Growing up

▲ *Small lemon sharks are often eaten by larger sharks. This is why they spend the first few years of their lives living along sheltered shorelines, such as this mangrove swamp.*

● **Many sharks** grow rather slowly and mature late in life. It can take a shark pup 10–20 years or more to mature into an adult.

● **This makes it difficult** for sharks to adapt quickly to new environmental conditions or to keep up their numbers when so many of them are killed by people.

● **Blue sharks** are among the fastest-growing. A pup grows about 20 cm every year.

● **A Greenland shark** grows very slowly, only increasing in size by about 0.5 cm a year.

● **As pups are small**, they are good targets for predators. The biggest danger comes from adult sharks. Pups may even be eaten by adults of their own species.

● **For every ten pups born**, only one or two will survive to be adults.

● **Many species** of pups live in 'nursery areas' – shallow parts of the sea close to the shore, where there are plenty of places to hide and smaller sea creatures to hunt.

● **Sharks are born** with a full set of teeth, so they can start to hunt straight away.

● **Adult sharks** don't look after their babies. Once the pup is born, or has hatched, it has to fend for itself.

● **A typical shark** lives for around 25–30 years, although some species, such as whale sharks and dogfish sharks, may live for 100 years or more.

● **Great white sharks** could live to be at least 73 years old.

● **Sharks keep growing** all through their lives, although they grow more slowly as they become older.

● **Sharks also grow** more slowly in cold conditions and when food is hard to find.

DID YOU KNOW?

Male great white sharks are about 26 years old before they are ready to mate; female great whites aren't ready to have babies until they are about 33 years old.

Friends and enemies

▲ *These remora fish feed on scraps and parasites from this lemon shark, as well as gaining protection from predators.*

● **There are several types** of sea creature that have a close relationship with sharks. These include some fish species and parasites that feed on the skin, blood or insides of sharks.

● **Small, crab-like creatures** called copepods attach themselves to a shark's eyes, gills, snout or fins. They nibble the shark's skin or suck its blood.

● **Copepods on the eyes** of Greenland sharks damage the surface of the eyes and make it more difficult for these sharks to see clearly. Sea leeches bite sharks on their undersides and suck their blood.

● **Many shark species** have tapeworms inside their guts. They feed on the shark's food.

● **Whale sharks** sometimes try to get rid of skin parasites, such as barnacles, by rubbing up against boats. The barnacles make the shark swim more slowly and may provide a route for an infection to get under the shark's skin.

● **Sometimes two species** can help each other. This kind of relationship between two animals is called symbiosis, which means 'living together'.

DID YOU KNOW?

Giant manta rays may spend several hours at a 'cleaning station', whereas sharks zip through in just 5–10 seconds.

● **Many sharks** visit 'cleaning stations' where small fish and shrimps remove dead skin and parasites from their bodies – even from inside their mouth or gills.

● **Basking sharks** are sometimes covered with sea lamprey fish, which use their suckers to grip tightly to the shark's skin. These sharks may sometimes leap out of the water and crash back down again to try and dislodge the lampreys.

● **Remoras or 'shark suckers'** are fish that attach themselves to sharks using suction pads on their heads. They hitch a ride on the shark's body and feed on leftover scraps of food.

● **Sharks open their mouths** to let tiny cleaner wrasse fish nibble lice and dead skin from between their teeth.

● **Small pilotfish** often swim alongside sharks, saving energy by keeping close to the bigger animal, which creates a sheltered 'pathway' through the water. The pilotfish is also protected by the bulk of the shark and able to eat leftover food scraps.

▼ *A Greenland shark with a parasitic copepod attached to its eye.*

Types of shark

● **There are more than 500 species** of shark and scientists divide them into eight large groups, called orders. They are then divided into about 34 smaller groups, or families.

● **Arranging species** into groups, or classifying them, helps scientists to study and identify them.

● **Scientists often disagree** about how to classify sharks, so there are several different ways to do it.

● **Shark orders** and families have long scientific names. For example, goblin sharks belong to the Mitsukurinidae family, in the Lamniformes order.

● **Some groups** have common names too. For example, species in the Lamniformes order are also known as mackerel sharks.

● **Each species** has its own scientific name, which is written in Latin. The first part identifies the genus (part of a family) to which the species belongs. The second part identifies the species within the genus.

● **Scientists decide** which group a shark belongs to by looking at features such as its body shape, markings, behaviour and DNA.

● **Sometimes**, very different-looking sharks can belong to the same group. Huge whale sharks and small, slender epaulette sharks are both in the same order.

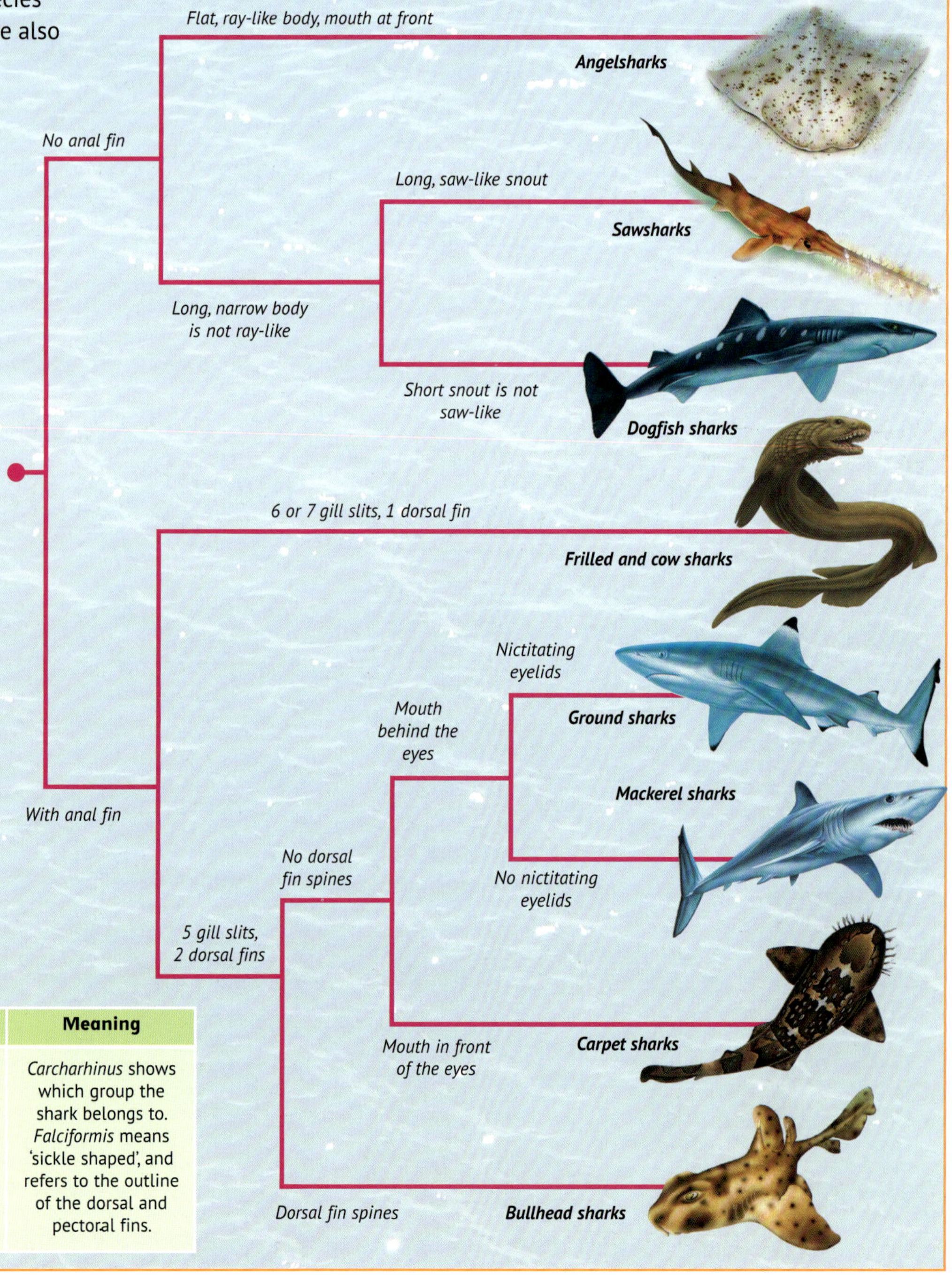

▶ *This diagram shows how different types of shark are thought to be related and the key characteristics of each group.*

▼ *Each shark species is given a two-part Latin name.*

Common name	Latin name	Meaning
Silky shark	*Carcharhinus falciformis*	*Carcharhinus* shows which group the shark belongs to. *Falciformis* means 'sickle shaped', and refers to the outline of the dorsal and pectoral fins.

Angelsharks

- **Angelsharks are named** after the wide, wing-like shape of their fins. There are at least 20 species of angelsharks.
- **Monkfish** is another name for angelsharks. People used to think their fins looked like a monk's robes.
- **Like wobbegongs** and other bottom-dwelling sharks, angelsharks are camouflaged with spotted, speckled skin patterns.
- **The ocellated angelshark** has 'eye spots' on its side fins and the base of the tail. These may help to divert attention away from the shark's real eyes.
- **These sharks** have flattened bodies. This allows them to stay close to the seabed. Most are about 1.5 m in length.
- **By burying themselves** on the seabed, angelsharks are hidden from passing fish and shellfish. They leap out to catch their prey with their small, sharp teeth.
- **Angelsharks can lie in wait** for over a week until their prey comes swimming past. One angelshark even managed to eat a cormorant – a type of large bird!
- **Female angelsharks** give birth to between one and 25 pups at a time.

▲ *The angelshark has very rough skin on its back, and patches of small thorns on its snout and between its eyes.*

- **The sensory barbels** on an angelshark's snout help it to detect and taste prey.
- **Angelsharks** draw in water through their spiracles and pump it out over their gills to keep them from getting blocked with sand. Their gill openings are on the sides of their head, not underneath.

DID YOU KNOW?

The biggest angelshark, the Japanese angelshark, reaches lengths of 2 m or more.

Sawsharks

- **Part of an order** of eight shark species, sawsharks have flat heads and saw-shaped snouts. They spend most of their time swimming or resting on the seabed.
- **The snout is called a rostrum**. It is pointed and has teeth, called rostral teeth, of various sizes sticking out all the way around it.
- **The snout of the longnose sawshark** can make up one third of the total length of its body.
- **At around 70–150 cm** in length, sawsharks are relatively small.
- **Sawsharks** use their saws for digging up prey such as shellfish from the seabed. They slash and jab at their prey before eating it.
- **Two long barbels** halfway along the snout help the sawshark feel its way along the seabed.
- **Most sawsharks** are grey, but the Japanese sawshark is a muddy-brown colour.

DID YOU KNOW?

Sawsharks aren't usually seen near the shore. They prefer to live at depths of up to 400 m.

- **Sawsharks also** use their long saws for defence or for competing with rivals during courtship.

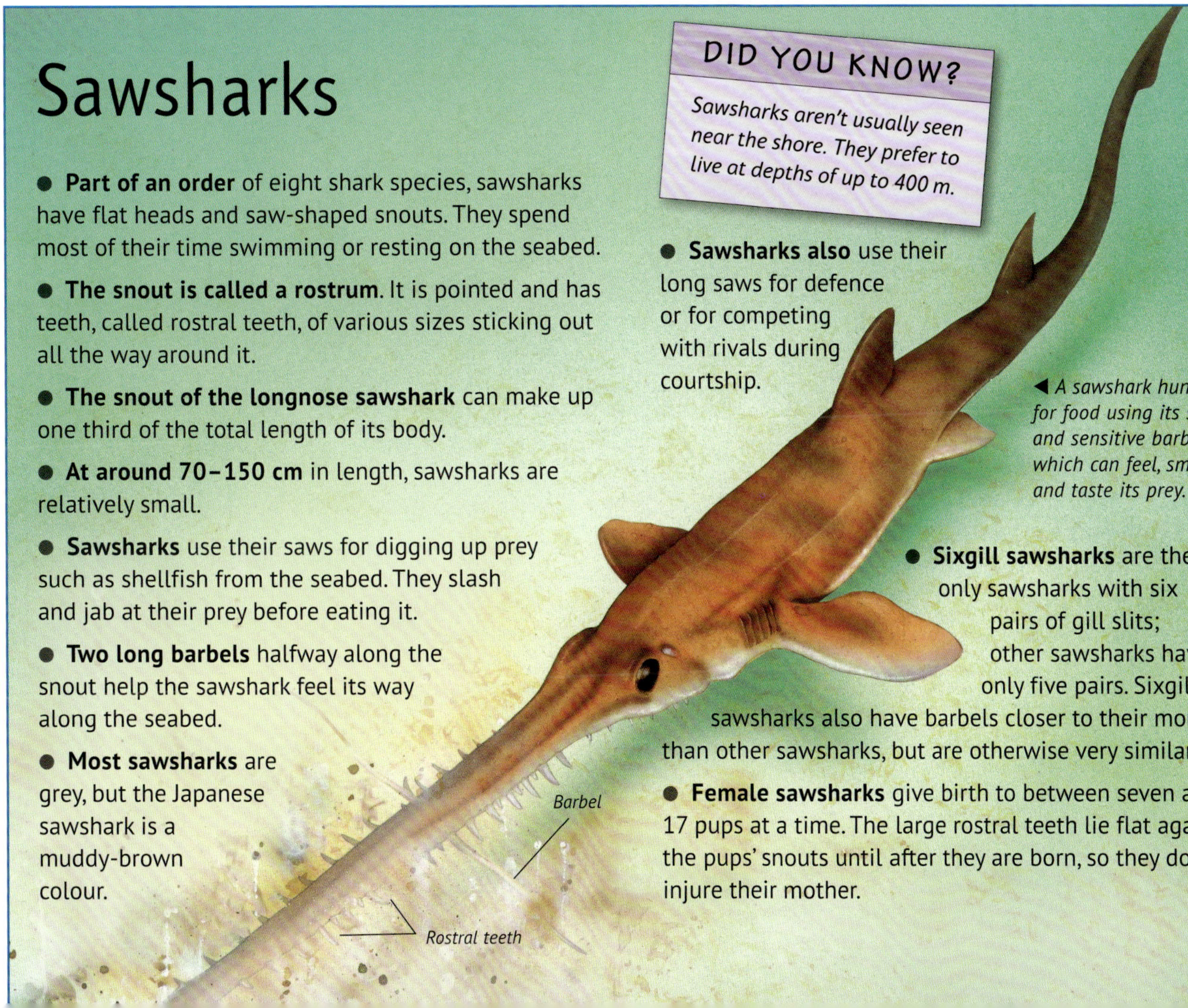

◀ *A sawshark hunts for food using its snout and sensitive barbels, which can feel, smell and taste its prey.*

- **Sixgill sawsharks** are the only sawsharks with six pairs of gill slits; other sawsharks have only five pairs. Sixgill sawsharks also have barbels closer to their mouths than other sawsharks, but are otherwise very similar.
- **Female sawsharks** give birth to between seven and 17 pups at a time. The large rostral teeth lie flat against the pups' snouts until after they are born, so they don't injure their mother.

Dogfish sharks

- **The dogfish shark order** (Squaliformes), consists of about 130 species in six families: dogfish sharks, gulper sharks, lanternsharks, sleeper sharks, roughsharks and kitefin sharks.
- **These sharks** usually have spines in front of their dorsal fins and they have no anal fin.
- **They may have** been named 'dogfish' because they are the most common sharks or because many types move in large groups, like packs of wild dogs.

- **Female dogfish sharks** give birth to pups. A single litter may have anything from one to over 50 pups.

DID YOU KNOW?

In America, spiny dogfish used to be caught, dried and burned as a fuel.

- **The spiny dogfish** has the longest known gestation period of any shark. Females can be pregnant for up to two years.
- **The smalleye pygmy shark** is one of the smallest sharks. It measures less than 10 cm in length at birth.
- **Gulper sharks** have huge green or yellowish eyes to help them see in deep, dark waters, up to 1500 m deep.
- **Sleeper sharks** are named after their slow, sluggish swimming habits.
- **The five species** of roughshark are named after their rough, tough skin. They have two high, triangular fins on the back, which look like the sails of a boat.
- **The kitefin shark** is an aggressive, deep-water predator, with powerful jaws and sharp teeth. The back edges of most of its fins are see-through.

◀ *A group of dogfish sharks on the prowl. They sometimes form schools of hundreds or even thousands of individuals.*

Greenland sharks

- **Although closely related** to dogfish, Greenland sharks are much bigger – they can grow up to around 6.5 m or more in length.
- **Greenland sharks** prefer cold water. They live in the north Atlantic, around Greenland, Iceland and Canada, and can stand temperatures as low as 2°C.
- **The Greenland shark** is a type of sluggish sleeper shark, which is related to another gigantic shark, the Pacific sleeper shark.
- **Alternative names** for the Greenland shark include ground shark, gurry shark, grey shark and sleeper shark. The Inuit name for this shark is Eqalussuaq.
- **Luminescent copepods** (tiny sea creatures) live in the eyes of the Greenland shark. They make the eyes glow in the dark, which may help lure prey towards the shark.
- **Greenland sharks eat fish**, squid, seals and sea lions, as well as scavenging on the dead bodies of whales.

▼ *One of the largest of all sharks, Greenland sharks are often characters in Inuit legends.*

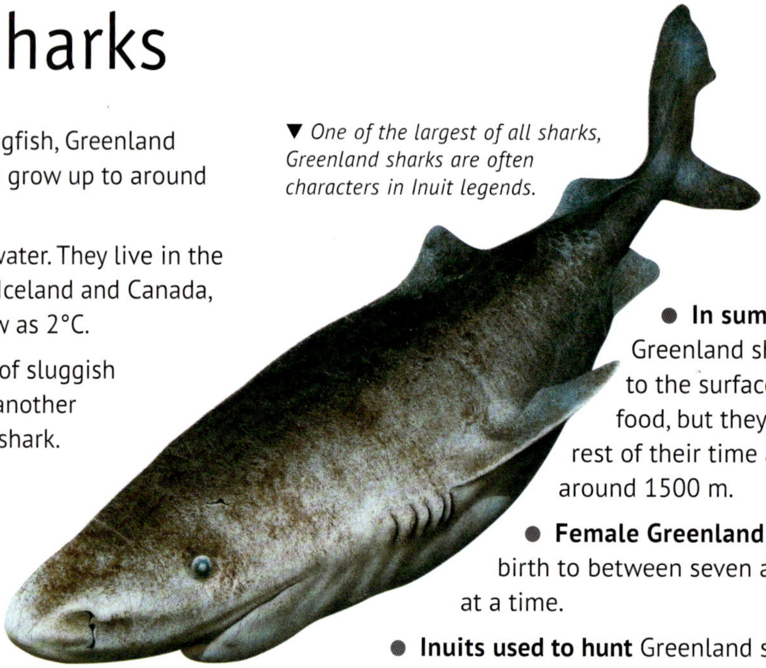

- **In summer**, Greenland sharks swim to the surface to find food, but they spend the rest of their time at depths of around 1500 m.
- **Female Greenland sharks** give birth to between seven and ten pups at a time.
- **Inuits used to hunt** Greenland sharks on lines through iceholes. They used the skin to make boots, and the teeth for knife blades.
- **Greenland sharks are** the longest-living vertebrates known on Earth.

DID YOU KNOW?

One female Greenland shark found was recently estimated to be around 400 years old.

Lanternsharks

◀ *The photophores (glowing spots) form distinct black marks on the abdomen, sides or tail of some lanternsharks.*

- **Lanternsharks** are the largest family of dogfish sharks, with over 50 species.
- **They live throughout** the oceans, near the bottom, at depths of 200–1500 m.
- **Lanternsharks** are named after their ability to glow in the dark. They produce light from glowing spots called photophores on their bellies, sides and fins.
- **There can be** as many as 500,000 photophores on just one shark! In a photophore, two chemicals are combined, causing a reaction that gives off light.
- **Lanternsharks use hormones** to switch their light spots on and off. The hormones stimulate pigment (colour) cells to cover or uncover the light spots.
- **The light spots** may help to camouflage these sharks against lighter surface waters, or even allow them to signal to other lanternsharks and find a mate in dark water.
- **Green dogfish** feed in groups. Their light patterns may help these sharks to find each other in murky water.
- **Some deep-sea lanternsharks**, such as the velvet belly shark, may use their lights to light up their surroundings in order to see prey.
- **The rough skin** of the granular dogfish is covered in denticles with sharp, hooked points, whereas the bareskin dogfish has a fragile, almost naked, skin with only a few, widely spaced denticles.
- **The lined lanternshark** has lines of dots and dashes along the top of its silvery-brown body, like Morse code.
- **The viper dogfish** has huge, curved, fang-like teeth to catch large fish, which it then swallows whole.

Cookie-cutter sharks

- **Found around the world**, cookie-cutter sharks are strange, deep-water sharks.
- **There are two species** – the cookie-cutter and the large-tooth cookie-cutter.
- **The large-tooth** is the smaller of the two, but it has bigger teeth. Its teeth are bigger in relation to its body size than those of any other shark.
- **Cookie-cutters** are brown in colour and have greenish eyes. They are about 50 cm in length.
- **To feed**, a cookie-cutter attaches itself to its prey by sucking with its mouth. Then it swivels its sharp teeth around in a circle until it has cut out a lump of flesh.
- **As cookie-cutters** don't need to catch their prey, they can feed on animals much larger than themselves.
- **Many sharks**, dolphins, porpoises and whales have permanent round scars from cookie-cutter shark bites.
- **The luminous underside** of the cookie-cutter shark can glow bright green and may help to attract its victims.
- **Although they are** relatively poor swimmers, cookie-cutter sharks probably migrate from deep water (2000–3000 m down) to mid-water levels or the surface at night.

▶ *The cookie-cutter has around 35 teeth in its upper jaw and 30 in its lower jaw.*

▲ *Cookie-cutters open their mouths wide to bite circular chunks out of their prey. They rarely kill their victims.*

Bullhead sharks

- **There are nine species** of bullhead sharks, including the horn shark, the Galapagos horn shark and the Port Jackson shark.
- **These stocky sharks** all have a pig-like snout and a small mouth in front of their eyes.
- **The prominent brow ridges** are polished smooth in species that rest by day in caves, or under ledges of rock or coral.
- **Bullhead sharks** are more active by night than by day.
- **They live in shallow coastal waters**, which are usually less than 100 m deep.
- **These sluggish sharks** wriggle slowly over the seabed hunting for prey, or clamber over the bottom on their paddle-like front fins.
- **Bullheads are small sharks**, growing to lengths of 1.2–1.7 m.
- **The sharp spines** on their back fins deter predators from trying to eat them.
- **Bullheads** have two different sorts of teeth. The pointed front teeth are used to hold prey, while the large, blunt back teeth are used for crushing shellfish and other small sea creatures.
- **Female bullhead sharks** lay eggs inside leathery egg cases, which are shaped like screws. They are such an awkward shape that it takes the mother several hours to lay each egg case.

◀ A male crested bullhead shark eating the egg case of another species, a Port Jackson shark.

Carpet sharks

- **The carpet sharks** are a varied group of about 40 different species of shark.
- **Species include blind sharks**, wobbegongs, nurse sharks, bamboo sharks and the zebra shark, as well as collared and long-tailed carpet sharks.
- **Many types** are less than one metre long, but this group also includes the whale shark, which is the biggest shark of all.

▼ The large, dark 'eye spots' may help to startle a predator or stop a predator from attacking this epaulette shark's real eyes.

DID YOU KNOW?

Collared carpet sharks can change colour to match their surroundings.

- **They live** in warm tropical seas, such as those around Australia, Indonesia and Arabia, and often inhabit shallow waters around reefs and sandbars.
- **Carpet sharks** often lie still on the seabed. Many species have a slightly flattened body shape that helps to camouflage them.
- **Most carpet sharks** feed on crabs, shellfish, octopus and sea worms.
- **Some carpet sharks** lay eggs in cases, while others give birth to pups.
- **Many carpet sharks** have beautiful speckled markings, which resemble the patterns of carpets or tapestries.
- **Part of the long-tailed carpet shark family**, bamboo sharks use their leg-like, muscular fins to clamber over coral reefs.
- **Bamboo sharks can survive** out of water for up to half a day, allowing them to feed in small pools on coral or rocky reefs.

Whale sharks

▼ *To catch food, a whale shark swims along with its massive mouth wide open.*

- **Whale sharks** are the biggest kind of shark and the largest fish on Earth. They grow to an enormous length of 14 m and have the same mass as a double-decker bus.
- **Their closest relatives** are zebra sharks and short-tail nurse sharks – not other filter-feeders such as basking sharks or megamouths.
- **The filter-feeding whale shark** sieves tiny plankton out of the water.
- **These huge sharks** are harmless to humans.
- **Although a whale shark** has around 3000 tiny teeth, they are of little use. Instead it uses bristles in front of its gills to trap food.
- **Scientists think** that some whale sharks could live to be 100 years old or more.
- **Whale sharks scoop up food** at or near the surface of the water, sometimes hanging vertically and bobbing up and down.
- **The whale shark** has an extra-large liver full of oil to help it float more easily. Oil is lighter than water so this giant shark can swim slowly along at the surface of the sea without sinking.
- **A whale shark's liver** makes up about 20 percent of its body weight and may weigh as much as a small car.
- **One female whale shark** was found with 300 pups inside her.
- **A whale shark's skin** is around 10 cm thick, making it the thickest of any living creature.

Nurse sharks

- **Unlike most carpet sharks**, nurse sharks don't have carpet-like markings. They are usually brownish-grey, and sometimes have a few spots.
- **Nurse sharks** hunt at night. During the day, they often lie on the seabed in groups.
- **These large sharks** can reach 4 m in length.
- **Nurse sharks** have two barbels beneath their noses. They use them to smell and feel for prey.
- **With a preference** for warm, shallow water (usually up to about 12 m deep), nurse sharks can be found in the east Pacific Ocean and the Atlantic Ocean.

DID YOU KNOW?

Nurse sharks are named after the loud sucking noise they make when feeding, which sounds rather like a human baby drinking milk from its mother.

- **Crabs, lobsters and sea urchins** are the preferred food of nurse sharks. They have broad, flat teeth to grind up hard shells.
- **If a nurse shark bites**, it hangs on with a clamp-like grip. It can be almost impossible to dislodge it.
- **The nurse shark** uses its snout to find prey and sucks food in rapidly. It can even remove conch snails from their shells.
- **The tawny nurse shark** is also known as the spitting shark because it spits water at an attacker as a form of defence. After spitting, the tawny nurse shark is said to grunt. It is one of the few sharks thought to make a noise.
- **Females give birth** to between 20 and 30 pups at a time, after a pregnancy lasting six months.

◀ *This nurse shark is using its strong pectoral fins to climb over rocks and coral on the seabed.*

Wobbegongs

● **Wobbegong sharks**, also known as wobbies, belong to the carpet shark family.

● **The name 'wobbegong'** was given to these sharks by the Australian Aborigine people. It is thought that the word means 'shaggy beard'. Wobbegongs are often found in shallow, sandy water around the coast of Australia.

● **Wobbegongs can be quite large**, and some, such as the tasselled wobbegong, grow up to 4 m in length. They all have large, flattened bodies to help them hide on the seabed.

● **Wobbegongs are powerful** seabed predators, feeding on smaller fish and other sea creatures, such as crabs, lobsters, octopus and squid. They suck in prey and spear it on their large teeth.

● **The strong jaws** of the wobbegong can easily bite off a person's hand or foot.

● **Wobbegongs sometimes bite** people who accidentally step on them. For this reason, they have a reputation as being dangerous. They may attack if they feel threatened.

● **Wobbegongs have** lots of whisker-like barbels around their mouths. The barbels of the spotted wobbegong are branched and frilly.

● **The tasselled wobbegong** has tassel-like barbels around its face, like a beard.

● **Wobbegongs use** their strong fins to clamber around on the seabed, sometimes even moving out of the water.

● **The female spotted wobbegong** has large litters of up to 37 pups.

◀ *The beautiful gulf wobbegong lives on coral reefs around the coast of southern Australia. It sometimes attacks divers.*

Mackerel sharks

● **The mackerel shark** family consists of 15 species. They are mainly active, fast, open-ocean predators that live near the surface of the sea.

● **The most famous shark**, the great white, belongs to this family, as do mako, salmon and porbeagle sharks.

● **Two filter-feeders** – the megamouth shark and the basking shark – are also in the mackerel shark family.

● **One very unusual mackerel shark** is the goblin shark, with its sensitive, blade-like snout.

● **The diet of mackerel sharks** varies from dolphins, seals, birds and turtles, to other sharks, rays, fish and small sea creatures.

● **Some of the larger mackerel sharks**, such as the great white, sometimes attack people.

● **Many mackerel sharks** live in groups and some, such as thresher sharks, hunt together.

● **Some mackerel sharks**, such as the shortfin mako, migrate long distances.

● **Mackerel sharks** give birth to pups rather than laying eggs.

● **Most mackerel sharks** are threatened by over-fishing.

▼ *Measuring up to 3.5 m in length, the porbeagle shark is warm-blooded and a fast swimmer.*

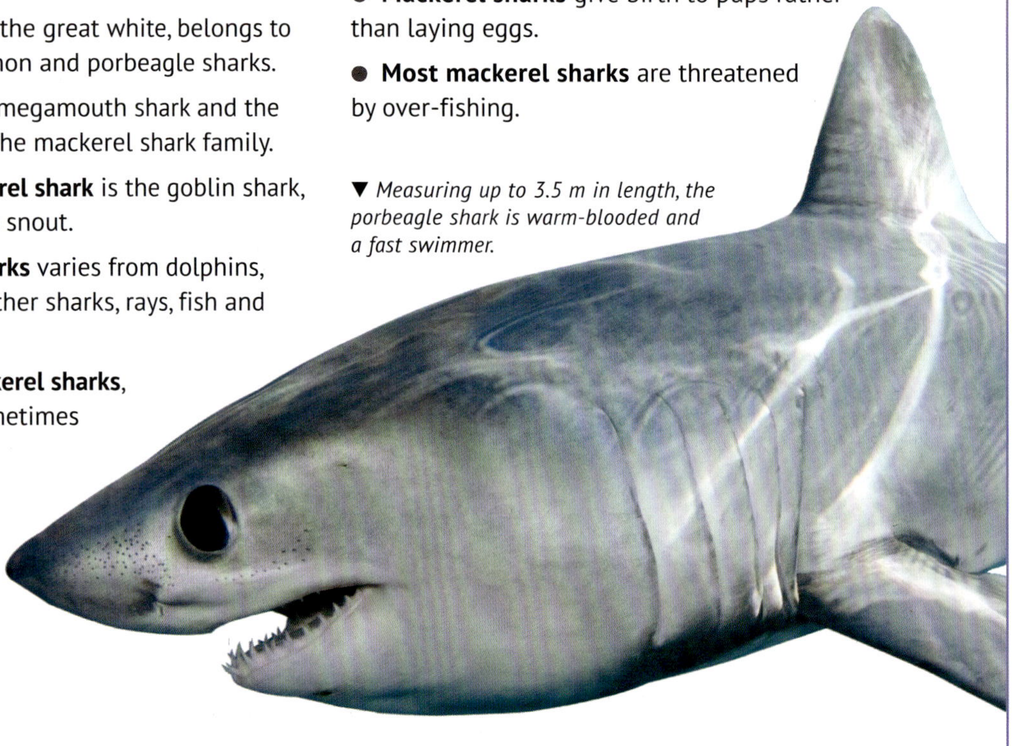

Goblin sharks

- **With its incredibly long**, flattened and pointed snout, the goblin shark looks very strange.
- **The long snout** looks like a weapon, but in fact, scientists think it helps the shark find prey using its sense of electrical detection.
- **Goblin sharks** have pale pink skin that is much softer and flabbier than the skin of most other sharks. It bruises easily.
- **Goblin sharks feed on fish**, squid and crustaceans such as crabs and lobsters.
- **Like many sharks**, the goblin shark pushes its jaws forwards as it attacks.
- **They have sharp teeth** at the front of their mouths for grabbing prey and smaller teeth at the back for chewing.
- **When they are born**, goblin sharks are 80–90 cm long, but they grow to lengths of at least 4 m.

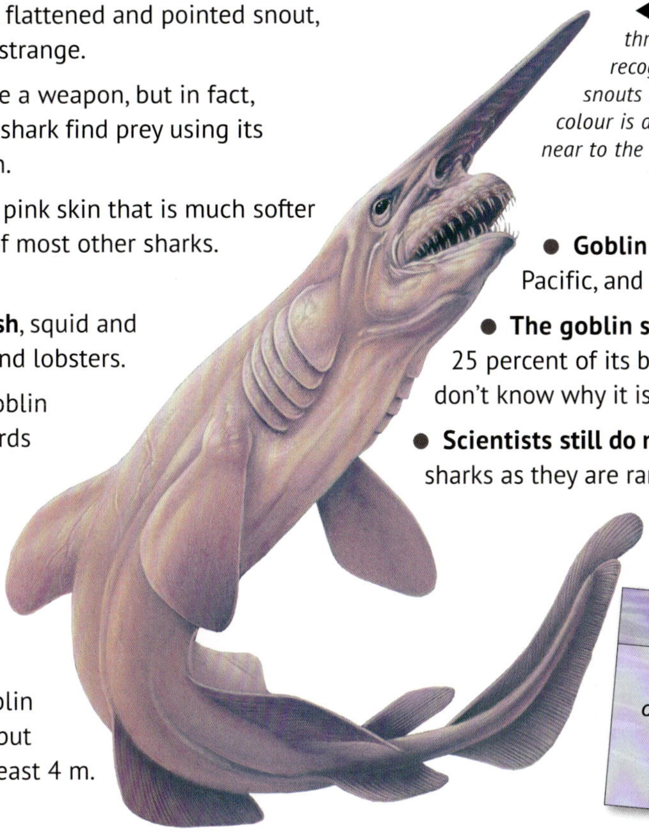

◀ *Even when their jaws are not thrust out, goblin sharks are instantly recognizable by their flat, sharp-edged snouts and bubblegum-pink colour. The colour is due to many small blood vessels near to the surface of a partly see-through skin.*

- **Goblin sharks** live in the Atlantic, Pacific, and western Indian oceans.
- **The goblin shark's** large liver takes up 25 percent of its body weight, but scientists don't know why it is so big.
- **Scientists still do not know** much about these sharks as they are rarely caught.

DID YOU KNOW?

Goblin sharks have survived on Earth for millions of years without changing very much at all.

Megamouth sharks

- **One of the most recently discovered** sharks is the weird-looking megamouth. It is probably one of the rarest species.
- **The first known megamouth** was caught in 1976, off the islands of Hawaii.
- **The megamouth grows** to more than 5 m long. It has a very thick, rounded, heavy body and a huge head.
- **Megamouths are filter-feeders**. They feed at night, cruising near the surface with their mouths wide open to filter plankton out of the water.
- **During the day**, megamouths swim down to depths of 200 m or more.
- **The megamouth** gets its name due to its huge mouth, which can be up to 1.3 m wide.
- **The scientific name** for the megamouth is *Megachasma pelagios*, which means 'huge yawner of the open sea'.
- **The mouth is at the front** of the snout, not underneath, as in most sharks.
- **The crocodile shark** is closely related to the megamouth shark but it is no bigger than a medium-sized dog and not a filter-feeder. Its main food is small fish, squid and shrimps, which it snaps up with its pointed teeth.

▼ *The megamouth traps small particles of food on finger-like bristles along its gills.*

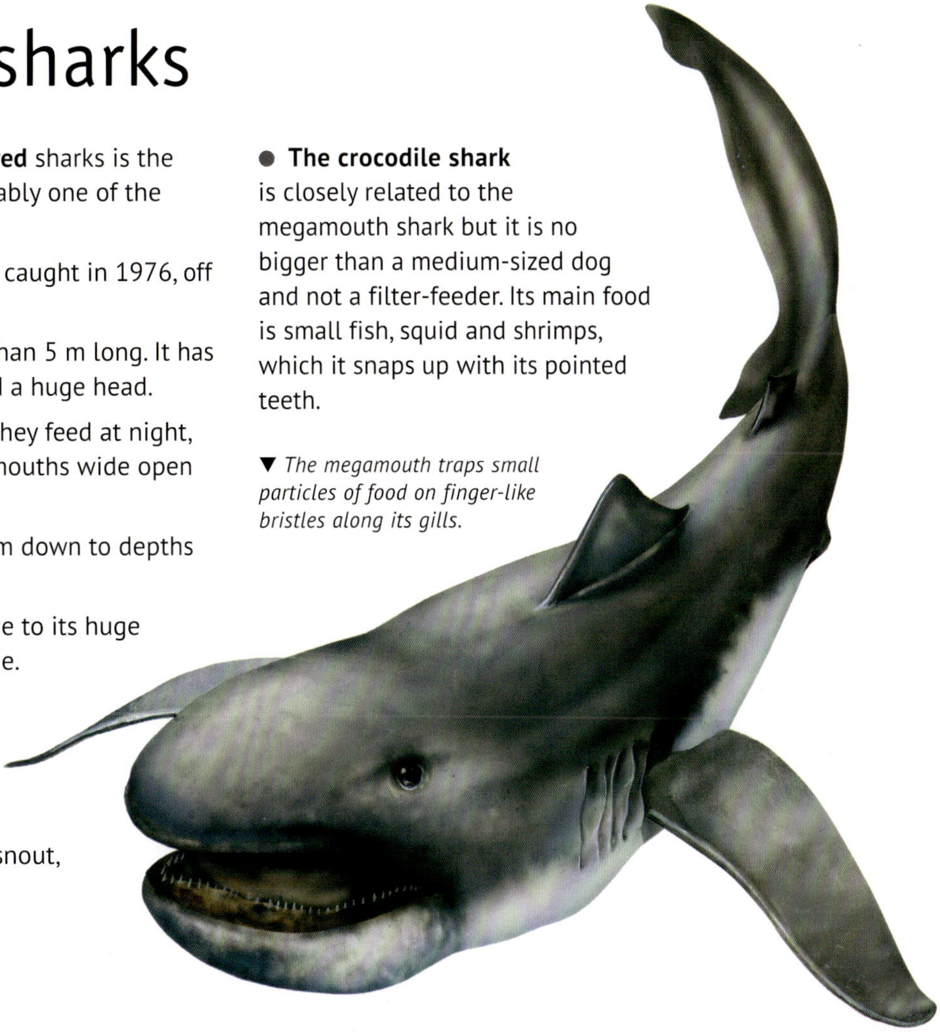

Sand tiger sharks

DID YOU KNOW?

Sand tiger sharks have been known to approach divers who are spear-fishing and grab the fish off their spears.

- **A typical sand tiger shark** is around 2–3 m long. It has brownish markings, but is not stripy like a tiger.
- **Sand tiger sharks** are not closely related to tiger sharks. They belong to a different order, and are more closely related to makos and great whites.
- **They are named after** their habit of swimming over the sandy seabed, and because of their large, sharp teeth.
- **Their diet is mainly fish**, but occasionally sand tigers kill and eat bigger animals such as sea lions.
- **Sometimes, sand tiger sharks** feed together, surrounding prey to make it easier to catch.
- **The sand tiger shark** has lots of gaps between its irregular, projecting teeth, giving it a 'snaggle-tooth' appearance.
- **Sand tiger sharks** can swallow air from the surface to help them hover at a particular depth in the water without using up a lot of their energy.
- **Male sand tiger sharks** guard females after mating, which gives their pups a better chance of surviving until they are born.
- **Female sand tiger sharks** give birth to two pups every other year after a pregnancy of between nine and 12 months. Pups hatch out of eggs inside the mother, and feed on the eggs and smaller pups that are produced after them.

▶ *A mouthful of sharp, pointed teeth helps the sand tiger shark to keep hold of slippery fish easily.*

Thresher sharks

- **There are three species** of thresher shark – the common, the pelagic and the bigeye.
- **Thresher sharks** are recognized by their extremely long tails. The upper lobe can be up to 50 percent of the shark's entire body length. Including the tail, these sharks can grow up to 6 m long.
- **They use their long tails** to round up shoals of small fish, such as sardines or herrings. Then they stun the fish by beating (or 'threshing') them with their tails before eating them.
- **Although threshers** are big, their mouths are small, so they only eat little prey.
- **Two or more thresher sharks** may work together to catch fish.
- **Thresher sharks** migrate away from the tropics to cooler waters in spring, and return to warmer waters in autumn.
- **Although thresher sharks** rarely attack humans, they have been known to injure fishermen by hitting them with their tails.
- **Common threshers** are the best-known sub-species, and are often seen near the seashore.
- **Pelagic threshers** get their name because they prefer to stay in the pelagic zone – the open sea – away from the seashore.
- **Bigeye threshers** often live in deep water. Their large eyes are up to 10 cm across – the size of a human fist.

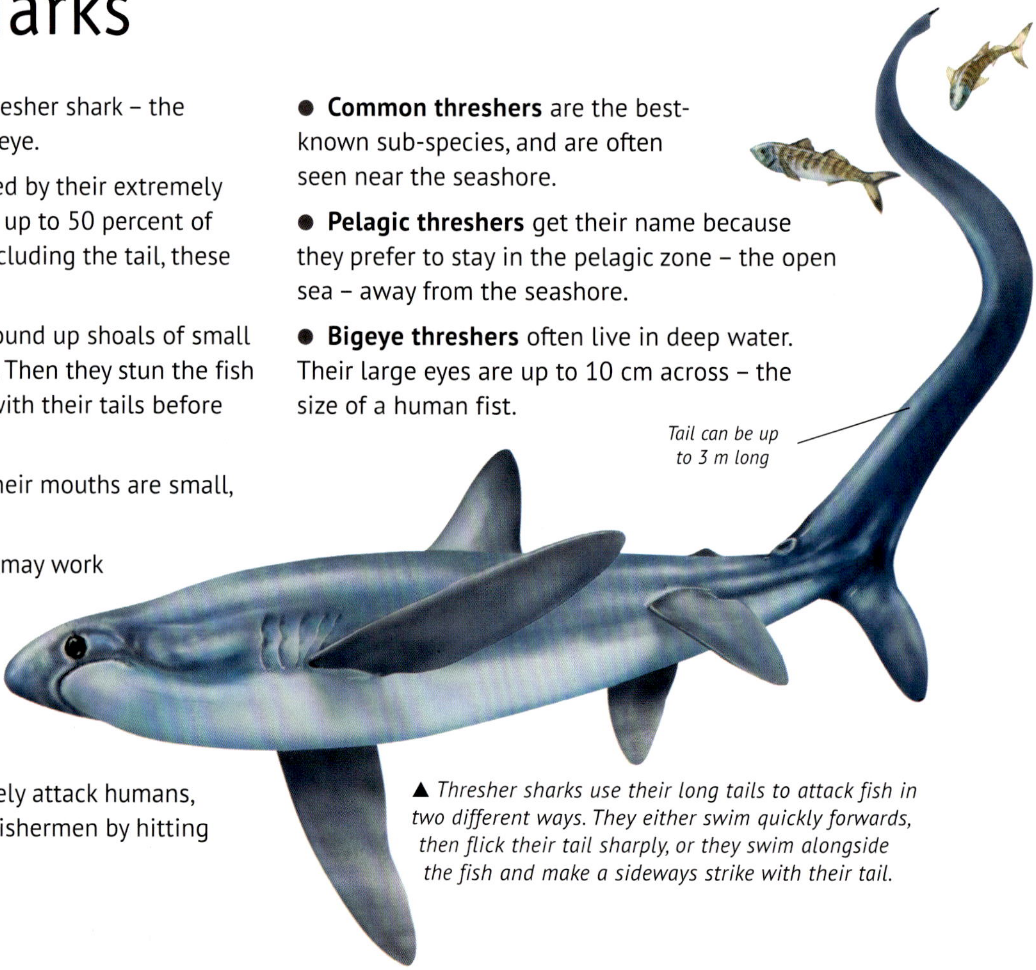

▲ *Thresher sharks use their long tails to attack fish in two different ways. They either swim quickly forwards, then flick their tail sharply, or they swim alongside the fish and make a sideways strike with their tail.*

Basking sharks

- **Basking sharks** get their name because they appear to 'bask', or lie in the sun, close to the surface of the sea when they are feeding.
- **They are the second-biggest shark** after the whale shark, growing up to 12 m in length.
- **Basking sharks** are filter-feeders, and feed by sieving plankton out of the water.
- **These placid animals** do not attack humans. They lack big teeth for biting or chewing.
- **Basking sharks** will sometimes leap right out of the water, and then fall back down with a huge splash.
- **Other names** for this species are bone shark, elephant shark, bigmouth shark, or sunfish – because people used to think they enjoyed lying in the sun.
- **Occasionally, basking sharks** have been seen swimming in large groups of 50 or more.
- **Basking sharks** probably live for more than 50 years.
- **The basking shark** filters over 1.5 million litres of water in one hour. That's as much water as there is in an Olympic-sized swimming pool!

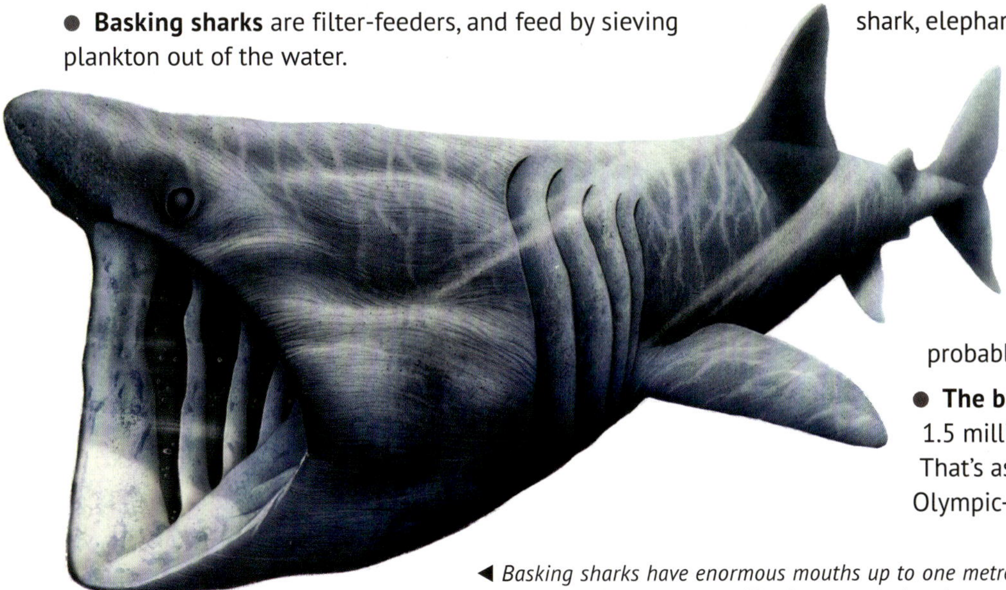

◀ *Basking sharks have enormous mouths up to one metre across, which they open widely when feeding. Their gill rakers are shed and re-grown at regular intervals.*

Great white sharks

DID YOU KNOW?

One great white shark swam 17,703 km from southern Africa to Australia in less than nine months.

- **The great white** is among the best-known of all sharks.
- **Belonging to the mackerel shark group**, great whites are fast, fierce hunters. They catch a wide variety of prey, from fish such as tuna, rays and smaller sharks, to marine mammals such as seals and dolphins, birds and turtles.
- **With large prey**, a great white may take a bite and then let go, leaving the animal to die from loss of blood before starting to feed.
- **A typical great white** is around 4–5 m long – slightly longer than a car. The biggest great whites on record were over 7 m long.
- **Great whites** are often found in medium-warm waters, such as those around Australia and Japan.
- **When swimming**, great whites will sometimes poke their heads out of the water or leap high into the air.
- **Great white sharks** are warm-blooded and keep a high body temperature, even in cold water.
- **This helps to speed up** their digestion, especially of fatty foods (such as seals), which are hard to digest but full of energy.
- **Female great whites** give birth to between two and 13 pups at a time after a pregnancy of about 12 months.
- **It is difficult** to keep a great white in captivity. If they are put into an aquarium, they live for only a few days.

▼ *A great white shark's body is sturdy, powerful and built for hunting.*

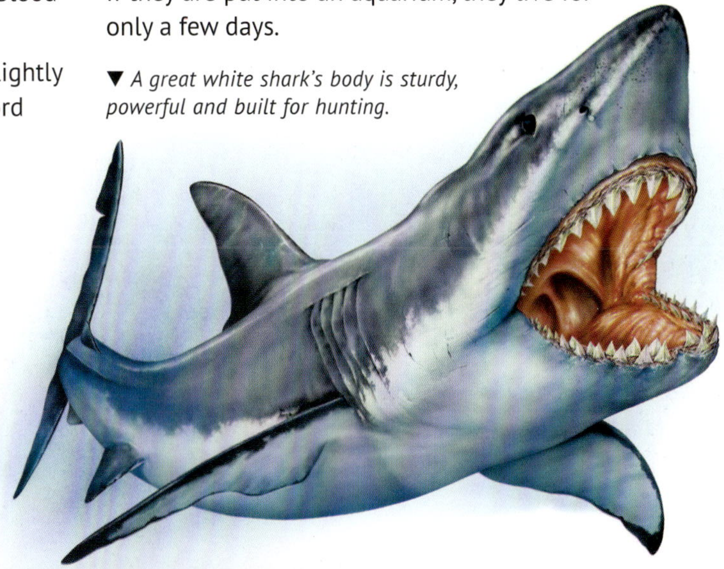

Mako sharks

▲ *A fast-swimming, active shark, the short-finned mako has large eyes, a long, pointed snout and large, dagger-like teeth. Its crescent-shaped tail fin enables it to swim at high speed.*

- **Swift and fierce**, makos are strong, muscular hunting sharks that can swim at great speed.
- **One shortfin mako** travelled over 13,000 km in six months, swimming to and fro between New Zealand and Fiji.
- **Makos are closely related** to great whites, and they live and hunt in a similar way. They will sometimes attack humans, but their diet is predominantly fish.

DID YOU KNOW?

There are two species of mako – the shortfin and the longfin. The longfin has longer pectoral fins and bigger eyes.

- **They have long**, streamlined, graceful bodies and pointed snouts, and can grow up to 4 m in length.
- **Known for their vivid colours**, makos are dark purple-blue on top and silvery-white underneath.
- **A mako's smooth teeth** are very narrow and pointed to help them grab slippery fish in their jaws.
- **The name 'mako'** comes from the Maori word for 'shark'. Makos are common around New Zealand, the home of the Maori people.
- **Female shortfin makos** have between four and 25 pups at a time. Each pup is about 70 cm long at birth.
- **People often fish makos** as sport and they are also caught for food.

Porbeagle sharks

- **Like great whites**, porbeagles are grey on top and white underneath. They also have a white mark on their dorsal fins.
- **Porbeagle sharks** grow up to 3 m in length. They have a second keel on their tails, which helps them to swim fast.
- **These sharks prefer** cooler seas, such as the north and south Atlantic Ocean. Porbeagles can keep their body temperature warmer than their surroundings.
- **Porbeagles are inquisitive** and may attack humans. However, attacks are rare because people don't usually venture into their cold water habitats.
- **Their diet is mostly fish** and squid. They will chase shoals of mackerel over long distances.
- **Porbeagles have long**, sharp teeth to spear prey and stop it from escaping.
- **Their smooth-edged teeth** cannot cut the flesh, so prey is usually swallowed whole.
- **Porbeagles migrate** with the seasons, moving to coastal waters near the shore in summer and swimming to deeper water for the winter months.
- **Female porbeagles** give birth to between one and five pups after a pregnancy of 8–9 months.

DID YOU KNOW?

The porbeagle shark may live for up to 65 years.

- **Porbeagles are among** the few fish that are thought to play. They roll over at the ocean surface, chase one another and wrap themselves in seaweed!

▲ *A porbeagle shark chases a shoal of fast-swimming mackerel.*

Catsharks

- **The largest shark family**, there are more than 160 species of catshark. Some have unusual names, including ghost catshark, bighead catshark, spongehead catshark and even Pinocchio catshark.
- **Catsharks are named** after their cat-like eyes.
- **They are usually** less than one metre in length, although some are only 30 cm long and a few reach 160 cm.
- **Catsharks eat** small fish and crabs.
- **Sometimes confused with dogfish**, catsharks can be identified by the lack of spines on their dorsal fins and are usually slimmer than dogfish.
- **Dogfish are usually** dull colours, but many catsharks have beautiful markings. The chain shark has patterns on its skin that look like silver chains.
- **Some catsharks** that live near the shore sleep in groups in rock crevices by day and come out at night.
- **Most catsharks lay eggs** in cases with long tendrils that curl around plants on the seabed.

- **A few catsharks**, such as the lollipop catshark and the African sawtail catshark, give birth to pups.
- **Catsharks are not dangerous** to people and some are kept in aquariums.

◀ *The coral catshark lives among the coral reefs of the western Pacific Ocean, from Pakistan and India to New Guinea and southern China. It hunts at night for small fish, shellfish and shrimp.*

Swellsharks

- **Also known as balloonsharks**, swellsharks are slow-moving sharks, about 50–100 cm in length.
- **This species** is named after its ability to swell to twice its normal size by pumping water into its stomach.
- **This skill** may startle or frighten a predator, giving a swellshark time to escape.
- **If in danger**, a swellshark puffs itself up into a ball inside a rocky crevice so it can't be pulled out of the rocks.
- **A closely related species**, the draughtsboard shark has dark and light checkerboard markings. It is said to bark like a dog as air escapes from its stomach.
- **Swellsharks** have long, wide mouths, which they use to gulp down mouthfuls of small fish before swallowing them whole.
- **They have up to 60 small, sharp teeth**, with dagger-like points, in each jaw.
- **Swellsharks catch prey**, such as small fish, in the dark by detecting the tiny electrical signals given off by the life processes of their prey.
- **Swellsharks hide in seaweed**, caves and rocky crevices by day and come out at night to hunt for fish, crabs, shrimps and prawns.
- **Very sociable**, swellsharks often rest together in groups during the day.
- **Female swellsharks** usually lay two eggs in large, purse-shaped egg cases.

▼ *The swellshark grows to a maximum length of about one metre. This sluggish shark is spotted and blotched all over, helping it to blend into a rocky seabed covered with seaweed.*

Houndsharks

● **There are more** than 40 species of houndshark, including the whiskery shark, the tope shark, the gummy shark and the leopard shark.

● **They are small** to medium-sized sharks, ranging from 40–150 cm in length.

● **Their oval eyes** have nictitating eyelids, which they can draw across their eyes for protection.

● **Most types live** on shallow seabeds, but there are a few deep-water species that swim at great depths, possibly deeper than 2000 m.

● **The whiskery shark** is the only houndshark to have long barbels on its nose. These help it to catch octopuses, which are its preferred food.

▶ *A spotted houndshark swimming over a sandy seabed near the Galapagos Islands. These stout houndsharks also live along the coasts of Peru and northern Chile.*

● **Instead of sharp, biting teeth**, most houndsharks have flat teeth for crushing prey, such as shellfish, crabs and lobsters.

● **Gummy sharks** were named because they seemed to have no teeth. They actually have flat, grinding teeth instead of sharp, pointy ones.

● **Female houndsharks** give birth to between one and 52 pups.

● **Tope sharks** may make long migration journeys to find food or safe places to have their young.

● **The leopard shark** may form schools with smoothhound sharks, spiny dogfish and bat rays.

DID YOU KNOW?

Larger leopard sharks nip the front fins of smaller individuals as a sign of dominance.

Weasel sharks

● **Most weasel shark** species are small, usually no more than one metre in length.

● **There are about** eight different species, including the hooktooth, the snaggletooth and the sicklefin weasel shark.

● **Weasel sharks live** in coastal waters of the east Atlantic Ocean and the west of the Pacific Ocean.

● **They have oval eyes** with nictitating eyelids for protection.

● **The hooktooth shark** has very long, hooked lower teeth, which stick out from its long mouth.

● **Straight-tooth weasel sharks** have pointed lower teeth, but they do not stick out of the short, arched mouth.

● **The Atlantic weasel shark** has a specialized diet of squid and octopuses.

● **It has a striking pattern** of yellow stripes along its back, which is light grey or bronze.

● **The female snaggletooth shark** gives birth to between two and 11 pups at a time, after a pregnancy of seven to eight months.

● **Most weasel sharks** are harmless to humans, apart from the snaggletooth shark, which is large enough to be a threat. It reaches a maximum length of 2.4 m.

▼ *Weasel sharks are related to bull and lemon sharks. They are recognized by the natural dent where the tail meets the body. This is called the precaudal pit.*

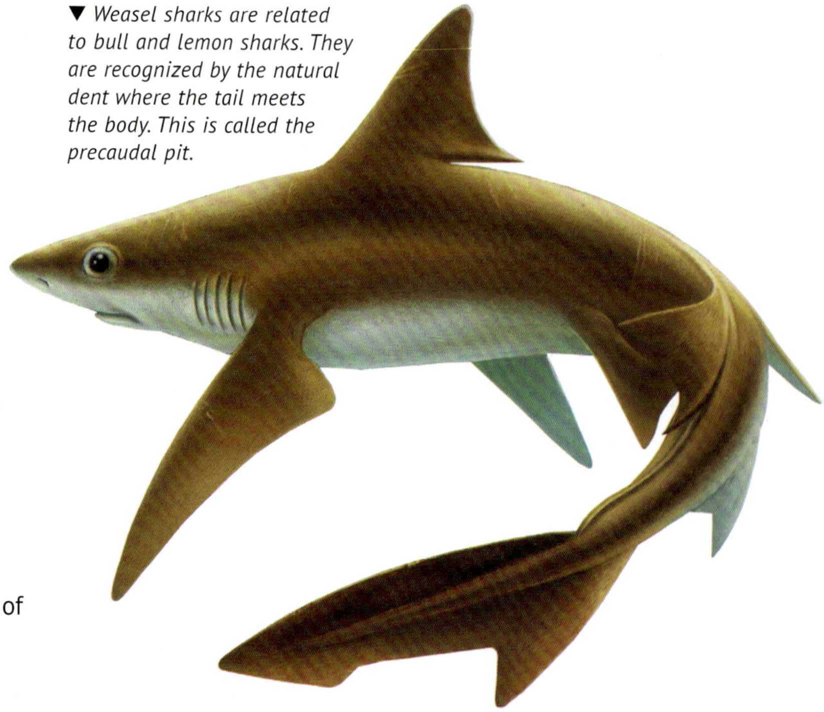

Requiem sharks

▲ *The bull shark is a fierce predator, which attacks sea creatures as large as itself. Smaller prey includes baby sharks, such as lemon shark and sandbar shark pups.*

- **There are at least** 56 species in the requiem shark family (Carcharhinidae). It was probably named after the French word for shark, *requin*.
- **The family includes** some of the most typical and well-known sharks, such as blue sharks, lemon sharks, tiger sharks, bull sharks and reef sharks.
- **Requiem sharks** are sometimes called whaler sharks.
- **Sharks in this family** are usually large and chunky-looking, with bodies 1–3 m long.
- **Their skin** is usually plain, without any patterns, although they are dark on top and light beneath. This countershading camouflages them from above and below.
- **Sharks in this family** have long, arched mouths with sharp, blade-like teeth.
- **Their eyes** are usually round with nictitating eyelids.
- **They have two fins** on their back. The second dorsal fin is usually smaller, and the top lobe of their tail fin is much larger than the bottom lobe.
- **Most requiem sharks** live in tropical waters, both near the shore and out in the open ocean, with most living in sunlit surface waters rather than the deep ocean.
- **A few requiem sharks** – the bull shark and the river sharks – are the only shark species that can live in freshwater for long periods of time.

Blue sharks

- **The streamlined shape** and long front fins of the blue shark allow it to move very fast through the oceans when hunting prey.
- **Named after its deep**, silvery-indigo colour on top, this shark has a pale underside.
- **Blue sharks** sometimes swim at the surface but reach depths of up to 335 m.
- **These sharks eat** mostly squid, although they will feed on any kind of fish or other sea creature.
- **The blue shark** has large, sensitive eyes to find prey and finger-like bristles on its gills to stop small prey escaping from its gill slits.
- **It may circle** round swimmers, boats and divers for some time before closing in and biting.
- **The skin of a female blue shark** is twice as thick as that of the male. This helps to protect the females from bites during courtship and mating.

DID YOU KNOW?

Blue sharks have large litters of pups, sometimes giving birth to more than 100 at a time.

- **This species** was once extremely common, and is found in almost every part of every ocean. The population is now falling because it is so heavily overfished.
- **Blue sharks** are often caught by accident on hooks or in nets intended for tuna and swordfish.
- **Experts have estimated** that ten million blue sharks are caught and killed every year.

▼ *Blue sharks are sleek, slim and graceful, and grow up to 4 m in length.*

Tiger sharks

▲ *Tiger sharks usually hunt alone, swimming slowly through the oceans until they spot a potential meal. This tiger shark is swimming in front of a group of lemon sharks, fighting for their share of food.*

- **The tiger shark** will attack almost anything, including humans, making it one of the most dangerous sharks.
- **These sharks** are usually about 3 m long, but they can grow up to 6 m.
- **They have massive heads** with a blunt snout, large eyes and a wide mouth.
- **The diet of tiger sharks** includes fish, seals, sea lions, turtles, shellfish, crabs, seabirds, dolphins, crocodiles, squid and jellyfish. They also take bites out of bigger animals such as whales, and have even been seen eating other tiger sharks.
- **Many unusual objects**, such as oil drums, tin cans, glass bottles, clothes, rubber tyres, coal, cushions, tools, and even pieces of armour, have been found in the stomachs of tiger sharks.
- **This species** is found in most of the world's warmer seas and oceans. It sometimes swims into river mouths.
- **Tiger sharks** are named after the striped markings of the young, which fade with age.
- **Females have large numbers** of pups. They are ovoviviparous and often have 35–55 pups at a time, but can have as many as 82 pups at a time.
- **Tiger sharks are strong swimmers**, able to reach speeds of more than 32 km/h in just a few seconds. However, they cannot swim this fast for very long.
- **Some tiger sharks** may travel many thousands of kilometres in one year, while others keep to a small stretch of coastline just 100 km long.

Bull sharks

- **The bull shark** is a powerful, aggressive hunter. It gets its name because its body is thick, stocky and muscular, like a bull.
- **This species** is not especially long – bull sharks usually grow to between 2–3 m in length.
- **They are among** the few species that can survive in fresh water. Bull sharks swim hundreds of kilometres up rivers such as the Mississippi in North America, the Amazon in South America and the Zambezi in Africa.

▼ *A very short, wide head, blunt snout and small eyes are characteristic features of the bull shark.*

- **Some bull sharks** have been found living in Lake Nicaragua, a large lake in Central America.
- **Bull sharks** are often known by other names, depending on where they live – such as the Zambezi River shark or the Nicaragua shark.
- **Some experts think** that bull sharks may be the most dangerous species. This is because they often lurk in shallow waters where humans swim.
- **Bull sharks** usually swim slowly near the seabed in water less than 20 m deep, but they are agile and quick when chasing prey.
- **They eat a wide range** of food, from fish and sea turtles to birds, dolphins and dead whales.
- **Bull sharks** have small eyes because they often live in shallow, muddy waters, where eyesight is not that useful for hunting prey.
- **Fierce and strong**, bull sharks probably attack more people than any other shark. They have huge jaws and large, sharp teeth.

Blacktip reef sharks

- **Blacktip reef sharks** have black tips on all their fins and are sometimes known as black sharks.
- **The black fin tips** may help to break up the shark's outline and improve its camouflage.
- **Like its cousin** the whitetip reef shark, the blacktip prefers warm, shallow water.
- **This shark has long**, slender teeth ideally suited to snapping up its main prey – fish that live around coral reefs.
- **Adults usually grow** to lengths of about one metre but some reach maximum lengths of up to 2 m.
- **Blacktip reef sharks** have small, oval eyes with a pupil like a vertical slit. Their eyes don't need to let in much light as they live in shallow, sunlit waters.
- **They are strong, active** swimmers, and their back fin often breaks through the surface in shallow water.
- **Blacktip reef sharks live** in the western Pacific Ocean, the Indian Ocean and the eastern Mediterranean.
- **They live alone** or in very small groups.
- **Females give birth** to between two and four pups at a time, after a pregnancy lasting 16 months.

▼ *The black fin markings of the blacktip reef shark contrast strongly with its pale skin.*

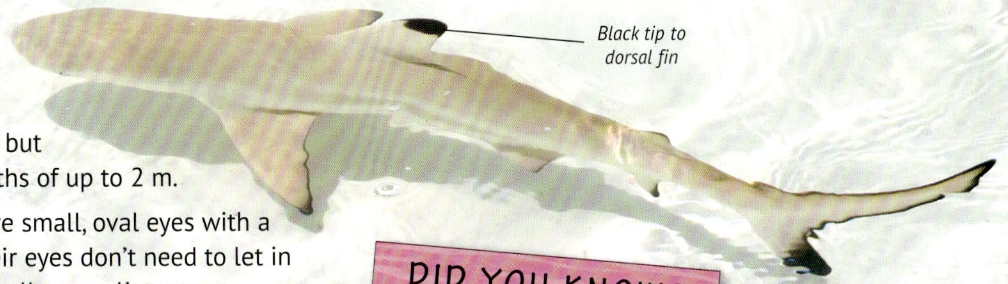

DID YOU KNOW?

Since the Suez Canal was built in Egypt, blacktip reef sharks have been able to swim through it from the Red Sea to the Mediterranean Sea.

Spinner sharks

- **This very active shark** is named after the way it spins through schools of fish with its mouth open when feeding.
- **It spins right out** of the water at the end of a feeding run, turning round and round up to three times before falling back into the water.
- **As well as fish**, spinner sharks also eat stingrays, squid and octopuses.
- **They have narrow**, pointed teeth in both jaws to help them keep a tight grip on slippery fish.
- **The narrow**, pointed snout of the spinner shark helps it to swim quickly and catch speedy fish.
- **Spinner sharks live** in warm to hot waters in the Atlantic Ocean, Mediterranean Sea and the western Pacific Ocean.
- **In the Gulf of Mexico**, spinner sharks migrate towards the shore to feed and breed as the water warms up in spring. In winter, they move into deeper water and may also travel further south.
- **Young spinner sharks** prefer lower water temperatures to the adults.
- **Females give birth** to between three and 15 pups at a time, after a pregnancy of 11–15 months.
- **Adult and young spinner sharks** have obvious black tips to most of their fins.

▼ *The spinner shark is sometimes confused with the blacktip shark because of its black fin tips. It has long gill slits in front of its pectoral fins.*

Night sharks

- **The night shark** is a deepwater shark, found at depths of between 275–365 m during the day, and 185 m at night.
- **There are no recorded attacks** on humans by this species.
- **The night shark** has a very long, pointed snout that is longer than the width of its mouth.
- **These sharks** live off the east coast of the Americas, from the USA south to Argentina, as well as off the west coast of Africa.
- **Although similar in appearance** to silky sharks and dusky sharks, unlike the night shark, neither of these species has green eyes.
- **Night sharks** are slim, grey-brown sharks, with small dorsal and pectoral fins.
- **There are 15 rows of teeth** on each side of the night shark's top and bottom jaws. The triangular top teeth have jagged edges, while the bottom teeth are narrow and upright.
- **The night shark feeds** on squid and small fish, including flying fish and sea bass.
- **Females give birth** to between 12 and 18 pups at a time. The pups are 60–72 cm long at birth.
- **Adults grow** to about 2 m long, reaching maximum lengths of 2.8 m.

▲ *Night sharks have large, green eyes, which probably help them to see in deep, dark waters.*

DID YOU KNOW?

The name of the night shark comes from the fact that it is usually caught at night.

River sharks

- **Only a handful of sharks** (about six species) can survive in the freshwater of rivers.
- **River sharks** live in parts of south and southeast Asia, and Australia. They grow up to 3 m in length.
- **River sharks** include the Borneo river shark, the Ganges shark, the New Guinea river shark, the speartooth shark and the Irrawaddy river shark.
- **All of these sharks** are very rare and in danger of dying out.
- **This is probably due** to people damaging their habitat and catching too many fish in the rivers where they live.
- **River sharks** have tiny eyes because eyesight is not an important sense in muddy river water. These sharks probably rely more on their electrical senses than their eyes.
- **The speartooth shark** is named after the tips of its lower teeth, which are shaped like tiny spears.
- **The eyes of the Ganges shark** point upwards.
- **As it swims** along the riverbed looking for prey, its upward-facing eyes may help it to search for prey in the water above.
- **River sharks** are secretive, mysterious creatures and scientists know very little about them.
- **Female river sharks** probably give birth to pups, but little is known about the details of their reproduction.
- **They probably** use their small, pointed teeth to catch fish.

◀ *The extremely rare speartooth shark lives in only a few rivers in New Guinea and the Northern Territory of Australia. It probably grows to lengths of 2 or 3 m.*

Hammerhead sharks

- **Hammerheads** are probably the strangest-looking sharks. The head is extremely wide and the eyes are at either end of the flat, streamlined hammer.
- **A hammerhead shark** has to turn its head from side to side in order to see forwards.
- **Experts think this head shape** may help the shark to find food (such as fish, other sharks, rays, squid and octopuses), by spreading out their ampullae of Lorenzini over a wide area.
- **The shark's nostrils** are also spread wide apart on its head, giving it 'stereo-sniffing' power and helping it to better detect the scent of prey.
- **The hammer-shaped head** also works like underwater 'wings' to lift the shark upwards as it moves through the water.
- **There are nine species** of hammerhead, including great, scalloped, smooth, winghead and bonnethead sharks. Each species has a head of a slightly different size and shape.

▲ *A bonnethead shark swallows a ray it has just found partially buried in the sandy seabed. It isn't affected by the ray's painful sting.*

▼ *The smooth hammerhead does not have a notch in the middle of its hammer-shaped head.*

DID YOU KNOW?

The great hammerhead is the biggest hammerhead shark and can grow up to 6 m in length.

- **During the day**, hammerhead sharks can often be seen swimming in large groups.
- **In hammerhead shark groups**, larger sharks tend to swim in the safest places in the middle of the group and smaller sharks around the outside. The sharks control their position in the group with displays, such as head shakes and swimming in large loops.
- **Hammerheads have taller dorsal fins** and smaller pectoral fins than most other sharks. This helps them to feed on the seabed.
- **Hammerhead females** give birth to pups. Scalloped hammerheads have 13–31 pups at a time after a pregnancy lasting eight to twelve months.

Shark relatives

● **Sharks are closely related** to two other groups of fish – the batoids and the chimaeras.

● **The batoids** include rays, skates, sawfish and guitarfish. They range in size from plate-sized skates to giant manta rays.

● **There are more** than 550 species of batoids – more than the number of shark species.

● **Most batoids** have wide, flat heads and bodies, and long, tapering tails. They look similar to some types of shark, such as angelsharks.

● **Most batoids feed** on bottom-dwelling sea creatures, such as clams, shrimps and flatfish, although manta rays feed on plankton and pelagic stingrays feed on squid.

● **Most batoids swim** by flapping their large, front fins. Some, such as sawfish, guitarfish and torpedo rays, use their tail for swimming, as sharks do.

● **Sharks are often difficult to catch** and keep in captivity, so scientists often study batoids instead. They are very similar to sharks, so they can provide clues to how sharks live.

● **Chimaeras are strange-looking**, long-tailed fish. Their name means 'a mixture', as they look a little like a cross between a shark and a bony fish.

● **The various species** of chimaera are also known as ratfish, ghost sharks, spook fish and even ghouls.

● **Like sharks**, batoids and chimaeras have light, flexible skeletons made of cartilage, instead of bone like other fish.

▶ *The smalltooth sawfish reaches an average length of 5.5 m.*

Rays

● **Rays are a type of batoid.** They are closely related to sharks.

● **Some rays** are wider than they are long because of their huge, flat, wing-like fins.

● **Most rays** use their wing-like pectoral fins for swimming. They look as if they are 'flying' underwater.

● **Many rays have** a long, whip-like tail. Unlike sharks, they don't use their tails to push themselves through the water.

● **Most rays are ovoviviparous** – they give birth to live young that have hatched from eggs inside the mothers' bodies, like some sharks do.

● **Rays live in seas** and oceans all around the world, from shallows near the shore to seabeds 3000 m deep.

● **Most species** are solitary and prefer to live alone. However some, such as golden cow-nosed rays, form huge groups of thousands of individuals.

● **There are two species** of manta ray – the giant oceanic manta, which can be up to 7 m wide, and the smaller reef manta. In both species, the wingspan is about twice the length of the body.

● **Manta rays** have a docile nature and are preyed on by killer whales and large sharks, such as the great white shark.

● **Many rays** have colourful patterns on their skin and live in shallow water. The Australian leopard whipray has leopard-like spots on its skin.

▼ *Rays have wide, flat bodies, which help them to skim closely along the seabed, searching for food.*

Electric rays

DID YOU KNOW?

The mouth of the Australian coffin ray is gigantic, which allows it to swallow prey half the size of its own body!

● **Electric rays** can generate electricity to give other animals a powerful electric shock. This ability can be used to deter predators or stun prey.

● **Some electric rays** produce as little as 37 volts or less, while Atlantic torpedo rays can generate as much as 220 volts of electricity.

● **The ancient Greeks** used the electricity from electric rays to numb the pain of operations and childbirth.

● **Short-nose electric rays** include some of the smallest rays, at less than 20 cm across. They are about the size of a pancake!

● **There are over 60 species** of electric ray, including Atlantic torpedo rays, the lesser electric ray and the marbled electric ray.

● **Electric rays** live in shallow waters, but can also be found in waters at least 1000 m deep.

● **Most electric rays** bury themselves under sand on the seabed during the day and come out at night to feed.

● **Electric rays feed** on fish, worms and shellfish. Adult Atlantic rays eat eels, flounders and even small sharks.

● **Lesser electric rays** have two pups at a time, while Atlantic torpedo rays may have as many as 60 pups at a time.

◀ *A lesser electric ray lives in shallow coastal waters. It can generate a voltage of around 37 volts in order to stun prey or defend itself from predators.*

Stingrays

● **Stingrays have a poisonous spine** (or sometimes two or three) in the middle of their tails. It is used mainly for defence against attack.

● **River stingrays**, unlike other rays, live in freshwater. They are found in rivers in Africa and South America, especially the Amazon River.

● **Round stingrays** have almost completely round, flat bodies, like dinner plates.

● **Spotted eagle rays** are covered with beautiful pale spots on dark skin, but are white underneath.

● **Most stingrays** live on the seabed. They feed on shellfish and crabs, which they crush with their teeth.

● **The eagle, duckbilled and cownose rays** are nicknamed 'nutcracker rays'. This is because their teeth are joined together to form plates, which they use to crush their hard-shelled prey.

● **The pelagic stingray** is different. It lives in the open ocean and feeds mainly on squid.

● **Most stingrays** only attack people in self-defence. If a person accidentally steps on a stingray buried in the sand, the stingray may flip up its dangerous tail to stab the person's legs or ankles with poison.

● **Females give birth** to between five and 15 young after a pregnancy of about nine months.

● **The mothers feed** the young a sort of 'milk' while they are developing inside their uterus (womb).

▶ *The bright blue spots of the blue-spotted stingray warn other animals that it has poisonous tail spines.*

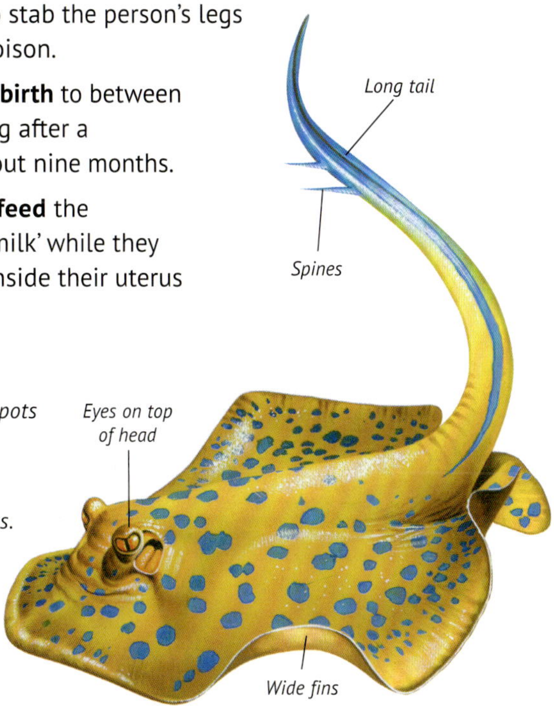

Inside a ray

- **Rays are nearly all** adapted for living on the seabed, where they feed on shellfish, shrimps and worms.
- **Unlike sharks**, which use their tails for swimming, rays swim by flapping their pectoral fins up and down like wings, or by rippling the edges of these fins.
- **On the inside**, a ray's body is supported by a skeleton made from flexible cartilage, or gristle, just like a shark's skeleton.
- **A ray also has gills** to absorb oxygen from the water and similar internal organs to a shark.
- **It has a large, oily liver**, which helps it to float because oil is lighter than water. The fat in its liver also provides a useful source of stored energy.
- **A ray's digestive system** consists of a tube from its mouth leading to its stomach, a short intestine (gut) and an opening called the cloaca for wastes to pass out.
- **Electric rays generate and store electricity** in kidney-shaped electric organs (rather like batteries) at the base of their front fins. They use their electricity to stun their prey, defend themselves from predators and communicate with each other.
- **Manta rays** have a spiral-shaped valve in their intestine, as do many sharks, such as the silky shark. The valve increases the surface area over which digestion takes place, slowing down the movement of food and allowing the ray to absorb more nutrients.

DID YOU KNOW?

Manta rays often visit feeding stations where small fish feed on the dead skin and parasites on their skin and gills. Both the mantas and the small fish benefit from this behaviour.

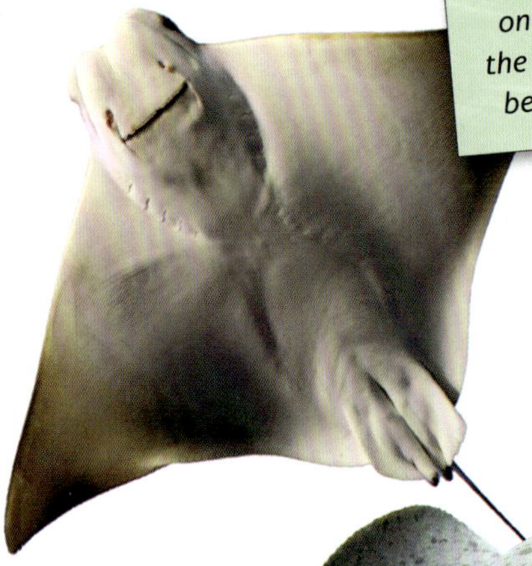

▲ *A ray has eyes and breathing holes (spiracles) on top of its body. Underneath its body are its mouth, gill slits and nostrils (nares). When they are buried in sand or mud on the seabed, rays use their spiracles to pump water to their gills, so they can keep breathing.*

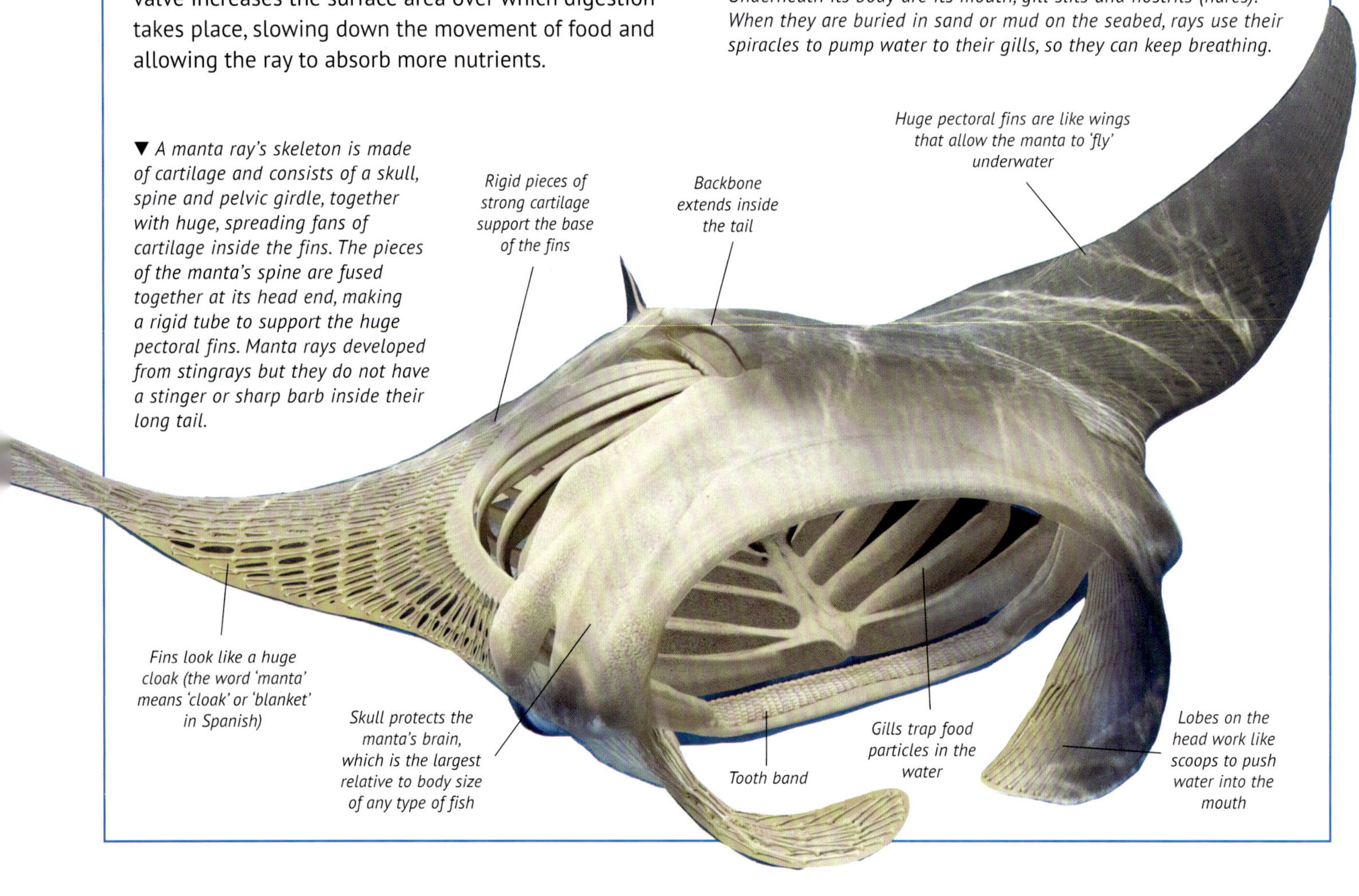

▼ *A manta ray's skeleton is made of cartilage and consists of a skull, spine and pelvic girdle, together with huge, spreading fans of cartilage inside the fins. The pieces of the manta's spine are fused together at its head end, making a rigid tube to support the huge pectoral fins. Manta rays developed from stingrays but they do not have a stinger or sharp barb inside their long tail.*

Skates

- **Skates are similar to rays**, but they tend to have straighter edges to the front of their pectoral fins, and shorter tails.
- **Most types of skate** live in deep water, as far down as 3000 m.
- **Skates usually lie** on the seabed waiting for prey such as crabs and shrimps to come close.
- **As its mouth** is on its underside, a skate does not lunge at its prey. Instead it swims over the victim and grasps it from above.
- **Like some sharks**, skates lay eggs with protective cases.
- **The egg cases** of the flapper skate are up to 25 cm long, and each contains as many as seven eggs.
- **Skate egg cases** have stiff spikes to help them stick into the seabed. They also have a sticky coating so that they soon become covered with sand or pebbles as a form of camouflage.
- **Skate is a popular food** in some parts of the world – especially the fins, which are called 'skate wings'.
- **The largest skate** is the flapper skate, which reaches lengths of up to 2.8 m.
- **The Texas skate** has two big spots, one on each 'wing'. These spots look like the eyes of a larger animal, and may deter predators.

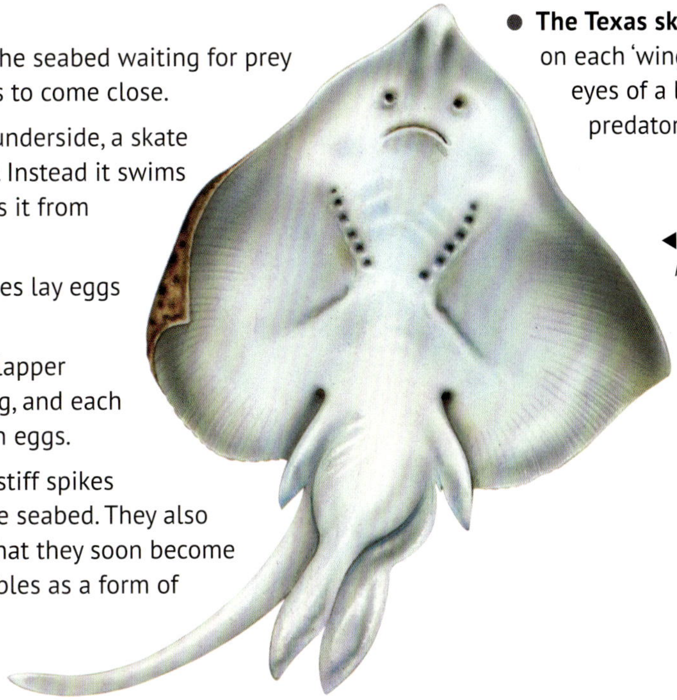

◀ *The common skate can be recognized by its long and pointed snout. This species is now usually called the flapper skate.*

DID YOU KNOW?

The flapper skate is critically endangered due to over-fishing and habitat destruction.

Guitarfish

- **Guitarfish** are a family of rays with over 40 different species.
- **The head** of a guitarfish is long, flat and guitar-shaped unlike the disc-shaped head of other rays.
- **The front fins** are smaller than those of other rays and they use their tails for swimming (like sharks).
- **The giant guitarfish** reaches lengths of up to 3 m. It is found in the Red Sea and Indian Ocean.
- **During the day**, the shovelnose guitarfish lays buried in the sand, with only its eyes sticking out, waiting to ambush crabs or flatfish. At night, it swims over the seabed, hunting for crabs, worms and clams.
- **Shovelnose guitarfish** crush crabs and shellfish with their many rows of pebble-like teeth.
- **The bowmouth guitarfish** (also known as the sharkfin guitarfish) has a mouth shaped like a longbow, and heavy ridges of sharp, spiky thorns on its head for defence.
- **It uses its large head** and front fins to trap prey against the seabed, then quickly gulps down its meal.
- **Female sharkfin guitarfish** have four to nine pups at a time. Each pup is about 45 cm long.
- **Young sharkfin guitarfish** have spots and bars on their skin, which gives them better camouflage than the adults, which are mainly grey.

DID YOU KNOW?

The shovelnose guitarfish has been living on our planet for over 100 million years.

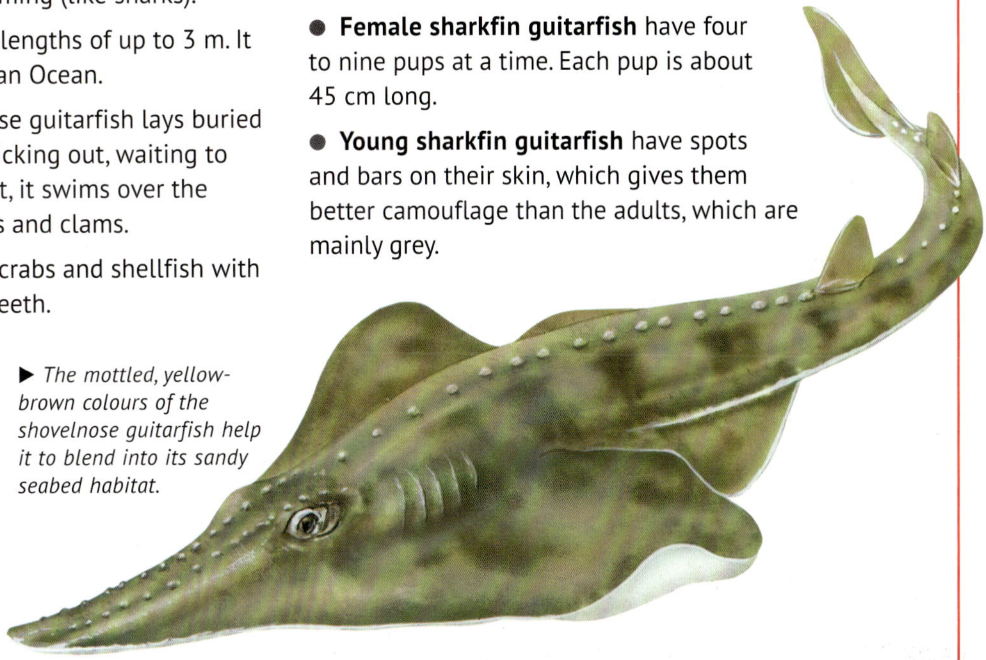

▶ *The mottled, yellow-brown colours of the shovelnose guitarfish help it to blend into its sandy seabed habitat.*

Sawfish

● **The seven species** of sawfish are a type of ray.

● **Sawfish get their name** from their long, saw-like snouts called rostrums, which are edged with sharp teeth, like those on a saw.

● **The green sawfish** grows to more than 7 m in length – longer than a great white shark.

● **Its saw** can account for up to one third, or more, of a sawfish's length.

● **Like rays**, sawfish have flattened bodies, but they look more like sharks than most rays do.

● **Although sawfish** resemble sawsharks, they are not the same. Sawfish are much bigger and lack barbels on their saws.

● **A sawfish uses** its saw to poke around the seabed for prey and to slice into shoals of fish.

● **When young sawfish** are born, their snouts are soft and enclosed in a covering of skin.

● **This protects** the inside of the mother's body from being injured by their sharp teeth. After birth, the protective skin soon falls off and the saw hardens.

● **All species of sawfish** are endangered, due to over-fishing by people and habitat destruction of coastal regions, such as mangrove swamps, where they live.

● **The large-tooth sawfish** sometimes swims up rivers in Australia.

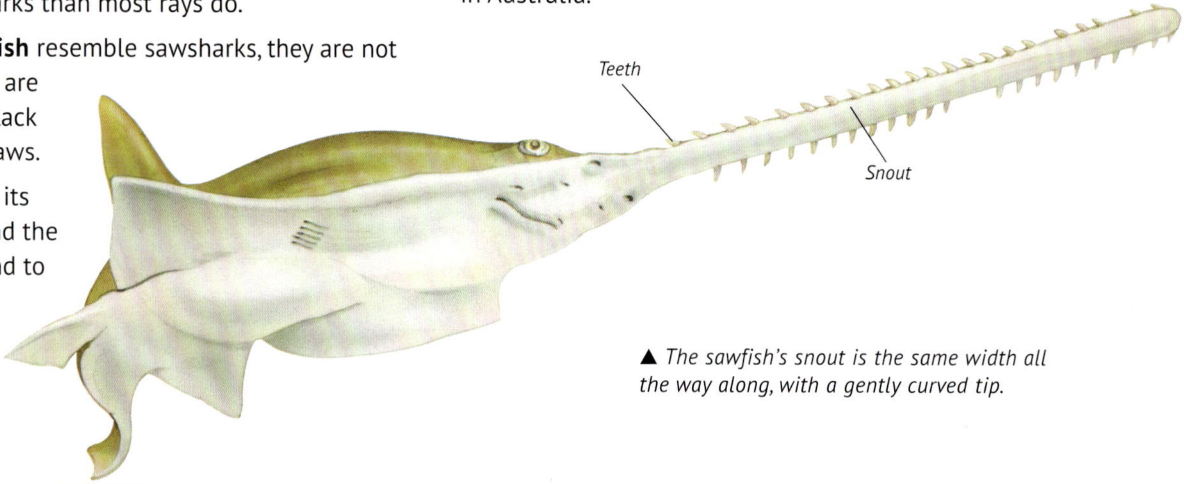

▲ *The sawfish's snout is the same width all the way along, with a gently curved tip.*

Chimaeras

● **Although they are related** to sharks and rays, chimaeras have evolved separately for nearly 400 million years.

● **There are over 40 species** of chimaeras. They live in water ranging from 500–2500 m deep.

● **The elephant fish** is a type of chimaera with a long, fleshy snout, which it uses to detect the electrical signals given off by buried shellfish.

● **Chimaeras have a plate-like gill cover** over their four gills (like bony fish).

● **To swim**, they flap their wing-like front fins, like rays.

● **Unlike sharks**, chimaeras cannot replace any teeth that are worn out or broken.

▲ *The spotted ratfish has large eyes and long fins. Unlike many sharks and rays, chimaeras swim very slowly. They stay close to the seabed, feeding on small fish and octopuses.*

● **With plate-like**, grinding teeth and large nostrils, a chimaera's mouth looks a bit like that of a rabbit. Another of their nicknames is rabbitfish.

● **The eyes of chimaeras** are usually green and very large, which helps them to pick up as much light as possible in the deep sea.

● **Most chimaeras** have a poisonous spine in front of their back fin.

● **Females lay eggs** with leathery egg cases.

◀ *The elephant fish has large green eyes high up on its head, and large front fins, which it uses for swimming.*

Dangerous or not?

● **It's a natural instinct** for people to be scared of sharks, as some are fierce hunters. Although sharks can be dangerous, attacks on humans are rare.

● **As well as attacking humans**, great whites have been known to attack small boats.

● **Great whites are deadly** to humans partly because we look similar in size and shape to their prey – seals and sea lions. The sharks simply get confused and attack the wrong prey.

● **Many experts think** bull sharks are actually more dangerous than great whites – but they are not well-known as killers because they are harder to identify. After an attack, bullsharks often escape unseen.

● **Sharks with spines**, such as horn and dogfish sharks, are not deadly but can inflict painful injuries on people.

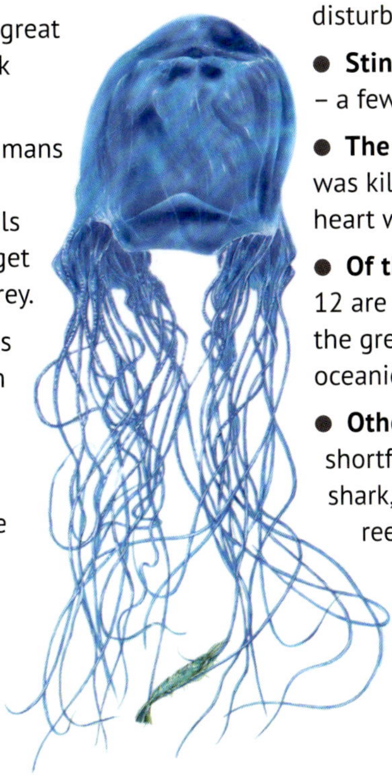

● **Not all dangerous sharks** are fast hunters. Nurse sharks and wobbegongs are usually placid and sluggish animals – but they can bite suddenly and hard if disturbed.

● **Stingrays**, which are related to sharks, can be killers – a few people die every year from their venom.

● **The wildlife expert** and TV personality Steve Irwin was killed in 2006, when a stingray barb pierced his heart while he was filming an underwater documentary.

● **Of the many hundreds** of shark species, only about 12 are usually dangerous to people. The top four are the great white, the bull shark, the tiger shark and the oceanic whitetip shark.

● **Other dangerous sharks** are the great hammerhead, shortfin mako, porbeagle, sand tiger shark, Galapagos shark, blacktip shark, Caribbean reef shark and grey reef shark.

◀ *More people have been killed by the box jellyfish than sharks and crocodiles combined. This lethal jellyfish can kill a person in just a few minutes.*

Attacks and survival

● **Every year** there are fewer than 100 reported cases worldwide of sharks attacking humans. Of these attacks, fewer than 20 are fatal.

● **Most attacks happen** in shallow water near the shore. This is because that's where sharks and swimmers are most likely to be in the same place at the same time.

● **Most incidents** happen off the coasts of eastern North America, South Africa and eastern Australia.

● **The danger of a shark attack** increases at night, when sharks move inshore to feed and are most active.

● **Sharks usually only attack** if they are hungry, if they feel threatened or angry, or if they mistake a human for prey. Divers may provoke an attack if they grab a shark by the tail.

● **People are more likely** to be killed by a lightning strike than a shark attack. Bees, wasps and snakes also kill many more people than sharks every year.

● **There are more deaths** from car accidents in one month than shark attacks in recorded history.

● **A great white shark** bit off marine photographer Henri Bource's leg while he was diving off the coast of Australia in 1964. He was soon back at work in the same job, and four years later another shark bit his artificial leg.

● **In 2003**, 13-year old Bethany Hamilton had her left arm bitten off by a tiger shark while surfing in Hawaii. She was surfing again within months and is still a top surfer.

● **In 2004**, while snorkelling in Australia, Luke Tresoglavic was bitten by a wobbegong. He had to swim to shore and drive to get help with the shark still attached.

◀ *Bethany Hamilton is still a top surfer, despite losing an arm in a tiger shark attack.*

DID YOU KNOW?

Experts have found that if a shark does take a bite of human flesh, it often spits it out or vomits it up later. Humans do not taste like a shark's normal prey.

Studying sharks

- **We know relatively little** about sharks. Scientists are trying to find out more about them.
- **The study of sharks** is sometimes called elasmobranchology.
- **Knowing more about sharks** – such as how they breed and what they need to survive – will help us to conserve them and stop shark species from dying out.
- **If you'd like to be a shark scientist**, choose subjects such as biology and chemistry at school, and study biology, genetics, oceanography or zoology at university.
- **Scientists also catch sharks** so they can study them in captivity. This lets them look closely at how sharks swim, eat and behave.
- **In laboratories**, scientists study shark blood, skin and cartilage to find out how their bodies work.

- **Some scientists study shark cells** to try to find out why they get so few diseases. This information could help to make new medicines.
- **In aquariums**, scientists test shark reactions to see how their brains and senses work.
- **Genetic analysis** of shark DNA helps scientists to identify closely related shark species, which look very similar and are difficult to distinguish from their appearance alone.
- **Dried shark tissue** from ancient sharks in museums can even be examined genetically to confirm the species and find out more about sharks that lived hundreds of years ago.

◀ *Some sharks, such as great whites, take an interest in diving cages, and seem to become more familiar with humans after coming into contact with them.*

Observation

- **To learn more about sharks**, scientists need ways of finding, following and catching them.
- **Most shark scientists** have to be strong and good at diving to get up close.
- **Scientists often use** diving cages or protective chainmail suits to study sharks underwater.
- **They can also study sharks** such as great whites without going in the water, using cameras on the ends of long poles.
- **Some shark scientists** dissect dead sharks to find out about their bodies or what they have eaten recently.
- **To follow sharks**, scientists use radio-tracking devices. They catch a shark and attach a transmitter that gives out radio signals. Wherever the shark goes, scientists can pick up the signals and work out the shark's location.
- **Scientists sometimes** attach tags to sharks they catch. The tag states where and when the shark was last caught. The same shark may then be found again somewhere else, giving scientists information about the shark's range.

▲ *A diver swims alongside a shark and records its movements and activities.*

- **A camera can be attached** to a shark to record its travels. The strap holding the camera gradually dissolves, and the camera floats to the surface to be collected.
- **Satellite tags** help scientists to track shark migration journeys by reporting the position of the shark to the satellite whenever the shark comes to the ocean's surface.
- **There is no evidence** that fitting scientific tags to a shark affects its survival in the wild.

Early sharks

● **The first fish** with a shark-like body shape lived about 450 mya (million years ago). They were not true sharks but had jaws and a lateral line similar to modern sharks.

● **By about 360 mya**, sharks of many shapes and sizes had developed. It was the golden age of sharks.

● **One of the earliest sharks** was *Cladoselache*, which lived about 370 mya. It was 1.5 m in length and had a powerful tail, like a modern mako shark.

▶ *The early shark Hybodus lived about 160 million years ago in the Jurassic Period, during the age of the dinosaurs.*

● ***Stethacanthus***, which lived about 350 mya, had a helmet of small teeth on its head and a spiny brush sticking out of its back. This may have been used during courtship or for defence.

● ***Tristychius* was similar** to a modern dogfish, but lived about 350 mya. It had a spine on each dorsal fin.

● **The unicorn shark**, *Falcatus*, had an L-shaped spine on top of its head. Only males had this spine, which may have been used to fight rival males or to attract females.

● **The whorl-tooth shark**, *Helicoprion*, did not lose its teeth. They moved along in a spiral and then were stored in a special chamber under its bottom jaw.

● **The giant scissor-toothed shark**, *Edestus giganteus*, had a mouth one metre wide. Its teeth were replaced in rows, but the old teeth stuck out in front of the shark's head and did not fall out.

● **About 150 mya**, sharks of the golden age began to die out. The ancestors of modern sharks, which were fast-swimming hunters, began to take over.

● **The biggest shark** was probably *Megalodon* from 20 mya. It was a colossal 20 m in length.

Shark fossils

● **Fossils are the remains** of, or the shape of, an animal preserved in rock. Often only the hardest parts of an animal, such as its skeleton, become fossilized.

● **When an animal dies**, its flesh and other soft parts start to rot. The harder parts, such as bone, rot more slowly and last longer. Over time, sediment layers settle on the remains. Minerals and salts replace the once-living parts and turn them and the sediments into solid rock.

● **As sharks have soft skeletons** made from cartilage, there are few whole shark fossils.

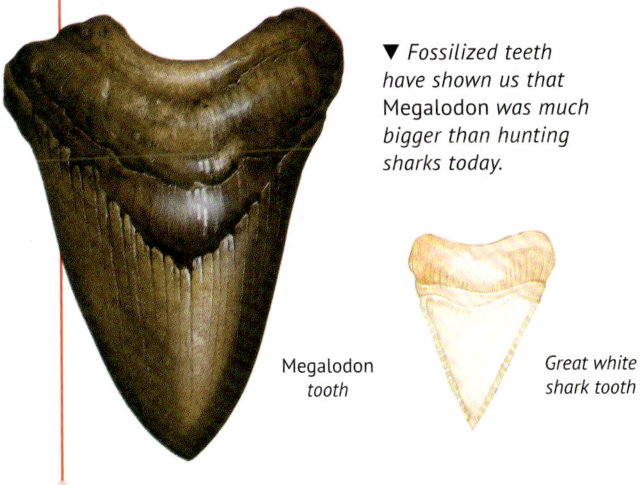

▼ *Fossilized teeth have shown us that Megalodon was much bigger than hunting sharks today.*

● **Scientists use shark fossils** to find out what sharks looked like long ago and how they lived. They often use tooth fossils to guess how big an entire shark was.

● **Shark fossils** are often found on land in places that used to be seas millions of years ago.

● **Some of the best shark fossil areas** are in parts of the United States, such as California, Maryland and Oklahoma.

● **Fossils of *Cladoselache***, one of the earliest known sharks, have been found with fish preserved in their stomachs.

● **Fossil shark teeth** are common because ancient sharks shed many teeth in a lifetime, like living sharks. Shark teeth are as hard as human teeth and do not rot away.

● **Fossil teeth** from relatives of today's mackerel sharks, such as ancient porbeagle sharks, have been found in rocks dating back 100 million years.

● **Fossil *Megalodon* teeth** date from over 15 mya ago to less than 2 mya.

Sharks in trouble

● **Shark populations are falling** mainly because of human activities, such as hunting, overfishing and the use of shark body parts in medicine.

● **Humans catch** over 100 million sharks every year, perhaps as many as 250 million.

● **Some shark species**, such as the spotted wobbegong, are still hunted for their skin. It is made into items such as belts, wallets, shoes and handbags.

● **Shark liver oil** has traditionally been used to waterproof boats, for lighting, cosmetics, paint, machine oil and as a source of Vitamin A in health supplements.

● **Sharks caught for sport** are usually released, but often die from exhaustion soon afterwards.

● **Sharks mature slowly** and don't always bear many young, so it can be hard for a species to build up their numbers again after being overfished.

● **Sharks are at the top of the food chain**. Poisonous chemicals from pollution collect in sea creatures, which the sharks eat. The poison then builds up in the sharks' bodies. Scientists think this may make sharks ill and make it harder for them to reproduce.

▲ *Many sharks die when they become tangled up in fishing or safety nets.*

● **Some sharks** live near the coast and young sharks often use shallow coastal waters as nursery areas. These areas are regularly polluted by human sewage and other waste, as well as by agricultural and industrial chemicals washed into the sea from rivers.

● **The demand for shark fin soup** in parts of Asia is responsible for the deaths of millions of sharks every year, including hammerheads, which have large fins.

● **The fins may be removed** from the shark, which is then thrown back into the sea while still alive. The shark dies soon afterwards because it can't get enough oxygen to breathe or hunt for food. This cruel practice is banned in about one third of shark-fishing countries.

Endangered species

● **An endangered species** is one that is in danger of dying out completely and becoming extinct.

● **Scientists try to find out** if a shark species is at risk by counting sharks seen in a particular area and measuring how much this changes over time.

● **Experts found** that sandbar shark sightings on America's east coast fell by 20 percent over 20 years. This shark is now classed as vulnerable.

● **Overfishing is the main reason** that sharks become endangered.

● **International organizations** such as the IUCN (International Union for the Conservation of Nature and Natural Resources) compile lists of endangered species to raise awareness.

● **According to the IUCN** over 50 shark species are now endangered, and 30 percent of sharks and rays are threatened with extinction in the wild. Several species of sawfish are critically endangered and may die out soon.

● **Great whites**, whale sharks, basking sharks, makos, porbeagles and threshers are just a few of those at risk.

▲ *Even though basking sharks are protected in some parts of the world, these large sharks are still at risk because they grow and mature slowly, and take a long time to reproduce.*

● **More than half** of all angelshark species are threatened with extinction because they are overfished.

● **Some sharks are threatened** when natural coastlines and estuaries are developed and built on. This destroys nurseries where sharks lay eggs or bear young.

● **Some of the rarest sharks** are river sharks, the daggernose shark and several species of angelshark. Several deep-water sharks, including the gulper shark and Harrisson's dogfish, are also vulnerable.

DID YOU KNOW?

Many shark species are so hard to study that scientists have no idea how many of them are left in the wild.

Saving sharks

◀ *A respected advocate for shark management, the Shark Trust is part of a global collaborative movement in shark conservation. It works to safeguard shark, skate and ray populations through science, education, influence and action.*

- **Ecotourism helps** to save sharks by encouraging local people not to kill them, as they can make money from sharks as tourist attractions.
- **Some shark-fishing** countries have imposed quotas to limit how many sharks fishermen can catch.
- **Governments can ban** the killing of some sharks altogether.
- **The UK has passed a law** making it illegal to catch or disturb a basking shark.
- **Some countries** have set up marine wildlife reserves where hunting wildlife is banned.
- **Conservation charities** such as the WWF (World Wildlife Fund) and Shark Trust work to educate people to help them avoid killing sharks unnecessarily.
- **By banning trade** in shark products, governments can help to stop unnecessary killing of sharks.
- **To help protect sharks**, people should avoid buying products such as shark fin soup.
- **Modern aquariums** and sea life centres help to explain the importance of shark conservation to their visitors. They also look after injured sharks, which can be returned to the wild when they recover.
- **Many sharks** could be saved from extinction if we work towards keeping the oceans clean and free of pollution, and try to preserve important shark habitats, such as coral reefs, near the shore.
- **More scientific** research into sharks would help us to better understand their biology and behaviour, and work out the best ways of helping sharks to survive in the future.

▼ *Tourists line up to take close-up photographs of blacktip reef sharks. The sharks have learned that they will get a free meal of fish if they swim in this area.*

INDEX

Index

A

aardvarks 156, 188, 218
aardwolves 230
abducent nerve 76
absolute zero 29, 50
absorption spectrum 32
acanthodians 135
Acanthostega 138, 139
acceleration 39, 44, 53
accentors 258
accessory nerve 76
acetic acid 61
Achilles tendon 96
acid rain 40
acids 61
acorn woodpeckers 285
acoustics 61
acraniates 134
actin 97
active transport 108
adders 145
Adélie penguins 271
adenine 112
adenoids 89, 120
adipose tissue 103
adjutant storks 279
adrenal glands 108, 110, 111
adrenaline 81, 111
Aegialornis 153
Aegyptopithecus 169
Aepyornis 152
aerosols 40
African buffaloes 224
African clawless otters 198
African crested porcupines 183
African elephants 194
African fish eagles 264
African green pigeons 254
African harrier hawks 255
African palm swifts 243
African pygmy kingfishers 266
African sawtail catsharks 337
African yellow-winged bats 223
afterbirth 118
ageing 115
Aglaophyton 128
agnathans 135
AIDS 119, 123
air 40, 138
  composition of 40
  density 36
  pressure 19
aircraft 25, 36, 39, 46
albatrosses 240, 250, 268, 271, 295
alchemy 50, 53
alcohol 43, 106
Aldabra brush warblers 275
Aldanotreta 133
algae 16, 126, 184
Algerian nuthatches 295
alimentary canal 102, 106
alkalis 24, 27, 61
alkanes 43
allergies 121
alligators 143
Allodesmus 159
Allopleuron 147
alloy steels 29
alpacas 204
alpha rays 31
Alphadon 157
alpine marmots 196
Altamira cave 179
alternating current (AC) 56
altricial young 259
alum powders 46
aluminium 46
aluminium oxide 46, 58
alveoli 90, 91
Amazonian manatees 203
Amazonian umbrellabirds 277
Ambulocetus 167
American badgers 200
American goldfinches 261
American plains bison 182
American robins 267
amino acids 98, 103, 105, 109, 112
ammonia 45, 109
ammonites 134
amniotic sac 117
amorphous carbon 62
amphibians 137, 138, 139, 140, 141, 142
Amphicyon 161
amps 21
ampullae of Lorenzini 313, 343
amylase 104, 106, 107
amynodonts 166
analogue 47, 58
anaphylactic reaction 121
anapsids 142
anatomy 68
Anchiornis 150
Anchiornis huxleyi 256
ancient murrelets 274
Andean cock-of-the-rock 277
Andean condors 277
Andean mountain cats 234
Andes fishing mice 236
Andrewsarchus 159
Andrias scheuchzeri 140
androgens 114
angelsharks 298, 302, 306, 307, 308, 314, 326, 327, 352
angiosperms 128
angular momentum 51
ant-thrushes 267
antacids 107
antbirds 263
anteaters 156, 182, 200, 205
antelopes 160, 163, 214, 227, 231
anti-particles 46
antibiotics 121, 123
antibodies 68, 88, 119, 120, 121, 122
antigens 121
antlers 189, 217, 233
anus 102
aorta 90
aortic valve 86
apes 169, 170, 187, 230
aponeuroses 96
appendicular skeleton 92
appendix 99

arachnids 131
arachnoid 72
Arandaspis 135
Araucaria 129
Archaefructus 128
Archaeopsittacus 153
Archaeopteryx 148, 150, 256
Archelon 144
Archimedes 56
Archimedes' principle 33, 56
Archimedes' screw 56
Arctic foxes 208, 219, 237
Arctic hares 208, 219
Arctic terns 250
Arctocyon 162
Ardipithecus kadabba 171
Ardipithecus ramidus 171
argalis 190
Argentavis magnificens 153
Argentavix 256
argon 27, 40
argus pheasants 265
armadillos 158, 212
armoured shrews 206
aromatics 43
arrhythmia 85
arteries 83, 84, 85, 86, 109
arterioles 83, 86, 87
arthritis 96, 100
Arthropleura 131
arthropods 131
artiodactyls 163, 167
Asian elephants 194
Asian sultan tits 254
Asiatic buffaloes 224
asses 191
astatine 23
asthma 90
astronauts 36, 41
astronomy 49
Atlantic torpedo rays 345
Atlantic weasel sharks 338
atmosphere 126, 138
atom bombs 55, 64
atomic clocks 13
atomic mass 27
atomic number 11, 14, 27
atoms 11, 14, 15, 18, 21, 25, 50, 109
  absorption spectrum 32
  bonds 13, 45, 63
  domains 19
  emission spectrum 32
  ions 11, 61, 109
  isotopes 11, 31, 52
  nuclei 11, 15, 34, 63, 64
  splitting 34, 52
  see also subatomic particles
atriums 84, 85, 90
auks 271, 272, 274
aurochs 212
Australian pelicans 283
Australian songlarks 275
Australian white-winged choughs 273
australopithecines 160, 169, 171
Australopithecus 170, 175
Australopithecus afarensis 172
Australopithecus africanus 171
Australopithecus anamensis 171
autoimmune diseases 100, 121, 122
autonomic nervous system (ANS) 69
aviation fuel 43
avocets 271
axial skeleton 92
axons 70, 71, 74
aye-ayes 208

B

B-cells 120, 121
babbling thrushes 267
babies 118
  birth 118
  fontanelles 72
  lanugo 101
  milk teeth 95
  miscarriages 118
  premature 118
babies (*cont.*)
  reflexes 75, 118
  skeleton 92, 95, 118
  sleep 82
  in utero development 117
babirusas 185
baboons 160, 216, 234
backbone 92, 93, 309
bacteria 16, 24, 44, 60, 81, 107, 120, 122, 123, 126
bacterial infections 123
Bactrian camels 198, 227
badgers 190, 199, 200, 209
bait balls 314
baking powder 61
balance 73, 76, 80
bald eagles 263, 264, 269
baleen whales 210, 224
ball skills 80
ball-and-socket joints 94, 96
balloon sharks *see* swellsharks
balloons 19, 34
bamboo sharks 302, 312, 321, 323, 330
banded mongooses 219
bandicoot rats 205
bandicoots 217
bar-headed geese 244
bar-tailed godwits 267
Barbary macaques 214
Barbary partridges 243
barbels 302, 308, 312, 327, 331, 332, 338
barbets 280
bareskin dogfish 329
barium 34
barn owls 250, 287
barred woodcreepers 270
baryons 37
basal ganglia 73, 80
bases 61
basking sharks 300, 301, 304, 310, 316, 319, 323, 325, 332, 335, 352
basophils 88

bat-eared foxes 237
bateleur eagles 264
batoids 298, 344
bats 148, 164, 199, 204, 216, 223, 228
batteries 21
bauxite 46
bay owls 287
baya weavers 251
beaked whales 210
bearded greenbuls 289
bearded vultures 289
bears 196, 199, 202, 207, 208, 221
beavers 162, 187, 192, 222
becquerels 60
bee hummingbirds 240, 269, 272, 290
bee-eaters 247, 269, 275
beetles 132
bell-magpies 280
beluga whales 204, 208, 210
Bengal tigers 186
benthic sharks 301
benzene 20, 21
beryl 26
beta rays 31
Big Bang 27, 41
big cats 196, 211, 215, 216
bigeye thresher sharks 298, 334
bighead catsharks 337
bighorn sheep 190, 228
bigmouth sharks *see* basking sharks
bilbies 190
bile 103, 106, 107
binary code 14
binturongs 219
biofuels 49
bioluminescence 298, 301, 317, 319, 328, 329
biosurfactants 24
birds 142, 148, 240–95
  baby birds 259
  beaks and feet 247
birds (*cont.*)
  camouflage 254, 255, 266, 285, 290
  courtship displays 241, 244, 247, 249, 251, 253, 256, 258, 262, 263, 264, 268, 272, 273, 276, 277, 278, 283, 289
  desert birds 292
  eggs 240, 272
  endangered 295
  feathers 151, 242, 256, 263
  flightless 151, 152, 252, 256, 260, 265, 278, 282, 285
  grassland birds 285
  migration 240, 250, 261, 267, 271, 275
  nests 269
  poisonous 247
  polar and tundra birds 271
  prehistoric 150–3, 256
  rainforest birds 265
  seabirds 152, 268, 269, 282
  senses 250
  songs and sounds 253
  species 240
  structure 242
  tool-use 273, 293
birds of paradise 244
birds of prey 247, 248, 255, 277, 283
bison 182
bitterns 290
bivalves 133
black bears 221
Black Death 123
black gibbons 230
black herons 290
black holes 41, 59
black kites 283
black panthers 211
black rats 205
black rhinoceroses 197
black skimmers 250
black swans 244
black vultures 277
black-backed jackals 232
black-capped chickadees 254
black-capped donacobious 259
black-capped vireos 295
black-footed cats 234
black-footed ferrets 209
black-headed ducks 241
black-headed orioles 280
black-naped blue monarchs 286
black-shouldered kites 269
black-thighed falconets 248
black-throated honeyguides 284
black-throated trogons 294
black-winged stilts 271
blackbirds 267, 294
blackbuck antelopes 231
blacknose sharks 302
blacksmith plovers 251
blacktip reef sharks 302, 304, 311, 317, 321, 341, 353
blacktip sharks 323, 349
bladder 96, 99, 109
blind mole rats 221
blind sharks 330
blood 73, 87, 99, 106, 109, 111
  cells 16, 68, 87, 88, 98, 112, 119, 120, 121
  circulation 83, 85, 86, 87, 309, 310
  clots 87, 105
  groups 87
  poisoning 123
  salt levels 108, 109
  transfusions 87
blood sugar 104, 107, 111
bloodhounds 201
blow moulding 22
blubber 185, 312
blue birds of paradise 244
blue chaffinches 261
blue sharks 298, 300, 304, 305, 310, 312, 319, 320, 323, 324, 339
blue tits 254
blue whales 196, 224, 316

blue-crowned hanging parrots 249
blue-crowned motmots 275
blue-footed boobies 282
blue-spotted stingrays 345
bluntnose sixgill sharks 301
boas 145
boat-billed flycatchers 245
bobcats 219, 225
body language
 mammals 214
 sharks 302, 319
body systems 68, 99
body temperature 42, 69, 82, 106, 228
bohemian waxwings 256
boiling points 17, 42, 46, 60
bone marrow 88, 91, 93
bone sharks *see* basking sharks
bones 18, 65, 91, 92, 94, 99, 105, 115
bonnethead sharks 306, 323, 343
bonobos 226
boobies 282
Borneo river sharks 342
Bose-Einstein condensates 17
bosons 46
bottle-nosed dolphins 216
bottle-nosed whales 210
boubou shrikes 253
bowel 103, 107
bowerbirds 262
bowhead whales 224
bowmouth guitarfish 347
brachial plexus 70
brachiopods 133
bradycardia 85
Brahminy starlings 242
brain scans 28, 39
brains 73
 and balance 80
 and co-ordination 80
 hominins 172, 173, 174
 humans 69, 70, 72, 73, 74, 75, 76, 77, 80–81, 99, 118, 177
 mammals 210
brains (*cont.*)
 and memory 81
 and moods and emotions 81
 primates 72, 177
 sharks 309, 311, 313
 and sleep 82
brainstem 72, 73, 82
brakes 26
bramble sharks 307
Branchiostoma 134
breastbone 92, 93
breathing
 fish 138
 humans 69, 89, 90, 91, 108
 through skin 138
 see also respiratory system
breech births 118
brittlestars 132
broad-billed rollers 241
broadbills 293
bromine 23
bronchi 90, 91
bronchioles 90
brontotheres 163
Brontotherium 163
bronze whaler sharks 314, 317
brood parasites 293
brown hyenas 230
brown kiwis 278
brown pelicans 283
brown rats 205
brown-headed cowbirds 295
Brownian motion 50
brubru shrikes 253
brush turkeys 259, 269
brush-tailed possums 217
bryophytes 126
bubonic plague 123
budgerigars 249, 292
buff-breasted kingfishers 266
buffaloes 224, 227
bulbuls 289
bull sharks 298, 300, 301, 314, 319, 339, 340, 349
bulldog bats 223
bullet-proof vests 24
bullfinches 261
bullhead sharks 298, 302, 304, 321, 326, 330
bumblebee bats 223
buntings 288
buoyancy 33
Burgess Shale 131, 134
burrowing owls 285
bush dogs 189
bush pigs 185
bushbabies 169, 222
bustards 153, 240, 255
butane 43
butcher birds *see* shrikes
butterflies 42
buttonquails 292
buzzards 244, 283
bytes 14

C

cactus wrens 259
Caenopus 166
Caesarian section 118
caesium 13
caimans 143
calcitonin 111
calcium 27, 65, 91, 111, 115
calcium carbonate 50, 58, 65
calcium hydroxide 65
calcium oxide 65
calculus 53
Californian sea-lions 222
calories 65
Cambrian Period 127, 132, 133, 135
camels 163, 190, 198, 227
camouflage
 birds 254, 255, 266, 285, 290
 guitarfish 347
 mammals 184, 186, 208, 219
 sharks 302, 308, 327
campo miners 270
Canada geese 244
candelas (Cd) 36

candles 43, 62
caniforms 159
canine teeth 95
Caninia 130
cannibalism
humans 172
sharks 314
Cantius 169
Cape clawless otters 198
Cape dune mole rats 221
Cape gannets 282
Cape hunting dogs 189
Cape weavers 251
capillaries 83, 87, 91, 109
capuchins 227
capybaras 192, 209
caracals 234
caracaras 248
carbohydrates 10, 103, 104, 106, 107
carbon 10, 21, 22, 29, 43, 62
carbon dioxide 40, 45, 68, 90, 91, 108, 310
carbon nanotubes 62
carbon reinforced plastic (CRP) 24
carbon-14 31
carbon-dating 31
Carboniferous Period 127, 129, 131, 132, 136, 139, 141, 142
cardinals 259
Caribbean reef sharks 136, 302, 349
caribou 189, 204
carotene 101
carpet sharks 307, 313, 314, 326, 330
cars 11, 23, 26, 38, 39, 40, 44, 49
cartilage 93, 95, 96, 115, 118, 303, 309
Caspian terns 250
cassowaries 247, 265, 278
cast iron 29
Castoroides 162
catalysts 13
catbirds 258, 262
cathode-ray tubes 15, 47
cats 159, 160, 214, 234
big cats 196, 211, 215, 216
domestic 235
catsharks 301, 302, 308, 321, 337
cattle 163, 212, 228
cattle egrets 285, 290
caustic soda 61
cave art 179
cave swiftlets 243
cedar waxwings 256
cells 98, 112, 113
active transport 108
diffusion 108
nuclei 98
osmosis 108
cellular respiration 16, 108
celluloid 24
cellulose 24, 103, 107
Celsius 42
cement 65
Cenozoic Era 127
central nervous system (CNS) 69, 70
Central Processing Unit (CPU) 14, 33
cephalopods 133, 134
cerebellum 73, 80
cerebral cortex 73, 74
cerebral hemispheres 73, 77
cerebrospinal fluid (CSF) 70, 72, 73
cerebrum 74, 77
Ceresiosaurus 146
cerulean warblers 294
cervical nerves 70
cervical spine 93
cervix 118
cetaceans 167, 182
chacma baboons 234
Chacoan peccaries 185
chaffinches 253, 261
chain reactions 64
chain sharks 337
chalcopyrite 55
chalicotheres 163
Chalicotherium 163
chalk 65
chamois 190
Chapman's zebras 237
Charnia 130
cheetahs 160, 195, 196, 216, 219
Cheirolepis 137
chelonians 144
chemical bonds 45, 63
chemical compounds 13, 14, 21, 45
chemical energy 11
chemical formulae 21, 45
chemical reactions 13, 24
chestnut sparrows 274
chevrotains 233
chicarees 196
chickadees 254
chickenpox 121, 123
chickens 153, 250, 263
chiffchaffs 275
chimaeras 321, 344, 348
chimpanzees 74, 169, 170, 214, 226
Chinese painted quails 243
Chinese water deer 233
chinstrap penguins 252, 271
chipmunks 196
chital deer 233
chloride 109
chlorine 23, 63, 107
chlorophyll 126
cholesterol 10, 103
chordates 134
choughs 273
chromosomes 112, 113, 114, 116
chyme 102, 107
cilia 119
cinnamon-breasted tody-tyrants 245
civets 219
Cladoselache 136, 351
clams 133
claspers 320, 321
cleaner wrasse 325

Climatius 135
cloaca 318, 320
clocks 13, 49, 58
cloning 44
clouded leopards 187
co-ordination 73, 80
coatis 229
cobras 145
coccygeal nerves 70
coccyx 93, 94
cochlea 78
cock-of-the-rock 277
cockatoos 249
cockles 133
cockroaches 132
coefficient of friction (CF) 26
coelacanths 137
coenzymes 106
coffin rays 345
colds 120, 122, 123
collagen 91, 95, 96, 99, 115
collared carpet sharks 330
collared lemmings 213
collared peccaries 190
colobus monkeys 214
colon 107
colour 42
  mixing colours 45
  primary colours 45
  spectrum 64
combustion 13, 49
common ioras 289
common miners 270
common thresher sharks 298, 334
communication
  mammals 214
  sharks 319
compact bone 91
complement 119
composites 24
Compsognathus 150, 256
computer games 14
computers 14, 35, 51, 62
concave lenses 48
condensation 17
conditioned reflexes 75
condors 277
conduction 34
conductors 12, 21, 29, 30, 55, 62
condylarths 162
Confuciusornis 151
conifers 129
connective tissues 97
Conocoryphe 131
conscious thought 77
convection 34
convection currents 34
convergent evolution 147, 157, 158, 265
convex lenses 48
cookie-cutter sharks 298, 301, 308, 318, 329
Cooksonia 128
coots 255, 269
copepods 325, 328
copper 30, 34, 46, 55
coprolites 154
coral catsharks 337
corals, coral reefs 130, 300, 302
cormorants 240, 269
cornea 78
coronal planes 68
coronary arteries 84
corpus callosum 73
cortex 70
corundum 46
cosmic rays 46, 60
cotingas 277
coughing 119
countershading 308
covalent bonds 63
cow sharks 326
cowbirds 294, 295
cownose stingrays 345
coyotes 232
coypus 209
crab-eater seals 197
crab-eating raccoons 229
crabs 131
crakes 255
cramp 109
cranes 20, 153, 262, 295
cranial nerves 69, 70, 76
cranial vault 72
cranium *see* skull
cream-coloured coursers 246
creodonts 159
crepuscular animals 315
crested barbets 280
crested berrypeckers 268
crested bustards 255
crested porcupines 183
crested tinamous 285
crested wood partridges 243
Cretaceous Period 127, 134, 139, 144, 145, 146, 149, 151, 152, 156
crimson topaz hummingbirds 290
crinoids 132
CRISPR gene editing 44
Cro-Magnon People 176, 178, 179
crocodile sharks 333
crocodiles 142, 143
crocodilians 143
crossbills 247, 261
crowned cranes 262
crowned eagles 257, 265
crows 259, 273
crude oil 22, 43
crustaceans 131
crystallization 26
crystals 26, 37
CT scanning 39
cuckoo shrikes 253
cuckoo weavers 251
cuckoo-rollers 241
cuckoos 153, 273, 293
cuprite 55
curassows 286
Curie, Pierre and Marie 37
curlews 267
cuttlefish 133
cyanobacteria 126
cycads 129
cynodonts 142, 184

cytoplasm 98
cytosine 112

D

dabbling ducks 241
Daeodon (*Dinohyus*) 164
daggernose sharks 352
darters 240
Darwin, Charles 158
decibels (dB) 55
declarative memories 81
deep-sea diving 63
deer 163, 217, 233
degenerative diseases 122
deinotheres 165
dendrites 71
Denisovan people 177
density 33, 36, 53, 56
denticles 307, 317, 329
dentine 95
dermis 100
Des Murs' wiretails 270
descending pathways 74
desert sparrows 274
desmans 206
detergents 24
deuterium 38, 52, 64
Devonian Period 127, 128, 132, 135, 136, 137, 139
dholes 189
diabetes 104
diamond 62
diana monkeys 214
diaphragm 88
diapsids 142, 147
diastole 85
Diatryma 256
Dichobune 163
dicynodonts 142
diesel engines 49
diet, human 103
diffusion 108
digestion
  herbivores 161
  human 68, 102, 107
digestion (*cont.*)
  rays 346
  sharks 318
digital broadcasting 47, 58
digital recording 58
Diictodon 142
Dimetrodon 142, 143
Dimorphodon 148
dingoes 189
Dinichthys 137
Dinictis 160
Dinilysia 145
Dinofelis 160
Dinornis 152
dinosaurs 127, 129, 142, 150, 156, 184, 247, 256
diodes 33
Diplocaulus 139
Diprotodon 157
direct current (DC) 56
diseases 122, 123
distance 20, 39, 41
distillation 43
diver birds 248
diving ducks 241
DNA 17, 26, 44, 98, 112, 113
dogfish sharks 298, 300, 301, 305, 308, 314, 315, 317, 319, 320, 321, 322, 323, 324, 326, 328, 329, 337, 349, 352
dogs 159, 161, 189, 199, 201, 214, 216, 227, 228, 232
dolphins 182, 210, 216, 219
donkeys 191
dopamine 71
dormice 199
dotterels 251
double helix 112
double-toothed barbets 280
double-wattled cassowaries 278
doves 254, 292
dowitchers 267
Draco 148
drag 26
dragonflies 132
draughtsboard sharks 337
dromaeosaurs 150
dromedaries 198
drongos 280
Dryopithecus 169
duck-billed platypuses 154, 182, 200, 313
duckbilled stingrays 345
ducks 151, 152, 241, 259, 265, 295
ductless glands 110
dugongs 203
Dunkleosteus 136, 137
dunlins 267
dunnocks 258
dura mater 72
duraluminium 46
dusky sharks 317, 323
dwarf cassowaries 278
dwarf lanternsharks 299
dwarf mongooses 219
dwarf sharks 301
dynamos 20, 56

E

eagle owls 287
eagle stingrays 345
eagles 184, 250, 257, 263, 264, 265, 269, 295
ears
  birds 250
  humans 78, 80, 89
  sharks 312
Earth
  atmosphere 40, 138
  core temperature 42
  formation of 126
  magnetic field 19, 196, 261, 305
  mass 36, 44
eastern phoebes 245
eastern yellow-billed hornbills 288
echidnas 154, 200
echinoderms 132
echoes 61
echolocation 210, 233, 246
eclipses 41

Edaphosaurus 142
Edestus giganteus 351
edible-nest swiftlets 243
egg cases 321, 322, 330, 347
egg-tooth 247
eggs
  amphibians 141
  birds 240, 272
  human (ova) 112, 116, 117
  mammals 154, 182, 200
  reptiles 141
  sharks 298, 321, 322, 330
  skates 321, 347
Egyptian plovers 246
eider ducks 241
Einstein, Albert 12, 13, 16, 30, 41, 59
elands 228, 231
Elasmosaurus 146
Elasmotherium 161, 166
elastic cartilage 95
elastic modulus 47
elasticity 47
elastin 96
Eleanora's falcons 248
electric circuits 21, 33
electric current 12, 19, 20, 21, 28, 56
electric motors 20
electric rays 345, 346
electrical charge 11, 12, 15, 46
electricity 12, 17, 33, 38, 56, 313, 345, 346
electrocardiogram (EEG) 85
electromagnetic fields 20, 28
electromagnetic force 10
electromagnetic radiation 18, 32, 48, 60, 64
electromagnetic spectrum 18
electromagnetic waves 32
electromagnetism 16, 28
electromotive force (emf) 21
electron microscopes 17
electronics 33
electrons 11, 12, 15, 17, 21, 23, 27, 30, 31, 32, 33, 34, 46, 47, 61, 63
elements 14, 21, 27
elephant birds 152
elephant fish 348
elephant seals 197
elephant sharks *see* basking sharks
elephants 165, 194, 216, 219
elf owls 292
elk 217
elementary particles 46
embryos 116, 117
emission spectrum 32
emotions 77, 81
emperor penguins 252, 271
emus 247, 259, 260
enamel, tooth 65, 95
endemic diseases 122
endocrine glands 110
endocrine hormones 111
endocrine system 110
endoscopes 32
endothermic reactions 13
energy 11, 13, 16, 18
  conversion 11, 57, 65
  food sources 103, 104
  thermodynamics 57
  transfer 11
  see also specific types of energy
engines 49
Entelodon 164
entelodonts 164
entropy 57
enzymes 24, 88, 102, 103, 104, 106, 107
Eocene Epoch 140, 151, 153, 159, 164, 168
Eohippus 168
Eomaia 155
eosinophils 88
Eozostrodon 154, 155
epaulette sharks 300, 306, 308
epidemics 123
epidermis 100, 101
epididymis 115
Epigaulus 162
episodic memories 81
epithelial tissue 99
Eryops 140
essential oils 43
ethanol 43
ethene (ethylene) 22, 43
ether 49
Eudimorphodon 148
euphonias 288
Eurasian badgers 199, 200
Eurasian blackbirds 267
Eurasian buzzards 283
Eurasian cuckoos 293
Eurasian hedgehogs 201
Eurasian nuthatches 291
Eurasian otters 198
Eurasian swifts 243
European bee-eaters 269, 275
European bison 182
European black vultures 289
euryapsids 142, 147
Eustachian tubes 78
Eusthenopteron 138, 139
eusuchians 143
eutherians 155
eutriconodonts 156
evolution
  convergent evolution 147, 157, 158, 265
  see also prehistoric life
excretion 107
exhalation 90
exocrine glands 110
exocrine tissue 107
exoskeletons 131
exothermic reactions 13
external combustion engines 49
extinctions, mass 133
extrusion moulding 22
eyelashes 78
eyelids 100
eyes and vision
  birds 250
  compound eyes 131

eyes and vision (*cont.*)
eye colour 114
humans 48, 78, 119
night vision 105
pineal eye 311
sharks 311

F

facet joints 93
facial nerve 76
faeces 102, 107, 108
Fahrenheit 42
fairy bluebirds 289
fairy terns 250
fairy-wrens 247
Falcatus 351
falconets 248
falcons 248
fallopian tubes 116
fantails 286
Faraday, Michael 20
fat-tailed dunnarts 190
fat-tailed dwarf lemurs 208
fats 103
fatty acids 103
feather stars 132
feather-tailed gliders 232
feathers
birds 151, 242, 256, 263
dinosaurs 150, 256
feeding frenzy 315
feet 94, 100, 247
feliforms 159
felines 160
femur 92
fennec foxes 196, 228, 237
ferns 129
ferret badgers 200
ferrets 209
ferrous compounds 29
fertilization 112, 116, 320, 321
fibre, dietary 103, 107
fibre optic cables 32, 35
fibreglass 22
fibrin 87
fibrous cartilage 95
field mice 236
fieldfares 267
figbirds 280
filter-feeders 133, 135, 210, 281, 310, 314, 316, 331, 332, 333, 335
fin whales 196
finches 261, 274
finfoots 291
fingernails 101
fingers 96
fins 136, 138, 302, 304, 306, 319, 343, 346
fire 13, 172
firecrests 275
firewood-gatherers 270
'First Family' 172
fiscal shrikes 253
fish
bony fish 137
breathing 138
cartilaginous fish 136
jawed fish 135
jawless fish 135
lobe-finned fish 137, 138, 139
prehistoric 135–7
ray-finned fish 137
sharks *see* sharks
fisher martens 183
fishing cats 234
fixed oils 43
flame robins 270
flamingos 152, 281
flapper skates 347
flerovium 30
floating 33, 56
flowering plants 128
flowerpeckers 268
flowerpiercers 288
flu 120, 122, 123
fluorescent lights 36
fluorides 23, 314
fluorine 22, 23
flutist wrens 259
flycatchers 245, 256, 270, 286
flying foxes 228
flying lemurs 232
flying squirrels 196, 232
foetus 117
follicle-stimulating hormone (FSH) 114, 116
fontanelles 72
force fields 10
forces 10, 12, 19, 20, 33, 44, 47, 53
fossa 219
fossil fuels 56
fossils 126, 154, 351
four-stroke engines 49
fourth dimension 12, 13
foxes 196, 208, 219, 228, 237
francolins 243
frequency 25, 57
friction 12, 20, 26
frigatebirds 240
frilled sharks 300, 301, 307, 323, 326
frogmouths 246
frogs 138, 140
frogspawn 141
frontal lobes 77, 177
fructose 104
fruit bats 204, 228
Fruitafossor 156
fulcrum 23, 56
fullerenes 62
fulmars 268
'funny bone' 70
fur seals 197

G

galagos 222
Galápagos finches 288
Galápagos horn sharks 330
Galápagos sharks 304, 349
gall bladder 99
Gallinuloides 153
gallium 27
gamma rays 18, 31
Ganges sharks 342

gannets 272, 282
gas exchange 89
gas lasers 25
gases 17, 36, 50
pressures 19
Gastornis 151
gastric juices 102
gastropods 133
gazelles 231
gear ratio 23
gears 20, 23
geese 151, 244, 259, 261
generators 21, 56
genes 44, 112, 113, 114
gene splicing 44
gene therapy 44, 113
genetic disorders 113
genetic engineering 44
genetically modified (GM) food 44
genets 219
genome 44, 112, 113
gentoo penguins 252, 271
Geocoma 132
geodes 26
germanium 27
germs 119, 120, 121, 122
gharials 143
ghost bats 223
ghost catsharks 337
ghost sharks 344
giant anteaters 205
giant armadillos 212
giant eland 231
giant ground sloths 158
giant guitarfish 347
giant hammerhead sharks 314
giant lanternsharks 299
giant otters 198
giant pandas 206
giant pangolins 212
giant petrels 278
giant scissor-toothed sharks 351
giant squirrels 196
gibbons 169, 230
gigabytes 14
Gigantopithecus 169
gila woodpeckers 292
gill arches 135
gill rakers 310, 316
gills 138, 139, 141, 310, 346
Ginkgo biloba 129
giraffes 163, 188, 219
glass 57, 58
glaucous gulls 279
gliding mammals 232
gliding reptiles 148
Global Positioning System (GPS) 35
global warming 40, 60
glossopharyngeal nerve 76
Glossopteris 129
glossy flowerpiercers 288
glossy ibises 281
glucagon 104, 107
glucose 16, 82, 90, 103, 104, 106, 108, 111
glycerol 103
glycogen 104, 106
glyptodonts 158
goats 163, 190
goblin sharks 300, 301, 307, 326, 332, 333
godwits 267
gold 11, 30, 34
goldcrests 275
golden cow-nosed rays 344
golden eagles 257
golden jackals 232
golden orioles 280
golden plovers 251
golden whistlers 247
goldeneyes 241
goldfinches 261
Golgi bodies 98
goliath cockatoos 249
goose bumps 100
gophers 162
gorgeted pufflegs 295
gorillas 169, 195, 214, 216
goshawks 255
grackles 294
granular dogfish 329
granulocytes 88
graphite 62
graptolites 133
grasping reflex 75
grass owls 287
grasshopper mice 236
grasshoppers 132
gravity 10, 36, 39, 41, 53
specific gravity 56
great argus pheasants 276
great black cockatoos 249
great black-backed gulls 268, 279
great blue herons 290
great crested flycatchers 245
great crested grebes 248
great curassows 286
great grey bowerbirds 262
great grey owls 287
great hammerhead sharks 301, 343, 349
great horned owls 235
great Indian hornbills 288
great jacamars 280
great kiskadees 245
great northern divers 248
great skuas 268, 271, 279
great spotted cuckoos 273
great spotted woodpeckers 285
great tits 254
great white pelicans 283
great white sharks 298, 299, 300, 303, 305, 306, 311, 312, 313, 314, 315, 317, 318, 319, 324, 332, 335, 349, 350, 352
great-tailed grackles 294
greater kudu 231
grebes 248
green broadbills 293
green dogfish 329
green sawfish 348
green-backed herons 290
Greenland sharks 298, 300, 301, 316, 324, 325, 328
Grevy's zebras 237

grey foxes 237
grey herons 290
grey matter 74
grey reef sharks 302, 306, 312, 349
grey squirrels 196, 199, 204
grey wolves 201, 229
griffinflies 132
grizzly bears 207
Grotte de Chauvet 179
ground sharks 326
grouse 258
guanine 112
guano 268
guans 286
Guianan cock-of-the-rock 277
guillemots 274
guinea pigs 158, 162, 192
guineafowl 243
guitarfish 298, 308, 344, 347
gulf wobbegong sharks 332
gulls 253, 259, 268, 271, 279
gulper sharks 301, 328, 352
gummy sharks 338
gums 95
gut 102, 106
gymnosperms 128, 129
gyrfalcons 248

H

hadrons 37
haemoglobin 83, 88
hagfish 135
hair 80, 100, 101, 115
halogens 23
Halysites 130
Hamadryas baboons 234
hammer-headed bats 223, 228
hammerhead sharks 299, 300, 301, 307, 311, 313, 314, 319, 323, 343, 349
hands 94
Hanuman grey langurs 214
hares 162, 193, 208, 219, 225
harpy eagles 184, 257
harriers 255
Harrisson's dogfish 352
harvest mice 218, 236
Hatzegopteryx 149
hawfinches 261
Hawking, Stephen 41, 59
hawks 153, 255, 259
hay fever 121
hearing
  birds 250
  humans 78
  sharks 312
heart
  heartbeat 80, 85
  human 83, 84–86, 91, 99, 115
  muscle 85, 97
  sharks 309
heart disease/failure 86, 103, 122
heart rate 76
heat energy 11, 13, 29, 57
  movement 34
hedgehogs 199, 201, 222
Helicoprion 351
Heliocystis 132
helium 25, 40, 42
helmet shrikes 253
helmeted hornbills 288
helper T-cells 120
Hemicyclaspis 135
hen harriers 255
Henodus 145
herbivores 161
heredity 44, 113, 114
herons 259, 269, 290
herring gulls 279
hertz (hz) 57
Hesperocyon 161
Hesperornis 256
hibernation
  birds 246
  mammals 199, 201
high blood pressure 109, 115
high-density polythene (HDPE) 22
hill mynahs 242
Himalayan monal pheasants 261
hinge joints 96
hinnies 191
hippocampus 73
hippopotamuses 163, 193, 218, 222, 228
histamines 100
HIV 119
hoary bats 223
hoatzins 293
'Hobbit people' 178
hog-nosed skunks 235
Holocene Epoch 127
holograms 54
hominids 171, 177
hominins 171, 179
Homo erectus 172, 174, 175, 177, 178, 179
Homo ergaster 177
Homo floresiensis 178
Homo habilis 173, 175, 177, 178
Homo heidelbergensis 174, 175, 179
Homo neanderthalensis 174, 176, 177, 178, 179
Homo rhodesiensis 174, 175
Homo sapiens 175, 179
Homo sapiens sapiens 175, 176, 177
honey badgers 200, 284
honeycreepers 288
honeyeaters 269
honeyguides 284, 285
hooded mountain tanagers 288
hooded pitohuis 247
hooded seals 197, 204
hooded skunks 235
Hooke's law 47
hooktooth weasel sharks 338
hoopoes 241, 259
hormonal system 68
hormones 82, 110, 111, 114
horn sharks 300, 304, 306, 317, 321, 330, 349
hornbills 265, 288
horned coots 269
horse bats 223

horses 162, 163, 168, 191
horsetails 129
houndsharks 338
house martins 264
house mice 236
house sparrows 274
howler monkeys 227
huias 280
human gonadotrophin (HCG) 116
humans
  brain 69, 70, 72, 73, 74, 75, 76, 77, 80–81, 99, 118, 177
  evolution 169, 170–176
  human body 68–123
  modern humans 176
hummingbirds 153, 240, 263, 269, 272, 290, 295
hump-backed dolphins 216
humpback whales 224
hunting
  early humans 179
  pack hunters 161, 189, 229, 232, 317
  sharks 315, 317, 319
Huygens, Christiaan 49
hyacinth macaws 247
Hyaenodon 159
hyaline cartilage 95
Hybodus 136, 351
hydro-electric power 56
hydrocarbons 10, 22, 43
hydrochloric acid 61
hydrogen 10, 14, 21, 22, 27, 36, 38, 40, 43, 45, 49, 61, 103
  bombs 38, 42, 64
  fuel cells 38
hydrophilic molecules 24
hydrophobic molecules 24
hydrostatics 56
hyenas 230, 260
Hylonomus 141
hyperlinks 51
hypoglossal nerve 76
hypothalamus 73, 82, 109, 110
Hyracodon 166
Hyracotherium 168, 191

I

ibises 281
Icaronycteris 164
Icarosaurus 147
ice 60
ice ages 127, 174
icebergs 60
Ichthyornis 152, 256
ichthyosaurs 147
Ichthyosaurus 147
Ichthyostega 138
icterids 294
icthyosaurs 142
ilium 94
image scanners 39
immune system 68, 81, 88, 110, 119, 121
  acquired immunity 121
  innate immunity 121
immunization 122
imperial woodpeckers 285
in vitro fertilization (IVF) 116
incisors 95
Indian vultures 295
Indochinese tigers 186
Indricotherium 197
indris 208
inertia 51
infertility 116
inflammation 96, 100, 119, 121
information superhighway 35
infrared (IR) 18, 64
inhalation 90
input/output 14
insects 131, 132, 148
  earliest 132
insulators 12, 34
insulin 104, 107, 111
integumentary system 68
interferons 119
internal combustion engines 49
internet 51
interneurons 70
intestines 97, 99, 102, 103, 107, 318
invertebrates, first 130
involuntary muscles 97
iodine 23
ionic bonds 63
ions 11, 61, 109
iridescence 42
Iriomote cats 234
iris 78
Irish elk 217
iron 11, 14, 21, 29, 58
iron oxide 29
Irrawaddy river sharks 342
ischium 94
islets of Langerhans 107
Isotelus 131
isotopes 11, 31, 52
itching 119, 121
ivory gulls 279

J

jacamars 280
jacanas 271
jackal buzzards 283
jackals 214, 232, 260
jackdaws 273
jaegers *see* skuas
jaguars 211
Japanese angelsharks 327
Japanese blue flycatchers 270
Japanese sawsharks 327
javelinas 190
jays 273
jellyfish 130
jerboas 192
jet engines 49
jet propulsion 53
joints 93, 96, 115
joules 65
Juramaia 155
Jurassic Period 127, 129, 140, 143, 147, 148, 149, 150, 155, 156

K

Kabylie nuthatches 291
kagus 291
kakapos 249
kangaroo mice 192, 236
kangaroo rats 190
kangaroos 157, 211, 213, 216, 217, 228
keas 249
Kelvin (K) scale 42
Kentish plovers 251
keratin 100, 101, 242
kerosene 16
kestrels 248
Kevlar 24
kidneys 87, 99, 108, 109
killer T-cells 120, 1119
killer whales 216
kilojoules 65
kinetic energy 11
kinetic theory of matter 17
king birds of paradise 244
king parrots 249
king penguins 252, 271
king of Saxony birds of paradise 244
king vultures 265, 277
kingfishers 266
kinkajous 229
kit foxes 196
kitefin sharks 328
kites 269, 283
kittiwakes 279
kiwis 250, 278
knee-jerk reflex 75
koalas 157, 225
Kodiak grizzly bears 207
kokakos 280
Komodo dragons 147
Koolasuchus 139
Krause's end-bulbs 79
krill 197, 224
krypton 40
kudus 231
Kuehneosaurus 148

L

La Brea tar pits 154, 160
labour, stages of 118
lactase 106
lactose 106, 107
lammergeiers 289
lampreys 135, 325
lanternsharks 299, 301, 317, 328, 329
lanugo 101
Lapland buntings 288
lappet-faced vultures 289
lapwings 251, 259
Large Hadron Collider 46
large intestine 99, 102, 107
large-tooth cookie-cutter sharks 329
large-tooth sawfish 348
larks 266
larynx 89, 90
Lascaux cave 179
lasers 25, 30, 36, 54
latent heat 29
lateral lines 312
laughing kookaburras 266
laughing thrushes 267
Lavoisier, Antoine 16, 28
law of conservation of momentum 51
Laysan albatrosses 271
leafbirds 289
least weasels 209
leeches 325
lemmings 192, 213, 218
lemon sharks 313, 315, 318, 319, 323, 324, 325, 339
lemurs 169, 208, 214, 232
lenses
  eye 78
  glass 48
leopard seals 197
leopard sharks 302, 308, 338
leopard whiprays 344
leopards 187, 211
Leptictidium 155
leptons 46
lesser electric rays 345
lesser horseshoe bats 223
leucocytes 88, 100
levers 20, 23, 56
lichens 126
life-forms, earliest 126
lifespan
  birds 240, 249, 262, 288
  elephants 194
  humans 115
  sharks 298, 324
ligaments 92, 94, 96
light 32, 54
  interference 42, 53, 54
  laser light 25
  primary colours 45
  sources 36, 48
  speed of 18, 34, 41, 54
  visible light 18, 48, 64
  white light 52, 64
light rays 48, 54
light waves 42, 49, 54, 64
lightbulbs 36, 42
lightning 12, 25, 42, 63
limelight 65
limescale 65
limestone 58
limpets 133
lined lanternsharks 329
Lingula 133
lions 160, 214, 215, 218, 219
Liopleurodon 146
lipase 106
lipids 103
liquid crystal displays (LCDs) 26
liquid molecules 50
liquids 17, 19, 25
  solutions 50
lissamphibians 140
little auks 274
little bustards 255
little grebes 248
little gulls 279

liver 87, 96, 99, 103, 104, 106, 304, 309, 323, 331
liverworts 126
lizards 142, 145, 147
llamas 204
lobsters 131
lobules 106
Loganograptus 133
loggerhead shrikes 253
lollipop catsharks 337
long-billed marsh wrens 259
long-billed wood partridges 243
long-eared bats 223
long-eared hedgehogs 201
long-tailed ducks 241
long-tailed dunnarts 217
long-tailed tits 254
long-tailed tree pangolins 212
longfin mako sharks 336
longnose sawsharks 327
lories 249
lorikeets 259
lorises 169, 222
low-density polythene (LDPE) 22
lowland streaked tenrecs 233
'Lucy' 172
Lucy's warblers 294
lumbar nerves 70
lumbar plexus 70
lumbar spine 93
lungfish 137, 138
lungs 83, 89, 90, 91, 99, 119, 138
lunula 101
luteinizing hormone 114
lux 36
lycra 24
lygase 106
lymph fluid 86, 120
lymph nodes 119, 120
lymphatic system 68, 86, 103, 119, 120
lymphoblasts 88
lymphocytes 88, 119, 120, 121
lymphokines 120
lynxes 225
lyrebirds 272
lysosomes 98
lysozome 119

M

macaques 214
macaroni penguins 271
macaws 247, 249, 265
machairodonts 160
machines 20, 65
mackerel sharks 301, 326, 332
Macrauchenia 158
Madagascar fish eagles 295
Maglev trains 28
magma 42
magnesium chloride 23
magnesium oxide 58
magnetic fields 19, 196, 261, 305
magnetic poles 19
magnets, magnetism 19, 20, 39, 46
  electromagnets 28, 56
magnificent riflebirds 244
magnox reactors 52
magpies 259
maidenhair tree 129
Maine Coons 235
mako sharks 298, 300, 301, 305, 306, 318, 323, 332, 336, 352
malachite sunbirds 268
Malayan tapirs 203
Malayan tigers 186
mallee fowl 286
maltase 106
maltose 106, 107
mammals 137, 182–237
  ancestors of 142
  Arctic mammals 208
  Australian 157
  camouflage 184, 186, 208, 219
  carnivores 159–161
  characteristics 182
  communication 214
  desert mammals 190
  endangered 186
mammals (*cont.*)
  fossils 154
  gliding mammals 232
  heat regulation 228
  herbivores 161
  hibernation 199, 201
  hoofed 162, 163
  marine mammals 182, 210, 216, 224
  marsupials 154, 157, 158, 182, 184, 211, 213, 217, 220, 225
  mating 222
  migration 196, 204, 227
  monotremes 154, 182, 184, 200
  nocturnal 196, 212, 218, 219, 222
  parental care 154, 182, 216
  placentals 154, 155, 158, 182, 184
  prehistoric 154–169, 184
  reproduction 154
  rodents 158, 162, 192, 205, 209, 221, 236
  sea mammals 203
  senses 196
  South American 158
  teeth 154, 182
  warm-bloodedness 155
mammoths 31, 154, 165, 166
manakins 277
manatees 203, 204
mandarin dogfish 301
mandrills 222, 234
maned wolves 227
manganese 46, 109
maniraptorans 150
manta rays 299, 325, 344, 346
Manx shearwaters 268, 278
marabou storks 279, 285
marbled catsharks 308
marbled electric rays 345
margays 234
marine otters 198
marmosets 227
Marrella 131
marrow 88, 91, 93

marsh hawks 255
marsh warblers 240
marsupial mice 222
marsupial moles 217
marsupials 154, 157, 158, 182, 184, 211, 213, 217, 220, 225
martial eagles 257
martins 264
masked boobies 282
mass 11, 33, 36, 44, 51, 53
 atomic 27
 molecular 45
matter, states of 17
Mawsonites 130
Maxwell, James Clerk 20, 28
mayflies 132
meadowlarks 294
measles 122, 123
mechanical advantage (MA) 20
mechanical energy 11
meerkats 236
megabytes 14
Megalodon 299, 351
megamouth sharks 306, 316, 332, 333
Meganeura 132
Meganeuropsis 132
megapodes 286
Megatherium 158
Megazostrodon 154, 155, 184
Mei 150
Meissner's corpuscles 79
melanin 100, 101
melatonin 110
melting point 58, 62
memory 73, 77, 81
menarche 114
meninges 72, 73
meningitis 72
menisci 95
menstrual cycle 114, 116, 117
mercury 30
Merkel's discs 79
'mermaids' purses' 322
Merychippus 168
mesites 292
mesoeucrocodylians 143
Mesohippus 168
mesons 37
mesonychids 167
Mesonyx 159
Mesopithecus 169
Mesozoic Era 127, 129, 134
Messenger RNA 98
metabolic rate 111, 242
metabolism 106, 111
metacarpals 94
metals 26, 30, 34
Metamynodon 166
metatarsals 94
methane 21, 40, 43, 107
Metriorhynchys 143
Mexican fishing bats 223
Mexican free-tailed bats 223
miacids 159
mice 162, 192, 196, 199, 218, 236
Microchiroptera 164
microphones 37, 47
microscopes 17
microwaves 18, 35
midbrain 73
migration
 birds 240, 250, 261, 267, 271, 275
 humans 176
 mammals 196, 204, 227
 sharks 305, 334, 341
 vertical migration 305
milk teeth 95, 154
millipedes 131
mineral oils 43
minerals 50, 103
mink 209
Miocene Epoch 140, 144, 145, 152, 153, 157, 159, 161, 163, 164, 169
Miotapirus 163
mirrors 48
miscarriages 118
mitochondria 98
mitral valve 86
moas 152
mobile phones 18, 35, 51
mockingbirds 258
Moeritherium 165
molars 95, 155
mole rats 221, 222
mole-lemmings 213
molecular mass 45
molecules 17, 21, 22, 24, 25, 29, 42, 45, 50
moles 206
molluscs 133, 134
momentum 51
monarch flycatchers 286
mongooses 219, 288
monito del monte 220
monitor lizards 145, 147
monkey puzzle trees 129
monkeys 74, 169, 214, 218, 227, 234
monkfish *see* angelsharks
monocytes 88
Monograptus 133
monomers 24
monotremes 154, 182, 184, 200
mood 81
Moon 36, 41
moonrats 201
moorhens 255
moose 217
Morganucodon 154, 155
mosasaurs 147
Mosasaurus 147
motion, laws of 44
motmots 275
motor cortex 74, 76, 80
motor nerves 69, 76
motor neuron disease 76
mountain gorillas 195
mountain lions 220
mountain tapirs 203
mountain zebras 237
mourning doves 292
mouse deer 233

mouse opossums 220
mousebirds 294
mp3 recordings 58
MRI scanning 39
mucus 90, 119
mud-nesters 280
mule deer 220
mules 191
multiple sclerosis 71
mumps 123
muons 46
muscles 97, 115
cramp 109
fibres 97, 115
humans 76, 87, 120
movement 97
sharks 303
muscovy ducks 265
music 57, 61
musk deer 233
musk oxen 190, 208
mussels 133
mustelids 200
mute swans 244
myelin 71
myofibrils 97
myosin 97
myriapods 131

N

nails 101
naked mole rats 221, 222
Namaqua sandgrouse 254
Namib golden moles 206
naphthenes 43
narwhals 208, 222
natural gas 43
Nautilus 134
Neanderthals 174, 176, 177, 178, 179
Neocathartes 153
Neogene Period 127, 144, 157, 166
neon 25, 40
neon lights 36
nephrons 109
neptunium 27
nerves 69, 75, 93, 108
nerve cells *see* neurons
nerve plexuses 70
nerve tissue 99
nervous system 68, 69
neurons (nerve cells) 71, 73, 74, 98
neurotransmitters 71
neutron stars 36
neutrons 11, 27, 37, 38, 46, 64
neutrophils 88
New Guinea river sharks 342
New World marsupials 220
New World monkeys 227
New World vultures 277
Newton, Isaac 44, 53
newtons (N) 10, 19
Newton's rings 53
newts 138, 140
Nicaragua sharks *see* bull sharks
nictitating membrane 311, 338
night monkeys 218, 227
night sharks 342
nightjars 246
nine-banded armadillos 212
nitrates and nitrites 63
nitrogen 10, 40, 45, 63, 126
liquid nitrogen 63
nitrogen dioxide 40
nitrogen oxide 63
nitrous oxides 40
noble gases 27
noctule bats 204, 223
nocturnal animals 196, 212, 218, 219, 222, 287, 315
noddys 250
North American porcupines 183
northern goshawks 255
northern harriers 255
northern jacanas 271
northern mockingbirds 258
northern wrens 259
nose 77
Notharctus 169
nothosaurs 145, 146
Nothosaurus 146
nuclear energy 11, 52, 64
nuclear fission 34, 52, 64
nuclear forces 10
nuclear fusion 52, 64
nuclear power stations 52, 60
nuclear reactions 64
nuclear reactors 52
nuclei 11, 15, 34, 63, 64, 98
numbats 205, 211
nurse sharks 300, 301, 302, 306, 312, 314, 319, 320, 323, 330, 331, 349
nutcrackers 273
nuthatches 291, 295
nylon 24, 47

O

occipital lobe 77
oceanic whitetip sharks 300, 311, 349
ocellated angelsharks 327
ocellated antbirds 263
ocelots 218, 234
octopuses 133
oculomotor nerve 76
odonatans 132
oesophagus 102
oestrogen 77, 111, 114, 116
oganesson 14
Ogygoptynx 153
ohms 21
oilbirds 246
oils 26, 43
okapis 188
Old World flycatchers 270
Old World monkeys 214, 234
Old World sparrows 274
Old World vultures 289
Oldfield mice 236
olfactory bulb 77
olfactory epithelium 77
olfactory lobes 311
olfactory nerve 76

Oligocene Epoch 151, 153, 157, 159, 160, 169
olive baboons 234
olive oropendolas 294
opaque 17, 48
openbill storks 279
opossums 157, 211, 220
optic nerves 72
optical fibres 32
optical microscopes 17
orang-utans 169, 187, 222
orcas 210, 216
ores 29, 30, 46
organelles 98
organic chemistry 10
organic compounds 10, 21, 43
organs 99
Oriental short-clawed otters 198
oriole finches 261
orioles 280, 294
oropendolas 294
Ororaphidia 132
Orrorin 170
Orthograptus 133
oryx 219, 228, 231
osmium 14, 36
osmosis 108
ospreys 240
ossicle bones 78
osteoblasts 91
osteocytes 91
Osteodontornis 152
ostriches 152, 240, 247, 250, 260, 272
otter civets 219
otter shrews 233
otters 183, 198, 200, 209
'Out of Africa' 176
ovaries 110, 111, 114, 116, 321
ovenbirds 270
over-fishing 332, 352
oviparous sharks 321
ovoviviparous rays 344
ovoviviparous sharks 323
ovulation 116
owl monkeys 218
owl parrots 249
owls 235, 250, 259, 271, 272, 285, 287, 292
ox-birds 197
oxidation 13
Oxyaena 159
oxygen 10, 16, 29, 87, 89, 90, 108, 117, 126, 138, 310
  in air 16, 40
  in blood 83, 86, 87, 88, 91
  liquid 16
  in water 21
oystercatchers 246
oysters 133
ozone 16, 40

P

pacemaker enzymes 106
pacemakers 85
Pacific sleeper sharks 328
Pacini's corpuscles 79
pain receptors 79
Pakicetus 167
Palaeocene Epoch 153, 157, 159, 161, 168
Palaeochiropteryx 164
Palaeomastodon 165
palaeontologists 128
Palaeopython 145
pale chanting goshawks 255
Paleogene Period 127, 128, 145, 152, 162, 163, 166
Paleothyris 141
Paleozoic Era 127, 133
palm civets 219
palm cockatoos 249
palm-nut vultures 289
palmchats 256
pancreas 99, 103, 104, 106, 107, 110, 111
pancreatic duct 107
pandas 206
pandemics 123
Panderichthys 138, 139
pangolins 212
Paraceratherium 163, 167
paradise flycatchers 286
paradise kingfishers 266
paradise whydahs 251
paraffin 43
paralysis 74
Paramys 162
paraplegia 74
parasites 325
parasympathetic nervous system 69
parathyroid glands 110
parietal lobe 77
Parkesine 24
parrots 153, 249, 253, 265, 295
particle accelerators 46
particle physics 46
particulate radiation 60
partridges 243
pascals 19
peacocks 276
peafowl 276
pebble mound mice 236
peccaries 185, 190
peewits *see* lapwings
'Peking Man' 172, 175
pelagic sharks 300, 301, 334
pelagic stingrays 345
pelagic thresher sharks 334
pelicans 247, 283
pelvis 92, 94
pelycosaurs 142
penduline tits 254
penguins 252, 271, 295
penis 115
Pentacrinites 132
penumbra 48
peptidases 106
peregrine falcons 244, 248
Periodic Table 14, 23, 27
peripheral nervous system (PNS) 69, 70, 76
perissodactyls 163
peristalsis 102

Permian Period 127, 132, 133, 139, 140, 142, 143
personality 77
Peruvian pelicans 283
PET scanning 39
Peteinosaurus 148
petrels 268, 278
petrol 42, 43, 49
petroleum 43
pH scale 61
phagocytes 119, 121
phalanges 94
pharalopes 267
pharynx 89
pheasant-tailed jacanas 271
pheasants 261, 265, 276
Phenacodus 162
pheromones 319, 320
Philippine falconets 248
Phiomia 165
Phorusrhacus 151
phosphate 91
phospholipids 103
phosphors 36, 47
phosphorus 10, 33
photoelectric cells 39
photoelectric effect 16, 30, 47
photons 18, 25, 30, 32, 36, 47, 48, 54
photophores 329
photosynthesis 40, 126
phrenology 72
Phyllograptus 133
pia mater 72
pianos 57
pied avocets 271
pied currawongs 280
pied fantails 286
pied flycatchers 270
pied wagtails 266
piezoelectric effect 37
pig-deer 185
pigeons 253, 254, 259
pigs 162, 163, 185, 190, 219, 228
Pikaia 134
pikas 193
pilotfish 325
pineal eye 311
pineal gland 99, 110
pinnae 78
pinnipeds 159
Pinocchio catsharks 337
pins and needles 70
pipits 266
pistons 49
pitch 57
pittas 293
pituitary gland 110, 111, 114, 116
placenta 117, 118, 323
placentals 154, 155, 158, 182, 184
placoderms 137
placodonts 145
Placodus 145
plains zebras 237
plains-wanderers 292
plankton 43, 135, 314, 316
plantcutters 295
plants
  angiosperms 128
  earliest 126
  gymnosperms 128, 129
  vascular 128
plasma (liquid) 87, 106, 120
plasma screens 47
plasmas (state of matter) 17
plastics 22, 24, 43
platelets 87, 88
platinum 30
Platypittamys 162
Plectronoceras 133
Pleistocene Epoch 127, 174, 179
Plesiadapis 169
plesiosaurs 142, 146, 147
Plesiosaurus 146
pleura 90
pliers 23
Pliocene Epoch 165
pliosaurs 146
plovers 246, 251, 269
plutonium 27, 52, 64
pneumonia 122
pochard 241
poison
  birds 247
  mammals 200, 206
  sharks 298, 308, 317
  snakes 145
  stingrays 317, 345, 349
polar bears 196, 202, 208
polecats 209
polio 122
pollution 40, 49
polonium 37
polycarbonate 22
polymers 22, 24
polysaccharides 104
polystyrene 22
polyvinyl chloride (PVC) 22
poorwills 246
porbeagle sharks 300, 301, 306, 332, 336, 349, 352
porcupines 158, 162, 183, 192
porpoises 182
Port Jackson sharks 301, 308, 314, 317, 330
Portuguese sharks 301
Portuguese water dogs 201
positrons 39
possums 217, 232
potassium 107, 109
potassium hydroxide 24
potential energy 11
potoos 246
power stations 52, 56, 60
power (work rate) 65
prairie chickens 258
prairie dogs 190, 209
pratincoles 246
precipitated solute molecules 50
precocial young 259
preening 263
prefrontal cortex 74
pregnancy
  humans 114, 116, 117
  sharks 323, 328

prehistoric life 126–79
first amphibians 138–139
first birds 150–151, 256
first fish 135
first insects 132
first invertebrates 130
first land-dwelling vertebrates 138
first life forms 126
first mammals 155, 184
first molluscs 133
first plants 126
first reptiles 141
timescale 127
premolars 95, 155
Presbyornis 152
pressure 19
pressure receptors 79
pressurized water reactors (PWRs) 52
prickly sharks 301
primary sexual characteristics 114
primates 169, 177
Primelephas 165
prions 278
prisms 53, 64
proboscideans 165
Proconsul 169
Procoptodon 157
Proganochelys 144
progesterone 111, 114
pronghorn antelopes 227, 231
propane 43
proprioceptors 76, 80
prostate gland 114
protease 106
proteins 103, 105, 106, 112, 113, 119, 121
protists 130
protons 11, 14, 27, 31, 37, 38, 39, 46
Protosuchus 143
Protungulatum 162
Psephoderma 145
pseudotooths 152
Psittacosaurus 156
ptarmigans 271
Pteranodon 149
pterodactyls 149
Pterodactylus 149
pterosaurs 142, 146, 148, 149
puberty 114
pubis 94
puffbacks 253
puffbirds 280
puffins 247, 274
pulleys 20
pulmonary circulation 83
pulse 85
pulsed lasers 25
pumas 220
pupil, eye 78
pups (sharks) 298, 319, 322, 323, 324
purple herons 290
purple martins 264
pygmy anteaters 205
pygmy falcons 248
pygmy hippos 193
pygmy kingfishers 266
pygmy marmosets 227
pygmy possums 217
pygmy seed-snipes 246
pygmy sharks 299, 315, 316, 317, 328
pygmy sunbirds 268
pygmy white-toothed shrews 206
Pyrotherium 158
pythons 145

Q

quadraplegia 74
quaggas 237
quails 243
quanta 30
quantum physics 30
quarks 11, 37, 46
Quartenary Period 127
quartz 26
quartz watches 37
Quetzalcoatlus 149
quetzals 265, 294
quicklime 65

R

rabbits 162, 193
rabies 235
raccoon dogs 189, 199
raccoons 229
racquet-tailed drongos 280
radiation 30, 31, 34, 37, 60
electromagnetic 18, 32, 48, 60, 64
particulate 60
ultraviolet 40
radio waves 18
radioactive decay 31
radioactive waste 52
radioactivity 31, 37, 60
radioisotopes 31
radium 31, 37
radon 60
rails 255
rainbow pittas 293
rainbows 53
rainforests 128, 265
random access memory (RAM) 14
Rapid Eye Movement (REM) sleep 82
rat opossums 157
ratfish 344, 348
rats 74, 162, 192, 205, 218
ravens 273
rays 136, 298, 299, 344–6, 352
razorbills 274
read-only memory (ROM) 14
receivers 35
reciprocating engines 49
red bats 223
red bishops 251
red blood cells 16, 87, 88, 98, 112, 119
red deer 233
Red Deer Cave people 177
red foxes 237

red kangaroos 211
red kites 283
red knots 267
red pandas 206
red squirrels 196
red-billed queleas 240, 285
red-billed scythebills 270
red-billed tropicbirds 268
red-breasted flycatchers 270
red-breasted geese 244
red-breasted nuthatches 291
red-eyed vireos 295
red-legged partridges 243
red-legged seriemas 285
red-necked grebes 248
red-vented bulbuls 289
red-vented malimbes 251
red-whiskered bulbuls 289
red-winged blackbirds 294
redpolls 261
redshanks 267
redstarts 293
redwings 267
reed warblers 293
reef sharks 300, 302, 304, 306, 311, 312, 315, 317, 319, 320, 321, 339, 341, 349, 353
reflexes 74, 75, 118
refraction 48, 49, 64
regent bowerbirds 262
reindeer 189, 204, 233
relativity 41
  general theory of 13, 16, 41
  special theory of 12, 16, 41
remora fish 325
Repenomamus giganticus 156
Repenomamus robustus 156
reproductive system 68
  female 116
  male 115
reptiles 137
  aquatic reptiles 145, 146–147
  eggs 141
  flying reptiles 148–149
  gliders 148
reptiles (*cont.*)
  prehistoric 139, 141–145
  sea reptiles 142
requiem sharks 301, 339
resonant frequency 57
respiratory system 68
  cellular respiration 108
  human 89
  see also lungs
restriction enzymes 44
resultant 10, 53
retina 78
reverberation time 61
Rhadinichthys 137
rhamphorhynchoids 148, 149
Rhamphorhynchus 149
rheas 247, 282, 285
Rhesus positive/Rhesus negative 87
rhinoceroses 163, 166, 197, 218, 222
Rhyniognatha 132
rib cage 93
ribbon-tailed birds of paradise 244
ribosomes 98
ribs 92, 93
rice tenrecs 233
rifleman 272
right whales 224
right-handedness 77
ring ouzels 267
ringed plovers 269
ringed seals 208
river sharks 298, 300, 339, 342, 352
river stingrays 345
roadrunners 292
rock wallabies 213
rock wrens 259
rocket fuel 16
rockets 10, 39, 41, 44, 49
rockhopper penguins 271
rockwarblers 247
rodents 158, 162, 192, 205, 209, 221, 236
rods and cones 78
rollers 241
rooks 273
Ross's gulls 279
rostrums 327, 348
rough-legged buzzards 283
roughsharks 308, 328
round stingrays 345
royal antelopes 231
royal flycatchers 245
rubber 12, 47
ruby-throated hummingbirds 263, 290
ruffed grouse 258
Ruffini's corpuscles 79
ruffs 267
rufous horneros 270
rufous scrub-birds 272
rufous-bellied niltavas 270
rust 21, 29

S

sabre-tooths 154, 160
Sacabambaspis 135
sacral nerves 70
sacrum 93, 94
saddle joints 96
saddlebacks 280
Sahelanthropus 170
St Bernard dogs 201
salamanders 140
saline drip 109
saliva 102, 104, 106
salivary glands 110
salmon sharks 305, 332
salts 23, 108, 109
  table salt 21, 63
sand cats 234
sand martins 264
sand tiger sharks 304, 315, 317, 318, 319, 323, 334, 349
sandbar sharks 352
sanderlings 267
sandgrouse 254, 292
sandhill cranes 262

sandpipers 267
sandwich terns 268
Sao Tomé giant sunbirds 268
sapsuckers 285
Sarcosuchus 143
Sarus cranes 262
satellites 35, 51
satin bowerbirds 262
saturated fats 103
saturated solutions 50
Saturn 49
satyr tragopans 276
Saurornithoides 150
savannah buffaloes 224, 227
sawfish 298, 344, 348, 352
sawsharks 301, 302, 307, 308, 312, 326, 327
saxophones 57
scalar quantities 53
scalloped hammerhead sharks 300, 313, 343
scalp 72
scaly-tailed flying squirrels 196, 232
scandium 27
scanning 28, 39
Scanning Microcopes 17
scarlet ibises 281
scarlet macaws 249
scaup 241
scavengers
  birds 153, 283, 289
  mammals 164, 230
  molluscs 134
  sharks 316
Schwann cells 99
sciatic nerve 70
scleractinians 130
screwdrivers 23
scrotum 115
scrub-birds 272
scrubwrens 247
scurvy 105
sea cucumbers 132
sea lilies 132
sea otters 183
sea urchins 132
sea-lions 159, 222
seagulls 152
seals 159, 197, 204, 208
seaweeds 126
sebaceous glands 119
sebum 114
secondary sexual characteristics 114
sedge warblers 253, 275
semantic memories 81
semen 115
semicircular canals 78, 80
senses
  birds 250
  human 68, 77–79, 115
  mammals 196
  sharks 309, 311–313
sensible heat 29
sensory memory 81
sensory nerves 69, 75
septum 84
seriemas 285, 291
serotonin 71
servals 234
sevengill sharks 301
sex cells 112
sex hormones 110, 111, 114, 116
sexual development 114
sexual intercourse 115, 116, 117
shadows 48
shags 240, 268
shark fin soup 352
sharkfin guitarfish 347
sharks 19, 298–353
  anatomy 303, 309
  attacks on humans 298, 340, 349
  camouflage 302, 308, 327
  in captivity 313, 335, 337, 350
  classification 326
  cold-blooded sharks 309
  communication 319
  conservation 353
  defences 308
sharks (*cont.*)
  digestion 318
  eggs 298, 321, 322, 330
  endangered sharks 298, 352
  fins and tails 306
  food and feeding 314, 316
  gills and breathing 310
  habitats 298, 300–302
  hunting 315, 317, 319
  intelligence 313
  lifespan 298, 324
  live young 298, 322, 323
  loners and groups 319
  male and female sharks 321
  mating 320
  migration 305, 334, 341
  observation and study of 350
  poison 298, 308, 317
  prehistoric 136, 317, 351
  records and statistics 298
  senses 309, 311–313
  shapes 307
  sixth sense 313
  size 299
  skin 307, 308, 320, 331
  speed 298, 303, 305, 310
  spikes and spines 308, 317
  swimming 304
  teeth and jaws 136, 314, 318, 330, 351
  warm-blooded sharks 300, 335
sharpbills 295
Shastasaurus 147
shearwaters 249, 268, 278
sheep 163, 190, 228
shells
  chelonians 144
  eggshells 65, 141, 272
ships 33
short-nose electric rays 345
short-tail nurse sharks 331
short-tailed pygmy tyrants 245
short-tailed shrews 206
short-toed eagles 264
short-winged grebes 248

shortfin mako sharks 298, 305, 332, 336, 349
shovel-billed kingfishers 266
shovelnose guitarfish 347
shovelnose sharks 308
shrews 206, 233
shrikes 253
shy-eye sharks 311
siamangs 230
Siamese cats 235
Siberian cranes 262
Siberian tigers 186
sickle-billed vangas 253
sicklefin weasel sharks 314, 338
sifaka lemurs 214
silica 58
silica aerogels 36
silicon 10, 29, 54
silicon chips 14, 33
silky flycatchers 256
silky sharks 307, 315, 317, 326
Silurian Period 127, 130, 135, 136, 137
silver 30, 34
silvertip sharks 302
singularity 41, 59
Sinoconodon 155
sinuses 72, 89
sirenians 203
Sivapithecus 169
sixgill sawsharks 327
sixgill sharks 301
skates 136, 298, 321, 347
skeletal muscles 97
skeletons
  human 68, 92, 95, 118
  sharks 303, 309
skimmers 250
skin 21, 99, 100, 115, 119, 307
skin cancer 18
skin colour 100
skuas 279
skull
  humans 72, 73, 92
  reptiles 142
skunks 196, 235
skylarks 266
slaked lime 65
sleep 82
sleeper sharks 300, 301, 328
sleeping sickness 122
sloth bears 218, 221
sloths 158, 184
slow lorises 222
slugs 133
small intestine 99, 102
smalleye pygmy sharks 328
smalltooth sawfish 344
SMEC Earthmover 20
smell, sense of
  birds 250
  humans 77, 118
  sharks 311
smiling 76, 81
Smilodectes 169
Smilodon 154, 160
smog 40
smooth dogfish 316
smooth hammerhead sharks 343
smoothhound sharks 300, 314
snaggletooth weasel sharks 338
snails 133
snake birds 240
snake eagles 264
snakeflies 132
snakes 142, 145
sneezing 119, 121
snipes 250, 267
snow buntings 288
snow finches 274
snow geese 244
snow hares 225
snow leopards 211
snowflakes 26
snowshoe hares 193
snowy owls 271
snowy sheathbills 279
soaps 24
sociable weavers 251
soda ash 58
sodium 24, 27, 63, 107, 109, 194
sodium bicarbonate 107
sodium chloride 21, 23, 63
solar cells 38
solar panels 16, 54
solar plexus 68
solenoids 28
solids 17
  density 36
  elasticity 47
  solutions 50
solutes 50
solutions 50, 61
solvents 50
somatosensory cortex 74, 75
song thrushes 267
sonic boom 25
soot 40, 62
sound 25
  measurement 55
  musical 57
sound waves 17, 25
South African grassbirds 275
south polar skuas 279
southern black-backed gulls 271
southern elephants seals 197
southern ground hornbills 288
space, dimensions of 12
space-time 12, 41, 59
sparrowhawks 255
sparrows 259, 274
speartooth sharks 342
specific heat 29
spectacled bears 221
spectacled flying foxes 228
spectral analysis 64
spectrum 53, 64
speed 39, 41
  of light 18, 34, 41, 54
  of sound 25
sperm, sperm cells 112, 114, 115, 116, 117, 320, 321
sperm whales 210, 216
spider monkeys 227
spiders 131

spinal cord 69, 70, 72, 74, 75, 76, 93, 309
spinal nerves 69, 70, 75
spinal process 93
spine *see* backbone
spined pygmy sharks 299, 317
spinner dolphins 216
spinner sharks 341
spinning tops 51
spiny anteaters 182, 200
spiny dogfish 298, 300, 301, 308, 315, 317, 319, 323, 328
spiracles 302, 310, 312, 327
spiral-horned antelopes 231
spleen 99, 107, 119, 120
splendid fairy-wrens 247
spongehead catsharks 337
spongy bone 91
spook fish 344
spoonbills 281
spores 128
spotted bats 223
spotted bowerbirds 262
spotted catbirds 262
spotted eagle rays 345
spotted flycatchers 270
spotted houndsharks 338
spotted hyenas 230
spotted ratfish 348
spotted seals 197
spotted skunks 235
spotted wobbegong sharks 352
Spriggina 130
springbok 227, 231
springhares 227
springs, coiled 11, 47
spruce grouse 258
spur-winged plovers 251
spy-hopping 216
squirrels 162, 190, 192, 196, 199, 204, 232
stalagmites and stalactites 50
star-nosed moles 206
starches 10, 103, 104, 106
starfish 132
starlings 242, 250
stars 13, 32, 36, 48, 62, 64
static electricity 12
Statue of Liberty 55
steam engines 49
steel 19, 29, 30, 33, 47
Stella's seacows 203
stem cells 88
Stephanoceras 134
sternum 93
steroids 110
Stethacanthus 351
Stictonetta 152
stilts 271
stingrays 317, 344, 345, 349
stomach 61, 99, 102, 119, 318
stone curlews 246
storks 153, 269, 279, 285
storm petrels 278
straight-tooth weasel sharks 338
strain 47
strap-toothed whales 210
stress 47
stretching and pulling 47
Strethacanthus 136
striped dolphins 216
striped hyenas 230
striped possums 217
striped skunks 235
stromatolites 126
strontium 13
subatomic particles 11, 17, 34, 46
  see also electrons; neutrons; protons
sucrase 106
sucrose 104, 106, 107
sugars 10, 103, 104, 106, 107, 111
sulphur dioxide 40
sulphuric acid 61
Sumatran rhinoceroses 197
Sumatran tigers 186
Sun 11, 36, 41, 54
  nuclear fusion 52
  surface temperature 42
sun bears 221
sunbirds 268
sunbitterns 291
sunfish *see* basking sharks
sungrebes 291
superb fairy-wrens 247
superb lyrebirds 272
superior vena cava 84, 90, 120
supernovae 14
surface tension 60
surfactants 24
swallow-tailed kites 283
swallows 261, 264
swans 244, 259, 263, 271
sweat 82, 108, 109
sweat glands 100
swellsharks 302, 308, 319, 321, 322, 337
swifts 153, 243
swivel joints 96
sword-billed hummingbirds 290
symbiosis 325
sympathetic nervous system 69
synapses 71
synapsids 142, 143
synovial fluid 96
synovial joints 96
synthetic materials 22, 24
Synthetoceras 161, 163
Syringopora 130
systemic arteries 86
systemic circulation 83
systole 85

T

T-cells 119, 120
tachycardia 85
tadpoles 140, 141
tails, prehensile 183, 219, 220, 227
takahes 255
talapoin monkeys 214
tamanduas 205
tamarins 227
tanagers 288
tapaculos 263
tapetum lucidum 311

tapeworms 325
tapirs 163, 203
tarsiers 169, 222
Tasmanian devils 217
Tasmanian wolves 192
tasselled wobbegong sharks 307, 332
taste, taste buds 76, 79, 118, 250
tawny nurse sharks 331
teal 241
tears 119
teeth and jaws
  amphibians 142
  fish 135
  humans 65, 92, 95
  mammals 154, 182
  pseudotooths 152
  reptiles 142
  sharks 136, 314, 318, 330, 351
Teflon 22
telecommunications 35
teleosts 137
telephones 35
television 18, 47, 58
temperature 17, 29, 42, 53
  body temperature 42, 69, 82, 106
temporal lobe 77, 81
tendons 76, 96
tenrecs 233
terahertz 18
terminal hair 101
terns 250, 259, 268
Terrestrisuchus 143
territory-marking 187, 219, 220, 225, 229
terror birds 151, 256
teslas 19
testes 110, 111, 114, 115
testosterone 10, 111, 114, 115
tetanus 123
tetrafluorethylene 22
tetrapods 138, 139, 141, 142
Texas skates 347
thalamus 73
therapsids 142
thermal energy 29
thermodynamics 57
thermonuclear weapons 38, 64
thermoplastics 22
thermoset plastics 22
thinking 77
Thoatherium 158
thoracic nerves 70
thoracic spine 93
thornbills 247
thrashers 258
Three Gorges Dam 56
three-banded armadillos 212
three-toed sloths 184
three-wattled bellbirds 277
thresher sharks 298, 301, 306, 308, 317, 323, 332, 334, 352
thrushes 267
thunder 25, 55
thylacines 157
Thylacinus 157
Thylacoleo 157
Thylacosmilus 158
thymine 112
thymus gland 110, 119, 120
thyroid gland 82, 110, 111
thyroxine 111
Tiaojishan Formation 155
tiger sharks 298, 306, 313, 314, 316, 317, 318, 323, 339, 340, 349
tigers 160, 186, 187, 219
time 13
  relativity 41
  time travel 59
timpkins 262
tinamous 282, 285
tissues 87, 99
Titan 49
Titanis 151
Titanis walleri 256
Titanoboa 145
titi monkeys 227
tits 254
toco toucans 284
todies 275
toenails 101
tongue 76, 79
tonsils 89, 119, 120
tool-use
  birds 273, 293
  early humans 173, 174, 178
  mammals 187, 226, 227
tooth decay 23, 122
toothed whales 210
tope sharks 338
torpedo rays 344, 345
torque 23
tortoises 142, 144, 245
tortoiseshell cats 235
toucan barbets 280
toucans 265, 272, 284
touch, sense of
  humans 79
  sharks 312
toxins 106, 123
Toxodon 154
trachea 89, 90, 91
tragopans 276
transducers 65
transformers 56
transistors 30, 33
translucent 48
Transmission Electron Microscopes 17
transmitters 35
tree kangaroos 213, 217
tremblers 258
Triadobatrachus 140
Triassic Period 127, 130, 143, 144, 145, 146, 147, 148
trigeminal nerve 76
triglyceride fats 103, 104
Trigonias 166
triidothyronine 111
trilobites 131
triodes 33
Tristychius 351
tritium 38
trochlear nerve 76

trogons 294
Troodon 150
troodontids 150
tropicbirds 268
trumpeter swans 244
trumpeters 262
tube-nosed bats 228
tuberculosis 123
tubules 109
tufted ducks 241
tundra swans 244, 271
tundra wolves 229
tungsten 23, 36
tunicates 134
turacos 293
turbines 49, 52, 56
turkey vultures 277
turkeys 258, 259, 269
Turkish Van cats 235
turning forces 23
turnstones 267
turtles 142, 144, 147
tusks 166, 185
tweezers 23
typhoid 123
tyrant flycatchers 245
tyres 19, 26

U

Uintatherium 161
ulnar nerve 70
ultrasound scans 117
ultraviolet (UV) 18, 36, 64, 248
ultraviolet (UV) radiation 40
umbilical cords 117, 118, 323
umbra 48
unicorn sharks 351
Universe
  Big Bang 27, 41
  energy 11, 57
  mass 36
  weight 38
ununhexium 14
upthrust 33, 56
uranium 31, 34, 37, 64
uranium dioxide 52
urea 109
ureter 109
urethra 115
urinary system 68
urine 108, 109
uterus 96, 114, 116, 117, 118, 321, 323

V

vaccination 121, 122, 123
vacuum moulding 22
vagina 115, 116
vagus nerve 76
valves, heart 84, 86
vampire bats 223
vangas 253
varanid lizards 145
Varanosaurus 142
vas deferens 115
vascular plants 128
vector charts 53
vectors 10, 53
vegetarian diet 103
veins 83, 84, 86, 109, 120
vellus hair 101
velocity 11, 39, 51, 53
velocity ratio (VR) 20
velvet belly lanternsharks 301, 317, 329
ventricles 72, 84, 85
venules 83
verdigris 55
vermilion flycatchers 245
Verreaux's eagles 257
vertebrae 92, 93, 96, 309
vertebrates 134, 138, 242, 309
vestibulocochlear nerve 76
vibrations 25, 57, 312
Victoria crowned pigeons 254
vicuña 204
violins 57
viper dogfish 329
vipers 145
vireos 295
Virginia opossums 220
viruses 119, 120, 122, 123
vision *see* eyes and vision
visual cortex 74
vitamins 100, 103, 105, 106, 107
vitreous humour 78
viviparous animals 154
viviparous sharks 323
vocal cords 90
Vogelkop gardener bowerbirds 262
voice box 89, 90, 99
voles 162, 213, 218
voltage 21, 56
volume 33
voluntary muscles 97
vultures 153, 256, 265, 277, 285, 289, 295
vulturine guineafowl 243

W

wagtails 266
wallabies 213
walruses 159, 185, 208
warblers 240, 247, 253, 275, 293, 294
warthogs 185, 195
wastes, bodily 70, 87, 91, 107, 109, 120, 318
water 23, 37, 60, 108
  in the body 107, 108, 109
  boiling/freezing point 42, 60
  chemical formula 21, 60
  insulator 34
  osmosis 108
  pH 61
  in space 60
  tap water 50
  water pressure 19
  water vapour 40
water buffaloes 212, 224
water mice 236
water opossums 220
water rails 255
water shrews 206

water voles 213
wattlebirds 280
wattled false sunbirds 293
wattled starlings 242
waxbills 251
waxwings 256
weasel sharks 338
weasels 200, 209
weaverbirds 269
weavers 251
web-footed tenrecs 233
weight 36
weightlessness 36
western capercaillies 258
western curlews 267
western tanagers 288
Westlothiana lizziae 141
whale sharks 298, 299, 300, 301, 306, 307, 311, 316, 321, 323, 324, 325, 330, 331
whaler sharks *see* requiem sharks
whales 167, 182, 196, 204, 208, 210, 214, 216, 219, 224
wheelbarrows 23
whiskery sharks 338
whistling swans 263
white blood cells 68, 88, 119, 120, 121
white light 42, 64
white pelicans 283
white rhinoceroses 197, 222
white sharks 311
white storks 279
white-backed vultures 289
white-billed divers 248
white-breasted mesites 292
white-browed fantails 286
white-eyed river martins 264
white-fronted nunbirds 280
white-headed ducks 295
white-naped swifts 243
white-plumed antbirds 263
white-tailed sea eagles 264
white-tailed tropicbirds 268
white-throated gerygones 247
white-throated jungle flycatchers 270
white-whiskered puffbirds 280
white-winged guans 286
whitespotted bamboo sharks 323
whitetip reef sharks 302, 304, 315, 317, 319, 320, 341
whooper swans 244
whooping cranes 262, 295
whorl-toothed sharks 351
whydahs 251
wild dogs 189, 216, 227, 232
wild pigs 185
wildcats 160
wildebeest 204, 227, 231
willie wagtails 286
willow ptarmigans 271
willow warblers 275
windpipe 89, 90, 91
winter wrens 259
wireless networks 18
wisdom teeth 95
wisent 182
wobbegong sharks 298, 302, 307, 308, 312, 321, 330, 332, 349, 352
wolverines 209
wolves 201, 217, 227, 229
womb *see* uterus
wombats 157, 211, 217, 225
wood mice 196
wood pigeons 253, 254
wood rats 205
wood storks 279
wood swallows 280
wood warblers 294
woodchucks 199
woodcreepers 270
woodlice 131
woodpeckers 259, 285, 292
work 20, 65
World Wide Web 51
wormholes 59
worms 130
wrens 259, 272
wrinkles 115
wrought iron 29
wrybills 251

X

X-ray crystallography 26
X-rays 18, 32, 39, 60
xenon 40

Y

yaks 212
Yalkaparidon 157
Yangtse dolphins 216
yapoks 220
yellow-billed oxpeckers 285
yellow-billed shrikes 253
yellow-breasted boatbills 286
yellow-eyed penguins 295
yellow-headed caracaras 248
yellow-vented bulbuls 289

Z

Zambezi River sharks *see* bull sharks
zebra sharks 308, 318, 321, 323, 330, 331
zebras 219, 237
zebu cattle 212, 228

Acknowledgements

All artworks are from the Miles Kelly Artwork Bank

The publishers would like to thank the following sources for the use of their photographs:

COVER: Fotolia.com Front (b) Creative images; Science Photo Library Front (br) Sebastian Kaulitzki; Shutterstock.com Front (tr) Jiang Hongyan, (tc) Sashkin, (tl) Farinosa, (bl) cbpix, (cl) Eric Isselee; Spine (t) TigerStock's, (b) Andras Deak; Back (tl) Aaron Amat, (tc) Kitch Bain, (tr) Jeff Grabert, (cl) Nataliya Osyka, (cr) Catmando, (cb) frantisekhojdysz

Alamy
10(bl) Image Source Plus; 21(cr) PhotosIndia.com LLC; 35(tr) Sueddeutsche Zeitung Photo; 139(br), 153(tr) & 162(bl) Stocktrek Images, Inc.; 179(bl) Dominic Robinson; 318(tc) WaterFrame; 332(br) Doug Perrine

Ardea
353(b) Valerie & Ron Taylor

Diomedia
150(cr) UIG Education; 184(t) Natural History Museum London UK; 232(br) Bruce Coleman International

Dreamstime
22(tr) Sebastian Czapnik, (bl) Shariff Che\'Lah; 33(bl) Victor Savushkin; 47(tc) K.walkow; 48(tr) Adam Gryko, (bl) Dan Klimke; 58(t) Alexei Novikov; 59(bl) Tamarwhite; 64(br) Theo Gottwald; 75(bc) Fragles; 82(c) Serban Enache; 104(bl) Cb34inc; 105(bc) Elena Schweitzer; 111(tc) Axel Kock, (b) Galina Barskaya; 115(bl) & 116(cl) Jelen80; 247(br) Steve Byland; 340(tr) Naluphoto

FLPA
221(b) Frans Lanting; 255(br) Roger Tidman; 293(bc) ImageBroker; 299(bl) Jeffrey Rotman; 302(cr) Peter Verhoog; 322(br) Steve Trewhella; 330(cl) Fred Bavendam; 337(cl) Fred Bavemdam, (br) Norbert Wu/Minden Pictures; 338(tc) Imagebroker, Norbert Prost/Imagebroker; 346(cr) Richard Herrmann

Fotolia.com
16(cl) Cre8tive Studios; 19(c) Fox; 23(tr) 2xSamara.com, (br) Juri; 25(br) photlook; 29(br) Canakris; 32(tc) Ericus; 54(br) Markku Vitikainen; 55(cl) Andreas Rodriguez; 62(cr) Cornelius; 65(bl) Ljupco Smokovski; 68(tc) Sebastian Kaulitzki; 96(tc) chrisharvey; 103(bl) NiDerLander; 105(tr) Celso Pupo, (bc) Elena Schweitzer; 241(cr) Steve Byland; 244(br) Keller; 250(c) Kaido Karne; 252(tr) Tersina Shieh; 254(tr) EcoView, (b) Nbgbgbg; 268(tc) David Thyberg; 271(tr) steve estvanik; 274(cl) KDImages; 285(br) javarman; 291(tr) marilyn barbone; 294(bl) Gregg Williams; 352(tr) Valamar

Getty
16(bc) Bettmann; 46(bc) Peter Ginter; 160(tl) Daniel Eskridge/Stocktrek Images; 171(bl) Régis Bossu; 310(b) Wildestanimal 2015; 313(bc) Luciano Candisani/ Minden Pictures; 314(cr) Tui De Roy/Minden Pictures; 324(t) Brian J. Skerry; 346(b) Todd Aki/Moment Open

Glow Images
173(bl) SuperStock; 304(cl) Norbert Probst/ImageBROKER

Image Quest Marine
341(b) 2009 Andy Murch; 348(bl) Kelvin Aitken – V&W

iStock
12(b) MvH; 20(tc) iariturk; 55(bl) travelpixpro; 57(bl) yenwen; 63(br) leezsnow; 94(tr) Raycat; 99(cl) cdascher; 106(cr) hartcreations; 190(bl) akarelias; 250(bl) Andrew_Howe; 256(bl) AlbyDeTweede; 271(b) & 276(br) Andrew_Howe

NASA
14(cr) Fred Deaton/MSFC; 18(tr) NASA/GSFC/MITI/ERSDAC/JAROS, and U.S./Japan ASTER Science Team; 36(b) MFSC/Nasa; 41(tr) NASA/Marshall Space Flight Center; 53(c) Jesse Allen/Earths Observatory/Modis Ocean Team/Remote sensing Group

National Geographic
157(t) Adrie and Alfons Kennis; 318(bc) Bill Curtsinger

NPL
284(tr) Roland Seitre; 300(bl) Michele Westmorland, (br) Doug Perrine; 310(tr) Alex Mustard/2020VISION; 314(br) Jeff Rotman; 317(br) Ian Coleman; 323(cr) Jeff Rotman; 329(tc) Florian Graner; 334(tc) & 343(bg) Chris & Monique Fallows; 352(cr) Alex Mustard/2020VISION

Oceanwide
298(t) C & M Fallows; 303(cl) & 317(tc) Andy Murch; 332(tc) Justin Gilligan

Photoshot
308(bl) Jeremy Stafford-Deitsch

Playstation
10(cl) Playstation

Rex/Shutterstock
28(tc) Granger/Rex/Shutterstock; 39(cr) Cultura/REX/Shutterstock; 41(br) Graham Eva/LNP/REX/Shutterstock; 44(b) Gerry Penny/EPA-EFE/REX/Shutterstock; 51(bl) Alex Segre/REX/Shutterstock; 303(tr) David Jenkins/ roberthcharding/REX/Shutterstock

Seapics
322(tr) Michele Hall; 323(tr) & 324(b) Doug Perrine

Shutterstock.com
3(bc) Eric Isselee; 7(tr 1) Spectral-Design, (tr 2) Alila Medical Media, (cr3) Ralf Juergen Kraft, (cr4) & (br5) Eric Isselee, (br6) cbpix; 8–9(bg) Egorov Artem; 13(bl) Evgeny Dubinchuk; 14(t) Steve Byland; 15(r) oorka; 17(tr) takasu; 18(bl) itsmejust; 20(bc) Georgios Kollidas; 21(br) James Steidl; 24(tc) Gwoeii; 26(bl) TOSP; 28(b) cyo bo; 29(tr) beboy; 30(cl) Sam72, (br) Dmitry Petrenko; 32(bl) lightpoet; 34(bl) Jeff Schultes; 35(br) sdecoret; 36(tl) Bedecs_HU; 37(tc) Everett Historical, (b) Designua; 38(cl) Takashi Images, (b) bankerwin; 39(br) Peter Bernik; 42(t) IM_photo, (cr) Jeff Grabert; 43(tr) FotoBug11; 46(cl) JetKat, (tr) Denis Selivanov; 50(br) Designua; 51(tl) Dziurek; 54(tl) Smileus; 55(cl) Tania Zbrodko, (c) Andrey Bayda, (c) Fesus Robert, (cr) Paul Drabot, (br) Shutterstock; 56(cl) Sukpaiboonwat, (cr) Andrii Zhezhera; 57(tl) hkhtt hj; 60(bl) Achim Baque; 63(cr) oorka; 65(tr) Yegor Korzh, (br) ifong; 66–67(bg) Magic mine; 69(bg) BlueRingMedia; 72(bc) Mega Pixel; 74(tc) Asier Romero; 75(cl) images72; 76(t) Galina Barskaya, (br) Harm Kruyshaar; 77(t) Ilike; 80(t) Air Images, (b) aastock; 81(tl) Valua Vitaly, (b) ESB Professional; 82(cr) Maridav; 85(tr) Alila Medical Media; 87(tl) Maridav; 88(tr) Mopic, (bl) sciencepics; 89(tr) Alila Medical Media, (b) Pete Saloutos; 90(tc) Alila Medical Media; 92(bg) Ralf Juergen Kraft; 93(tc) Sebastian Kaulitzki; 95(tr) Guido Vrola; 95(bc) & 96(bl) Alila Medical Media; 103(tr) ifong; 104(cl) Nattika; 107(tr) decade3d – anatomy online, (bc) Gordon Bell; 108(cr) Markus Mainka; 109(tr) Hans Christiansson, (bc) Tefi; 110(tr) CLIPAREA l Custom media; 113(tr) Lisa F. Young; 115(tr) CroMary; 117(bl) FamVeld; 118(cl) Alila Medical Media, (br) Africa Studio; 119(c) Alila Medical Media; 121(tl) hartphotography; 122(tr) michaeljung; 124–125(bg) Michael Rosskothen; 126(c) Rob Bayer, (bl) BergelmLicht; 127(cl) leonello calvetti; 129(cl) Madlen, (bc) Petr Salinger; 130(bl) Paul Vinten; 132(cr) Amanda Nicholls, (bl) MarcelClemens; 133(cl) Suphatthra China; 136(t) Rich Carey; 138(br) izarizhar; 141(bc) Nicky Rhodes; 143(tc) leonello calvetti; 146(bc) Andreas Meyer; 147(cl), 148(b) & 149(t) Michael Rosskothen; 150(br) Catmando; 154(tr) Rich Koele; 158(tc), 161(bl) & 164(tc) Ralf Juergen Kraft; 166(tc) Ozja; 167(tr) Catmando; 176(tr) Procy; 180–181(bg) Eric Gevaert; 182(tr) Dave Pusey, (bc) Olivier Le Queinec; 183(cl) neelsky, (br) tratong; 184(br) worldswildlife wonders; 185(cl) BMJ, (bc) Jason Prince; 186(tr) & 187(c) Eric Gevaert; 187(bl) BMJ; 188(tc) Eric Isselee,

(bc) Harm Kruyshaar; 189(cl) Sean Nel, (br) Sylvie Bouchard; 190(tl) Bildagentur Zoonar GmbH, (cr) TOMO; 191(b) Coprid; 193(tl) Sergey Uryadnikov; 194(tr) Johan Swanepoel, (b) Four Oaks; 195(cr) Eric Isselee, (bl) Mike Price; 196(tc) Tatiana Volgutova, (br) dangdumrong; 197(t) PicturesWild, (bl) Don Fink; 198(t) DR Travel Photo and Video, (bl) Worldswildlifewonders; 200(tc) Worldswildlifewonders, (br) Kyslynskyyhal; 201(c) ANP; 202(tl) Ilya Akinsin, (b) Fotokon; 203(br) ylq; 204(tr) Eric Isselee, (bl) Nadezhda Bolotina; 205(c) Shcherbakov Ilya, (br) Vladimir Wrangel; 206(tr) Khoroshunova Olga, (bc) Santia; 207(tr) Greg and Jan Ritchie, (b) Scott E Read; 208(tl) Outdoorsman, (b) Henk Bentlage; 209(tr) Steve Meese, (b) Miroslav Hlavko; 210(cr) Luna Vandoorne, (b) RKB; 211(tl) Smileus, (br) Leslie Crookes; 212(cl) Heiko Kiera, (b) Oscity; 213(tr) Rafael Ramirez Lee, (bl) Andy Poole; 214(bl) smokyme; 215(tr) Eric Isselee; 216(bl) Iv Nikolny; 217(cl) Josef Pittner, (br) Robyn Butler; 218(tl) elitravo, (b) Carl Dawson; 219(tl) Nailia Schwarz, (b) Ryan M. Bolton; 220(c) Donna Heatfield, (bl) Baranov E; 222(tc) Blue Orange Studio; 223(tr) Jason Prince, (bl) Michael Lynch; 224(t) idreamphoto, (b) Serge Vero; 225(tl) Geoffrey Kuchera, (br) covenant; 226(tr) Kitch Bain, (b) Sergey Uryadnikov; 227(tr) Gail Johnson, (bc) BMJ; 228(cl) Christian Musat, (br) Erik Zandboer; 229(c) LazyFocus, (bc) Eric Isselee; 230(tr) Setaphong Tantanawat, (bl) Daniel-Alvarez; 231(t) Johan Swanepoel, (br) Shutterstock; 232(cl) John Carnemolla; 233(cr) Arto Hakola, (bl) Mark Bridger; 235(cl) LeniKovaleva, (bc) Ultrashock; 236(cr) niall dunne; 237(tc) Pim Leijen, (br) Jamen Percy; 238–239(bg) Eduardo Rivero; 240(cr) Jenny Leonard; 242(tl) Hydromet; 245(bl) Rafael Martos Martins; 246(cl) Lovely Bird; 248(cr) Brian Guest; 249(tr) Butterfly Hunter, (b) Alan Jeffery; 253(tl) Victor Tyakht, (cr) Alta Oosthuizen; 258(bc) Chepko Danil Vitalevich; 259(tc) tntphototravis; 262(br) Luke Shelley; 268(br) Four Oaks; 275(tc) aaltair; 276(t) Sergei25; 281(tr) worldswildlifewonders, (b) Anna Om; 286(cr) Super Prin; 287(tr) Kaido Karner; 290(cl) mlorenz; 292(tl) francesco de marco; 296–297(bg) Matt9122; 298(b) nicolasvoisin44; 299(c) Krzysztof Odziomek; 300(cr) ilolab; 301(br) Greg Amptman; 302(bl) frantisekhojdysz; 304(b) Fiona Ayerst; 306(cr) cbpix; 308(cr) NatalieJean; 311(cr) Dray van Beeck, (bl) Matt9122; 312(bl) Pommeyrol Vincent; 313(cr) Matt9122; 314(bc) Photon75; 315(bg) A Cotton Photo; 316(tr) Dudarev Mikhail; 319(cl) Brandelet; 325(tl) Greg Amptman; 330(bl) iliuta goean; 331(bl) Sergey Dubrov; 339(cr) Florian Graner; 340(bl) Ian Scott; 341(t) Micha Rosenwirth; 344(b) Durden Images; 345(cl) Ethan Daniels; 348(cr) Greg Amptman; 349(bc) Gustavo Miguel Fernandes; 350(tc) kbrowne41, (cr) Greg Amptman; 354–355(bg) Michael Rosskothen

Shutterstock & Artwork
305(bl) ilolab

Science Photo Library
13(tr) Andrew Brookes, National Physical Laboratory; 17(bc) Lawrence Livermore; 38(tr) US NAVY; 40(br) Thomas Deerninck, NCMIR; 44(tr) Makoto Iwafuji/Eurelios; 45(br) Russell Kightley; 60(tl) Patrick Landmann, (br) Russell Kightley; 61(tl) Brian Bell; 62(tc) Russell Kightley; 62(bl) Victor Habbick Visions; 78(bc) Jacopin/BSIP; 79(cr) Clouds Hill Imaging; 85(bl) Ria Novosti; 86(tr) Zephyr; 87(br) Medical RF.Com; 91(b) Mikkel Juul Jensen; 93(bl) & 94(cr) Sebastian Kaulitzki; 98(bc) Jacopin; 100(cl) Russell Kightley; 114(br) BSIP, JACOPIN; 119(tr) Kateryna Kon; 121(bl) Gavin kingcome; 123(tr) Hybrid Medical Animation, (bl) Russell Kightley; 136(b), 144(b), 145(tc), (br), 146(t), 151(bl), 152(tc), (bl), 153(br) & 154(bl) Jaime Chirinos; 155(cl) Millard H. Sharp; 156(b) Jose Antonio Penas; 157(bl) Mauricio Anton; 161(tr) Mark Hallett PaleoArt; 162(tr) Natural History Museum, London; 170(tr) Christian Jegou Publiphoto Diffusion; 171(tc) & 172(tc) Mauricio Anton; 172(bl) Christian Jegou Publiphoto Diffusion; 174(cr) Raul Martin/MSF, (bl) Mauricio Anton; 175(l) Natural History Museum, London; 176(b) Claus Lunau; 177(tc) Ria Novosti; 178(cr) Mauricio Anton; 179(tr) Christian Jegou Publiphoto Diffusion

Topfoto
49(tr) & 53(br) Granger, NYC

Every effort has been made to acknowledge the source and copyright holder of each picture. Miles Kelly Publishing apologizes for any unintentional errors or omissions.